The MOUNTBATTENS

The Last Royal Success Story

ALDEN HATCH

Random House : New York

FIRST PRINTING

© *Copyright, 1965, by Alden Hatch*

All rights reserved under International and Pan-American Copyright Conventions. Published in New York by Random House, Inc., and simultaneously in Toronto, Canada, by Random House of Canada Limited. *Manufactured in the United States of America by The Book Press, Brattleboro, Vt.*

DESIGNED BY MARGARET F. PLYMPTON

Library of Congress catalog card number: 65-11283

Acknowledgements

A BIOGRAPHER is constantly surprised and heartened by the courtesy, even enthusiasm, shown him by busy men and women who are willing to lend their valuable time to him for the sake of enlightening him concerning the great affairs in which they have taken part. Such assistance is for the most part purely unselfish, and done out of respect for historical truth. Among the many people who helped me with this book I am particularly grateful to: His Royal Highness Prince Bernhard of the Netherlands; former Prime Minister Earl Attlee; the Earl and Countess of Airlie; Lt. Col. the Earl of Romney; Field Marshal the Viscount Slim; General of the Army Dwight D. Eisenhower; Lt. General Sir Frederick E. Morgan; General Sir Michael West; Vice-Admiral Sir Edward Parry; Air Marshal Sir Charles and Lady Strafford; Lt. General Sir Cecil M. Smith; former Minister of Defence the Honorable Harold Watkinson; Vice-Admiral John Durnford; Admiral Royer Dick; Vice-Admiral John Godfrey; Rear Admiral Ronald V. Brockman; Lord Malcolm Douglas-Hamilton; Sir Mark Norman, Bart; Sir Esler Denning; Captain S. W. Roskill, R. N.; Major General Sir Kenneth Strong; Princess Wiesemsky; Dorothy, Lady Bruntisfield; Lady Lambe; Dame Elizabeth Murdock; Mrs. Andrew Kerr; Mrs. M. A. Liddell and Miss Kerr; Mrs. Eiler Donald; Miss Noreen Parks; the Countess of Brecknock; Colonel Philip Cochran; Messrs. Robert Cecil and Robert Ford (of the Foreign Office); and Messrs. Randolph Churchill; Jeremy Hutchinson, Q. C.; G. R. Rougier, Q. C.; A. J. (Rocky) Wilkins; C. J. Asbury; Stephen Fry; Mr. and Mrs. Maurice Zinkin; Charles Pick; Gordon Fellows-Morgan, and Justus Baldwin (Jock) Lawrence.

In addition I owe an especial debt to my research assistant Mrs. Joan Saunders and to Lord Mountbatten's literary executor, Mr. Alan Campbell-Johnson; to the former Director General of British Information Service in the United States, Mr. Peter Hayman; and to the tireless and efficient staff of the Library of the British Information Service, as well as to the staff of the Admiralty Library in London.

ALDEN HATCH

SOMERLEAS
CEDARHURST, LONG ISLAND
JANUARY, 1965

Contents

PART I. Prince Louis

PART II. Lord Louis

PART III. Prince Philip

I

PRINCE LOUIS

Chapter 1

THE MAGNIFICENT
MOUNTBATTENS

"IT'S A FUNNY THING," Lord Attlee said, taking a sip of sherry, "those Mountbattens are the only members of the Royal Family who have ever shown great ability."

"All three of them," he added. "Prince Louis, a great sailor who was done in by the *Globe* in 1914; Dickie (Lord Mountbatten), who became Chief of the Defence Staff in spite of being royal, not because of it; and Philip, I think—if he had a chance."

The former Labour Prime Minister may have been somewhat unkind to some other members of the Royal Family, who have shown considerable ability—when they had a chance—but he was completely correct about the Mountbattens. They are the most important family in Great Britain, not because of their relationship to royalty, whom they far outshine, but because of their brains, guts, and energy.

They are also one of the most unpopular families in the Kingdom, despite their having served their adopted country brilliantly and well for the better part of a century. They are disliked, partially because nothing upsets a traditional Englishman more than seeing a member of the Royal Family doing something constructive, and also because when Lord Mountbatten sees a thing that needs doing, he does it regardless of whose

(3)

feelings are hurt. His nephew, Prince Philip, has the same energetic disregard of people's sensibilities—particularly those of reporters. The Queen and her Government hold a tight rein on this prince, who knows himself capable of great things, and so his frustrations erupt in small ways.

In the Carlton Club, the ultimate stronghold of conservatism, and the drawing rooms of the West End, the Mountbattens are discussed in lowered voices as "very dangerous." "How are they dangerous?" one may ask; and the answer is, "Because they are so powerful and so ambitious. Because they have tried to move in on the Throne, and have *succeeded* in controlling the Defence Establishment." Then comes the clinching argument, "Because Dickie Mountbatten is practically a *socialist*."

This picture of Lord Mountbatten as the evil genius of England is far from a universal opinion. Ask any man who served under him in H.M.S. *Kelly* or who was on his staff in Southeast Asia or who was a member of his brain trust in India; ask his servants and the pensioners he cares for tenderly; ask Clement Attlee, who begged him to accept the onerous task of presiding over the dissolution of the British Empire—the Tories will never forgive Mountbatten for that unpopular but essential public service; or if you could, ask Nehru, for example, and you would get a very different answer.

Both answers are partly right. Lord Mountbatten is humorless, arrogant, vain, and absurdly proud of his insignificant royal ancestors. He is intensely ambitious—a driven man powered by an unshakeable desire to avenge the wrong his father suffered. He is ruthless of purpose, even though the purpose is usually good.

But—he is a superb leader of men, fearless, loyal, loving, and kind beyond the call of conscience to those who serve him. He is, rare combination, a brilliant naval technician and a farsighted, imaginative statesman possessed of great common sense combined with daring initiative and real concern for humanity. He is a dedicated Englishman. He is quite a man.

Incidentally, Prince Philip, in his faults and his virtues, is a chip off the avuncular block, but only a chip. Though they are both dashing, handsome, and loaded with charm, neither of them has the open-hearted warmth that made their father and grandfather, Admiral of the Fleet His Serene Highness Prince Louis of Battenberg, one of the best-loved officers of the Royal Navy. Prince Louis' amiability did not indicate any lack of decision, daring, or seamanship. Lord Fisher, the Father of the modern British Navy, noted in 1911, "I propose that he [the new First Lord of the Admiralty, Winston Churchill] take as his First Sea Lord

Prince Louis of Battenberg, the very ablest admiral, after Sir Arthur Wilson, that we possess, both afloat and ashore. [*Private*] *Wilson is no good ashore.* . . . He [Battenberg] is more English than the English. . . ."

In *The World Crisis* Churchill himself wrote, "So much of my work in endeavoring to prepare the Fleet for war was dependent on the guidance and help I received from Prince Louis of Battenberg. . . . Prince Louis was a child of the Royal Navy. . . . The deck of a British warship was his home. All his interest was centered in the British Fleet. . . . He had a far wider knowledge of war by land and sea, and of the Continent of Europe, than most of the other Admirals I have known. . . ."

In October, 1914, Prince Louis, who was in fact First Sea Lord of the British Admiralty, was forced to resign because of the hysteria that made the English suspect of treason anyone with a German name. Even dachshunds bore the stigma and it was frightfully unpatriotic to have German measles. By 1917, with thousands of young Englishmen dead in the mud of France, this feeling became so virulent that King George V, on the advice of Prime Minister Lloyd George, changed his family name from Wettin to Windsor and the Battenbergs became Mountbattens.

Incidentally, it is fortunate that Americans did not succumb to this panic in World War Two. What would they have done for generals without Eisenhower, Spaatz, Grunther, Eichelberger, Wedemeyer, and their brilliant colleagues? In this connection Vice Admiral Sir Edward Parry tells of encountering American Admiral Schnackenberg, commanding in the Mediterranean in 1946. Somehow the talk turned to names and the American admiral remarked wryly, "If I were in your navy my name would be Mountschnacken."

Battenbergs or Mountbattens as you will, these three men, father, son, grandson, have played great and constructive roles in the history of England. All three did so with such picturesque dash and magnificent disregard of public opinion that each in turn became extremely controversial. Because he was and is the most powerful and dynamic of them, Lord Mountbatten is hated the most bitterly. His plan for unification of the British Defence Establishment did nothing to lessen this enmity. When he abolished the First Lord of the Admiralty he infuriated the Navy; and reducing the Royal Air Force to a mere section of the Department of Defence made the airmen livid. The fact that most of them recognized that it enormously increased the efficiency of the British Armed Forces hardly assuaged their injured feelings.

Perhaps the most exasperating thing about the Mountbattens is that while they were performing their unique services for England they had a splendid time. Riding the crest of their royal wave, they fully enjoyed all the perquisites of their position. Glittering with diamond stars and garters (as well as small, simple medals earned for valor) at great court functions or lavish private parties, playing polo or hunting in far-off swamps and mountains, roughing it lustily and living in splendor and loving it, they pursued pleasure as strenuously as they sought fame and honor, and as successfully.

Since the Battenbergs had little money of their own, they achieved magnificence by judicious marriages. Prince Louis married Queen Victoria's granddaughter. His son restored the Mountbatten's ebbing fortunes by marrying lovely Edwina Ashley, who brought him wonderful companionship, social grace—without which he might not have gone so far—and $30,000,000. Prince Philip, of course, topped them both by marrying the future Queen of England.

However helpful to gracious living may have been the fact of the Mountbattens' relationship to virtually every royal house in Europe, it cannot be emphasized too strongly that it was no help at all to the naval careers of Prince Louis and Lord Mountbatten. Quite the contrary. Up to a point their eminent connections did smooth their way—up to let us say the rank of captain, after which they became suspect by reason of their birth. The old sea dogs, who came up from the gunroom the hard way, growled, "Entrust half a billion pounds' worth of battleships to a royal whelp who was born with an admiral's stripes in his pocket? Not bloody likely!"

So father and son had to prove, doubly and trebly, that they could be trusted with all those handsome ships. Not only that, but they had to be so much better than their rivals for command that they sank prejudice and forced the professionals to say grudgingly, "He is the best we've got."

The fact that this was done twice in two generations—and almost a third time in three—how it was done and the complex, brave, brilliant, arrogant, pleasure-loving, dedicated, hard-working men who did it make an extraordinary story of royal achievement against the tide of history.

Chapter 2

PRINCE ALEXANDER
FOUNDS A FAMILY

THE EARL MOUNTBATTEN OF BURMA, Knight of the Garter, Grand Cross of the Bath, Grand Cross of the Star of India, Distinguished Service Order, etc., etc., (some thirty-five et ceteras), considers himself the forty-first generation in descent from Duke Ydulf, a Frankish nobleman who "flourished" in 600 A.D. In an enormously erudite work entitled *The Mountbatten Lineage* (privately printed in 1958) Mountbatten painstakingly traces his ancestry from duke to duke and king to king down through the Grand Dukes of Hesse and the Rhine to the present day. Why he devoted so much energy to discovering ancestors, few of whom played as great a role in history as he, seems like an aberration in an otherwise brilliantly modern mind. Alan Campbell-Johnson, his close friend and literary executor, says that Mountbatten collects ancestors as other men collect postage stamps—for relaxation. In any event he acquired some rare specimens of royal progenitors, ranging from several Frankish kings called Clovis through Charlemagne to Queen Victoria, all duly authenticated by the College of Heralds.

Royal and ancient though the Battenberg-Mountbatten lineage may be, the name of Battenberg itself is newer than that of most commoners.

The family was founded in 1851 by Prince Alexander of Hesse and the Rhine. It had a rather romantic origin.

The Old Palace at Darmstadt was in an uproar in the spring of 1841. The grand duchy was a rich little principality—with rugged mountains, tall forests, and lush valleys—spanning the Rhine and bordered by the Main just west of the Kingdom of Bavaria. The reason for the excitement in the turreted medieval castle was that Princess Marie, the sixteen-year-old daughter of Grand Duke Louis II of Hesse and the Rhine had just been affianced to the Tsarevitch Alexander Nicholaevitch, eldest son of Tsar Nicholas I of Russia.

The princess, a plump little German girl whose pudding face was surrounded by eight fat sausage curls, was naturally scared silly at the prospect of leaving the *Gemütlichkeit* of her father's relatively cozy court for the barbaric splendors of the Winter Palace. To reassure her, Tsar Nicholas invited her next older brother, Prince Alexander, who incidentally was his godson, to come with her and live at the Russian Court. So the two children (Alexander was only seventeen) went to St. Petersburg where Marie was married with tremendous state, in the alien rites of the Orthodox Church, to the future Tsar Alexander II of all the Russias.

Life in St. Petersburg was not as bad as the little princess feared. She was, of course, used to the punctilio of court life. Her husband was young and gay, kind and liberal-minded; and her brother, who was as close to her as a twin, was the confidant of her hopes and worries. Prince Alexander had a very good time indeed. At that age he was rather short and dandified, with a small mustache and finely cut features. But he was a spirited young chap, who longed for military glory. The Tsar saw to that. On the day of Alexander's christening he had made his godson a lieutenant in the Imperial Russian Army. When Alexander reached St. Petersburg the Tsar promoted him to colonel and soon afterward to major general.

Naturally Alexander fell in love—with the Tsar's daughter, Grand Duchess Olga. But Nicholas's benevolence did not go that far; he had other plans for Olga. So Alexander went off to the wars, not as a major general but as a volunteer in the expedition to put down a rebellion in the Caucasus, led by the Mohammedan, Shamyl. It was a highly satisfactory substitute for puppy love. Alexander proved himself a man in the cut and thrust, billowing black-powder smoke and sifting yellow dust of battle. He won the Order of St. George (fourth class) for valor and scooped a nice souvenir off the littered battlefield—the late Shamyl's own Koran.

Back at Court he found that his sister had a pretty new lady-in-waiting, Countess Julie Hauke in the peerage of Poland. Julie was an orphan, for her aristocratic mother had died young, and her father Maurice, Count of Hauke, General of Artillery in the Imperial Russian Army, and Minister of War in the satellite government of Poland, had been killed defending the palace in Warsaw against rebellious Polish cadets in 1830. He died saving the life of the Governor General of Poland, Grand Duke Constantine, brother of the Tsar. The latter gratefully brought up General Hauke's two orphaned daughters in his own household, which is how Countess Julie happened to move in such exalted circles. Unlike most Russian generals of the time, Hauke had achieved his rank by sheer ability. His only known ancestor was his father, Frederick Hauck, a Hessian from Mainz. When the Tsar made the General a Polish count, he changed the spelling of his name to the slightly more artistocratic Hauke. Naturally the Haukes receive short shrift in *The Mountbatten Lineage*.

Julie was a remarkably pretty girl. There is a portrait of her painted some years later, which shows her wearing her dark brown hair parted in the middle under a headdress shaped like a flat pillbox, with ropes of pearls looped around it and pearl clusters in her ears. A certain strength of character appears in her long straight nose, but her mouth is small and sweet, and her large brown eyes under lightly penciled brows are warm and wistful.

Prince Alexander must have found her sufficiently enchanting to outweigh rank and royalty, and fear of imperial displeasure. In ten years he had reached a place very close to the pinnacle of Russian military life. A painting, done during that summer of 1851, shows him commanding a review of the Imperial Russian Chevalier Guards at the Summer Palace, Tsarskoe Selo. Tsar Nicholas is there, plumed and mounted on a charger, while the Tsarina watches from an open carriage as the young prince in an eagle-crested silver helmet gallops by at the head of the Emperor's Guard.

The denouement was triggered by a kindly thought of Tsar Nicholas, who told Alexander that he was destined for the honor of marrying the Tsar's own niece, the Grand Duchess Catherine Michailova. Alexander faintly expressed his appreciation of the honor, but his luxuriant sidewhiskers bristled with horror. There followed a lovers' flurried conference, a noble Victorian decision to lose the world for love, and a midnight dash in the traditional droshky, its three horses at a dead run, over the muddy road from Tsarskoe Selo to St. Petersburg.

Then across the endless, ocean-flat plains of western Russia and Poland they rattled, in a train pulled by a bell-mouthed, wood-burning locomotive. With the sense of the Tsar's hot breath on their necks, they probably took to a droshky again to avoid Warsaw; and so, after several harassed days and uneasy nights, they crossed the Russian border to Breslau where they were properly married by a nervous priest on October 28, 1851. They telegraphed the happy news to their august relatives.

Tsar Nicholas considered himself a patient man, but such ingratitude—and stupidity—threw him into an imperial tantrum. His language ripped the fragile, artificial elegance of Tsarskoe Selo, as lightning tears a summer night. With a stroke of the Imperial Pen he stripped Alexander of his military rank and kicked him out of the Imperial Russian Army.

Fortunately for the impulsive young prince, his father had died three years before, and his older brother now reigned in Hesse-Darmstadt as Grand Duke Louis III. The Grand Duke was scarcely pleased at his brother's escapade; but he was a fat, amiable gentleman, who decided to make the best of it. Of course, there could be no question of regarding this misalliance as a royal union. It must be a morganatic marriage, which, while valid in the sight of God, was limited under the laws of men: Countess Julie and her children could enjoy no perquisites of her royal husband's rank, not even his name. But the poor girl had to have *some* name; so Grand Duke Louis looked into his file and dusted off a lapsed title for his new sister-in-law. A week after the marriage, on November 5, 1851, he created her Countess of Battenberg, an insignificant town in the mountainous northern part of the grand duchy. Seven years later, when she had given birth to a daughter and several handsome sons, he elevated her into the twilight zone of royalty as Her Serene Highness the Princess of Battenberg. The children, of course, became serene highnesses, too.

Meanwhile Prince Alexander was out of a job. He pushed on with his bride to Geneva, then as now the refuge of the affluent dispossessed, and let it be known that a former major general of the Imperial Russian Army sought suitable employment. After a year or so, his young cousin, Emperor Franz-Josef of Austria, decided to make him a major general in the Austrian Army, in command of the Cavalry Brigade.

Improbable as it may seem, Prince Alexander turned out to be an excellent general, though destiny played him the dirty trick of always putting him on the losing side. In 1859, he commanded an Austrian infantry division in the brief war against France and resurgent Italy. In three hot weeks in June he fought in two great battles—Magenta and Solférino—in which the Austrians were badly beaten; of all their generals only Alexander emerged with an enhanced reputation. At Solférino, after nearly sixteen hours of desperate fighting, in which the casualties of both sides totaled a staggering 38,000 men, the Austrian Army broke and ran. Prince Alexander averted a total rout by seizing the two-headed-eagle banner of his imperial cousin and galloping through his disorganized division, rallying them for a desperate charge that checked the triumphant French just long enough to safeguard the Austrian retreat.

Emperor Franz-Josef gratefully promoted Alexander to lieutenant general in 1861, and gave him the rare Order of Marie Thérèse, the Austrian equivalent of the Victoria Cross.

The following year Prince Alexander retired and went home at last to live in Hesse-Darmstadt, taking Julie and their five children with him. All five had been born in different places: Princess Marie in Geneva in 1852; Prince Louis at Graz in Austria in 1854; Alexander's first cry echoed from the storied piazza of Verona in 1857; Henry in Milan in 1858, while his father commanded the Austrian garrison; and Franz-Josef, born in 1861, could claim Padua as his native city. However interesting his pursuit of glory made this peripatetic life for Alexander, one may imagine how weary Julie was of gypsying around Europe, even though her caravan usually was drawn by four horses and her tents had marble halls.

Her husband brought her home to Schloss Heiligenberg, a fanciful country house with towers like Italian *campanili,* which stood in a wooded valley under a towering pine-clad mountain in the heart of Hesse-Darmstadt. Alexander had inherited it when he was thirteen, and it had remained empty for twenty-six years. Its crisp, pine-scented air, its stillness and serenity, its lawns and little lake, cleared farms and silent woods, and its many hospitable rooms made it a wonderful place to raise a family. It was Julie's first and only home; and though he became an Englishman, and took an English name, it was the place Prince Louis of Battenberg also thought of as "home."

Since Prince Louis was only eight when the family moved to Heiligenberg, he must have had but fragmentary memories of all those other houses, castles, villas, and army barracks he had lived in up to then. Heiligenberg formed the pattern of childhood for him even though he lived there only for six summers, for in winter the Battenbergs lived in the Alexander Palace in Darmstadt.

It was a gay and carefree life except on Sundays, which were rather awful. On that day Louis and his brothers were dressed up in the Russian national costume—loose collarless embroidered blouses of sky-blue or crimson silk and baggy black velvet breeches stuffed into high boots of soft red leather. In the morning the whole family went to church and then to Sunday dinner with the Grand Duke. From twenty to forty people sat down at an enormously long table loaded with heavy silver, and consumed a long succession of heavy meats served by lackeys in scarlet and gold. The Grand Duke, a mountain of flaccid flesh, over-flowed a thronelike armchair at the head of the table, while his guests were ranked in strict order of precedence down to the children at the end. Such a meal required at least three hours to consume and by that time the day was over.

Weekdays more than made up for Sunday's penance. Within the safety of their forest preserve the boys could fish and, when they grew older, shoot, a life-long love of Prince Louis. He also had a little Arabian mare from the King of Wurtemberg's stables to ride. Plenty of young visitors came to play with them, children of the Austrian and French ministers to Hesse-Darmstadt and their own royal cousins from all parts of Europe. Everyone was at least trilingual, and they babbled in English, French, and German interchangeably.

Once every summer Tsar Alexander II, who had inherited Russia in 1855, came with his family to Heiligenberg. It was more in the nature of a visitation than a visit. All the Battenbergs moved into a wing of the Slosh, as their English governess called it, so the Tsar could have their rooms. Though Prince Alexander was very glad to see his beloved sister again, and the young cousins had a wonderful time together, especially the little Romanovs free from the omnipresent secret police, it must have been a relief when they all went home.

However, no one grudged Tsar Alexander and his sweet wife their happy days at Heiligenberg. Ruling Russia was the most dangerous profession in the world. Though Alexander was a kind and liberal Tsar, who in 1861 took the revolutionary step of abolishing serfdom, he, like his predecessors and successors, lived in fear; and despite his benevolence he was assassinated by nihilists in 1881.

Even the tranquility of Heiligenberg was not as secure as it seemed. The people of Hesse-Darmstadt thoroughly disliked their indolent but autocratic Grand Duke. Beneath the grand duchy's fairytale landscape of turreted castles and picturesque villages, their discontent rumbled gently; however, prosperity and the army kept things from getting out of hand.

Meanwhile, the House of Hesse and the Rhine was still doing well in the matrimonial line. Young Louis' first cousin, Prince Louis, the heir of childless Grand Duke Louis III, married Queen Victoria's second daughter, Princess Alice of England, at Osborne on July 1, 1862. The Queen, deep in mourning for her beloved Albert, called it "the sad marriage," and, indeed, Princess Alice, though really in love with her husband, habitually wore a melancholy expression on her plain face. Young Louis grew very fond of her and she had a decisive influence on his life.

In the summer of 1866, the pleasant pattern of Louis' life was briefly interrupted by yet another war. Prussian Chancellor Prince Bismarck's insatiable ambition for his country led him to declare war on Austria. The little kingdoms and principalities of Saxony, Hanover, and Hesse ill-advisedly sided with Austria and raised an allied army. Prince Alexander was offered command of an army corps, and though he foresaw the dismal outcome, he felt duty-bound to accept it.

So on a lovely summer day Prince Louis watched his splendid father stride out onto the portico of Heiligenberg in the full panoply of a lieutenant general. Prince Alexander had grown from weedy youth to strong middle age. His luxuriant side-whiskers and long, curving mustache gave a proper military menace to his thin, intellectual face. The breast of his gold-laced tunic was a blaze of orders—fine targets for enemy sharpshooters. The prince patted his children's heads and kissed Julie tenderly. Then clapping on his plumed helmet, he swung himself onto his charger and cantered, clanking quietly, off to war.

Seven weeks later he rode home, honorably defeated once again. The amateur armies of the princely states never had a chance against Bismarck's superbly trained divisions, who smashed the Austrians at Königgratz and then brushed off the German Allies at the not very bloody battle of Aschaffenburg. The Prussians goose-stepped into Darmstadt with bands blaring, and pillaged the city and outlying villages in their customary lovable manner.

But Prince Alexander knew he had done his best, and he now retired for good—with no fewer than twenty-five grand crosses of different European orders in testimony to his gallantry and skill. His son was very happy to have him safely home; and those Englishmen, who later thought that Prince Louis of Battenberg must be pro-German because of his name, should have remembered that the first threat to his boyhood security was Prussia.

Boys grew up fast in the nineteenth century. They did not usually dawdle through a university, prolonging childhood by the artifice of education while making up their minds as to what they wanted to do. By the time he was twelve, Prince Louis knew exactly what his career would be. His decision, rather odd in his circumstances, was shaped by his cousin by marriage, Princess Alice.

Prince Louis dearly loved his British cousin and her two pretty baby daughters, Vicky and Ella. Whenever they were together they talked in English about England. Though Princess Alice spoke English with a German accent, as did her whole family, she was ardently British. She considered the Royal Navy a most glorious institution, and Louis listened for hours to her tales of tall ships and gallant men. He was especially interested in her brother Alfred, Duke of Edinburgh, who had decided to make the Navy his career.

Then Alfred himself arrived to visit his sister. Tall and broad-shouldered, in the long blue frock coat and heavy golden epaulettes of a post captain, with his golden hair, curly sidewhiskers, ruddy cheeks, and bright blue eyes, he was the beau ideal of a British sailor. Now Louis heard at first hand about the scrapes and fun and hardships of a midshipman's life. Alfred told him about storms at sea with a great ship knocked on her beam ends while her straining sails burst like cannon shots and waves smashed over her decks, about great battles of other days, about the new steam, iron-clad warships being built for Queen Victoria's Navy. He raised Louis' pulse as he described the great traditions of the service and the honor of being part of them. Before Alfred left Darmstadt, Prince Louis had made up his mind. He would be a sailor.

Though he was a spindly lad with a long triangular face, big solemn brown eyes, and a gentle manner, when Prince Louis made up his mind it was next to impossible to unmake it. His father tried and so did his other German relatives. They thought the whole idea was silly. As they pointed out, none of the German states had a navy worth mentioning, whereas their armies were the finest in Europe. That, they said, was where he belonged.

Prince Louis firmly reiterated his determination to seek honor on the sea. In that case, his father suggested, why not join the Austrian Navy? His cousin, Emperor Franz-Josef, would arrange everything. Prince Louis said he saw no reason to join a second-class fleet, when the greatest navy the world had ever known belonged to England. Prince Alexander patiently said, "To do that you would have to give up your German citizenship and become a British subject."

Prince Louis answered respectfully, "That is what I intend to do, sir."

And that is what he did.

Chapter 3

IN SPITE OF
ALL TEMPTATIONS...

WHEN PRINCE ALEXANDER FINALLY yielded to his son's determination, he did so right royally. He had two English tutors come to Hesse to coach Louis for his examinations. Mr. Everett of Magdalen College, Oxford, and an assistant, spent the summer of 1868 at Heiligenberg, cramming the necessary information into the boy's receptive mind.

By the end of summer Louis was fourteen and a half, then the usual age for cadets to enter the Royal Navy. On September 25, he left for England escorted by his devoted father and Mr. Everett. The North Sea gave their paddle-wheel packet quite a tossing, and Louis, who felt fine, was delighted when poor Mr. Everett rushed to the rail and gave up his lunch. In England Doctor Burney of Alverstoke cramming school took charge of things. He examined Louis and found that he was ahead of English boys his age in most things, but behind in the language itself.

On October 14, 1868, Louis went before the public notary at Gosport and swore the solemn oath of allegiance to the Queen of Great Britain and Ireland; he then signed a paper and became a British subject. After that, His Serene Highness Prince Louis of Battenberg was entered as a naval cadet in the British Navy and assigned to the *Victory* at

Portsmouth. Then came the delightful business of buying his uniforms and gear under the tutelage of Doctor Burney.

When they were ready Louis put on his monkey jacket with its rows of brass buttons, tight-bottomed trousers, and peaked cap, after which he was ceremoniously presented at Admiralty House to the Commander in Chief Portsmouth, Admiral Sir Thomas Pasley. Finally he reported for duty aboard *Victory*.

Prince Louis' first duty was a tour of the ship in charge of a petty officer. It was superb indoctrination had he needed any. The famous old ship-of-the-line looked very small to have carried so heavy a freight of history. Reverently Louis looked up through the intricate rigging at the masthead, from which had flown the great admiral's last immortal signal, and along the shadowy gundeck at the same cannon that had banged and bellowed at Trafalgar. The plate marking the spot where Nelson fell was holy ground to him.

As has been said, royal blood did smooth the first part of the way for a princely naval cadet. In those delightfully undemocratic days a glow of that divinity which still hedged a king illuminated even the person of a small serene highness. An early indication of this was that Prince Louis was invited to dine at Admiralty House with his commander in chief and the admiral's three old-maid daughters. A more important instance followed.

Prince Louis had been slated to join the training ship *Bristol*. Instead, he was ordered to the frigate *Ariadne* in which the Prince and Princess of Wales were to make a tour of the Mediterranean. Louis was not entirely pleased by this jolly prospect, for he reckoned that he would learn far less than he would have on the *Bristol*. Though he could hardly beg off the assignment without offending the next King of England, he realized that this was a hazard of birth and a forerunner of the sort of thing he would have to fight all his life if he was to have a serious naval career. But it was great fun.

Louis spent a happy German Christmas at Darmstadt, proudly wearing his new uniform all the time and lording it over his brother, Sandro (Alexander), who had only the glittering uniform of a captain in the Hessian Hussars, which both knew was play-acting, while Louis' ugly, dark blue uniform was the Real Thing.

Then Prince Alexander took his son to Trieste where, on January 20, 1869, Louis was rowed out in a howling gale to join *Ariadne*. She was an old-fashioned, square-rigged frigate whose design had hardly changed since Trafalgar, except that an auxiliary steam engine had been added; she was considerably faster under sail than under steam.

Much has been made of the hardships of a midshipman's life, and no doubt Prince Louis suffered some of them. In *Ariadne*, as in Nelson's navy, the midshipmen were quartered in the gunroom just aft of the forecastle on the lower deck. It was dark and cramped and smelled of sweat and sewage. A hammock is about as uncomfortable a place to sleep as man has invented, and the food was appalling. Almost until the present generation of pampered sailors, senior officers delighted in describing the slimy slumgullion and iron-hard, weevily biscuits they ate in their youth. How they loved those weevils in retrospect—they even broke them out of the biscuits and held weevil races. It was all part of the legend of wooden ships and iron men that never really died until the coddled crews of the steel ships of World War Two, like Mountbatten's *Kelly*, fed on ice cream and shown first-run movies every night, proved that it is not what is put into them that gives a man the guts to keep the guns firing as his ship is blown to glory.

Whatever the discomforts of *Ariadne*'s gunroom, Prince Louis soon enjoyed some dazzling changes of pace. On January 27, the Prince and Princess of Wales came alongside in the pretty paddle yacht *Psyche*, all gleaming in white and gold paint and shining brass. That first night Prince Louis was invited to dine with them in the spacious cabins specially built in *Ariadne* for their accommodation. If the food had not had a rating astronomically higher than that of the gunroom, one can be sure that Edward, Prince of Wales, would personally have keel-hauled the cook.

From then on Prince Louis alternated between gastronomic heaven and hell with dizzying speed. In Egypt the royal couple invited him to sail up the Nile with them. Their convoy included a large paddle steamer, which towed a specially built houseboat and was followed—to avoid the heat and smell of cooking—by a kitchen steamer. Right behind her came the provision ship loaded gunwale-deep with exotic food and a thousand bottles of champagne, three thousand claret, ten thousand beer, and twenty thousand soda water. She towed a stable-barge housing enough Arabian horses to mount a regiment of sheiks. The Duke of Sutherland and a convivial group of friends tagged along in a Nile steamer he had borrowed from the Khedive of Egypt.

It was a liberal education, though not exactly the sort Louis had sought. They toured ancient tombs and temples, hunted the local game, galloped their quick-footed Arabs madly across the desert, and had a banquet every night.

In Cairo, the famous iron man of Egypt, the Khedive Ismail Pasha, feted them extravagantly and presented decorations to all—including, of course, Midshipman Battenberg. Then they went in a special train to Suez where Count de Lesseps was finishing his canal, which was opened six months later.

The entire cruise was a series of wildly extravagant pageants—in Turkey and the Crimea, where Prince Louis and the whole glittering company charged over the course of the Light Brigade, in Greece, and in Italy. When the cruise finally ended in May, 1869, the jovial Prince of Wales had become very fond of his young kinsman, which was to cause several interruptions in his career. After a short leave at home Prince Louis was posted to the *Royal Alfred*, one of the newest ships in the Fleet.

Between them, Prince Louis of Battenberg and Lord Mountbatten served in the Royal Navy for nearly a hundred years, during which time two tremendous revolutions took place in sea warfare: the father went from wooden frigates to dreadnoughts; the son saw the dreadnoughts made obsolete by aircraft.

When Prince Louis entered the Navy in 1868, the first revolution was shivering the timbers of the Board of Admiralty. Only six years before, the naval battles of the American Civil War had proved that the largest wooden ship-of-the-line did not stand a chance against even a small steamer with improvised armor; and John Ericson's invention of the revolving turret mounting twin cannon for the U.S.S. *Monitor* had made obsolescent the conventional broadside arrangement of smooth-bore guns. However, the American ships could only fight in calm water.

Even more worrying to the sea lords was the French seagoing iron-clad *Gloire*, launched in 1859. They had nightmares of the *Gloire* and her ugly sisters sinking Her Majesty's entire navy. Confidential reports stated that, "The First Lord is very anxious, mortified and vexed by the progress of the French Iron-clad."

To meet this threat the British hastily produced a series of im-provised iron-clads. The *Royal Alfred* was one of these hybrids. She had been laid down as a wooden line-of-battle ship and switched in mid-building to an iron-clad. Her wooden sides were sheathed with 6-inch cast-iron armor, and she was armed with ten 9-inch rifled cannon, five on each broadside, and eight 7-inch rifled guns trained fore and aft. She was a full-rigged ship of 3,230 tons, with 29,000 square feet of canvas. Though she had an 800-horsepower steam engine, everything was arranged so she could go under sail in a hurry. The tall funnel amidships was collapsable and her drive shaft was ingeniously hinged so the propellor could be hauled up out of water when she was under sail. Like most mongrels she was ugly with an uncompromising, straight bow and a bobtailed stern in which, however, the mullion windows of a state cabin looked like an anachronistic vestige of a Spanish galleon.

In 1869, the *Royal Alfred* was flagship of the British West Indies Squadron. Prince Louis joined her at Halifax and served in her for four years and seven months. During that time he went home only once, in the summer of 1870, when he went to Darmstadt on leave in order to be confirmed in the Lutheran Church.

Those were the years when he learned to be a real sailor. This was no royal junket around an inland sea, but the normal routine of a foreign-station ship, with hard, any-weather sailing from the tropics to the near-Arctic north. In spite of steam and iron plating, this was the old navy still. Officers were supposed to be so rugged that they did not even have overcoats until Prince Alfred introduced them in 1874.

Possibly to keep warm, or cool off, everyone drank a great deal; rum was served even to the midshipmen. Louis appears to have sold most of his ration to other officers in order to buy sweets, but he saw some heroic drinking parties. Once when the *Alfred*'s midshipmen entertained their fellows from five other ships of the squadron, Prince Louis could not participate, being officer of the watch. Foreseeing the inevitable he chalked the names of the other ships at intervals along the deck. As the party drew to a close the unconscious bodies of the guests were carried up on deck and laid carefully in the allotted areas so there would be no trouble sorting them out and loading them in the proper boats.

Flogging had not yet been abolished. Prince Louis recorded that it was "a grewsome sight," the first time he saw a man spread-eagled on a grating to get seventy-two lashes for a minor insubordination.

The gunroom of the *Royal Alfred* was even worse than *Ariadne*'s. It was below the water line, so it had virtually no air or daylight. Aboard ship there was no favoritism for royal blood. Prince Louis ate those weevily biscuits for weeks at a time, and clambered up the high rigging in blazing sun and furious equinoctial storms. Scampering like a monkey over the sloping decks, battered and soaked by seas slamming over the bulwarks, while senior officers roared orders through megaphones, he learned the art of handling those clumsy yet wonderfully responsive creations of wood and copper rivets, eighty-foot tree trunks, and acres of canvas, so that when his time came to command he felt instinctively the mood of a ship as a fine horseman senses the capability of his mount.

By actual practice, trial and error—and the tactful, *sotto voce* suggestions of an old boatswain's mate—he learned how to handle eight-oared whaleboats in a tide-rip, how to handle men in a crisis, and above all how to handle himself under any circumstances.

During that time he was studying the theory as well as the practice of his profession under the tutelage of the ship's officers. In October, 1869, he passed his examination for midshipman. The next hurdle was the intermediate examination to become a senior midshipman, which he passed in April, 1872. With this he graduated from the childish monkey jacket to the double-breasted, long-skirted frock coat of an officer. He continued to study hard for the next grade, sub-lieutenant, and to absorb enthusiastically the rough lessons of practical seamanship for which theory is no substitute.

Service in the *Alfred*, nonetheless, was far from being all hard work and no fun. Among Prince Louis' twenty-six fellow midshipmen he made many life-long friends—who nicknamed him "P.L." by which he was henceforth known throughout his years in the Navy. Chief among these friends was a gay blade named Frederick Spring-Rice. On cruises Louis amused himself by making excellent drawings of the picturesque scenes he witnessed, and he also made music—there was a piano in the captain's cabin on which he frequently played duets with the bandsmen or accompanied Captain Nicholson as he sang in a fine voice whose tremendous volume resulted from issuing orders to the topmen through a megaphone.

Though Prince Louis had a lowly place in the hierarchy of command on shipboard, ashore he was still a royal prince who ranked—in the eyes of the ladies at least—next to or above his commander in chief, Vice-Admiral Edward Fanshawe. He was asked to all the balls, banquets, and other entertainments offered to the officers of the squadron, and a good many others as well. When the *Royal Alfred* came into port the newspapers were apt to feature the midshipman. In Barbados the local paper inaccurately announced: "The Prince of Brandenburg [sic], the brother of the Empresses of Austria and Russia, is serving in the flagship as a midshipman." That set all the mothers in town planning. There was no segregation in Barbados and Prince Louis wrote home that his partners at the balls were white, black, and colored. "All were very nice," he added.

He generally took his leaves when the ship was in Quebec or Halifax, going down to the United States because they interested him. In September, 1872, he and another midshipman rode the rattlebang steam cars as far west as St. Louis, taking in Detroit, Chicago, Cincinnati, Toledo, Cleveland, and Buffalo as well. That, too, was an important part of his education, for, as late as 1904, many senior British officers, including the great Admiral Lord Fisher, disliked and distrusted Americans.*

The *Royal Alfred* roared home across the North Atlantic before a winter gale, and anchored at Spithead on January 3, 1874. Louis went home to Darmstadt on leave. The family waiting for him at the station did not recognize the broad-shouldered, bronzed six-footer who stepped out onto the platform. Prince Louis noted that they all looked smaller than he remembered.

Back in England, he was assigned for a month to the Port Guard ship *Wellington*, so he could cram for his examination for promotion. The president of the Board of Admirals who examined him said that he had passed the best examination in the history of the ship. The admirals were especially impressed by his logbooks illustrated with his professionally drawn sketches and plans.

Sub-Lieutenant Battenberg went on to gunnery school, in Portsmouth, where he made an equally brilliant record. While there he weekended with Queen Victoria at Osborne on the Isle of Wight and with the Prince of Wales at Sandringham. From gunnery school he went to the Naval College at Greenwich to brush up in the classics and languages. It was here that he first encountered trouble because of his German name. The professor of French was still burning with indignation over the defeat of his country in the Franco-Prussian war only three years before. Though Prince Louis spoke the language well, and his fellow students hardly knew *dame* from *vache*, the professor ranked him way down on the list. This kept him from getting another "First."

By now Prince Louis had been studying ashore for nearly eighteen months, interrupted, however, by frequent leaves. He had worked hard, but the courses seem rather cursory when compared with the four years of intensive study required at the United States Naval Academy. The result appears to have been that the young American officers of the late nineteenth century had considerably more theoretical knowledge than the British, who received more experience in seamanship.

Throughout this period of schooling Prince Louis was officially attached to H.M.S. *Excellent*. Of all the strange craft in which he served during this era of naval evolution, *Excellent* was the weirdest. Used for experimental gunnery she was about the size of a large tugboat; just forward of her stubby mast was a huge 9-inch rifled cannon (nearly half as long as the ship) mounted in an impromptu revolving turret.

---

*Lord Fisher later became frantically pro-American, and worked furiously for an Anglo-American federation. [See p. 64.]

How she could float, let alone move through the water, was an esoteric mystery of naval architecture. Had she ever fired that gun broadside she might well have been knocked bottom up. Presumably Prince Louis did firing practice in her; if so, he must have learned several things not in the books.

During his long stay in England Prince Louis also added to his experiences by falling in love. He would have had to be inhuman to avoid it, for English girls were quite as much attracted to this up-standing young lieutenant, with his light brown mustache and the promising beginnings of a fine curly beard, as the young ladies of Barbados had been. True, he had very little money, but who needed money with his resplendent relatives?

P.L. thought that the loveliest of them all was the Honorable Violet White, daughter of Lord Annalay. She was, indeed, an authentic Irish beauty with the lilt of Irish laughter in her voice. And she was very much in love with him.

Prince Louis asked her to marry him and she accepted. It was rather naïve of him to do so without consulting his own family; but Louis was then, and all his life, pleasantly indifferent to the importance generally attached to his royal connections. He thought of himself quite simply as a naval officer and wished other people would do the same. Thus he was astonished at the storm in his own family generated by his engagement. England joined Hesse and the Rhine in opposition. Everyone agreed that it would have to be a morganatic marriage, and two such in succeeding generations were too many. Even Prince Alexander, though he did not regret his own, urged his son not to follow his example. No doubt the Prince of Wales had a long serious talk with his young protégé; and from Osborne came the rumblings of even more august displeasure, for Queen Victoria was the greatest snob of her remarkable era.

There is no documentary evidence as to just how the matter was settled; but the logic of character is a key to the solution. Prince Louis was a young man with a high sense of loyalty and honor, and very little regard for rank. He was also extremely stubborn. It is unthinkable that he yielded to threat or to logic. On the other hand, the Irish are a proud and touchy lot, especially touchy when it comes to being patronized by the English. So it is reasonable to assume that Lord Annalay said he would be damned if there would be any morganatic monkeyshines about his daughter's marriage, and that the spirited Miss White herself broke the engagement.

The extraordinary and pleasant feature of this otherwise sad little episode is that friendship was not broken. All his life Prince Louis remained on warmly affectionate terms with Violet White, who later married Lord Percy St. Maur, and with her older sister, the Countess of Leicester. An interesting comment on times changing for the better is that Lady Leicester's grandson, Angus Ogilvie, married H.R.H. Princess Alexandra of Kent with the enthusiastic approbation of the Queen of England, and Princess Anne as a bridesmaid.

Perhaps as a consolation prize for being a good boy, perhaps to remove him from temptation, the Prince of Wales commanded Prince Louis to accompany him on his tour of India in 1875–76. This was no more likely to forward a naval career than was the trip of 1869, but again it was impossible to refuse. So he reported aboard *Serapis* on September 7, 1875.

To board the ancient troopship was to take a step backward in time. Full-rigged with a spacious main deck uncluttered by armament, her engine power was obsolete even then. But she was remarkably comfortable, having been rebuilt inside for the accommodation of Prince Edward and his suite, who joined the ship at Brindisi on October 16.

Like most of Prince Edward's chosen companions they were a gay company, except for a few circumspect individuals like Canon Duckworth, sent along by the Queen to preserve a semblance of decorum. The Duke of Sutherland was among them and several other rich young peers, as well as W. H. Russell representing *The Times*, and Mr. Simpson, an artist for *The Illustrated London News*. Perhaps the most interesting from Prince Louis' point of view was Lord Charles Beresford, who also had a passion for the Navy. In addition to being a superb officer destined for the highest rank, Lord Charles was immensely charming and a great wit, whose imitations of famous people set the company roaring with laughter. Incidentally, it was his most famous imitation of Majesty Herself, which later provoked Queen Victoria's crushing, "We are not amused."

Beresford's combination of technical brilliance, dedication to the service, and social grace won the heartfelt admiration of the young man who hoped to follow in his footsteps and who, in fact, did. Beresford responded warmly, as he always did, to youthful hero worship, and a friendship grew that was to flourish until the time when an embittered old sailor, beached in a London club, treacherously struck it down.

The Indian Tour of the Prince of Wales made his previous trip around the Mediterranean look like an economy-class Cook's Tour. Though Prince Louis was only an officer of the *Serapis* and not an official member of the suite, Edward took him along on all the junkets.

From Calcutta they crisscrossed the length and breadth of India, Nepal, and Kashmir, traveling seven thousand miles in a special train, with two other trains to carry food and servants. Where the rails did not yet run, as in the Princely State of Gwalior, they traveled in carriages drawn at a gallop by teams of four artillery horses; the teams were changed every six miles. In Lahore they rode in charabancs pulled by six dromedaries mounted by liveried postilions.

The whole trip was one tremendous *durbar* after another—levées, state banquets, state balls, garden parties, inspections, cornerstone layings, and municipal luncheons. The Indian princes vied with each other to see who could entertain Prince Edward with the most riotous magnificence. Cities of gorgeous tents, with silver-plated tent poles and luxurious furniture sprang up, manned by five thousand servants and retainers. Full orchestras played every night and thousands of gallons of champagne were consumed by a company whose brilliant, multicolored raiment, dazzling decorations, and jeweled ornaments would have made King Solomon look like a Puritan.

Nor was sport neglected. There was pig sticking, in which, on horseback and with lances, they pursued wild boars over the rocky terrain. Prince Louis, on a small Arab as handy as a polo pony, got his pig, but another boar got him. It charged his horse, overturning it. Prince Louis was found unconscious with a broken collarbone. He said later, "My brain was somewhat shaken. . . ." Nonetheless, he came off better than poor Beresford, who had all his front teeth knocked out as he leaned down to drive his spear into a boar which inconsiderately bucked it back into his face.

The inevitable tiger hunts were more spectacular, but far less dangerous, with eight hundred elephants directed by bugle calls, and battalions of beaters driving the game. Only the Prince of Wales was allowed to shoot lest someone shoot him in the excitement; so Louis was a mere spectator, sitting in a howdah with his arm in a sling. On another hunt, however, Prince Edward's elephant, frightened by a tiger, dashed under a tree and knocked down a bee's nest; while Prince Edward fought off the bees, Louis shot the tiger.

After four frenzied months in India it must have been pleasant indeed for Louis when the party rejoined *Serapis* at Bombay. He immediately resumed his normal duties—"I kept the middle watch that night."

While living in enormous luxury, Prince Louis never had more than a few pounds in his pocket. This anomalous situation, which would have been galling to a man of a different temperament, apparently bothered him not at all. However, he never lost a chance to make a little—honest —money on the side. At Bombay Mr. Simpson of *The Illustrated London News* got a telegram ordering him to China if he could find an artist to take his place. Prince Louis offered his services, and he found wonderful material for his pen on the voyage home. The ship was a floating menagerie, for Prince Edward had been presented with a variety of wildlife ranging from a Bengal tiger to ostriches and peccaries. The hold was full of beasts and the less dangerous were exercised on deck. Louis' delightfully humorous sketches made a hit with the editors. He wrote, "They very nearly filled a copy of the paper. I made quite a lot of money and Simpson had me elected Honorary Member of the Institute of Painters in Water Colours. . . ."

Twice more in this period Prince Louis was tempted by the devil of distraction. At Bombay he received a letter from the Duke of Edinburgh inviting him to join his ship, H.M.S. *Sultan,* which was not temptation but a call to duty, for the Duke was an excellent and hard-driving captain. The Prince of Wales begged Louis not to accept, but instead to go on half pay for a while and join his entourage at Marlborough House. This action would have opened a vista of endless gaiety and advancement in royal favor, but Prince Louis politely yet firmly turned it down.

In 1878—when Bulgaria, having gained her freedom from Turkish misrule during the Russo-Turkish war, was constituted as a semi-independent principality by the Congress of Berlin—came the devil's second, more resplendent offer. A principality without a properly royal prince was an anomaly in those king-conscious days, so the Bulgars went shopping for a sovereign.

To his considerable astonishment Prince Louis was offered the throne of Bulgaria by emissaries from the new principality and the Congress of Berlin. With even less hesitation than in the case of Prince Edward, to whom he was devoted, Louis turned the offer down. "The deck of a British warship" was, indeed, his home. The Bulgars turned to Louis' brother, Prince Alexander of Battenberg. He accepted and thus became the first of the Battenberg men to rise from Serene to Royal Highness.

Chapter 4

POWER POLITICS

—OLD STYLE

The *Serapis* ANCHORED in the Solent on May 11, 1876. Two days later the Prince of Wales rewarded her officers with promotions, and Prince Louis now could drop the sub from lieutenant. In July he joined the *Sultan* commanded by Captain H.R.H. Prince Alfred, Duke of Edinburgh, in Besika Bay in Turkey.

The *Sultan* was the biggest, most modern ship in which Prince Louis had yet sailed, but she was still an evolutionary hybrid. Her armament—eight 10-inch rifled guns mounted on her broadside and four 9-inchers mounted in side ports, so they could fire forward or back at an angle—was murderous for her time. She was thick-skinned with nine inches of armor backed by twelve inches of teak outside the thin iron hull protecting her vitals. The bow and stern were largely unprotected on the theory that the central citadel would keep her afloat, even if her extremities were shot full of holes.

However, the *Sultan* still showed the Admiralty's indecision between sail and steam.* At a time when transatlantic liners had only

---

*There was a reason behind this insistence on sail power. Because of the distances British warships had to cover in guarding their world-wide trade, it was essential that they be able to reach the scene of action without depleting their limited supply of coal. Not until Britain had established coaling stations all over the world was the Royal Navy freed from dependence on the wind.

vestigial rigging, the *Sultan* was bark-rigged with two tall masts forward and a stumpy mizzenmast aft; two tall funnels were set abreast, just behind the foremast. She was slightly faster under steam than sail, since her reciprocating engine could drive her at fourteen knots. Under both sail and steam in a good blow she could probably manage 16 knots, but she was an anachronistic sight, with her black slab-sided hull and the black smoke pouring from her funnels between the straining white sails. Her long bowsprit, carrying a cloud of staysails, jibs, balloon jibs, and flying jibs, slanted upward far beyond her ugly straight-cut bow, while the galleon-like windows of her state cabin broke the armored defenses of her bobtail stern. One further reminder of the good old days: Prince Louis' small cabin was infested with rats.

Cruising the Mediterranean with Queen Victoria's son as your captain might sound like another soft job. It was not. According to Prince Louis' biographer, Admiral Mark Kerr, he was made "signal mate [he had become an expert in this field in the *Royal Alfred*] in addition to which he relieved the officer of the Morning Watch when he went down to change his clothes (for breakfast); kept the First Dog Watch at sea; was the permanent Officer of the Guard in harbor and took the place of any lieutenant who went sick or on leave." As though this were not enough, Prince Alfred named Louis his equerry. P.L. was forced to accept the appointment much against his will. He thought it was a mistake for there was a lot of hard work involved, including answering Prince Alfred's mail, and he always had to eat with the prince, which, of course, kept him apart from his fellow officers.

Under the heading of "pleasure" was playing piano accompaniment to the Duke of Edinburgh's violin. Since the Duke had an uncertain ear, he often flatted excruciatingly. It was better when he conducted the massed bands of the Fleet for he could, at least, keep time.

Another of Prince Louis' jobs was as messenger and intermediary between the Duke and his executive officer who were not on speaking terms. But P.L. was finally convinced of the error of being an equerry when the Duchess of Edinburgh, who was his Cousin Marie (the daughter of Tsar Alexander II) and her two little girls came aboard at Malta for a cruise to Villefranche. It was a rough passage during which the duchess and both nurses collapsed. There was no one but his less-than-Serene Highness left to feed, wash, and dress the babies. Prince Louis, however, was indirectly compensated. While at Villefranche he went to Monte Carlo where he put two louis ($8) on the red, which came up nine times in succession. His winnings amounted to $4,096, less his original stake.

During his service in the *Sultan* Prince Louis saw and took part in the implementation of power politics—old style. The Mediterranean was, in effect, a British lake. Her Majesty's Government proposed to keep it so, for they regarded it as the life line of the Empire. By far the strongest of the British fleets was stationed there, based on Malta. At that time the Admiralty considered France the most dangerous possible enemy, with Russia second; hence British naval policy called for a navy easily able to defeat the French and Russian fleets combined. The new German Empire, founded in 1871 by bringing all the small German states like Hesse-Darmstadt under the sovereignty of Prussia, had the strongest army in Europe, but no navy worth bothering about.

In the 1870s the Russian menace loomed large in British thinking. Her policy aimed to take Constantinople from the decadent Turkish Empire in order to secure an ice-free port and a window on the Mediterranean. The main object of British policy was to prevent this, even though it meant supporting the "unspeakable Turk." "Unspeakable" was justified when one considers the way the Turks treated their Christian subjects in Bulgaria and their other Balkan provinces. This behavior lent a moral sanction to Russia's political ambitions and damaged Britain's position. Christian indignation finally brought about a conference between the Great Powers and Turkey in Constantinople in 1876. The Powers agreed on demands for better government for the Sultan's Christian subjects, but when the Turks refused them, Russia had a green light.

During the entire time Prince Louis served in the *Sultan*, the danger of a Russian thrust toward Constantinople called the tune to which the British fleet danced back and forth in a sort of seagoing minuet. When the Russians assumed a threatening pose the fleet advanced to Besika Bay; then Russia would draw back and, when tension relaxed, the ships retired to Malta.

In 1877, the Russians finally declared war on Turkey. Their enormous army steamrollered through the Balkans, right up to the gates of Constantinople. The fleet had, of course, moved to Besika. The two admirals and those officers who were horsemen, including Prince Louis, were fox hunting when a messenger came galloping across the rugged Turkish landscape with a dispatch ordering the fleet to Chanak, the main Turkish defense of the Dardanelles. Hounds were whipped off a hot scent and everyone tore back to the beach, where horses, hounds, kennels, kennelmen, and hunt servants were hastily loaded in the ships, which, thus prepared for any eventuality, sailed for the Dardanelles and a possible war.

When they reached the strategic strait the Turks, whom they had come to help, refused them permission to enter—the Turks distrusted the British only a little less than they distrusted the Russians—and for three days the ships circled around like hounds at fault. Then orders came from the Admiralty to go in anyway and help the Turks whether they liked it or not.

The ships were cleared for action; the horses, hounds, and huntsmen were marooned ashore. Early on a bitterly cold and lowering morning the line of black-hulled ships steamed slowly between the fortified headlands. This was the first time Prince Louis had felt the tension of war. No one knew whether the Turkish forts would open fire or not. The ships' guns were trained and gunners stood tensely by with lanyards in hand. Prince Louis, as signal mate, was on deck peering through a spyglass at Admiral Sir Geoffrey Phipps Hornby's flagship *Alexander*, to get signaled orders, and at the forts, for the flash and smoke of cannon.

At this critical moment the iron-gray sky dissolved in snow that blotted out the forts. The fleet moved blindly on until *Alexander* shuddered to a stop on a sand bar. *Sultan* sheered off quickly and anchored, as did the rest of the fleet. An anchor cable was sent to the flagship, who managed to heave herself off. As she floated free the snow stopped as suddenly as it had begun. To their horror the British officers saw that the fleet had anchored directly under the huge cannon of Fort Medjedieh.

Fortunately, the Turks only fired off a note ordering the British out, to which, of course, the British paid no attention. They continued to Gallipoli, where the Admiral detached a couple of battleships to help the unwilling Turks defend this vital position, and the rest of the fleet steamed on through the Sea of Marmara and anchored ten miles from Constantinople.

That was about all there was to it. Tsar Alexander II saw that he was not going to get Constantinople this time. Though his large army could easily have overwhelmed the Turks, once it got within cannon-shot of the fleet its light field pieces would have been helpless against the big guns of the armored ships. He started peace talks with the Turks.

While England and Russia were on the verge of war it occurred to no one in the fleet to doubt Prince Alfred's loyalty, because he was married to the daughter of the Tsar, or Prince Louis', even though his uncle by marriage, Alexander II, was personally commanding the Russian Army and his brother Sandro was fighting with the Russian cavalry. The fact is that as against the Turks both Alfred and Louis were strongly pro-Russian, but they were also loyal Englishmen—and if England's interest required them to fight *for* the Turks *against* the Russians they were prepared to do so with all their hearts.

During the peace talks, the Admiral gave Prince Louis permission to go through the lines and bring his brother back aboard the *Sultan*. When Prince Alexander arrived, the Admiral gave a gala dinner for him and the Duke of Edinburgh aboard the flagship. A few days later Prince Louis was similarly entertained by his brother and the Grand Duke Nicholas in the Russian camp.

Though professional soldiers and sailors understand that family affection does not imply treason, civilians are often less broadminded. When news of the interchange of hospitality reached London it caused a tremendous row. Even Queen Victoria, who was passionately pro-Turk, was furious, and wrote a hot letter to her son and an admonition to Prince Louis. The public reaction forced the Admiralty to order an investigation, but after hearing the facts they rather grudgingly cleared of wrongdoing the Duke, Prince Louis, and all concerned. The fact remains that it was very bad public relations on their part.

The "life line" secured once more, the fleet returned to Malta, where life must have been very pleasant. Both Prince Louis and his son, in his time, loved this picturesque island. When the fleet was in, the Duke and Duchess of Edinburgh lived at the San Antonio Palace, high on the hill above the harbor of Valletta. Prince Louis, in his capacity as equerry, lived there with them, going down to the *Sultan* with the Duke early every morning to perform his duties as a naval officer. The long hot afternoons were often free.

When P.L. first came to Malta the game of polo was just being introduced on the Mansa Parade Ground by army officers who had served in India. It looked like great fun to the young man, who loved horses next to ships. He bought a small polo pony named Snowflake, and enthusiastically took up the game; he was probably the first naval officer to do so. What a rare sight he must have been, careening madly over the field with his long legs almost touching the ground, his whiskers combed by the wind, and his eyes flashing with zest for sport and danger.

In April, 1878, Prince Louis went on leave and was then posted to H.M.S. *Agincourt*, an older ship than *Sultan*, hence representing no advance in naval design. He served in her until April, 1879, when he yielded to the affectionate insistence of the Prince of Wales and served in the Prince's yacht *Osborne* throughout the summer. Since her congenial commander was Captain Lord Charles Beresford it was a pleasant interlude. Among other things Prince Alexander of Battenberg, P.L.'s younger brother who had just been elected reigning Prince of Bulgaria, came to pay his respects to Queen Victoria. The British made a great to-do over him, and of course Prince Louis had a prominent part in all the festivities.

When autumn came the Prince of Wales wanted him to remain in the *Osborne*. Once again Prince Louis had to be disagreeably firm. He told the Prince that such service was doing his career no good; that he would rather go on half pay until he got another ship. Apparently the Prince realized his good sense, for he took no offense. In fact, he was so fond of P.L. that from 1876 until his marriage, Prince Louis had his own room at Marlborough House. He used it a lot that year, for he remained on the inactive list until August, 1880, when he was appointed to the *Inconstant*.

She was an iron frigate, so well designed that, in spite of her engine and propeller, she was a better sailer than the famous old wooden frigates. In company with four other ships known as the Flying Squadron, commanded by Admiral Lord Clanwilliam, she set off on a cruise around the world. The voyage was expected to last about a year, but it was two years before *Inconstant* anchored off Spithead again.

Prince Louis had many exciting and amusing adventures on the cruise of the *Inconstant*, but only a few of them are relevant, although each added to the sum total of his vast experience of men and ships and foreign lands. One apparently insignificant note at the time was the presence aboard of a very small and pink-cheeked midshipman named Mark Kerr. Prince Louis took a great liking to the boy, who fairly worshiped him. In time Mark Kerr became his flag-captain, his biographer, and perhaps his dearest friend. Another midshipman who went on the cruise also played an important role in Prince Louis' future. He was the son of the Prince of Wales Prince George, afterward King George V. With his older brother, Prince Albert Victor, later Duke of Clarence, who died in 1892, Prince George was in the *Bacchante*.

The Flying Squadron sailed first down the east coast of South America, then, on hurried orders from the Admiralty, crossed to South Africa, where the newly restless Boers had started a small rebellion, nearly twenty years before the Boer War. By the time the ships arrived the Boers had been quelled, for the time being, so after a pleasant stay at Cape Town, the Squadron headed eastward for Australia.

Flying before the wild westerly gale that blows constantly around the world in the Roaring Forties, *Inconstant* ran right out of sight of the other ships. She shortened sail and the others finally lifted their masts over the horizon, all except *Bacchante*. When days passed and she did not appear, Lord Clanwilliam and his officers began to worry. Prince

Louis was in a state of great anxiety for the young princes whom he had known and loved since childhood. He had reason to be.

As *Bacchante* tore along at 15 knots before the gale, coasting down the huge following seas like a tremendous surfboard and wallowing in the valleys between them until the next wave came to lift her stern high and drive her forward in a surge of foam, her rudderpost broke and she swerved out of control. The sharp report seemed like the crack of doom to every man aboard, for all knew that if she broached broadside to those forty-foot waves she would be swamped. Her captain, Lord Charles Scott, was an old-style sailor who remembered a trick that hardly ever had been used during the nineteenth century. Bellowing mightily through his megaphone he ordered the whole watch on deck into the forward rigging—the jib stays and the foremast yards and shrouds. Two hundred men obeyed, and their bodies acted like an enormous headsail on which the pressure of the wind forced *Bacchante*'s bow to leeward and held her stern to the gale. Meanwhile the men of the port watch worked madly to rig a jury rudder. So *Bacchante* was brought under partial control again and, driving still before the wind, came safely to the small Australian port of Albany. While *Bacchante* was being repaired, the royal midshipmen were transferred to *Inconstant*. Thus Prince Louis was for several months a shipmate of his future King.

The cruise of the *Inconstant* continued around the Pacific Ocean. Judging from his letters and diaries Prince Louis thoroughly enjoyed every place he visited. He described with gusto the pioneering society of Australia, the barbaric Fiji Islands, the sophisticated art of China's ancient civilization, and the startling contradictions of old ways and new in Japan, which was emerging from the chrysalis of her ancient isolation into a modern nation. The reception of the Squadron in Japan far exceeded the welcome it received anywhere else. The Son of Heaven himself received the English princes in a gold-embroidered tent, and gave a great dinner in their honor in his double-moated palace in Tokyo. Though in his diary Prince Louis poked gentle fun at such pathetic efforts to copy European customs as the garish pink and blue uniforms and comic-opera decorations of the Japanese military, he was alive to the beauty of the land and the charm of its people. He carried away a small bit of Japanese art—a fiery dragon tatooed on his left arm.

Inconstant did not go around the world after all, but retraced her course to the Cape of Good Hope and thence to St. Helena and the Cape Verde Islands. There, power politics diverted her homeward course once again to Egypt. Arabi Pasha had revolted against Khedive

Ismail Pasha and set up a military dictatorship. France and England reacted to this threat against the Suez Canal by sending an allied fleet to
Alexandria "to protect their nationals." The immediate result was that a
lot of their nationals were promptly murdered in the streets, and Arabi
Pasha began to strengthen the fortifications.

When the British admiral demanded that the work stop, Arabi
Pasha told him where to go. At this, "the French ships sailed away in
dismay," but the Royal Navy was not bluffed that easily. The fleet
sailed in and blew the stuffing out of the old forts. Arabi Pasha and his
army left town hurriedly.

Inconstant arrived too late for the bombardment, but Prince Louis
was ordered to take a company of bluejackets ashore to guard the
Khedive who had been locked up in his palace. With little Midshipman
Kerr as his second in command and two of the newly invented Gatling
guns to strengthen his fire power, Prince Louis marched his men through
the deserted streets of Alexandria and bedded them down in the
Khedive's harem—from which the women, unfortunately, had fled. It
was a neat little military operation, but no special danger had been involved.

Two weeks later a small British army captured Arabi Pasha and
restored dear old, corrupt Ismail Pasha as Khedive. Prince Louis wrote,
"My picnic . . . suddenly came to an end and we reembarked."

On October 16, 1882, *Inconstant* anchored at Spithead, exactly two
years after she had left.

Chapter 5

BALKAN DETOUR

PRINCE LOUIS SPENT the winter and spring of 1883 on half pay. A proper snowy Christmas at Darmstadt was followed by a trip to Bulgaria in March to see his brother, Prince Alexander, in his new principality.

Sandro was having a stormy passage. He had been just twenty-two when he assumed the throne in 1879. Although in theory Bulgaria still owed a shadowy allegiance to Turkey, in practice she was a Russian satellite. Prince Alexander believed that he should rule for the benefit of the Bulgars not the Russians. Early in 1880 Sandro went to St. Petersburg to visit the Tsar. His father and Prince Louis, who was between ships, were due to arrive one evening just before dinner. Their train was a little late so Alexander II ordered dinner delayed while Sandro went to the station to meet them. As the Tsar was impatiently awaiting his guests, a time bomb exploded in the dining hall of the Winter Palace, totally wrecking it and killing over a hundred guardsmen quartered on the floor above. Had the train been on time the bomb would have killed the entire Imperial family and both Battenberg brothers as well.

Alexander II felt very grateful to his nephew, and Sandro had no difficulty persuading the Tsar to allow him a fairly free hand with the Bulgars. As long as the liberal Alexander II lived there was no trouble. But the odds against a Tsar were multiplied in exact ratio to the number of attempts on his life. In 1881 his luck ran out as a nihilist bomb found its mark.

Sandro went to St. Petersburg again in 1882 for the coronation of his cousin, Tsar Alexander III, who had been shocked into an autocratic frame of mind. There would be none of this liberal nonsense of his father's. Sandro was told he would have to follow orders, and the cousins quarreled heatedly.

When Sandro came back to his capital, Sofia, he found that the two Russian generals whom he had appointed as regents had issued some oppressive decrees. He promptly fired the generals and rescinded their decrees, which made him extremely popular with the Bulgars, and intensely unpopular with the Tsar.

When Prince Louis reached Sofia the following year, the situation was uneasy. As they drove together through streets lined with Sandro's cheering subjects, Louis did not doubt his brother's popularity; but he knew that the Tsar was conspiring against Sandro. Since the Prince owed his throne, and Bulgaria owed its very existence, to the force of Russian arms, it was a perilous position.

Very foolishly, but at least bravely, Sandro decided to pay a visit to his theoretical suzerain, the Sultan, in an attempt to balance Turkey against Russia. He invited Prince Louis to go with him as counselor and friend. The brothers drove halfway across Bulgaria to the Black Sea in an open carriage, and then went by yacht to Constantinople. The visit was outwardly successful. The Sultan could not do enough for the princes socially; but he could do nothing politically, simply because his corrupt and decaying country did not have the military power to challenge Russia.

Had Prince Louis had the political sagacity of his later years he indubitably would have dissuaded his brother from a course that was bound to inflame the Tsar. But he was less than thirty and his brother was only twenty-six. They were babes in the political woods, pushed by birth into positions of power without adequate preparation; and they were under all sorts of pressures: from Alexander's subjects, from French and English diplomats cynically playing the power game, and even from Queen Victoria, who was emotionally governed by her dislike of Russia, and kept writing to them to stand firm. They had not learned the maxim, "Statesmanship is doing what is politically possible in the right direction." So hapless Sandro tackled the impossible, and Prince Louis egged him on.

After the Turkish visit the brothers parted, Louis to return to Darmstadt, Prince Alexander to his increasingly difficult role in Bulgaria, where his relations with Russia went from bad to worse. In 1883 he became secretly engaged to Princess Victoria of Prussia, daughter of

Crown Prince Frederick of Germany who was married to Queen Victoria's eldest daughter. Her parents were delighted with the match, but the sapient old German Chancellor, Prince Otto von Bismarck, the cornerstone of whose policy was to keep Russia on friendly terms with Germany, violently opposed it on the theory that to give Bulgaria a Prussian princess would be "like throwing a marshal's baton over the walls of a besieged fortress." Bismarck won, even though Queen Victoria also favored the match as a way of putting a spoke in Russia's wheel.

Meanwhile, unlucky Prince Alexander got into further difficulties. The southern part of Bulgaria, still a Turkish province, revolted successfully and asked to join Bulgaria. The Prince rashly granted permission without consulting the Tsar, who furiously declared the union illegal and ordered the senior Russian officers, who held all the field commands in the Bulgarian Army, to resign. England and France gaily supported Prince Alexander's action—anything to annoy Russia. This threw the Tsar into such a fury that, as his grandfather had done to Alexander's father after the elopement, he struck the Prince's name from the Russian Army lists.

This did not cause Sandro much concern, but the loss of the Russian officers left his army thoroughly disorganized and with no officers above the rank of captain. Taking advantage of this situation, King Milan of Servia deliberately picked a quarrel with Bulgaria and declared war in November. The Tsar sat back happily and waited for Alexander to call for help.

Some Battenbergs were brighter politicians than others, but they were all good fighters. Prince Alexander took personal command of the Bulgarian Army and, with his youngest brother, Franz-Josef, who had left the Prussian Guard to join him, he hastily reorganized it, promoting captains to generals and lieutenants to colonels. Commanding this jerry-built war machine he marched to face the professional generals of Servia.

The small armies met at Slivnovitz near the Servian frontier. As occasionally happens in the unpredictable art of war, the amateurs outgeneraled the old pros. King Milan and his troops were chased back over the border, and Prince Alexander was given an almost Roman triumph by his hilarious subjects on his return to Sofia. The Tsar was not pleased.

For a few years more the young Prince balanced precariously on his throne, pulled, hauled, and jostled by the competing Great Powers, supported only by his subjects. But his cousin in St. Petersburg played the subtle game of those who cannot achieve their purpose by straightforward bullying. First there was an apparent rapprochement, and some of the Russian officers returned to help train the Army. Then, in the summer of 1886, the Tsar sent a secret message to Alexander that King Milan was preparing for war again. Acting promptly on this intelligence Alexander sent his best troops to the frontier, despite warnings from his loyal Bulgarian officers. When Sofia was nearly bare of troops, the Russian officers engineered a *coup d'état:* With a couple of regiments of unreliable Bulgarian troops they stormed the palace and took Alexander and Franz-Josef prisoner.

Naturally no harm was done them, for royal blood was more sacred in those romantic days than it has ever been before or since. The princely brothers were escorted to the royal yacht at Rachovo on the Black Sea. She took them to a Russian port from which they were shipped overland in a special train to Limburg in Austrian Galicia. Prince Louis and their father came dashing up from Darmstadt to meet them. Also greeting them was the news that Alexander's loyal subjects had retaken Sofia and kicked the Russians out. They wanted him to come home.

Father and sons held a council of war in Limburg. Sandro honestly desired to do what was best for his Bulgars. But what was best? He knew his people loved him, he knew that there were many things he could do for them, chief of which was giving them an honest, pro-Bulgarian government. He also knew that his return would bring down on them the Tsar's implacable enmity, and he knew that Russia was all powerful in the Balkans. Had he the right to expose them to such harassment as they could then expect?

His father answered, "Yes." More important, Prince Louis answered, "Yes!" He had no doubts of the right course, for his training and his temperament urged bold action. He probably honestly believed that his brother's return would be best for the Bulgars. He knew it was better for England to have Alexander, rather than a Russian puppet, on the throne, and he was, above all, a patriotic Briton. Furthermore he carried powerful arguments in his dispatch case—a personal message from Queen Victoria urging Alexander to return to Sofia, and a similar one from the Crown Princess of Germany.

The prestige and power of these appeals, supported by the charm and logic of the older brother he adored, overcame Prince Alexander's better judgment. He knew the English Queen's writ ran no further than a cannon shot from the sea, and that Prince Bismarck would never do anything to alienate Russia, no matter what the Crown Princess thought. Nevertheless, the messages gave him hope that perhaps diplomatic pressure could be brought to bear on the Tsar and that with England and Germany on his side things might not be too difficult. Perhaps the clinching word was spoken when Prince Louis said, "If you'll go back, I'll go with you!"

So the three brothers came to Sofia where there was a welcome home for Alexander that brought tears to all their eyes; Bulgarian Prince, Prussian Guardsman, and British naval officer—they were all sentimental German youths.

Of course it did not last. The Tsar formally announced to all the Great Powers that as long as Alexander remained her Prince, Bulgaria would be his enemy. Alexander had no answer to that except to abdicate; to remain would have been an act of selfish egotism of which he was incapable. For the last time he drove through the streets of his capital with tears in his eyes. And his people wept with him.

The rest of Alexander's story is anticlimactic. The project of his marriage to Princess Victoria of Prussia was revived, but Bismarck remained obdurate, probably to thwart Victoria's mother, the Crown Princess, whom he detested; Queen Victoria withdrew her support; Princess Victoria's brother, Prince Wilhelm, soon to be Wilhelm II of Germany, angrily denounced the marriage. So the off-again-on-again engagement was finally broken.

In 1889 Prince Alexander wearily renounced his rank and titles in favor of a morganatic marriage to Johanna Loisinger, a young opera star of the Darmstadt Court Theatre. His cousin, the Grand Duke Louis IV, gave him the non-royal title of Count Hartenau. To have something to do, this former ruling prince, commander in chief, and general entered the Austrian Army as a lieutenant colonel. Wearing the insignia of his comparatively humble rank and the grand crosses of thirty-six different orders, which kings and emperors had given him in his days of glory, he must have been an unusual and pathetic sight.

Alexander died in 1893 at Graz, where Prince Louis had been born. He was only thirty-six. His widow outlived him by fifty-eight years, dying in Vienna in 1951.

Chapter 6

TWO ROYAL
WEDDINGS

WHILE THE FORTUNES OF Prince Alexander were rising and falling, two
of his brothers were consolidating the family position in the hierarchy
of royalty. It has been noted that in 1883 Prince Louis spent a great
part of his long wait between ships in Hesse-Darmstadt, where there
had been considerable change. In 1877, the porcine, autocratic Grand
Duke Louis III died and was succeeded by his amiable nephew, Louis
IV. The following year, the new Grand Duke's wife, sad, sweet Princess
Alice, caught diphtheria from her children and died. Her eldest daughter, Victoria, age fifteen, became head of her father's household and
brought up the younger children.

In Darmstadt, Prince Louis lived with his father and mother at the
Alexander Palace or Heiligenberg, but he spent a great deal of time at
the Grand Ducal Palace and his cousin's favorite country house, Wolfs-
garten. There he fondly watched Vicky grow up as she assumed her
responsibilities. His feeling for her had been elder-brotherly affection
until he returned from the long cruise in the *Inconstant*. In 1883, Vicky
was twenty, a tall, handsome girl with great poise derived from having
acted as her father's hostess for five years. She had a quick, inquiring
mind. Like her mother she always talked with Louis in English which
she spoke very fast with a heavy German accent. He enjoyed her com-

pany, and his rather patronizing affection changed and deepened, first to admiration and then to love.

As for Vicky, she was no more immune to Louis' gaiety, warmth, and good looks than the young ladies of Barbados and London had been: She frankly adored him. When he proposed to her in the summer of 1883, she accepted him gladly, subject, of course, to the approval of all the people who had to approve a royal marriage.

So much for romance. From a practical point of view, Prince Louis could hardly have been unaware of the prestige he would acquire by marrying Queen Victoria's granddaughter. Looking at it from the Grand Duke's viewpoint, Prince Louis was not an especially brilliant match, but on the other hand Louis IV had three other daughters for whom to find husbands. Finally, Vicky had inherited her maternal grandmother's strong will. She wanted Louis and her father was not the man to oppose her.

So much was then agreed upon; but it all depended on what the Widow at Osborne said. Queen Victoria, who was very much a woman, had also been charmed by Prince Louis. She warmly approved the marriage and offered him a post in the Royal Yacht *Victoria and Albert*, which, under the circumstances, he could hardly refuse.

Prince Louis married Victoria in Darmstadt on April 30, 1884. It was a great occasion, made greater by the fact that Queen Victoria came bringing her youngest daughter, Princess Beatrice. Naturally Louis' parents were there, and his three brothers. His mother was still a handsome, vigorous woman, but the prince with whom she had eloped so long ago had aged to a silvery simulacrum of that dashing young gallant. Even so, he was very proud and gay.

Other royal relatives came from all over Europe. The Grand Ducal Palace—a huge series of buildings, ranging in style from dour medieval fortress to the charmingly delicate new wing where the family lived—was crowded with them. Lesser royalties were billeted in the Grand Duke's many country castles all over Hesse.

It was as different as possible from the "sad marriage" of Vicky's mother, Princess Alice. Darmstadt was a small and friendly city where there was no need for the stultifying state of the English Court. Since virtually all the guests were related to each other, they could relax and enjoy themselves in familial intimacy; and the obvious happiness of the bridal couple induced a current of joy in them all.

Prince Louis wore the splendid dress uniform of the Hessian Artillery. He described it in a high-spirited letter to Spring-Rice in which he enclosed two photographs of himself: "The one in uniform is the last one taken and I thought it might amuse you to see what I look like when got up as an (honorary) defender of the 'Fatherland.' I regret that the focus did not include the extremities in the shape of high boots and spurs and a 'pickel-haube' with flowing black plumes. As I am still considered a renegade by most of my countrymen, I have to do this as a sop to them when I appear on State occasions at home. At any rate it has the advantage that I need not mount a war-horse in naval rig, which is never pleasant. . . ."

The aging Queen of England, well on her way now to becoming the "Grandmother of Europe," was also in high spirits. She even beamed approvingly when she noticed that Louis' younger brother Henry and Princess Beatrice seemed attracted to each other. This led to the second, and most effulgent, of the Battenbergs' royal marriages.

The Battenberg brothers were all attractive men, but their ability seemed to diminish in order of seniority. Without doubt, Louis was the ablest of the family. Alexander had brains and energy, but he had the misfortune to come to power too soon. Franz-Josef, the baby, never amounted to much. Prince Henry, whom the family called "Liko," was the middle one, at this time an officer in the German Emperor's Household Cavalry. Handsome and intelligent like his brothers, he lacked their driving energy and ambition, but he was amiable and lovable.

Princess Beatrice, a year younger than Henry, was a tall girl with the hourglass figure so admired by the Victorians. She had curly dark brown hair and an almost perfect Grecian profile with a rather long straight nose. Though she was mildly talented in painting and music, she, too, lacked the fire and intelligence of her older sisters. She and Prince Henry were thus well matched.

Queen Victoria evidently approved of the alliance from the first. She invited Prince Henry to spend Christmas with her at Windsor Castle, and when he asked her permission "to pay his addresses to her daughter," she gave him her blessing after making one important proviso: If they married they would live with her.

This was the key to the old Queen's amiability. Prince Henry was no more a great match than his brother had been, but Victoria was not concerned by that. All her other children had married and moved away. Beatrice was a devoted daughter and her constant companion—whom she had no intention of losing. That Henry had no obligations in foreign countries and little ambition made him the perfect husband for Beatrice. As the Queen wrote to the Duke of Grafton: "[Prince Henry] can therefor understand that it would have been quite *out of the question* for [Beatrice] ever to leave the Queen, and she would never have *wished* it herself. . . . Prince Henry of Battenberg is, however, ready to make England his home, and the Princess will continue to live with the Queen as heretofor. He is very amiable, very unassuming and sensible, and in addition very good-looking."

Prince Henry gladly agreed to the Queen's terms. Possibly he was so much in love with Beatrice that he did not mind what Lord Mountbatten later referred to as "the tiresome undertaking" of living with the Queen. More likely he was so beglamored by the prospect of becoming Queen Victoria's son-in-law that he swallowed it.

The wedding took place on the Isle of Wight on July 23, 1885, at one in the afternoon. At that hour the Royal Family, with the exception only of Crown Prince Frederick of Germany, drove from Osborne House to Whippingham Church through the lovely summer weather. The Queen and her daughter came last in an open carriage drawn by four grays with outriders. The old stone church was filled with two hundred members of the Government and nobility of England, who were also accommodated in grandstands built in a covered passage through the churchyard. The front pews were filled with royalty including, of course, Prince Louis of Battenberg and his bride. Five gold and white chairs were placed in front of the altar for the Queen, the exquisite Princess of Wales, the Grand Duke of Hesse and the Rhine, Prince Alexander of Hesse, and the Princess of Battenberg—how proud Julie Hauke must have felt that day.

According to *The Illustrated London News*, "The Bridegroom was supported by his two brothers, Prince Alexander I of Bulgaria and Prince Francis Joseph of Battenberg." He wore the dress uniform of the Household Cavalry with high jackboots and an eagle-crested silver helmet. Crossing his tunic was the blue ribbon of the Garter, which the Queen had just given him. His bride was radiant in a low-necked gown of white satin draped with Honiton lace and a gossamer-thin lace veil, and, like her bridesmaids, she carried a bouquet of orange blossoms the size and shape of a Roman shield.

However handsome the bridal couple looked, Queen Victoria stole the show as she came in on the arm of the bearded Prince of Wales. She had been seen so seldom in public since her husband's death, that people could not look enough. She wore a full-skirted, low-necked gown of black satin and delicate lace, crossed by the bright blue Garter ribbon. On top of her white widow's cap and veil was a tiny jeweled imperial crown; around her bare throat cascaded diamonds, centering on the fires of the Koh-i-Noor, the great Indian diamond whose name means "Mountain of Light."

When the Archbishop of Canterbury had pronounced the final blessing they all returned to Osborne House, and to what was perhaps the gayest party ever held there. The big, rambling house, with its strange medley of architecture from the Victorian gingerbread of its long verandahs to its Italian *campanile* from which flew the Royal Standard, had been the favorite summer residence of young Queen Victoria and her Prince Consort; and after his death, it became the melancholy retreat of the inconsolable widow. Now gloom was banished: The house was full of flowers, and its tall windows were open wide to the sweet, salty breeze. The superb lawns were crowded with strolling couples, the women in elaborate, bustled gowns and flowered bonnets; they all twirled matching parasols. The men for the most part wore the gaudy nineteenth-century livery of war so much better suited to a fete than a battlefield.

Scattered over the grounds were large tents and pavilions in which the guests lunched and drank champagne, while the bands of the Marines and the 93rd Highlanders alternated in providing a continuous blare of sound. The Queen with the bride and groom and their families lunched in the Royal pavilion. Late in the afternoon the bridal couple left in an open carriage for Quair Abbey, six miles away, which the Queen had lent them for their honeymoon.

Their departure hardly interrupted the festivities. According to *The Illustrated London News*, as darkness fell, "The view from the north front of the brilliantly illuminated palace was very beautiful. As the Royal and noble guests wandered in and out among the bronze statues, the air was sweet with the odour of flower-beds and fresh with the scent of the neighbouring sea. In the centre of the great lawn rose a fountain hung with many-coloured lamps, and countless glow-worms of light were festooned from upright stanchions between the fountains. The sounds of laughter made pleasant echoes in the night, and strains of music from the bands mingled with the distant plash of oars plying the sea. Upon the guard-ship, the Queen's yachts and a couple of gunboats the fireworks gleamed and paled, and died out in the darkness. . . ."

At Quair Abbey the bride and groom were not so distant that they could not hear the boom of the bombs or see the multicolored stars of the rockets fired in their honor. It was almost as far as they ever got from their possessive mother and Queen.

Prince Louis' service in the *Victoria and Albert* entailed frequent attendance on the Queen, who, though recovered now from her be-

reavement of twenty-odd years before, was as self-centered and demanding as ever. In fact, since Prime Minister Benjamin Disraeli had
made her Empress of India in 1876, she had acquired even greater notions
of the respect due her. At Windsor, Osborne, or Balmoral none of the
courtiers in attendance could leave the house, go to bed, or even light a
cigar—even though they might be several corridors removed from
Majesty—until at about eleven o'clock an usher gravely informed them
that the Queen had retired for the night.

The Queen insisted on the utmost formality of dress. At dinner
everyone was required to be in full fig with the ribbons and stars of their
orders, except that at Windsor the members of the Household wore the
"Windsor Coat," which was black with gold buttons and scarlet lapels
and cuffs. Yet the dinners themselves were surprisingly gay, for contrary to the general impression Victoria had a sense of humor, or at least
of the ridiculous, and in the presence of her family and intimates she
let herself go a bit. Sometimes when Prince Louis sat beside her relating
anecdotes of his cruises she would laugh so hard that her widow's
cap would go awry and her face purple.

When Louis and Vicky visited at Balmoral, life was rather more
informal. There were frequent picnics, which the Queen loved, and the
men went stalking the Highland stags nearly every day. The Queen
took a great interest in the sport and always got a full account of who
had shot what and how far. Prince Louis was a fine shot, but Franz-
Josef was indifferent at hunting as he was in most things. One evening,
according to Sir Frederick Ponsonby's *Recollections of Three Reigns*,
Franz-Josef, having been out stalking, proceeded to give a rambling
account of his day's sport, unconscious that the Queen knew every
detail.

"All would have been well had he left it at that, but he went on to
say it was a pity everything was so badly done—the stalkers didn't know
much about stalking. Then the Queen turned on him and she asked him
how many shots he had and when he replied he could not remember, she
asked him if he had had seven and missed them all. She asked how far
the stags were when he fired and he replied he was no judge of distance, whereupon she said, 'I suppose about a hundred yards.'

"It then dawned on him that she knew exactly what happened, and
he shut up like an umbrella."

Since "Victorian" is a synonym for prudish decorum, the morals
of the Court were of the highest, with one remarkable exception: The
Queen had no objection to men drinking and provided the means so
lavishly that her liquor bills must have been astronomical. No doubt the

gentlemen attending her needed this antidote to boredom, but it was small help to Prince Louis who seldom drank heavily.

At Balmoral he was astounded by the gigantic consumption of the wine of the country—Scotch whiskey. The Scottish guides, stalkers, estate workers, and everybody else apparently got drunk almost every night. A fresh bottle of whiskey was always put in the Queen's carriage—the coachman got it after the drive. Each guest who went stalking was provided with a full quart of Scotch; any that was left belonged to the guide. Of course the annual Gillies' Ball was a scene of drunken revelry. Queen Victoria, who always attended, took no notice; apparently she thought it was just natural.

One of the greatest sprees at Balmoral was the annual ceremony on Prince Albert's birthday, which was held in front of the statue the Queen had erected in his memory; everyone on the estate was expected to attend, the men in formal attire. The Queen would drive up in her pony chair at eleven o'clock, and the rather touching ceremony was held. As soon as she drove away the entire company made a break for the great tent lined with barmen and bottles. By early afternoon the entire countryside was littered with the bodies of Scotsmen in top hats and frock coats happily sleeping it off.

The two years Prince Louis spent in the *Victoria and Albert* were the last long hiatus in his naval career. He was uneasily conscious of passing time. At one point there was a war scare with Russia, and he thought enviously of the exciting activities of his colleagues in the fleet. After it was over he wrote wistfully, "I was sharpening my cutlass ready to ask for immediate transfer. . . ."

In the autumn of 1885, he insisted to the Queen that he must get on with his career, and that he would go on half pay until appointed to another ship. The Queen was content in the company of her daughter and Prince Henry, who had become "the ideal son-in-law no less than the ideal husband. He got Tosti to arrange musical evenings for [the Queen], and for London companies to act at Windsor, and did much to break up the heavy atmosphere of her widowhood. . . ." She saw Prince Louis' point and made no difficulty.

Of his service in the Queen's Yacht Prince Louis wrote to Spring-Rice, "It was a mighty fine 'loaf' in the *Victoria and Albert*, and I should not care ever to go back to her."

Chapter 7

TOWARD THE
ZENITH

$\sim$

WHEN HE LEFT THE Queen's Yacht Prince Louis was made a commander, his final promotion resulting from royal favor. He spent most of the next two years on half pay with such occasional employment as a brief stretch in the cruiser *Cambrian*, duty in the Gunnery School ship *Excellent* again, and in the *Vernon* studying the latest development in Whitehead torpedoes, then in their erratic infancy. Development in these fields was being pushed forward fast by brilliant young Captain John F. (Jackie) Fisher, the Director of Naval Ordnance. On July 29, 1887, Battenberg joined the *Dreadnought*, as her commander (executive officer).

This was not the famous *Dreadnought*, which gave her name to the modern battleship and was the ninth ship of that name in the Royal Navy, the first having fought the Armada under Drake. Prince Louis' *Dreadnought* was the eighth. Technically known as an "iron-clad turret ship," she was a compromise between the American Monitors and the sea-going British iron-clads. She had two enormous round turrets each very heavily armored and armed with two 12.5-inch, 3-ton rifled cannon. They were fully revolvable, and both could fire in any direction, except her after turret could not fire dead ahead nor her forward turret dead aft. To make this possible the superstructure was cantilevered out from a narrow conning tower so that it overhung the main deck; the turret guns had a wide arc of fire *under* it. The overhanging upper deck and bridge were an unholy clutter of ventilators, life boats, stays, ropes, small-caliber guns, twin funnels, and a stubby mast—the sails were gone at last.

Dreadnought was an extremely large and powerful ship for her time—325 feet long, 10,829 tons displacement, and 8,200-horsepower engines whose twin screws drove her at 14.5 knots. With fourteen-inch armor protecting engine rooms and conning tower, and eight- to six-inch armor the rest of her length, she was the most heavily armored ship ever built for the Royal Navy and the last to have overall armor like a true iron-clad. She was the first ship in the British Navy with artificial ventilation and longitudinal bulkheads. *Dreadnought* was, in fact, another of those strange aquatic sports of naval evolution. Armored, ugly, and ungainly, she should have been called *Dinosaur*, even though she foreshadowed the design of her famous namesake.

Prince Louis' service in her marked a great advance in his technical knowledge of his profession. As her commander he was responsible for all the supervisory minutiae, from gunnery to maintenance, from personnel to fuel and food. His position could be compared with the manager of a business with the captain as president concerned with overall policy and ultimate executive decisions.

It was constant hard work with few let-ups. For example, he wrote a description of coaling ship in Smyrna, when a thousand tons of coal were hoisted aboard from a collier in eleven hundred bags. The job took from 4:30 A.M. Saturday until Monday morning. "During all that time," he wrote, "I was in my clothes, having my meals almost always standing, and only lying down on the deck, all dirty and greasy, for an hour's sleep at a time. . . ."

The men worked in two-hour shifts, one on and one off, in choking clouds of coal dust under a burning sun that heated the deck plates to frying temperature. Prince Louis was with them constantly, cheering them on and "humouring them a good deal." He noted that it was very hard on them. As for himself, he wrote, "On the third day I was so worn out that I could hardly drag myself along."

During Prince Louis' entire service in her, *Dreadnought* was part of the Mediterranean Fleet, which, as before, was the crack outfit of the Royal Navy. The best ships and officers were stationed there, and from the shop talk of officers exchanging visits between ships and ashore in Malta, Prince Louis got an intimate insight into the latest naval thinking about the problems of an evolving service.

Naval thinking, at the highest level of the top brass, was decidedly ossified. So bound were they by tradition that any deviation from Nelsonian tactics and principles met armor-plated opposition. For example, in 1879, when young Jackie Fisher (afterward Admiral of the Fleet Lord Fisher of Kilverstone) wrote a paper urging the abandonment of sails, the reaction at the Admiralty was, "Who is this young whippersnapper?" And he was passed over for promotion.

One "modern" school of thought favored going all the way back to the tactics of the Roman triremes. They thought that armored ships were so impregnable to gunfire that fleet actions were impracticable and would be replaced by individual ship fights in which the opposing vessels would try to sink each other by ramming. For this reason, through the 1890s, warships were built with a steel ram projecting underwater from their bows. Although the new rifled guns had ranges of 10,000 yards, target practice was held to 1,500 yards at most, and nobody cared much whether they missed or not. Some captains even dumped the extra ammunition overboard rather than dirty their beautiful white paint with powder smoke. As a result a record of 27 per cent hits at a *stationary* target was considered a good performance.

But under the crust of conservatism new ideas were bubbling among such younger men as Fisher, Beresford, A. K. Wilson, John Jellicoe, and many others. Prince Louis closely associated himself with their thinking. He knew what the big guns of the *Dreadnought* could do if they were properly handled, and he also did some very constructive thinking about maneuvering large fleets in action. In line with this was his intensive study of new signaling methods, since to keep control of a fleet in action the commander in chief must be sure his orders are properly transmitted. Thus in his evolving philosophy of naval tactics Prince Louis belonged to what later became known as the "Blue Water School."

During part of Prince Louis' service in *Dreadnought*, he once again had young Prince George, now a lieutenant, under his command. The younger son of the Prince of Wales was immensely keen, ready for any hardship. For example, he worked just as hard as Battenberg when they coaled ship. He was determined to rise by his own merit in his chosen profession. Like Prince Louis, "The deck of a British warship was his home," and when he became King, he was acutely nostalgic for the naval life.

Princess Louis lived ashore in Malta like the other officers' wives. Because the Battenbergs had very little money they did not live even as well as some of the more affluent naval families. They had a little daughter, Princess Alice of Battenberg, who was born in Windsor Castle in February, 1885. Their second daughter, Louise, was born in July, 1889.

Vicky threw herself into life on Malta with enthusiasm. Her husband wrote to Spring-Rice that, "She is a regular sailor's wife, and takes an immense interest in all naval matters. She knows all my naval chums and all about them, including yourself, of course. . . . She is ready to go anywhere with me. . . ."

Prince Louis got his first command on October 3, 1889, the *Scout*. She was called a torpedo-cruiser, but gunboat was more like it, for she was actually much smaller than a modern destroyer, weighing only 1,580 tons. Naturally he was immensely proud of her and took great care to make her the smartest and most efficient little ship in the fleet. His hard work and good sense were noticed by Vice-Admiral Sir Anthony Hoskins, Commander in Chief Mediterranean Fleet.

Besides winning his Admiral's approval, Prince Louis impulsively got himself into trouble and thereby changed the rules for relations between the British Foreign Office and the Admiralty.

Scout was anchored in the Red Sea off Jeddah one blazing hot afternoon, when the lookout saw a black head swimming toward the ship. He called the captain. With the whole watch on deck, Prince Louis watched the swimmer's painfully slow progress across the shining water. When he finally reached the ship two sailors got a rope around him, and hauled a thin, exhausted, naked Negro to the deck. Spent and starved though he was, the man evidently had acquired some surprising knowledge of international law. Standing in a pool of water on the deck, he pointed to the White Ensign flying from the stern and said in broken English that he was a slave and claimed the protection of the British flag.

Soon after him came a steam launch bearing the British consul, in a solar topee and whites. The consul, anxious only to have no trouble in his area, explained to Prince Louis that the slave's owner had come to him and demanded the return of his property. Louis was rather hazy about the legal rights of the matter, but in no doubt about the moral right. "I shan't give him up," he said, and tried to reason with the consul.

"I demand that you surrender him to me," the consul said furiously. "According to regulations, you must do as I say." Red faced, eyes blazing, Prince Louis shouted, "I demand that you get off my ship, and *I* have the power to make you."

The upshot of the business was that the consul complained to the Foreign Office, which went in turn to the Admiralty. Prince Louis was summoned before his commander in chief. With a smile Sir Anthony said, "It is my painful duty to inform you that the Admiralty finds that you have acted contrary to regulations and has ordered that you be officially reproved."

Then the Admiral's smile broadened to a grin as he went on, "I have also been instructed to inform you that the regulations in question will be changed." And so they were. The Admiralty put such pressure on Prime Minister Lord Salisbury that it was ordered in Cabinet that in the future the Navy was to be free of consular authority.

Near the end of his Mediterranean Tour, on December 31, 1891, Prince Louis was promoted to captain. Admiral Sir Anthony Hoskins, who was going to Whitehall as Second Sea Lord, was looking for a chief of staff to accompany him. It is more than likely that Prince Louis' name was suggested to him by his flag lieutenant, Mark Kerr. Whether this is so or not, Sir Anthony not only liked Prince Louis immensely, but had decided for himself that he was one of the outstanding young officers in the fleet. So the Admiral invited him to come to Whitehall as Assistant Director of Naval Intelligence and Head of the Mobilization Department, as well as his chief of staff.

Prince Louis had to wait on half pay until November to take the appointment. During that time his first son, Prince George of Battenberg, was born on November 6, 1892. On November 23, he moved into his new offices in the Horse Guards on Whitehall. The large, gloomy, high-ceilinged rooms had been used by the Duke of Wellington.

Hardly had Prince Louis tried on his three hats than the powers above gave him two more. He was made Naval Adviser to the War Office and Chief Secretary to the Joint Naval and Military Committee of Defence, which had the task of trying to work out some sort of cooperation between the two highly antagonistic services. Finding him enormously energetic, intelligent, and Teutonically painstaking, his superiors and colleagues piled the work on him. Not only was he given much of the paper work of his five posts to do, but he was asked to serve on seven other important committees including the Royal Artillery and Engineers Committee (forts and minefields throughout the Empire); Committee on Invasion of Great Britain; War Office Torpedo Committee; subcommittees on Submarine Mining, Electric Light, and Armaments; and as Naval adviser to the Colonial Defence Committee. The unspoken phrase in Whitehall appears to have been, "Let Louis do it!"

And Louis did. How he managed to get through the mass of paper work without benefit even of typewriters is quite incredible. Like Napoleon, he must have needed at least seven secretaries writing furiously—in the elaborate copperplate script of official documents—to keep abreast of him. How he even managed to read and retain the masses of information that crossed his desk is remarkable enough. He not only did so, but found time for long inspection trips besides. On one of these he is said to have "christened a thousand forts in a thousand hours."

Luckily he was at the peak of physical condition. His powerful frame seemed indestructible, his energy unquenchable. Of course he stoked his fires with an amazing amount of food. Lord Esher wrote: "Prince Louis was a big man and had a big appetite. At breakfast he began on porridge, then fish, then eggs and bacon or a meat dish, then a plate of cold ham, then hot muffins or crumpets, then a lot of toast and butter and jam, and finished on fruit. His meal would have fed an officers' mess."

If he started the day like that, one can imagine the devastation he wrought in one of those ten-course Victorian dinners. Yet he never developed the paunchy look of so many of his contemporaries. The weight he carried was muscle-hard. Though he drank so little by the standards of his time, he could, if so disposed, knock back a magnum of champagne without a stagger.

Another aspect of his ability to cope with this prodigious amount of work was his intense interest in it, for his position afforded him a professional education available to few men. All the ramifications of that immensely complicated organization of ships and sailors—armies, forts, mines, torpedoes, guns, shipyards, factories, installations, and the literally thousands of different activities that combined to form the defenses of the Empire—were touched on in that flood of documents, many of them marked, "Most Secret. Most Urgent."

Nor was Prince Louis unaware of the leverage of his position, so much greater than its titles implied. It was the classic situation of an underling who more or less can mold events, because he has the subject at his fingertips and can subtly direct the attention and thinking of his superiors. Even though the naval designers might know more about ships than he, the ordnance experts about guns, the Army about strategy, and the experts on torpedoes, mines, forts; and so forth about their specialties, he was dealing intimately with all these things and therefore was familiar with their interrelationships. Finally, and this was a special obligation, his superiors trusted him.

Prince Louis' modus operandi was always to attempt conciliation between opposing factions without sacrificing any essential principles. His soft answers, logical reasoning, and charm—which he used at forced draught in sticky situations, accounted for his remarkable success. Of course, his royal connections did no harm, for even the most ardent democrat tends to be a trifle more polite when speaking to the kin of kings.

Because Prince Louis always worked behind the scenes it is difficult to determine which changes his influence brought about. One definite thing is that he succeeded in having the antiquated muzzle-loading guns in all the coastal forts replaced by modern breech-loading, rifled cannon.

But more than any single achievement, it was his pervasive influence toward modernization and "Blue Water" thinking that was important. Like many of his fellow officers his ideas were strongly affected by *The Influence of Sea Power in History*, by Captain Alfred Thayer Mahan of the United States Navy, published in 1890, and Mahan's *The Influence of Sea Power Upon the French Revolution and the Empire*, published in 1892. These two books opened the eyes of the English to the strategic role of their Navy and marked the real inception of "Blue Water" thinking. Battenberg's enthusiasm for Mahan undoubtedly infected many of his superiors, and played an important if little known part in the design and function of the large number of new ships laid down during the "Navy Scare" of 1893–94, brought on by the Alliance signed by France and Russia in 1893, at which time the entire Board of Admiralty threatened to resign unless the British Navy was brought up to parity with the combined fleets of both powers. The result was that, replacing the weird evolutionary accidents of the 1880s, came the first modern battleships—the Royal Sovereign Class designed by Sir William White, which were copied by all the navies of the world.

A notable instance of Prince Louis' foresight was that at a time when most British officers, including Jackie Fisher, thought of France and Russia as the great enemies, Prince Louis was seriously concerned by the German fleet being built by his cousin, Emperor Wilhelm. Perhaps the fact that he knew "Willie," as the family called him, so well and was able to evaluate his megalomaniacal tendencies, gave him an edge over strategists who thought of Germany purely in terms of land power.

Prince Louis' preoccupation with maneuvers as opposed to single-ship actions led him to invent the Battenberg Course Indicator at this time. It was a comparatively simple instrument that enabled squadrons of ships to maintain their relative courses accurately at high speed. It was officially adopted by the British Navy in 1894, and copied by all the other navies in the world. Ultimately its principles were adapted to early bombsights for airplanes.

A very important aspect of Prince Louis' work at the Admiralty was bringing about better relations with the Army. In those days the two services were generally contemptuous of each other, and this feeling was at one of its bitterest peaks when Battenberg went to Whitehall in 1892. Within one week of taking office he settled amicably one long-standing acrimonious dispute between the Army and the Admiralty. During his two years on the Joint Naval and Military Committee of Defense, he won the admiration and affection of his military colleagues. When, late in 1894, he left to take command of the *Cambrian*, he received touching letters of regret from many of the Army's ranking officers, including Lord Sandhurst, who headed the committee. The Commander in Chief of the Army, H.R.H. the Duke of Cambridge, said, "You have produced a mutual feeling of goodwill and unanimity that I have long wished to see established. . . ." And Adjutant General Sir Redvers Buller wrote, "I suppose you like a ship better than a joint secretaryship, but . . . you will seldom do better or more valuable work than you have done in the past two years. Whatever I have done, I feel I owe greatly to your ability and energy, and the very conciliatory spirit you have infused into all differences. . . ." This accolade came from one of the Army's most uncompromising characters.

While Prince Louis was at the Admiralty, the Battenbergs rented a house at Walton on Thames, near Hampton Court. It was open country then, though only a short trip by train to Waterloo Station. In 1894 Vicky's sister, Princess Alexandra of Hesse and the Rhine, was staying with them, when the Tsarevitch Nicholas came to England on an informal visit. The shy and sweet-tempered son of Tsar Alexander III spent a great deal of time in the easy, informal atmosphere of Prince Louis' house, and fell in love with his first cousin Alix. In all likelihood it was arranged this way; royal marriages of that magnitude don't just happen. Certainly it was a disaster. Although the two were apparently happy as man and wife, Princess Alix was a strong-minded woman who developed a strain of religious fanaticism. In the final, stormy days of the Russian Empire, she fell under the hypnotic, evil spell of the monk, Rasputin, and carried her weak husband into that mystic circle which finally undermined his tottering throne.

In addition to playing *deus ex machina* to this ill-starred marriage, Prince Louis was called on every so often to help settle some family difficulty. In 1890, when he was on leave from the Mediterranean, he received a summons from the Queen to come to Osborne House and "put a very troublesome matter right." It is interesting that she should turn to him rather than to one of her immediate family.

The tempest centered about one of the Queen's Mohammedan Indian servants, Abdul Karin. Victoria liked to have a close confidant among her household servants, and John Brown, her Scottish gillie, who had performed this role for many years, to the irritation and scandal of her appointed officials, had died in 1883. Increasingly beglamored by being Empress of India, the Queen had replaced him by Abdul, of whom she became very fond. She promoted him to *Munshi*, and began to ask his advice about confidential letters and dispatches from India. This shocked the Queen's official Household and caused an uproar in the Government.

Prince Louis arrived at Osborne House determined to defend the Queen's right to ask advice of anyone she pleased, but he discovered that the right was on the other side. Government officials explained to him that investigation had shown that the *Munshi* was corresponding with an Indian revolutionist; and Lord George Hamilton, Secretary of State for India, wrote that he could not conscientiously send highly confidential papers to the Queen if she continued to show them to the *Munshi*.

It was one thing for Prince Louis to recognize the necessities of the situation, but quite another to convince his imperial grandmother-in-law. This he did most skillfully in a man-to-woman talk in which he pointed out that with her great knowledge of Indian affairs she must realize that her Hindu subjects would strongly resent a Mohammedan being placed in the position of her advisor. Furthermore, he added, the Indian princes could not possibly understand allowing an Indian of inferior birth to see her confidential papers.

This was the kind of reasoning Queen Victoria could understand and accept. She was intensely jealous of the British Government's interference in her private life, but she was proudly conscious of the sensibilities of her Indian subjects. She promised Prince Louis to show no more confidential papers to the *Munshi;* but to prove her independence of the Government she announced that he would henceforth be known as her "Indian Secretary."

Another, sadder family duty devolved upon Prince Louis when Prince Albert Victor, Duke of Clarence, the eldest son of the Prince of Wales, died in 1892. Not only was he very fond of the young Prince, but his close friendship with his father and mother brought him into the stricken circle at Marlborough House. He advised on the naval aspects of the funeral ceremonies and did his best to comfort the grieving parents. Perhaps the saddest moment of all was when young Prince George came to him almost in tears: "You know what this means," he said. "Now that I am in the direct line for the throne, I'll have to give up the Navy."

"I know," said Prince Louis gently.

"I don't know how I can do it," the Prince said miserably. "All my training, all my ambitions were for a naval career. I love the Navy."

"You could have no better training for your new responsibilities,"

Prince Louis told him. "And with your knowledge of naval affairs you can exert a tremendous influence for the welfare of the Navy when your time comes to be King."

On October 16, 1894, Prince Louis took command of the light cruiser *Cambrian*, a ten-gun, twin-crew ship of 4,360 tons and 9,000 horsepower. She was capable of 19 knots, a great speed in those days. *Cambrian* was the prettiest ship in which Prince Louis ever served with her graceful black hull and white superstructure. Her two funnels and short, slender masts were slightly raked. Her lines were almost yatchlike, and, in fact, her captain cherished her with such loving care that she was known to the Mediterranean Fleet as "Prince Louis' Yatch."

He took Mark Kerr with him as his commander, and together they set out to make *Cambrian* the smartest ship in the fleet. They had the help of two brilliant young lieutenants—Osmond de Brock who went on to become Admiral of the Fleet, and later, the Honorable Horace L. A. Hood, who was a rear admiral in the *Invincible* when she blew up at the Battle of Jutland.

As captain of one of the smallest ships in the fleet Prince Louis could hardly have expected to make a great record in the inter-fleet sporting events, but he did. It was not due just to his inspiring leadership, but also to crafty planning. He and Mark Kerr carefully selected their crew from among the best available athletes, or at least men who looked likely. They made sure that they kept in superb physical condition and that they practiced assiduously for each event. Finally, the enthusiasm of their captain and commander aroused a like spirit in the men.

As a result the crew of the little *Cambrian* won inter-fleet contests that included the Duke of Edinburgh's Challenge Cup for twelve-oared cutters (never before won by a small ship), the *Undaunted* Field Gun Cup (previously always won by the Royal Marines), and cups for sailing at the Nice Regatta, the Mediterranean Rifle Cup, the Light Weight Boxing Championship, and such extracurricular events as the Racquet Challenge Cup. When Prince Louis left her, the *Cambrian* had won practically all the cups on the station except the Veterans Cup, and had the greatest record in the fleet for games of all kinds. She also had the lowest percentage of punishments, which was only 1.4 per cent of her crew.

In *Cambrian* Battenberg broke down some of the traditional class distinctions of the Royal Navy by having the gunroom mess—warrant officers and midshipmen—eat at a table in the wardroom, instead of on the lower deck. He and Mark Kerr frequently joined the gunroom mess.

A few months after arriving in the Mediterranean *Cambrian* was ordered to Algiers. To Prince Louis' delight, the American cruiser *Chicago* was at anchor in the small, mole-protected harbor. In command of her was Captain Mahan and Battenberg lost no time in inviting the author of *Sea Power* to dinner. They hit it off at once. While both ships were in harbor their captains dined together and talked shop almost every night. In the exciting give-and-take of discussion and argument Battenberg honed his mind to a sharp edge of knowledge.

Less interesting, though pleasant nonetheless, was *Cambrian*'s next duty as guardship to Queen Victoria, who liked to spend the early spring at a hotel in Nice. Since that city had no harbor, *Cambrian* anchored in the long narrow harbor of Villefranche, enclosed as securely as a Norwegian fjord by its steep, villa-dotted hills. Here Prince Louis used a little royal pull to get the Queen to review his ship's company on one of her afternoon drives around the hills. It went off splendidly to the great enjoyment of the men, except that the chaplain, who in those days did not wear naval uniform, turned out in court dress. At the sight of his incongruous figure standing beside a dusty road in the bright sunshine the Queen snorted, whether from suppressed amusement or annoyance no one was sure.

Naturally, Prince Louis saw a good deal of his royal relatives. When the Prince of Wales paid a dutiful visit to his Mama, he was happy to escape for a congenial lunch aboard *Cambrian*. Battenberg got along more easily with the Queen than her son did, probably because he was not so closely related to her. Near the end of her stay she said affectionately, "I wish you and Vicky lived more in England. Would you be willing to take command of the *Victoria and Albert?*" For the last time Prince Louis politely declined, pointing out that it would be a dead end to his career. The Queen respected his ambition, and later appointed him to the honorary post of her Personal Aide.

When she came to Nice the following spring, 1896, she again asked for *Cambrian*. This time Prince Louis told her he had put in for leave to attend the coronation of his brother-in-law, Tsar Nicholas II of Russia, whose father, Alexander III, had died of Bright's disease. Relations between Great Britain and Russia were in their usual acute condition, and the Queen saw an opportunity to use Prince Louis' charm to oil the wheels of diplomacy. Cables flew back and forth to Prime Minister Lord Salisbury, who commissioned Battenberg to talk with Russian Prime Minister Prince Lobanoff-Rostofsky and try to calm his Slavic suspicions of England's intentions. A modern British Prime Minister would have rejected indignantly such a suggestion as royal meddling with affairs of state, but in that enlightened era it was rightly considered a proper function of the monarch and his family to propose and perform diplomatic errands for the good of the realm and the peace of the world.

In a genial talk with Lobanoff-Rostofsky, Battenberg discovered that the Russians were agitated about the possibility of the British closing the Suez Canal to Russian shipping in the event of some crisis. Since England had no intention of breaking her commitments on the neutrality of the Canal, it was a simple matter to soothe this particular sore spot on the body of international relations.

Prince Louis again "meddled" in affairs of state in regard to the British consular service. At that time most British consuls were nationals of the countries in which they represented England. They were entrusted with various confidential documents. Aware of the European moral code in the matter of spying, Prince Louis considered this rather naïve of the Foreign Office; and he was horrified to discover that the Frenchman who was British consul at Toulon, the great French naval base, had been sent a secret paper concerning British naval strength. On his own initiative he sent one of *Cambrian*'s lieutenants to trick the consul into giving back the paper. When he reached England he talked Lord Salisbury, who had been delighted by his success in Russia, into making a change of policy and henceforth appoint only Englishmen to important posts in the British Consular Service.

During this period the Battenbergs lived with their children in a pleasant villa on Malta. Prince Louis and Vicky were working on his history of the names of British warships, which are repeated through the centuries; it was published in 1897. Those were happy days but they were darkened by personal sorrow. Louis' father, Prince Alexander, had died in 1888. This was sad but not a shock, because Alexander had simply faded away. But when Louis' gay, vital mother died suddenly in September, 1895, he was deeply grieved.

Family deaths seem often to come in series. Only four months later Prince Henry died on a troopship off the African coast, where England was engaged in one of her "little wars" against the Ashanti tribesmen in West Africa. Prince Henry, tired of playing the palace poodle, had asked the Queen to let him volunteer. He was backed strongly by Princess Beatrice, who realized that her husband needed to prove his manhood. The Queen consented reluctantly and Prince Henry joined General Sir Garnet Wolsey's expeditionary force. He caught a virulent fever and died in the troopship bringing him home. His princess showed her moral courage at this time. When Queen Victoria said, "He should never have gone," Princess Beatrice answered firmly, "No! It was right for him to go. That he died was God's will."

In June, 1897, Prince Louis was given command of the battleship *Majestic*, flagship of the Channel Squadron. He did not take up his post immediately because of the celebration of the sixtieth year of Queen Victoria's reign—the Diamond Jubilee, the radiant zenith of the British Empire.

From the barbarous, fog-shrouded island conquered by Julius Caesar, the way had led steadily upward for nearly nineteen centuries, gradually at first, with dips and rises, and finally, during the reign of one great Queen, in an ever steeper rush up the slippery pinnacle of imperial power. On the other side of that great divide, it fell more steeply still, so that very month of June, 1897, is marked more sharply than the peak of Everest as the apex.

To Britons, and to all the world, the symbol of England's rise and greatness was the small, stout, yet majestic figure of the Queen-Empress. During her long years of sovereignty Victoria had been arrogant and warmhearted, selfish and self-immolating, sometimes foolish, sometimes wise; but always steadfast, always brave, always true to the right as she saw it, and always regal. She had been alternately popular and disliked; cheered at, booed at, even shot at. But now there was nothing but acclamation. The squadrons of saluting warships that crowded her harbors; the marching troops from every corner of the world, uniformed in all the hues of the rainbow with skins of all the colors of humanity; the brassy bands, the squealing pipes, the native drums and oriental flutes; the horses, ponies, mules, camels, oxen, and elephants that carried her gold-cuirassed Household Cavalry, turbaned Sikhs, caftaned Bedouins, or dragged the great guns—the whole variegated assemblage, representing almost every breed of men, were there to honor her. For this was the apotheosis of Victoria. She had become in her own person England and the Empire.

By virtue of his kinship to her and his post as Naval Aide, Prince Louis was close by the side of the Queen through all this stunning pageantry, and though a minor figure, he was notable. Winston Churchill later called him "The beau-ideal of a British Naval officer," and in truth he seemed to personify the virtues and spirit of the Royal Navy. His frock-coated blue uniform was shaped to the waist by the belt from which hung a long, gold-hilted sword. His breast was covered by such an array of glittering orders that, with the heavy gold aigulettes looped over his shoulder, might have overwhelmed a smaller man but only enhanced his tall, stalwart figure. The full, pointed beard and curving mustache, big straight nose, high brow, and calm, friendly eyes, gave an impression of serene confidence. As he walked beside his Queen's carriage you could know that he was proud without being pompous, proud to be part of his splendid service, his country and the Empire—the Empire over whose liquidation his son, with equal devotion, would one day preside.

Nothing seemed more remote a possibility in those hot, happy days of June, 1897. They were all sailing, riding, marching confidently toward a still more glorious future. None in the ranks or the cheering crowds saw the steep slope beyond; none but a sallow, bespectacled little man who wrote:

> Far called our navies melt away,
> On dune and headland sinks the fire. . . .

Chapter 8

WITH FISHER
AND THE
MEDITERRANEAN
FLEET

PRINCE LOUIS SERVED ABOARD *Majestic* for two years under a dyspeptic admiral who tried his amiability almost to breaking point. It was at this time that he was first troubled by gout, possibly induced psychosomatically, but more probably a result of those gargantuan meals.

In 1899, he was made Assistant Director of Naval Intelligence. That sounds as if he were helping to direct the activities of navy spies, but actually the misnamed Office of Naval Intelligence was the housekeeping section of the Admiralty set up to manage the mobilization of the naval establishment, and, later, its strategic planning. The actual gathering of information concerning the naval activities of foreign powers was a small and rudimentary part of its function, because the *gentlemen* who ran the Royal Navy in those days considered spying rude and dishonorable.

As Assistant D.N.I., Battenberg's principal efforts were directed toward trying to reform the Navy's system of promotions, in order to get younger men as captains and admirals—the average age at promotion to rear admiral was fifty-three and a half. He also worked to improve the command structure of the various fleets and wrote some thoughtful papers on the functions of an admiral's chief of staff. Mark Kerr's uncle, Lord Walter Kerr, was First Sea Lord. He was a pleasant gentleman to work with, but since he belonged to the old school it was difficult to get things changed.

Meanwhile the Battenbergs were living far more elegantly than ever they had. Queen Victoria had lent them Frogmore House in Windsor Great Park—a large, pleasant country house with its own lovely gardens embellished—in the Romantic taste—by an ivy-clad fake ruin. So close that it was part of Frogmore grounds was the Royal Mausoleum where Prince Albert lay waiting for his Queen to join him, as indeed she longed to do.

At Frogmore, in 1900, there took place an event of little apparent importance in the increasing roar of history moving into high gear for the twentieth century. Yet even in the year of the Relief of Ladysmith and Mafeking, of the German Navy Act, which marked the Kaiser's decision to contest England's dominance of the oceans, and of the movement in the United States to develop its enormous latent strength as a great naval power, it also had a special significance for England. On June 25 Prince and Princess Louis' second son was born. Queen Victoria drove across the park in her pony chair to look him over, and a month later returned to hold him in her arms as he was christened Louis Francis Albert Victor (for the dead Duke of Clarence) Nicholas of Battenberg. Most ungraciously, he knocked her glasses off—his first impact on the Royal Family.

At about this time little Louis' proud father also had an embarrassing experience: He contracted a severe case of measles. Not only was he a very sick sailor, who lost eighteen pounds, but the agony of the rash under his luxuriant whiskers must have been almost unendurable. The Navy being what it always was, Prince Louis, a gallant and dignified figure, had to take a bit of teasing from his fellow officers. Fortunately his sense of humor was as applicable to himself as to other people, and he accepted it all with a broad grin.

Prince Louis had been in Whitehall only a few months when the Boer War broke out in October, 1899. To the amazement and anguish of the British, the small amateur armies of embattled Dutch farmers inflicted a series of disastrous defeats on the "invincible" British regulars. It was 1776 all over again—with British discipline and training offset by inept generalship and an enemy who skillfully made use of their familiarity with the terrain and local conditions. As Ladysmith and Mafeking were besieged and relieving columns commanded by Sir Redvers Buller suffered bloody repulses, the glory of two years before began to dim. Though no Englishman would admit it, the unsettable sun of Empire was over the yardarm.

Of course, unlimited resources eventually turned the course of the war, and by October, 1900, the situation in South Africa was well in hand, though it took another two years of anti-guerrilla warfare before the Boer Republics finally surrendered. The effect of the war on the British Army was profound and salutary; it shocked it into modernization. Dead wood was cleared away; ancient officers who had bought their commissions were retired; tactics and weapons systems were overhauled. One shudders to think what might have happened in Flanders some fourteen years later had this revamping not taken place. It was well for England that the Boers fought so valiantly.

The Boer War had only an indirect effect on the Royal Navy, because no one, after all, challenged Britain's rule of the waves. The only active participation of the fleet was providing cruisers to escort the troopships to South Africa, and supplying some units of Royal Marines and naval guns for the land battles. Nevertheless, the Admiralty took a new look at itself in view of what had happened to the Army.

Furthermore, all the Great Powers were intensely sympathetic to the Boer Republics. England was depicted in their newspapers as the great bully using her enormous power to crush the aspirations of a small, gallant people. Kaiser Wilhelm of Germany was particularly outspoken; he openly encouraged the Boers and implied that he would have helped them if he could, which he could not, because of lack of sea power. However, his government put the German Navy Act of 1900 through the Reichstag which provided for a large program of building battleships and lesser ships of war. With England thus isolated and faced by a hostile Europe, the climate of the Admiralty was prepared for change. It awaited only the coming of a strong man—and he was on his way in the person of Sir John Fisher.

On September 10, 1901, Prince Louis was made Commodore Second Class and given command of the brand-new battleship *Implacable*, one of the ships designed by Sir William White. Though she still had the bulging ram bow beloved by the ram-and-sink school of thought, she was almost the final word in naval design before the all-big-gun dreadnoughts. Her two modern turrets fore and aft were armed with a pair of 12-inch guns, and she had a strong secondary armament of 6-inch guns. She was heavily armored with nine inches of case-hardened steel for 218 feet of her length, which made a citadel fifteen feet deep extending four and three quarter feet below the water line. Each of her steel masts had two fighting tops—for that improbable close action. When Prince Louis commissioned her she was probably the most powerful battleship afloat.

Implacable sailed immediately to join the Mediterranean Fleet whose commander in chief was Admiral Sir John Fisher. Prince Louis knew Jackie Fisher well, and admired him as the leader of the young rebels who aimed to shake the Navy out of its long-time lethargy. A rather short and stocky man, he had a round, brown, bulldog face with features of a slightly Oriental cast, which led his enemies to say that he was the illegitimate son of a Singhalese princess. Actually, his parents were lower-middle-class English.

Fisher was a wild man, a super-egotist, a bounding enthusiast, a fanatical patriot, a furious belligerent, and a naval genius who was far ahead of his time. The surge of his energy was equaled only by the intensity of his emotions. He lived at full speed ahead and there was never a shade of gray in his thinking. He either loved a man dearly or hated him ferociously. He signed his headlong letters, "Yours 'till hell freezes" or "Yours 'till the angels sing," which meant, Yours 'till you disagree with me. Not that he refused to listen to argument or even to change his mind; but once a policy was established, anyone who openly opposed it was either a blithering ass or a black-hearted traitor.

This 160-pound package of cordite was about to blast the Royal Navy out of its snug harbors and into the twentieth century. When Prince Louis' ship joined the Mediterranean Fleet, Fisher was putting some of his ideas into effect—he had already invented, and named, the "destroyer" to cope with the small, fast torpedo boats of the era. The fleet was accustomed to maneuvering at half speed in a sort of formal naval quadrille, rather like infantry drill on a parade ground. Fisher ordered that every ship should move at full speed and that their evolutions simulate battle conditions. Gunnery was emphasized; the range for target practice was raised, first to a sensible 6,000 yards, and then even further. Accuracy improved fantastically, and soon the big guns were scoring twice as many hits at 6,000 yards as they had at 1,500. Finally, realistic war games were introduced.

Prince Louis was delighted with what he saw, and joined in the great game with gusto. He became one of the group of ardent young captains who backed Fisher's policies against the dead hand of moss-backed bureaucracy. Fisher in turn had a high regard for Battenberg. In 1901, he wrote to the First Lord of the Admiralty, the Earl of Selborne: "The two best officers in the whole British Navy are . . . Captain W. H. May . . . and Prince Louis of Battenberg, and what they don't know no one else can teach them. . . ."

However, though Battenberg strongly admired his chief, he was not blind to his idiosyncrasies. For example, Fisher's flagship was the *Renown*, an elderly battleship with comparatively light armament but very comfortable admiral's quarters. Prince Louis wrote to Captain George King-Hall: "As to *Renown* she should not be the flagship; in fact, she ought to be in China. We want the biggest and best in the Mediterranean; J.F., of course, won't part with his 'yacht,' but it is quite wrong...." That gibe about a yacht returns an echo of *Cambrian*.

Battenberg also disagreed with Fisher about the United States. At this time the Admiral considered America a real menace. He wrote: "The late Lord Herschell who was out here ... was, I am sure, of the opinion the Yankees are dead against us. Only ¼ of the population of the United States are what you may call natives; the rest are Germans, Irish, Italians, and the scum of the earth...." And he sent Battenberg a memorandum on war plans in which he envisaged: "War with a German-American Alliance" and "War with a Russian-American Alliance." Prince Louis, who knew the "Yankees" better, was not alarmed. When Fisher's son married a charming American girl and the Admiral went over there for the wedding, he came about on the other tack and ardently advocated an Anglo-American federation [see p. 21 and 21n].

Battenberg and Fisher worked closely together on plans for improving the administration of the Admiralty. Prince Louis wrote a long memorandum proposing sensible changes aimed at relieving the First Sea Lord of the growing mass of routine duties. He advocated creating a fifth Sea Lord, who would be charged with strategic planning—a sort of chief of the general staff. Fisher enthusiastically adopted the proposal of a fifth Sea Lord and forwarded it to Lord Charles Beresford under his own name with the comment, "Battenberg has invented a magnificent name for him—'THE WAR LORD.'"

However, when Fisher himself became First Sea Lord he fought the idea of a chief of staff, and wrote: "War is a case of *ONE* man and *ONE* mind and *ONE* voice!"

Prince Louis' old shipmate in the *Serapis*, Lord Charles Beresford, was second-in-command in the Mediterranean. This charming Irish aristocrat, with his pleasant, clean-shaven face and merry wit but easily muddled mind, was a tremendous favorite with all ranks from the lower deck to the commander in chief. Fisher said of him, "None better"; and Beresford loved Fisher's dash. But Fisher, with his genius for making enemies, was already laying the foundation for the famous feud. According to Marder, when Beresford's flag captain bungled bringing the battleship *Ramillies* into Malta Harbor Fisher signaled Admiral Beresford: "Your flagship is to proceed to sea and come in again in a seamanlike manner." Such public humiliation is hardly endearing to a touchy subordinate.

Prince Louis had always liked Lord Charles. They became even closer friends during this time.

While he was in command of *Implacable*, Prince Louis once again had Mark Kerr as his second-in-command. They set out as usual to make her the best ship in the fleet, picking their men as before. The result was that she soon rated top of the fleet in games, smartness, cleanliness, and shooting. Her record with the big guns speaks for itself:

After Turret 12-in guns

Right gun	6 rounds	6 hits
Left Gun	7 rounds	5 hits
Total:	13 rounds	11 hits (84.5 per cent)

6-in Guns

1. Best gun one minute's run 8 rounds 8 hits (100 per cent)
2. Best gun two minutes' run 14 rounds 13 hits (93 per cent)

(An absolute record for both types of guns.)

In the maneuvers of September, 1902, Prince Louis got his first chance to command a fleet. The combined Mediterranean and Channel Fleets were "fighting" a smaller squadron commanded by Rear Admiral Burges Watson, which included *Implacable*. Soon after the maneuvers started Watson was taken ill and Prince Louis was ordered to succeed him in command. His fleet was blockaded in Argustoli Harbor in the eastern Mediterranean, and his problem was to escape from the greatly superior blockading fleet. On a dark night Battenberg sent his destroyers out to drive the "enemy" destroyers off shore. Then he sent out his cruisers, rigged out to look like battleships, and ordered them to turn south. The whole enemy fleet took off in gleeful pursuit, whereupon Battenberg took his battleships out at full speed and turned *north*. The blockaders never even saw them until they reached safe anchorage in Cagliari.

Just before these maneuvers, Sir John Fisher had been ordered to Whitehall as Second Sea Lord. In spite of his being a hell-raising curmudgeon, or perhaps because of it, the whole fleet adored him; and when he left, their spontaneous demonstrations of affection were unequaled in its history. Sir John was even more deeply moved. As Prince

Louis and Admiral Watson came into his cabin in the *Renown* to say good-bye, Fisher glared silently at them for a long moment—and then bolted out of the room to hide his tears.

The crews of all the ships were topside as *Renown* weighed anchor and pointed her bow toward the narrow entrance of the harbor. True to his nature Jackie Fisher took her through the fleet at full speed with great white waves curling from her bow and her guns firing a farewell salute that was almost drowned out by the full-throated cheers of twenty thousand sailors clinging to every vantage point to watch their admiral leave.

In January of 1901, while Prince Louis was serving in the Mediterranean, he was summoned home by a telegram telling him that Queen Victoria was dying. When he joined Vicky at Osborne House he learned that it was only a matter of hours. The great, gloomy mansion was crowded by all the members of the Queen's family, who could make the trip—among them, thirty-seven great-grandchildren of whom little Louis of Battenberg was the youngest.

Of them all the most sorrowful was Victoria's grandson, the German Emperor. Although he had said harsh things about England and comforted her enemies, that had nothing to do with his feeling for her. On January 22, 1901, for the last two hours of her life, Kaiser Wilhelm supported the dying Queen in his arms, never moving from that position lest he disturb her. It was a feat of superb physical endurance and of love, and when her last sigh ended her ordeal he was still holding her.

All Englishmen and all of her subjects throughout the Empire, whatever their politics or national aspirations, mourned Victoria. They knew somehow that they were weeping not for her alone, but for the passing of an age. Especially did her beloved Indians mourn. Sir William R. Lawrence wrote from Calcutta: "From my verandah in the early morning of February 2, 1901, I saw a sight that set me thinking. I saw the greater part of Calcutta's dense population file solemnly past on their way to the great park to sit all day without food, mourning for the great Queen-Empress who had made them her children."

In his capacity as her Naval Aide Prince Louis' place was beside Victoria's coffin, throughout the sorrowful pageantry of death. He accompanied it to the dock at Osborne and aboard the *Victoria and Albert* which steamed slowly through the great fleet whose guns were firing their farewell salute to the Queen who had been so proud of them. He rode on the funeral train to London and walked beside the gun carriage drawn by the eight famous cream-colored horses through the cold gray streets, black now with people standing silent in the falling snow; then, to another station and the last short stage to Windsor.

The train reached Windsor an hour and a half late. The heavy coffin was unloaded and placed on another gun carriage drawn by four artillery horses, which had been waiting all that time in the bitter weather. When the order to start was given they lunged forward, rearing and plunging. As the traces broke, solemn order was replaced by wild confusion. The coffin rocked as though about to topple to the ground; the soldiers were trying to control the frantic horses and people scattered in all directions for fear of their flying hooves.

King Edward VII was standing at some distance talking to the Kaiser, the King of Greece, and Prince Louis when the Queen's secretary, Sir Frederick Ponsonby, rushed up wild-eyed to describe the disaster. The horses were clean off their heads; there was no more harness; no one knew what to do.

As the King hesitated, Prince Louis said, "May I make a suggestion, sir? We can improvise drag ropes and let the naval Guard of Honor draw the gun carriage in the customary naval way."

"That is an excellent idea," the King said.

"Then I have your permission to give the necessary orders?"

"Certainly!"

Prince Louis hurried to the scene of confusion. He saw Navy Lieutenant Percy Nobel standing with the guard of a hundred sailors who in the old rugged tradition wore no overcoats. "Ground arms and stand by to drag the gun carriage!" he commanded.

Noble repeated the order and the men started the evolution. "I didn't tell you to go through the whole manual of arms," Battenberg said.

Then he helped unharness the horses, and with a sailor's skillful hands, spliced traces, reins, odd bits of rope, and the communication cord from the Royal Train into drag ropes. One can imagine him, working furiously with his long sword banging against his calves, his cocked hat awry, and the snowflakes frosting his whiskers.

Meanwhile the Army people were furious at the usurpation of their prerogative. Battenberg paid no attention to them, so Colonel Bigge rushed up to the King and complained bitterly. Edward was in no mood for nonsense. "Right or wrong we're doing it this way," he said. "We'll never get on with it otherwise."

In about fifteen minutes the ropes were ready and the sailors tailed on to them; without orders the Military Guard hustled into columns of fours in front of them, and the kings and princes fell in behind. The sailors gave a great heave and the gun carriage moved forward at a slow march. "Looking like a really good gun crew," they drew the coffin through Windsor Town, up High Street and Park, and then turned toward the enormous gray mass of the castle above. Through the gates of the Long Walk they went, and slowly up the hill. It was heavy going, but the men were on their mettle and never broke their slow, steady step until at last they stopped in front of St. George's Chapel.*

The coffin remained in the chapel overnight, guarded by immobile sentries with their heads bowed and their hands folded on reversed arms.

The next day was still cold and snowy. After a simple service in the chapel, attended by the Royal Family, great officers of state, and the foreign kings and special envoys, the Queen's coffin was once again placed on a gun carriage drawn by a more manageable team. The band led the way, followed by the Guard of Honor. Then came the gun carriage, with Prince Louis and the Queen's other aides walking beside it, followed by the King of England and Victoria's royal descendants.

The procession moved slowly across the snowy park to the heavy beat of a funeral march until it reached the gates of Frogmore. There the band fell out and lined the drive, while the Queen's Own Pipers took their places at the head of the cortege. At that moment the whole mood of the occasion changed; the thrilling ululation of the pipes playing "Flowers of the Forest" echoed wildly in the icy air, lifting everyone's heart. Now, everyone moved more briskly, remembering, perhaps, how the Queen had loved the Highland music, thinking that she must be glad to be coming home to its strains to her beloved Albert. So, almost gaily, they laid her to rest by his side.

Louis and Vicky and their children walked the short distance home to the comfort of an open fire in Frogmore House.

---

* The bluejackets made such a fine show, according to Lord Mountbatten, that Prince Louis was able to persuade King Edward that the Royal Navy should provide gun crews at all future funerals of sovereigns. Mountbatten says that most of his father's Army friends cut him dead in the clubs for months afterward.

Chapter 9

FISHER MEN

THINGS CHANGED FAST when King Edward VII came to the throne. Even before six months had passed and Vicky could put off her official court mourning—a full black cashmere dress trimmed with crepe and folds of white chiffon around the neck, worn with a peaked Mary Stuart cap and long flowing crepe veil even indoors, and very becoming to her it was—the atmosphere of the Court changed from somber virtue to sophisticated high living. Though Victoria's grandson, the Kaiser, truly sorrowed for her, it is likely that her eldest son felt a sense of relief and liberation.

The relationship between them had been formal, if not strained—this had been due to faults on both sides. After the death of the Prince Consort the Government had proposed to the Queen that she allow the Prince of Wales to consult with her on affairs of state. She resolutely rejected the suggestion and refused to show him so much as a single dispatch or state paper—she trusted him less than the *Munshi*. The fact that her son liked horse racing, beautiful women, and international society—including American millionaires—convinced her that he was too frivolous for the serious business of government.

All these things were true—the heir to the throne had even been named co-respondent in a divorce case. But the Queen had misjudged his ability to understand and act wisely in matters concerning the welfare of the Empire, as he showed when he became King. Knowing his own worth and having very strong ideas about many aspects of the realm,

Edward lived in a state of frustration for nearly forty years. Having nothing serious to engage his energy undoubtedly made him even more frivolous.

Now he was King and the Empire was in his hands, not that he greatly changed his manner of living. He still loved racing and staying with millionaires—the Jewish banker Sir Ernest Cassel acquired a superb mansion at Newmarket, largely to have a place to entertain the King during the racing season. The unofficial position of the King's mistress continued to be filled by lovely Alice Keppel. Nevertheless, the King took a very serious view of his responsibilities and influenced the course of British policy far more than any monarch since has had the ability or temerity to do.

His principal interest was in foreign affairs, about which he probably knew more than any of his Cabinet Ministers. Though the German Emperor spoke English with less accent than the King of England, Edward clearly recognized Germany as his country's most dangerous rival, and set out, with personal charm and a conciliatory spirit, to win France and Russia as allies. More than any other statesman he was the architect of the Triple Entente of France, Russia, and England that was to save Europe from German domination.

The King also took great interest in the Royal Navy, which the Queen had taken for granted. Yet here too she had frustrated him. In 1840 the young Queen had written to the War Office and the Admiralty proposing that her husband be made a Field Marshal and Admiral of the Fleet. The War Office said, Yes, the Admiralty, No. Then, in 1862, after the Prince Consort's death, the Admiralty tentatively proposed giving the Prince of Wales that highest naval rank. The Queen replied in effect that since they would not do it for Albert they could not have her son. Much later she compromised by allowing Edward to be made an *honorary* Admiral of the Fleet, the only rank he ever held in the Royal Navy.

Edward had always loved the Navy despite this, and, recognizing it as the great tool of British foreign policy, made it his personal business to look after its welfare. His first move was to appoint Prince Louis his personal Naval Aide. So Battenberg added E.R. to the initials V.R. on the shoulder straps of his aiguillettes; eventually he added a third set of kingly initials, those of George V.

As a sign of his interest King Edward told Prince Louis to arrange for him to sign all naval commissions. Battenberg went to the Admiralty who told him that it was legally unnecessary for the King to do so; in fact they would not allow it. Battenberg argued, and the Admiralty finally admitted that it would be nice for the officers to have His

Majesty's autograph; so they agreed to allow him to superscribe his signature across the top of the commissions, which King Edward did from then on.

Because the King had such a high opinion of Prince Louis' ability, as well as a great fondness for him, he depended on him for advice on all naval matters. This was important because of the revolutionary changes about to be inaugurated by Admiral Fisher. Battenberg might be said to have tutored the King in the intricacies of the new naval policy, and to have had a great deal to do with making Edward, like himself, a "Fisher man."

The importance of this is shown in a letter written in 1907 by Admiral Fisher to King Edward, in which he said, "When Your Majesty backed up the First Sea Lord [Fisher] against the unanimous naval feeling against the *Dreadnought*—when she was first designed—and when Your Majesty launched her, went to sea in her, witnessed her battle practice—which surpassed all records—, it just simply shut up the mouths of the revilers as effectively as those lions were kept from eating Daniel! *And they would have eaten me but for Your Majesty. . . .*" [Fisher's italics.]

Though Prince Louis had no scruples against pulling royal wires in order to modernize the Navy, his intimacy with the King troubled him for fear it might bring him undeserved advancement. In 1904, when he was promoted to rear admiral, he wrote to Admiral Fisher that he would be greatly distressed to receive any promotion due to "the influence of the King, my uncle."

On November 15, 1902, soon after Fisher became Second Sea Lord, Prince Louis was recalled to Whitehall as Director of Naval Intelligence; one can see the fiery little admiral's hand quite clearly here. Battenberg succeeded Captain (later Admiral) Reginald Custance, and spoke of his fear of proving "unequal to succeeding a man of Custance's calibre," and "regret at leaving the Fleet and the ship."

As Second Sea Lord in charge of personnel, Fisher introduced drastic reforms in the treatment of the lower deck. In addition to more important changes, the sailors were to be supplied with plates and cutlery and would no longer have to eat their miserable rations out of tin basins with their fingers. Naturally, the old hard-shell admirals roared that this would make sissies of them. Other Fisher reforms included the nucleus crew system, to keep the ships of the reserve fleet in condition to fight, and a great change in educating naval officers. He abolished those old hulks, the schoolships *Britannia* and *Hindustan*, and replaced them with two naval colleges. King Edward disliked Osborne House, which he had inherited, and gave it to the nation. Fisher had shed-like dormitories built where the vast stables had been and sent the midshipmen there for their first two years of training. He built a modern school at Dartmouth on the mainland, where they went for two years more before going to sea. Thus they received four years of education instead of only two.

At the Department of Naval Intelligence, Prince Louis co-ordinated with Fisher and did some important renovating on his own. He too worked to make the reserve fleet "a real Home Fleet," not just a collection of mothballed hulks. He also wrote a badly needed directive on commerce protection—the first on the subject since the introduction of steam—and urged that merchant ships be armed for self-defense, which caused great agitation among the sea-lawyers, and took nearly ten years to effect. As late as 1914 Winston Churchill observed that he could not imagine any civilized power attacking merchant ships with submarines.

Battenberg also proposed government insurance of merchant vessels in wartime, because the excessive rates private insurance companies would have to charge would cause shipowners to lay up their vessels just when they were needed most. It took nearly twelve years to effect this sensible proposition; Prince Louis drove it through when he was First Sea Lord in 1913, just in time to keep the merchant navy on the seas in World War One. When it wound up its affairs at the end of the war the Government War Risk Insurance Office, instead of costing the taxpayers money, showed a large profit.

In addition to all this, Prince Louis greatly expanded the department's defense-planning work, which he had inaugurated in 1900, until it began to resemble a true planning staff. He wrote: "The Navy has only copied one thing from [the Germans], the best of all—'the true organizer of Victory'—the General Staff. . . . We thus have the skeleton at hand. . . ."

In order to put flesh on the "skeleton," in the form of officers educated for staff planning, Battenberg backed the "War Course" at Greenwich; this developed eventually into the Imperial Defence College, which became the postgraduate school for future admirals.

Lord Selborne, who was First Lord, relied on Battenberg to advise him about naval appointments. Considering what happened later, it is notable that when the post of Commander in Chief Mediterranean fell vacant Prince Louis advised the appointment of Lord Charles Beresford. He wrote, "Beresford trains the Flag-Officers and Captains under him, but Wilson [Rear Admiral Sir Arthur Wilson] does not . . . Fisher's case is peculiar . . . He does everything himself, like Wilson; but unlike him, he employs a large number of young officers as his staff . . . The

Mediterranean must always remain our big training ground. What we want there is a C. in C. who will train and teach . . . his staff."

So Beresford got the prize post he wanted so much.

Prince Louis enjoyed a pleasant interlude from this hard work and strain when his oldest daughter, Princess Alice, married Prince Andrew of Greece in October, 1903. Though his loyalties were English, Prince Louis still thought of Darmstadt as home, and so the wedding took place there. It was the last occasion on which the whole family joined together in a completely carefree celebration.

As they began pouring in from all over Europe, Darmstadt was in a frenzy of excitement, its streets crowded with fine carriages filled with radiant royalty. Every train had to be met with clanking cavalry escorts for kings and queens and princely heirs apparent. The bridegroom's parents, King George and Queen Olga of Greece, arrived with most of their children, including the Duke and Duchess of Sparta (later King Constantine I of Greece). King Edward's exquisite, fragile Queen Alexandra, her daughter, Princess Victoria and Princess Beatrice represented England. Tsar Nicholas and the Tsarina Alexandra brought their four young daughters; and Grand Duke Paul was also among the Russian contingent. The Kaiser's brother, Prince Henry of Prussia, who had married Vicky's little sister, Irene of Hesse, came, as did minor royalty from all over Germany. Since most of them brought their children the palaces of Battenberg's brother-in-law, Grand Duke Ernest, who had succeeded his father in 1892, overflowed. Prince Louis, who had inherited Heiligenberg from his father, took his whole family there, including three-year-old Louis, and it, too, was filled to the dormers with gay young cousins.

How very young and gay even the elders were! The parents of the bridal couple were almost the oldest, and they were only in their early fifties; Tsar Nicholas and Grand Duke Ernest were only thirty-five; most of the others scaled down from there. The tall, thin, awkward groom was twenty-one, and his bride was just eighteen—a pretty girl with the golden hair and sparkling blue eyes, though she had an unfortunate birthmark. It must have seemed to her—to all of them—the very morning of life, ambient in beauty, golden in serenity, radiant in promise.

Since it was a family affair and Darmstadt was such a small friendly place there was little rigid ceremony, though of course they did things right. The Tsar brought the Imperial Russian Choir with him to sing their stirring national songs and superb Gregorian chants; artistic Grand

Duke Ernest had so carefully nurtured the Darmstadt Opera Company that its gala performance of *The Sunken Bell* was something to remember. There were, of course, the proper ceremonials in connection with the weddings—all three of them: the German civil ceremony, a Protestant ceremony that took place in the palace, and the elaborate rites of the bridegroom's Greek Orthodox Church, with bearded patriarchs chanting sonorously and attendants holding jeweled crowns over the heads of Prince Andrew and Princess Alice, like figures in a Byzantine mosaic.

But after the rituals, formality went by the boards. Grand Duke Ernest gave the bridal dinner in the great baroque dining hall of the Old Palace. The suites were not invited—just family. While bands played and scarlet-liveried servants dashed in and out of the cavernous kitchen, everyone tore into one of those enormous ten-course dinners of hors d'oeuvres, soup, fish, roast, a Roman punch (to cool overheated stomachs for further effort), game, salad, ices, cakes, and cheese savories. With the ices came the toasts: to the bride, to the groom, to both; to Hesse, to Greece, to Great Britain, to Russia, to Germany, to half of Europe, and maybe even to America.

Prince and Princess Louis were alight with happiness and pride in their lovely daughter; Battenberg drank his magnum of champagne and perhaps a bit more. Finally dinner was over, the six-tiered wedding cake cut, and the bride with her chirping bridesmaids went up the great double staircase to change into her traveling clothes, while the rest of the party milled around in the great hall.

By that time they were almost all a bit tight; and since nearly all were related and had no outsiders to worry about, they were skylarking, as Mark Kerr writes, "like a Bank Holiday on Hampstead Heath." Little princes and princesses were racing around, sliding and slipping on the stone floor as children in such a state of excitement must or bust, while their elders did a little roughhousing, too. Young Prince George of Greece thought it would be funny to clap a man's gold-laced hat on the Grand Duchess Vera's ultra-modern bobbed head, and in the process knocked her glasses off; while he slipped away, she began to beat innocent Mark Kerr over the head with the hat while Queen Alexandra almost collapsed from laughter.

Gayest of all was the young Tsar. To those who remember the sad last picture at Ekaterinberg, and think of him only as a tragic figure, it is pleasant to glimpse him that night, his eyes sparkling with mischief as he roamed around making jokes and thinking up devilment.

Meanwhile everyone had been supplied with bags of rice and old slippers. The ten-foot-high oak doors were thrown open, and in front of the portico under bright new electric lights a landau waited, a cockaded coachman on the box and a footman standing at the heads of the Grand Duke's finest pair of grays. Everything was ready. Then came the inevitable, the seemingly interminable wait.

At last came a clatter of footsteps echoing to the vaulted roof, and the young couple came running down the staircase in a storm of rice, while everyone shouted at the top of his lungs. Out the great doors they went, with the whole crowd after them. They leapt into the carriage, horses' hooves struck sparks from the cobblestones, the footman scrambled desperately to his seat, and off they went around the court toward the gates.

Suddenly the Tsar shouted, "Come on! We can catch them again outside!"

At a dead run he cut across the court toward a side gate, with children hanging to his coat tails and the royal mob after him, swords banging against legs, Orders glittering, women lifting up their long skirts and running like hares with diamond necklaces swinging wildly, coronets and diadems askew. The German detectives with umbrellas and the Tsar's secret police took off after them but never caught up.

The street outside was lined six deep with Hessian burghers and their wives—presenting a solid wall of flesh—waiting to see the newly-weds drive by. Leading his pack the Tsar hit the line like a football player and, shedding children, charged through just as the carriage came along with Princess Alice bowing and smiling radiantly to the crowd, as a well-schooled princess should.

Nicholas took aim at close range and threw his bag of rice right into her face. Then, running along close behind the carriage, he threw a satin slipper. Princess Alice caught it expertly, leaned over the back of the carriage, and, shouting, "You're a stupid old donkey!" she conked the Tsar of all the Russias on the head with the heel.

Nicholas stood in the middle of the street between rows of astounded burghers, bellowing with laughter, so weak from mirth he could hardly move. Alice resumed her seat, and with unruffled poise began bowing and smiling radiantly to the crowd as a well-schooled princess should.

On October 21, 1904, Admiral Fisher, cap rakishly aslant and pale gray eyes shining with excitement, sailed into the office of First Sea Lord at the Admiralty. He had deliberately chosen Trafalgar Day for his inauguration, and it became the occasion of another memorable victory.

For Fisher carried the plans for the *Dreadnought* in his brief case. This was the design of the all-big-gun ship—ten 12-inch guns in five turrets, 17,900 tons, 21 knots. She was the prototype of the modern battleship, and remained the basic design for fifty years until the battleship joined the Roman galley in the graveyard of obsolete ships of war. Fisher also brought plans for the *Invincible*, an all-big-gun cruiser— eight 12-inch guns in four turrets, 17,500 tons, speed 25 knots. To obtain this speed she was lightly armored. The Invincible Class came to be called battle cruisers. Fisher intended them to protect commerce, destroy enemy cruisers—"They'll lap them all up like an armadillo let loose on an ant hill!"—and scout at high speed for the battle fleet. They were *not* intended to engage battleships, and when they did so at Jutland three of them blew up. They were badly designed and were one type of British ship never copied by the American Navy.*

To save money and provide crews for his "huge" new ships Fisher ordered the scrapping of 154 old ships, from gunboats to slow unarmored cruisers, which he called, "Ships that could neither fight nor run away." They were "showing the flag" all over the world, and Fisher believed they were no longer needed. Prince Louis backed him up with a long and carefully drawn paper on the problem. Yet both Fisher and Battenberg were wrong—for those ships would have been most useful fighting submarines in World War One.

When Fisher's plans became known all hell broke loose. *Dreadnought,* said his critics, would make every battleship in the Royal Navy obsolete and thus destroy its carefully built supremacy. Such ships were a wild extravagance; they were mistakenly designed, and would sacrifice protection to gain speed, according to report. Even Captain Mahan in America took a crack at them—but every nation copied them.

However, the row over the *Dreadnought* was nothing compared with the clamor over scrapping the gunboats and slow cruisers. On this point the agonized wails of Navy conservatives were reinforced by a howl from the Foreign Office that British policy would be impaired if there were not a ship in every part of the globe to enforce it.

Fisher rode roughshod over every objection. More than his actions, the *way* he acted—impatiently, arrogantly, contemptuously—was like a forced draft under the roaring flames of controversy. Battenberg, while backing Fisher's ideas, tried to soothe the combatants. It was hopeless. The "Band of Brothers" that had been Nelson's ideal of the Navy, became a pack of wolves snarling at each other. In a few years, as Fisher

---

* The American Navy started to build two of the world's largest battle cruisers, but Treaty of London restrictions forced conversion of these to the aircraft carriers *Saratoga* and *Lexington*.

continued his innovations—most of them absolutely right and farsighted —the Royal Navy was split right down the middle.

Fortunately, before he became too deeply involved in this internecine struggle, Prince Louis was ordered to sea. In an atmosphere as roiled as a river in flood, he left behind him at the Admiralty nothing but affection and admiration. It was said that, "Directly he had arrived his influence as a revered leader was established. . . . His departure from the Admiralty to hoist his Flag at sea left a blank and a sense of deep regret throughout the building."

Chapter 10

THE GRANDEST
CRUISE

IN 1902 PRINCE LOUIS HAD PROPOSED to Lord Selborne, First Lord of the Admiralty, the formation of two flying squadrons of fast armored cruisers. His proposal was accepted and, in January of 1905, to his utter delight, he was ordered to hoist his rear admiral's flag aboard the cruiser *Drake*, in command of the Second Cruiser Squadron. He immediately secured Captain Mark Kerr as his flag captain and chief of staff, and this congenial pair set forth on the grandest cruise they ever made.

Drake, the twenty-third ship of that name in the Royal Navy, was one of those beautiful, fast, four-stacker armored cruisers that were useful right into World War One. She was 500 feet long and displaced 14,100 tons. Her 31,400-horsepower engines driving twin screws gave her a speed of over 24 knots. One 9.2-inch gun was mounted in each of two turrets forward and aft, with twelve 6-inch guns on her broadside. She had two slim military masts crossed by the anachronistic yards for the sails it was still thought cruisers needed. With her long, slim lines and high speed she was as lovely a "yacht" as ever an admiral took to sea.

The rest of the squadron consisted of five cruisers of the County Class—*Cornwall*, *Bedford*, *Essex*, *Berwick*, and *Cumberland*. They were smaller than *Drake* (9,800 tons) but almost as fast.

Nothing but pleasant things happened to Prince Louis while he was in the *Drake*. First of all, on February 27, 1905, King Edward and Admiral Fisher visited her at Portsmouth, and the King spent the night aboard. The ship was dressed in a gala array of signal flags throughout the rigging, with the Royal Standard flying from the mainmast and Prince Louis' two-starred flag from the fore. At dinner that night the food was superb and ample to feed a fleet. Prince Louis, with an assist from Captain Kerr, provided King Edward's favorite brandy, which was exactly a century old, having been distilled in 1805, the year of Trafalgar. According to Flag Lieutenant Gerald Sowerby, "Excepting that the King lost at bridge [to Mark Kerr], which he did not seem to mind, the evening went well."

Drake then sailed to join the Channel Fleet under Admiral Sir William May at Gibraltar. Being in a ship with Prince Louis meant that one would see a good deal of royalty. Queen Alexandra, who was sailing around the Mediterranean in the *Victoria and Albert*, came aboard for tea on March 29; the next day Kaiser Wilhelm steamed into Gibraltar in the liner *Hamburg*, which he was using as a yacht. When the Kaiser announced his intention of visiting *Drake*, Mark Kerr told Prince Louis that to please his navy-proud kinsman, the Kaiser should be treated, not as an Emperor, but as an Admiral of the Fleet. So Battenberg transferred his own flag to the *Berwick*, and as the Kaiser came aboard hoisted the Imperial Standard and the Union Jack (the flag of a British Admiral of the Fleet) at the main. When the Kaiser left he was honored by the nineteen-gun salute of an admiral instead of the twenty-one guns due an Emperor, which pleased him enormously.

On April 18 Prince Louis became a grandfather, as Princess Alice gave birth to a daughter. There was a gay dinner party aboard *Drake* that night. A few days later, by a very unremarkable coincidence, the Second Cruiser Squadron was ordered to Greece. On May 8 they sailed into sunny Phalerum Bay from which they could see the creamy Parthenon on its yellow hilltop.

On the dock to greet her husband was Vicky, together with Prince Andrew, who was as thin and gawky as ever, but whose monocle fairly glittered with paternal pride. Princess Margarita of Greece was christened in the barn-like royal palace at Athens two days later.

The squadron sailed around the Mediterranean for a while, then through the Pillars of Hercules to Lisbon, where King Carlos and Queen Amelie spent a lot of time aboard *Drake*. They all went to one of those charming Portuguese bullfights, in which no one, not even the bull, gets hurt; Prince Louis did not like the real Spanish type.

In spite of the holiday air of this voyaging, Battenberg and Kerr were bringing the squadron up to the same peak efficiency they had achieved in their individual ships. Prince Louis' keenness for communication and fleet maneuvers soon had his ships tuned to split-second accuracy in all sorts of evolutions, which were invariably carried out at high speed. They also took part in fleet maneuvers. According to report, Battenberg was pretty tricky. In one sham battle he succeeded in boxing Admiral Hedworth Lambton's flagship between four of his cruisers. The defeated admiral signaled, "Are you rehearsing for the Battle of Trafalgar?"

Prince Louis' squadron sailed for North American waters on August 1, 1905, for the purpose of "creating good feeling between the United States and Great Britain and cementing the friendship between Canada, Newfoundland and the Mother Country." They could not have picked a better man. The squadron went first to Quebec, sailing up the St. Lawrence in a fog so dense it stopped all other navigation—Battenberg believed that nothing should stop the Navy. After festivities there, the ships scattered to show the flag in different Canadian ports: *Drake* went to St. Johns, Newfoundland. There the Governor and Mr. R. G. Reid, who owned the only railroad, invited Prince Louis and some of his officers to go caribou hunting. Naturally, he accepted, and off they went in a special train, complete with Pullmans and a diner, which parked on a siding deep in the wilderness. The caribou did not co-operate, but they had a fine hunt.

While at Halifax, a little later, Battenberg and Kerr went moose hunting, camping in a log cabin beside a lake in the brisk, sweet air and blazing autumn foliage of the untouched forest. Getting up every day at dawn, tramping through the woods honking his moose-call, Prince Louis felt never a twinge of gout, but had never a shot at a moose either. However, Mark Kerr got one, and they ate well.

On his return to Halifax Prince Louis received his first American fan letter. It was from an Irish-American gentleman in Chicago, who hoped the Prince "would come to our fair city so I can plaster your royal puss with rotten eggs." Roaring with laughter Prince Louis pasted it in a special page of his scrapbook.

Despite this inauspicious beginning for the attempt at international amity, things went well when they reached Annapolis on November 1. Ignoring the waiting pilot boats—the British Navy never used pilots except on Indian rivers and in Bermuda—Prince Louis brought his squadron up Chesapeake Bay at nineteen knots during the night. They anchored off Annapolis in the morning, and were welcomed by the American Cruiser Squadron and the American Atlantic Fleet's jovial commander in chief, Rear Admiral Robley Evans—who, because of his

exploits in the American Civil War and the Spanish-American War, was
known to all as "Fighting Bob Evans."

There was a regular love feast at Annapolis between British and
American officers. Prince Louis greatly admired the United States Naval
Academy, with its mellow buildings set on a green peninsula between
the Severn River and Chesapeake Bay. Since the Academy had been
founded in 1845, this was one place where American tradition was far
older than British, for Osborne Naval College was only two years old.
If the traditions were old Battenberg found the curriculum very up-to-
date, and far more thorough than anything yet attempted by the British.

On the other hand the Americans expressed amazement and delight
at British seamanship in the fast night run up the Chesapeake. Indeed,
they were so impressed that the following year they sent Commander
(later Admiral) William Sims, USN, to England to study Battenberg's
methods of training for maneuvers and gunnery. Another American,
Admiral Cameron Winslow, once remarked, "We've got to thank
Prince Louis for that [new fleet maneuvers]. For if we had not seen
the way your squadron worked, I don't suppose we would have worked
as a fleet even now."

While in Annapolis, Prince Louis called on Governor Warfield of
Maryland—a great uncle of the Duchess of Windsor. He was delighted
by the eighteenth-century executive mansion and the governor's informal Southern hospitality: "It is so homelike," he said, "so comfortable and cosy, and that is what I like in a house above all things." When
Governor Warfield brought in his six-year-old daughter Emma, Prince
Louis said to her, "I have a little boy about your age."

"What's his name?" Emma asked.

"He has six names, one of which is Louis," the prince said smiling
at her. "But we call him Dickie."

On November 3 Prince Louis and his captains went with Admiral
Evans to Washington for several days of lush entertainment, which culminated in an official dinner at the White House. Unlike most such
functions this was great fun. Though the White House could hardly
be called cosy, dynamic young President Theodore Roosevelt and his
rambunctious family of two girls and four boys made it "informal and
homelike." At dinner in the large, walnut-paneled dining room decorated
with broad-antlered mooseheads and other lugubrious specimens of
Roosevelt's prowess and the taxidermist's art, Prince Louis sat on the
President's right. They got on, as Roosevelt might have said, like a house
afire.

The vigorous young man, who was leading a vigorous young nation
from parochial isolation to a great place in the comity of nations, was

boiling with ideas. With his blue eyes snapping behind thick-lensed pince-nez and his strong white teeth snapping under his sandy mustache, Roosevelt fired questions like a gatling gun, and just as rapidly volunteered forthright opinions on naval affairs and world politics. Battenberg found himself talking almost as fast as the President in an atmosphere of intellectual excitement and mutual interest. When they had left the White House after dinner, Prince Louis said to Mark Kerr, "I'm hungry. Let's get something to eat."

"Why we just had a wonderful dinner," Kerr exclaimed.

"I had practically nothing," said Prince Louis. "The President and I were talking so hard and he was so interesting that I just motioned the food away."

On Sunday, November 5, Prince Louis returned to the White House for a family luncheon that was even more pleasant. Then they all went back to Annapolis. On Tuesday the Atlantic Fleet of 8 battleships and 4 cruisers sailed for New York, and the following day the Second Cruiser Squadron sailed to join them there.

On the morning of November 9, which happened to be King Edward's birthday, the British cruisers rounded Sandy Hook and, ignoring the white-winged pilot schooners, tore along through the Lower Bay at 19 knots. These were no drab gray ships of war. Wearing their peacetime dress of black hulls, white topsides, and tall buff funnels and spars, they were a gay and gallant marine picture. In shallow Ambrose Channel they slowed down a bit so that their wake would not wash out the shoreline. In the deep water off the Battery, backed by the incredible, sky-piercing towers of Manhattan, they went full ahead again. With black smoke pouring from their tall funnels and flashing white bones in their teeth, they rounded into the Hudson River and headed for their appointed anchorage.

It had been arranged that the British ships would anchor in line, two cable lengths apart, just behind the American Fleet. Prince Louis and Mark Kerr gleefully planned to pull off their favorite maneuver. The ships never slackened speed until they reached the appointed place. Then, at a signal from *Drake*, all ships dropped anchor simultaneously. Engines went full astern to check their speed, and the entire fleet brought up standing, exactly in position. As the anchors hit the water every cruiser dressed ship with hundreds of signal flags. The great, armorial Royal Standard streamed out from *Drake's* mainmast and the guns of all the ships began firing the Royal Salute in honor of the King's birthday. The American Fleet saluted the Royal Standard at the same time. As Mark Kerr observed, "All this rather complicated the difficult maneuver the Admiral was carrying out. . . ." But it was spectacular!

In New York Prince Louis proceeded to the task of "creating good relations" with enormous vigor and bonhomie. Official visits, banquets, and entertainments were interspersed with innumerable private parties. It seemed that every one of New York's opulent "Four Hundred" wanted to entertain His amiable Serene Highness. With all the unavoidable high living Prince Louis' gout struck hard, and he could hardly hobble; but his smile never lost its spontaneous warmth. Even when the Mayor of New York took him for a long and painful walk through an unfinished tunnel under the streets and showed him the beginning of a subway, he kept his serenity. "There, Your Highness! I guess you never saw a railroad underground in the Old Country," the mayor said proudly. "Marvelous!" exclaimed Battenberg, who for years had been commuting to work on the London Underground. "What will you people think of next?"

Two or three speeches a day added strain to Prince Louis' already arduous round, for he hated speech-making, but the genuine friendliness of the Americans made it all worth-while. At a time when Admiral Fisher was fretting about a possible German-American alliance Prince Louis, at a naval dinner in New York, could say from his heart, "Words fail me to describe to you, my brother officers of the American Navy, our feeling at the cordiality of your reception of us. . . ."

And American Admiral Coghlan replied, "We need not a written treaty of alliance. Our feeling of good fellowship is enough. . . ."

To repay his prodigal hosts Prince Louis gave a tremendous bash aboard *Drake* on November 14. The ship was moored alongside one of the Cunard Line's Hudson River piers. Twelve hundred people were invited and they all came, filling every inch of deck and cabin space. Truckloads of flowers from their American friends turned the ship into a conservatory, an orchestra played dreamy waltzes and jerky two-steps, the flood of champagne almost equaled the Hudson's broad tides. It was *the* party of the year.

On November 20 there began what was perhaps the most remarkable feature of this eventful cruise. Shortly after noon the squadron weighed anchor and sailed in column down the Hudson and out to the Lower Bay. As they passed Sandy Hook Lightship, Prince Louis signaled them to form line abreast. Then a gun was fired from *Drake*— that was the start of a *race* back to Gibraltar.

The Admiralty had not sent enough good Welsh coal for all six ships so Prince Louis handicapped *Drake*, by using American coal, which the British considered inferior. In spite of this *Drake* was leading

Berwick by five miles on the sixth day out, when a leak developed in a high-pressure cylinder, which required that one engine be shut off. While the engineers worked like madmen *Berwick*, followed by *Cumberland*, pulled abreast of *Drake*. At this point repairs were complete, steam went on, and the three splendid ships almost abreast tore through the rough wintry seas nearly rolling their tall stacks out. Men of all grades were working in short shifts the stokehole, and now the younger officers joined them, heaving coal into the roaring fires as fast as they could shovel.

So, almost neck and neck, they came to the Straits of Gibraltar. *Drake* was three-quarters of a mile ahead as they went by Tarifa Point, but *Berwick* was gaining. With everybody not working in the engine room on deck cheering her on and Prince Louis dancing a sort of nervous hornpipe on the bridge, *Drake* crossed the finish line a few lengths ahead of *Berwick*, with *Cumberland* only two hours behind. Statistically, *Drake* and *Berwick* both beat the transatlantic record for warships by over half a knot—3,327 miles in 7 days, 7 hours, 10 minutes for an average speed of 18.504 knots.

What seems extraordinary today about this race is that it happened at all. Certainly Prince Louis must have obtained permission from the Admiralty, although it is equally certain that he dreamed it up himself. No doubt it was justified as a high-speed test of ships and men to determine what they could do in an extreme emergency. It could also be considered a morale-builder. But when you get right down to it the thing was a sporting event; and those full-speed dashes through crowded harbors were just showing off to impress the natives of New York! They risked some of the best cruisers in the British Navy—the *Cornwall* narrowly missed sinking a crowded ferryboat in New York—for what must have been great fun for all concerned. Furthermore these risks were taken during a serious diplomatic crisis involving France, England, and Germany, over French advances in Morocco. The Algeciras Conference was about to meet across the Straits from Gibraltar, and the Great Powers nervously awaited its outcome with their fingers on the triggers.

All of which points up the fact that, until World War One proved, once and for all, that war is not a game and forced the English people to take it as seriously as say business or railroading, the naval and military establishments were run in a sporting spirit by gifted amateurs. There were exceptions, of course, though the only professional who comes to mind is Sir John Fisher, who lived and breathed and thought only of the Navy and shocked his gentlemanly contemporaries by his brutal pronouncements that war must be fought with the utmost violence. At the

Hague Peace Conference of 1899, he said: "Humanizing war! You might as well talk of humanizing Hell. . . ." This is Fisher on how to fight a war: "Hit your enemy in the belly and kick him when he's down and boil your prisoners in oil (*if you take any*) and torture his women and children, then people will keep clear of you. . . ." Fisher intended this to be taken as hyperbole; it turned out to be a simple statement of fact.

When, in 1904, Fisher suggested to King Edward that it might be a good idea to attack and sink the growing German Navy without warning, the King's reaction was, "My God, Fisher, you must be mad!"

When, in 1909, Fisher made the same suggestion, the King only looked thoughtful.

Certainly Admiral Fisher was not always right, as Prince Louis frequently pointed out; but those who opposed his reforms did so on sentimental rather than practical grounds. For example, they opposed the scrapping of little old ships, because these "showed the flag" and not because they would be useful in antisubmarine warfare; they condemned Fisher's plan for training line officers and engineers together—because it would destroy the class distinction between them and not because in dealing with increasingly complex mechanisms a certain amount of specialization was necessary. Finally, they opposed the *Dreadnought*— because she was big, expensive, and unconventional, and not because her all-big-gun armament left her rather defenseless against attacks by the fast new torpedo-boat destroyers.

In other words the arguments were emotional, based on sentiment and tradition rather than logic. Fisher was a highly emotional man himself, and he reacted to criticism by flying into a rage rather than with persuasive argument. Thus the split in the Royal Navy deepened, because the gentleman sailors tended to cling blindly to the old ways and the great professional was not quite professional enough to disregard personalities for the sake of principles.

Prince Louis was sufficiently aware of the facts of modern life to favor a strongly progressive naval policy. And yet, for all his great technical knowledge and dedication to the service, he must be classified among those gifted, very gifted, amateurs. This does not mean that his brilliance and the profundity of his knowledge, as well as the diligence with which he pursued his profession, were not far above his contemporaries'. But his pervading spirit, his attitude toward the Navy and even toward war itself were molded by chivalrous ideals and a romantic conception of naval life. Given his training and royal birth, and the euphoric thinking of people in that innocent era that had never seen a war fought with modern weapons, he could not have been otherwise.

Chapter 11

THE CAPTAINS
AND THE KINGS

WHEN PRINCE LOUIS LEFT THE *Drake* on February 4, 1907, she was, as usual, top ship of the Royal Navy in gunnery, and the Second Cruiser Squadron was top squadron. Battenberg was promoted to acting vice-admiral and made second-in-command of the Mediterranean Fleet. His new flagship, the battleship *Venerable*, was a pre-dreadnought type, similar to the *Implacable*. She was moored at the mole directly behind *Drake*. When the moment came for Prince Louis to leave, *Drake's* crew deserted their ship. Without orders they formed up in a double line from gangway to gangway, and in a storm of cheering Prince Louis walked between the lines to take up his new command.

It was a most unusual tribute to an admiral. Captains often win the love and loyalty of their crews, but admirals are usually considered a nuisance aboard a ship, because of the extra work entailed by their presence. The tribute was due to Battenberg's unique personality, combining courage with kindness, ability with humor, and finally the fact that he was such a fine figure of a sailor. Standing tall on his bridge, with the wind combing his whiskers and his keen eyes focused far away, he dressed up a ship like the Royal Standard at her main.

Prince Louis only served in *Venerable* for six months, at which time he was given command of the important Atlantic Fleet and shifted his flag to the *Prince of Wales*. She was a fine new pre-dreadnought battleship armed with four 12-inch guns, twelve 6-inch guns, and a lot of smaller weaponry. But her speed was only 18 knots, and the launching of *Dreadnought* in 1906 made her obsolescent almost before she was commissioned.

Prince Louis took great pride in his new flagship and worked to bring her to the usual peak of perfection. Mark Kerr tells the story of Battenberg making one of his thorough inspections. As always he poked his nose into everything, including a locker used to store cleaning rags. As he lifted the lid, he and his staff saw printed on it in large letters: NO ONE BUT A BLOODY FOOL WOULD LOOK IN HERE! While the staff turned purple, Prince Louis burst out laughing.

In the maneuvers of 1909 the Atlantic Fleet became the Blue Fleet, which, with the White Fleet, was pitted against the superior Red Fleet commanded by Admiral Sir William May from the *Dreadnought*. Mark Kerr had the *Invincible* under Sir William. The "battle" took place around the British Isles from Scapa Flow to the Irish and Channel ports. According to Admiralty documents, in spite of their general inferiority —and also in spite of the fact that Mark Kerr was advising May about what he could expect Battenberg to do—the Blue and White fleets trounced the Red, which had twenty-four ships "sunk," compared to a loss of only thirteen ships of the combined Blue and White fleets.

From the bridge of the *Prince of Wales* one summer morning Prince Louis happened to witness an event of greater historical importance than he realized. Like most naval officers he was an early riser, and that day he was up at dawn. The lookout had been alerted that he might see Louis Blériot attempting the first cross-Channel flight. It was an absolutely clear morning with so little wind that the sky was mirrored in the still water. Sure enough, at about five A.M. they saw small white wings, yet bigger than any bird, and heard the sharp *put-put* of a motor where none had ever been before. Battenberg saw the mothlike machine head first for Deal, then, dropping one wing toward the water, turn sharply left. The monoplane was less than a hundred feet in the air, and through his telescope Louis could see the small figure of a man sitting above the wings between the wire stays. On the strand below the white walls of the cliffs Prince Louis saw a man violently waving a large French flag.

Blériot came toward the flag, flying below the top of the cliff. Battenberg saw the propeller stop turning and the plane slide gracefully down the slope of air and skim over a small flat meadow below Castle Hill. Three men picking mushrooms were in the way and Battenberg noted, "To avoid them at the last moment he [Blériot] put his helm hard aport, which made the machine, then very near the ground, run its nose (on which was fixed a windmill-like propeller) against a rather steep grass bank and smashed the blades. . . ."

Prince Louis must have gone ashore to examine the machine, for he wrote a very detailed description of its three-cylinder motor, wings "like a pair of skiff's sails," rudders, pilot's stool-like seat, and controls. He finished this account by saying somewhat optimistically: "It is perfectly safe as, if the motor stops, the fixed wings (curving slightly like a bird's, concave downward) act as a parachute. One could make it for £20, I should say."

He did not live long enough to learn that twenty pounds' worth of wood, cloth, and wire doomed his great steel ships looming like fortresses on the morning tide.

Despite his splendid new command, the days of fun were just about over for Prince Louis. This was due, not only to the lowering war clouds streaked by the lightning of frequent crises as tensions between the British and German empires built up like huge electrical charges, but also to the bitterness within the Royal Navy. The battle was now fully joined between the naval officers who sided with Admiral Fisher and those, called "The Syndicate of Discontent," led by Lord Charles Beresford. They violently opposed Fisher's reforms, and on his return to England in 1908 Prince Louis was shocked by the virulence with which the "Band of Brothers" attacked one another. Beresford's group used leaked interviews to their favorite newspapers to attack the Admiralty, or rather, First Sea Lord Fisher, since he was, in effect, the whole show.

Fisher in turn was equally violent. The quarrel deepened to the point that Beresford, commanding the Channel Fleet, would not speak to Rear Admiral Percy Scott, the commander of his cruiser squadron who was a Fisher man. Lord Charles was egged on by his second-in-command, Admiral Custance, who is supposed to have borne a personal grudge against Fisher and who was generally regarded as the brains of the opposition of which Beresford was the figurehead. Generally speaking, outward civility was maintained until May 11, 1908. At the King's Levée in St. James's Palace that day, Fisher and Beresford met. The First Sea Lord extended his hand; Beresford publicly turned his back on his superior officer. In those days and in that place courtesy and honor were still so highly regarded that this was an unforgivable insult.

But it is not to be supposed that Beresford's group was entirely wrong and entirely unreasonable. For example, in their attacks on the *Dreadnought* in favor of more numerous smaller ships they were undoubtedly wrong, but they did have the support of such eminent naval authorities as Admiral Mahan and Sir William White, who had designed the last pre-dreadnoughts. On the other hand they were probably right in criticizing Fisher's disposition of the Home Fleet, and they were certainly right in claiming that naval officers who did not belong in the "Fish Pond," as the First Sea Lord's disciples were called, were discriminated against. In fact, Fisher himself said of these "traitors" that, "their wives should be widows; their children fatherless, their homes a dunghill."

Though in the main he supported Fisher, Prince Louis was horrified by the ruthlessness with which the First Sea Lord treated his opponents. In a letter written in 1909 to King-Hall, he spoke of a plan he had proposed two years earlier to combine the Nore Division of the Home Fleet, the Channel Fleet, and the Atlantic Fleet into one command under "an Admiralissimo."* "I believe it would have been accepted then," he wrote, "but J.F. [Fisher] was determined that Beresford would not have so big and honorable a command. I think C.B. has been badly treated . . . No wonder since he is surrounded by a crowd of admirers who openly compare him to Nelson . . . You know how much I admire J.F. He is a truly great man and almost all his schemes have benefitted the Navy. But he has started this pernicious partizanship in the Navy—there is no denying it. Anyone who opposed J.F. went under. His hatred of C.B. has led him to maintain for the past two years an organization of our Home forces which was indefensible. . . ."

Even the Royal Family took sides. King Edward strongly supported Fisher who had become his close friend; and because, as Fisher observed, "Without question . . . the King now molds public opinion," his loyalty kept Fisher in office.

On the other hand Prince George, the Prince of Wales, inclined toward Beresford's group, though his main desire was to see peace restored in the Navy.

To compound the Navy's difficulties, the Tory Government, which had ruled in England with hardly a break for twenty years, fell in 1905. They were succeeded by a Cabinet composed of idealistic liberals, headed first by Sir Henry Campbell-Bannerman and later by Herbert H. Asquith, among whom were radical reformers like Lloyd George and John Burns, and dewy-eyed pacifists like John Morely. They pro-

---

* This was eventually done.

posed to slash the Navy Estimates (budget) in order to have more money to spend on social reforms. Young Winston Churchill, who joined the Cabinet as President of the Board of Trade in 1908, belonged to the small-navy group. The First Lord of the Admiralty was Lord Tweedmouth, whose name is descriptive of his ability; he suffered a mental breakdown in 1909. Reginald McKenna, "a kindly little man," who was sensible and honorable, took over in 1908. Poor McKenna was caught in the middle of the political row that was piled on top of the naval dissensions.

This was the disarray of the British Empire as it faced its greatest challenge. No longer was there a question of a British Navy able to defeat any combination of two powers; the last time that was mentioned was in the report of the commission headed by Prince Louis in 1904, since which time the Russian Fleet had been virtually eliminated by the Japanese Navy in the Russo-Japanese War, and the French had become dependent for their very existence on their informal alliance with England, largely engineered by King Edward. Even Fisher had decided that England would never fight the United States. Now there was only a desperate race to keep ahead of Germany's booming fleet of dreadnoughts and battle cruisers.

Fortunately the English people were alerted to their danger. *The Riddle of the Sands*, a novel by Erskine Childers about a "bolt-from-the-blue" German invasion, had enormous popularity. The First Lord sent a copy to Prince Louis and asked what he thought of it. Battenberg replied: "As a novel it is excellent; as a war plan it is rubbish." Nevertheless it stirred the English up no end.

Even so, the radical pacifists in the Cabinet might have been able to keep the naval budget dangerously low had the Kaiser himself not helped the big-navy exponents. The impetuous German Emperor roared around, rattling his sabre and flaunting his fleet in warlike speeches, while provoking a series of diplomatic crises that kept the British in a state of alarm and forced even Lloyd George to accept the principle that England must build two dreadnoughts to Germany's one. Had the Germans ever learned to keep quiet until they were fully prepared to fight they might have won either or both World Wars.

Still, the surface of English life reflected only the pageantry and serenity of Britain's wonderful century of unchallenged security. The Battenbergs continued to live at Frogmore, with occasional delightful holidays at Heiligenberg. In August they were almost always invited aboard the King's Yacht during Cowes Week. Edward did things even more spectacularly than Victoria. At lunch aboard the *Victoria and Albert* the King sat at one end of the long table, with its gold service and masses of roses, and Queen Alexandra, still as fragile and delicate as a piece of Sèvres porcelain, sat at the other, ringing a tinkly golden bell to summon the servants as each course was furnished. On the deck outside the Marine Band played softly in order not to interrupt the conversation, which was always stimulating.

The Kaiser envied King Edward for many things, not the least of which was the *Victoria and Albert*. One of their last truly cordial meetings was when the King went to Kiel in the yacht to visit the Emperor in June of 1904. Sir Frederick Ponsonby described the party aboard the *Victoria and Albert* as, "an odd mixture. There was Baron de Constant, a French Pacifist; . . . the Prince of Monaco, a scientifically minded man who cared only for deep-sea fishing; Prince Louis of Battenberg, a popular admiral of the British Navy who was a great friend of King Edward; Lord Selborne, the First Lord, as Minister in Attendance. There were about fifteen others. . . ."

The *Victoria and Albert* came alongside the dock at Kiel, which was bristling with soldiers with fixed bayonets, at night in a pouring rain. The Kaiser came aboard with a slicker over his dress uniform to greet his uncle, the King. They all went out on the dock in the dark and rain to stand at attention while the band *oomphed*, "God Save the King," after which they inspected the Guard of Honor. Prince Louis, tramping along behind the monarchs, shook the water from his whiskers and wished the Kaiser had fewer soldiers. When they had splashed through all the puddles, they boarded the Kaiser's yacht, the *Hohenzollern*. Compared to the gracious luxury of the *Victoria and Albert*, *Hohenzollern* seemed Germanically crude. She was a converted navy ship and looked it, from her cramped public rooms to her cabins whose white-painted walls showed rivets and pipes. The Kaiser seemed a bit apologetic—he always had an inferiority complex when his uncle was around.

But in spite of this dank start, it was a gay evening. King Edward was always mellowed by good food and wine, which was plentiful. The Kaiser bounced back into tearing-good spirits. No one could be more charming when he was in the mood. There was only one slightly sour note. The Kaiser clapped Prince Louis on the shoulder and said, "What are you doing in that uniform? You should be wearing that of your own country, of the German Navy."

In properly respectful tones but with a glint in his eye, Battenberg replied, "Sir, when I joined the Royal Navy in 1868, there was no German Empire."

More changes came in 1910. On January 25 Admiral Fisher struck his flag: the pressures had become too great. His work was done and would stand up—the all-big-gun ship, water-tube boilers, nucleus crews, the great naval building programs, the advance from 12-inch guns to 13.5-inch guns, and the introduction of submarines, which Beresford called "Fisher's toys," all were his. Now it was time to heal the scars. Reluctantly the Cabinet eased him out and had the King create him Lord Fisher of Kilverstone as a sop. His place was assumed, but not taken, by Admiral Sir Arthur K. Wilson.

"Tug" Wilson was the old sea-dog type, stocky and sturdy, with a curly gray beard and bright blue eyes that squinted as though he were forever "looking into the spindrift whipped from the wavetops." He proved that though splendid at sea, he was, as Fisher wrote, "no good ashore." This he knew himself, and King Edward had to persuade him to take on the job. His chief asset was that he was not involved in partisanship and was highly respected in the Navy; his trouble was that he was secretive, unable to delegate authority, and, as the King once said, "One of the most obstinate men I ever came across."

It was well that Fisher left when he did, for a few months later, in May, 1910, his great protector, King Edward, died. Again Prince Louis walked the long sad miles beside his sovereign's coffin, and nine kings followed it. In a few years one would have been hard-pressed to find nine reigning kings anywhere. The Kaiser was there, of course, but not very sorrowful; he had loved his grandmother, but had come to hate his uncle. Those "damned alliances" of Edward's closed the ring around him, around Germany, thwarting her splendid onward surge, frustrating her every move. Wilhelm felt boxed in. It made him frantic, quite frantic.

So King George V came to the throne, a kinder, gentler man than his father, if less intelligent; hoping for a gentle, peaceful reign....

The great change at the Admiralty, which precipitated Prince Louis into the realm of policy-making, both naval and international, was brought about by the Agadir Crisis in the summer of 1911. This last and sharpest prewar crisis was caused by a French expedition to Fez, which foreshadowed a move toward the annexation of Morocco. Germany countered by sending the gunboat *Panther* to the west coast port of Agadir "to protect her nationals" in the unsettled conditions prevalent there. The logical conclusion that the Kaiser was feeling for a naval base on the west coast of Africa—which would threaten Britain's line of communication to the Cape of Good Hope and South America—sent chills and fever racing through the body of the Admiralty and the British public as well. It occurred just as the small-navy radicals seemed to be winning their demand for cutting the dreadnought-building program; here is another instance of the German's providential short-sightedness.

It had the effect of uniting the British Cabinet. The radical Lloyd George made a speech in which in effect he announced to the world that if Germany brought on a war, Britain would stand by France. The German Government replied with a communication to England that Foreign Minister Sir Edward Grey told Winston Churchill was "so stiff that the Fleet might be attacked at any moment." A warning message of impending war was sent to every British ship. Churchill wrote: "It is nothing . . . It is foolish, too fantastic to be thought of in the twentieth century. Or is it fire and murder leaping out of the darkness at our throats, torpedoes ripping the bellies of half-awakened ships, a sunrise on a vanished naval supremacy, and an island well-guarded hitherto, at last defenceless?"

In the midst of this panic, Churchill, who was now Home Secretary, discovered that the Navy's reserve supplies of cordite at Chattenden and Lodge Hill magazines were unguarded and the Home Office was responsible. He tried to get the Admiralty to send Marines. They refused. He then asked Army Secretary Lord Haldane for a company of troops to supplement his own police reserves. They were promptly sent. Churchill also uncovered a network of German spies in British ports.

At the height of the crisis, on August 23, 1911, Prime Minister Asquith called a secret meeting of the Committee of Imperial Defence. In the morning General Sir Henry Wilson, Director Military Operations, graphically presented a complete plan for landing six divisions of the Army in France to help her defense in case Germany attacked her.

In the afternoon First Sea Lord Sir Arthur Wilson was called upon, but he would tell the Committee nothing definite. The plan for naval action was locked up in his mind, and *no one else knew it;* it probably was not even written down. But he did imply that he thought the Army plan was crazy and that he had made no provision for guarding the transport of troops to France. The Committee realized that Wilson was worse than Fisher in his obsession for one-man control; Fisher at least had told his plans to Wilson. Wilson told no one.

The Agadir Crisis blew over as did all the others until—the last one. But Asquith realized that something must be done about the Admiralty. There must be a planning staff and co-ordination with the Army. First Lord McKenna, committed to Fisher and Wilson, was resolute against it; so McKenna must go. Asquith decided to shift him to Home Secretary, and appoint, of all people, the small-navy advocate, Winston

Churchill, First Lord of the Admiralty. He had first to placate King George who did not trust Churchill with his precious Navy.

The Navy was appalled, but they little knew their man. Asquith had called Churchill to Archerfield in Scotland to offer him the Admiralty. Churchill, who had once called it a poor ambition, now accepted it enthusiastically. That night from his bedroom window he saw against the evening sky the serrated silhouettes of two battleships steaming stately down the Firth of Forth. He wrote: "They seemed invested with a new significance to me." From that moment Churchill in his powerful imagination became part of and dedicated to the British Navy. And remained so all his life.

Churchill exchanged offices with McKenna on October 25, 1911, and he immediately took some elementary precautions "to enable me to sleep quietly in my bed." These included a *naval* guard for the cordite magazines; orders that naval officers, instead of just a sleepy clerk, must remain on duty at the Admiralty all night and holidays so that never a moment should be lost in giving an alarm, and that one of the Sea Lords must always be on duty in or near the Admiralty to receive it. He then set about reorganizing the whole place.

First he sent to Italy for his old friend Lord Fisher to come home and advise him. He found the man "a veritable volcano of knowledge." For a time he considered asking Fisher to return as First Sea Lord, but his desire to end the feuds that had rent the Navy finally determined him to look elsewhere for a new First Sea Lord. However, he made Fisher his unofficial, confidential adviser.

In a letter to be shown to Churchill, Fisher wrote: "I propose that he [Churchill] should take as his First Sea Lord Prince Louis of Battenberg. The very ablest Admiral, after Sir Arthur Wilson, that we possess, both afloat and ashore. . . . He is the most capable administrator in the Admirals List *by a long way*. . . . I think this should please the Liberal Party—they will say what better proof could we give of our confidence to Germany than by selecting a man as First Sea Lord with German proclivities. In reality he is more English than the English. Captain Mark Kerr should be Winston's Private Secretary, as he's the ablest Captain on the Navy List and he's a bosom friend of Battenberg. . . ."

Other Fisher suggestions were Sir George Callaghan for Second Sea Lord and, "SIR JOHN JELLICOE IS THE FUTURE NELSON —he is incomparably the ablest sea admiral we have—perhaps better than Battenberg— . . . so it's important to get him as Second-in-Command of our main Fleet. . . ."

Although King George pressed hard for the appointment of either Admiral Sir Hedworth Meux, who as Hedworth Lambton had been in Beresford's camp, or Admiral Sir John Durnford, Churchill was inclined to accept Fisher's advice and name Prince Louis. However, according to Lord Esher's diary, Lloyd George "was horrified at the idea of a German in the supreme place," and Asquith told Churchill that "L.G. is an excellent foolometer and the public will take the same view." It was a tragically accurate prediction.

In the end Churchill decided to appoint Admiral Sir Francis Bridgeman as First Sea Lord and Prince Louis as Second Sea Lord. In that post he would be in charge of personnel and thus in a strategic position to heal the wounds of the Fisher-Beresford feud by pouring on the balm of his good will and charm.

Churchill invited Battenberg to dinner in London and broke the news to him. Though it was a promotion, Prince Louis accepted it charily. He was commanding the Third and Fourth Divisions of the Home Fleet in the *King Edward VII* and loving it. Ashore, he and his growing family were living in mellow Admiralty House at Sheerness. That summer he wrote, "Our two 'Battles' outside were grand. I placed myself in the centre as umpire and signalled to the ships continuously the damage they were supposed to have sustained. Nothing of the kind had ever been tried before and there is much talk and excitement. . . . How strange that the Admiralissimo [Bridgeman] should all this time be wearing full dress and firing salutes!" It was indeed strange and a sign that the Navy still needed modernizing.

Prince Louis threw himself into his new job vigorously, and enthusiastically bombarded Churchill with long, carefully thought-out letters about the organization of the fleet and the new General Staff, but he must have been sad at leaving his superb dreadnoughts for the desk work and politics of Whitehall. He would have been heartbroken had he realized that, except for a few weeks borrowed from the Admiralty, he would never again command a fleet at sea.

Chapter 12

SECOND SEA LORD

WHEN ON DECEMBER 6, 1911, Prince Louis took up his post as Second Sea Lord, the Admiralty was vibrating with new life and buzzing with the inevitable dissensions always caused by a new broom in a bureaucracy. Winston Churchill, an energetic fireball, had set out to make himself the world's greatest expert on naval affairs. He wrote, "The Admiralty yacht, *Enchantress*, was now to become largely my office, almost my home, my work, my sole occupation and amusement. In all I spent eight months afloat in the three years before the war. I visited every dockyard in the British Isles and in the Mediterranean, and every important ship . . . I got to know what everything looked like and where everything was, and how one thing fitted into another. . . ."

Wherever he went Churchill invited officers of all ranks aboard *Enchantress* and shot searching questions at them. He learned a great deal, but he upset many officers of flag rank, who thought lieutenants should be seen and not heard. There had never been a First Lord like this, they said, quite truly.

However Churchill had no time to complete his naval education before getting action. He felt that "a great danger had passed very near us; that there was a breathing space before it would return; that we must be better prepared next time. . . ." He began those preparations immediately.

Although he had made Sir Francis Bridgeman First Sea Lord,

Churchill says he relied heavily on Prince Louis to advise him on the necessary changes. "[He] was on the whole my principal counsellor, as Second Sea Lord from January, 1912 to March, 1913.* . . . And as First Sea Lord thenceforward to the end of October, 1914. . . ." Of course Fisher, in Italy, was in full eruption, pouring forth a torrent of letters of advice, most of it good.

Prince Louis' first task was the creation of a naval war staff—a planning staff we would call it. Churchill states that all the details were worked out by Battenberg and approved by the First Sea Lord. It was based partly on a paper furnished by General Sir Douglas Haig, which described the military doctrine of staff organization. It was also necessary to train officers for staff work, so in 1912 the Royal Navy Staff College was started at the Naval College at Portsmouth. These changes were long overdue. The Royal Navy had done very little thinking about strategy. British naval officers were not required to study naval doctrine and had contributed virtually nothing to naval literature since Nelson's day. As Churchill put it, " 'The Silent Service' was not mute because it was absorbed in thought but because it was weighted down by its daily routine."

A weakness of Battenberg's plan was that the War Staff was purely advisory. Progressive officers felt that it should have real authority and be headed by the First Sea Lord. To this Prince Louis objected, because it was a planning body and not the executive. He made the point in rather stuffy fashion when he was First Sea Lord, that he would not "lower the position of my office by becoming Chief of Staff to a civilian First Lord."

The new War Staff did not have time to begin functioning properly before war came. Churchill and Battenberg reckoned that it would take fifteen years to become really efficient and they had only thirty months. But viable war plans were produced and circulated among the commanders in chief, an arrangement far better than having them a secret between one man and his God.

Rear Admiral Ernest C. F. Troubridge, one of the few Englishmen who had had experience in modern naval warfare while Naval Attaché in Japan during the Russo-Japanese War, was selected by Battenberg as Chief of the War Staff. Other good Churchill-Battenberg appointments were Vice-Admiral Sir John Jellicoe as second-in-command of the Home Fleet, and Rear Admiral David Beatty as Churchill's naval secretary. The First Lord was warned against Beatty as being rash and too

---

* Churchill's memory faltered. This should read January, 1912, to December, 1912.

unconventional, by several senior officers, but the moment Beatty reported to him, Churchill recognized a kindred soul and decided to appoint him on the spot. Beatty, not Jellicoe, turned out to be "The Nelson" of World War One.

Three other appointments were made with Prince Louis' advice in his successful effort to bind up the Navy's wounds. These were Admiral Sir Hedworth Meux as Commander in Chief Portsmouth; Admiral Sir Archibald Berkeley Milne, Commander in Chief Mediterranean; and Admiral Sir Reginald Custance to head the important Committee of Inquiry into the entry and education of cadets and midshipmen. All three were Beresford men; Lord Charles himself had reached the age of retirement. Their appointments caused the Fisher volcano to blow its top. "They are preparing for disaster," he wrote to Gerard Fiennes, the naval journalist; and to Churchill he wrote, "I regret that in regard to . . . what you have done in the appointments of Sir Hedworth Meux, Sir Berkeley Milne and Sir Reginald Custance, I fear that this must be my last communication with you on any matter at all. I am sorry for it but I consider you have betrayed the Navy. . . . I am going to transfer my body and my money to the United States. . . . Adieu, Yours, Fisher."

To Lord Esher he wrote that it was all the King's doing. His Majesty's sycophants were playing hell with him and, "Winston, alas! . . . feared for his wife the social ostracism of the Court and succumbed to the appointments of two Court favorites* . . . *a wicked wrong in both cases*—and Bridgeman and Battenberg are to blame. They ought to have left the Admiralty—but I suppose they both funked. . . ."

Esher replied, "I hear that Winston thinks Battenberg a sort of St. Vincent.† . . . If that *is* his view he will have a rude awakening one of these days. The man is just above average that's all." Fisher answered, "You are right about B. I told Winston that he was only a superior sort of *commis voyageur*, but quite *excellent* at *details* of organization, which is what you require of a Second Sea Lord. . . ."

This was Fisher at his worst, roaring with wounded pride. Hell froze over at the first wind of opposition, and he forgot that he had called Battenberg "the very ablest admiral." Of course he soon simmered down. Far from being disastrous the appointments of these excellent officers did much to repair the break and restore the "Band of Brothers" feeling in the Royal Navy. Only Beresford, in spiteful retirement, continued to rage against whoever held the place his burning ambition had coveted.

---

* What poppycock! Imagine Clementine Churchill caring, or King George V being so small!

† Admiral Lord St. Vincent, of Nelson's era.

Although no man could foresee the ultimate effect of aviation on naval strategy, and Prince Louis certainly did not, he was very interested in the aeroplane's possibilities for scouting; and, backed by the adventurous Churchill and with Lord Fisher's distant approbation, he strongly promoted aviation in the Navy. By 1911 an "aerodrome" had been established at Eastchurch and several machines acquired from the French and Americans to be used in training young officers as pilots. In the two years since Blériot's flight aeroplanes had improved to the point where they could carry a passenger in addition to the pilot.

Eastchurch had been part of Battenberg's Home Fleet command in 1911, and "to get the feel of it" he liked to fly with the pioneer aviators. The first time he went he took Dickie (little Louis) with him. It was quite difficult to get the bulky Admiral properly strapped into the extra seat perched on the edge of the biplane's lower wing, and with all that weight aboard the little machine could barely stagger into the air. But as it slowly climbed, and the circle of the horizon widened from three miles to thirty, Battenberg enthusiastically decided that he could see a lot farther than from the crow's-nest of a ship, with all that that implied.

When Prince Louis landed, Dickie begged his father so hard for a ride that he allowed the pilot, Lieutenant Arthur Longmore, to take his son up—he was still over-optimistic about the safety of flying. With the small, thin eleven-year-old aboard, the plane fairly bounded into the air, and Dickie had a better flight than his father.

Mark Kerr also became infected with air fever and helped to develop the world's first aircraft carrier, the *Hermes*, which was commissioned in 1913. She could accommodate only three seaplanes, which could not return to the ship. Unfortunately, she was abandoned as a carrier just before the war. At the Battle of Jutland those three little planes might have enabled Jellicoe to find and destroy the German Fleet.

However, aeroplanes were still a minor matter compared with the tremendous step taken by the Board of Admiralty in 1912. This was the decision to build five new dreadnoughts with *15-inch* guns and a speed of 25 knots, with engines fueled by *oil*. Churchill is generally supposed to have proposed it, but for once almost everybody in the councils of the Navy supported him. Fisher wrote wildly enthusiastic letters from Italy; Bridgeman and Battenberg were strongly for it. It was a bold proposal. Although an experimental 15-inch gun was being built no one was sure how well it would work. No matter! The Board unanimously approved the program, and the result was the Queen Elizabeth Class of super-dreadnoughts which magnificently proved their worth at Jutland.

Strangely enough the German Navy could have eliminated these superb ships without firing a shot. Churchill was still worried about the enormous expense of the naval race with Germany. The Naval Estimates for 1912–13 were £45,070,000 (about $220,000,000), which seemed an horrendous sum to those innocents who had not learned to think in billions. Churchill determined to try to do something about it. With the concurrence of Foreign Minister Lord Grey and Prime Minister Asquith he sent Sir Ernest Cassel to Berlin to try to negotiate a cutback of both building programs. Sir Ernest was a sort of minor Rothschild, with many international connections including a close personal friendship with the Kaiser and his intimate friend Herr Albert Ballin, head of the Hamburg-Amerika Line. He was a man of great good will, devoted to peace.

Sir Ernest's feelers were so well received that the British Government sent an official mission to Berlin headed by Lord Haldane. Their negotiations came to nothing, and instead of reducing their naval building program the Germans actually increased it. Churchill tried again, proposing a Naval Holiday for the year 1913, "a blank page in the book of misunderstanding," in which neither country would build any capital ships. This proposal too was rejected by the Kaiser.

In July, 1912, Prince Louis took a busman's holiday from his onerous work at the Admiralty. He appointed himself Commander in Chief of the Blue Fleet, which was to "fight" the Red Fleet in the annual maneuvers. This made sense because it was assumed that, in the event of war breaking out, the Second Sea Lord would become Commander in Chief of the Grand Fleet* as did Admiral Jellicoe, who was Second Sea Lord in July, 1914. On July 13, while commanding the Blue Fleet, Prince Louis was promoted to admiral. For once, however, he was beaten in the maneuvers, the only time on record. Beaten or not, he had a splendid "holiday" with the salt air blowing the fug of Whitehall out of his lungs.

There was also a tremendous review at Portland in 1912, of the combined fleets, flying the flags of a dozen admirals and the pennants of as many commodores. King George was present in *Victoria and Albert*, with the Admiralty Flag flying from her foremast, the Royal Standard from her main, and the Union Jack from her gaff. Churchill, of course, was there in *Enchantress*.

One day the entire fleet put out to sea in a dense fog, for battle firing practice. The ships were virtually invisible to each other and kept station by whistle signals and other means developed largely by Prince Louis in his experiments while in command of his cruisers and the

---

* According to Lord Mountbatten, but not necessarily so.

Atlantic Fleet. Suddenly the fog lifted and the targets were visible in the thin sunshine. The fleet was steaming in one long line of battle and twenty-four dreadnoughts opened fire in turn. As each ship fired her broadside of ten huge guns she disappeared momentarily in smoke and flame, and actually staggered sideways from the recoil.

Though Sir George Callaghan and not Prince Louis was in overall command, the fleet returned to harbor in true Battenberg style. Each of the three eight-ship battle squadrons formed in a line abreast. With cruisers and destroyers ahead, behind, and on their flanks they tore along at twenty knots—bows cutting the water in lines as straight as the Guards on parade, battle flags stiff in the wind of their speed. Never slackening speed the armada of a hundred fifty ships passed between the wide headlands of the harbor. The foreign observers aboard *Enchantress* with Churchill watched with bulging eyes as, still in formation, the fleet raced toward the rocky shore, seemingly bent on hurling itself to destruction. Churchill estimated that the leading ships were five minutes' run from the beach; then four, then three. At the peak of tension, bright signal flags broke out from the flagship *Neptune*'s mast, and at that exact moment a hundred fifty anchors splashed into the bay, cables roared through hawseholes, and white water boiled under counters as the engines went full astern. In less than a minute all the ships were at rest, their ordered, ruler-straight ranks covering many square miles of water in the broad bay.

Winston Churchill and his First Sea Lord were not getting on at all well, that summer of 1912. Bridgeman was upset by Churchill's active interposition in the details of running the Navy. The constant suggestions of the First Lord of the Admiralty, his habit of leaping blithely out of official channels to seek advice from every grade, from lieutenants on up, and of making statements without consulting Bridgeman, irked the tradition-minded Admiral no end.

On the other hand Churchill considered Bridgeman old-fashioned, an ineffective advocate of naval policies in meetings of the Committee of Imperial Defence (he was, in fact, a poor speaker), and both wishy-washy and inflexible at the wrong times. The two men were on stiffly formal terms and Churchill asked advice only from Prince Louis. He sought a way to get this Old Man of the Sea off his back.

The opportunity came in November, 1912, when Bridgeman had an appendectomy followed by two severe attacks of bronchitis. Though the Admiral recovered quickly, Churchill seized his chance and, in a firm but courteous letter, he informed the First Sea Lord that he should retire, because, "if, by any misadventure, we were to be involved in war, I feel that the burden might be more than your health could sustain. . . ."

Bridgeman was upset and pointed out to Churchill that his health was lately much improved and that his doctor gave him a clean bill of health. He also suggested that differences of opinion on policy was the real reason he was being asked to resign.

With the diplomatic mendacity the most upright politician must occasionally employ, Churchill replied that, "there is absolutely no truth in this idea. . . . Honestly I only thought about your health and the European situation and what would happen if war began and you broke down."

So Bridgeman was out and Churchill, with relief, appointed Prince Louis First Sea Lord on December 9, 1912. But that was not the end of the matter.

Bridgeman complained bitterly that he had been "fired without warning" because he did not agree with Churchill. The Conservative press raised a hue and cry. King George, who had never approved of Churchill and now liked him even less, made no secret of his sympathy for Bridgeman. The Conservative Party, ever alert for a handy axe with which to bludgeon the Government, leapt to Bridgeman's defense. Andrew Bonar Law, the Conservative Leader, spoke angrily in the House of Commons of "the brutal ill usage" Bridgeman had suffered, and Lord Charles Beresford, who had been elected to Parliament, joyfully gave tongue. Even Churchill's own party, who regarded him as a rather erratic young fellow, were distinctly distressed.

Churchill, of course, could take care of himself in such clashes, and fortunately he was able to produce letters Bridgeman had written in November to various friends, including Prince Louis, telling them how ill he felt and speaking of resigning of his own accord. This took the wind out of the opposition's sails, but did not reconcile them.

Though none of this was Prince Louis' doing, he felt the backlash of the storm. He was what he had longed to be—First Sea Lord; but he came to the post in a fog of political controversy. However, in the Navy they were saying about Battenberg, "He was born a royal prince but lived it down."

Chapter 13

FIRST SEA LORD

PRINCE LOUIS WAS REPORTED to be "in the seventh heaven of delight," when he took over as First Sea Lord, the post for which he had been working all his life. Arthur J. Marder, in *From the Dreadnought to Scapa Flow*, after describing Battenberg's good qualities, says, "But he was inordinately ambitious and made no bones of it. . . ."

Inordinate ambition is so rare among royalty that one wonders what driving force motivated Prince Louis and, indeed, his male descendants; for they, too, were driven men, with the exception of George, his eldest son. The spur in Battenberg's flank may have been the cloud of morganatic marriage dimming slightly the radiance of true royalty. Or perhaps it was the lowly Hessian blood of the Haucks, transmitted through the dashing Countess Julie, which produced this plebeian drive for self-advancement. Whatever the cause, it was no mean ambition but a desire to prove himself in his own right as a sailor and as a servant of his adopted country.

Nor did Prince Louis attain first rank by ruthless tactics. He never knocked his enemies down and kicked them in their bellies as advocated, though seldom practiced, by Lord Fisher. Nor did he ever play politics and connive and trim to gain place. In fact, being related so closely to the Royal Family, he went out of his way to avoid getting anything he felt he had not earned. Though there was a small and disgruntled group of naval officers who jealously sought to knife him, he remained apparently oblivious to their conspiracies though he was, in fact, well aware of them. On one occasion he even went to the rescue of a fellow admiral who *he knew* had intrigued against him a short time previously. In contradistinction to these ill-natured few were the sailors of all ranks who admired him extravagantly. In 1911 Rear Admiral Sir Charles L. Ottley wrote to Lord Esher, "There are literally hundreds of naval officers who would be quite willing to believe that black was white if [Battenberg] issued a memo to that effect."

Now that he was First Sea Lord only one goal was left for Prince Louis—to be the best First Sea Lord the Navy ever had. He did not quite make it, but he came close. The pursuit of this ambition and his absolute integrity resulted in a series of clashes with the exuberant First Lord. But, to the credit of both men, these disagreements in no way diminished Churchill's confidence in Battenberg—rather they enhanced it—nor Prince Louis' loyalty to his civilian chief.

The first of these clashes was brought on by one of Prince Louis' earliest acts upon taking office. He telegraphed to Mark Kerr, who was commanding the new dreadnought *Prince of Wales,* to come to see him at once. When Kerr arrived Battenberg said, "The war plan now in effect calls for a close blockade of German ports, parading our battle fleet in two separate squadrons up and down the North Sea off the German coast just as though submarines, mines, destroyers and aircraft did not exist. It's just plain suicide!"

Prince Louis told Kerr to draw up a new plan for a distant blockade similar to a plan Captain Kerr had submitted to the Admiralty two years before. "Bridgeman was sick for two months," Battenberg said. "He left so much back work that I haven't time to do this myself. No one knows my thoughts as well as you. Do it!"

Kerr's plan was to patrol the North Sea with destroyer flotillas, keeping the capital ships far out of harm's way. The battle cruisers were to be based at Minch on the northwest coast of Scotland, the battle fleet at Bantry Bay in Ireland, and the heavy armored cruisers like the *Hogue, Cressy Euryalus,* etc., at Scapa Flow in the Orkney Islands. Light cruisers, destroyers, and submarines were to be stationed along the east coast and Channel ports, to patrol the waters from the Norwegian coast to the Dover Straits.

Prince Louis presented this sensible plan, as written, to the First Lord and a council of admirals. The admirals were enthusiastic, but Churchill, who had absorbed the theory that "Our first line of defence is the enemy's ports," was against it. It contravened his every instinct for offensive action, for coming to grips with the enemy as soon as possible or keeping him bottled up tight. This was just what the

Germans hoped for, as it would allow them to wear down the British Fleet by sudden sorties in force.

Churchill also proposed a hair-brained scheme for "an offensive at the outset." He proposed to blockade the mouth of the Elbe and hold Heligoland Bight with the entire destroyer flotilla, strongly supported by the fleet, for a week, while the Army went to France. The Admiralty replied that in that week 50 per cent of the destroyers would be lost to mines, torpedoes, and enemy sorties, and the fleet would be endangered. As opposed to the cork-in-the-bottle theory, the Admiralty wished to give the German High Seas Fleet every opportunity to come out, and then destroy it in blue water.

The upshot was a compromise on the Kerr plan—a not very distant blockade. The battle fleet was to be stationed in the north of Scotland at Scapa Flow and Cromarty, and at the Firth of Forth. The heavy cruisers were to be used in patrolling—with unhappy results in the event—and the destroyers, light cruisers, and submarines were to operate more or less as planned. Like all compromises, this one had grave weaknesses, but in the end it served.

One of its worst features was that although the Channel ports were well fortified, those on the east coast were almost totally undefended. They were supposed to be the Army's responsibility, but the generals felt that what means they had must be used to build up the strength of their mobile forces. Their budget was far smaller than the Navy's and they were not about to spend any money to make their rival service feel secure. Rival, and not sister service, is the correct word; so it has always been in every country with two or more services competing for the public purse, until the guns actually begin to shoot and often even then.

Seeing that they could hope for nothing from the Army, Churchill and Battenberg decided, "in desperation," that the Navy would have to do something. They had the means to defend only one port and they chose Cromarty. Naval guns were set up on the headlands, Marines were sent to garrison the works, and a rather amateurish defense against submarines and torpedoes was begun. It was extremely rudimentary compared to the great German ports bristling with all manner of defense and totally invulnerable to attack by sea. Scapa Flow, which became the main anchorage of the Battle Fleet when war was declared, was completely naked save for a few pathetic batallions of Territorial artillery, roughly analogous to our National Guard.

Another excellent move made almost immediately by Prince Louis when he became First Sea Lord was to raise the range for target practice with the big guns from 10,000 yards to a realistic 15,000. Later he increased it again to 16,000. This was particularly fortunate, because the one great naval battle of the war, Jutland, was fought at ranges up to 22,000 yards.

To replace Battenberg as Second Sea Lord, Churchill had brought Vice-Admiral Sir John Jellicoe to Whitehall. A small, slight man, careful and meticulous, he was ideally suited to the job. The whole Navy respected him as a brilliant technician. Yet he lacked the commanding presence of a great leader and the daring, offensive spirit of the Nelsonian tradition. Soon he and Battenberg were involved in another spirited clash with Winston Churchill.

Jellicoe furiously resented Churchill's custom of taking an active part in the technical direction of the fleet—"meddling," he called it. His resentment reached the flash point in November of 1913 over the affair of Captain Gerald W. Vivian of the aircraft carrier *Hermes* and a young lieutenant of the Naval Air Service. They had an argument about a minor matter concerning an air base on the Medway. The lieutenant laid the matter before Churchill, who was on one of his inspection trips, "quite improperly," according to naval tradition. Churchill was impressed and ordered that it be done the lieutenant's way, and the lieutenant cheekily told Captain Vivian that if it were not, he would write to the First Lord of the Admiralty.

Such a breach of discipline set the fat on fire. Vivian wrote to his superior, Admiral Sir Richard Poore, and the Admiral sent Jellicoe, who was in charge of Naval Air, a hot protest. Somehow Churchill got wind of the business, saw the correspondence, and danced with rage, while Jellicoe smoldered like a volcano. Churchill said he was going to fire Poore, Jellicoe threatened to resign, taking the Third and Fourth Sea Lords with him. The matter went up to Prince Louis who was at his best in this sort of situation. He told Poore and Jellicoe humorously that the First Lord of the Admiralty was off his rocker and they should take no notice of him. Then he sent for the lieutenant and talked to him like a Dutch uncle, which in a way he was. The upshot of it all was that the lieutenant apologized to Captain Vivian, the Admiral reluctantly withdrew his letter and expressed regret, Jellicoe withdrew his resignation, and Churchill soon forgot the whole thing.

The only reason to mention this teapot tempest is to show that it took a very special sort of commander to work with Winston Churchill. In their sober afterthoughts most naval officers admitted that much of Churchill's "meddling" was good for the Navy, but they found it damned annoying at the time. His self-confidence and original thinking negated their cherished theories, short-circuited their sacred channels, and upset their dignity. This same theme runs through all British military writings in World War Two, but by that time Churchill was the indispensable man and his commanders on land, sea, and air were expendable; so they had to put up with it.

Things were far different in World War One. Not only was Churchill young and untried, but he was even brasher then. Almost everyone, including the King and most of the Cabinet, distrusted Churchill's erratic brilliance. Because Battenberg also had an adventurous mind and a keen sense of humor about himself, he appreciated Churchill's great qualities, and never stood pompously on his dignity. His method of handling Churchill with persuasive argument and the light rein of humor led Professor Marder to call him "not forceful," and Fisher, when he became disenchanted, to refer to Battenberg as "the Jelly Fish." On the contrary it made for a wonderful partnership in which Churchill's flashing impetuosity was channeled but not frustrated by Battenberg's superior technical knowledge and gentle guidance.

Though the First Lord and the Sea Lords were at odds over these trivialities they were solidly in accord on the main points of naval policy. In particular they were unanimous on the Naval Estimates for 1913–14 of—£46,309,000. In order to maintain a ratio of 60 per cent over the German Fleet, they provided for the building of five super-dreadnoughts, which became the Royal Sovereign Class. Like the *Queen Elizabeth*, they were to be armed with eight 15-inch guns, and fourteen 6-inch guns to defend against the big new German destroyers—all-big-gun Fisher didn't like that. They were nearly 2,000 tons smaller than the Queen Elizabeth Class (25,750 compared to 27,500), and were coal burning* with a speed of only 21 knots. This retrogression was made in the interests of economy, and when Churchill announced the figures in March, 1913, the usual political Donnybrook began. The big-navy Conservatives said it was not enough; the radical wing of Churchill's own party said it was too much.

However, this row was nothing compared to the howl that went up when, in December, 1913, the 1914–15 Estimates of £50,700,000 (about $250,000,000) were announced. This included only four super-dreadnoughts, eventually to become the battle cruisers *Repulse* and *Renown*. The increase was accounted for largely by the rise in maintenance costs, increase in numbers of personnel and pay, and so on. At this point Churchill became the hero of the Conservative Party, the villain of his own. Radical Socialists like Ramsay MacDonald started an out-and-out pacifist campaign. Chancellor of the Exchequer Lloyd George published an interview in which he said Anglo-German relations were much friendlier and reminded Churchill that his own father, Lord

---

* Later changed to oil.

Randolph Churchill, had resigned rather than accept "bloated" armament expenditures. He called the naval race "organized insanity." This statement was regarded generally as an insult to Churchill. It looked as though the Liberal Government were about to blow up.

The press and the nation took sides, exchanging acrimonious prophecies of disaster. Pressure groups formed to propagandize pro and con. But the real fight took place in the Cabinet meetings in January, 1914. Churchill was backed by Foreign Minister Sir Edward Grey and several others. Prime Minister Asquith was also on his side, but was more interested in holding the party together. However, eight members of the Cabinet, including former First Lord McKenna, vociferously backed Lloyd George's demand that only two battleships be built. In despair Churchill said, "My back is against the wall."

Help came from outside the Government. Prince Louis and the other three Sea Lords let it be known that they would resign with Churchill if the Estimates were slashed. Finally, King George V, who was *not* afraid to intervene in politics when he conceived it to be his patriotic duty, made clear in rough, salty language that he was on the sailors' side. Though his remarks were made in private they were widely known and carried great weight.

Because of the united front presented by the Admiralty, the support of the King—who had completely reversed his opinion of his First Lord of the Admiralty—and thanks to some inept German diplomacy, Churchill won out. By March he could write exultantly, "In all these months of bickering we had only lost three small cruisers and twelve torpedo-boats for harbor defense."

Meanwhile a non-partisan committee had been formed to examine the condition of Britain's defenses against a bolt-from-the-blue invasion. The committee consisted of ten Cabinet ministers, Conservative Leader Arthur J. Balfour, Battenberg, Sir John French (Chief of the Imperial General Staff), and a number of other admirals and generals. To everybody's surprise and pleasure, these men of divergent views actually produced a unanimous report, early in 1914, on how to meet the danger—by the adoption of a new military scheme for Home Defence, which envisaged local forces to take the first shock and a strong mobile central force to deliver the *coup de grâce*. It also evaluated the probabilities of such an attempt and the naval dispositions to meet it, and came up with the conclusion that an invasion was unlikely and in any event the invading force could not be larger than 70,000 men. Its evaluation proved to be correct.

Much less prescient were the Admiralty conclusions about the use of submarines as commerce raiders. In January, 1914, Fisher warned Churchill that such use was likely. The First Lord of the Admiralty observed that, "It is inconceivable that any civilized nation" would so use them. The Admiralty officially expressed the opinion, in 1912, that the submarine had "the smallest value of any vessel for the direct attack upon trade," because the crews were not large enough to man ships taken as prizes and the submarine had no means of "removing passengers and other persons if she wishes to sink one."

Prince Louis concurred in this view—"Unthinkable," he said to Fisher. He was too gentle a man even to consider the possibility that the Germany of his childhood memories might adopt a policy of *spurlos versunken* (sunk without a trace). For all his progressive thinking, he was too humanitarian to function efficiently in a world whose bright tomorrow would be lit by such infernal fires.

But if Prince Louis, like the vast majority of British naval officers, was euphoric about submarine warfare, he had no illusion about the possibility of a surprise German attack on the British Fleet in the midst of peace. Though Germany had signed the Hague Convention of 1907, which expressly provided for a formal declaration of war before hostilities began, Louis was not willing to bet the survival of Britain against Germany's keeping the agreement. Japan had started the Russo-Japanese War by a sudden attack on the Russian Fleet at Port Arthur. With far higher stakes to gain, Germany might be tempted to do the same.

Throughout the years of Prince Louis' service at the Admiralty this terrible anxiety never left his mind by day or night—especially by night. As Winston Churchill points out in *The World Crisis*, the Continent was like a vast powder magazine that "one hellish spark" might ignite. But a surprise attack against the Continental powers was impossible, because armies must be mobilized and concentrated on the frontier and that cannot be done secretly. Yet, all the German Navy had to do was get up steam and steal up on their unsuspecting victim under cover of fog and darkness. The danger of the British Fleet being destroyed by gunfire was not too great, since they could reply to that on a few moments' notice, but the torpedo was the weapon of surprise and treachery that could destroy a dozen dreadnoughts before their sleepy crews could man the guns. Had this happened to the Royal Navy, as it did to the American Fleet at Pearl Harbor, England would have lost the First World War before ever she began to fight. The United States, secure on her vast continent behind great oceans, had time to recover and fight back. The English island, cut off from the Empire and all sources of supply, would have fallen into the enemy's lap like a coconut severed from its stem.

It was impossible to guard completely against this possibility. The great ships could not always be kept moving at full speed, with lookouts posted, guns manned, and destroyers screening them. In fact they had to spend most of their time at anchor, often in unprotected roadsteads. They had to have training cruises followed by periods of refitting and leave for their crews. But what could be done, Battenberg did.

He kept the fleet in a state of constant alert. Wherever the battleships were anchored, small fast sentinel ships patrolled the approaches. The fleet never went off to its customary cruises in the Atlantic unless the First Sea Lord knew with certainty that most of the German Fleet was in drydock for its winter refits. When the grand maneuvers were held in the North Sea, they were so timed and arranged that, afterward, plenty of coal remained in the bunkers and only a small percentage of the fleet was recoaled or in drydock at a given time. Above all, the position of every unit of the fleet was charted and so disposed that at any given moment it could muster enough strength to ward off an enemy attack.

Winston Churchill, his restless mind forever imagining all possible and impossible contingencies, was, if anything, even more anxious than Battenberg, but even he was satisfied that everything possible was being done to safeguard his beloved ships, so powerful yet so vulnerable, on which the life of England depended. To test their readiness Churchill, on arriving at the Admiralty, often would send for Prince Louis and his staff and shoot the sudden question, "What happens if war with Germany begins today?" He writes, "I never found them without an answer which showed that we had the power to effect our main concentration before any portion of the Fleet could be brought to battle."

As shown by captured German documents, Churchill and Battenberg, though completely justified, acquired a great many needless gray hairs. The German Government never even contemplated this particular act of treachery. Perhaps old Admiral Alfred von Tirpitz, who masterminded the later *shrechtlichtkeit*, might have liked to try it, but Kaiser Wilhelm had not yet been so far corrupted by the Prussian militarists. After all his upbringing had been much the same as that of Prince Louis. Words such as chivalry, faith, honor held the same meanings for him and, until desperation drove him to renounce it, he lived by the same creed. True, he could be persuaded by the Imperial General Staff to break the treaty guaranteeing Belgian neutrality. But at least he sent the Belgians an ultimatum beforehand and did not treacherously take them by surprise. Like all the other gentlemen who were guiding the destinies of the great nations, the German Emperor had no conception of modern war.

. . .

There was never a lovelier summer in Europe than that of 1914; and none so fine again until 1939. In London, gentle May ceded to radiant June. Flowers lighted the parks with rainbow beauty, and window boxes in the serene squares—Belgrave, Grosvenor, Eaton—bloomed brightly with geraniums and spring flowers, decorating the classic houses, great and small. There were several balls every night, and pink-cheeked young Englishmen and happy debutantes rushed from one to another while their elders, sparkling with all the jewels an Empire could furnish, arrived in high-topped Daimlers, glittering Rolls-Royces, and fine broughams drawn by high-stepping horses with cockaded coach-men and footmen on the box. Prince Louis saw the Derby won by Durbar II, and Royal Ascot never was so regally superb. Even the climate of international relations seemed to take its cue from terrestrial meteorology. There was, for once, not a cloud of crisis in the sky.

The Battenbergs were living in London that summer at Mall House, the official residence of the First Sea Lord. It was big and ornate, with great echoing corridors and a tremendous marble staircase, designed for official functions and not for comfort. But the Battenbergs did not mind too much; they were accustomed to palatial inconvenience. Also they were very blessed in their domestic life; they were a close, con-genial family. There is no recorded evidence that Prince Louis ever had any impulse to stray as did so many of his contemporaries at Court and in naval circles. Vicky had, of course, changed considerably from the plumply pretty princess he had married. Her Royal Grand Ducal Highness Princess Louis of Battenberg had become rather stout and overpowering. She still talked incessantly in heavily accented English with complete confidence that what she was saying was too important to be missed. The children of their friends found her a little frightening. Prince Louis found her refreshingly blunt and loved her dearly.

Alice was living happily in Greece with Andrew, whose eldest brother was now King Constantine I. They had four girls but as yet no son. Louise, an agreeable young lady of twenty-two, was still living at home; both boys were in the Navy. George was a lieutenant in the battle cruiser *New Zealand* and Dickie had just completed his first term as a naval cadet at Osborne. Prince Louis went to inspect it in his capacity as First Sea Lord, and as he strode along the ranks of little boys standing rigidly at attention, he was both amused and infinitely touched by the proud, adoring eyes of his younger son.

In June, 1914, good feeling between England and Germany reached the highest point since Kaiser Wilhelm had decided to build a fleet to challenge Britain's supremacy on the sea. Oddly enough, the occasion was the festive reopening of the Kiel Canal, which had been widened and deepened to permit the big new German dreadnoughts to go from the mouth of the Elbe on the North Sea to Kiel on the Baltic Sea without exposing themselves by going outside, around the Danish coast and through the narrow Kattegat Straits between Denmark and Norway. The sixty-mile inland route across the neck of Schleswig-Holstein gave Germany unchallenged control of the Baltic, since the feeble Russian Fleet could do nothing against them, and the British dared not risk the Grand Fleet in those confined waters. It was hardly a pleasant prospect for the Royal Navy, but so amicable were the feelings of the two countries that the British Government decided at the invitation of the German Emperor to send a squadron of warships to Kiel to take part in the ceremonies. They also sent a squadron to Russia's Kronstadt Naval Base on the Baltic in order not to hurt the Tsar's feelings.

Herr Ballin wrote to Sir Ernest Cassel, who was still working for disarmament, that if he could get Winston Churchill to come to Kiel and talk with the Emperor and Admiral von Tirpitz, he was sure something could be accomplished because the Admiral in a mellow mood had expressed a desire to discuss things, not with the diplomats, but with naval people. Of course Winston was anxious to go, but the Cabinet would not let him. Quite evidently they thought him too impulsive to be trusted in the handling of a diplomatic matter. For one thing, with his round, pink-cheeked face and eager eyes, he looked too *young* to be trusted.

So without Churchill but with the Kaiser there hobnobbing with British admirals in the last days of June, 1914, some of the finest ships of the Royal Navy lay peacefully at anchor beside the new German dreadnoughts, surrounded by a holiday crowd of yachts, chartered liners, and all sorts of smaller vessels. The sun shone brightly; every day there were races and other sports, and at night banquets with speeches of good fellowship and toasts to all concerned. The Kaiser was at his most charming, and really enjoyed himself with the technical navy talk.

When a German airman was killed flying a British seaplane the chief officers of both fleets attended the funeral, standing bareheaded as platoons of German and British sailors fired the farewell volleys over his grave.

The officers in the lower echelons of both navies entertained each other in an atmosphere of pure *Gemütlichkeit*, while the wardrooms rang to their drinking songs as they hoisted steins of strong German beer that everybody admitted was better than any British brew. The sailors of both fleets, given generous leave, strolled arm in arm through the friendly city sparking the girls and getting gloriously drunk in the rustic beer halls.

Only one slight shadow fell on that sunny scene. On June 28 word was received that the Archduke and Archduchess Franz-Ferdinand of Austria had been assassinated by a crazy Servian at the Bosnian city of Sarajevo. The Kaiser left hurriedly for Berlin.

If the international scene was serene, the United Kingdom was not. The Liberal Government of Prime Minister Asquith had at last made good their promise of passing a Home Rule Bill for Ireland. The Catholic south of Ireland was delighted; the Protestant north was angry and terrified at the thought of being a minority governed by the "wild Fenians" of the South. The Ulster leader, Sir John Carson, had raised and armed a private army pledged to fight such a move; the southern Irish were also arming. Civil war seemed imminent.

When, in March, 1914, the British garrison at the Curragh Base was alerted to march into the north of Ireland and take possession of the arms depots there, all the officers announced they would resign rather than do so. This came to be known as the Curragh Mutiny, and it shook the British State to its foundations. Never had the country been split so wide. The Conservatives cried that the Liberal Government had planned a massacre of Ulstermen, frustrated only by the patriotism of the Army. The Liberals claimed that Ulster was planning open rebellion to nullify the constitution and had seduced the army officers from their allegiance to the Crown.

King George was frantic. His fury against the Liberal Government could hardly be contained by the constitutional imperative to remain above the battle. "If they keep on," he said, "I'll have no army left."

The political battle raged through May and June, and in July it worsened. Acting on his own initiative, though with Prime Minister Asquith's assent, the King summoned a conference of Conservative, Liberal, and Irish leaders to Buckingham Palace on July 20. They came, they met, they fought fiercely with no compromise possible. After three days of angry wrangling the conference abruptly ended. The German Embassy in London informed the Foreign Office in Berlin that the British were so deeply divided that they were incapable of acting in international affairs. This opinion was absolutely valid by any logical standard. But neither the English nor the Irish are logical people.

.   .   .

There are times in their recorded history when the Almighty seems to take special care of the British. Whether by His interposition or just dumb luck—it was certainly not foresight—such a situation occurred in July, 1914. Back in the autumn of 1913, Churchill and Battenberg were discussing every possible way to save money. One suggestion, which probably came from Churchill, was to omit in 1914 the annual Grand Maneuvers, which cost a tremendous amount of money, and substitute a trial mobilization of the Third Fleet, the entire Royal Fleet Reserve, and all the reserve officers. There had previously been partial mobilizations but never before in history had the fleet as a whole been involved. To make it official, Churchill wrote to the Sea Lords proposing it on October 22, 1913. Prince Louis agreed enthusiastically. Since his days as Director of Naval Intelligence he had been especially interested in personnel problems and had worked with Fisher on the system of reserves. It appeared to him more valuable to try it out than to hold the maneuvers, and there certainly was not money enough to do both.

The test mobilization began on July 15, 1914. It had no relationship to the crisis over the assassination of the heir to the Austrian throne. Indeed, that emergency seemed to be simmering down. Austria was angry and threatening, and there had been ominous rumblings from Russia, but diplomacy appeared to be succeeding. The situation was not nearly as bad as it had been at Agadir. The Kaiser was so untroubled that he had gone on a yachting holiday off the coast of Norway. This was unfortunate, because while he was away his admirals and generals got in over their heads.

Since no state of emergency was declared there was absolutely no legal obligation for the British naval reservists to answer the Admiralty's call to mobilize; but almost all of them did. Over 200,000 men reported at the different naval depots. Officers from the Admiralty were sent to all the bases to study the procedure and make notes on how it could be improved next time. But there was no next time. Churchill and Battenberg went together to the great Chatham Base. They watched the reservists draw their kits and proceed to their designated ships. It was not done without confusion, but on the whole it went well. The old battleships and cruisers of the Third Fleet got up steam and sailed for Spithead to join the magnificent new ships of the First and Second Fleets in a grand review.

Prince Louis and Winston Churchill boarded *Enchantress* and sailed to join them. When they arrived the Royal Yacht was already there and the waters of the roadstead were covered by hundreds of warships of every size and type. It was the greatest assemblage of naval power the world had ever seen or ever would see again.* In the deep, blue water under the cloudless sky of that fine summer it was enough to churn the emotions of any man who loved the sea.

On July 17 and 18 the ships lay at anchor, while the King, Churchill, and Prince Louis inspected as many of them as possible. On the morning of July 19 the fleet put to sea for various exercises. The *Victoria and Albert* had stationed herself out at sea with the Royal Standard flying and the King on the bridge. Nearby lay *Enchantress.* Since these were not war maneuvers but a review, the fleet came out in gala dress, every ship decked in all her signal flags, the bands playing madly and officers and men in dress uniforms crowding the decks. As each ship went by, it fired the Royal Salute—the bark of guns, a haze of smoke, the tremendous roaring cheers across the water.

Steaming at 15 knots it took that great armada six hours to pass the Royal Yacht. The King was nearly delirious with joy. The First Lord of the Admiralty recorded the scene in poetic prose charged with emotion. Prince Louis of Battenberg was the proudest man in the world, with the possible exception of one small naval cadet, standing on the deck of an old battleship straining his eyes through the haze of her guns for a glimpse of that splendid figure on the bridge of *Enchantress.*

---

* The great American armadas of World War Two in the Pacific may have been more numerous, but they largely represented air power rather than pure naval might.

Chapter 14

THE GREAT
DECISION

WHILE THE CABINET WRANGLED, the Irish armed and the English fumed over the trouble in Ireland, and the Kaiser sailed among the Norwegian fjords in his white schooner yacht *Meteor,* the soldiers and diplomats of Europe somehow got themselves caught in a tremendous current of events that carried them, struggling unavailingly, toward the catastrophe of war. Of that wonderful century of unchallenged security, during which England had grown great, there remained a scant ten days. In order to understand the problems of Prince Louis and the other British military commanders it becomes necessary to evaluate the civilians who governed England as she faced the greatest threat since her sentinel ships in the Channel had seen ten thousand campfires of Napoleon's *Grande Armée* waiting at Boulogne for the Emperor's order to cross the narrow strait.

Actually there was hardly ever a group of men more ill-equipped— by temperament, training, and inclination—to conduct a modern war than were the Liberal Government of England in July of 1914. They were idealists of the great Liberal tradition who had come to power after twenty years of tough Conservative rule. With shining eyes and happy hearts they intended to mold their world nearer to mankind's desire.

They functioned in a rose-colored ideological haze that stemmed back to Jean-Jacques Rousseau and Robert Paine, Richard Cobden and John Bright. Gladstone was their exemplar and John Stuart Mill their prophet. Their philosophy was profoundly pacific.

Prime Minister Asquith was a man of noble character, absolute integrity, high ideals, and charming manners, whose memoirs show his utter inability to cope with harsh reality or assay the worth of his human tools. An example is the entry in his diary of March 25, 1915, concerning Winston Churchill: "It is a pity that Winston has not a better sense of proportion. I am really fond of him, but I regard his future with misgivings. I do not think he will ever get to the top in English politics with all his wonderful gifts."

Foreign Minister Sir Edward Grey was a great gentleman and diplomatist of the old school, with a profound knowledge of foreign policy as practiced in the chess-like moves and minuet figures of the nineteenth century. As long as the old diplomacy was practiced he played his part skillfully and coolly. When it broke down, he became less valuable. War was not his métier.

Then there were the radicals, Lord Morley, John Burns, and their fellows, bred in the tradition of Fabian Socialism as propounded in the drawing rooms of Chelsea by Edward Pease, Bernard Shaw, and Annie Besant, under the egis of Beatrice and Sydney Webb. It visualized a never-never land of social equality and a state-run economic order as unreal as Dante Gabriel Rosetti's "Blessed Damozel leaning over the Gold Bar of Heaven." They could not know that it would take Bolshevist brutality to make socialism work. These radicals permitted Sir Edward Grey to commit England's honor to the defense of France if she were attacked, yet said they would resign if England declared war on Germany. And did!

Of them all, two men alone had the steely temperament and ruthless mentality necessary for the conduct of war—Lloyd George and Winston Churchill. But the latter was as yet too unseasoned, too brusque, bravura, and callow to hold the balance between the daring and the fantastically rash. Lloyd George had enough low cunning and common sense, unhampered by chivalrous tradition, to learn his trade. But so little did he know of it in 1914 that on July 23, the day the Austrians sent to Servia the ultimatum that precipitated World War One, he made a speech in which he prophesied that future differences between nations would be settled by arbitration. He needed two years to learn his lessons, and he did not emerge as the necessarily Draconian leader until 1916.

To these, perhaps, should be added Lord Haldane, who had rebuilt the Army and negotiated the tentative arrangement with the French military leaders for the dispatch of a British Expeditionary Force to France in the event that his colleagues in the Cabinet decided to honor their commitment to defend her. He was a big, burly man with a certain mental toughness. Unfortunately for England he, like Prince Louis, became the victim of Germanophobia. Because he had once referred to Germany as his "spiritual home," there arose against him, in Asquith's words, "one of those fanatical and malignant outcries which from time to time disgrace our national character." On this account Asquith was reluctantly forced to dispense with his valuable services in May, 1915.

As somewhat related to these well-meaning idealists we must, perhaps, place Prince Louis of Battenberg. Though he was more knowledgeable in European politics and, by training, more alert to the danger and more warlike than they, he also was too idealistic and too civilized to be completely successful in the profession of arms as practiced by the new barbarians. He would be dismissed as First Sea Lord for a ridiculous reason. Yet perhaps a deeper truth prevailed. His successor, Lord Fisher, the son of an obscure army officer, could see more clearly than a great gentleman who could not bear to look.

On the other hand, given the character of First Lord of the Admiralty Winston Churchill, Battenberg might well have functioned more effectively than Fisher. It is one of those unresolvable ifs of history.

Prince Louis was in his office at the Admiralty at six o'clock on the evening of Friday, July 24, 1914, when Winston Churchill, in a state of agitation, hurried in from a Cabinet meeting. The conference at Buckingham Palace had broken up that day, and they had been despairingly debating the Irish Question when a King's messenger handed Sir Edward Grey a "most immediate" dispatch. As the Foreign Minister read it aloud, the Irish Question was forgotten. It was the text of the ultimatum sent to Servia by the Austrian Government. Churchill brought a copy of it to the First Sea Lord. "Read that!" he said. Prince Louis read the document with unbelieving eyes. It was the most brutal, domineering demand that, as far as he could remember, any government had ever made upon another. He could not see how any nation great or small could accept its terms and keep her self-respect.* He agreed with Churchill's excited statement: "There is a real danger of war."

That Friday night Churchill dined with Herr Ballin at Sir Ernest

---

* By modern standards set by Communist diplomacy the Austrian ultimatum was a polite, even courtly document; but by the customs of a more civilized era, Prince Louis' judgment was correct.

Cassel's great house on Park Lane. Ballin was on a fishing expedition for the Kaiser to find out if England would stay out of war if Germany guaranteed not to annex any French territory. Churchill gave him no hope of such a deal, but Ballin recorded that as Churchill was bidding him good-bye, the First Lord pressed his hand, and with tears in his eyes, said, "Let's not have a war!"

The following morning the situation looked considerably worse. Russia was not taking kindly to the position in which her little Slavic ally had been placed. Churchill came to the Admiralty, where he and Battenberg took stock of the Navy's situation. It was good. True, all the regular reservists had been paid off and the old ships of the Third Fleet left with skeleton crews. But the First Fleet was concentrated at Portland and the ships of the Second Fleet were at their home ports still fully manned by their nucleus crews plus the Immediate Reserve. Both Fleets were ready for battle, and they were to remain so until Monday morning when the First Fleet would disperse by squadrons for their normal occasions and the Second Fleet would begin to discharge the reservists in their crews. So the First Lord and his Sea Lord reckoned that at any time until Monday morning a wireless message to the Commander in Chief Home Fleet, Sir George Callaghan, would keep the main British Battle Fleet intact and ready to fight.

After giving Battenberg a list of things to be done, Churchill explained that he had planned to spend the weekend with his family in the country at Cromer, and hurried off. Prince Louis watched him go with a look of irony in his eyes.

All that afternoon and evening Battenberg remained at the Admiralty, reading the dispatches that poured in from the great European capitals. Word came that Servia had accepted the Austrian ultimatum with minor reservations. Somewhat easier in his mind Prince Louis went home to a late dinner.

He was at the Admiralty by eight the next morning. Churchill rang up about nine and said he was going to the beach with his children and would call again when he got back. The messages from Vienna, St. Petersburg, Paris, Berlin, and Belgrade began to pour in. Austria had not accepted Servia's acceptance of the ultimatum, which was to expire at 6 P.M. She wanted complete abasement and control of her little Balkan neighbor. The other messages were not too alarming in themselves, but they all added up to dangerously rising pressures.

Sitting in the great echoing building, alone except for a skeleton staff, Prince Louis anxiously read the dispatches, and reflected between readings on the peculiar insouciance of the English. Though the European powder keg might explode at any moment, not one important

Cabinet minister had canceled his weekend plans. Asquith, Grey, Haldane, and Lloyd George were all off at country houses. The First Lord of the Admiralty was playing in the sand with his children. Prince Louis noted, "Ministers with their week-end holidays are incorrigible. . . ."

At about noon Churchill telephoned again. Prince Louis' summation of the situation sounded so threatening that the First Lord decided to give up his sacred Sunday afternoon. "I'll be with you by nine o'clock," Churchill said. "Meanwhile I authorize you to do whatever is necessary."

If Prince Louis smiled a little grimly as he hung up the receiver, it was because he knew the buck had been passed. There was no doubt in his mind that war was as close as the next tick of the clock. That being the case, the fleet must be kept together for the safety of England. If he should let slip the providential gift of time, granted by its fortuitous mobilization, he could only consider himself a traitor to his adopted country. On the other hand the pacific gentlemen of the Cabinet would probably regard an order to alert the fleet as a usurpation of the civil power and, what was worse, an incitement to Germany. If the international situation looked calmer in the morning, they would say he had acted rashly and would have his head. Churchill's vague grant of authority meant nothing; he could easily say that he had not intended to authorize an act that Germany could consider warlike. The others, especially the radicals, would be furious, and the career Prince Louis had loved would end in a flurry of polite protestations of regret that his resignation must be accepted. They might even advise the King to give him a peerage. But in his case it would mean nothing. What do you create a serene highness? It would mean nothing anyhow. All he cared for was the Navy.

Prince Louis decided to wait until the Austrian ultimatum expired at 6 P.M.—that much grace he could safely allow himself. Eagerly he snatched the dispatches out of the red boxes sent over by messenger from the Foreign Office. They gave him small hope. Late in the afternoon there was a lull. He sat looking out of the window at the gentle sunshine lighting the peaceful trees and flowers and green English grass. Such a lovely day! . . .

Down in Parliament Square Big Ben's chimes rang loudly in the Sunday stillness. Prince Louis walked from the window to his desk, while the sonorous reverberation of the famous clock six times shook the quiet air. In Vienna old Emperor Franz-Josef had broken off diplomatic relations with Servia and ordered his army mobilized. Prince Louis reviewed the position once again.

It would have been so easy to play it safe from his personal point of view. There was still another twelve hours before the fleets would begin to disperse. Battenberg could certainly have reached Asquith or Grey or Lloyd George to get official authorization to order the fleets to remain mobilized. He had no intention of trying. They would most probably say, No!

Churchill was out of reach on the train, but would be at the Admiralty by nine o'clock. That still left plenty of time to send the message to Callaghan. With Churchill there Prince Louis would be in the clear. But he had misgivings about the volatile First Lord. Churchill's reputation among his colleagues for impetuousness and lack of judgment had already put him in a weak position. For him to take the onus of issuing this order—which almost amounted to mobilization for war with the resultant shock to the strained fabric of international relations— would confirm their opinion and perhaps force his resignation as First Lord of the Admiralty, thereby ending his political career. Would Churchill be willing to take the risk? Would he not insist on consulting his colleagues? Prince Louis feared this would mean that the order would not be sent. Even if Churchill were willing to risk political extinction, should he be asked for the sacrifice?

There were too many ifs. Prince Louis was convinced that the safety of England depended on the readiness of the fleet. He had lived too long with the specter of surprise attack to risk it now. He saw that to play it safe for himself was exactly antithetical to playing it safe for England. He knew his own German people, knew that they might strike like lightning at their chosen moment, while the British Cabinet debated. Someone must save these naïve English from themselves, even if it took a German to do it. So, to hell with the constitution! And to hell with the Cabinet! To hell with the Kaiser and old Tirpitz! To hell with all of them! And to hell with his career. The British could easily find another First Sea Lord, but not another fleet.

Rapidly Prince Louis wrote a wireless to the commander in chief, ordering the First and Second Fleets to remain mobilized, ready to fight. Firmly he signed it: Louis Battenberg.

It was an act of supreme loyalty.

Winston Churchill came in at nine as he had promised. When Prince Louis showed him the order to Admiral Callaghan he gave his instant approval. Then Churchill went to call on Sir Edward Grey, who happened to have rented the Churchills' house on Eccleston Square.

Sir Edward was alone with Sir William Tyrrell of the Foreign Office. He too endorsed Prince Louis' act as necessary. The members of the Cabinet might have hesitated to approve such an order, but they could not rescind it. Certainly they had the legal power to do so, but it was politically impossible. If anything went wrong they would be responsible for having reversed the decision of the First Sea Lord; and that they dared not do.

Furthermore, Sir Edward proposed to make the news public. It might, he thought, have a sobering effect on Germany. So Churchill hurried back to the Admiralty where he and Prince Louis drafted a carefully worded communiqué:

ORDER TO THE FIRST AND SECOND FLEETS

Orders have been given to the First Fleet, which is concentrated at Portland, not to disperse for manoeuvre leave for the present. All vessels of the Second Fleet are remaining at their home ports in proximity to their balance crews.

This was not quite the truth, since the reserve crews were kept aboard the ships. It cleverly softened somewhat the implication of mobilization while at the same time indicating to the public—and to Germany—that the fleet was in a state of readiness.

On Monday, July 27, there was a long and indecisive Cabinet meeting. In fact there were one or two equally indecisive meetings every day that week. In his memoirs Asquith says that three quarters of the Cabinet were dead against intervention under any circumstances, even though they had gone along with that quasi alliance (*entente*) with France; and the French, relying on it, had withdrawn all their large ships to hold the Mediterranean on the understanding that the Royal Navy would guard the French ports on the Channel and the Atlantic. The Prime Minister himself appears to have been quivering like an oscillograph between the factions of his Cabinet, ready to do almost anything to hold it together. Sir Edward Grey and Winston Churchill were firm for the honorable course of defending France if she were attacked. Sir Edward said he would resign if the pacifists prevailed. Helplessly Asquith wrote: "Of course if Grey went I should go, and the whole thing would break up."

On July 28 Austria declared war on Servia. Though there were still some who hoped for peace—Grey was working adroitly to bring about a general European conference with some chance of success—this was the overt act. To mobilize is threatening but not final, since troops can be demobilized. It is almost impossible to undo a declaration of war.

When the news reached them Prince Louis and Winston Churchill held a private council of war at the Admiralty. Battenberg and his

Chief of Staff Rear Admiral Frederick Sturdee, were resolved that the fleet must go to its War Station. It must go at once and secretly before the Germans could attack it or mine the narrow Dover Straits. Churchill needed no convincing, but he faced the problem of having to handle the pacific Cabinet. The only way was simply not to tell them. Churchill wrote, "Because I knew the Cabinet would not act it was necessary to take peculiar and invidious responsibility for things that had to be done." Prince Louis went even further than Churchill in taking responsibility which was more "invidious" because he was acting extra-constitutionally.

Churchill, however, did tell the Prime Minister of the decision to send the fleet to its War Station. Asquith gave his consent both to the order and to keeping his colleagues in the dark. So the order was sent for the First Fleet to sail secretly for Scapa Flow and the Second Fleet to assemble in its place at Portland.

Shortly after midnight the great dreadnoughts, battle cruisers, cruisers, destroyers, accompanied by mine sweepers, trawlers, and other craft, silently weighed anchor and steamed out of harbor. With no lights, in utter silence, they moved swiftly up the center of the Channel. Like a long snake, deadly yet vulnerable, eighteen miles of warships passed the Dover Straits unseen at high speed, though they could see the lights of France and England on either hand.

That was probably the most anxious night Prince Louis ever spent. For, though there was no reason to suspect it, he could not be sure that the Germans had not foresightedly laid a trap of submarines and mines into which the fleet might blunder to disaster in the darkness. If it did, the responsibility was his alone. For he had advised the First Lord, he had signed the orders, he had assumed the risk. It was he who staked the very life of England on the safe passage of the fleet through that narrow gateway to the North Sea. So he sat all night at the Admiralty, outwardly as calmly composed as his noble portrait by De Laszlo, inwardly volcanic, waiting for the dire message that fortunately never came.

The message that did come the next morning as he was holding the daily staff meeting with Churchill and the other Sea Lords was a report from the flagship *Iron Duke* that she and the entire fleet were safely out in the blue water of the North Sea.

Then came the repercussions. The German ambassador, Prince Lichnowski, who was honestly working for peace, went mournfully to Sir Edward Grey to lodge his Government's angry protest. Grey told him with official correctness that, "The movements of the Fleet are free of all offensive character, and the Fleet will not approach German waters."

But he knew and Tirpitz knew, and Prince Louis joyfully knew, that the strategic concentration of the fleet had been successfully effected. Whatever happened, Britain was in a position to control events on the sea. No one could rob her now of that advantage by surprise or by treachery. At the first clang of danger the ships could slip quickly from the unconfined Scottish bases to lose themselves in the vast mass of mist-shrouded northern waters from whence a wireless from the Admiralty could send them racing to ward off a blow or strike overwhelmingly at an enemy. In Churchill's exuberant phrase, "The King's ships were at sea!"

The move of the British Fleet to the War Station does not appear to have made the international situation any worse, but then nothing much could since it was almost as bad as it could be. The statesmen, kings, and emperors had lost control of events. The generals had the bits in their teeth and were hell-bent for war. When the Kaiser got back from his ill-timed Norwegian holiday he honestly tried to stop the rush toward war. It was too late. The truth appears to be that the tremendously powerful German General Staff had decided that this was the most favorable moment for them to crush France, nullify Russia, and assume the hegemony of Europe. They were still certain that because of her Liberal Government and internal dissensions England would not come to France's aid. It was a sad miscalculation.

But everyone was miscalculating. For example, the majority of the British Cabinet believed that Germany would not attack France and that if she did she would not go through Belgium, whose neutrality had been guaranteed in 1839 by England, Prussia, France, Austria, and Russia, and that if she did the Belgians would not resist. This same majority did not want to go to war even though Germany did all those things. The financiers in the City of London were dead against it. No wonder the Germans guessed wrong, when not even the English thought they would fight.

Meanwhile the rush of European lemmings toward the precipice of war continued. On July 29 Austrian artillery began shelling Belgrade, the Servian capital. On July 30, Russia mobilized and Germany promptly sent her an ultimatum to desist. Asquith got the King out of bed at 1:30 A.M. to send the Tsar a "Dear Nickie" telegram begging him to stop the mobilization. The poor weak Tsar wanted to, but he could not. Strong Kaiser Wilhelm was just as helpless under the pressure of his generals. On August 1 Germany mobilized and declared war on Russia. France mobilized. On August 2 Germany declared war on France and invaded Luxembourg.

Meanwhile the British Cabinet were still debating. The leaders of the Conservative Party, Andrew Bonar Law and Arthur J. Balfour, assured them of their loyal support if war became inevitable.

The indecision of the Cabinet was unfortunate for the preservation of peace. The certain knowledge that Britain would fight just might have given the German General Staff pause. It also put Prince Louis and England's military leaders in a very difficult position, since now they must prepare for war without seeming to. Battenberg did all that could be done. On Monday, July 27, telegrams had been sent alerting the commanders of all British squadrons and ships throughout the world, and ordering them to shadow possible enemy vessels. The situation was especially dangerous in the Far East where a small British force was menaced by a squadron of powerful German cruisers under daring Admiral Count Maximilian von Spee. Prince Louis ordered mobilization of the old battleship *Triumph*, which was acting as depot ship for gunboats on the Yangtze River. She was too slow to keep up with the cruisers, but they could scuttle under her wings for protection. The China Squadron was ordered to concentrate at Hong Kong. Though Prince Louis had full responsibility for these decisions, they were made at staff meetings usually attended by the Second Sea Lord, Admiral Sir John Jellicoe. Under Battenberg's leadership there was absolute unanimity on all of the Admiralty's decisions.

On July 29, after Austria had declared war on Servia, Prince Louis sent out the official "warning telegram" to all ships. He also urged Churchill to obtain the Government's permission to order full mobilization of the fleet, because the Third Fleet's deactivated old ships were needed. Churchill's impassioned plea to the Cabinet was rejected on the ground that it was provocative. However, he secured authority to put "Precautionary Period Regulations" into effect. Naval harbors were cleared, bridges were guarded, steamers were boarded and searched. Thousands of watchers, both servicemen and volunteers, lined the coasts scanning the quiet sea.

By one more fortunate coincidence two powerful dreadnoughts being built for the Turkish Government were almost completed. On July 30 Churchill ordered Prince Louis to prepare to seize them if war was declared. Later these ships joined the fleet as the *Canada* and the *Erin*. It was about the last bit of good luck the Royal Navy had for a long time.

Also on that day Admiral Jellicoe was relieved as Second Sea Lord and ordered to join the fleet as second-in-command. The next day he came to the Admiralty to say good-bye, and found himself in a secret meeting with Churchill and Battenberg. To his amazement and real consternation they told Jellicoe that in the event of war he would probably be ordered to take over from Callaghan as Commander in Chief of the Grand Fleet, as the combined First and Second fleets were to be called. Jellicoe objected violently to this superb promotion. Loyalty to his old friend Callaghan was his principal motivation, but he also anticipated the possible effect of a change of command at that time on the morale of the fleet, and the confusion that might result.

Prince Louis was adamant. He felt that these risks must be taken for sound reasons. Callaghan was an old man in somewhat uncertain health, who was due to retire October 1. But Callaghan's health was only part of the reason. Battenberg had great confidence in Jellicoe. He wanted a young and vigorous man in command of the fleet, and, though he grieved at the thought of the blow this would be to an old and valued friend, he would not be ruled by sentiment. He chose the best man for the job. Though Jellicoe did not completely fulfill his hopes there was no other admiral as good with sufficient rank.* He sent Jellicoe a sealed envelope to be opened on order of the Admiralty.

The Cabinet finally consented to full mobilization of the fleet on Saturday, August 1—for once no one had left town for the weekend. The next day, Sunday, August 2, as Germany declared war on France, Asquith finally made his personal decision as to what England should do. He decided, somewhat speciously, that England had no obligation either to France or to Russia, and that an expeditionary force was out of the question at the moment. There would be no intervention of any kind as long as (1) Germany did not send her fleet through the Channel, and (2) she respected the neutrality of Belgium. Germany was willing to abide by the first condition. She decided the second by sending an ultimatum to Belgium demanding passage for her armies.

That afternoon Winston Churchill and Prince Louis invited the French naval attaché, the Comte de Saint-Seine to the Admiralty and informed him of Asquith's decision. Then Battenberg worked with him on agreements as to the disposition of French and British ships, and the Allied command of fleets, and gave him the secret signal books to be distributed to the French naval commanders. They made it clear, however, that these arrangements were to come into effect only in the event that Britain decided to go to the assistance of France, which was a matter of policy that could only be decided by the Cabinet.

---

* Vice-Admiral Sir David Beatty, commanding the Battle Cruisers, though a better man, was too junior to be acceptable to the Navy.

Instead of caving in as most of the English, including Winston Churchill, thought she would, Belgium prepared to defend her neutrality. On August 3 King Albert appealed to England for aid. That made the issue clear. England's honor as a guarantor of Belgian neutrality was at stake.

At a stormy meeting, the Cabinet decided to send Germany a note demanding to know if she would respect Belgian neutrality. Even this half measure was too much for John Burns and Lord Morley. In a moving scene, anger forgotten, they explained that conscience forced them to resign. The sticking point for Morley was that, "To bind ourselves to France is to bind ourselves to Russia," which country he regarded as a monstrous medieval tyranny. Lord Beaumont and Sir John Simon also wanted to resign, but Asquith and Lloyd George persuaded them to stay.

That night Prince Louis telegraphed to Admiral Jellicoe to open the sealed envelope containing his orders to assume command of the Grand Fleet. The transfer was effected in a typically British meeting of the two admirals at dawn of August 4, on board the *Iron Duke* at Scapa Flow. Callaghan was a big man with a sad bull-terrier face above the old-fashioned, high, wing collar he wore even at sea. Jellicoe, small, neat, and dapper, looked even sadder, for he was filled with distress at the thought of Callaghan's anguish at losing his great command at this glorious moment. Callaghan, though stunned by the news, which he had not suspected until he also received a telegram from Prince Louis, "behaved," in Jellicoe's words, "as always, as a most gallant officer and gentleman, and his one desire was to make the position easy for me, with entire disregard for his own feelings."

So, with stiff-lipped formality beneath which their surging emotions were known only to each other, the two admirals went through the ceremonial of exchanging command. Sir George Callaghan struck his flag, and an aide folded it carefully and held it under his arm. As Callaghan went down the accommodation ladder to his barge, Admiral Jellicoe's four-starred flag was hoisted over the *Iron Duke*. A short time later in obedience to another telegram from Prince Louis, Jellicoe led the gray steel mass of warships past the rocky headlands into the enveloping mists of the Arctic Ocean.

In that same dawn the German Army plunged over the Belgian border, sweeping resistance aside. It was on hearing this news that Prince Louis had sent the telegram ordering the fleet to sea. The Cabinet met and, with the ancient courtesy they still observed, instead of declar-

ing war immediately, sent the Imperial German Government an ultimatum giving them until midnight German time to order the recall of
their troops from Belgium.

That was a wearing, anxious day. Except during Cabinet meetings
Churchill stayed with Prince Louis at the Admiralty. They were no
longer uneasy about the Grand Fleet. Their special concern was the
Mediterranean, where the powerful German battle cruiser *Göben* and
her consort, the fast light cruiser *Breslau*, under the command of
Admiral Douchon, were roaming—a menace to the transports bringing
the French Algerian Army back to fight in France. Shadowing *Göben*,
but shackled by their lack of authority to attack, were the British battle
cruisers *Indomitable* and *Indefatigable*. The *Invincible* was also in the
Mediterranean. Early that morning Churchill appealed to Asquith and
Grey for permission to order the Commander in Chief Mediterranean,
Sir Berkeley Milne, to take action if *Göben* attacked the French transports. They agreed but said they would tell the Cabinet. Churchill then
told Prince Louis to send the telegram he had already prepared:

IF GÖBEN ATTACKS FRENCH TRANSPORTS YOU SHOULD AT ONCE ENGAGE
HER. YOU SHOULD GIVE HER FAIR WARNING OF THIS BEFOREHAND.

German armies were already far into Belgium. Their huge howitzers were smashing the Fortress of Liège. All the world knew they
would not stop; could not be stopped now. Yet when the Cabinet heard
of Prince Louis' order to Milne they demanded it be rescinded. No act of
war must be committed before the expiration of the ultimatum. They
felt that, "The moral integrity of the British Empire must not be compromised for the sake of sinking a single ship."

Churchill accepted the Cabinet's decision as correct, but he wrote
later, "Little did we know how much this honourable spirit of restraint
was to cost us, and all the world."

Actually, the *Göben* had no intention of attacking the French. She
was heading eastward toward Turkey, with whom Germany had con-
cluded a secret alliance two days before.

Meanwhile Italy, the third partner of Germany and Austria in the
Triple Alliance, had issued a declaration of neutrality. In view of this,
Prince Louis proposed to Churchill that he telegraph to Admiral Milne,
"Acquainting him with Italy's announcement and enjoining him to re-
spect this rigidly and not allow a ship to come within six miles of the
Italian coast." Churchill replied, "So proceed. . . ."

Through that long summer afternoon Churchill and Prince Louis
sat in the Admiralty War Room under the huge maps that showed the
positions throughout the world of every unit of the Royal Navy, think-

ing with anguish about those great ships steaming slowly through the sunny Mediterranean. The British battle cruisers were holding close to *Göben*, less than 10,000 yards, with their crews at battle quarters, their guns loaded and trained on her. At a word from the Admiralty they could have blown her out of the water with their superior weight of metal. Churchill writes, "We suffered the tortures of Tantalus." In fact, his round face was no longer boyish but strained with weariness and anxiety, his round eyes out on stalks. Prince Louis, apparently calm, went about the business of his office. A servant brought them tea in the big quiet room, just as he always did. They drank it wordlessly, looking out the window at the sunshine slanting down on busy, peaceful London.

Big Ben struck five. Battenberg made a quick mental calculation of the time left until sundown in the Mediterranean. His tremendous self-control cracked just a little. Like a small boy hinting for something he knows he will not get, he said, "We still have time to sink her before dark." Churchill's eyes blazed and went dead. Quite unable to speak he imperceptibly shook his head.

As darkness came down on the southern sea the *Göben* increased her speed to 24 knots. *Indefatigable* and *Invincible* strained to keep her in sight, slashing white scars through the dark satin sea. Unknown to the British, *Göben* was capable of a sudden short burst of tremendous speed. She went to 26 knots, then 27, and disappeared in the darkness.

Meanwhile, at 5:50 P.M. another message was sent:

ADMIRALTY TO ALL SHIPS

GENERAL MESSAGE. THE WAR TELEGRAM WILL BE ISSUED AT MIDNIGHT AUTHORIZING YOU TO COMMENCE HOSTILITIES AGAINST GERMANY, BUT IN VIEW OF OUR ULTIMATUM THEY MAY DECIDE TO OPEN FIRE AT ANY MOMENT. YOU MUST BE READY FOR THIS.

Now was a time of waiting. The orders were given; every squadron, ship, and captain, every naval base, coaling station, and fortress throughout the Empire was alert and ready. It was extraordinarily quiet in the Admiralty War Room, so quiet you could hear the mahogany grandfather's clock tick off the lagging seconds. Telegrams, delivered by soft-footed aides, continued to pour in from ships and bases. At his desk Prince Louis dealt silently with them, occasionally showing one to Churchill who sat uneasily in an armchair nearby. Through the tall open windows came the strangely soft murmur of vast crowds in Parliament

Street and the Mall. There was an almost religious quality to the hush; it was as unthinkable to speak loudly here as in church.

At about nine o'clock an aide came in and reported to Prince Louis that the French admirals, who had crossed from Calais to confer on naval co-ordination, had arrived. He got up quickly and went to greet them with his chief of staff. He brought them to the War Room and presented them to Churchill who found them, "fine figures in uniform and very grave." Their arrival raised the tension another notch. The English, whose country had never been invaded since 1066, were aroused yet confident of England's security; the Frenchmen, remembering 1870, knew that France was fighting for her life.

There was a quick, intricately technical discussion between Prince Louis and the French admirals at which many things, whose negotiation might have lasted weeks in peacetime, were settled in minutes. At one point the French said they would like to use the great British base at Malta, which in 1803 had caused a war between England and France. Prince Louis looked questioningly at Winston Churchill, who spoke directly to the French admirals saying, "Use it as you would Toulon."

The French left at about 10:30 P.M. and quiet settled over the room again. The small group of admirals, captains, and admiralty clerks sat or stood speaking in low voices or not at all, waiting for the ultimatum to expire at eleven o'clock, which was midnight German time. Prince Louis and Winston Churchill behaved according to their habit—Battenberg apparently serene, Churchill jumping with nerves.

The chimes of Big Ben rang out, followed by the first deep bong of the striking hour. Prince Louis nodded and there was a sudden burst of activity in the room. Through the windows surged the indescribably thrilling sound of many hundred thousand voices singing "God Save the King."

Before the verse was ended or Big Ben's eleventh stroke sounded, the message was flying to all units of the Royal Navy, wherever in the world they were:

COMMENCE HOSTILITIES AGAINST GERMANY.

LOUIS BATTENBERG

Chapter 15

THE WIDE AND NARROW SEAS

WHAT WAS PERHAPS THE GREATEST TRIUMPH of the Royal Navy in World War One was completely bloodless. It was the transportation of the British Expeditionary Force of four infantry divisions and one cavalry division, consisting of 80,000 men and 30,000 horses, 315 field guns but only 125 machine guns (!) across the Channel to France without the loss of a single man or even one horse.

This extraordinary feat was due to superb planning on the part of the British naval and military leaders, greatly assisted by stupidity on the part of the German General Staff, who did not understand the uses of sea power. The Germans were so dominated by the idea of British superiority at sea that they ordered their superb High Seas Fleet to remain supine in harbor instead of challenging the Royal Navy and, perhaps, stopping the movement to France of the British Army, which in the event played the decisive role in wresting from them the quick, complete victory for which they had planned so carefully and so long. This was extraordinarily short-sighted, for never again would the High Seas Fleet have such a favorable opportunity. The British had twenty-four dreadnoughts in home waters against Germany's sixteen, but Germany had nearly twice as many destroyers. Since the Germans could have taken the initiative as to when and where to attack, the odds were not as bad as they may seem. From that time forward the ratio of strength between the fleets mounted steadily in favor of England.*

In spite of their dangerously small numerical superiority the British Admiralty remained supremely confident. Prince Louis attended the Great War Council on the afternoon of August 5, at which were present the entire Cabinet and all the high military commanders, including Field Marshal Sir John French, who was slated to command the British Expeditionary Force, and General Sir Douglas Haig. Also present was retired Field Marshal Lord Kitchener of Khartoum, the greatest living British soldier, looking rather odd in civilian clothes as soldiers often do. He was soon to be made Minister of War with dictatorial authority over British strategic planning. There, too, was fiery little Earl Roberts of Kandahar. When the question arose as to whether to send four infantry divisions to France, or all six divisions of the regular Army in England, Prince Louis advised Churchill to speak in favor of sending all six, assuring him that, "The Navy can defend England against invasion, except for hit-and-run raids."

The decision to hold the BEF to four divisions for the present was taken contrary to the Admiralty's advice.

The huge cross-Channel movement began on Sunday, August 9, and was completed on August 22. The entire fleet in home waters was engaged in guarding it. These were the days of highest tension. Winston Churchill and Prince Louis, as well as virtually every officer of the Royal Navy, believed that Germany's High Seas Fleet would come out to try to stop this reinforcement of France. What else was a Navy for? But what the British did not know was that the Kaiser himself had ordered his fleet to run no risks, and the German General Staff agreed that it was not worth-while to bother about Britain's "contemptible little army."

On August 15, 16, and 17, when the movement of troops was heaviest and the transports made a veritable bridge of ships across the Channel, submarines and destroyers formed a cordon across the mouth of Heligoland Bight, from which the German Fleet must emerge if it ever did. Behind them, risking the narrow North Sea waters from Dogger Bank to the Horn Reef, steamed the Grand Fleet, tempting and taunting the High Seas Fleet to come out and fight. Bitter was the disappointment of the Royal Navy, from Prince Louis to the stokers on the oldest, slowest destroyer, when they did not stir.

.   .   .

---

* At that time the German General Staff had effective control of the German Navy. They told Minister of the Navy von Tirpitz nothing of their plans. The admirals wanted to fight; the generals would not let them.

In terms of global strategy the war at sea went well. The excessive fears of some admirals that Germany would loose a swarm of fast, armed liners to raid British commerce proved unjustified. Of forty-two German ships suitable for the purpose, all but five were bottled up either in Germany or in neutral ports. The merchant ships on which the life of the English island depended sailed almost unchallenged on the seven seas, while not a German merchantman dared move except in the Baltic Sea.

This did not occur by chance. On the wall maps in the War Room Prince Louis and his staff played a tremendous game of naval chess, moving their pieces here and there on the blue waters, trying to anticipate enemy moves and counter them in advance. The world was their board, the places where the sea lanes converged and crossed were their squares, the very life of England was the stake.

Cruisers were sent to watch the German liners in New York; others searched the Indian Ocean for the German cruisers *Dresden* and *Karlsruhe;* the hunt for *Göben* and *Breslau* continued in the Mediterranean, and in the Pacific British squadrons hunted for Admiral von Spee's big, fast cruisers *Scharnhorst, Gneisenau, Nurnberg,* and *Emden.* In addition, troop convoys from New Zealand, Australia, India, and Canada had to be organized and guarded. They all reached England safely.

But if the big plans went well, lesser matters went terribly wrong. It was these that made the headlines. The great movements of armies and fleets were silent and secret until their purposes were accomplished, but the mischances were hot news. Inevitably some merchant ships were captured or sunk by the few German cruisers still eluding the British net. Naturally, these made the news, not the thousands that safely completed their voyages.

More important were the *Göben* and the *Breslau,* though at the time this problem seemed small in comparison with the big picture. After they had been lost the night of August 4, they were pinpointed coaling at Messina in the straits between Italy and Sicily on the afternoon of August 5. From there they could go west to attack the French transports or east toward the Dardanelles and safety. They chose to go east. Though Admiral Milne had three battle cruisers, four large armored cruisers, and several light cruisers, he let them slip through his fingers. Because he misunderstood his orders to stay between the German ships and the French transports, he kept *all* his capital ships to the westward. Excessive caution and lack of energy might also have been responsible. When he heard of it Lord Fisher said half seriously, "They should shoot Milne to encourage the others."

But it must be remembered that neither Milne nor the Admiralty knew of Turkey's secret alliance with Germany. They assumed that if

the German warships reached the Dardanelles the Turks would intern
them. Nor was Prince Louis blameless in the matter, since his order to
Admiral Milne to keep six miles off the Italian coast was a contributory
factor. When he learned that the *Göben* was at Messina he should have
issued specific orders to the commander in chief to enter the straits, even
at the cost of annoying Italy, or at least to blockade *both* exits. Instead
he trusted to Milne's judgment—with fatal consequences.

How fatal can be seen from the results. When *Göben* and *Breslau*
reached the Dardanelles, Turkey "bought" them from Germany but left
the German crews on board and made Admiral Souchon Commander in
Chief of the Turkish Navy! Bulwarked, or bullied, by the German
battle cruiser, Turkey soon came into the war on Germany's side. The
Dardanelles were closed to Allied merchant shipping, and there went
Russia's last ice-free ports on the Black Sea, her supply line from the
west. In winter the Allies could send her supplies only through Vladi-
vostock in the Pacific, from whence they must travel more than 7,000
miles over the single-track Trans-Siberian Railway to the armies fighting
Germany.

This strangulation of Russia contributed greatly not only to her
ultimate defeat but also to the success of the Bolshevist Revolution. Even
as late as 1930, when he published *The World Crisis*, Winston Churchill
could not know how terrible the cost of "honorable restraint" would
be for England and the world.

Prince Louis' frustration over this episode and his anxiety over
potential catastrophes were further compounded by the Commander in
Chief of the Grand Fleet. Up in Scapa Flow, Admiral Jellicoe was as
nervous as your Aunt Nellie. A perfect stream of messages from him,
demanding all manner of reinforcement and material impossible to provide, poured into the Admiralty. Someone must have told him that he
was "the only man who could lose the war in an afternoon," and he
was having nightmares.

In justice to him it must be admitted that Scapa Flow was undefended and open to torpedo attack by submarines and destroyers. But
Jellicoe was forever fighting phantoms. He would suddenly take fright
and order the Grand Fleet to Ewes on the west coast of Scotland or
Lough Swilly in Ireland, leaving the North Sea exposed to the enemy.
Battenberg never knew where his ships would be next day; fortunately,
the Germans did not know either.

One misty night at Scapa a destroyer's gun crew fired at what they
thought was a periscope—some people say it was a seal. Half the fleet

opened up with small-caliber guns, and in the middle of the racket Jellicoe pushed the panic button and took the whole great armada flying out to sea. "The future Nelson" hardly seemed to be acting the part. Prince Louis soothed him with a stream of reassuring telegrams and as much reinforcement as could be spared from England's global needs. In fact he sent too much, thereby courting disaster in the Pacific.

Bad news came to England from land as well as sea. On August 23 the proud armies of France, shattered by the crushing power of the superior German Wehrmacht, began their retreat to the Marne. On that same day the British Army had their first test of battle. At Mons, in Belgium, 160,000 Germans under General von Kluck, with a vast superiority of cannon and machine guns, attacked 70,000 British entrenched along the Mons Canal. For nine hours the British stood them off. Then they retreated to Le Cateau where they fought again on August 25. The glory of Mons and Le Cateau has become a legend. Outnumbered and outgunned, the British took on the best troops the Kaiser had and fought them to a standstill. But glory cost 10,000 casualties. And, with their right wing left in the air as the French were thrown back, the British joined the great retreat.

Sir John French thought the game was up, but fell back in good order keeping contact with the French. His despairing dispatches made even Churchill lose hope, and, as the casualty lists poured in and the lines on the newspapers' war maps inched back toward Paris, the British public were stunned. They badly needed a shot in the arm. The Royal Navy provided it.

Heligoland Bight is a bay or gulf of the North Sea, formed by the curving coasts of Germany and Denmark, guarded by the heavily fortified island from which it takes its name. The High Seas Fleet was based at Wilhelmshaven and other ports at the apex of the Bight. Because it was so easily defended it was considered German water. Churchill, who was anxious to take some offensive action in the Bight, convened a meeting with Prince Louis and Admiral Sturdee. It was attended as well by Commodore Reginald Tyrwhitt, "a brilliant officer and a grand fighter," who commanded the Harwich Striking Force of light cruisers and destroyers, and Commodore Roger Keyes of the Submarine Service. The two commodores proposed a simple but daring plan, which was refined and adopted at the meeting.

On the night of August 27–28 Commodore Tyrwhitt led the

light cruisers *Arethusa* and *Fearless* and two squadrons of new destroyers silently into the Bight. Six of Keyes's submarines operated with them, and backing them up were the battle cruisers *New Zealand* and *Invincible*. In a rare burst of enthusiasm, Jellicoe sent three more battle cruisers and six light cruisers from the Grand Fleet—just in case. Churchill recorded, "He did more. He sent Sir David Beatty."

The misty dawn of August 28 found Tyrwhitt's little squadron close inshore. As their shapes became dimly apparent the big coast-defense guns on Heligoland opened fire, but missed. Once the alarm was given a confused fight began in the patchy fog. British staff work was incredibly bad—Tyrwhitt was never informed that Beatty was there with three more battle cruisers, and Beatty did not know where Keyes's submarines were operating and might have been torpedoed by them. But for once luck was with the English and that is better than staff work any day.

For nearly ten hours the British squadron went rampaging around Germany's home waters. Ships dashed in and out of fog banks, shooting at half seen enemies; fighting in single combat, by twos and three, and sometimes by squadrons. In Wilhelmshaven the German Admiralty were in the sort of flap the Pentagon would know if enemy warships were shooting up Long Island Sound.

In general, Tyrwhitt had managed to get between the German destroyer patrols and their base. As the German flotillas began to suffer, light cruisers raced to the rescue. The English destroyers ran for it, and lured them into range of the British battle cruisers, which Beatty with typical audacity had led far into the Bight. The great 12-inch guns of *New Zealand*, *Princess Royal*, *Invincible*, and Beatty's flagship *Lion* smashed the light German cruisers *Ariadne* and *Köln* like eggshells. The *Mainz* was sunk by a concentration of smaller British cruisers, and a German destroyer went down. Other German cruisers and destroyers fled for home in various states of dilapidation.

True to his chivalrous instincts, if not to the technology of modern war, Commodore Keyes in the destroyer *Lurcher* stopped near the sinking German ships and, in the midst of the battle, lowered boats to haul German sailors out of the water. Other British vessels hurried up to help. According to German Admiral Scheer, "The English ships made the greatest efforts to pick up survivors." *Lurcher* brought 234 German prisoners back to England, among them a son of Grand Admiral von Tirpitz. But over a thousand German sailors died, including the admiral commanding the cruiser squadron. British losses were 35 killed and 40 wounded.

The Battle of Heligoland Bight was actually only a skirmish, but it did far more than merely cheer up the English. It confirmed the German inferiority complex concerning the Royal Navy. The Kaiser was so upset that he issued a ban forbidding major units of the German Fleet to put to sea without his personal permission. Thus the High Seas Fleet was shackled still further to impotent inactivity. Only its few submarines still roamed unfettered. Otherwise not a ship stirred for two vital months. But for every plus there seemed to be a minus. In this case it was that the Germans began to concentrate on building more submarines. At the beginning of the war they had only twenty-seven, while the British had sixty-five. This ratio was soon drastically changed.

August 28 was a day of high glee at the Admiralty. As the reports of the battle came in, Churchill was beside himself with delight and Prince Louis' usual serene mask was shattered. He stood in the War Room snatching the wireless messages from the hands of the decoders, his eyes sparkling and his whiskers split by a broad grin. Late in the evening, as more detailed information came in he was particularly pleased by reports of the splendid shooting by *New Zealand*'s No. 1 (forward) turret commanded by Lieutenant Prince George of Battenberg.

It was one of his last happy hours.

Early in September the most decisive battle of the war was fought. The French and British armies stood on the Marne, bringing the great German advance to a bloody halt. Then they counterattacked and drove the Germans back, halfway to the border. The front was stabilized along the line of the Aisne River.

But the joy of victory at Heligoland Bight and the Marne was soon dissipated by disaster in the North Sea. According to Kerr's plan for naval strategy no large ships were to be used in patrolling the narrow seas. But because of the shortage of light cruisers and destroyers, and also because the latter could not keep the sea in heavy weather, the big old armored cruisers of the Bacchante Class, rather like Prince Louis' four-stack *Drake*, had been used for the purpose since the war began.

Prince Louis opposed this because of the danger of submarine attack. But most of his colleagues thought this was nonsense, and in view of the enormous demands on smaller ships for duty in the Channel—another division was being sent to France, followed by the Brigade of Marines to the Belgian coast—he foolishly allowed himself to be overruled. On September 18 he and Churchill finally decided that patrolling with the heavy armored cruisers had become too dangerous, and he ordered them to the western end of the Channel to be replaced by Arethusa Class light cruisers, supported by battleships based on Sheerness. He locked the stable door just too late.

On September 19 the North Sea was whipped by an equinoctial gale. Commodore Tyrwhitt's destroyers, rolling their rails under the steep, choppy seas, were ordered back to harbor. In view of this, Rear Admiral Henry H. Campbell commanding the cruiser squadron proposed that the armored cruisers *Aboukir*, *Hogue*, and *Cressy* be allowed to continue their patrol between Yarmouth in Suffolk and the coast of Holland without destroyer escort. Battenberg demurred, but when the War Staff pointed out that submarines could not operate in that weather he consented reluctantly.

The morning of September 22 was clear and calm after the storm. Tyrwhitt's destroyers were on their way to rejoin the cruisers, which were plodding along at 10 knots in line abreast just as though the sea were as peaceful as it looked. The sun rose, sharply silhouetting *Aboukir* in the periscope of the submarine *U-9*, which was skulking down the Dutch coast. It was such an easy shot, it was not even sporting. The first *Aboukir* knew of her danger was the stunning shock and roar of flame as a torpedo exploded in her vitals.

If you stop in battle to rescue enemy sailors, what do you do when your own men are drowning? *Hogue* and *Cressy* closed on the sinking *Aboukir* and lay dead still on the sunny sea lowering their boats—two big fat sitting ducks. "Fire two! Fire three!" ordered Captain Weddigen of *U-9*.

Of the three British cruisers there remained only a litter of wreckage, a few boats, a mass of men struggling in the sea. There had been more than 2,000 men aboard them—mostly reservists and young cadets from Osborne posted to the old cruisers for safety—1,459 perished. About 800 were saved.

When they brought the news to Prince Louis at the Admiralty he said bitterly, "I should not have given in to them!" (his naval advisers).

In France the two great armies deadlocked on the Aisne were trying to outflank each other by extending their lines westward toward the Channel. As they neared the coast it became essential to hold the Channel ports of Havre, Boulogne, and Calais if the British were to maintain and supply an army in France. In order to do this the Belgian fortress city of Antwerp must hold out at least until the French and British could extend and consolidate their line to the coast covering these harbors. The remnant of the Belgian Army was concentrated around Antwerp, under the personal command of brave King Albert. Queen Elisabeth and the Belgian Government were in the city.

On September 28 the Germans attacked Antwerp, firing on its ring of forts with the enormous 17-inch howitzers that had smashed the forts at Liège and Namur. Four days later, on October 2, the situation became desperate. Two of the forts had fallen. Late in the evening a telegram was received in London from the British Minister to Belgium stating that the Belgian Government had decided to flee to Ostend the next day and that the King at the head of the Army would begin the retreat hoping to link up with the Allies somewhere on the coast.

The British Cabinet were shocked by this inexplicable Belgian despair. Lord Kitchener and Winston Churchill felt that if Antwerp were to fall now, the Germans could sweep up all the Channel ports before Field Marshal French could get there. French forces were hurriedly ordered to reinforce the Belgians. The British Brigade of Marines was sent from Ostend to the trenches around Antwerp. Best of all Winston Churchill himself dashed over to the temporary Belgian capital. He was worth a division at least.

Churchill arrived in Antwerp at 3 P.M. on October 3. His dynamic determination and stirring oratory decided King Albert and the Belgian Council to hold out. Churchill seemed to be everywhere at once, racing to the farthest outposts, getting shot at by everything from Big Berthas to machine guns and snipers. Glorying in danger, he had a perfectly wonderful time, and his presence reanimated the Belgians. Indeed, Asquith said that, for a couple of days, "Winston was running the Belgian Government."

Before he left for Antwerp, Churchill had asked the Cabinet to give Prince Louis full charge of the Admiralty during his absence. Such was their confidence in Battenberg that they agreed without hesitation. So Prince Louis now had "sole responsibility" for all Admiralty decisions, civilian as well as naval. The pressures became enormous.

A deluge of telegrams came to Prince Louis from Churchill in Antwerp, demanding that he accomplish the impossible. First, Churchill ordered that the two Naval Brigades made up of naval reservists in training be sent over at once. Vast quantities of ammunition must go with them. Immediately after this he persuaded Kitchener to send the 7th Division, made up of regular Army units scraped up from all the outposts of the Empire and concentrated in England. It consisted of 18,000 men and 63 guns, and was to be accompanied by the 3d Cavalry Division of 4,000 men, 12 guns, and 4,000 horses. The Naval Brigades totaled 8,000 men. He also called for armored trains with naval guns.

Prince Louis had to organize transport for this multitude on the spur of the moment—not only great numbers of merchant ships but also cordons of light cruisers, destroyers, and submarines to guard their precious cargo. Three days later, on August 6, a triumph of improvisation, it was done. The naval brigades were fighting beside the Belgians. The 7th Division arrived, without the loss of man, horse, or gun, even before it was expected, and made secure the line of the Belgian retreat, in the event retreat became necessary.

Unfortunately it did. The exhausted Belgians gradually were pushed back; when the German siege guns came within range of Antwerp's superb ancient buildings and 400,000 civilians King Albert felt he could ask no more of his people. The retreat was ordered. Belgians, French, and British all got away safely except for two and a half battalions of the British Naval Brigade, which wandered over the Dutch border by mistake and were interned for the duration.

There was harsh criticism in England for what they called "Churchill's Antwerp adventure." Forgotten was the tremendous feat of moving 30,000 men, with their horses, guns, and equipment, across the Channel in four days. The English people knew only that Antwerp had fallen and the fine young men of the Naval Brigade had been slaughtered—for nothing as they saw it. Unknown to the public was the fact that ten days were needed for Sir John French to establish a line in front of the vital Channel ports; that ten days had been bought by Belgian and British blood.

The only proper target for criticism was Churchill's order, and Prince Louis' agreement, to the use of the two reservist Naval Brigades. The men were hardly half-trained—some of them did not even know how to fire their guns. As a result their casualties were much higher than would have been those of fully trained troops. It is doubtful if they contributed enough to the battle to justify their losses. The use of the 2,000 regular Marines is another matter. They fought superbly, and because of this and the effect of their presence on Belgian morale, their contribution was far beyond the proportion of their numbers.

As to the necessity for defending Antwerp, most historians now agree that the delay caused the Germans did, in fact, save the Channel ports.

Meanwhile, withdrawal from Antwerp brought no lessening of Churchill's demands on the First Sea Lord. The sort of thing he required is shown in an order dated October 10, 1914.

1 5,000 to 6,000 Royal Navy Brigade and nearly 2,000 marines at Ostend are to be embarked for Cherbourg after dark "tomorrow the 11th."

2   1,500 Belgian recruits to be embarked "at once" for Dover.

3   Transportation of *15,000* Belgian recruits and reservists from Dunkirk to Cherbourg, "to continue without intermission as rapidly as possible. . . ."

4   Enough transports to embark 7th Division and 3d Cavalry "to be kept in immediate readiness with steam up in Ostend, Dunkirk, Dover and the Thames . . . Flotilla arrangements to be made accordingly . . ." [all this in case the Germans should cut off the British troops].

5   Marine and Naval details at Dunkirk to be re-embarked. . . .

6   Three monitors to be ready to cover a crash re-embarkation.

7   The Transport Department to furnish ships to carry stores, ammunition, and matériel to the Belgian Army. . . .

8   8,000 to 10,000 Belgian wounded to be brought from Ostend to England.

In addition to these demands, as the armies came down to the sea at last Prince Louis had to supply large numbers of old battleships, monitors, and lighter ships to take part in the land battle by bombarding from the sea the German troops fighting their way along the coast toward the Channel ports. These ships played a decisive role in stopping the German advance at Ypres.

Writing of Antwerp and its aftermath in *The World Crisis* Churchill says, "It would not have been possible to deal with these complications—themselves only one subsidiary part of our task—unless Prince Louis and I, working in complete accord, had the power to give orders covering the whole business which were unquestioningly obeyed. Yet some of these orders left me with misgivings that we were asking more than they could do. . . .

"It was with a feeling of relief and admiration that I saw all these immense demands smoothly and punctually complied with. . . ."

Chapter 16

"A FANATICAL AND MALIGNANT OUTCRY"

THE WAR HAD GIVEN the English people a psychological shock greater than we, who are accustomed to living in danger, can imagine. A hundred years of serenity had left them with no memory of a time of actual peril to their country. Nor did the first weeks of war arouse their fears, for England always won. The Navy was an impregnable bulwark behind which they could organize for war. The "magnificent Army" of France, the "Russian Steamroller," and "Our gallant Soldiers of the King" would soon flatten the *pickelhaube*d, goose-stepping troops of the megalomaniacal Kaiser. So the English believed.

When it did not happen that way—when the Russian Steamroller bogged down at Tannenberg and the French came within a whisker's width of losing the war in the first five weeks; when the casualty lists took columns of fine print and the *Illustrated London News* carried page after page of pictures of handsome young British officers "Dead on the Field of Honour"; when the Royal Navy seemed to be cowering at

Scapa Flow apparently impotent, as mines and submarines took their toll
—the English people gave way to a burst of hysteria.

Mons and Le Cateau were England at her finest. The "fanatical and
malignant outcry" at home did indeed disgrace the national character,
and it took the form of an almost insane hatred of anything German. It
was fed by the admittedly brutal behavior of German troops in Belgium,
though rumor grossly exaggerated even this—no one ever saw Belgian
babies with their hands hacked off by German bayonets, but everybody
believed such tales. Anybody in England with a Germanic name, even
of the third and fourth generation, was subject to insult. No orchestra
dared play a Wagnerian note and dachshunds were hissed in Hyde Park.
Spies were ubiquitous, treason rampant. Prime Minister Asquith was
castigated for not interning a German maid who had served him for
three decades. And, above all, in the febrile agitation of the public mind,
the man responsible for the strategic disposition of the fleet, that last
rampart of the beleaguered Empire, was a German prince.

Through August and early September Prince Louis was not especially disturbed by this anti-German feeling. But the sinking of the
Aboukir, Hogue, and *Cressy* focused public distrust upon him. There
was, there must be treason at the top for such a disaster to befall the
Royal Navy. Because they were "most secret," no one knew of Battenberg's brilliant arrangements for ferrying the BEF to France, or of his
wise and careful dispositions of the fleets to meet enemy action on all the
seas. What they did know was that the Navy had suffered a grievous
loss. The pictures of the handsome little boys, the midshipmen who had
perished in the North Sea, turned their hearts to ice and their heads to
fire. They wondered darkly if someone very high up had not betrayed
the unguarded presence of those ships to the German Admiralty.

Despite the reputation of the English as an unimaginative people,
they manufactured rumors that exceeded the wildest feats of Verne or
Poe: Russian troops were "seen" passing through England to bolster the
Western Front; submarines were "sighted" in every river mouth and
cove, receiving supplies and information; all sorts of things were said
about Cabinet officers and military commanders. Prince Louis of Battenberg was the subject of one of their most fantastic inventions.

As early as October 3 Lord Fisher wrote, "One of the queer
canards that are flying around London is that Prince Louis of Battenberg, First Sea Lord of the Admiralty, is 'confined in the Tower of
London.' . . ." Fisher did not believe a word of that, but he added the
opinion that the first of our "damnable difficulties" was that "Our
directing Sea Lord [is] played out." The very day he wrote that letter
the Cabinet had shown their confidence in Battenberg by entrusting him

with the "sole responsibility" for the Admiralty while Churchill was in Antwerp.

Prince Louis had not yet lost his sense of humor. As he came into one of his clubs a friend called out to him, "What are you doing here, Admiral? I thought you were in the Tower."

"You're 'way behind the times, old man," Battenberg answered gaily. "I was shot last Thursday."

Wit notwithstanding, it is easy to imagine the strain and sadness he felt as the knowledge of public distrust was piled upon the enormous responsibilities of his position. For he knew only too well what people were thinking and were saying in those very clubs. He could not help but notice the conversations that broke off as he approached and the fellow members who greeted him in strange, embarrassed voices.

Embittered Lord Charles Beresford led the pack that were trying to hound Prince Louis out of the Royal Navy. So outrageous were Beresford's statements, that Winston Churchill wrote him an angry letter* saying in effect that if he did not stop defaming the First Sea Lord, Churchill personally would see to it that Beresford's ambition to be made an Admiral of the Fleet (Retired) would never be realized. It never was.

As October darkened toward winter, things got worse. The light cruiser *Hawke* was torpedoed, and *Emden* and *Karlsruhe* were sinking merchant ships in the Indian Ocean. Von Spee was still cavorting in the Pacific. What was the Navy doing?

The newspapers were receiving floods of letters about the First Sea Lord, ranging from dignified suggestions that, although Prince Louis was undoubtedly an honorable, patriotic man, he should resign, because as a man of German birth he could not have "that keen animosity which we as Britishers should wish the head of our Navy to have at this critical juncture" to bald charges of treason and explosions of naked hatred.

Prince Louis sorrowfully was considering whether he should resign, not because of lack of animosity, but because public distrust embarrassed his functioning and hampered his decisions by clouding strategic thought with personal considerations. On October 26 he wrote to Lord Walter Kerr: "My responsibility and constant anxiety in this great office are very heavy, and being continuously attacked and yet quite helpless—although assured afresh of the Government's confidence—I feel sometimes that I cannot bear it much longer. . . ."

For a time the press restrained itself admirably, simply consigning the letters to deserved oblivion. But pressure was rising dangerously,

---

* According to Randolph Churchill who found it in his father's unpublished files.

and on October 26, while Prince Louis was writing to Lord Walter, *The Globe* exposed the whole business in an editorial stating that its editors had received hundreds of letters protesting against Prince Louis' remaining as First Sea Lord. While affirming their own confidence in his integrity and patriotism, they felt that in view of the public uneasiness and "for sake of the First Sea Lord himself, no less than for that of the nation . . . we ask that some authoritative statement shall be issued of a nature so emphatic and so unqualified as to remove at once and forever every cloud of doubt, and to silence every breath of rumour."

No such statement was issued. The Winston Churchill of 1940 would have blasted the rumormongers with a thunderbolt of invective and an affirmation of Prince Louis' honor in phrases so magnificent that the sorry business would have been ended. But in 1914 Churchill himself was in trouble. Distrusted by his own colleagues, blamed by the public for the failure of the "Antwerp adventure," which in his own words became "a cause of fierce reproach," as well as for other mishaps, he was clinging to the position of First Lord of the Admiralty by his eyebrows. There is reason to believe that he may already have discussed with the Prime Minister and King George recalling Lord Fisher to the post of First Sea Lord.* Certainly he was not prepared to stake his political life on defending Prince Louis.

The *coup de grâce* was delivered on the morning of October 27, when Prince Louis dashed unceremoniously into Winston Churchill's office. His face was gray, his eyes defeated. "The *Audacious* has struck a mine off Lough Swilly, and is believed sinking," he said.

Churchill read the wireless from Jellicoe, and assayed the news. *Audacious* was one of the finest new dreadnoughts in the Grand Fleet, and her loss would seriously impair its ratio of strength over the German Fleet. Jellicoe had taken the fleet to Ireland for target practice and safety. Unknown to him a German mine layer had dropped her eggs in the Irish Sea hoping to sink merchant shipping out of Liverpool. By extraordinary bad luck *Audacious* had struck one of them. Another wireless from Jellicoe confirmed that she had sunk after all her crew had been saved. The Admiral urgently requested that the loss be kept secret. This was done.

But how long can such a secret be kept? All the newspapers knew of it, and although they agreed to suppress the news, they did so reluctantly. Next day, as a direct result, *The Globe* printed a fistful of letters calling on Prince Louis to resign.

Now this was in all their minds. When the loss of the *Audacious*

---

* See Lord Fisher's notes on his reappointment as First Sea Lord.

became known the hue and cry against Prince Louis would rise to a clamor. Bitterly he assessed his position, which he knew now would became untenable unless the Government gave him full support—and he knew they would not. All the fires of ambition urged that he remain; and a nobler motive, his belief that with the whole vast complex of naval strategy at his fingertips he could best serve his country in his present post, also argued, Stay.

On the other hand the fierce outcry against him would probably impair if not destroy his usefulness. If that were true, he had no choice but to serve his country best by ceasing to serve her at all. During a terrible sleepless night Prince Louis went over and over the pros and cons again and again. Relentless logic forced him toward the conclusion that patriotism demanded that he resign. Yet he could not quite force himself to the decision to quit the service he had loved all his life under a cloud that seemed to dim his honor. He knew in his heart what the decision must be, but he needed a little more time. Before he could form his resolution the matter was taken out of his hands.

A deliberate veil of obscurity has been thrown over the exact circumstances of Prince Louis' resignation. In *The World Crisis*, Churchill implies that it was Battenberg's own decision. After describing the ugly rumors, Churchill writes, "I was therefore not surprised when, toward the end of October, Prince Louis asked to be relieved of his burden." Even Mark Kerr, in his biography of Battenberg, accepts this version, saying only that, "It was owing to the fact that we had no statesman of the very first rank that Prince Louis' resignation was accepted, thereby causing great detriment, not only to his own country, but to the world at large. . . ."

The real truth becomes apparent only on reading Prime Minister Asquith's informal notes jotted down each day:

> October 28. The sinking of the *Audacious* . . . is cruel luck for Winston, who has just been here pouring out his woes. . . . Winston's real trouble, however, is about Prince Louis and the succession to his post. He must go, and Winston has had a most delicate and painful interview with him. Louis behaved with great dignity and public spirit, and will resign at once. . . .

Here stands the naked fact. There can be no doubt that the Cabinet was determined that the First Sea Lord walk the plank; and to Churchill was delegated the horrid task of telling him so. Though no description of that "delicate and painful" interview has ever been given by either of the principals, one can easily imagine the feelings of these two friends. Prince Louis must have felt the blow like a round shot in his midriff.

But he bore it without flinching. Nor did he, even in his secret heart, blame Churchill for a thing that his own reason had already accepted. But Churchill blamed himself; and never afterward forgot. The fact that he carried a sense of guilt is shown by his extraordinary efforts to forward the career of Prince Louis' younger son, Lord Louis Mountbatten, in World War Two. This was so evident that it was remarked upon by the chief of the Imperial General Staff Sir Alan Brooke and by numerous contemporary writers.

Once decided upon the thing was done handsomely, with every consideration and honor by all concerned. Prince Louis wrote:

October 28, 1914

Dear Mr. Churchill,

I have lately been driven to the painful conclusion that at this juncture my birth and parentage have the effect of impairing in some respects my usefulness on the Board of Admiralty. In these circumstances I feel it to be my duty, as a loyal subject of His Majesty, to resign the office of First Sea Lord, hoping thereby to facilitate the task of the administration of the great Service to which I have devoted my life, and to ease the burden laid on H. M.'s Ministers.

I am,
Yours very truly,
Louis Battenberg,
Admiral

As Prince Louis was writing this letter his nephew, Prince Henry's son Prince Maurice of Battenberg, was killed fighting with the King's Royal Rifle Corps in the desperate battle at Ypres. The news of his death and Prince Louis' letter of resignation were published the same day.

Churchill replied:

October 29, 1914

My dear Prince Louis,

This is no ordinary war but a struggle between nations for life or death. It raises passions between races of the most terrible kind. It effaces the old landmarks and frontiers of our civilization. I cannot further oppose the wish, you have during the last few weeks expressed to me, to be released from the burden of responsibility which you have borne thus far with so much honor and success. . . .

The Navy of today, and still more the Navy of tomorrow, bears the imprint of your work. The enormous impending influx of capital ships, the score of thirty-knot cruisers, the destroyers and submarines unequalled in modern construction which are coming now to hand are the result of the labours which we have had in common, and in which the Board of Admiralty owes so much to your aid.

The first step which secured the timely concentration of the Fleet was taken by you.

I must express publicly my deep indebtedness to you, and the pain I feel at the severance of our three years' official association. In all the circumstances you are right in your decision. The spirit in which you have acted is the same in which Prince Maurice of Battenberg has given his life to our cause and in which your gallant son is now serving in the Fleet.

I beg you to accept my profound respect and that of our colleagues on the Board.

> I remain,
> Yours very sincerely,
> Winston S. Churchill

Thus Prince Louis left the Admiralty, saying good-bye to his friends and colleagues with a noble sadness in his eyes, and far more serenity than the others could command. There remained the final duty of taking leave of the King.

He arrived at Buckingham Palace at four o'clock in the afternoon of October 29, just as the Prime Minister was leaving. The King received him in his "writing room"—with its sentimental Victorian pictures on the wall, the ornate, crowded desk, small tables covered with bibelots and mementos, and the handsome clock on the mantelpiece marking the exact minute by Naval Observatory time. For this was no formal audience, but a meeting of two very troubled men who were bound together by ties of friendship and strong family affection.

King George was evidently deeply moved. Perhaps he was remembering the days when he served as a midshipman in the *Inconstant* with young Lieutenant Prince Louis. Almost certainly he thought of Battenberg's family advice and counsel when his older brother died and he faced the responsibility of kingship and the necessity of giving up his naval career. He was, in fact, uniquely constituted to understand Prince Louis' emotions—for he too was a loyal Englishman who bore a German name, and he too had been forced to leave the service he loved.

The two men talked for a moment in constrained formal phrases and then the King burst forth his sympathy and belief in his cousin's loyalty in highly emotional language mixed with profane comments on his enemies. It was too much for Prince Louis. The self-control he had preserved throughout melted and collapsed before the love and loyal friendship of his King. In that small and cluttered room where there was no one to see him but his Sovereign, the Admiral broke down and wept.

Moved to comfort him at any cost, with typical generosity and impulsive disregard of whether his ministers approved or not, King George said, "To show my trust in you, I'll make you a member of my Privy Council."

And he noted in his diary, "Which pleased him. . . ."

Prince Louis' resignation was a shock to the service and, in spite of all the talk, to the country as well. Telegrams and letters poured in. The Commander in Chief Grand Fleet wired: :

HAVE RECEIVED WITH THE MOST PROFOUND SORROW THE INFORMATION CONTAINED IN YOUR TELEGRAM. THE WHOLE FLEET WILL LEARN THE NEWS WHEN PUBLISHED WITH THE DEEPEST POSSIBLE REGRET. WE LOOK TO YOU WITH THE GREATEST LOYALTY, RESPECT AND GRATITUDE FOR THE WORK YOU HAVE ACCOMPLISHED FOR THE NAVY.

JOHN JELLICOE

Former First Lord of the Admiralty Lord Selborne wrote to *The Times* that he would "as soon mistrust Lord Roberts as Prince Louis . . . That anyone should have been found to insinuate suspicion against him is nothing less than a national humiliation." Even J. H. Thomas, the leader of the Labour Party, wrote a long and indignant letter to *The Times*, extolling Prince Louis, whom he know only by reputation, and saying that if this sort of thing continued, "it will indeed be difficult for public men to endeavor to serve their country in the manner we have a right to expect." Many other public men of all parties and shades of opinion wrote to Prince Louis and to the newspapers to express their regret and dismay.

Having done the damage the British press burst forth in laudatory articles showing a sense of guilt and shame. *The Times*'s indignant editorial on the subject was accompanied by the letters mentioned above. The *Daily Mail* called Prince Louis, "a loyal and noble figure," and termed his decisions, "wise and even chivalrous"; while *The Globe*, which had triggered the explosion, printed a column of excuses for having done so, together with a nauseatingly fulsome tribute to Prince Louis and his "very noble act of self-abnegation."

Yet despite all the encomiums and regrets, there were many who felt that a change was due at the Admiralty, not because they doubted

Prince Louis' loyalty, but because they felt he was not tough enough to meet the brutal necessities of war. So the results must be examined impartially.

Churchill, and practically the whole press, had already decided that Lord Fisher was the only possible replacement for Battenberg, the one man who could restore the country's confidence in the Admiralty. King George disagreed, for he disliked Fisher and feared that as First Sea Lord he would reopen the old scar of controversy. Thus the King did everything in his power to prevent Fisher from being named First Sea Lord. Lord Fisher states that the King's secretary, Lord Stamfordham, presented to Churchill the names of at least six different men, all of whom the King preferred to Fisher. This is not verified; but the King's angry interview with Churchill on October 29 is. That morning, in his hailing-the-bridge-in-a-storm voice, King George used every argument he had against Fisher's appointment. Among other things, he said, "At his age [seventy-four] the job will kill him." To which Churchill replied, "Sir, I cannot imagine a more glorious death." When Fisher heard of it he wrote, "Wasn't that lovely!"

When Churchill left, the King was still unconvinced; but Asquith went to the King that afternoon, just before Prince Louis, and insisted on Fisher's appointment. Finally the King said, " I cannot constitutionally oppose my ministers, but I feel it my duty to record my protest."

Asquith diplomatically suggested, "Sir, perhaps a less severe term, 'misgivings,' might be used by Your Majesty."

So the King wrote, "while approving the proposed appointment of Lord Fisher as First Sea Lord, I do so with some reluctance and misgivings. I readily acknowledge his great ability and administrative power, but I cannot help feeling that his presence at the Admiralty will not inspire the Navy with that confidence which ought to exist. . . . I hope my fears may prove groundless. . . ."

Despite the King's "misgivings" the change was good—at first. Very early on the morning of October 30, 1914, Lord Fisher went to pray in Westminster Abbey. When he rose from his knees he said exultantly, "Resurrected! Resurrected! Resurrected again!"

Then he hit the Admiralty like a rotary plow. Senescent admirals and other dead wood came flying out, along with the worn-out carpet from the First Sea Lord's office—the carpet had not bothered Prince Louis, but it seemed that Fisher could think properly only on an Oriental rug. Furthermore he seized the nettle of authority firmly and would not be turned from his course by public clamor, political considerations, or the pleading of his commanding admirals.

Two days after Fisher took office, for example, von Spee's cruisers in the Pacific met a British squadron of smaller cruisers under Admiral Sir C. Cradock near Coronel off the coast of Chile. Instead of retiring to the protection of the old battleship *Canopus*, as Prince Louis had suggested that he do in such a contingency, Admiral Cradock engaged the enemy. The result of his ill-considered gallantry was that two big old British cruisers, the *Good Hope* and *Monmouth*, were sunk. Admiral Cradock went down with his ship. There were no survivors.

Immediately on hearing of this disaster Fisher took two battle cruisers, the *Invincible* and *Inflexible*, from the Grand Fleet and sent them off under Admiral Sturdee to hunt von Spee. A third battle cruiser, *Princess Royal*, was sent to watch the Panama Canal. Von Spee's squadron was caught and sunk off the Falkland Islands on December 8.

When *Princess Royal* was taken away from the Grand Fleet, Jellicoe's lamentations poured in upon the Admiralty in a flurry of telegrams and letters, and even the dashing Beatty joined the woeful chorus. Prince Louis might have heeded them; Fisher did not.

The King's misgivings about Fisher's age were not entirely justified. Churchill has described the "formidable energy" with which the septuagenarian First Sea Lord hurled himself into his work. Fisher arose at 4:30 A.M. and did an immense amount of work before the rest of the world awoke. But like all old men his strength faded in the afternoon and he usually went to bed exhausted at eight o'clock, by which time, however, he had accomplished more than most younger men. Nor were the old scars reopened. Lord Fisher's bitterest enemies rallied loyally to his support.

But ultimately King George was proved right and Churchill wrong, because of a clash between Churchill and Fisher. As Churchill wrote, "Clearly the First Lord's ability to acquit himself of his duty depends on the character, temperament and capacity of both the First Lord and the First Sea Lord. They must settle it between themselves, and if they cannot agree wholeheartedly on the momentous problems with which they are confronted . . . another combination must be chosen by the Sovereign on the advice of his Prime Minister."

When Prince Louis was First Sea Lord, Churchill said, "The conduct of the Admiralty resolved itself into the intimate comradeship and co-operation of the First Lord and the First Sea Lord with the chief of staff [Sturdee] standing by their side. . . . The machine worked very smoothly. . . . Beside our regular meetings the First Sea Lord and I consulted together constantly at all hours. . . ."

The situation was quite different between Churchill and Lord Fisher, for these two men could not work together. The clash of their temperaments neutralized the great qualities each possessed, and resulted first, in an unfortunate stalemate, and finally in a disastrous rupture. It had been another matter when Fisher was merely advising Churchill without any official position—Churchill could take the advice or leave it. But when Fisher took over as First Sea Lord he began to get megalomaniacal aspirations toward a dictatorship as complete as Lord Kitchener's at the War Office. Any orders or suggestions made by Churchill infuriated Fisher, and as the First Lord habitually poured out a steady stream of them, Fisher was constantly on the verge of apoplexy. As early as December 20 Fisher wrote, "Winston has so monopolized all initiative at the Admiralty and fires off such a multitude of purely departmental memos ... [that] the consequence is that the Sea Lords are atrophied ... and I find it a Herculean task to get back the right procedure, and quite possibly I may have to clear out, and I've warned Winston of this. ..."

So they had begun fighting already, and the situation steadily got worse. They differed about nearly everything, from the types of new ships to be built to the disposition of the old battleships Churchill was using for guarding distant harbors and for bombardment, which Fisher wanted scrapped. Most of all they differed on the grand strategy of how the war should be fought. In fact in this respect Fisher was out of accord not only with Churchill but with the whole Cabinet, all the generals, and a good part of the Royal Navy. He "resigned" almost every other day.

The final blow-up came over the Dardanelles expedition. In January, 1915, the Russian Government called desperately for a diversion to take the crushing weight of German and Austrian armies in the Caucasus off their faltering troops. For this reason, and because of the enormous political and logistic advantages of opening the Dardanelles, the British Government discussed the possibility of forcing them by a squadron consisting of the new 15-inch-gun dreadnought *Queen Elizabeth* and eleven old British and French battleships and heavy cruisers. Churchill was eager for it, but Fisher had decided as early as 1904 that it was impossible for ships to force the Dardanelles, and age had hardened his mental arteries.

The matter was decided at a War Council on January 28, 1915, which was attended by Lord Kitchener, Fisher, and Admiral Sir Arthur K. Wilson, as well as Churchill, the Prime Minister, and most of the Cabinet. While the discussion was in progress Fisher sat, as stony as a basilisk, saying never a word. His excuse was that nobody asked his opinion, and the First Lord already knew his views. After the meeting he walked out determined to resign. Kitchener rushed after him and persuaded him not to.

Once the die was cast it behooved Fisher to support the expedition

Founders of the Family. Prince Alexander of Hesse and the Rhine and his bride, Countess Julie Hauke, later created Princess of Battenberg. (*Radio Times Hulton Picture Library*)

The Governor of Bombay taking leave of Edward, Prince of Wales, aboard H. M. S. *Serapis* after his tour of India in 1875–76. (Sketch by Prince Louis of Battenberg, by courtesy *The Illustrated London News*)

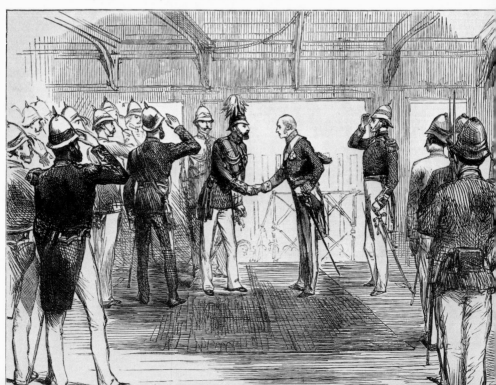

Loading an ostrich, a Maharajah's gift to the Prince
of Wales. (Sketch by Prince Louis of Battenberg, by
courtesy *The Illustrated London News*)

The *Serapis* was a floating menagerie.
(Sketch by Prince Louis of Battenberg,
by courtesy *The Illustrated London
News*)

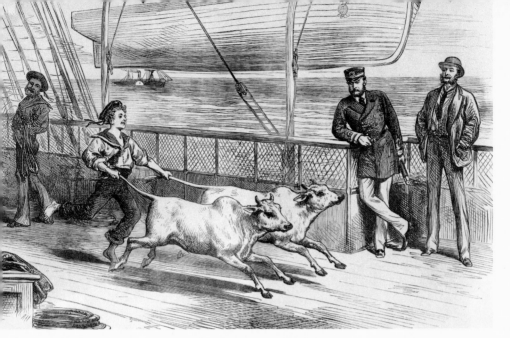

Ship's boy exercising young buffalo. (Sketch by Prince Louis of Battenberg, by courtesy *The Illustrated London News*)

Prince Louis' bride, Princess Victoria of Hesse, in her wedding dress. (*The Illustrated London News*)

The wedding of Queen Victoria's granddaughter Princess Beatrice to Prince Henry of Hesse and the Rhine. Queen Victoria and the Prince of Wales are in the background. (*The Illustrated London News*)

Osborne House on Princess Beatrice's wedding day. (*The Illustrated London News*)

Admiral Prince Louis of Battenberg, First Lord of the Admiralty.

Admiral of the Fleet, the Earl Mountbatten of Burma, K.G., P.C., G.C.V.O., D.S.O., etc., etc. (*Photograph by Karsh, by courtesy of Camera Press*)

Sir Ernest Cassel—whose money made it all possible—shooting at Newmarket. (*P. A.-Reuter*)

Edwina Cynthia Annette Ashley at the time of her marriage to Lord Louis Mountbatten. (*Radio Times Hulton Picture Library*)

Lord and Lady Louis Mountbatten aboard the *Majestic* their honeymoon. (*Radio Times Hulton Picture Library*)

"She went down with all guns firing." Captain Lord Louis Mountbatten's flagship, H. M. S. *Kelly*. (*Imperial War Museum, London*)

Lady Louis Mountbatten with her daughters—Pamela, age twelve, and Patricia, age seventeen—in New York, November, 1941. (*Wide World*)

Supreme Allied Commander, SEAC, Lord Louis Mountbatten between Chiang Kai-shek and Madame Chiang. Others (l. to r.) General Ho Yin-chen, Lt. Gen. Brehon Somervell, and Lt. Gen. Joseph Stilwell. (*Wide World*)

The Supreme Allied Commander with an Afridi leader. (*Wide World*)

Home from Burma. Lord Louis with Edwina and Patricia at their London home, 1946. (*Wide World*)

with all his energy; instead he fought it tooth and nail. He grudged every ship that was sent, even the slow old battleships for which, he had said, "The scrap heap cries aloud!" Once, when Churchill begged for further reinforcements, he replied that he could not "spare a single dinghy."

The bombardment of the outer forts of the Dardanelles was begun on February 19, 1915. By March 2 they had been destroyed, and the Allied Fleet moved on to attack the inner and intermediate defenses, which were protected by extensive mine fields. The decisive attack took place on March 18. That day the inner forts were heavily punished; but the old battleships *Bouvet*, *Ocean*, and *Irresistible* were sunk by mines, and the *Inflexible* and *Gaulois* were severely damaged. Admiral Sir John de Roebeck decided, with Fisher's approval, against further attacks until an army could be landed at Gallipoli to take the forts from the land. As is well known, this effort also failed, and resulted in terrible losses. The result was that in May, 1915, Fisher finally resigned in a fury, bringing down Asquith's Cabinet. A coalition Government was formed and Churchill was forced out as First Lord of the Admiralty, to be replaced by Arthur J. Balfour. Thus the Royal Navy lost the service of its most brilliant and progressive civilian chief.

But, oh! what might have been. Long afterward Churchill wrote, "Not to persevere—that was the crime." Turkish records found after the war prove that on the night of March 18 the Turkish forts were in ruins and their great guns had fewer than a half dozen rounds of ammunition left; the Turkish Government was in disorder and the Sultan was packing to leave Constantinople.

Had the fleet gone in the next day they would have found the road through the strategic Straits as open as The Mall on a summer Sunday. They could have sailed in like a review at Spithead, smashed the *Göben* at her anchorage, and made themselves masters of the Black Sea. With Russian ports open to the world again, her grain would have flowed out and supplies would have poured in from England and America to resuscitate her matériel-starved armies. The tide of war might well have turned and, most important of all, the Bolshevist Revolution might never have taken place—with all that implies for today's world.

In fairness to Lord Fisher it must be said that the three other Sea Lords, as well as Sir John Jellicoe and even Sir David Beatty, concurred in his opinion that the Dardanelles could not be forced by ships alone. But there can be little doubt that had Prince Louis remained at the Admiralty, working "in intimate comradeship and co-operation" with Churchill, he would have supplied that small extra margin which would have made the difference between defeat and glorious victory.

Winston Churchill's son, Randolph Churchill, commented, "That is undoubtedly true. But if we had won the Dardanelles my father would have become Prime Minister. So we would not have had him when we needed him most, in World War II. After all, you can't be Prime Minister in two wars."

This appears to be a formidable non sequitur, but an interesting one.

Chapter 17

ADMIRAL OF THE
FLEET

THE FINAL CHAPTER OF Prince Louis' life is as melancholy as the last act of *Cyrano*, played in a misty setting of falling leaves and dripping sky; though just at the end it has a glorious sunset. There is nothing quite so unhappy as a retired admiral. Retired generals still live and function as they always have—on land. But an admiral is torn from his chosen element. No longer can he sway to the lift and surge of a strong ship breasting the sea; never again will he face the keen, salt wind while balancing on a heaving bridge. Rose bushes in a suburban garden are a poor substitute.

Unhappy beyond even this normal fate was that of Admiral Prince Louis of Battenberg. He was only sixty years old, hale and vigorous; his mind was at its peak of performance, his energy undiminished, his courage youthfully high. All the qualities which could serve his country in these perilous days were wasted—good for nothing.

The Battenbergs' first task was to vacate Mall House and find another place to live. This problem was solved by the kindness of Princess Louise,* to whom Queen Victoria had left Kent House on the Isle of Wight. Princess Louise in turn had provided in her will that it should

---

* Queen Victoria's daughter, married to the Duke of Argyll.

go to Princess Vicky, but when the Battenbergs suddenly found themselves homeless, she gave it over to Vicky immediately. Within a few days the Battenbergs went there to live, they thought, for the rest of their lives.

Kent House was a moderate-size, Tudor-style mansion, with many bays of mullion windows overlooking blue water, and tall, intricately designed brick chimneys. When the sea mists swirled around it, one could imagine it a setting for one of Charlotte Brontë's tales of murder and hauntings, but when the sun shone on its ivied walls and the soft summer wind blew off the Solent, it became a charming haven for retirement. It is probable that, under the circumstances, Prince Louis was as happy there as he could have been anywhere. At least he could see and smell the sea.

But the days must have been interminable. Wrenched from the bustle and the exciting pressures of his eighteen-hour days in Whitehall, he suddenly had nothing significant to do. He spent a great deal of time with the wounded men who were convalescing in the naval hospitals on the Isle of Wight, some of whom he took home with him to live at Kent House. In a further attempt to fill the lagging hours he began to catalogue his large collection of medals commemorating famous naval battles; he also secured and listed replicas of medals he did not own. Thus the catalogue became a compendium, which was to develop into a three-volume naval history of which his son, Lord Louis Mountbatten, wrote: "To my father this work meant much more than the mere cataloguing of his collection of medals, and in truth he produced a Medallic History of all navies, a perpetual memorial to the great traditions of the sea. . . ." Meanwhile Prince Louis read in the newspapers of history being *made* by lesser men.

Occasionally Battenberg journeyed to one of the great naval bases to see his son George, who was still in the *New Zealand;* Dickie was at Dartmouth Naval College. He paid one such visit, on January 15, 1915, to the Battle Cruiser Squadron at Rosyth on the Firth of Forth where he stayed in the *New Zealand* at the invitation of Rear Admiral Gordon Moore. Prince Louis was still aboard her on Saturday, November 23, when a telegram came from the Admiralty stating:

FOUR GERMAN BATTLE CRUISERS, SIX LIGHT CRUISERS AND TWENTY-TWO DESTROYERS WILL SAIL THIS EVENING TO SCOUT ON DOGGER BANK [about 200 miles west of Heligoland]. . . . ALL AVAILABLE BATTLE CRUISERS, LIGHT CRUISERS AND DESTROYERS FROM ROSYTH SHOULD PROCEED TO A RENDEZVOUS AT 55° 13′ N, 3° 12′ E, ARRIVING AT 7.00 A.M. TOMORROW. . . .

Admiral Moore gleefully showed the telegram to Prince Louis, and said, "Come along with us. We may have some fun!"

Battenberg's eyes lit up with delight at the prospect; then the lights went out: "No," he said, "I am suspect, you might get into trouble taking me. Send me ashore."

So he went ashore in the admiral's barge. Near the dock he found an old friend, Mrs. Andrew Kerr, Mark Kerr's sister-in-law. He sat in the car with her in the fading light watching the black oil smoke pouring from the great warships' funnels as they got up steam. Darkness fell but still they sat, until the signal lights began to wink. White water frothing under the battle cruisers' sterns, the rattle and clank of anchor chains through the frost-still air—and the long dark shapes began to move, imperceptibly, then faster. With a lace of foam at their bows Beatty's battle cruisers slid under the high bridge, heading for the North Sea and the Battle of Dogger Bank.

That was where capital ships of the Royal Navy and the High Seas Fleet first met in battle. Beatty succeeded in sinking the powerful German cruiser *Blücher;* and the great battle cruisers *Seydlitz, Moltke,* and *Derfflinger,* the newest and fastest ship in the High Seas Fleet, were being badly mauled by Beatty's big guns when his flagship *Lion* took an armor-piercing shell in her engine room that cut his speed to 15 knots. Command of the rest of the squadron—*Princess Royal, Tiger, Indomitable,* and *New Zealand*—devolved on Admiral Moore. He failed to see Beatty's last Nelsonian signal, "Keep closer to the enemy," and continued on a previously ordered course, with the result that the other enemy battle cruisers escaped; one wonders if they would have had the master of cruiser tactics been standing beside him on *New Zealand's* bridge.

Another frustrating experience for Prince Louis was when, a little over a year later, he could only read in the papers about the Battle of Jutland, the one full-scale battle between the Grand Fleet and the High Seas Fleet. It would take a book to describe the action in detail; but the salient point is that, three times in the course of the battle, Admiral Jellicoe had to choose between a daring, even reckless, maneuver and a prudent course allowing the German Fleet to put more distance between itself and the British. Three times he opted for prudence. As a result the German Fleet, though badly battered, escaped destruction. Three British battle cruisers, *Indefatigable, Invincible,* and *Queen Mary,* were sunk.

The old cliché is always dusted off in Jellicoe's defense: He was "the only man who could lose the war in an afternoon." But it is never pointed out that he not only could, but he *did* lose the war that afternoon, by failing to destroy the High Seas Fleet. Had he not failed, the British could have greatly hampered the U-boat campaign by close blockade, or possibly by taking Heligoland. By 1917, with the German Fleet still in being German U-boat sinkings of merchant ships actually had England at the point of starvation, and only the intervention of the United States, with its huge fresh fleet and limitless resources, saved the Allies from defeat.

It must have been agony to Prince Louis to read of that lost opportunity for a modern Trafalgar. In fact, he so expressed himself. It was equally agonizing for Lord Fisher, by now also in retirement, whose motto was, "Rashness in war is prudence, as prudence is criminal."

The anti-German hysteria in England did not abate. In the dismal days of 1917—as Russia fell into the chaos of revolution, the exhausted French Army was on the point of mutiny, and the British Island so beleaguered by U-boats that survival seemed only a matter of weeks— Germanophobia reached its zenith. The whispers reverberated that the King must be pro-German, since his family all had German names. When someone finally dared to repeat this to the King, according to Lady Maud Warrender, "He started and grew pale." It is likely that he also loosed some choice lower-deck language. Then he called for his secretary and asked if it were true. Stamfordham admitted it was, and when the King asked his advice he hesitantly suggested that His Majesty might change his name.

"I wouldn't mind that," King George said, "I'm not sure what my name is in any case." Neither was the College of Heralds. When Mr. Farnham Burke of that omniscient institution was consulted, he replied that he was "not quite positive." He was sure it was not Stuart, and doubted if the generally accepted Guelph was correct. "My surmise," he said, "and it is no more than that, is that His Majesty's name is either Wipper or Wettin."

"Then we'll change it," said King George.

And so there began at Buckingham Palace a very serious parlor game. Members of the family had different suggestions—Tudor-Stuart (bad connotations), York, Plantagenet (affected), England, Lancaster, even D'Este and Fitzroy (sounds illegitimate). Finally Lord Stamfordham came up with the winner. He discovered that King Edward III had once been called Edward of Windsor. The King liked that, and Windsor it was.*

Lord Rosebery wrote to Stamfordham, "Do you realize you have christened a dynasty? There are few people in the world who have done this, none I think . . . I admire and envy you."

All other members of the Royal Family living in England were invited, which is to say commanded, to follow the King's example. There is reason to believe that Prince Louis of Battenberg thought it was nonsense, but he had to go along with it. He chose Mountbatten, which was not only a literal translation of Battenberg, but also the name of an island fort in Plymouth Sound. In fact all his new names derived from the sea. The King proposed to create him a marquess in lieu of serene highness, and he took the title Milford Haven, a former Royal title (dating from 1706) which came from a fine harbor on the Welsh coast. For his second title, which his eldest son might wear by courtesy, he became the Earl of Medina after the river near Kent House; his third title was Viscount Alderney, after a Channel Island. His cousin Prince Henry's son, Prince Alexander of Battenberg, became Alexander Mountbatten, Marquess of Carisbrooke.

When Lord Stamfordham went to the Party leaders at Westminster to present the King's list of new titles he was a bit nervous about what the Labour Party would think of Prince Louis' being made a marquess, so he kept this news for the last. As he hesitated before saying it, Labour Leader J. H. Thomas asked, "What about Prince Louis?"

Stamfordham said, "He becomes Marquess of Milford Haven, Earl of Medina, and Viscount Alderney."

In his forthright way Thomas said, "Well, I don't think that's half enough, and neither does the Labour Party. What that man has done for our Navy . . . intelligence and many other things is almost beyond belief, and the way he was kicked out at the beginning of the war was a scandal. I wrote him about it at the time and he wrote me back a fine manly letter with never a word of complaint. I shall keep that letter all my life."

Prince Louis duly took his seat in the House of Lords, with all the color and splendor of its traditions. Walking between his sponsors, the Marquess of Crewe and the Marquess of Lansdowne, he was a splendid figure in his ermine-trimmed robe ablaze with twenty-seven grand crosses of different orders, ranging from the Legion of Honor to the

---

* When the Kaiser heard of this he said, "Fine! Next time we play Shakespeare we'll call it, "The Merry Wives of Saxe-Coburg-Gotha."

Rising Sun of Japan. The glossy brown of his hair and beard were barely touched with gray, his face was still ruddy from the sea winds, and his eyes sparkled with, perhaps, a faint touch of amusement as they placed the four-pointed coronet of a marquess on his head.

What he really thought of the whole business was expressed in a flash of wit when the name changes were first announced. He happened to be staying at Keavil in Dunfermline with his son George, who had recently married Countess Nada, daughter of the Grand Duke Michael of Russia. In the visitors' book at Keavil he wrote:

> July 9th. Arrived Prince Hyde.
> July 19th. Departed Lord Jekyll.

The final twist of irony to the name-changing is that today, in those very clubs where the cabal against him started, in the Carlton and Boodles and the Turf, the name of Battenberg, meaning Prince Louis, has a hallowed ring, while the name Mountbatten wakes scurrilous old echoes.

On a Monday in July of 1918 Prince Louis and his wife went down to the dock at East Cowes to meet the ferry on which their cousin, Princess Marie-Louise of Schleswig-Holstein, was arriving for a visit. As the boat was tying up Prince Louis leapt aboard and began to look for his guest. The moment he saw her, her long face very pale, her big eyes seeing ghosts, he knew something terrible had happened. "Louis," she said. "Thank God you came aboard. I don't think I could tell Vicky."

"What's happened?"

"The Bolsheviki have shot Nicky and Alix and all their children."

"All of them, all—?"

"Yes. I have a letter from the King for Vicky. He's holding up the news until I could tell her."

"Give it to me," Prince Louis said gently. "I'll break it to her when we get home."

No one knows how Prince Louis told his wife the news of the ghastly mass murder at Ekaterinberg. With royal self-control she came out of her room a few minutes later to thank Princess Marie-Louise for undertaking the difficult task of bringing the tragic message. They talked of it for a few moments but it was so incredible that there was little to say. According to the Princess, Vicky seemed stunned to numbness. After about half an hour she said, "Let's go out and work in the garden. There's any amount of work to be done, and one gardener can't do it alone."

They worked, not only that day, but every day—all day long, gardening or picking blackberries and mushrooms, as though by exhausting herself Vicky could shut her mind to what had happened now and have only the happy memories of the gay young Tsar and her young sister and their pretty little daughters in those happy summers in Darmstadt back in another age that was only five or six years ago.

A short time later Vicky learned that another sister—Ella (Elizabeth), wife of Grand Duke Serge of Russia—had also been assassinated by the Bolsheviki. Ella's body was smuggled out of Siberia by a devoted Orthodox priest and taken to Shanghai. Two and a half years later, in January, 1921, it was arranged for her body, together with that of a faithful little nun named Marvara who had died with her, to be taken to Palestine for burial in the Russian church built by her brother-in-law Tsar Alexander III on Calvary, where Christ was crucified. The Battenbergs went there to attend the ceremony and Prince Louis described the journey in a letter to his brother's widow, Princess Beatrice.

The Battenbergs met the boat from Shanghai at Port Said. The bodies were accompanied by the same priest who had taken them out of Russia, "a handsome man with long hair and a beard." After a night at Port Said the small freight car containing the two teak coffins was ferried across the Suez Canal, and the Battenbergs walked across on a bridge of boats, accompanied by General Lord Allenby and the Stroukoffs, a Russian couple who had been part of the Grand Duchess's suite before they escaped from Russia, and were devoted to her.

Allenby had arranged for them to travel to Jerusalem in a private railway car. They arrived there at about one in the afternoon. All the Orthodox clergy in black and silver funeral vestments met them at the station and held a brief service on the platform. Then they went by motor to the foot of Calvary.

Prince Louis wrote: "At the foot of the Mount the coffins were lifted out and carried up the steep, stony, zig-zag road to the church. Most of the carriers were Russian peasant women, stranded pilgrims, who staggered under the tremendous load, sobbing and moaning all the time, and almost fighting to get at some part of the coffin. I clung to one of the handles, and once had to climb over the body of one of the women, who had tripped over a stone and fallen full length. One huge priest, with hair like a lion's mane, was, happily, at the head end, but it was a relief when we reached the church safely.

"A service was held at once, the congregation overflowing outward through the open doors. . . . Tomorrow the last [service] will be held by the Patriarch, a splendid old white-bearded man. . . .

"The Stroukoffs you know are Ella's Private Secretary and the former Lady-in-Waiting, Kitty Kaglianioff. The latter had accompanied Ella and Serge in 1888, when they came to inaugurate this very church. . . ."

That strange funeral marked the end of sadness for Prince Louis. The year 1921 was a good year, a happy year. True the Battenbergs had lost most of their money, the equivalent of a quarter of a million dollars, which he had invested in a platinum mine in Russia; it was lost to the Bolsheviki. He had sold Heiligenberg after the war for approximately $150,000, but that, too, vanished in the wild inflation of the mark. All that remained was their property in England and Prince Louis' half pay as a retired First Sea Lord. He gave up Kent House in 1919 and went to live in Fishponds, a cottage on the grounds of Netley Castle owned by Colonel Charles Crichton, whose wife was the daughter of Mark Kerr's uncle, Admiral Lord Frederick Kerr.

Prince Louis did not seem to mind the loss of grandeur. The good things that happened in 1921 more than made up for having to take buses instead of taxis and live in a pretty little house instead of a beautiful big one. The first of these good things occurred on July 21, when he was asked to take the chair at the annual dinner of the Royal Navy Club. These dinners were usually attended by fifty to eighty members. Hearing that Prince Louis was to preside on this occasion, about eight hundred members came from all parts of the Kingdom and even from distant lands. The First Lord of the Admiralty, Lord Lee of Fareham, offered a toast to Prince Louis, in which, as he wrote, "I took the opportunity, which I had long desired, to express publicly my sympathy with Lord Milford Haven on the stroke of Fate which had befallen him, and my belief that the trust and affection with which he was regarded, by both officers and men, throughout the great Service to which he had devoted nearly his whole life, had never wavered and were as strong as ever."

As Prince Louis rose to answer the toast there was a roar of cheering that shivered the crystal chandeliers of the United Services Club and lasted for five minutes. When it ended, because the only people in the world more sentimental than old soldiers are old sailors, there was more mist in their eyes than there is on the North Sea.

Partly as a result of this ovation, which he described as "most remarkable and significant," Lord Lee wrote to the King proposing that Prince Louis be promoted by a special Order-in-Council to the rank of Admiral of the Fleet on the Retired List. Lord Stamfordham answered that the King, "Has read your letter . . . with much satisfaction, and is delighted to give his approval of your proposal to promote Admiral the

Marquess of Milford Haven to the rank of Admiral of the Fleet on the Retired List to date from August 4th, 1921.

"His Majesty has always felt keenly for Lord Milford Haven, whose distinguished service terminated under circumstances which, as you say, can only be regarded as tragic. Nevertheless, Lord Milford Haven bowed to his fate without murmur or complaint, and with that dignity worthy of his generous nature.

"The King is sure that this recognition of his services will be welcomed by the Navy at large."

So they did their best to make amends, and Prince Louis welcomed the gesture as generously as he had abided by the necessity for his downfall. Yet knowing the man one may be sure that he would have given all his stars and orders and honors, and possibly life itself, for the chance of commanding the fleet for a few hours on a misty May afternoon off the Jutland Peninsula.

Later in that happy August, the captain of the battle cruiser *Repulse*, in which Lieutenant Lord Louis Mountbatten was serving, invited the new Admiral of the Fleet to take a cruise with them. Prince Louis accepted gladly and joined the ship at a Scottish port.

Repulse was the last word in battle cruisers; indeed, she was almost the last one ever built. Designed under the guidance of Lord Fisher and launched in 1916, she was the ultimate expression of his favorite theories about the very fast all-big-gun ship. Armor and even gun power were sacrificed for speed. She could hurl her 26,500 tons through the water at 32 knots or about 40 miles an hour. Her armament was six 15-inch guns, two having been sacrificed to gain more speed. She also had seventeen 4-inch guns to defend herself, inadequately, against destroyer attack. Anti-aircraft guns were added as an afterthought. She was long and low and lean, and looked like the greyhound she was. Unfortunately she shared the greyhound's vulnerability.*

Repulse sailed northward in the crisp salt breezes of those chilly seas. Reveling in the sway of her deck, and the sounds of creaking rivets, and the soft purr of the powerful engines of this great ship, Prince Louis relived his youth; as he studied the latest navigational and aiming devices with which she was equipped, he looked a little way into the future—fortunately, for his peace of mind, not too far.

The company of fellow sailors in the captain's cabin and the wardroom was pure delight, further enhanced by the company of his hand-

---

* *Repulse* was sunk by Japanese aircraft in about ten minutes off the coast of Malaya in 1941.

some younger son. Dickie was now a shade taller than his father, a string-bean of a fellow, with strong, straight features and a devilish light in his eyes that promised the daring which he later displayed. Prince Louis loved him dearly, and what's more, he *liked* him very much.

That was a fine cruise, almost as fine as the one in the *Drake* before the world collapsed. Prince Louis returned to London on Saturday, September 10, and put up at the Naval and Military Club Annex. Vicky and their daughter Louise were staying at a nearby hotel, preparatory to going to Scotland. Prince Louis was looking forward to going to Constantinople to see George, who was serving in H.M.S. *Cardiff*.

He was not feeling very well, and with characteristic reluctance, he asked Vicky and Louise to stay over one night until he felt better. Of course they did, and on Sunday they sent for a doctor, but none of them was really worried.

That afternoon they sat with him while the club's housekeeper brought him up some tea and toast, which he ate. Then they went out to pick up some medicine the doctor had prescribed. When they returned the housekeeper met them weeping. She had gone in to fetch the tray and found Prince Louis dead. They ran up the stairs and burst into his room.

The Admiral was leaning back on the pillows against whose white his beard and hair still showed traces of glossy brown. His eyes were closed and his high forehead was serene. He looked as though he were having a pleasant dream.

Perhaps he was. Certainly, in spite of the one harsh blow fate had dealt him, he had had a wonderful life. For sixty-one of his sixty-seven years, including the last one, he had been supremely happy. Not only had he enjoyed the good things of the world with tremendous zest, but he had been able to use his great abilities to the full in the service he loved, for the country he had made his own—something few royal princes, however great their talents, are allowed to do. Without vanity he could know he had done a good job.

More satisfying even was the knowledge that he had won the respect and love of his fellow sailors, from the lower deck to the admiral's bridge. And he had, too, pride in his two sons who were striding along the same path of fearless excellence.

Finally God had granted him the ultimate boon that neither fore-thought, science, nor character can command—a quick and easy death.

II

LORD LOUIS

Chapter 1

BOY AND MAN

STEPHEN FRY WAS A NAVAL CADET at Osborne in 1914. Because of its
drama, he always remembered a dreary day in late October of that
year. News had come that the First Sea Lord, Prince Louis of Battenberg, had been forced to resign because of his German name and origins.
As Fry came out of the main hall, Queen Victoria's erstwhile coach
house, he saw a small cadet standing stiffly beside the flagpole which was
rigged like a ship's mast and flew the White Ensign and the commanding
admiral's two-star flag. The boy evidently thought himself quite alone,
for he was staring into the drizzle, making no effort to conceal the tears
raining down his cheeks.

Fry recognized Dickie Battenberg, and with quite remarkable tact
in a boy of fourteen, ducked quickly out of sight. Though he was not
especially fond of Battenberg, who was a bit of a loner, he felt sorry for
him. Like almost everyone else in the Royal Navy, even lowly cadets,
he thought that Prince Louis' forced resignation was a scandal and a
shame; and like all the other fellows at Osborne he knew how proud
Dickie was of his glamorous, brilliant father.

Fry was not too young to recognize that he had witnessed a moment
of genuine tragedy, but what he could not know was that he had seen
the psychological rebirth of the Earl Mountbatten of Burma. Lord
Mountbatten, and everyone who knows him, agrees that the beclouded
resignation of his splendid father was the turning point of his life. Few
people can point to so clearly marked a moment in the formation of

(167)

their character and destiny. The futures of most men are shaped gradually by their interests, talents, and environments. Of course, young Battenberg had some natural predilections; after all, he was committed to a career in the Royal Navy. What he lacked until then was determination.

During the miserably unhappy days that followed, his rage against a world that could so dishonor a most honorable man was like the white heat of a blast furnace forging the steel of character; not only forging it but giving it the cutting edge, the ruthlessness, that could and did trample every thing and every person that stood in the way of Dickie's blazing ambition to vindicate his father in his own person by someday becoming First Sea Lord.

Surely he had thought of it before; daydreamed schoolboy fashion of coming back to Osborne, wearing the insignia of the highest rank, as had Prince Louis a few months earlier, to review the naval cadets of that infinitely distant day. But it had been only a daydream not a promise. Now it became a vow, a quest, and, bitterly, a holy war against the world. Battenberg became the sort of person who never relaxes and never, never forgets.

Dickie appears to have been sweet, feckless, and rather timid as a child. It was natural that he should be, for he was the son of his parents' middle age, an unexpected accident of the sort that occasionally overtakes people who think they have completed their families. His brother George was eight years older than he. Louise was eleven when he was born and his sister Alice married Prince Andrew only three years later.

Generally speaking he was probably somewhat spoiled, at least by royal standards, which are the strictest of any walk of life—they have to be, because princes are on parade even in their prams. From the moment Dickie knocked off Queen Victoria's spectacles he probably got away with murder. Of course his mother was never a woman to be trifled with, and she tolerated no nonsense. But she had time to lavish more love on Dickie than she had on the others. Prince Louis was away so much of the time that when he came home he reveled in family affection and especially in the open adoration of his gentle towheaded son. Yet he did not blindly worship Dickie. It is likely that he had more respect for George, who was far more brilliant as a boy and seemed more stable. But love begets love, and the bond was very close.

By any normal standards Dickie's upbringing was wildly irregular. All sailors' children are accustomed to follow their fathers wherever they may be stationed. Dickie's travels were compounded by the Battenbergs' royal connections in almost every European country. His family were continually on the move—from Austria to Corfu, where his sister and Prince Alexander had a villa by the sea, unimaginatively called Mon Repos; then on to stay with Cousins Nickie and Alix in the great echoing summer palace of Tsarskoe Selo, or with Cousin Ena in one of the castles of her husband, King Alfonso, in Spain. Admiralty House at Sheerness was familiar territory, as was Casa Medina at Malta. Perhaps Heiligenberg was the nearest thing to a home he ever had, but even this was in a foreign country for Dickie was definitely British.

The brief summer weeks the Battenbergs spent in their ancestral home were sheer delight to Dickie. He knew every corner of the big old house, its towers and turrets and crazy mixture of architectural styles that somehow blended harmoniously with the steep, pine-clad hills looking down a valley of bright meadows.

At Heiligenberg he could run wild, as his father had, roaming about the meadows, collecting small animals or lizards and turtles as pets—Mountbatten had a houseful of pets all his life. And if he chose he could explore the woods back of the house, where the pine trees made endless cathedral corridors through which he could run on springy, sweet pine needles—although he seldom did so, for there might have been wild animals there. He also had a pony, which he liked as he did all domesticated animals, but he did not ride a great deal.

Tsar Nicholas and Tsarina Alix sometimes came to stay at Heiligenberg, bringing their four pretty daughters and later their delicate baby son, the Tsarevitch. Naturally this caused much the same dislocation and confusion as when Tsar Alexander II visited in Dickie's grandfather's day, and it was just as much fun.

The intimacy of the Romanovs and Battenbergs was the cause of Mountbatten's incongruous nickname. At first the Battenbergs called their baby son Nicky, since Nicholas was one of his five names, but when the Tsar's family came to visit there were too many Nickys. So his sisters and brother changed it to "Dickie," and Dickie it remained.

Dickie's Russian cousins also were probably responsible for one of his childish fears. Until he was five or six he was afraid to go to bed alone in the dark.

"It isn't the dark," he explained. "There are wolves up there."

"Why, Dickie, there are no wolves in the house," said Prince Louis, laughing.

Logically Dickie said, "I dare say there ar'n't, but *I* think there are."

One can picture the little grand duchesses filling his head with traditional Russian tales of a droshky fleeing through a howling snowstorm, while somebody heaved the baby out to distract the pursuing wolf pack.

The fact is that Dickie was very cautious. There is an account, possibly apocryphal, of his Aunt Alix asking him what he wanted to be when he grew up. "I haven't decided yet," Dickie answered.

"How about being a soldier?"

Dickie shook his head. "Soldiers always get shot."

"A sailor then, like your father?"

"No. Ships are always sinking."

Thinking of a safe civilian occupation the Tsarina proposed an engine driver.

Dickie thought that over, but again his decision was negative—the engine might "go over the embankment."

True or not, the story is completely in key with his character—until the time of radical change.

Next to Heiligenberg Dickie probably liked living in Malta, where in fact some of the happiest days of his adult life also were spent. A sensitive small boy could be aware of the beauty of the place. From their hilltop villa he could see old castles and fortifications, gold in the sunset, the creamy-white buildings of Valletta, orange trees in the valleys, the raw tops of the baked hills—and at the end of every view the incredible blue Mediterranean water, covered by the triangular sails of the fishing boats and, what he loved best, the great ships of war, his father's ships, with their tall masts, buff funnels, and black guns against the peacetime white of their superstructures, and the White Ensign flashing over them.

When Prince Louis was second-in-command of the Mediterranean Fleet he often took seven-year-old Dickie aboard his flagship *Venerable*, and turned him over to some old quartermaster to be amused, while the Admiral conducted his business. Those were great times, for British sailors are notoriously fond of children, and they went to extraordinary lengths to entertain him. As for Dickie, he always got on wonderfully with the lower deck—better, in fact, than he ever did with the wardroom.

Malta has always been a place for Sunday picnics and these, too, were great fun. They would drive out to the country in one of the local carrozzas pulled by horses with gaily colored headdresses, made of pheasants' tails, used to scare away the devil. Somebody, usually Dickie, always had to ride on the box with the coachman so the devil could not slip into the empty seat beside him; through the Maltese servants Dickie possessed intimate knowledge of his Satanic majesty. The picnics were held on a cliff by the sea or a slope in the hills, where the servants spread a white cloth on rocky ground and strewed cushions for the grownups.

The food was superb, especially the oranges and other semi-tropical fruits that were hard to obtain in England.

Everyone loved to dress up in those days. As if their customary costumes—the men's brilliantly colored uniforms and gold or silver helmets with cascades of cockfeathers, the ladies' elaborately lacy gowns and cartwheel hats—were not enough, they held numerous fancy-dress balls at which they wore elaborate and authentic costumes from their ancestors' closets. There is a picture of one such group at Malta, in which Prince Louis is splendidly sinister in high black boots and a knee-length black tunic with a huge golden Russian Imperial Eagle blazoned on its front; his full mustache curls fiercely upward toward his high-peaked black headgear. Dickie, pale and thin, is standing beside him engulfed by the dress uniform of a Cossack officer, with the same high black boots, a long-skirted coat with cartridge pouches, a high astrakhan cap, and a gold-hilted dagger at his waist.

Dickie was given many other uniforms by his reigning relatives— those of the Hessian Life Guards, the pleated skirts of the Evzon Guards of Greece, and of course uniforms of various British regiments. He was generous about lending them to his friends, but he was also a stickler for form. If one of the boys turned out with a cartridge box on the wrong side or a belt improperly fastened, Dickie gave him a dressing-down. His uniforms were always absolutely correct, a characteristic that persisted. From the storm-lashed coast of Norway to the steaming Burmese jungles Mountbatten miraculously managed to look neat, crisp, and perfectly appointed for the occasion.

Dickie's education during his peripatetic youth was surprisingly systematic, and this was due entirely to his mother, who may have been a schoolteacher *manquée*. She liked to inform people, and she had a methodical German mind and a strong sense for the seriousness of learning. She taught Dickie at regular times and insisted that his homework be completed punctually. Of course he had a governess as well, but Vicky was undoubtedly the moving spirit. She must have been seriously disappointed to discover that he was no scholar; George had been a great deal more interested in his lessons.

Through most of his boyhood Dickie came up against these unfavorable comparisons with George, who was not only a better scholar, but a better athlete as well. This was especially true when, at age ten, he went to Lockhurst Park Preparatory School. George had gone to Cheam in Surrey, where he had been a leader in sports and studies. Dickie was definitely in the ruck at Lockhurst Park.

In fact he showed so little aptitude or ambition that Prince Louis became worried, but he realized there was not a great deal he could do about it, besides encouraging his son to apply himself to his studies, particularly mathematics, his weakest subject. As to Dickie's ineptitude at sports, there was nothing much anyone could do about that; one either has the right reflexes or one does not, Prince Louis thought. He did not realize that determination sometimes can overcome natural deficiencies.

It was during his holidays from Lockhurst Park that Dickie took that first ride in an aeroplane. He was hardly frightened at all, for he was imbued with his father's false confidence in the safety of aerial navigation. In fact he loved it, for though he lacked proficiency in games and horseback riding, Dickie had a natural affinity for mechanical vehicles—he became expert with fast cars, fast motorboats, and planes.

Dickie duly entered Osborne in the autumn of 1913. Since Prince Louis' day the entering age had been lowered to thirteen, because of Lord Fisher's theory that to "catch 'em young and treat 'em rough" was the way to make a good sailor. The theory did not work very well in practice, since most boys were not quite up to it. There was so much illness that the following year the entering age was put back at fourteen.

Merely getting in was quite an accomplishment, because in those days it was fashionable to be a naval officer; thus there was hot competition for admission. First came a proper physical examination, quite different from the casual one Prince Louis had passed; then a rather stiff written test which eliminated about half the applicants. Most important of all was the oral examination before a board composed of an admiral, several senior captains, and commanders. It is possible that they were inclined to favor the son of an officer as popular as Prince Louis, but it would be less than fair to Dickie to suppose that, with his long indoctrination in naval lore and his shy but engaging personality, he would not have passed in any case.

As soon as Dickie got the notice that he had passed into the Royal Navy Prince Louis took him down to the best-known naval tailors, Messrs. Gieve, Mathews, and Seagrove, who worked as hard giving him a perfect fit as they would have for an Admiral of the Fleet—Dickie was as particular as if he were one. He was immensely pleased with the result and his father took a snapshot of him standing under one of the gray stone arches of the Admiralty. Here for the first time can be seen signs of the famous Mountbatten charm. Though still quite small he was beginning to grow up to his long straight nose, which became him so well when he achieved his full height. His short, brass-buttoned cutaway blue jacket and the naval cap with its gold fouled-anchor-and-crown insignia were immensely becoming. Most charming of all were the merry eyes, and broad, delighted self-conscious grin of a little boy in his first *real* uniform.

It is doubtful that he was as happy when he reached the Isle of Wight; life at Osborne must have been pretty grim. Queen Victoria's ornate villa was now a house for naval pensioners, and the college consisted of a series of hastily built, temporary wooden buildings in the old stable yard. One was about six hundred feet long, extending back from the fancy coach house which was the main hall. It formed a corridor from which other temporary structures extended at right angles about every twenty yards. Their outer walls were so flimsy that the boys could —and did—kick holes in them. Those on the left were long dormitories, in each of which about forty boys slept in cots, with a sea chest at the foot for their clothes and kits. At the far end of each dormitory were lavatories and a plunge bath about three feet deep. Every morning at 6:30 A.M. the little boys were roused out of bed by a clanging gong. Naked, they ran down the length of the dormitory, tore through that icy water, and on the other side, dried themselves with skimpy towels, while their teeth chattered like watchmen's rattles.

Doors on the other side of the corridor opened into similar buildings, used as study halls. Southeast of the dormitory sheds was a barnlike wooden building housing the huge raftered mess hall and classrooms. It was appropriately called Nelson, and in bold brass letters on the crossbeam supporting the gallery was his motto: THERE IS NOTHING THE NAVY CANNOT DO.

The sick bay, usually well filled, was at the end of the row of dormitories. Parents complained constantly that Osborne was unhealthy because of the effluvia of the old stable yards, but this is dubious. The plain truth is that little boys, sent from comfortable homes to live in those damp, unheated buildings through which the Channel wind whistled, were bound to get sick. Add to that the Spartan regime of long hours of study and enforced exercise in any weather, the badly cooked, ill-chosen food, plus homesickness—it is a tribute to the stamina of the English people that most of the boys survived.

His Serene Highness Prince Louis of Battenberg was entered in Exmouth Term, Frobisher Gun Room, Port Watch—the bright boys were in the Starboard Watch. His name on the list was the only mention of his royal rank; his instructors addressed him as Cadet Battenberg, and the boys called him Battenberg or Dickie. He got no preferential treatment, and he was not sufficiently royal to arouse the animosity of his fellows. He was just another naval cadet.

Dickie did not receive a very good education, for there was no

attempt at Osborne to broaden minds, as there was at the United States
Naval Academy, where the entering age was eighteen and the courses
were similar to those in a university. The curriculum at Osborne was
strictly utilitarian. The boys were not taught the classics, as at the great
English public schools, and history was taught with reference to the
Royal Navy. The emphasis was on mathematics, seamanship, signaling,
rowing, sailing—and tying knots! Engineering was taught rather thoroughly at the engineering shops down by the River Medina, and the
cadets got somewhat cursory instruction in English grammar and one
foreign language, a choice of French or German. Dickie chose French;
he already spoke German very well.

Of course there were organized sports on the extensive playing
fields that had been the lawns of Osborne, and as at Lockhurst Park,
Dickie was unplaced. Recreation was decidedly limited. The major
weekly event was the day on which the cadets received their spending
money—one shilling. A mad rush for the sweet shop followed. But the
small amount of money was not as bad as it sounds; the boys could buy
quite a bagful for threepence. Then there were the Saturday night
dances, of which Stephen Fry says, "No girls, of course. We danced
with each other. The Marines provided the orchestra. If you were
really honored you got to dance with the term lieutenant. I remember
dancing with him and he smelled dreadfully of whiskey. It wasn't an
awful lot of fun!" We can hardly blame the lieutenant for bracing himself.

Dickie's inevitably low morale got a tremendous lift during his
first term when his father became First Sea Lord. When he came home
for his first Christmas leave it was to Mall House. The grandiose official
residence of the First Sea Lord had the ugly, stodgy furnishing and
cold atmosphere characteristic of official residences of the top brass
everywhere. But Dickie appears to have found it an agreeable place to
live. Throughout his life, whenever he had a choice of habitation, he
invariably selected the largest, the most magnificent, attaining his ideal
in the Viceroy's House at New Delhi.

Because of Prince Louis' wide-ranging interests a brilliant variety of
guests poured through Mall House. Aside from the various naval officers
whose names were about to go down in history, such as neat, precise
Jellicoe and dashing Sir David Beatty, with his cap slanted over one eye
and his cock-of-the-walk stride, Dickie met British statesmen of both
parties—Arthur J. Balfour and Herbert Asquith, Lloyd George and
Bonar Law—the whole gamut of the rulers and would-be rulers of the
Empire, including legendary Lord Kitchener. The most frequent visitor
was, naturally, the First Lord of the Admiralty, Winston Churchill.
Youngest of them all, he had a boyish zest he never lost, even when he

became the oldest, and so he knew how to get on with boys. Dickie adored him and by natural reaction he clearly liked Dickie, for beyond the barrier of age there was a compatability. Both were great romantics, with a naïve but engaging love for the color and splendor of naval life and deeds of valor. Dickie was outgrowing his youthful timidity, and though not yet exactly daring, he was a hero-worshiper and quite aware of Churchill's reckless gallantry in the Sudan and the Boer War. Of course the main object of Dickie's hero-worship was still his father.

He spent two more pleasant vacations at Mall House, and on two occasions elsewhere during the spring and summer of 1914, reached the pinnacle of youthful pride and pleasure. The first time was when Prince Louis reviewed the naval cadets at Osborne, and Dickie stood in the ranks, trembling with excitement, his soul in his eyes.

The second was that greatest of all naval reviews, the one at Spithead in July, 1914. The naval cadets were sent in batches in the old battleships of the Third Fleet—it was superb indoctrination. Dickie and his friend George Rougier were among those assigned to the *New Zealand*—not the new battle cruiser *New Zealand*, in which Prince George was already commanding the forward turret, but the old predreadnought ship of the same name. She was somewhat similar to the *Venerable*, and since Dickie was familiar with that ship, he was able, for once, to assume the leadership of his group and show them about the ship, while explaining things with a knowing air.

If that review caused a surge of emotion in the hearts of grown men, like Churchill and Prince Louis and the King, one can imagine the pitch reached by a fourteen-year-old boy actually taking part in it and wearing the uniform of that great service. The long ruler-straight lines of great ships cutting through the blue water, wheeling and maneuvering in intricate formations at high speed in precise response to the hoists of signal flags that kept going up and down the flagships' masts, were surely a sight beyond which there could be but one more stirring—those same ships in actual battle.

Then came the climax, the fleet in column, dressed in all their bright battle flags, passing the Royal Yacht and the *Enchantress*, while the 4-inch guns cracked out the Royal Salute, and their smoke drifted back with the exciting smell of burnt cordite. It aroused in Dickie an intensity of patriotism, a sort of holy pride in King and Country, the Royal Navy, and his magnificent father, that without sacrilege could be compared to religious exaltation.*

·   ·   ·

---

* Like his father, Dickie burst into print as an illustrator. Some photographs he took of this review were printed in the school magazine, bringing him a pleasing if temporary prominence.

Less than three weeks later war came, bringing a turbulence of emotions, of hope and fear, pride again; and pity, as the first wounded came back to the Isle of Wight. Finally to Dickie there came humiliation and a deeply understanding sympathy for his father, and rage against the world's injustice, as Prince Louis, in his own words, came to the "ignominious end of a lifetime of loyal service to the Royal Navy."

George Battenberg did not take it nearly as hard for the forward turret of *New Zealand* at Scapa Flow, with the ever present alarms and dangers of war, was much further from home than Osborne. Also George was so much older that he had experienced some of life's injustices and was armored with a more philosophical attitude; also his temperament was far less intense than Dickie's.

But he too had one moment of deep emotion—when the gun crews of his turret, with whom he had worked and fought at Heligoland Bight, came to him solemnly in a formal delegation. Their spokesman, an old petty officer, said, "Sir, we have come to express our horror at what has happened to your father, and our belief in his loyalty."

Dickie at Osborne had the sympathy of his fellow cadets, though in the code of boys they did not try to express it. Had they tried, Dickie would have been terribly embarrassed. As Rougier said, "We tactfully avoided the subject."

So Prince Louis' younger son suffered, very much alone. In those few terrible days he became a man.

Chapter 2

PRINCE LOUIS' FOOTSTEPS

LATE IN 1914 THE SENIOR CLASSES of Dartmouth Naval College were called out to man the mushrooming Fleet. The boys of Battenberg's term were pushed ahead to fill the gap. Passing out of Osborne he ranked thirty-fifth in a class of eighty—his new resolution had not had time to affect his standing.

Dartmouth was a more comfortable and suitable place than Osborne, having been designed and built as a naval college during the two years when the two first classes were going through Osborne. A handsome red-brick building trimmed with stone, it had proper appointments, spacious social rooms, comfortable dormitories, study halls, laboratories, and a chapel. There was also a Captain's House, a gymnasium, and a swimming pool. The College was situated halfway up a gentle hill above the River Dart in Devonshire. A long series of stone stairs led down to engineering shops at Sandquay and the dock, near which the hulk of the old *Britannia* lay.

The food was better at Dartmouth, with Devonshire cream for Sunday tea, the legacy of a kind old lady who liked boys. In his time off Battenberg could go boating on the creeks or ramble over the rolling countryside. At the Saturday night dances there were actually women to dance with—the wives and daughters of officers on the station.

Young Battenberg came into his own at Dartmouth. By intense application he gradually climbed up the academic ladder. He was made one of twenty-four cadet captains, and he placed second in fencing with the single stick—a rough and unpopular sport once favored by Robin Hood and Little John.

Perhaps his greatest triumph of guts over inadequate flesh was the two-oared cutter race on the Dart. He and his best friend, Cadet Stopford, won it when they were only juniors in competition with teams of older and heavier boys—the first time ever juniors had won.

George Rougier, who slept in the cot next to Battenberg at Dartmouth and who was perhaps his next-to-best friend, affectionately describes him at this time as "rather gay and gallant."

Dickie's leaves were spent with his parents at Kent House, not much of a change of scene, but a most welcome change of environment. In 1916 Prince Louis was still fairly affluent, and he provided his son with his first automobile, a racy white touring car, glittering with brass like a fire engine; but since he was not allowed to use it at night, it had no headlamps. Dickie had tremendous fun, and learned to drive it very expertly.

When Battenberg passed out of Dartmouth, early in 1916, he had risen to eighteenth out of eighty in his class. He took a final intensive three-month course in Keyhams, and he came out of that top man.

Midshipman Prince Louis of Battenberg was ordered to report aboard Admiral Beatty's flagship *Lion*, the crack ship of the Royal Navy. Royal rank or more likely the Navy's affection for Prince Louis may well have procured him this favored assignment. The famous battle cruiser, armed with eight 13.5-inch guns and a speed of 27 knots, had fought in all the naval battles in the North Sea. When Battenberg joined her in July, 1916, she had great patches in her hull and armor—honorable scars of combat. One entire forward turret was new. A German shell had burst in the original one at Jutland, killing its entire crew. With his dying breath the turret captain ordered the flooding of the magazines deep below it in the hull. This was the only thing that saved *Lion* from blowing up as did her three sisters—*Queen Mary*, *Indefatigable*, and *Invincible*—after similar hits.

Unfortunately from the Battenberg point of view, the *Lion* had seen her last great fight. After Jutland the High Seas Fleet never again challenged the Royal Navy in force. In a sense they had won a technical victory at Jutland, but they realized that only the fortunes of war had saved them from total destruction.

Midshipman Battenberg arrived aboard *Lion* wearing a ribbon on the breast of his uniform, commemorating his attendance at the coronation of King George V. Since many of her officers, who had served in all the big naval battles in the North Sea, wore no ribbons at all, this was a typical bit of swank not calculated to make him popular. But Dickie's attitude toward decorations was similar to Diamond Jim Brady's toward diamonds, "Them that has 'em wears 'em."

If his seniors were slightly irritated by that egregious ribbon, they could not complain about Midshipman Battenberg's diligence. Men who served in the *Lion* with him still remember the intensity with which he went at his studies, and his energetic pursuit of all sorts of extraneous information concerning naval techniques. "He was frightfully keen and enthusiastic," they recall. He was on his way.

In October, 1916, Admiral Jellicoe was made First Sea Lord and Admiral Beatty at last succeeded to the command of the Grand Fleet. These were the right spots for both, since Jellicoe was an excellent administrator and Beatty was a first-class fighting admiral.

Admiral Sir William Pakenham took over the battle cruisers from Beatty. The staff he brought with him to *Lion* included Lieutenant Prince George of Battenberg, so the two brothers had the pleasure of serving together in the same ship. It was by no means all hard work. The day of shipboard movies was still distant, but the officers got up amateur theatricals to break the monotony of long tours of duty. Dickie made quite a hit as a principal girl in a musical comedy. "He was damned attractive, too," one of his shipmates recalls. No one could be gayer than Dickie and no one more morose when black moods struck. However, his depressive cycle produced not withdrawal but demonic energy.

In February, 1917, both brothers were transferred to Beatty's flagship, the superb 25-knot, 15-inch-gun super-dreadnought *Queen Elizabeth*. It was during this time that the famous name change took place; Prince Louis becoming the Marquess of Milford Haven and Prince George the Earl of Medina. It is probable that Dickie liked it even less than did his father, for he set great store by rank and it was definitely a social demotion. Now, instead of being a prince and a serene highness, he had no legal title. Only by courtesy was he, like the younger son of any marquess, called Lord Louis Mountbatten. Perhaps this, too, drove him to make it more resplendent than any hereditary title in the world.

Young Lord Louis saw no actual fighting in World War One. When, in April, 1917, the United States entered the war, and the great

American dreadnoughts, with their 14-inch guns and their strange wire-basket masts, reinforced the Grand Fleet, there was no longer a chance that the Germans would come out to be clobbered. Nevertheless, he saw some hard service.

In 1918 Mountbatten was transferred from *Queen Elizabeth* to the submarine *K-6*. She was small, cranky, and uncomfortable compared to her modern counterparts, and even compared to the seagoing U-boats of the German Navy. But patrolling under the North Sea in her was more exciting and gave him a greater sense of participating in action than did the big super-dreadnought.

Mountbatten's service in *K-6* lasted only long enough for him to get the feel of submarining. Then he was promoted to sub-lieutenant, and transferred to second-in-command of H.M.S. *P.31*, one of the small, fast patrol boats used to hunt submarines in the narrow seas and to protect the convoys going to France.

Lord Louis loved her. At eighteen years of age he had the responsibility of command whenever the captain was not on the bridge, and in his mind she became *his* ship, and therefore, like all *his* ships, the best damn ship in the Royal Navy.

The work was hard. September and October of 1918 were the months of the last great Allied push that ended the war. British reinforcements were pouring across the Channel in a steady stream of troopships, and the patrol boats were run ragged guarding them. *P.31* sometimes made two round trips in twenty-four hours—which, with refueling, waiting for the convoys to be loaded, and other delays, meant that nobody aboard her got any sleep at all. One night when Lord Louis was on the bridge and his ship going 20 knots he blacked out. He had gone to sleep on his feet.

Then suddenly it was all over—the Kaiser in flight to Holland; the great German Army rapidly falling back into Germany; red flags of revolution hoisted over German dreadnoughts in Kiel by mutinous sailors; and the sad, black-coated emissaries of the new German Government signing the surrender in a railway car in the forest of Compiègne.

Ten days later, on November 18, 1918, the High Seas Fleet put to sea for the last time. It consisted of ten dreadnoughts, eight battle cruisers, a number of cruisers, and fifty destroyers. Admiral Beatty, accompanied by King George and the Prince of Wales, met them with the Grand Fleet off the Firth of Forth. Slowly the German ships passed between the splendid double line of British and American warships, into the Firth of Forth where silently watching crowds stood along the banks. At sunset the flags of the Imperial German Navy were lowered, never to be raised again.

.   .   .

On a fine November day in 1918 both of Prince Louis' sons came home on leave. As a souvenir of the occasion all three were photographed in uniform in the doorway of Kent House. The Admiral, still stalwart and handsome, stands proudly between his two sons; Lord Louis has reached his full height and tops his splendid parent by a scant inch; George, Earl of Medina, is smaller and slighter (to make himself nearer the height of the other two he is surreptitiously standing on tip-toe).

The Royal Navy was demobilized in a great hurry, for Britain was broke. Every day counted. All but four of the P boats were ordered mothballed—"in care of maintenance," the British called it.

P.31 was one of the lucky four. Then orders came to demobilize her. The captain rushed up to Whitehall to find out what was happening, ordering Mountbatten to hold everything until he returned. While he was gone Admiral Bernard, commanding at Portsmouth, announced that he would inspect the patrol boats to see if the orders had been properly carried out.

Lord Louis acted with typical ingenuity in evading orders. He bundled the crew with all their gear into a boiler room, shut the door, quickly painted it, and hung a sign: FRESH PAINT. When Admiral Bernard came aboard there were only Mountbatten and a few maintenance men in sight. The Admiral asked if the ship was in care of maintenance. "She's next door to it, sir," Lord Louis answered. He reckoned it was not a lie because the ship in the next birth was in that condition.

The captain got things straightened out at the Admiralty, and *P.31* was back in full commission the next day. Lord Louis served in her for nine months more.

The drastic reduction of the fleet left many young officers unemployed. To solve the problem of what to do with them, someone at the Admiralty had the sensible idea that it might be a good thing to educate them a bit. So in 1919 Mountbatten received orders to attend Cambridge University, where he entered Christ's College.

The move to Cambridge represented one of those abrupt changes of environment Mountbatten always enjoyed because he had the gift of being able to adjust quickly to any circumstances—variety truly spiced his life. It was a rip-roaring year at the ancient university. Many of the undergraduates had served in the war. They were men, not boys. Having returned unscathed from Flanders' deadly fields they felt they were living on borrowed time and should make the most of it. Lord Louis, released from the discipline he had known all his life, burst out in his first playboy phase.

At first almost the only men he knew at Cambridge were his cousins, Prince Albert (later, King George VI) and Prince Henry (later Duke of Gloucester), who were at Trinity College. He saw a good deal of them, but both were restrained by their position, and in Albert's case by a retiring nature. Mountbatten sought wider vistas. His enthusiasm for life and quick, easy charm made him popular. In no time he had a large circle of friends. He was elected to the Pitt, a very social club where he spent many evenings drinking and talking about everything, from the state of the world to the future of Art, about which he knew nothing at all. But he was a quick study and soon acquired a glib patter.

Though superficially he was just a light-hearted undergraduate, his dynamic purpose was undiminished. Since the way to eminence at Cambridge was intellectual, he sought attainment in that hitherto unexplored area. His night-owling did not interfere. Having reached his full strength, he exhibited the extraordinary physical endurance that astonished—and exhausted—three generations of his countrymen. He attended lectures all day, talked and drank half the night, and studied hard the rest of the time. When he slept is uncertain.

Students at the great English universities are very interested in politics. Lord Louis was not, but to serve his purposes he made himself so, temporarily. In his first term he wangled an invitation to join the Union,* and was not only the first active naval officer ever to do so, but also was chosen to lead the debate against Oxford. This was an extraordinary feat, for he had no experience at all in public speaking let alone debate, and was never too comfortable on his feet. But determination and a quick wit are very helpful attributes.

Having been chosen, he pulled off a typical piece of Mountbatten razzle-dazzle. According to the rules the leader could invite one outside guest. Lord Louis wondered, "Who is the best debater I know?" The obvious answer was Winston Churchill, at that time serving in Lloyd George's postwar Conservative Government as Secretary of State for War. His eminence might have given another youth pause. Not Mountbatten. He rang up the Secretary and asked him to the debate. Churchill accepted—he would do anything for Prince Louis' son.

The subject of the debate was, "Resolved: The Time is Ripe for a Labour Government." Cambridge had the negative. The earnest young

---

* The Unions at Cambridge and Oxford are famous debating clubs where future statesmen try their oratorical wings.

men of both universities presented their formal arguments and counter arguments in the elegant language and ornate style of the old parliamentarians whom they sedulously aped. Then Lord Louis took the floor, wearing the mess jacket of a naval officer and on whose breast quite a few more service ribbons had joined the coronation medal. Standing very tall and slim, with deviltry in his eyes, he respectfully addressed the Chair: "Sir," he began, "in my humble opinion everything that has been said so far by the speakers on both sides is tripe."

The gasps of horror were drowned by a tremendous snort of glee from His Majesty's Secretary of State for War.

The Season of 1919 was the first postwar blooming of society. The dammed-up debutantes came out in droves, and people of all ages reveled in the release from the drab austerity years. To add to the season's brilliance were three bachelor princes of the House of Windsor, headed by the altogether charming Prince of Wales. Lord Louis Mountbatten ranked next to them in the social pecking order, and the fact that he had no income beyond his small naval pay was no drawback. Good looks, gaiety, and kinship to the King were enough for the man-hunting mamas of the debutantes. Invitations poured in to him.

Since Cambridge is only an hour by train from London he came up every weekend. And now for the first time in his life, he could indulge in innocent gaiety enhanced by all the adjuncts of wealth and elegance. In the great mansions, Crewe House, Wimborne House, Chesterfield or Londonderry House, and forty or fifty foreign embassies, dinner was still served on gold plates by footmen, wearing powdered hair and knee breeches. In that last year before the Roaring Twenties social life was still innocent. Liberty had not degenerated into license and some Victorian restraints survived—all the girls were carefully chaperoned.

In Lord Louis' eyes the prettiest of them all was Audrey James. She was half English, half American, and altogether beautiful, with masses of dark brown hair flying around a delicate intaglio face, and a figure that looked far more ethereally fragile than it was. She was vivacious and intelligent.*

Lord Louis fell in love with her, and after two weeks of full-ahead courtship, they became engaged. But even first love could not swerve Mounbatten from his appointed course. In December, 1919, the Prince of Wales returned from a highly successful trip to Canada and the United States. His description of his adventures made Mountbatten envious. "What fun!" he exclaimed. "I wish I'd been along."

* The writer was personally acquainted with Miss James at this time.

"Come with me on the next trip," the Prince said casually. "I'm going to Australia in the spring."

Mountbatten determined to do just that. Not only did he want very much to see the world, but Prince Louis had made a similar trip, and he was carefully planting his feet in each of his father's footsteps.

But no further mention of it was made, so on the last day of the Christmas vacation he decided that something must be done. The Court Calendar in *The Times* stated that H.R.H. the Prince of Wales would attend a ball that night given by Lady Ribblesdale at 18 Grosvenor Square. Mountbatten called up a somewhat older friend, and asked, "How well do you know Lady Ribblesdale?"

"Rather well. Are you going to her party tonight?"

"No, but I want to," Lord Louis said. "David's going to be there and I absolutely have to see him."

"What about?"

"I can't tell you now, but it's vital."

"If it's that vital, I'll have a go at it."

Lady Ribblesdale was happy to include Lord Louis Mountbatten in her guest list. He went, and put pressure on "David," who good-naturedly agreed to have him appointed Flag Lieutenant to Admiral Halsey, his naval aide. On March 16, 1920, Mountbatten sailed from Portsmouth in the battle cruiser *Renown*, flying the Prince of Wales' Standard at the fore, for a seven-month cruise to the South Pacific. What he told his fiancée is not known, but it was probably something about "line of duty" and "royal command." Miss James does not appear to have swallowed it.

Renown, a sister ship to *Repulse*, had been remodeled inside to make her comfortable for the long cruises on which the astute Lloyd George sent the boyishly charming Prince of Wales to knit the raveled edges of the Empire. Her first stop was Bridgetown in Barbados, where Midshipman Prince Louis had wowed the local belles of all colors nearly half a century earlier. Thence she went through the Panama Canal and north to San Diego, California.

Her one-night stay in San Diego provided a footnote to history. At a dance given at the Officers Club a striking young matron named Wallis Warfield Spencer was briefly presented to H.R.H. Neither of them felt any particular emotion, and Mrs. Spencer noted: "Last night I met the glamorous Prince of Wales and the magnificent Mountbatten."

Mountbatten looked anything but magnificent as *Renown* crossed the equator, for he had to pay the neophyte's obeisance to King Neptune by being dumped backward into a tank of water and thoroughly ducked by the Sea God's minions. In fact he looked like a skinny drowned rat.

In New Zealand and Australia Lord Louis partook of both the pleasures and pains of a royal progress—the endless receptions, reviews, luncheons, dinners, balls, shouting thousands mobbing the Prince (as English crowds are too well bred to do), the social throat cutting and hurt feelings, the pompous politicians seeking publicity, the miles of simpering schoolgirls holding bouquets. It was almost a relief one night in western Australia when the special train went off the tracks and, as little Dickie of long ago had feared, over the embankment. No one was hurt, but one particularly pompous politician, heartily disliked by the Prince and Mountbatten, got stuck in the toilet, whence his unhappy howls sounded like a native dingo.

Four months and 162 cities, towns, and villages later, they headed north again in *Renown*. They stopped in the Fiji Islands, where their reception was exactly like Prince Louis' description of his long ago. Then to Samoa, Hawaii, the Canal again, and some island hopping in the Caribbean to appease the people the Prince had missed on the outward voyage. *Renown* made a final call at the oldest dominion, Bermuda. On October 10, 1920, she steamed into Portsmouth Harbor in a perfectly beautiful English fog, or so it seemed to one traveler who, temporarily, had had his fill of tropical suns.

But it was all well worth-while. Not only had Lord Louis learned a great deal about a part of the world he would be seeing again, but he had established a firm, one might say conspiratorial, friendship with his princely cousin. In his subdued memoirs the present Duke of Windsor has written: "Dickie . . . was, at nineteen, a vigorous and high-spirited young man who became the instigator of many an unexpected diversion outside of the official program." Which statement leaves considerable scope for the imagination.

Chapter 3

SIR ERNEST CASSEL'S
GRANDDAUGHTER

SOMEWHERE OUT IN THE South Pacific Lord Louis had received a letter from Audrey James, who had decided to marry Major Dudley Coates. In London, her switch from a man of royal lineage to a mere millionaire gave rise to the quip that Audrey "preferred the arms of Coates to the coat of arms." Lord Louis' heart does not appear to have been devastated, though his pride almost certainly was lacerated.

On his return from India Lord Louis was posted to the battle cruiser *Repulse*. During his frequent leaves he resumed his gadding in London, which was gayer than ever—gray toppers were back in fashion and the Guards Brigade had shed wartime khaki for their brilliant dress uniforms.

As the Season of 1921 progressed Mountbatten found himself invited to a very grand ball at Claridge's, given by the American hostess, Mrs. Cornelius Vanderbilt, whose daughter Grace was seeing a good deal of Prince Albert, Duke of York, thereby arousing unjustifiable hopes in her mother's ambitious bosom. At the ball Lord Louis met Edwina Ashley, who had made her debut while he was away. The combination was a natural from the first.

Edwina was a veritable English beauty with the rose-and-cream skin that the English climate seems to nourish. She had the then fashionable slim, boyish figure, soft, reddish-brown hair, and the biggest, brightest blue eyes in London. What was not immediately apparent was that she also had a first-class mind—which, she always said, "I inherited from my Jewish ancestors"—and a warm, sympathetic heart.

Sir Ernest Cassel, who had worked so hard to prevent the war, was Edwina's grandfather; his great friend King Edward had been her godfather. Though so lucky in his friends and his investments, Sir Ernest was terribly unlucky in those he loved most. He married Annette Maxwell, daughter of Mr. Robert Thompson Maxwell of Croft's Hall, Darlington. He adored his fragile, gentle wife, who, after the birth of their only daughter, Maud, contracted tuberculosis. So deeply did Sir Ernest love her that when she was dying he forsook his religion and became a Catholic convert so that, as she said, "We may be together in heaven."

After his wife died, Sir Ernest transferred his love to Maud, who had inherited her mother's delicate constitution. In January, 1901, she married Major Wilfrid Ashley (later, Lord Mount Temple), a grandson of the Earl of Shaftsbury. He had noble ancestors, including by an odd quirk the American Indian, Princess Pocahontas; he also had very little money, but a magnificent estate, Broadlands, in Hampshire, which his great-grandmother, the Countess Cowper, had inherited from her second husband, the famous Lord Palmerston. Thus Broadlands was not tied up in the Shaftsbury entail, and was Wilfrid Ashley's legacy from his father, the Honorable Anthony Evelyn Melbourne Ashley. The munificent marriage settlement Sir Ernest made on Maud enabled the Ashleys to live there in style. Their daughter, Edwina Cynthia Annette Ashley, was born on November 28, 1901.

Edwina had a rather unhappy childhood, though her adult life was more than compensation for it. Like Lord Louis, she grew up on the run as her parents followed Grandfather Cassel from Moulton Paddocks at Newmarket, to his villa in the Riederfurks in Switzerland; or to Biarritz when King Edward went there. There were other relatives to visit as well. In summer they spent a few weeks on the wild west coast of Ireland, at Classiebawn Castle which Ashley had also inherited. Between moves they lived at Broadlands.

Edwina's sister Mary was born in 1904. From that time Maud Ashley was never well. The inherited predisposition to tuberculosis became manifest. In spite of all the money Sir Ernest spent on doctors and nurses, hiring half a hotel in Egypt, and chartering a liner to bring her home, his beloved daughter died in 1910. Edwina was nine years old.

In the next three years the Ashley children were even more discombobulated. Brought up mainly by governesses and servants, they were constantly sent to visit relatives, probably to keep them out of their father's way. Sir Ernest Cassel's sister, Mrs. Minna Cassel,* whom they called "Auntie Grannie," tried her best to take their mother's place, and Edwina became very fond of her. But she missed her pretty mother, who in spite of her physical weakness had always been gay and loving. Edwina compensated for her loss by lavishing her love on numerous pets.

Though no one will say so definitely, it is evident that there was little affection between Edwina and her father. He was a slim, handsome man, with a Guardsman's mustache and a good deal of charm. In World War One, he commanded a battalion of the King's Liverpool Regiment in Flanders, and then was elected a Member of Parliament. He was Minister of Transport in Baldwin's Conservative Government, 1924–29.

Though Ashley was a conscientious public servant he was stuffy and had the limited sort of mind that regards anything new as unfortunate. Lord Attlee, who knew him well in later years though they were politically at opposite poles, described him as "a nice old Tory, not very bright, but one of the nice old boys." He was not good with children.

In that fine summer of 1914, when so many worlds fell apart, Edwina received a crushing blow. Her father called her to his study at Broadlands and told her that he was going to be married to Mrs. Mary (Molly) Forbes-Sempill. To his twelve-year-old daughter, whose memory of her mother had become beautiful beyond reality this seemed disloyal. She was childishly, romantically unfair about it.

Molly Ashley never had a chance to become friends with her oldest stepdaughter. For if Edwina had little affection for her father, she absolutely detested her stepmother, who responded predictably. Edwina had inherited the steely will that had enabled her grandfather to rise from obscure poverty to enormous wealth and international repute. Even at twelve her brain was the best at Broadlands. A clash was inevitable. Mary Ashley was so much younger than Edwina that she hardly remembered her mother, and since her mind was less brilliant and her will less strong, she got on very well with Molly Ashley.

When Major Ashley went to war, life became so uncomfortable at Broadlands that something had to be done about Edwina. She was sent to school at Eastbourne. It was a perfectly decent girls' school, but like most such establishments in England at that time, dark, cold, dreary,

---

* Mrs. Cassel had been divorced and had resumed her family name for herself and her two children, Sir Felix Cassel and Anna Cassel Jenkins.

and educationally uninspired. Edwina had lived more luxuriously than most English girls, even those of her own class. She hated it.

When Mary's turn came to go to school she softly persuaded her stepmother to send her to a much more fashionable—and comfortable—establishment; whereupon Edwina raised such hell that the Ashleys said she could go to another school, and Molly Ashley chose the first Domestic Science College in England. It was housed in a great country mansion, where the girls did all the work, including the cooking. This was supposed to teach them to be housewives or teachers of domestic science. Just why Mrs. Ashley thought Edwina should waste her fine brain learning how to cook and scrub floors is unexplained; it may have been pure malice. Yet it did turn out for the best. The experience Edwina acquired in menial chores came in handy during World War Two.

When the first war ended Edwina made a strong plea to her family to let her go to Italy instead of to a "finishing school." They agreed that she could, accompanied of course by a governess. One suspects that Sir Ernest footed the bill, but it was a worth-while expenditure. Only a very insensitive and unintelligent person cannot get something from a country where nature and art are rivals in beauty and history walks hand in hand with philosophy and religious exaltation. Since Edwina was neither, she profited greatly.

Then she returned to Broadlands. What to do with her now? Sir Ernest, whether prompted by her or not, solved the problem by inviting her to live with him at Brook House and act as his hostess. The Ashleys consented with sighs of relief.

Edwina had taken on a stupendous task. Brook House at Park Lane and Upper Brook Street, though not the largest, was probably the grandest mansion in London. Sir Ernest, who bought it from Lord Tweedmouth in 1905, had set out with Oriental extravagance to make it a visible symbol of his wealth. Eight hundred tons of Serravezza marble from Michelangelo's quarry in Tuscany went into it—even the six kitchens were marble-lined. The huge dining room, where a hundred guests could eat comfortably, was paneled in polished oak and crammed with massive gold and silver plate. In fact the whole house was full of the most expensive *objets d'art* Sir Ernest could find. The walls were covered like pages in a stamp album with old masters, which he acquired with the assistance, but not necessarily the guidance, of Sir Joseph Duveen. Tables and cabinets were crowded with fine crystal, rare porcelain, china, and the largest collection of jade in London.

The full magnificence hit Sir Ernest's guests in the eye as they entered his house. First they entered a lobby, paneled in lapis lazuli and cream-colored marble veined with moss green. Then, bang!, the great hall, sheathed in white marble extending upward four stories to a glass dome. Corinthian columns twenty feet high supported the gallery, and the broad stairway was a cascade of marble. It was the realized dream of a poor Jewish boy, who now could show the world how rich he had become. Edwina's young friends used to call it "The Giant's Lavatory."

Purse-pride was indeed one of Sir Ernest's less attractive characteristics. One English lady told how she received a necklace of lapis lazuli; on the first night she wore it she encountered Sir Ernest Cassel, whom she knew fairly well. "How do you like my new necklace?" she asked proudly. Sir Ernest fingered it. "Very pretty stuff," he said. "I've got a room made of it."

Edwina and her grandfather lived alone in Brook House, except for Sir Ernest's secretary, Miss Underhill, and about twenty servants. To be chatelaine of this remarkable mansion was quite an undertaking for a girl of eighteen, for however much the great world might make fun of Sir Ernest's taste, they gladly accepted his invitations. This was due, not entirely to his money and superb entertainment, but also because he was known as a man of integrity, ability, and good will—in large if not in small matters.

So Edwina sat at the head of her uncle's table when around it were such figures as the Asquiths, the Churchills, Lord Balfour, and other leaders of both parties, as well as the great bankers, and a resplendent collection of peers and various members of the Royal Family. She soon learned to be at ease with them, and her young beauty and fresh, spirited point of view enchanted these distinguished older men. Even their wives liked her, because she put on no side.

Getting on with her grandfather may have been more difficult. In his last years Sir Ernest was embittered by his sorrows and by wartime persecution because of his German birth. Though, with Lord Reading, he had negotiated the half-million-dollar American loan for the Allies in 1915, he, like Prince Louis, was accused of disloyalty—and finally he wrote his one and only letter to *The Times*, saying in part, "Nearly half a century of my life has been spent in England, and all my interests—family, business and social—are centered here. All my male relatives of military age are serving with the King's Forces. My unfailing loyalty has never varied or been questioned, and while affirming this, I also desire to express my deep sense of horror at the manner in which the war is being conducted by the German Government. . . ."

This did not silence his critics. The chauvinistic Anti-German League brought an action in court to have him removed from the Privy Council. The suit failed, but he was deeply hurt. When the war ended people forgot, but he did not.

At home he was a martinet, rather like Elizabeth Barrett Browning's impossible Victorian father. Bearded and bald, short, fat, and pompous, he burst into terrible rages at the drop of a spoon. Why the servants put up with him, were even devoted to him, is a mystery explained only by the quality of the man under his harsh exterior.

Edwina recognized his quality, too. And while they had some dreadful rows, they were akin, and they knew it. The strong foundation of their relationship was a basic compatibility, reinforced by mutual respect and genuine love.

Edwina made her debut in the spring of 1920. Sir Ernest gave his taste for splendor full rein. The ball at Brook House was a night to remember, even in a time and place of lavish entertainment. Edwina wore a pale gold dress, and shapeless though it was, in the mode of the era, she carried it off triumphantly. Indeed, Edwina looked beautiful in everything she wore, whether full court dress or khaki shorts and shirts in a Burmese jungle.

Once "out," she plunged into a vertiginous social swirl of balls and dinners, country weekends, yachting parties, racing at Ascot, and boat weeks at the universities—the whole range of pleasure. She was lonely no longer, for she met literally hundreds of young people. They were a gay and rather reckless lot, just bursting out of the gyves of old conventions. The men were mad for her. They would have been, in any case, but in addition the newspapers always referred to her as "The Greatest Heiress in England," which she probably was.

Yet Edwina was not extravagant at this stage. The story is that her grandfather gave her an annual allowance of the equivalent of $1500 and made her buy her own clothes out of it. This is nonsense—the proper attire for Ascot Week alone would cost half of that. But Sir Ernest did pinch pennies in strange little ways—he is said to have given up wearing starched white waistcoats with his business suits when the price of laundering them went up to thirty-five cents. So he kept Edwina rather strapped for ready cash.

He was as strict with her in other areas as circumstances permitted. She never went anywhere unchaperoned, and he personally investigated and approved every invitation she accepted. But obviously he could not keep a constant watch on her. The techniques of evading chaperones were becoming a fine art among the debutantes, and in that social scramble opportunities for mischief were limitless. Not that Edwina did anything really naughty; but she certainly did many things her grandfather would have thought outrageous. Bursting with vitality and high spirits she was a leader of "the wild young things." She had a glorious time, but she did not fall in love.

As autumn dripped down on England Sir Ernest began to get the bronchial afflictions chronic in older people living in that climate. His doctors ordered him to the south of France, and Edwina dutifully went with him. They left at just about the time that *Renown* steamed into Portsmouth Harbor. After a dull winter on the Riviera, Edwina Ashley returned to England ready for anything. It was then that she met Lord Louis Mountbatten.

Though Lord Louis and Edwina saw a great deal of each other during June and July, 1921, their romance does not seem to have gone into high gear until the yachting event of the year, Cowes Week, early in August. She went to stay with Sir Godfrey and Lady Baring, while Lord Louis had a snug berth aboard the big, three-masted schooner yacht *Atlantic*, in which General and Mrs. Cornelius Vanderbilt were cruising during the month of August.

Mrs. Vanderbilt must have seen how the wind was blowing. One can imagine her telling her dapper little husband, with his neat Vandyke beard, that Dickie Mountbatten seemed interested in the Ashley girl, and wouldn't it be nice for both of them if something came of it. She invited Edwina to join them in *Atlantic* for a short cruise to Le Touché and other ports on the French coast. It was one of her few successful efforts at matchmaking.

The long, graceful yacht held the record for sailing ships from New York to Land's End. With her large, creamy sails, narrow black hull, and polished bright work she was indeed a fair argosy for romance. Though the Vanderbilts' manner of yachting was almost as luxurious as Cleopatra's, the sea inevitably brings its own opportunities for hardihood. Lord Louis discovered that Edwina was a wonderful companion in sport as well as frivolity. Actually, of the two, she was the better natural athlete, and she could swim and ride rings around him. As for Edwina, she unquestionably fell in love, head over heels, hell for leather, full speed ahead and damn the torpedoes, which was ever her way of doing things.

Lord Louis did not ask her to marry him aboard *Atlantic;* he had the shyness of the once bitten. Besides, the Prince of Wales had invited him to go to India in the autumn, and he had no intention of leaving another fiancée behind to make a fool of him. But he was thinking about it so seriously that he took Edwina to see his parents at The Fishpond.

For the second time in a month Edwina fell madly in love with a Mountbatten, but of course Prince Louis was already married.

Then Mountbatten rejoined *Repulse* for that halcyon last cruise with his father, the memory of which he treasured all his life. When she anchored in Invergordon, Prince Louis left for London full of plans for his trip to Constantinople to see George. Lord Louis went to spend a few days with the Duke and Duchess of Sutherland at Dunrobin. By no chance at all Edwina was there.

It should have been another happy interlude, but its memory was forever tragic. As they were sitting down to dinner on the evening of September 11 a footman handed Lord Louis a telegram telling him of his father's death that afternoon. It was almost impossible to realize that the gay, beloved man—with whom he had been cruising so joyfully only a few days before—was gone. It was the first deep sorrow of his life.

Lord Louis left that night for London to take part in the heart-rending pomp with which his country honored one of its most faithful servants. Edwina returned to London four days later. In the cavernous confusion of Liverpool Street Station Miss Underhill met her with the news that a footman had found her grandfather sitting at his big cluttered desk, his head fallen among his business papers.

The next day Lord Louis went to see Edwina. Brook House, never a place of warmth, now was as dead as a pharaoh's tomb. In the rosewood library, where she waited for Lord Louis, Edwina somehow seemed smaller than life.

They were both forlorn young things, in a real sense orphaned and forsaken. Though Lord Louis felt filial affection for his mother, his father had been the focal point of his life. And to Edwina her grandfather was seemingly an immutable rock of refuge. However much she might have desired to escape from his adoring tyranny, he had been the sure foundation and omnipotent presence in her life. Nothing very terrible could happen to her as long as he was there to put things right.

Though Edwina did not feel the same piercing sorrow for her grandfather as Mountbatten did for Prince Louis, she was more lost than he. After all he still had his career; he knew where he was going, more resolutely now than ever. And beyond these days of sadness, the *Renown* lay waiting in Portsmouth Harbor to carry him and the Prince to India. But as Edwina must have told him, she had no place to go but Broadlands, where she felt unwelcome; and the only person who could make her future bearable was going away for eight months—which must have seemed to her like eight centuries. If she cried like a little girl in his arms no one would be surprised.

Lord Louis must have been deeply moved. However hard his surface he had a strong strain of German sentimentality and an even stronger loyalty to those who depended on him. He may even have toyed with the idea of giving up the trip to India; but that would alter the charted course of his destiny, which he would not do. Instead he had a happier inspiration.

He knew that Lord Reading, Viceroy of India, had been a close friend of Sir Ernest Cassel. He asked Edwina if the Viceroy had ever suggested that she and her grandfather pay him a visit, and when she said he had, Mountbatten sprang his suggestion: "Why don't you come while we're there?" he asked. "It would be a tremendous lark!"

That opened a new and dazzling prospect for Edwina, for them both. Sorrow was forced into the background and youth looked toward a radiant future. First making sure he really meant it, Edwina said that she would try. She had no idea of just how she would manage it, but she knew she would get there somehow.

Chapter 4

HOLLYWOOD
HONEYMOON

Sir Ernest Cassel's net estate after taxes amounted to about £6,000,-000 (nearly $30,000,000). He had given away over £2,000,000 during his lifetime. He divided his estate into shares and left one eighth to his niece, Mrs. Anna Jenkins, and one quarter to his nephew, Sir Felix Cassel. The remaining five eighths he left in trust, two eighths of the income going to Mary Ashley and three eighths to Edwina, with the remainder to their children. He already had given his sister, Mrs. Minnie Cassel, large sums of money, but he left her £30,000 a year, together with Moulton Paddocks and Brook House for life, after which they were to go to Edwina. Her share of the estate amounted to over £750,000 ($3,500,000) and her income was £60,000 a year, or £45,000 after taxes ($225,000). But she was to be paid only a small allowance until she married or reached the age of twenty-one.

Estates of that size take a long time to settle. When Edwina went to Portsmouth on October 26, 1921, to see Lord Louis off in *Renown*, she still did not know where she would get the money to follow him to India, though Lord Reading had promptly provided an invitation. She was sure of one thing: financial aid would not come from her father. Her reception at Broadlands had been even chillier than she had anticipated, for Mrs. Ashley was rather bored by reading, in *The Sketch* and *The Tatler*, about her glamorous stepdaughter's doings.

From Portsmouth Edwina went directly to Auntie Grannie at Bournemouth. One of her great regrets was that she had not told her grandfather about her love for Lord Louis. The only member of her family she had confided in was her favorite cousin, Marjorie Jenkins. Mrs. Cassel was not surprised, nor was she unreceptive to the idea of having a cousin of the King in the family. She agreed to lend Edwina £100 for her round-trip fare to India. Considering Edwina's prospects she might have been a bit more daring and made it £200, but she, too, had that unexpected Cassel frugality about small things.

Edwina's father and stepmother agreed that she could go to India, provided she was chaperoned on the trip. Going through the passenger list of the Pacific and Orient liner, she found a lady she knew slightly who agreed to take care of "dear Edwina." It was a rather nebulous arrangement, but faced by the possibility of Edwina at Broadlands in a raging fury the Ashleys accepted it. So Edwina sailed for Bombay in a second-class, inside cabin on the P. and O.

Meanwhile Lord Louis was arriving at "the Gateway of India" under very different circumstances. This time *Renown* was commanded by Captain the Honorable Herbert Meade, a son of the Earl of Clanwilliam, who had commanded the Flying Squadron in which Prince Louis had sailed the Pacific in 1880, a coincidence which pleased Mountbatten greatly.

With all her flags flying the battle cruiser steamed into Bombay Harbor in a thunder of cannon saluting the Prince of Wales. On the Apollo Bunder stood Lord Reading, tall and thin, his long face eroded by time and shaded by a white topee. With the Star of India blazing on his gray morning coat he looked the prototype of English aristocracy; but actually he was the liberal son of a ship broker, and was taking the first tentative steps toward the dissolution of the Empire over which Mountbatten was to preside. Behind the Viceroy were massed the reigning princes of India, a royal rainbow of multicolored shimmering silks and jeweled turbans.

After the welcoming ceremony in a domed pavilion with gilded minarets built for the occasion, the Prince's party drove in open landaus to Government House on Malabar Point, escorted by the Governor's Indian Bodyguard, sunlight glinting on the polished steel tips of their lances. Though Mahatma Gandhi had called for a *hartal*, a boycott of the Prince, the streets were crowded with people, and for the first time

Lord Louis heard the immense susurration of multitudinous delight and the advancing ripple of applause with which Indian crowds greet a popular personage.

After three days of ceremonies in Bombay the party started on the tour. It was just as Prince Louis had described *his* long-ago tour with a Prince of Wales. There were three special trains, led by a pilot train containing reporters and a traveling post office. Then came the elaborately decorated royal train, with its luxurious private car for the Prince and almost as comfortable accommodations for his retinue of nearly a hundred people. It was followed by a long mixed passenger-and-freight train consisting of coaches crowded with Indian servants, flatcars carrying the open carriages for state entrances, and cattle cars for the horses as well as for the chargers the Prince and his staff would ride at reviews, and twenty-five polo ponies lent by the maharajahs for the Prince's pleasure.

So in splendor they rolled through India—Baroda, Rutlam, Udaipur, Jodhpur, Bikaner, and Lucknow, famous for the heroic stand of the British men and women in the Indian Mutiny. Only in sacred Benares, and in Allahabad, where Nehru was sitting in a British jail, was the *hartal* effective and the streets deserted; but even there twenty thousand happy Indians turned out to watch the Prince play polo and cheer every shot.

Lord Louis had no intention of missing the fun of these polo games, arranged at almost every stop. In his book, *A King's Story*, the Duke of Windsor wrote: "Although . . . [Dickie] had scarcely ridden before, he was determined to learn to play polo, and his initial appearance on a polo pony startled the Indian Cavalry officers and my staff. But Dickie was nothing if not analytical; and undaunted by his inexperience he persevered."

Next they went to Nepal for an elaborate tiger shoot and here Mountbatten was more in his element, for he had always been a fine shot.

Whether mounted on polo ponies or elephants they had lots of fun despite the tight official schedule. Except for a few senior stuffed-shirts, the Prince's staff were a rollicking lot—horsemen all and fellows in mischief to the royal cousins: the Honorable Bruce Ogilvie, younger son of Lord Airlie; Colonel Revers Horgan of the 20th Deccan Horse—an eight-goal man at polo and a spectacularly snappy dresser ahorse or afoot; nonchalant Colonel C. D. Harvey of the Central India Horse, another elegant centaur; and Colonel Edward Dudley "Fruity" Metcalf, an Irish Dragoon straight out of Charles Lever.

But underneath all the fun, the colorful spectacles of imperial pomp, and the remarkably complex logistics by which the royal caravan was moved from place to place, with smooth precision and split-second timing, both the Prince and Lord Louis were uneasily aware of the yeast of revolution fermenting in the souls of 300,000,000 people. Even that first day in Bombay they had heard the crack of rifles above the blare of brass and thump of drums as Ghandi's more extreme followers, forgetting their spiritual leader's creed of non-violence, tried to break up the crowds watching the Prince and were repulsed by British troops.

And they knew that there was a deep split among the British themselves. Lord Reading had come to India determined to implement the British Government's promise to give Indians a greater share in the government of their country, with the long-range objective of eventual independence. Everything he tried to do was blocked by the barricaded bureaucracy of the British military and civilian Government of India, who regarded him as a Bolshevik and a renegade. Though he had little interest in politics at this time, Mountbatten, taking his lead from the Prince of Wales' outspoken liberalism, supported Lord Reading's objectives, and had no sympathy for the human roadblocks to progress.

Eventually, the three royal trains pulled into Calcutta where the Prince's party boarded the Royal Indian Mail Steamer *Dufferin* for a trip to Burma. From her bridge Mountbatten for the first time saw Rangoon, shimmering in the tropical heat with Schwe Dagom Pagoda crowning its hilltop in a golden flame of reflected sunlight. He went with the Prince up the Irrawady to Mandalay and back to Rangoon with never a premonition of how many would die to clear the way next time he made that journey.

The entire party returned to India, arriving at Delhi in mid-February, where the Viceroy laid on a welcome of imperial splendor including a formal dinner in the great banqueting hall for 150 Indian princes and 1,350 other people.

The Prince and his staff, including Lord Louis, stayed with the Viceroy in the Viceregal Lodge in the old city. New Delhi, which was to be the magnificent capital of the Indian Empire, was just being built. When Lord Louis first saw it, its five square miles were a wilderness of sand heaps, half finished roads, and roofless shells of monumental buildings, over which thousands of workmen swarmed in seemingly utter confusion.

The Viceregal Lodge had been the temporary residence of the

Viceroys in Delhi when Calcutta was the capital of India, and it was decidedly crowded by the Prince's retinue. Hardly had they settled in when Lord Louis received a frantic telephone call from Edwina—stranded in Bombay. "I've only got money enough for third-class fare," she said, "but the stationmaster says I must not travel that way—only Indians do. Why shouldn't I travel with Indians, Dickie?"

The idea of his almost-fiancée traveling in one of the hot, dirty, wooden-benched cars—jammed with Indian families carrying their household goods, bedding, and cooking equipment—which he had seen through the plate-glass windows of the royal train, stunned Mount-batten—the contrast seemed ridiculous. But knowing Edwina's dislike of pomposity, he was careful not to show it.

"Indians are all right," he said, "but you'd be frightfully uncomfortable. Leave everything to me. I'll fix it up."

Edwina arrived in Delhi the next day—first class. She had traveled over 12,000 miles, counting the return trip, to be with her Dickie for six very crowded days.

A fair sample of the Prince's schedule would go something like this: 8:30 A.M., breakfast with the Viceroy and guests; 9:30, review troops; 11:30, visit hospital; 1:30 P.M., civic luncheon; 3:00, polo match; 6:00, reception; 8:30, dinner and a ball. Since Lord Louis had to accompany the Prince on most of these occasions there was little time left for Edwina; and since the Viceregal Lodge was teeming with people there was hardly a place they could be alone together.

But Mountbatten found the place and made the time. He no longer doubted the durability of Edwina's love for him; and his own ardor was considerably warmed by the pressure of competition from virtually every unmarried Briton in Delhi who met Edwina. In what is now Room 13 of Delhi University, which the Viceregal Lodge has become, he formally asked her to marry him. In her forthright way she said of course she would.

Everyone was delighted. A cable was sent to King George asking the Monarch's permission, which as an heir to the Throne, however distant, Lord Louis required. Back came a warm royal blessing. The engagement was announced by the Viceroy, and congratulations poured in.

The Prince of Wales, one of history's great, if misguided, romantics, relieved the congestion at the Viceregal Lodge with a magnanimous gesture. Lady Reading extravagantly had ordered a bungalow built on the grounds so the Prince could escape from the insatiable hordes who surrounded him. He was, of course, the first person Lord Louis told about his engagement. The Prince gave his favorite cousin his warmest congratulations and the key to his bungalow. Lord Mountbatten still has the key.

In six days it was all over. Lord Louis left with the Prince to complete the tour of India and go on, as his father had, to Ceylon, Malaya, Hong Kong, and Japan, where Crown Prince Hirohito entertained them extravagantly, but adroitly foiled Mountbatten's professional eagerness to inspect a Japanese super-dreadnought. Meanwhile Edwina sailed home in a freighter.

A lot of sentimental nonsense has been written by the Mountbattens' biographers about the marriage of Edwina Ashley and Lord Louis Mountbatten. This much is true: They were indubitably in love with each other. And why not? Both were extraordinarily attractive young people. Mountbatten, slim, handsome, and elegant, had sparkling high spirits and a boyish enthusiasm for all phases of existence, which complimented rather than diluted his steely ambition and real ability. Though consciously an aristocrat, he unconsciously covered his sense of superiority with a humorously deprecatory manner that was as beguiling as his spontaneous, eye-crinkling smile. Edwina was mad for him, and so were half the girls in England.

Enough has been said of Edwina's beauty, but she had also a tremendous zest for living. Another trait they shared was enormous energy and magnificent health; they seemed never to tire. They were, in fact, superlatively mated—how well even they did not learn for nearly twenty years.

But it is absurd to pretend that this intelligent and sophisticated pair were unaware of the material advantages each gained by their marriage. Lord Louis had extravagant tastes and no money, and Edwina's great fortune not only would enable him to live in the style to which he wanted to become accustomed, but, if it were not absolutely essential to the realization of his ambition to become First Sea Lord, it would certainly help. Nor was Edwina unaware of the social advantages of being closely related to the Royal Family, but without any of their onerous responsibilities.

All London agreed it was a wonderful combination. According to Ray Murphy in *The Last Viceroy*, Lord Louis' mother, who was now living in an apartment in Kensington Palace assigned to her by the King, objected because Edwina was too rich. This does not sound in the least like Her Grand Ducal Highness, and there is no documentary proof of any such reservation on Vicky's part; but if she had any it was because of Edwina's lack of royal quarterings and not her abundance of money.

Renown returned to Plymouth on June 20, 1922. Mountbatten found vigorous preparations for the marriage under way. In fact Edwina had even efficiently procured the marriage license. Now that it was settled that she was to make such a spectacular match, Sir Ernest's executors deposited thousands of pounds to Edwina's credit in the bank. One of the first things she did with it was to buy her fiancé a wedding present certain to enthuse him—a sporty gray Rolls-Royce.

Then the wedding presents began to pour in to Brook House where Edwina was living with Auntie Grannie. They were on a royal scale. Edwina, who had never had much jewelry, was given magnificent pieces by everyone, from Queen Alexandra to the Aga Khan. There were jeweled rings, pins, and necklaces; diamond tiaras and lorgnettes—she was a little near-sighted. In spite of her sometimes simple tastes she loved them, for it was her nature to go headlong in any direction. She liked to rough it in shaggy old things, but she also liked to go to a ball glittering like the Ice Princess.

If Mountbatten and his bride had not had the rugged constitutions of Siberian ponies they could not have survived the next four weeks. There seemed hardly a minute and never a meal that was not bespoken by some London hostess anxious to honor them and bask in their reflected glamor. The entertainments included a rather overpowering family luncheon at Buckingham Palace, which Edwina took in easy stride—she had not been Sir Ernest Cassel's hostess for nothing.

There was a pleasant interlude when she took her fiancé to Broadlands to present him to her family, whom he had never met. Lord Louis loved the classic simplicity of the house which has been called "the ideal small great house." For once its atmosphere was warm with hospitality, and whatever reservations or jealousy the Ashleys may have felt were quickly dissipated as Mountbatten effortlessly turned the charm up full blast to win their friendship.

The wedding, at St. Margaret's, Westminster, on July 18, 1922, was an extravaganza that must have delighted Sir Ernest's soul in his Catholic heaven. Edwina, in frosted silver, looked angelic. Besides Mary Ashley, who was her maid of honor, her bridesmaids included the four Greek princesses, daughters of Lord Louis' oldest sister,* wearing delphinium-blue dresses and modish Dutch-style hats of silver lace shaped like in-

---

* Their brother, Prince Philip, was only one year old.

verted basins. The whole Royal Family were there, from King George, Queen Mary, and Queen Alexandra to the youngest prince, as well as royalty from all over Europe, and some eight hundred other guests. Twenty thousand Londoners stood behind the barricades in Parliament Square.

Lord Louis' ushers were all naval officers. The Prince of Wales, looking engagingly young and slightly overpowered by his admiral's uniform, was best man. Lord Louis, in the long blue frock coat and golden epaulettes of a naval lieutenant's dress uniform, with his father's gold-hilted sword at his side, looked very tall and thin. He seemed years older and much more forceful than the Prince, who was six years older than he.

Lord Louis added a typical Mountbatten touch to the proceedings. As he and Edwina came out of the church under the traditional arch of swords held by the cocked-hatted ushers, she saw that a guncrew of twenty-five bluejackets were tailed on to their limousine. Grinning at her surprise, her husband opened the door for her and leapt in after her, adroitly managing his dangling sword. The warrant officer shouted commands, the bluejackets heaved on the ropes, and off they went at a smart dogtrot around the corner and up Victoria Street in a typhoon of cheers from the crowd.

Even Brook House was almost burst at the seams by the crowd of guests. The odor of flowers, perfume, and people was overpowering. Mountbatten methodically counted that he and Edwina shook five hundred hands, leaving three hundred or more unshaken, before the King and Queen graciously left and he felt free to say to Edwina, "Go up and change your clothes, and let's get out of here!"

The Rolls was waiting in Upper Brook Street. Edwina in an airy, coral-colored dress and matching summer coat dashed with her husband through the stinging rice. He shoved her in, jumped behind the wheel, and took off in effortless, silent speed through Knightsbridge and Kensington to the Great West Road, heading for Broadlands, which Colonel Ashley had lent them for the night.

When two very young, spoiled, strong-willed people marry, storm warnings fly from every headland. The more alike they are, the stronger the cyclonic disturbances set up in the marital atmosphere. So it was with the young Mountbattens. Their first row occurred on their honeymoon, and it was a notable skirmish.

Due to his naval training and Germanic temperament Lord Louis was an indefatigable planner. He had meticulously worked out the schedule for their motor trip around the Continent, even to which inn and at what hour they would have tea every day. Edwina hated regimentation. She wanted to drift along according to caprice. As they left Paris in the Rolls her husband yielded to her whim.

They got as far as Tours that night to find every hostelry filled with American and German tourists. It took all Mountbatten's persuasion to get them into an attic room with a single bed. The night was hot, the bed was lumpy, and these were not small people. They tossed and turned, cursed, and laughed wryly. Finally Mountbatten dropped into a light doze and fell out of bed.

That did it. He sat in a hard chair for three hours, instructing Edwina in a pedantic voice edged with anger on the folly of improvisation. By that time it was daylight, so they dressed wearily and went their way. For the rest of the trip Edwina let her husband make all the arrangements. He had won the first battle but not the war.

Lord Louis' itinerary included an old-fashioned Grand Tour with visits to all his royal relatives, from Hesse-Darmstadt to King Alfonso and Queen Ena of Spain, his first cousin. Having "done" Europe, Mountbatten, who had six months' leave, looked across the Atlantic. They crossed the ocean in a verandah suite of the *Majestic*, and the United States in a private car lent them by their new friend, Colonel Robert M. Thompson of Baltimore—in those days virtually every American tycoon owned one of these status symbols. Though the car was borrowed it cost the Mountbattens approximately $2,000 to have it hauled from New York to Los Angeles via Washington and the Grand Canyon, and back by way of Chicago and Niagara Falls. The latter detour was Lord Louis' idea, for he had heard it was the thing to do on an American honeymoon.

The American trip was a tremendous jaunt, and the Mountbattens appear to have successfully avoided the attentions of New York's Four Hundred society families and the West Coast imitation of same. Instead they mingled happily with the greats of stage, screen, and sport. In their preference for bohemian rather than social people they were in complete accord. Nothing bored either of them more than pretense, and it must be admitted that in this era most of America's first families were crashing snobs.

So they dined with Jerome Kern in New York, met Babe Ruth and rode the roller coaster at Coney Island (Mountbatten is reported to have done it eight or nine times), dropped in on President and Mrs. Harding at the White House (the Four Hundred considered the Hardings "awfully provincial"), hobnobbed with Will Rogers, and in Beverly Hills stayed with the Douglas Fairbankses at their "stately home," Pickfair. To quiet the apprehensions of their relatives, who read of their doings in the international press, their letters home described the luxury and elegance of the Fairbanks ménage. They did not describe their adventures in Hollywood, then going through its most Babylonian phase.

Edwina was still young enough to be dazzled by glamorous men and women with famous names, and her husband thoroughly enjoyed their reckless abandon and unconventionality. In that gay hegira they acquired a liking for America and Americans which they never lost.

In December they sailed for home. Like his father, Lord Louis had allowed himself three years of extracurricular frivolity. They had not been wasted, any more than had Prince Louis' youthful fling. But in the liner going home Mountbatten found himself pushing her along. The banked fires of ambition roared and crackled. He wanted urgently to get back to work.

Chapter 5

NAVAL OFFICER IN
PEACETIME

IN JANUARY, 1923, LORD LOUIS was posted to the dreadnought *Revenge* of the Royal Sovereign Class. Since they were the last battleships designed before the war (completed in 1916) she had not benefited by its lessons. In fact she was something of a retrogression, as her speed was 21 knots compared to the *Queen Elizabeth*'s 25, though she too was armed with eight 15-inch guns.

The accidental as well as the deliberate parallelism between Lord Louis' career and his father's appeared again as he joined *Revenge* at Constantinople, where the Mediterranean Fleet was holding the Dardanelles against a possible attack by a resurgent Turkish Army which had lately thrown the Greeks out of Smyrna. No dependents were allowed to go to Constantinople, so Edwina was left in London, the first of many such separations. She took it philosophically—having married a naval officer she knew what to expect.

Lord Louis was undoubtedly glad to be back in the world of men again, with his mental propeller biting deep water instead of racing in the social froth. He was less easy in the company of women than men, especially sailors, and never quite comfortable unless he was working hard.

The Turkish crisis was settled by the Treaty of Lausanne and *Revenge* was pulled back to Malta. Lord Louis spent a short leave in a small country house in Dorchester which Edwina had rented. Then he rejoined his ship. *Revenge* was in Funchal Bay in Madeira on February 14, 1924, when the Mountbatten's daughter, Patricia, was born in London. Her godparents were the Prince of Wales, Lady Patricia Ramsey— the famous Princess Pat—and her grandmother, Lady Milford Haven.

Lord Louis' tour of sea duty ended in the summer of 1924. He came home to find Edwina ensconced in Brook House—by courtesy of her aunt, who preferred Bournemouth. She had vastly improved it by tasteful redecoration. After a hectic trip to the United States with the Prince of Wales in September, Mountbatten, at his own request, was ordered to take the Long Signals course at the Royal Naval Signals School at Portsmouth. This was partly conscious emulation of Prince Louis and partly his own tremendous interest in the latest electronic gadgetry, especially as it applied to naval communications.

Edwina promptly rented Adsdean in the nearby countryside. Standing in a charming, tree-shaded park, it was a large neo-Tudor house, built in romantic Victorian times—rambling, roomy, and comfortable. Edwina staffed it with eighteen servants, most of whom were shuttled back to Brook House when the Mountbattens went to London. The hundred-yard-long stables were filled with horses—polo ponies for Lord Louis, hunters for Edwina, whose favorite was a big gray named Searchlight. The house was full of pets, ranging over the years from a lion cub to a pair of wallabies and a most unpleasant anteater named Schnozzle, who once fell into the toilet.

Mountbatten made methodical preparations for his new assignment. He even went so far as to ask his older naval friends whether it would be more tactful for him to drive to school in a Morris than a big car. They told him it would; so he bought a huge new Hispano-Suiza sports model, with a silver signalman on the radiator cap. He also imported a Gar Wood speedboat. "Insufferable ostentation" was the verdict of the senior officers.

His classmates, however, seem to have taken him in stride. Lieutenant (now Rear Admiral) Royer Dick who became Mountbatten's close friend at the Signals School describes him at this time: "He would have gone ahead in the Service without any pull. He was the sort of man, to quote Kipling, 'Who filled the unforgiving hour.' "

One thing that always struck me about him was his ability to compartment things in his mind. He'd work on the wireless thing, say until six o'clock, and then put it clear out of his mind and think about polo. But trying to interrupt his train of thought was like trying to stop the Flying Scotsman with a penny whistle.

Far from being difficult or pompous, Mountbatten was one of the easiest men ever to get on with, especially when he was young. People liked and admired him. The fact that he had plenty of cars and fast motor boats had nothing to do with it.*

At the Signals School Mountbatten really bit the bullet. He scheduled his days with mathematical precision. Up at 7:30, he started for school at 8, worked hard until 4:30, and went home for exercise—golf on the small, private links in the park, or practicing polo shots from the back of a wooden horse named Winston. From 5:45 to 6:30 he played with Patricia. Then he usually dashed back to the school to work on his inventions until 9:30 or 10, when he came home to eat a late dinner and to "be agreeable to Edwina's guests." He began answering his large correspondence at 11:30 P.M.

It was a highly educational period both for him and for the Signals School, for Mountbatten had the rare type of mind that creates as it learns. The abrasion of other men's thoughts caused his intelligence to shoot out a spark-shower of new ideas. To state an accepted rule or formula was to produce a challenge from him, and if nine sparks died in air the tenth brought new illumination. Since wireless signaling was a backward branch of the Navy Mountbatten had plenty of scope.

He was never content with things as they are but constantly sought to improve them. This hobby extended all the way from inventing household gadgets to redesigning his clothes. He is credited with the introduction of zippers on men's trousers and elastic shoelaces that enabled him to slip his feet into a pair of oxfords without untying them. He sold the zipper idea to the Prince of Wales, himself a sartorial innovator, and as a result the fashion spread from Bond Street to all the world.

Graduating at the top of his class, Mountbatten was appointed flag lieutenant to the commander of the Reserve Fleet, Vice Admiral Sir Rudolf Bentinck in the old dreadnought *Centurian* in April, 1926. This was not his cup of tea. He took the "Dagger Course" in advanced electronics at the Royal Naval College in Greenwich, and meanwhile used all his connections, until six months later he got the job he wanted—Assistant Fleet Wireless Officer to Admiral Sir Roger Keyes, Com-

---

* Admiral Dick in conversation with the writer. [Hereafter, this symbol (§) will be used to denote information obtained by the author in conversation or correspondence.—Ed.]

mander in Chief Mediterranean Fleet. As has been noted, royal kinship has certain advantages.

Knowing they would be in Malta for a long tour Edwina rented the Casa Medina on a hillside in Valletta; later she bought it. At the top of a narrow street of ancient houses built of golden Maltese stone, it had a superb view of the harbor. It was tall, sunny, and airy. She hung yellow curtains at the windows and kept the rooms full of flowers, which she loved as her grandfather had. While the Mountbattens lived there the Maltese called it, "The Lord's House."

Part of Mountbatten's job was instructing midshipmen in the fundamentals of wireless. He was a wonderful teacher, who could induce interest in his pupils' minds by the current of his own enthusiasm. His explanations were clear and simple; he never used technical jargon if a plain word would do. To demonstrate the principle of a radio transmitter he made a model of one with glass tubes, instead of wires, through which ran different colored inks. He had a fine time pouring the inks into it, making his white uniform a chromatic mess. He also wrote a textbook which he referred to as "a child's guide to wireless." It was widely used in the Navy.

Later, in 1929, Mountbatten taught the Long Signals Course at the Signals School in Portsmouth and also was in charge of examining the petty officers and ratings who were qualifying as wireless operators. By then he had become a very fast telegrapher himself. "We never could put anything over on him," one of his pupils said.

Naturally such things as being responsible to a large degree for wireless communications in the fleet and teaching young men the rudiments of radio were not sufficient to use up Mountbatten's energy. He also set out to perfect his French. In 1919 he had spent some time in Paris working on his French pronunciation with a sort of elderly governess. Now he insisted on talking French at all meals. Edwina, who had an excellent accent, was a great help, but despite his heroic efforts Mountbatten never quite succeeded in getting the sound right; to this day he speaks French with an Oxford accent. However he mastered the technical aspects of the language so well that he wrote and published a French-English dictionary of naval terminology.

Malta was one of the fonts of polo, so naturally Lord Louis had at it. He still looked like a sack of flour on a horse, but when he got to the ball he could hit hard and accurately. In addition he formed a polo team, the Bluejackets. It consisted of Lieutenant E. G. (Teddy) Haywood-Lonsdale, at No. 1; Captain D. A. B. Neville of the Royal Marines, No. 2; Mountbatten, No. 3 and Captain, of course; and his best friend in the Navy, Lieutenant Commander Charles E. Lambe, Back.

None of them played very good polo, but Mountbatten made the whole much greater than the sum of its parts. He handled it like a military operation, holding strategy meetings over tea at Casa Medina with his teammates after each game, discussing mistakes, working out new tactics and combinations, studying all the books on the game and translating theory into practice. But his real contribution was leadership. He had, then and always, afloat and ashore, in battle or in sport, the magic gift of inspiring men to do better than their best. It meant more than all the intense mental calculations he was so fond of making.

In 1931 this quartet of beginners with zero handicap took on the 17th/21st Lancers, rated at thirteen goals and the finest regimental team in the British Army, in the finals of the Malta Handicap Tournament. The match was played on the Marsa Ground where Prince Louis had galloped, far more gracefully in his day. So inspired were the Bluejackets that when the final bell rang the real score was 7 to 7. Since the Lancers had to allow their full handicap of thirteen goals the official score was Bluejackets 20, Lancers 7.

That was Bluejackets' year. They played the Royal Air Force Team in the Duke of York's Cup with no handicap. As the last chukker began Bluejackets were two goals behind. Riding with necks for sale, led by a rampaging desperado whose mind nevertheless remained as cold as a computer, the Bluejackets actually scored three goals in seven and a half minutes, to win the match.

But Lord Louis could not rest at playing the game, he had to leave his mark on it. He wrote an excellent *Beginner's Guide to Polo*, which he wittily signed "Marco"; and designed a new mallet head, which really gave improved performance and was sold all over the world; he turned over his royalties to the Royal Navy Polo Association, which he had founded.

In 1928 Lieutenant Lord Louis Mountbatten was appointed Flotilla Signals Officer in the destroyer *Stuart*. This meant that he was constantly off on cruises. Edwina was extraordinarily restless, and she kept running off to London and all over Europe. When she was in Malta she "followed the Fleet." In April, 1929, she motored to Gibraltar to join her husband. He and Charles Lambe got a brief leave, and though Edwina was expecting her second child in a few weeks, the three of them dashed across the Straits for a weekend in Morocco. The roads were rough, and returning in a chartered launch the sea was even rougher. The flotilla's next stop was Barcelona. Edwina drove the Rolls there to meet them.

When Mountbatten and Lambe joined her at the Ritz Hotel, she said, "Oh, Dickie, the baby's coming. You'd better get a doctor."

For all his efficiency, the only doctor Mountbatten could find in Barcelona was a throat specialist. Desperately he rang up his cousin Ena in Madrid; she was out, so King Alfonso took the call.

"Edwina's having a baby," Mountbatten told him. "We need a doctor."

"Wonderful. Congratulations, Dickie!" said the King.

"I need help," Mountbatten repeated, "a doctor."

"I don't know any in Barcelona," the King said, "but I'll send a regiment right around to guard dear Edwina."

"Couldn't you find out?"

"Don't you worry about a thing. The guard will be there in twenty minutes!"

So they were. They cordoned off the hotel and stood like statues in the corridor, getting in everybody's way, while Pamela Mountbatten was delivered by the throat specialist and a gray nun. King Alfonso was her godfather.

After his tour of duty teaching at the Signals School, Mountbatten was made Fleet Wireless Officer, Mediterranean Fleet, in 1931, which gave him a real opportunity to put his ideas into effect. At headquarters in the Castile, which had been the fortress of the Knights of Malta, he installed a communications center far in advance of the time. All wireless communications of the fleet were monitored and analyzed; radio silence, when ordered, was tightened up. He also devised a system whereby all thirty destroyers of the Mediterranean Fleet were able to acknowledge receipt of a message in turn within one minute. Drills were held of communications in a fleet action.

A Signals School was also established, where young officers gave instruction to fleet operators. Mountbatten instituted practice in decoding by sending a coded message to all ships to be decoded against time. The winning ship received an award of merit. Slow ships were given special training.

Using his influence at the Admiralty Mountbatten got the pay of naval radio operators raised in line with their efficiency. Meanwhile he had visited each of a hundred-odd ships of the fleet in order to meet their radio operators. Back in the Castile he analyzed their techniques from the undulator record and sent them personal messages of advice or praise. The discipline and morale of the fleet wireless operators soared.

Lord Louis spent half his time afloat in his office aboard Sir W. W.

Fisher's flagship, that grand old veteran of the Dardanelles and Jutland, the *Queen Elizabeth*, in which he had served as a midshipman.

Another effort which enormously increased Lord Louis' popularity with the lower deck was getting motion picture equipment aboard all the ships; in 1931 only a few of the largest ships had movies. Sound equipment for the new "talkies" cost about £400 (nearly $2,000). Mountbatten knew that this was more than the Admiralty would allow or the ships' companies themselves could afford, so he designed a loudspeaker system himself, which could be built for £85 from spare parts carried in the Fleet Repair Ship, and he actually went to many of the ships himself to install it.

Later he organized the Royal Naval Film Corporation and got the Duke of Kent to act as its patron. Through Mountbatten's friendship with British and American movie magnates the corporation was able to get new films for the fleet, sometimes before they were shown in London or New York.

Lord Louis had been promoted to lieutenant commander at the age of twenty-seven, and in 1932, he was promoted to commander. He was very young to attain these ranks in the peacetime Navy. His early advancement was due partly to the fact that he had entered the Navy at thirteen and a half, just before the age limit was raised, but mostly to his own energy and ability. His royal connections may have helped some, but most officers with whom this question was discussed agree that Mountbatten deserved advancement.

In 1934 he was given his first command, the brand-new destroyer *Daring*, with a designed speed of 36 knots; he actually got her up to 38.2 knots.

She became his darling and his baby. Like Prince Louis and Mark Kerr in the *Cambrian*, who had, of course, told him all about it, Mountbatten hand-picked his crew with a view to athletic excellence. He had his executive officer make a card file of the ship's company, and studied it until he knew all their names and backgrounds. When he was going to inspect any particular section he gave himself a refresher course in the men he expected to see. Calling them by name and asking about their duties and home problems gave them the feeling that he knew and cared about them, which indeed he did. Furthermore he intended to make *Daring* Cock of the Fleet.

Then his sailing orders came. He was to sail with the flotilla to Singapore and exchange ships with the flotilla on station there. It was a bitter blow because that group were comparatively slow, old destroyers built at the end of World War One.

During a long voyage out he worked the crew and his ship as hard as though he would have her forever. When the exchange took place, the comparison between *Daring* and the cramped old-fashioned *Wishart*, to which he transferred, was even worse than he had anticipated. But he did not remain in the dumps long. *Wishart* was now *his* ship; and by a peculiarity of his temperament anything that belonged to him was the best—or he would make it so. Besides, he still had his splendid crew, who by now were completely devoted to him.

Edwina traveled to be with him in Singapore, which was following the fleet with a vengeance. When he sailed for home, she went off to look at Java, leaving a honey bear to be brought home in *Wishart*.

The voyage to Malta took five weeks, during which time Mountbatten worked out his most significant invention of that era. Prince Louis had invented a course indicator; his son devised an instrument to enable ships to keep station. Captains of ships, especially destroyers, maneuvering at high speeds, had constantly to determine what number of engine revolutions would enable them to move up or fall back as required in a formation. Mountbatten's gadget was brilliantly simple. The captain had only to move a dial on the bridge to the number of yards he needed to gain or lose, and the equivalent in revolutions was registered in the engine room.

Getting the Admiralty to accept "Dickie's toy," as they called it, was almost beyond even his powers of persuasion. Among the first destroyers equipped with it was his own famous *Kelly*, commissioned in 1939.

Inventing was night work. Lord Louis spent the long days getting his men into peak physical condition and training them for the gunnery and communications exercises, and the boat races, swimming, football, and other sporting events of the Mediterranean Fleet. This was not just for fun, but because he believed that "a ship . . . with the will to win is a ship who has a healthy morale bred in her . . . and the guts so valuable in time of war."

In addition to sweating it out with the officers' boat crew on the rowing machine, Lord Louis trained for his favorite sport. He had a wooden horse and screened well built on *Wisthart*'s deck, and he practiced polo shots for hours on end. He was completely aware of his athletic limitations: "If you are a natural you can throw the book away," he often said, "but if you're not you can make up for it, by studying techniques and constant practice."

The *Wishart* had the will to win. In the regatta at Malta, when the last two races came on, her boats tied for first place with those from a battleship. As the petty officers' crew rowed off Mountbatten told them that if they lost he'd de-rate the lot of them. They won. Then came the officers' race. With Lord Louis stroking the boat there was not much doubt about the result. *Wishart*'s boat won by fifteen lengths.

So, as Mountbatten had planned, his little ship became Cock of the Fleet. When he left her he told his crew, "I said we would win every trophy there was to be won. As you all know, the *Wishart*'s teams triumphed in every game but football. In that we lost every match. This was my fault, because I did not specify which trophy we were to win, the silver cup or the wooden spoon [the booby prize]. We won the spoon, so our record is clear."

When he left his ship after nearly two years, it was not in his captain's motor gig. In the traditional gesture of respect and affection his officers manned the oars of the whaler, and rowed him off in a wild storm of unorganized cheering from the crew. The next time that happened to Mountbatten six admirals were at the oars.

In 1936 one of the usual interservice rows was in progress in Whitehall, between the Admiralty and the Air Ministry over the Fleet Air Arm, which was under their dual control. As everybody should have foreseen this arrangement led to bitter disagreement and hopeless inefficiency. The Admiralty wanted full control. Hoping to enlist Mountbatten's persuasive charm—and his eminent connections—in their struggle, the Admiralty appointed him to the staff of the Fleet Air Arm at Whitehall. They were not disappointed.

Lord Louis never had any compunctions about using his royal pull, his charm, and Edwina's money for the good of the service. The First Sea Lord, Prime Minister Stanley Baldwin, and First Lord of the Admiralty Sir Samuel Hoare found themselves meeting other Navy and Air people and various Members of Parliament of both parties, including Winston Churchill, and even the King at intimate little dinners at Brook House or informal weekends at Adsdean. In the warm atmosphere created by the Mountbattens difficulties often seemed to melt away, and minds met freely, as they always do, under the influence of good wine, good food, and good will.

From his office Mountbatten turned out brilliant briefs for his superiors to argue at official meetings where the ultimate decisions were made. As a result the Admiralty eventually got most of what it wanted. The Fleet Air Arm came under its control although not Coastal Reconnaissance or Convoy Protection. Whether this division of responsibility for aircraft is a good thing or not is still moot, in both England and America today. No matter! Lord Louis had done his job according to his orders and his beliefs. His superiors did not object.

The most important single thing Mountbatten did for the Royal Navy is little known and almost forgotten. He virtually forced the Admiralty to accept a new invention—not his own but another man's— the supreme importance of which he instantly recognized. By 1936 Nazi Germany was re-arming, and Hitler had announced his intention of making her the most powerful military nation in Europe. The Luftwaffe, the German Air Force, seemed to spring almost full grown from the aircraft factories. British Intelligence had information concerning a secret plane, the dive bomber; but little or nothing was being done to counter it.

One day Lord Louis was sitting behind an old-fashioned mahogany desk in his small, crowded office in a back corridor of the Admiralty when his friend, Captain George Ross, R.N., dropped in, bringing with him a short, stocky, bouncy man whom he introduced as Mr. Anthony Gazda.

Gazda was an Austrian engineer who had left his country for Switzerland to escape the increasing drift toward fascist totalitarianism. Through his connections in Germany he had learned about the new dive bomber, the Stuka, and sought a defense against it. He found it in a 20-mm. machine cannon built at the Oerlikon Works near Zurich. He acquired the rights to the gun and redesigned it to fire at the rate of 500 shells a minute.* He offered it first to the United States Naval Ordnance Department. Though its little shell could pierce armor plate, it didn't even dent American skepticism.

Then he took it to England, where he found the British Admiralty even more blockheaded. He could not convince a naval officer of either nation that any warship could be sunk by aerial bombing. When Gazda said, "Even battleships are not immune," they roared with laughter. Lord Louis was his last hope.

Gazda told the author that the moment he met Mountbatten he felt the sudden current of mutual attraction that on rare occasions presages a lasting friendship. He had never told his story so well as he did then, prompted by Lord Louis' searching, intelligent questions. In the end Mountbatten was not only convinced but fired with enthusiasm; he

---

* In its final refinement the Oerlikon-Gazda gun fired at the rate of over a thousand shells a minute.

had been worrying over the problem of defending ships against dive bombers. "I think you had better meet my boss," he said to Gazda.

He took the Austrian to lunch with Captain Grey, Chief of the Naval Air Division. They talked for five hours. Captain Grey was convinced, but he said, "Mr. Gazda, I believe you're on the right track, but you're in the wrong department. We are the Air. You must go to Anti-Air."

That did not stop Mountbatten. Swinging his influence with all his might he introduced Gazda to the Commander in Chief Home Fleet, Sir Roger Backhouse, who was slated to become First Sea Lord. He also rounded up the top brass—including the comptroller of the Admiralty, the Third Sea Lord, the Assistant Chief of Staff, and the Chief of Ordnance—to attend a film-lecture by Gazda. On the appointed day Gazda was in despair; he had laryngitis and could not speak above a whisper. According to Gazda, "Lord Louis said, 'Don't worry I'll do it!' He studied my notes briefly and then, while the film ran, he delivered my lecture far more brilliantly than I could have."

After that splendid start things bogged down. Gazda had to return to Switzerland. On the morning he was to leave Mountbatten asked him to breakfast at Brook House. "I'm going to bat for that gun of yours,"* he said, "but I want something from you."

"What is this?" Gazda asked.

Speaking with unusual intensity Lord Louis said, "I want your sacred word of honor to offer the gun to no one else until we reach a final decision."

"You have my promise," Gazda said.

It was a very difficult promise to keep, for the totalitarian nations were after the gun, and so were the Japanese. Prince Chichibu, the Emperor's brother, went to Zurich and offered Gazda $2,000,000 plus royalties for it. If he had not promised Lord Louis, Gazda said, he would have accepted. He thought he was a fool not to.

For two years more, while the Nazi terror grew blacker—*Anschluss* with Austria, and Czechoslovakia and Munich—Gazda, energetically backed by Mountbatten, fought to get his gun accepted by the Admiralty. He gave dozens of demonstrations and convinced many people. But the road was blocked by three things: Bureaucratic inertia, the lobbying by the great British armament firm of Vickers, Ltd., and the implacable opposition of the new Chief of Ordnance, Captain John C. Leach, R.N. There was no question of Leach's integrity; he honestly

---

* It was then the fashion, introduced by the Prince of Wales, to use American slang.

believed the Oerlikon-Gazda gun was no good, and he blocked every effort to get it accepted.

When Lord Louis' friend Admiral Backhouse became First Sea Lord things began to move. On April 1, 1939, the Admiral telephoned Gazda that the gun had been accepted. The guns were immediately put into production, and were first mounted on British warships in September and October, 1939, among them H.M.S. *Kelly*.

The guns proved to be the most effective defense against aerial attack the Navy had. They were mounted not only on virtually every British warship but also on all the ships of the vast fleet the United States built during World War Two.

It is certain that if Mountbatten had not had the imagination and foresight to use his great personal influence, with reckless disregard of his seniors' opinions, to force the gun on the Admiralty, it would have gone to England's enemies.

Chapter 6

"IN HONOUR BOUND"

MANY PEOPLE WHO ARE MAGNIFICENT in times of war or crisis seem bound to get into trouble in periods of tranquility. Such were both Lord Louis and Edwina Mountbatten. Though he was so utterly wrapped up in his career that he frequently bored his dinner partners by talking nothing but Navy, Mountbatten could not find enough fully to engage his enormous capacity for work. Activities that would have left most men glad to fall into bed and sleep, hardly dimmed his vitality. He used up the excess in all-night parties in London and all sorts of extra-curricular activities as he cruised around the world. Despite his strenuous pursuit of his career, he well earned his reputation as a playboy.

Edwina had, if anything, more energy than he, with no career to use up any of it. With a husband who was frequently at sea, nurses and governesses to take care of her children, plenty of money, and electric beauty she was possessed by an almost demonic restlessness. That same glamorous combination made her fair game for the sensational press of England and America, which magnified her escapades beyond probability.

One of the Mountbattens' earliest encounters with unfavorable publicity was on their trip to the United States in 1924. The Prince of

Wales had suggested that they all go over to watch the International Polo matches on Long Island. What began with high expectations and a light-hearted ocean voyage in the *Berengaria* ended in a shambles of bad weather, bad temper, bad behavior, and bad polo. Though the Mountbattens were reasonably circumspect throughout, they got their share of opprobrium.

September on Long Island is usually a time of halcyon weather, warm enough for summer sports, but with the tingle of autumn cutting the muggy miasma of August. In September, 1924, it poured rain almost every day, and this undoubtedly contributed to the debacle. Mr. and Mrs. James A. Burden had lent the Prince their beautiful Georgian house at Syosett on the rich, rolling North Shore of Long Island. The Mountbattens and Edwina's friend, the Honorable Mrs. Richard Norton, stayed with their new friends the Joshua Cosdens on a huge estate nearby. All around were the great country houses of wealthy Americans in as perfect an English setting as they could manage. They planned a series of magnificent parties for the young man whom they romantically idealized as the very prototype of Prince Charming.

The trouble began because the Prince was not at his most charming. He and his companions were looking for a high old time in the America of prohibition, bootleggers, and bare-kneed flappers. His hosts envisioned a stately pageant in which they would show these English aristocrats that America had reached the Age of Elegance. As a result the Prince and his cohorts began slipping away early from balls given in his honor, at a cost of fifty to a hundred thousand dollars, and disappearing into the raucous speakeasies and illicit night clubs of New York. He also developed a marked preference for bathtub gin over French champagne smuggled in at enormous cost. The Americans, who are at heart far more puritanical than English Society, took it exceedingly amiss. The papers headlined: PRINCE DISAPPEARS AGAIN! or PRINCE HOME WITH THE MILKMAN.

The British Polo Team, following this august example, also caroused more than they practiced. When rain postponed the games for a week such an unholy row broke out among them that Lord Wimborne, who had financed the team, left for England in a huff on the very day of the first match. He spared himself a painful afternoon. The British made a pitiful showing; at half time the score was America 10, England 1. The Prince gave his countrymen a tongue lashing during the interval, after which they played much better, scoring five more times. The American spectators felt so sorry for them that they wildly cheered every English goal, and were silent when their own team scored.

Meanwhile, after a wild little party for the Mountbattens at the Cosdens', a burglar shinnied up the Corinthian columns and ransacked the rooms in which everyone was sleeping it off. He got about $200,000 worth of Mrs. Cosden's jewels and $30,000 worth of Edwina's wedding gifts.

Back in England, and glad to be there, Edwina worked hard re-decorating Adsdean, while her husband plunged into work at the Signals School. The following Season she launched her sister Mary, who was a rather pallid copy of herself, at a ball in Brook House in the grand Cassel manner, with royalty abounding.

In 1930 she and her cousin Marjorie Jenkins, who had married the Earl of Brecknock in 1920, went to America again. This time Edwina managed to avoid American Society even more successfully. The two women had a splendid time in Hollywood, where they stayed with the Fairbanks, and Edwina even acted in home movies with Charlie Chaplin.

In New York they spent many late nights in Harlem, and gossip in England made much more of this than it deserved. In those days, before race relations became so strained in America, it was the fashion for perfectly proper people to go to Harlem after the theater, and take a box at the Cotton Club or the Savoy Ballroom from which to watch the hilarious proceedings. Both places had magnificent Negro jazz bands led by such fine musicians as Duke Ellington or Cab Calloway. The dancing of the young Negro couples who jammed the floor was not in the least vulgar; rather it was violently athletic and joyously exuberant. It was great fun to watch.

In 1932 the attacks of the sensational papers on Edwina reached such a pitch that she determined to put a stop to it by a libel action against Odham Press, Ltd., proprietors of a rag called *The People,* and Mr. Harry Ainsworth, its editor. Edwina and Lord Louis returned from Malta to prosecute the action before the High Court of Justice.

The following quotations are taken from the solid, unsensational report of the proceeding in *The Times* for July 9, 1932.

The libel complained of in the action appeared on May 29 [1932]. It was the most monstrous libel of which counsel had any knowledge. The usual practice in such cases is not to read the libel to avoid giving further publicity, but in the present instance, after most careful consideration, and, indeed, at the express request of Lady Louis Mountbatten, he was supposed to read the libel so its full enormity might be known. . . . And so the whole world might know that foul and lying rumors had been taken out of the region of hints and suggestions into the light of publicity. . . .

The Words Complained Of.

The libel was written by "The Watcher." He wrote: "I am able to reveal today the sequel to a scandal which has shaken Society to the very depths. It concerns one of the leading hostesses of the country, a woman highly connected, immensely rich. Her associations with a colored man became so marked that they were the talk of the West End. Then one day the couple were caught in compromising circumstances. The sequel is that the Society woman has been given the hint to clear out of England for a couple of years to let the affair blow over, and the hint was from a quarter which cannot be ignored."

"The Watcher" named no names but everything possible was done to identify Lady Louis Mountbatten. . . . It is scarcely necessary to say there was not one syllable of truth in the horrible allegation. The publication caused Lady Louis Mountbatten and those closely connected with her unspeakable anguish.

She had been informed by a friend of the identity of the colored man supposed to be referred to. She had never even met him and never had anything to do with him in any shape or form. When that fact is remembered, there were no words in which counsel could characterize the infamy of such a publication.

The Defendants never for a moment sought to defend the action. [They made a full apology.] Lady Louis demanded no indemnity although she could have had the heaviest sort of indemnity according to the article. There was no limit to the sum which a jury might have awarded her. . . .

Lord Louis Mountbatten then went into the witness box and said [that he was ordered to Malta in August 1931]. Ordinarily such an appointment lasts two years, and they [officers] arrange for wife and children to go with them. Lady Louis Mountbatten giving evidence, said that last August, she had gone to Malta to join her husband. Mr. Birkett [counsel for the Mountbattens] said: "The libel speaks of a colored man. Is there any syllable of truth in these allegations?" Answer: "Not one word of truth. In fact, I have never, in the whole course of my life, even met the man referred to."

It was quite evident that the Lord Chief Justice thought there should be a prosecution for criminal libel, as he said, "There are some libels which are crimes on the part of everybody concerned.

What am I asked to do?" Mr. Birkett [speaking for Lady Louis] said, "I ask that the record should be withdrawn on the terms I mention." [Full public apology by the Defendants.]

This sordid story is given here not only because it shows the sort of thing the Mountbattens were subject to but also because her behavior was so typical of Edwina Mountbatten. Her courage in asking that the libel be read is matched by her charity in not demanding the huge damages she could have had and not permitting criminal prosecution of those responsible.

King George and Queen Mary gave dramatic proof of their sympathy for the Mountbattens. On the very day that *The Times* carried the account of the libel it was announced that, "The Dowager Marchioness of Milford Haven and Lieutenant Commander the Lord and Lady Louis Mountbatten visited their Majesties and remained for luncheon."

Other people were not as kind to the Mountbattens. A group of ultraconservative old families disliked them intensely because of their free-wheeling ways, and this became a real annoyance to Lord Louis. Always craving for every badge of social distinction he wanted to join the Royal Yacht Squadron, the pre-eminent yacht club in England, whose yachts alone are allowed to fly the White Ensign of the Royal Navy. The ruling clique were annoyed by his flamboyant character and even more disgruntled by his fast motorboats roaring through the anchorage, setting their yachts leaping wildly and smashing expensive crockery. Twice Mountbatten was put up for the Squadron and twice blackballed.

The third time he thought he had everything fixed. Pressure had been brought on the entrance committee from High Quarters, and Lord Louis had conducted himself with remarkable discretion and proper humility in their presence. The vote was to be taken after lunch on Sunday of Cowes Week. Edwina, who thought the whole business ridiculous and the members of the Squadron extremely stuffy, did a very naughty thing that day.

At eleven o'clock that Sunday morning the old *Victoria and Albert* lay at anchor in the roadstead, flying the Royal Standard at her mainmast and the Church Flag from the fore, indicating that their Majesties were attending Divine Services aboard. By tradition the waters for a hundred yards around the Royal Yacht were sacred to the privacy of the King. As King George's voice joined loudly in the chorus of the first hymn it was drowned out by the roar of an engine at high speed.

Out from among the anchored yachts flew a mahogany hull between white wings of foam. Behind it on a surfboard—water skis had not been invented—rode Edwina. In a two-piece silver bathing suit that hid nothing of her slim, boyish figure and long handsome legs she was the epitome of grace and beauty—and mischief. Skillfully following the curving wake of the motorboat she circled the Royal Yacht several times, then disappeared standing like a Nereid between the tall plumes of spray.

After the meeting that afternoon a friend asked her how the voting on Lord Louis had gone. "It was lovely," she said. "When they opened the ballot box it looked like the inside of a rabbit hutch!"

For the record, Lord Louis was elected to the Royal Yacht Squadron at a later date.

Now began Edwina's great travels. Her restlessness intensified as her marriage reached the point so many do when she and her husband got on each other's nerves. The more they were apart the better they liked each other.

Edwina's first excursion, in 1931, took her to the West Indies and Mexico. In 1932 she went on an archaeological tour of Persia with her sister-in-law, Nada Milford Haven, traveling in an ancient hired car and a small chartered plane. In 1934 she and Marjorie Brecknock roamed around South America, where the acme of their journey was crossing the Andes on horseback through violent storms, without even a tent. There followed the trip to the Far East when she met her husband's destroyer at Singapore. Going home she was the first commercial passenger to fly from Australia to England. In 1936 she crossed Communist Russia alone on the Trans-Siberian Railroad. Next came a motor tour through almost the length of Africa.

Edwina's greatest prewar adventure started early in 1939 in Southeast Asia, taking her through all the places she later came to know so well. From Lashio she went 770 miles over the newly finished Burma Road in an ancient and dilapidated truck, with a driver and a Chinese handyman. The trip took a week.

Between Edwina's travels and Lord Louis' naval service the Mountbattens were not in England very much. When they were, their activities were equally frenzied. The parties they gave at Brook House were famous for uninhibited gaiety and an exciting mixture of the social, artistic, and theatrical worlds. It was at this time that Noel Coward, at the peak of his fame, became one of Lord Louis' most intimate friends.

Ordinary parties did not provide sufficient thrills, and this rather wild group of which Edwina was a leader invented the Treasure Hunt and the Scavenger Hunt. In the latter you were required to bring in certain unlikely objects, such as a black garter from an old lady in Piccadilly. Suddenly the midnight calm would be blasted by the roar of high-powered motors driven by men and women in full evening dress, racing down the broad avenue at reckless speed until they sighted their prey. Tires shrieking they skidded to a stop and surrounded the old lady, pulled up her skirts, and, if she had black garters, tore them off; then they dashed away at sixty miles an hour, while the police looked on benevolently at the aristocracy amusing themselves.

On the other hand, at a dinner at Buckingham Palace no one could look more regal than Edwina, in her glittering tiara and superb jewels, or behave more sedately. Afterwards they might all go down to Covent Garden and, with their jeweled tiaras slung over their arms to take the weight off their heads, walk through the confusion of great vans unloading produce from the garden counties and fragrant stalls overflowing with fruits and vegetables, stopping to pick up an exceptionally fine box of strawberries or an armful of roses from one of Eliza Doolittle's colleagues; thence to a teamsters' all-night restaurant for supper of sausage and scrambled eggs. Even though she conformed to Court etiquette Edwina set her own fashions. In the thirties when skirts went down, hers remained short; she had no intention of concealing her lovely legs.

By 1935 Brook House was becoming obsolete, for it cost Edwina nearly $100,000 a year to maintain. She finally succeeded in maneuvering it out of the Cassel Trust, and sold it. A large modern block of flats was built on its site. The Mountbattens reserved the two top floors for themselves—the first penthouse in London.

It consisted of thirty rooms and was perhaps the most fabulous flat that city ever saw. Assisted by her American friend, Mrs. Cosden, who had become a professional decorator when her husband lost all his money, Edwina skillfully blended the best pictures and furniture from Brook House with a light, airy, modern décor. Lord Louis had a wonderful time fitting it out with such modern gadgets as panels between the reception rooms, that folded back to make a big ballroom, and a fully automatic elevator from the private entrance on Upper Brook Street. That lift was the terror of London. Once when Queen Mary came to tea, it got out of control and shot up and down several times while Mountbatten frantically pushed the buttons; and the Queen, who was a splendid sport, regarded him with calm amusement.

Under her frivolity Edwina was beginning to feel the stirring of the ardent humanitarianism that marked her later life. The hopeless poverty, disease, and abject misery she had seen on her travels and in the East End of London shook her. Since capitalism could produce such horrors, she turned to socialism as the only remedy. Her more conservative friends regarded her as an outright communist. One evening when she was on her way to a Court function, in full regalia, her Rolls with two men on the box stopped at a red light. A man she knew slightly stuck his head in the open window and said, "So that's what a communist looks like!"

Edwina was never a member of the Communist Party, but she did sympathize with its objectives. When Lord Attlee was asked if he believed she was a communist at this time, he replied thoughtfully, "She was very, very left." This coming from a former Labour Prime Minister is significant.

Lord Louis, on the other hand, was completely apolitical, as a good naval officer should be. His personal thinking definitely favored Labour rather than the ultra-Conservatives of the Prime Minister, Mr. Stanley Baldwin's, type, but he did not express his views publicly or let them influence his actions.

Because of his close friendship with the Prince of Wales, Mountbatten was emotionally involved in the extraordinary and tragic events that shook the Monarchy and the Empire in 1936. On January 20 King George V died, and the Prince of Wales succeeded to the Throne as King Edward VIII. The result was an even more violent change in the customs and morals of the Court than when Edward VII succeeded Queen Victoria. In fact the parallel was striking. Like his grandmother, King George was extremely conservative and averse to change—even at quite small dinner parties at Buckingham Palace the gentlemen were required to wear knee breeches—and like Victoria he distrusted and disapproved of his son and heir. There is the well-authenticated story of the occasion on which a palace official heard him giving his son a dressing down. In his best storm-at-sea voice the old King roared, "You dress like a cad. You act like a cad. You *are* a cad. Get out!"

Feeling as he did, the King never allowed his son to see Government dispatches nor discussed affairs of state with him. He even regarded the Prince's real contributions as "Ambassador to the Empire"—his arduous state visits to all the Dominions—with some disapprobation. Despite his occasional admittedly indiscreet behavior, Edward was genuinely proud of his accomplishments in strengthening the bonds between the restive overseas Empire and the Throne. He also had learned a great deal about trade and industry, the economic needs and the political viewpoints of those distant countries. He had strong ideas about how to modernize the Monarchy to conform to them. Now that he was King he tried to effect these things.

But England under Stanley Baldwin was governed by the most reactionary Cabinet since the days of the Marquess of Salisbury. They regarded King Edward's innovations with incredulous horror. When he was photographed crossing the street, from St. James's Palace to a nearby building, carrying an umbrella their toes curled up at his lack of royal dignity, and when he told the unemployed Welsh coal miners that something must be done about their pitiful condition, howls of anguish at this entry of the King into politics could be heard emanating from the Cabinet Room at Number 10 Downing Street. Despite the Government's unconcealed disapproval, the King persisted in his efforts to do away with some of cumbersome trappings of tradition and bring the Monarchy closer to the people. He might have succeeded, had it not been for a fatal weakness in his own character.

Ever since 1931 Edward had been deeply in love with Mrs. Ernest A. Simpson. At first he was frequently a guest at the Simpsons' small, pleasant flat in Bryanston Court; later Mr. Simpson faded from the scene, and Wallis Warfield Simpson became the Prince of Wales', and then King Edward's, constant companion. Clear-eyed as he was about economics and the democratic trend in the world, Edward appeared to be living in a romantic dream world in which he, in the role of Prince Charming, could marry the woman he loved—and get away with it. The trouble was that Mrs. Simpson, who had been divorced from her first husband and would have to be divorced from Mr. Simpson to make his dream come true, hardly fitted the role of Cinderella. When, in October, 1936, she filed divorce proceedings against Mr. Simpson the whole delicate fabric of their idyll was shredded. Baldwin's Cabinet, ashen at the possibility of the King, Defender of the Faith, marrying a twice-divorced woman, moved for a showdown.

Mountbatten was posted to the Naval Air Arm early in 1936, and was in London during the entire constitutional crisis. The new King had appointed him his Naval Aide, as King Edward VII had Prince Louis of Battenberg.

Ever since 1931 the Mountbattens had seen a good deal of the controversial couple—at small parties in London night clubs, like the Embassy and the Kit Kat Club, and at Edward's beloved private residence, Fort Belvedere overlooking Windsor Great Park. The Prince had even brought Mrs. Simpson with him when he visited the *Wishart* while Lord Louis commanded her. During 1936 this intimacy continued.

Though Lord Louis was not politically involved in the short dramatic struggle between the King and his ministers, which culminated in King Edward's abdication on December 10, 1936, he was deeply moved and personally concerned. When it became evident that the Duke of York would have to become King, he went to Mountbatten for advice. With tears in his eyes he said, "This is terrible, Dickie, I don't know how I can do it. My training has been as a naval officer, not for kingship. That is all I ever wanted, and I'm afraid I'll fail the people and my family."

Almost in the very words his father had used to comfort King George V when the death of his elder brother had put him in direct line for the Throne, Lord Louis said, "Bertie, a naval officer's training is the best possible preparation for the job. I know you will make a splendid King."*

Meanwhile Mountbatten was having a personal battle with his own conscience. Certainly he was too sophisticated to have shared the King's delusion that he could marry Mrs. Simpson and still reign in England. But he had never faced the bleak possibility of abdication. Now that it was about to happen the long friendship between them and the many kindnesses and unwavering support the King had given him through the years, and the memory of the happy voyages they had made together, demanded loyalty in return. Lord Louis was painfully aware that the gesture he contemplated would in all probability wreck the career that meant everything to him. Realizing that, he decided that he could do no less. He called the King at the Fort and offered to go into exile with him.

However lonely and forsaken King Edward felt on that last terrible day of his reign, he was far too kind and understanding to accept such a sacrifice. In a tone of authority, whose very abruptness showed the emotion that it cloaked, Edward categorically refused to allow his cousin to join his enforced pilgrimage.

Only twice in his life did Mountbatten do anything to imperil his great ambition. In pursuing it he was often as ruthless as has been claimed. But above and beyond the driving force that conditioned his whole life he placed the obligations of loyalty. Say what you will of his opportunism, his arrogance, his vanity, but remember that, whatever the stress of temptation, he never defaulted the motto on the scroll beneath his coat of arms: *In Honour Bound.*

.   .   .

* King George VI appointed Lord Louis Mountbatten his Naval Aide.

The last two years before the war were somewhat more sober for the Mountbattens. In 1938 Lord Louis' brother George, Marquess of Milford Haven, died, and was succeeded in the title by his nineteen-year-old son David. Everyone agrees that George Mountbatten was more brilliant than his younger brother, but he lacked the drive and the capacity for taking infinite pains that were the foundation of Lord Louis' genius. Because his rather temperamental Russian wife could not live on his small income and his pay as a naval officer, George had retired from the Navy in 1932 to try to make money in business. He joined an American company, Sperry Gyroscope, and was reasonably successful.

His death brought a new responsibility to the Mountbattens, because George had undertaken the care and education of his nephew, Prince Philip of Greece, son of his sister Alice and Prince Andrew. Now this brilliant young man became, in effect, Lord Louis' ward, and in spirit the son the Mountbattens never had.

On July 3, 1939, Edwina's father died. He had been created Lord Mount Temple in 1932 for his services to the Government. He left Broadlands and Classiebawn Castle to Edwina.

But it was not so much these family tragedies that took the edge off the Mountbattens' zest for living, as it was the greater tragedy that loomed over all the world. Lord Louis' role in war, if it came, was of course predetermined. Now Edwina began to prepare herself for the part she was to play. As early as 1938 she organized first aid classes in the penthouse apartment and joined the newly formed Women's Volunteer Service. Her gay friends thought it rather silly of her to be so intense about it all. But Edwina went to work as an auxiliary nurse in Westminster Hospital, doing all the menial chores she had hated in school, and worse things, like handling bedpans, comforting the dying, and accustoming herself to the sight of blood in the operating theater.

Just before the war she joined the St. John Ambulance Brigade in which she was to reach her apex of heroic service, as her husband did on the sea.

Chapter 7

"HAS ANYBODY HERE SEEN KELLY?"

THE THING LORD LOUIS MOUNTBATTEN LOVED BEST in all his life was a ship —H.M.S. *Kelly*. Well did she deserve his devotion, for in her he attained his finest moments and the emotional climax of his life.

In his foreword to Kenneth Poolman's biography of the *Kelly*, Mountbatten wrote: "I was the only captain she ever had, and I knew and loved her from the time of her birth when her keel was laid until the keel was the last thing visible as she sank beneath the waves. . . .

"The *Kelly* was sunk on May 23, 1941, in the Battle of Crete. No one left their posts when the end came. She went down with all her guns firing and all her men at their action stations. We did not leave the *Kelly*, it was she who finally left us. . . ."

The *Kelly* was designed as the flotilla leader of the K Class destroyers. Mr. A. P. Cole began work on her plans in 1936, almost at the same time Mountbatten returned to the Admiralty from commanding the *Wishart* in the Mediterranean. He worked closely with Cole on the *Kelly*'s design, proposing numerous refinements including a new type of bridge and more comfortable crew's quarters.

She was a single-stack destroyer of 1,695 tons. Her geared steam turbines of 40,000 horsepower were designed to drive her at 36 knots—

she went about 2 knots faster—and her armament consisted of six 4.7-inch guns mounted in pairs in two turrets forward and one aft, and ten 21-inch torpedo tubes in two banks of five. Two heavy machine guns were mounted amidships, and for additional defense against aircraft she had a 2-pounder pom-pom—later she was equipped with two Oerlikon-Gazda 20-mm. machine cannon. Naturally, she was also equipped with Mountbatten's station keeping device. Her crew consisted of 240 officers and men.

The *Kelly*'s keel was laid down on August 26, 1937, at Hebburn-on-Tyne, by Messrs. R. & W. Hawthorn, Leslie & Co., Ltd., of Newcastle. She was launched on October 25, 1938, and named for Admiral of the Fleet Sir John Kelly, the only ship of that name ever carried on the lists of the Royal Navy. She hoisted the White Ensign on August 23, 1939.

During the building of the *Kelly*, Mountbatten, who had been promoted to captain in 1937, was constantly turning up at Hebburn to see how she was getting on. Early in 1939 he was posted to her in command of the Fifth Destroyer Flotilla to consist of the K Class destroyers *Kingston*, *Kipling*, *Kashmir*, *Kandahar*, *Kimberly*, *Khartoum*, and *Kelvin*. He was utterly delighted, but probably not very surprised, though he called it "unexpected good fortune." It was what he wanted; and what Lord Louis wanted, he usually got.

Mountbatten went immediately to Hebburn and spent most of the next few months in that rather dismal Tyneside town. He said that he has never known such "a happy relationship" between ship and builder as there was between the *Kelly* and Hawthorn-Leslie, and that he established "a life-long friendship" with the Managing Director, Sir John Rowell.

Captain Lord Louis Mountbatten prepared for his command with the same methodical exactitude that he displayed in every enterprise, from supreme command to polo. He watched over the progress of all the other K Class destroyers wherever they were being built. Their future commanders were invited for a weekend at Adsdean, where Mountbatten held a seminar with them on organization, strategy, tactics, and a hundred other aspects of operating the flotilla. Then he invited the engineer officers to Adsdean and with them took a short course, under Rear Admiral Dight at Haslar, on the expected mechanical characteristics of their new ships and how to get the best out of them.

On the day Mountbatten took command of the *Kelly*, August 23, 1939, she looked her prettiest. Long and low in the water, with a knife-like stem and flaring bow, she was painted pale green—for Mediterranean service. Her raked funnel bore the black stripe of a flotilla leader.

After her final trials Mountbatten signed the receipt for her. The Red Duster came down and the White Ensign of the Royal Navy was hoisted in its place. Then with a skeleton crew she sailed for Chatham.

Far more important events occurred on August 23 than the acceptance of the *Kelly*. That day German Foreign Minister Joachim von Ribbentrop and Russia's Vyacheslav M. Molotov signed the Non-Agression Pact between Germany and Russia, which relieved Hitler of the danger of fighting on two fronts. War was only a matter of days.

Mountbatten had long been sure it would come. While Prime Minister Neville Chamberlain and his Cabinet desperately tried to stave it off by appeasement at Munich and talked of "peace for our time," Lord Louis was visiting Chartwell and listening to the fiery warnings of Winston Churchill, who was laying bricks for the kitchen floor of the cottage he and Mrs. Churchill planned to occupy during the holocaust he foresaw.

Almost no one else in England paid any attention to the former First Lord. Throughout the 1930s, Churchill, like his father, Lord Randolph Churchill, "was ploughing his lonely furrow," disliked and distrusted by the leaders of all three political parties. His warnings of approaching war and pleas that Britain prepare to defend herself, were unnoticed by those who were deaf because they did not want to hear. It is true that during the summer of 1939 the British politicians began to have an uneasy suspicion that Winston was right after all. Nevertheless the publication of the Russo-German treaty was a stunning shock to them. Mountbatten was not stunned; only spurred to enormous activity.

He took the *Kelly* into Chatham on August 25. The Admiralty had sent out its warning alert and called up the reserves. The next morning the rest of the *Kelly*'s crew marched out of the barracks and lined up on the dockside in three rows. Seventeen-year-old Charles J. Asbury, listed as a "boy," says, "I remember seeing Mountbatten standing on the quarterdeck of *Kelly* surveying us. I thought how handsome he looked. Then he came around and inspected us—especially the boys. He instilled into you the feeling that he knew exactly what he was doing. When things got pretty dusty later, we all felt that he would get us back home somehow, that the dangers were not so bad as long as he was in command. It's a trust I never had in the captain of any other ship I ever served in."

Then Asbury added with the shine of memory in his eyes, "Mountbatten was so damn good-looking. There was something about the way he carried himself. He seemed a cut above everybody else!"

Mountbatten spoke to the men lined up on the dock and to those already aboard the *Kelly*, saying, "I have always found that you cannot have an efficient ship unless you have a happy ship. That is the way I intend to start this commission and that is the way I intend to go on.

"We have come to Chatham to store and ammunition ship. Now normally we are allowed three weeks by the Admiralty to complete this operation. I have decided it must be completed in three days. I expect you all to play your part. . . . We have a job to do. Let's do it!"

Then he said, "The motto I have chosen for the *Kelly* is *Keep On*. I expect you to live up to it!"

The *Kelly* was ready in three days. On August 29, she sailed on a moonlit sea for Portland and her "working up" trials—gunnery, signals, boat drills, general training, which usually take at least a month.

On the morning of September 3, 1939, Mountbatten was nearing the end of a lecture to the officers and petty officers on the use of his station keeper, when a telegram was handed him by Chief Petty Officer Primrose. He read it and said, "At this point I usually say, 'If war should break out at this moment you know enough about it to work it.' Well, at this moment war has broken out!"

Going to the public address system he then gave the news to all his men ending with, "So when we leave this harbor we shall be right in the face of the enemy who will be out to destroy us. We must find him and destroy him first!"

There was no question now of the *Kelly* going to Malta. The best and newest ships would fight in home waters. After hooking up the radio so all hands could listen to Chamberlain's rather pathetic speech, everybody went to work painting the *Kelly* black-gray for northern waters. Mountbatten, typically turned out in elegant white overalls, stood on a stage between two seamen, painting more furiously than anyone.

That night a three-word message that made morale shoot up like a rocket came in the clear from the Admiralty:

TO ALL SHIPS
WINSTON IS BACK.

To Lord Louis the knowledge that Winston was once again First Lord of the Admiralty was good news beyond believing. Confident in himself, his ship, and his crew, he could now be confident of energetic imaginative direction at the top. He knew, too, that progressive ideas, his own included, would have a hearing.

Beyond that may have flashed the thought that this would do his own career no harm; but this should imply no unworthy selfishness. For from that moment ambition was fused with patriotism and blazed with a single ardent object—to find the enemy and destroy him. To this quest he dedicated all his enormous energy, his intense concentration, and his romantic concept of honor. He pursued it with extreme, some say reckless, violence. But remember this was not like World War One, when a case could be made for caution in order to conserve acknowledged superiority on the sea. This time England was facing a far more formidable foe. She was short of ships and short of men. And her western approaches were ringed by U-boats. Above all she was short of aircraft which, as Mountbatten was one of the few naval officers to recognize, had drastically tilted the balance of sea power. She was, though she did not know it yet, the underdog. To win she had need of men who would take improbable chances against improbable odds with high hearts.

The *Kelly*'s war began the very next day. Rather to his surprise Mountbatten found that he had not exaggerated when he told his crew that the moment their ship left harbor they would be "right in the face of the enemy." Accompanied by the destroyer *Acheron* and a motor anti-submarine boat,* they left harbor in a fine, still dawn for anti-submarine exercises in Weymouth Bay, between the sheltering arms of Portland Bill and St. Alban's Head. The water was rippled blue, vacationers were sunning on the beach at Torquay. Home waters! In the midst of a maneuver Mountbatten received a message from the M.A.S.B.: TORPEDOES APPROACHING YOU.

Instinctively he rang for full speed and gave the routine orders that swung *Kelly*'s stern to the M.A.S.B. Then he did a double take. "Anybody who sees a torpedo yell to bridge," he shouted into the public address system.

A man ambled up the ladder, saluted, and asked, "You didn't mean those torpedoes fired by the M.A.S.B. did you, sir?"

"You God damned fool, M.A.S.B.'s *don't carry torpedoes!* This is the *real thing!*"

Lord Louis swung *Kelly* around and, with the M.A.S.B. and *Acheron*, began to quarter the bay like a hound at fault. Lieutenant Commander Burnett got a ping on the Asdic.† He gave Lord Louis the course, and *Kelly* went for it. Depth bombs were flung from the stern; the sea rose up in shaggy white columns. Around came the *Kelly* again, and as she sliced back, the surface of the water was thick with

---

* Like our P.T. boats, but with depth charges instead of torpedoes.

† A listening device similar to sonar.

fish floating bellies-up and slick with fuel oil. The Admiralty scored it a probable.

On September 11 Mountbatten got a hurry call to Whitehall. Orders so secret they could not be telegraphed were handed to him at the Admiralty, and as he read them Mountbatten must have smiled. The First Lord had a great sense of drama.

The next day the *Kelly* picked up Major Randolph Churchill, the First Lord's son, and raced across the Channel to Le Havre. On the way Mountbatten, as was his custom, informed the crew of their mission. They had already guessed it!

At Le Havre Major Churchill jumped onto the heavily guarded dock. Under the shaded lights Mountbatten saw him returning with his passengers. The crew stood at attention and the boatswains' squealing pipes echoed among the wharf sheds, as Lord Louis at the gangway welcomed his former King aboard.

While the *Kelly* leaped and zigzagged across the Channel at full speed with Commander Evans on the bridge, Mountbatten had dinner with the Duke and Duchess of Windsor and Major Churchill. It was a gay party. The ship, trembling with speed and careening at abrupt changes of course imbued them all with a sense of exciting urgency. The Duke, alight with enthusiasm and the hope of being able to serve his country once more, seemed years younger than the last time Lord Louis had seen him.

They came safely to Portsmouth where Mountbatten expertly brought his ship alongside darkened Farewell Jetty. As the hawsers were made fast, a few lights came on, glinting on the fixed bayonets of a khaki-clad honor guard. Edward shook his cousin's hand with an extra hard grip, and went quickly down the gangway with Wallis. They paused to wave good-bye to the cheering crew and the Duke said, "God bless you and keep you safe!"

Then, after a second's hesitation, he went on. The wartime security, the haste, the very absence of ceremony pitched emotion high as the former King stepped onto English soil.

So far it was a very gay war, but not for long. The Germans had stationed most of their available submarines around the British Isles before war was declared. The Royal Navy was trying desperately to shepherd merchant ships through the deadly ring, using every destroyer they could muster; even risking aircraft carriers in the narrow seas. In addition the British Expeditionary Force was crossing to France and had to be guarded. The destroyers were kept going night and day, until trawlers and other auxiliary craft could be equipped for convoy duty.

Six days after landing the Duke, the *Kelly* was patrolling off Land's End when an SOS came from the aircraft carrier *Courageous*, which had been torpedoed. Full speed again—*Kelly* seemed always to be moving at full speed. By the time she arrived on the scene *Courageous* had sunk, but men were still struggling in the water, while two neutral liners and some destroyers stood by. Threading his ship through rough seas, wreckage, and floating bodies, Mountbatten picked up a few survivors, among them his friend, Commander Abel Smith, who two weeks before had been in Buckingham Palace as Equerry to King George VI. The Captain of the *Courageous* and five hundred men were drowned.

The next day, September 19, the *Kingston*, second of the Ks to be commissioned, joined the *Kelly*. Lord Louis now had two ships of his flotilla. They worked out of Plymouth on escort and patrol duty for a month. During this period the *Kelly* got one U-boat certain and several probables. On October 20 they were ordered to join the fleet at Lock Ewe, and thence to Scapa Flow, which was being used as an advance destroyer base. The fleet had been withdrawn after the dreadnought *Royal Oak* had been torpedoed by a submarine which had sneaked into the anchorage. Until the new anti-submarine defenses could be installed everyone at Scapa was in an advanced state of jitters. "Every floating broomstick is a periscope here," wrote Bob Knight, the *Kelly*'s "reporter."

Patrolling out of the Orkneys, north beyond the Arctic Circle and east to the Norwegian coast, was sea warfare at its most arduous. Three or four hours of daylight was the most that could be expected—if the faint glimmer filtering through storm-black clouds could be called daylight. Through huge, smashing seas, through snow and hail and icy rain or opaque fog, the *Kelly* pitched and rolled. The safety lines on the open decks were never unshipped.

The mess deck had no central heating and no one, including Mountbatten, had proper winter clothing, because the *Kelly* had been slated for Malta. Her crew improvised; some wore flash-proof suits meant for fire-fighting, woolen socks on their hands for mittens, and towels wrapped around their heads. Lord Louis served rum early and often. "It was the only way you could keep warm," says Asbury.

Yet morale was high, partly because the *Kelly* had a magnificent crew, but also in great measure due to her captain. "You felt he had everybody's problems at heart," Asbury said; and Commander Jeremy Hutchinson, who joined the *Kelly* on her second commission, added,

"He was no aloof captain. He was so modern and up-to-date, and he made you feel that you were not an amateur—that you were good. He took everyone into his confidence. He would always ask you for your views on how to solve some problem. 'We're very dead set in our ways,' he'd say to you. 'You may have some new ideas. If so let's hear them.'"

Most inspiring of all, perhaps, was the fact that Mountbatten fought gaily. No matter what the hardships or exhaustion, nor how great the peril, he was clearly having a tremendous time, living at the peak of exhilaration. The worse things got, the higher soared his spirits. His particular type of humor, not subtle but schoolboyish, went over well with the lower deck. They called him "Louis," though not to his face; and they said, "Louis doesn't expect miracles, but he's bloody disappointed if he doesn't get them."

In late October word was flashed from the Admiralty to Scapa Flow that the American Merchantman *City of Flint*, captured by the German pocket battleship *Deutschland*, had reached Murmansk with a prize crew and three hundred British prisoners of war. She was trying to sneak down the coast of neutral Norway to a German port. Destroyers were ordered out to intercept her if possible, but without violating Norwegian neutrality. Mountbatten was not too concerned about Norse sensibilities and he took *Kelly* right up to the rocky Norwegian coast. One dark night he was in the very jaws of a fjord when a spunky little Norwegian gunboat shot out of the mist and signaled, "Get out or I'll open fire!"

Lord Louis was not prepared to start a war with Norway. However, he ordered *Kelly* close aboard the gunboat, and through a megaphone he called to her captain, "Please give my regards to my cousin Crown Prince Olaf, and tell him I hope he's keeping well!"*

With her boats smashed and her taffrail carried away by a winter storm, the *Kelly* was sent back to Hebburn to refit. The crew were given a two-week Christmas leave. On the night before she was to sail again the renegade Englishman who called himself Lord Haw-Haw announced over the Berlin radio, "And where is your Lord Louis Mountbatten? Don't think we don't know. He is in the Tyne. But he will never leave it."

The *Kelly* sailed next day. Orders came to attack a U-boat that had sunk two merchantmen in the mouth of the harbor. Mountbatten protested that it had probably mined the estuary. His protest was dis-

---

* The *City of Flint* never reached Germany. She was interned at Bergen and her prisoners were freed.

allowed. Off went *Kelly* at full speed again, just missing a freighter as she passed Jarrow Staits. As Mountbatten maneuvered toward a burning tanker he felt a horrid grinding-bumping under *Kelly*'s keel which he was sure was a mine. Three times it scraped the hull, then hit a propeller. In a blast of flame and up-boiling water the stern of the destroyer rose several feet and dropped. She lay dead in the water.

In that frightful period of suspense, Mountbatten's crew stood to their posts—all except one. A young stoker, knowing he had no chance below, panicked and broke for the deck.

The *Kelly* was towed back to the shipyard. There Lord Louis spoke sternly to his crew: "Today we have been through one of the most trying experiences that can befall a ship in war—the suspense of feeling a mine bumping along the bottom—waiting for it to explode. Luckily it was not a very good mine and didn't go off until it hit the propellers. Out of two hundred and forty men aboard two hundred and thirty-nine behaved as they ought to have—as I expected them to. But one panicked and deserted his post—and his comrades—in the engine room.

"When he was brought before me, he told me himself that he knew the punishment for deserting his post was death. You'll be surprised to know that I am going to let him off with a caution, and a second one to myself for having failed in four months to impress my personality and my principles on each and *all* of you. . . .

"From now on I expect *everyone* to behave the way the two hundred and thirty-nine did. I will under no circumstances whatever tolerate again the slightest suspicion of cowardice or lack of discipline and I know that none of you will fail me."

Then Lord Louis relaxed and smiled at them, his eyes crinkled with delight. "You're the luckiest crew in the Navy," he said. "You get two Christmas leaves, while we repair ship. Now I know that having just come back from leave you're all broke. But I've been talking to Lady Louis on the telephone and she asked me to tell you that her Christmas present to you is a round-trip ticket for every man to his home."

There was no Christmas leave for Lord Louis. He and his personal staff commanded the Fifth Flotilla from the newly completed *Kelvin* until *Kelly*'s repair was completed in February, 1940.

When she sailed again from Hebburn with a brass band on the dock to play her off, the *Kelly* ran into her least glorious moment. She had been "degaussed"—that is fitted with electric cables to neutralize the newly invented German magnetic mines, which were exploded by the magnetic field of a ship without touching it. Before putting to sea she ran her degaussing trials, a straight run down river and back.

She completed the first run and began to turn. Asbury on the bridge beside Mountbatten heard him order "Full astern!" Somebody blundered. The *Kelly* went full ahead. Mountbatten, fairly dancing with rage, kept shouting "Full astern, damn it!" Too late! *Kelly*'s bow crashed into an oil tanker alongside a dock. Then the order took effect. She shot backward and hit a drifter coming up river. Unfortunately no record was kept of the historic remarks made by Lord Louis Mountbatten.

As the *Kelly* limped back to her dock the bandsmen were just putting their instruments away. Grinning broadly they hastily uncased them. The Band Master raised his baton and "Has Anybody Here Seen Kelly?" blared forth.

Back the *Kelly* went to Scapa Flow and more patrolling in dirty weather. But she was still a gay ship with much singing, aided by Seaman Rogers and his ukelele. Lord Louis even persuaded blond film star Frances Day to come aboard and do a turn for the crew.

Then, patrolling in a snowstorm so thick Mountbatten could not see the bow from the bridge, the *Kelly* ran into the destroyer *Ghurka*, which was far off course. Most of the crew never even saw her and the radio operator flashed, HAVE HIT MINE, KELLY. Back came a message: NOT MINE BUT ME, GHURKA.

This time the *Kelly* was repaired in the London Graving Dock. While there she had lots of company. King George and Queen Elizabeth, with the little princesses, paid her a visit and Edwina came often. This was *her* ship as well as Dickie's. Though women are considered unlucky on ships the crew loved Edwina. She did not stay in officers' country, but prowled around talking to everybody. Wherever the *Kelly* was, Edwina's thoughts followed. Sacks full of heavy clothing appeared mysteriously, and crates of oranges, more precious than gold in wartime Britain, would arrive for her crew. Any sailor who had family trouble was sure to get help either from the captain or the captain's wife.

It would not have been a Mountbatten ship without mascots, so there were a calico cat and mongrel dog named George. One day in London Lord Louis noticed one of the ship's company was missing. "Where's George?" he asked a seaman.

"I don't know, sir. Looks like he jumped ship and got lost."

"Here's two quid," Mountbatten said. "Now you get lost until you find him."

George was found.

While the *Kelly* was in London the strange pause in the fighting on land—which the Americans called "The Phoney War" and Churchill poetically named "The Twilight War"—ended on April 9, 1940, with a thunder of tanks, the reverberation of artillery, and great ships fighting up and down Norwegian fjords half seen through blinding snowstorms as the Nazis scooped up little Denmark and treacherously invaded the southern part of neutral Norway. Prime Minister Neville Chamberlain's Government, already tottering from public distrust, tried desperately to retrieve the situation by landing troops in northern Norway. Ill conceived and ill equipped—no air support, no tanks, very little artillery—the expedition had no chance against the Germans. Within three weeks the Royal Navy was ordered to rescue the remnants of a force which had landed at Namsos under Major General Carton de Wiart.

On April 29 Lord Louis in the *Kelly* arrived at Scapa Flow. He was called immediately to a Commanding Officers' Conference, which was planning the evacuation of Namsos. They put him in command of a flotilla consisting of four British destroyers and the French destroyer *Bison*. That same day they sailed for Namsos, screening the fleet commanded by Rear Admiral John Cunningham. On April 30 they rendezvoused at Kya Light, seventy miles south of Namsos. Dense fog kept the cruisers and transports from going on, but Mountbatten signaled for permission to make a sortie with his destroyers, reasoning that the fog would protect him from enemy bombers. Permission granted!

He led his five destroyers up the Norwegian coast by dead reckoning. Suddenly the fog lifted for a moment and yells of "Land dead ahead!" came from the bow. The whole flotilla wheeled seaward just in time to escape running head-on into a rocky promontory. It was sheer luck that Lord Louis did not lose them all. But one has to be lucky in that kind of war.

On the afternoon of May 1 the fog lifted. Admiral Cunningham ordered the cruiser *York*, five destroyers, and three transports to dash up Nansenfjord to Namsos. The *Kelly* led the way.

As the squadron entered the fjord Lord Louis ordered the *Kelly* to make 26 knots. She left the other ships to follow and rushed alone through the still water in the eerie twilight between the tall green hills where in springtime night never falls. The memory of that lovely scene, of the sweet smell of land strong in his nostrils after weeks at sea, moved Mountbatten to one of his few lyric outbursts: "One could see the magnificent snow-capped hills and fertile valleys with their friendly, peaceful farmhouses. I said to myself, 'This can't be war. War never came to so quiet and innocent a spot. . . .' "

Yet he was facing the most difficult feat of seamanship he ever performed and, with the exception of the Battle of Crete, the most dangerous. Once in the narrow fjord there was no turning back for the *Kelly* or any of the ships strung out far behind her. In single line they followed the twists and turns of the deep channel until around a bend it opened out into the harbor, lighted by the glare of burning Namsos. The whole town was a sea of fire, houses, churches, warehouses, piles of stores on the jetties, and ships in the anchorage. Black silhouettes against red flames, over 5,000 troops stood waiting to be taken off.

The troopships tied up to the docks and the destroyers nuzzled against the embankment while soldiers jumped onto their decks. Then they ferried the men out to the *York* lying in the harbor, and went back to shore for more. *Kelly* picked up the French *Chasseurs Alpines*, who leaped aboard followed by their beautiful, long-haired dogs, half-husky, half-Alsatian. In that fierce light ships and men were sitting ducks for air attack. Mountbatten said, "I simply cannot understand why the Germans did not bomb the hell out of us."

The evacuation began at 10:30 P.M. At 2:20 A.M. the last soldier jumped onto the destroyer *Afridi,* and they started back down Nansen-fjord. Though the Luftwaffe had not attacked, Mountbatten knew they would be in for it at dawn. Sure enough, at the first light, the planes came—reconnaissance first, then high-level bombers plastering their patterns on the ships in line, then the dive bombers, almost straight down out of the sky with their unearthly screaming. *Kelly*'s pom-pom got one amid wild cheering in which Lord Louis joined.

Wave after wave came the Luftwaffe, from 8 A.M. to 3 P.M., following the ships far out to sea. English luck held pretty well; none of the transports were hit; but the *Bison* was smashed to a blazing hulk and *Afridi,* trying to pick up swimmers, took two bombs, rolled over, and sank. The rest of the squadron sailed safely home.

No rest for the *Kelly.* After refueling she was ordered to join the cruiser *Birmingham* and a destroyer force under Rear Admiral Glennie searching for a German mine-layer and some E-boats—Motor Torpedo Boats—in the North Sea close off the German coast. They were joined by their new sister ship, the *Kandahar,* which had aboard Lord Louis' young nephew, David Milford Haven.

Visibility as usual was almost zero. A submarine alarm was followed by gunfire on the horizon. As the *Kelly* and *Kandahar* turned toward it the destroyer *Bulldog*, which had strayed from her own flotilla, joined them. The three destroyers tore through the descending darkness. Then somebody yelled, "Torpedo!"

Mountbatten straining his eyes from the bridge saw nothing in the heaving, misty sea. Then came a *thump*. "Thank God it was a dud!" he said.

His words were lost in a terrible crash and a sheet of flame higher than the bridge. The *Kelly* was lifted clear out of the sea and fell back, seething with steam and flames. *Bulldog* radioed, KELLY TORPEDOED, and came close aboard.

In that roaring inferno nobody knew how badly the ship was hurt, but nobody lost his nerve. Commander Evans fought his way below with a damage-control party. From the bridge Lord Louis called through a megaphone, "Don't jump overboard until I give the order. Don't panic. We're not sinking!" It was more hope than conviction.

Kelly lay dead in the water, her starboard rail awash. Mountbatten ordered depth charges and torpedoes set to "safe" and jettisoned. Then he called for volunteers to heave ready-use ammunition overboard. Coming down from the bridge to help, he found Bob Knight badly burned. He took off his long blue overcoat and wrapped it around the petty officer. In an improvised hospital Pharmacist's Mate Herbert Male was operating on the wounded by the light of electric torches—it looked like the cockpit of the *Victory* at Trafalgar.

About 11 P.M. the *Bulldog* got a line aboard and began to tow the *Kelly* very slowly, with the *Kandahar* standing by. *Kelly's* steering mechanism was smashed, but she could be steered from the emergency tiller aft. A chain of men relayed orders from the bridge to the crew working the tiller.

At ten minutes past midnight Mountbatten was alone on the bridge when he heard the roar of gasoline engines. Out of the darkness shot a German E-boat at 40 knots. She hit the *Bulldog* a glancing blow and, machine guns blazing, careened along the towrope. She crashed against the *Kelly* and actually leaped up on her listing deck, then skidded aft carrying everything left standing with her. Lord Louis heard German voices yell in panic. Then the E-boat slid off the stern and blew up.

Long afterward Mountbatten admitted that he was pretty embarrassed by his own reaction. When the E-boat appeared spitting fire at twenty yards, "I ducked down behind the bridge screen," he said. "It was a very silly thing to do, for it would not have kept out a rifle bullet. Then I suddenly felt frightfully ashamed and very glad I was alone on the bridge so that no one had seen me duck. I said to myself, 'Never again will I permit myself to show when I am afraid.' "

At early dawn the *Kandahar* came alongside and took off the wounded. Lord Louis read a brief service over the dead, and they were buried at sea. The *Kelly* was slowly settling deeper in the water. The other destroyers took station around her as an anti-aircraft defense, and two British planes appeared just in time. The German air came over bombing. *Kelly's* gun crews aimed their guns manually, while other men brought up ammunition from the magazines. There were no hits.

Toward evening the weather got worse. The towline kept breaking. The *Kelly* had settled so deep that she "looked more like a submarine than a destroyer." The sea was sloshing through her boiler room. At this point Admiral Glennie in the *Birmingham* signaled: ABANDON SHIP, I'M GOING TO SINK YOU.

Lord Louis signaled back, TRY IT AND I'LL BLOODY WELL SINK YOU!

However, he decided to tranship most of the crew to lighten ship. He remained aboard with five other officers and twelve men. When night fell and the *Kelly* seemed about to break up, they, too, left.

But in the morning the *Kelly* was still there—her motto was "Keep On." Mountbatten and his volunteers went back aboard. Two Navy tugs sent by the Admiralty arrived and took the destroyer in tow. Slowly, incredibly, they hauled her across the sullen sea, bombed again and yet again by Nazi planes. Ninety-one hours after she was torpedoed the *Kelly* came home to the Tyne. Slowly, between wildly cheering crowds, she was towed up river to Hawthorn-Leslie's dry dock. There the ninety-foot gash in her side was revealed, with a writhing mass of twisted steel sticking out like intestines. It had taken incredible seamanship, leadership, and "the faith and fire of a Nelson," to bring her home through stormy seas and enemy bombing.

As soon as the *Kelly* was safe, Lord Louis gave the crew home leave—all but the twenty-seven of them who would never see home. As he stood on the station platform watching the cars of their special train slide by, they were leaning out of the windows singing, "Has Anybody Here Seen Kelly?"

Chapter 8

ALL GUNS FIRING

It TOOK SEVEN MONTHS to repair the *Kelly*. Indeed she was virtually a brand-new ship when she left the Hebburn yard. Meanwhile she missed Britain's blackest hour—and finest, as Winston Churchill, who became Prime Minister on May 10, 1940, rightly called it. The German blitz of Holland and Belgium was followed by the miraculous evacuation of the British Expeditionary Force from Dunkirk, the fall of France, and Italy's declaration of war, which forced England to detach more ships from her hard-pressed Home Fleet to guard the Mediterranean.

Then as England, her Allies defeated, stood alone, came the Battle of Britain—when the Luftwaffe attempted to knock out the Royal Air Force preparatory to the invasion of England, and were themselves knocked out of the English skies by that small devoted band of R.A.F. fighter pilots. As the dark months came, October, November, December, the Germans began the ultimate horror of massed night-bombing raids on English cities.

Though the *Kelly* was out of it during those stormy months, Mountbatten was in the thick of it. After a brief leave at Broadlands with Edwina, during which he made everybody miserable by moping over the *Kelly*, he resumed command of the Fifth Flotilla from various sister ships of the J Class—*Jackel*, *Jupiter*, and *Javelin*. They were based on Plymouth in the narrow Channel that was now the front line of

Britain's defense. While he was in the *Javelin*, Lord Louis fought his most criticized action.

At 5:40 A.M. on the morning of November 29, 1940, between Land's End and Start Point, the *Javelin*'s radar screen picked up five enemy ships. By Aldis lamp—the ship's radio had broken down—Mountbatten ordered the flotilla to converge on the enemy. They attacked in quarter line—a staggered formation. Mountbatten signaled, ABOUT TO INTERCEPT ENEMY DESTROYERS BEARING STARBOARD. Then he fired a star shell.

There were the enemy destroyers, big and black in the white light, only 900 yards away. *Javelin*'s first broadside missed by a mile. Mountbatten personally gave the range for the next broadside, and watched shells burst on the leading German destroyer. He ordered the helm to port to fire torpedoes. At that instant in a blinding flash and roar, the *Javelin*'s bow disappeared. Seconds later another torpedo hit the stern, exploding the after magazine and blowing *Javelin*'s stern clear off. Her midsection lay dead in the water.

In the confusion the flotilla's second-in-command in the *Kashmir* failed to take over. Though they went on at full speed with all guns blazing, the flotilla was disorganized. The Germans laid down a smoke screen and got away.

They got away—that was the point of criticism. It was called "a disgrace." Mountbatten was criticized for not opening fire sooner, for engaging in quarter line instead of Fisher's line ahead, for getting himself torpedoed, for getting too close to the enemy; for all sorts of things a Monday-morning quarterback can see.

Lord Louis took it hard. He felt that he had failed, though he could not see how. Others did not agree. In the New Year's Honors List of January 1, 1941, Captain Lord Louis Mountbatten was awarded the D.S.O., Britain's highest decoration for valor, after the Victoria Cross.

Senior officers were already beginning to be jealous of Mountbatten. His dash, his fame, his royal blood, and his flamboyance led some of them to denigrate his exploits as recklessness and his habit of having ships shot out from under him as bad seamanship. In this connection General Sir Frederick Morgan tells of the first time he met Mountbatten:

> I was commanding the defences in the West Country, when their Majesties the King and Queen came with King Haakon of Norway to inspect Plymouth. Captain Dickie Mountbatten, who was in Plymouth, joined them when the Royal Train came in. I remember it well, because that night after the King and Queen

left, Plymouth was absolutely wrecked by bombs. It was so bad in the morning light that to show our defiant spirit I ordered all the flags hoisted and sent to Essex for a band, and we all danced on the Hoe. I danced with Nancy Astor, who was Mayoress of Plymouth. The place was so badly smashed, there was nothing else to do.

To get back to Mountbatten. I thought him frightfully attractive. After he had gone I said to the local Admiral, "Mountbatten is doing a fine job, isn't he?"

The Admiral said, "Yes, but it's getting pretty expensive to mount Dickie."

That was a rather gentle, really humorous crack, yet it showed the wind direction like the telltale on a racing yacht's mast. As the war went on and Mountbatten's rank rose like a rocket while stars clustered on his shoulder straps, the comments of his former superiors became less funny and more acid.

In regard to Mountbatten's seamanship let a man who dislikes Lord Louis have the last word. Captain S. W. Roskill, R. N. (Ret.), the official historian of the Royal Navy in World War Two, said(§) "When you have abundant evidence of personal vanity it is difficult to not attach too much importance to that. But there was never any good grounds for criticism of Mountbatten's handling of the Fifth Destroyer Flotilla. Certainly getting the *Kelly* back to harbor after she was torpedoed was a remarkable feat of seamanship. The First Sea Lord, Sir Dudley Pound, felt it rated the D.S.O."

The *Kelly* was recommissioned on December 15, 1940. When the call for former *Kelly* men to rejoin went out through the fleet most of them volunteered, leaving much safer billets on battleships and cruisers. "It was sort of crazy," says Asbury, "but you felt you had to do it."

Good new men joined, too. Rocky Wilkins came aboard to handle one of the new Oerlikon-Gazda anti-aircraft guns. Sub-Lieutenant Jeremy Hutchinson was in charge of the pom-pom. The new first lieutenant was Lord Hugh Beresford, a nephew of Admiral Lord Charles Beresford, who had "done in" Prince Louis of Battenberg. He was an intense, mystic young man who could write of "running a ship under God's orders . . . I have a strong feeling that our success or failure during these coming months depends directly on my listening to Him and following out His instructions calmly and coolly."

Taffy Davies, a naïve young boy, was another new crew member.

He had never heard of the *Kelly*, and said that he thought she'd be a nice safe ship because his mother had said, "Captain Lord Louis Mountbatten is a cousin of the King, and those people are never allowed to take chances."

A coarse hoot came from the veterans in the crew and somebody said, "How wrong can you be? Louis's a real death-and-glory boy, he is."

When Mountbatten addressed his new crew he gave evidence that he had not changed. "Always steer toward the sound of guns," he said. Then the *Kelly* sailed for Scapa Flow. In January, 1941, she joined the *Kipling*, *Kashmir*, and *Jersey* at Plymouth on the Channel patrol. As Greece fell to the Nazis and the Germans tightened their grip on the Mediterranean, the Fifth Flotilla was ordered to Malta. The *Kelly* sailed from Plymouth in April, 1941, with fifty seasick commandos as passengers.

Although the narrow waist of the Mediterranean between Sicily and German-held Tunisia had been almost closed to British ships by the German Air Force, the *Kelly*'s flotilla safely reached Malta. But as he stood on the bridge leading them into Valletta's Grand Harbor, Mountbatten could hardly believe that this was the gay, beloved island of his memories. The steep, narrow streets were filled with the rubble of the charming golden houses; the docks were a shambles and the rusting masts and blackened superstructures of a dozen ships stuck up from the blue water of the harbor. The black-clad Maltese, lining the shore to cheer the flotilla in, looked like wraiths.

The *Kelly* berthed alongside one of the few working docks. As her last hawser was secured the air raid sirens howled. The Luftwaffe, based on the Sicilian airfields a little over a hundred miles away, had been ordered to extirpate this last British outpost in the central Mediterranean. They came over at all hours, by day in screaming Stukas, by night in massed formations of Heinkel high-level bombers. To fight them off there were only the anti-aircraft guns on ships and shore and a few devoted Hurricane fighters of the R.A.F. Though Hitler's planes had been denied England, at least by daylight, he virtually owned the blue Mediterranean sky.

The flotilla was at Malta for three tortured weeks. Almost every night they went out to sweep the ship lanes between Sicily and Tunisia in order to break up the German supply lines to Rommel's Afrika Korps. Every day without fail they were bombed in harbor. Lord Louis remarked, "It is unpleasant being bombed at sea, but far more unpleasant in harbor where one is a sitting target."

He ordered that half the crew of each ship should go into the rock shelters in cliffs around Grand Harbor. With typical frankness he said, "I gave the order, but I had not the moral courage to obey my own order. There was nobody to give me the order so I stayed on board.

"I hated it every time we were bombed, but I was more frightened of what my friends would say if my ship were sunk while I was in shelter."

The crew agreed with their captain about harbor bombings. Dangerous as were the night operations, they liked them better than the days. At least some of them could get a little sleep.

One night the flotilla was ordered to bombard German shipping in the harbor of Benghazi. All authorities agree that Mountbatten carried out the bombardment with great skill and daring, taking his little ships right up to the entrance to the breakwater, under the cannon of the shore batteries. His guns were already set for the range and direction. With rapid broadsides he smashed most of the German ships in port, and got away before the shore batteries found his range.

On another morning, however, as Mountbatten was leading the flotilla back to port, the fourth ship in line, the *Jersey*, hit a mine and sank. Mountbatten had the moral courage to refuse to take the flotilla out again until the Channel was properly swept of mines. They were in harbor for ten days during which time Mountbatten stated, "We were bombed forty-seven times."

On May 20, 1941, the Germans launched the air-sea invasion of Crete, lying about seventy-miles off the tip of Greece. British forces on the island were 28,600 men, most of whom had been rescued from Greece. They had very little artillery, about 25 tanks, and insufficient transport. However, the killing statistics were in air power. The British had 6 Hurricane fighters and about 20 obsolete planes of other types; against these the Germans launched 610 bombers and fighters and 530 transport planes. Including other types, the total of German aircraft taking part was 1,280. The Germans sent in 16,000 superbly equipped paratroopers by air. Another 7,000 were sent by sea, but the Royal Navy saw to it that the seaborne contingent never reached the battle. Nevertheless, the British on Crete did not have a chance.

On May 21, 1941, Captain Lord Louis Mountbatten returned from a staff conference on Malta. As was his invariable custom he called the *Kelly*'s crew together and told them what they were going to do. Crete was under heavy German attack and the flotilla had been ordered to join Admiral Rawling's fleet guarding the island from seaborne attacks. Hiding nothing, he told the men, standing in their white singlets and shorts under the hot sun on the forward deck, how nasty it would be.

German planes from nearby Greek airfields would be bombing them all day. There would be no aircraft to counter them. He ended by saying, "I know you'll do what I expect of you."

That evening the *Kelly* sailed, followed by the *Kashmir, Kipling, Kelvin,* and *Jackal.* Through the night and the next morning the flotilla raced over a quiet sea, pausing only to knock off a German U-boat they happened upon. Lord Louis never left the *Kelly*'s bridge. Every few hours a mess boy brought him a slice of thick bread and butter and a can of sardines. Presumably he dozed occasionally sitting upright.

At 4 P.M. on May 22, Mountbatten saw the main fleet ahead under heavy air attack. As the *Kelly* aproached, the old battleship *Warspite* was hit by a Stuka's bomb, but her heavy armor prevented serious damage. The cruisers *Gloucester* and *Fiji* and the destroyers *Greyhound* and *Juno* had been sunk, and the cruisers *Carlyle* and *Naiad* put out of action. Nearly every ship in the squadron had been hit. The previous night, however, they had sunk an entire German troop convoy with 4,000 men aboard.

The Fifth Flotilla took station with the fleet. Almost immediately Admiral Rawlings ordered Mountbatten to take the *Kelly, Kashmir,* and *Kipling* back toward Crete to pick up survivors from the *Gloucester* and *Fiji;* but these orders were countermanded by an order to patrol the northwestern coast of Crete. In the narrow Kíthira Channel between Crete and the Greek islands, the *Kelly*'s radio operator picked up a message from General Bernard C. Freyberg, commander of the beleaguered troops on Crete: NAVAL BOMBARDMENT OF MALEME AERODROME WOULD BE APPRECIATED. Right on its heels came a message from Admiral Rawlings: TO CAPTAIN D5. COMPLY WITH G.O.C. SIGNAL.

The Germans had taken Maleme Airfield, which was on a bluff close to the shores of Crete. As Mountbatten swung his column in that direction the *Kipling* reported steering-gear trouble. He went on, accompanied by the *Kashmir.* The *Kelvin* and *Jackal* were on detached patrol. Mountbatten did not need them so he signaled their commanders: AM BOMBARDING MYSELF. He was teased in the Navy about that "extraordinary feat" for years.

As the *Kelly* tore along, at full speed as usual, her radar picked up a ship. "Open shutters!" ordered Lord Louis. Searchlight beams flashed out and fingered the sea until they picked up a caïque—a large sailing schooner—crammed full of German troops. A couple of broadsides from the destroyers at point-blank range sank her, while German soldiers in battle equipment jumped overboard shouting "Heil Hitler!" A little further on they shot up another caïque, this one loaded with

aviation gasoline, which went up in a pillar of fire. "To be honest these
. . . were large sailing ships and it was rather murder," Mountbatten
commented later.

Then he took his two destroyers to within 1,200 yards of the rocky
coast and plastered Maleme Airfield with a barrage that temporarily dis-
rupted the German troops holding it.

Just as the first light of morning cracked the sky Mountbatten
received an order from Admiral Rawlings to "withdraw forthwith toward Alexandria." It was high time; in fact, past time.

At 30 knots the *Kelly* and *Kashmir* headed for safety. They did
not go flat-out because they were perilously low on fuel. A crystalline
Mediterranean dawn broke—scarlet and gold, changing through the
spectrum of pink and green to gentle blue. Not a breath of wind stirred
the water, though the 30-knot gale of her speed cooled the *Kelly*'s decks.

Between six and seven o'clock two formations of high-level bombers
attacked the two destroyers. But they had only anti-personnel bombs
and did no damage. Then at 7:55 A.M. the *Kelly*'s radar reported, "Large
formation of aircraft approaching astern." To Mountbatten on the
bridge the ugly black Stukas must have looked like a swarm of ptero-
dactyls as they came in low over the water. There were actually twenty-
four dive bombers. He ordered evasive action, and both destroyers
began the desperate twisting and turning all knew to be almost useless
against dive bombers.

Mountbatten saw two Stukas peel off and dive on *Kashmir*. She
disappeared in a great belch of flame and smoke: "*Kashmir*'s gone!"

Then the Stukas were diving on the *Kelly*. "Full starboard rudder!"
Mountbatten ordered. The destroyer began a sharp turn at 30 knots,
leaning outward from centrifugal force. The high, horrible scream of
the German plane almost drowned the noise of *Kelly*'s guns, all firing
at once. Mountbatten saw the fat, thousand-pound bomb leave the
Stuka's belly, and fall unerringly. Gunner Ted West on an Oerlikon got
onto the aircraft, which disintegrated.

Then the bomb hit, well aft of the funnel. It went right through the
deck and exploded in the *Kelly*'s vitals, blowing half her bottom out and
raising a blast of smoke and flame, pieces of steel, and human bodies.
Lord Louis grabbed the megaphone and shouted, "We've been hit.
Keep the guns firing."

The engines were still running. The *Kelly* never slackened speed.
But she careened further and further to port until she capsized still
going at 30 knots. All her guns were firing, every man was at his post
until the water rising over the port side washed them away. Rocky

Wilkins was firing an Oerlikon to which he had tied a pair of baby shoes, for luck. "The first thing I noticed was that I had to keep raising my sights to keep on the plane," he said. "Then I didn't know a thing until I came up to the surface of the sea. I had my baby's shoes in my hand. I don't remember grabbing them."

Mountbatten stood on the bridge, hanging onto a stanchion until the rail come down to the water. Then bracing his feet on his own direction finder, he dove into the sea.

Charley Asbury says, "I was asleep in the shell room with my head resting on my arm. We were practically out of ammunition so the shell room was absolutely empty. The guns and the explosion seemed to happen all at once. As the ship went over I slid down the deck and up the bulkhead and escaped through a hole in the bottom of the ship. I stood on the *Kelly*'s keel for a few minutes, then I dove overboard and swam to a Carley float. I'm a strong swimmer."

Poor Rocky Wilkins was not. He was flailing the water with his arms when Lieutenant Dunsterville, the signals officer, came along and towed him to an empty beer crate.

The *Kelly* was now floating upside down. "You could see her whole keel from stem to stern. The propellers were still turning." Both Wilkins and Asbury describe Lord Louis and Beresford diving repeatedly into the oily sea and dragging survivors back to the Carley float. The other officers who were still alive were also rescuing seamen. Later, when Asbury was wounded in the arm by a machine-gun bullet Lieutenant Hutchinson took off his life preserver and gave it to him.

The *Kelly* floated for quite a while. By the time she began to settle all the swimmers the rafts could hold had been hauled to them. Others clung to floating debris or treaded water in life preservers. As he saw his ship about to sink, Mountbatten called in a shaky voice, "The *Kelly*'s going. Give her a cheer, lads!"

They raised a pitifully jagged cheer as their beloved ship tilted by the stern and slid out of sight.

Mountbatten knew how awful they felt, for he felt worst of all. But this would not do. "Give us a song!" he yelled. In a strong, harsh voice he started, " 'Roll out the barrel, we'll have a barrel of fun.' "

Gallantly they joined in. Asbury says, "I tried to sing but only made a terrible noise. We could just see Crete in the distance and there was no sign of any other ship."

Then the black, reptilian German planes came back, diving down on the rafts loaded with survivors; raking them with machine guns. Either started by Mountbatten with his sense of irony, or perhaps spontaneously, everyone began to sing, " 'We're poor little lambs, who have lost our way. Baa! Baa! Baa!' "

Three hours later Mountbatten saw the tripod mast and single stack of a sister destroyer lift above horizon. It was the *Kipling* coming up fast. She checked and nosed slowly among the survivors throwing over Carley floats and life preservers, draping landing nets over her side. Then she stopped and lowered her whaler. The men who still were strong enough to swim made for her; others were picked up by the small boat. Mountbatten climbed aboard. It was one of those exquisite ironies that a ship named for the master poet of the British Empire in India rescued the man who was destined to liquidate that empire.

Lord Louis immediately joined Lieutenant Commander St. Clair-Ford of the *Kipling* on the bridge. German planes came in again squirting machine-gun bullets. Disregarding them Mountbatten told Commander Ford to lower the *Kipling*'s fast motorboat, which was still on the davits. As the boat reached the water, but was still attached to the falls, a Stuka dove on the *Kipling*. Her captain ordered, "Full speed ahead!"

Mountbatten called to the men lowering the boat, "We're going ahead. Cut the falls."

In the confusion the ropes at the boat's bow were cut first. As the destroyer started ahead the small boat was whirled around. Mountbatten yelled, "You bloody fools cut the *after* falls!"

Lord Charles Beresford and First Lieutenant Bush of the *Kipling* leaped to obey. As they hacked at the ropes *Kipling* surged forward under the drive of 40,000 horsepower. The tremendous drag of the swamped boat tore the after davit out of its socket. Tangled in the ropes, Beresford and Bush were crushed to death and pulled overboard.

Wild with grief and rage Mountbatten said he was taking command of the *Kipling*. He was a captain and the overall commander of the flotilla. Though only a lieutenant commander, St. Clair-Ford resisted— the *Kipling* was *his* ship. A brief, blazing row took place on the bridge. Ford appears to have kept control of the ship's actual maneuvers, but when the dive bombers made a renewed attack and the question arose as to whether the *Kipling* should make for Alexandria or stay and try to pick up the remaining survivors, Mountbatten gave the order to stay. They stayed.

He devised a pick-up-and-run technique of rescue. When the Stukas were attacking, the destroyer dodged and circled at full speed with guns blazing. Whenever there was a lull she dashed in and gathered up the isolated clumps of *Kelly* men. On one of these runs the *Kipling* hit the wreck of the *Kelly*, which was still floating under water, and tore a gash in her side which reduced her speed to 20 knots. But not until Mountbatten was sure that every living man had been saved did he give the order to head for Alexandria, four hundred miles away.

It was a rough passage. Limping along at 20 knots, leaking oil through her torn side, the *Kipling* left a broad slick of oil behind her. It was easy for enemy bombers to pick up that trail. They came baying down it again and again. Luckily the crippled destroyer was soon beyond the range of the Stukas, but high-level bombers took their place.

Mountbatten would be the first to admit that Commander Ford handled his ship superbly. Even at comparatively slow speed he seemed able to outguess the Germans and dodge the patterns of bombs. Shuddering from the blasts of near misses the *Kipling* snaked between columns of white water as the sea was heaved up all around her. The Luftwaffe made forty attacks before she got beyond their range. To the men aboard it seemed a miracle that she passed through unscathed.

Though Lord Louis had not been to bed since leaving Malta—three days and nights—he remained on the bridge of the *Kipling*. It was the ultimate test of his incredible endurance. He went below only to talk to his crew, the *Kelly* men. With a pencil and notebook he walked among them, talking with the most critically wounded—many of whom died on the voyage—and writing messages for their families. His men always had thought he really cared about them; now, as they saw him torn by grief, filthy from the oil-smeared sea, his face lined and his eyes sunken from fatigue, they knew he loved them.

That night the *Kipling* ran out of oil. But she had radioed for help, and the fleet tanker *Protector* found her and refilled her fuel tanks. In the bright afternoon sunshine they sailed into Alexandria. Those men of the *Kelly* who could still stand lined the rails. Standing beside the white-clad crew of the *Kipling*, they were a weird and ragged lot. Some had only dirty khaki shorts, others had borrowed mismatched garments from their rescuers. One man wore nothing but a black and gold kimono that a member of *Kipling*'s crew had bought for his girl.

Word of their exploits had preceded them. As the ship passed through the lock gates to the inner harbor they saw the great ships of the Mediterranean Fleet—battleships, aircraft carriers, cruisers and destroyers and submarines, many just returned from the Battle of Crete—all with their crews ranked on their decks to cheer them in. There were no measured hip-hip hoorays, but an enormous spontaneous ovation whose sound reverberated from ancient buildings and filled the hot dome of the sky.

The wounded were met by ambulances at the dockside, and the others went aboard the repair ship *Resource*. Mountbatten went in the *Kipling*'s motor launch to the main base. As he came up to the dock the first person he saw was Midshipman Prince Philip of Greece, who had been aboard the battleship *Valiant* in the battle. Philip looked affectionately at Lord Louis' oil-smeared face and said, "Hello, Uncle Dickie. You look just like a nigger minstrel."

Even after reporting to the commander in chief, Admiral Sir Andrew Cunningham, Mountbatten did not go to bed. "Boy," Asbury says, "before they even had time to clean my wounds in the hospital, Mountbatten came to see us."

Of the 240 officers and men of the *Kelly*'s crew 130 went down with their ship or died of their wounds. Before he left for England on orders from the Admiralty, Mountbatten went to No. 46 storage shed where his crew were housed to say good-bye. They were still a pretty ragged looking lot, for uniforms were in short supply in Alexandria, but they all sported brand-new white topees which had been issued to them.

As they lined up to hear him, Lord Louis' sentiment almost got the better of him. When he spoke his voice quivered with emotion and sometimes almost failed him.

"I have come to say good-bye to the few of you who are left," he said. "We have had so many talks, but this is our last. I have always tried to crack a joke, and you have all been friendly and laughed at them. But today I am afraid I have run out of jokes, and I don't suppose any of us feel much like laughing.

"The *Kelly* has been in one scrap after another, but even when we have had men killed the majority survived and brought the old ship back. Now she lies in fifteen hundred fathoms, and with her more than half our shipmates.

"If they had to die, what a grand way to go, for now they all lie together with the ship we loved, and they are in very good company. We have lost her but they are still with her.

"There may be less than half the *Kelly* left, but I feel that each of us will take up the battle with a stronger heart. Each of us knows twice as much about fighting, and each of us has twice as good a reason to fight.

"You will all be sent to replace men who have been killed in other ships, and the next time you are in action remember the *Kelly*. As you ram each shell home shout, '*Kelly!*' And so her spirit will go on inspiring us until victory is won.

"I should like to add that there isn't one of you I wouldn't be proud and honored to serve with again. Good-bye. Good luck. And thank you all from the bottom of my heart."*

---

* Though the Battle of Crete was lost, Churchill called it "a Pyrrhic victory" for the Germans, because the only crack German paratroop division was so badly mauled that it never again was able to undertake a large-scale action.

Chapter 9

TRIPHIBIOUS MAN

WHEN MOUNTBATTEN RETURNED TO England, he was given a month's leave and posted to command of the aircraft carrier *Illustrious*, which had been badly bombed in the Mediterranean and was being repaired in the United States Navy Yard at Norfolk, Virginia, under Lend-Lease. During his leave he and Edwina lived in a small house she had rented in Chester Street, staffed only by a cook, Mrs. Cable, Edwina's personal maid, Jessie, and a houseboy-valet named John Dean. It was as different as could be from the great penthouse on Park Lane.

At the outbreak of war Edwina had given up the penthouse. It was not only sensible but very, very lucky, for the Brook House apartment was blown to bits early in the Luftwaffe's blitz of London. Like many English children who were cared for in hospitable American homes, Patricia and Pamela Mountbatten were living in America with Mr. and Mrs. Cornelius Vanderbilt.

Edwina had turned Broadlands into an annex of the Royal Southampton Hospital with eighty beds, an operating theater, and the latest medical equipment, reserving only a small apartment for herself and Lord Louis. She was elected the first woman president of that ancient institution.

Though he was living at home Lord Louis saw all too little of his

Lady; for during the war Edwina achieved what is no exaggeration to call her apotheosis. All her latent humanitarianism and her splendid energy were utterly committed to her incredibly strenuous service. Like the *Kelly*, she seemed always to be going "full ahead."

Since 1922 Edwina had belonged to the Order of St. John, and was vitally interested in its world-wide field of work, "for the good of Humanity." The Order had been founded in the eleventh century. Originally crusaders and defenders of Malta against the infidels, the Knights and Brothers of St. John now devoted themselves to humanitarian and lifesaving work. Their first ambulance units had worked in the Franco-Prussian War of 1870; and the St. John Ambulance Brigade had been formally organized in 1877. Just before the war Edwina left the W.V.S. and became an auxiliary nurse with St. John Brigade. In 1940, having passed her examinations, she became a member of the Kensington Nursing Division of St. John, and was made an officer of that unit. She rapidly rose to deputy superintendent in chief of St. John Nursing Division, in charge of all St. John personnel staffing the London A.R.P. service in ambulances, air raid shelters, and first aid and medical posts.

When the blitz burst over London in October Edwina showed her quality. She worked all day in her office, and spent most of her nights in the air raid shelters under the rotten old houses of London's East End. Those dismal relics of Dickensian squalor took the worst beating of all; their inhabitants lived nightly in the dank, rat-infested cellars, tunnels, vaults, and crypts of churches, while their miserable habitations were blown to rubble above their heads. In her plain, dark-blue uniform and perky blue and white hat, Edwina was as beautiful and electric as ever. Wherever she passed and paused to chat and encourage, a wave of rising morale followed her like an induced current of enthusiasm.

To get from one shelter to another she, of course, had to go above ground through the inferno of roaring flames, falling walls, and the terrifying blast of 2,000-pound bombs. Just after she left one shelter a direct hit killed everyone in it. It never seemed to bother her in the least. She had no more fear than Lord Louis on the bridge of the *Kelly*, or if she had she showed it no more than he.

And like her husband she had no reluctance about swinging all her influence for a good cause. When the divisional superintendent of A.R.P. in the Stepney District told her that all appeals to the Ministry of Health to improve conditions in the air raid shelters had gone unanswered, she said through tight lips, "Something will be done at once!"

She went straight to the Minister of Health, Mr. Malcolm J. MacDonald, and laid it on the line. Rats disappeared, while benches, blankets, and makeshift toilets appeared in the shelters forthwith.

In Edwina's executive function the latent organizational ability she had inherited from her grandfather suddenly blossomed. She had an amazing memory for figures, and could reel off reams of statistics without notes. Those who worked with her have said that they would make a game of trying to catch her in a mistake—a game they never won.

About the time Lord Louis came back from Alexandria, Edwina was asked to represent the Joint War Organization Committee (The British Red Cross and St. John) on a fund-raising tour in the United States. Lord Louis decided to use the last part of his leave to go with her.

Though the war separated the Mountbattens physically it brought them closer together than they had been since the first days of their marriage. Gone were the tensions and mutual irritations, for they were both so dedicated, and each was filled with admiration for the splendid job being done by the other. They valued every moment they had together and would go to any length to help each other in their work.

They crossed the Atlantic in one of the slow but comfortable Pan American flying boats, which had begun the first passenger service to England in 1939. On the plane Edwina, who was much more frightened of strange audiences than bombs, said, "Dickie, will you read the speech I've written out and see if you think it's all right?"

Mountbatten carefully read through the rather stilted phrases of the manuscript. When he finished he grinned at her and tore it up. "Just speak from your heart, my dear," he said, "and you'll wow them."

They had a week together with the girls at the Vanderbilts in Newport. Beaulieu, the great stone château set among cropped lawns and glorious flowerbeds overlooking the famous Cliff Walk and Sakonnet Bay, was still running full blast, staffed by twenty or thirty servants. To the Mountbattens being there was like going back in time to a lovely long-ago era. Do not suppose that because of their heroic services and passionate commitment they did not revel in all that luxury.

Then they parted, Edwina to go on a speaking tour that took her 28,000 miles in the United States and Canada, and Lord Louis to join his ship. He was very proud as he took over command of the *Illustrious*, and he planned to forge a spirit in her that would make her into an infinitely more powerful *Kelly*. In the event, he spent very little time in the great aircraft carrier.

In the autumn of 1941 the New World was at last, "with all its power and might, stepping forth to the rescue and liberation of the Old." The Lend-Lease Act had placed the full resources of American industry at Britain's disposal. At their dramatic shipboard meeting in August,

1941, Winston Churchill and President Franklin D. Roosevelt had signed the Atlantic Charter, which stated the aims and sealed the alliance between the great English-speaking nations. The United States was at war with Germany in everything but name, and the American President was determined to make it a shooting war just as soon as he could lead the American people the last step of the way.

Lord Louis Mountbatten found the American scene very much to his taste. He had always liked Americans for their enterprise, their free and easy attitude toward rules and regulations, and for their willingness to try anything once. Now he admired the fighting spirit that he saw generating in all her armed services.

When Lord Louis and President Roosevelt met, there flashed between them one of those instantaneous friendships which endure the longer for having happened suddenly. They had much in common. Both loved ships and their respective navies more than anything else in the world. Both were ahead of their time in social planning in human affairs and in military and naval innovations. Both were born fighters. Both were aristocrats, who met at ease on equal ground; and, with their inborn sense of security, they did not give a damn what other people thought about them. It was a friendship that served England well.

Their sudden intimacy produced an invitation to Mountbatten from Admiral Harold H. Stark, Chief of Naval Operations, to fly out to Pearl Harbor. Lord Louis was keen to inspect the big fortress of the Pacific, which was the greatest of all American Naval Bases.

He arrived in Pearl Harbor early in October, 1941. He was shocked by what he saw. To a man who had experienced modern war and knew too well the effectiveness and fury of aerial attack the American defenses seemed pitifully amateurish. Admiral Husband E. Kimmel, who held the unfortunate title of CINCUS (Commander in Chief United States), and his opposite number, Lieutenant General George V. Strong, to whom he was not speaking, complacently showed Lord Louis over the forts and batteries with their great coast defense rifles pointing out to sea, which did indeed make the base impregnable to naval attack. But they also showed him the meager anti-aircraft batteries, the few slow and unreliable P-40 fighter planes, and the half-trained troops who manned the defenses. Looking down from a lush green hill on almost all the mighty capital ships of the United States—aircraft carriers and 16-inch-gun dreadnoughts—moored in pairs in the narrow roadstead, Lord Louis had a horrid picture of what dive bombers could do. "Why even the communication wires of the fighter control system are run above ground!" he exclaimed.

As politely as possible Mountbatten tried to point out some of these deficiencies. Nobody paid him any heed, for American naval officers were just as impregnable to new ideas as those of the Royal Navy had been before the Germans taught them some painful lessons.

On October 10, while Lord Louis was at Pearl Harbor, he received a coded cable from London:

PRIME MINISTER TO LORD LOUIS MOUNTBATTEN:
WE WANT YOU HOME HERE AT ONCE FOR SOMETHING WHICH YOU
WILL FIND OF THE HIGHEST INTEREST.

Churchill also cabled President Roosevelt's alter ego, Harry Hopkins, breaking Mountbatten's date to spend a night at the White House. It was rather a pity. For Roosevelt's mind was wide-open to new suggestions, and had Lord Louis been able to talk to him in confidence things might have been very different two months later at Pearl Harbor.

Mountbatten started home to England in a fury, and went at once to Chequers to see Winston Churchill. The last thing in the world he wanted to do was to give up *Illustrious* which he dreamed of making a super-*Kelly*. Smiling like a paternal kewpie the Prime Minister told him of his new appointment. He was to head Combined Operations, the organization which was directing the commando raids on France, and creating the apparatus—the landing craft, amphibious tanks, and all the other special equipment—as well as training the men of the three services in the co-ordinated maneuvers necessary for the invasion of Fortress Europe.

Mountbatten laid his ears back. "I'd rather go back to *Illustrious*," he said stubbornly.

Churchill growled, "Have you no sense of history? You fool! What will you do if you turn your back on this great enterprise? Go back to sea and repeat your last achievement, and get yourself sunk in a bigger ship."

Then with all the eloquence at his command the Prime Minister outlined his vision of what Combined Operations should do. That night England was only a hand-span above her lowest ebb, but Churchill told Mountbatten, "Your primary object will be the invasion of Europe for unless we return to the Continent and beat the Germans on land we shall never win the war.

"All the other headquarters in this country are thinking defensively. Your job is to be offensive; train for the offensive; work out the craft, the equipment, the tactics, the administration and everything needed to sustain the offensive. . . . The south of England is now a bastion against invasion; you will turn it into a springboard from which to launch *our invasion!*"

Mountbatten recorded that he was amazed at this wonderful fighting spirit. In that dark hour hardly another man in England thought of anything but hanging on. Lord Louis later said, "I knew at once that he was right. I left the room inspired. I stopped grumbling."

Within an hour he was at work beginning to plan the invasion of Europe.

Admiral of the Fleet Sir Roger Keyes, the intrepid, imaginative sailor who had been the instigator of the successful sortie into Heligoland Bight in World War One and the hero of the Dardanelles and of the great raid on Zeebrugge, had gotten Combined Operations off to a good start. But the British Chiefs of Staff had thwarted him at every point. At seventy years of age, Admiral Keyes had lost none of his dash, but a good deal of his flexibility. An Admiral of the Fleet, he did not relish being snubbed by men who were his juniors in age and rank. He had resigned in a huff, and Churchill had let him go, feeling that a younger man might be able to work things out better.

Concerning his appointment of Mountbatten to this vitally important job Churchill wrote: "Lord Louis Mountbatten was only a captain in the Royal Navy, but his exploits and abilities seemed to me to fit him in a high degree for the vacant post."

There was a good deal more to it than that. What Churchill wanted as head of his pet project was a young man with no preconceptions, a man of imagination who would avidly embrace new ideas of tactics and new inventions, instead of automatically rejecting them. He wanted a man of reckless daring, for only such a man could even contemplate a direct attack on Hitler's frowning beaches. Above all he wanted a friend who would confide in him, and whom in turn he could influence toward unorthodox measures.

Because of Lord Louis' royal connections and supreme self-confidence, some called it arrogance, Churchill correctly judged that he would not be daunted by official cold shoulders; nor would he have too much respect for the sacred channels of command. And because of his charm he might be able to get away with it. In fact Mountbatten's mission was an end run around the Chiefs of Staff Committee.

He was promoted to acting commodore, and given the official title of Adviser, Combined Operation. This was downgrading the post in deference to the Chiefs of Staff, for Admiral Keyes had been Director of Combined Operations. Mountbatten was to sit in on Chiefs of Staff meetings when anything to do with Combined Operations was discussed. He threw himself into his new work with typical abandon, and pretty soon it became the be-all of his life. He had three main objectives, the first, to get along with the Chiefs of Staff in order to wheedle them into giving him as much support as possible. With the Mountbatten charm turned up high and that pleasantly self-deprecating manner of putting forth suggestions, which he could assume so gracefully when it forwarded his purpose, he was highly successful. Of course, if he met unreasonable opposition, such as the refusal of an Army general to attach an engineering section to Combined Operations on "administrative grounds," he swung the bludgeon of his influence with the Prime Minister with a mighty *whoosh*. But this was rare.

His second intention was to make sure that no scientist or inventor who had anything good to offer was turned down, and that every possible proposal was given a chance. In this he exceeded the bounds of reason and sponsored a lot of absolutely crackpot schemes. On the other hand, he backed some extremely valuable additions to the arsenal of modern war, including the amphibious tank and the "Mulberry" floating harbors used on the Normandy beaches. His own fertile brain created a number of useful devices, including the flexible pipe line "Pluto," used to pump oil under the Channel from England to the Continent, and the command ship. This was a floating headquarters for amphibious operations, equipped with every possible means of communication, from which a commander in chief could keep in touch with his forces on sea, land, and in the air. It was used by both the British and Americans in all the major assault landings from Sicily to the islands of the Pacific.*

Finally, and most important of all, Mountbatten was determined to make Combined Operations a truly integrated body. Sailors, soldiers, and airmen were to submerge their loyalties to their individual services and work together in single-minded devotion to the team. When America came into the war, U.S. Army Chief of Staff General George C. Marshall went to England and inspected Combined Operations. He was impressed by the extraordinary degree of integration of the three services. "How do you do it?" he asked.

Mountbatten did not want to describe the terrible time he had had getting the services to work together so he remarked, "Well, after all, they all speak the same language." Then with that charming eye-wrinkling smile he added, "And come to think of it, you speak English, too, of a sort. Why don't you send me a few American officers?"

---

* Captain Roskill says, "If Mountbatten had twenty-five ideas, five were completely crazy; you could throw fifteen away, but five were really useful."

This was done, and gradually even national loyalties were sub-ordinated to the team spirit. Combined Operations thus became the prototype of such great Allied headquarters as Eisenhower's SHAEF and Mountbatten's own Southeast Asia Command.

Mountbatten made many other innovations in his headquarters, in-cluding bringing in scientists to form a research department, much against the wishes of his naval officers, who called them "absent-minded professors" and "mad Moriaritys." Another thing they disliked was the informality he fathered, such as the combined mess for men and women. Already the old admirals had their knives out for him; but the morale of his headquarters soared.*

However brilliantly he succeeded Lord Louis had a very serious fault as an executive—an obsessive passion for detail. He would drive his people crazy by insisting on personally directing the minutest details of the work. In London he practically redesigned his headquarters in Buccleuch House on Richmond Terrace himself, going so far as to choose the color of paint for the offices. Later, in Southeast Asia, he insisted on personally redesigning the uniforms worn by the WRENS. He had to run the whole show and wasted a lot of his own—and other people's—valuable time. To counterbalance this he could, and did, make lightning-fast decisions, not only in minor events, but on great and perilous occasions when the lives of thousands of men and victory or defeat hung in the balance.

Now that he was permanently stationed in England Lord Louis' intimacy with Winston Churchill deepened. He was often summoned to Number 10 Downing Street and was frequently invited for weekends at Chequers. Through those long Saturday nights the Prime Minister drank his ten or twelve highballs, while his mind roved familiarly through all the far-flung intricacies of global warfare, drawing on his vast knowledge of history and his vivid imagination to forecast the future from the lessons of the past. Lord Louis profited enormously—as what intelligent person would not?—storing up knowledge and *élan vital* to serve him in the future.

He also had the opportunity to expound his own iconoclastic views and promote his pet projects. Time and again General Sir Alan Brooke (later Field Marshal Lord Alanbrooke), who became Chief of the Im-perial General Staff in November, 1941, wrote in his diary, "Dickie is spending the night at Chequers. What will they come up with now?"

The nervousness of the Chiefs of Staff was well grounded. Ray Murphy contends that Mountbatten always scrupulously got instruc-

---

* Lord Louis called Combined Ops: "The only lunatic asylum in the world that is run by its inmates."

tions from the C.O.S. before going to Chequers. No doubt this is true when official matters were discussed. But what those two wide-ranging minds dreamed up in their after-dinner sessions might be considered nightmares by an orthodox military man.

The Chiefs were, in fact, very orthodox. General Sir Alan Brooke, with his stocky figure, his stolid face, grizzled mustache, and spectacles, looked like a small-town banker. He was a fine military technician and a fearless soldier; but, like most of England's professional generals who had served in the 1914–18 war, he was reduced to a defensive mentality by the remembrance of that ghastly slaughter and of the desperate days of 1940 in France. Dulled by defeat, he was always preaching caution.

The First Sea Lord, Admiral of the Fleet Sir Dudley Pound, was silvery-old and failing fast. He regarded the C.O.S. meetings as rest periods and slept through most of them. If anyone mentioned the Navy he woke up and said, "No!" Then he went back to sleep again. Air Chief Marshal Sir Charles Portal was, in Sir Frederick Morgan's words, "The king pin of the C.O.S., the brightest of the lot." Being an airman he was decidedly more adventurous than the others, but he was far from having the wild-blue-yonder spirit.

The other member of the Chiefs of Staff Committee was the Prime Minister's Special Representative and Military Adviser, General Sir Hastings Ismay. "Pug" Ismay was beloved and respected in all the British Services, and by the Americans, too. He had a merry round face and merry round eyes, and the expression of an alert, amiable terrier. He also had a remarkably clear, unprejudiced mind and an understanding of the political as well as the military implications of global strategy. As he said himself, "For all those years I was in the center of the web."

He regarded himself merely as Churchill's agent on the C.O.S., and generally confined himself to expressing the Prime Minister's views, often toning them down in the interests of peaceful coexistence between Churchill and his generals. He was, in fact, the great mediator. It was not an easy job.

To get a little ahead of chronology, on March 9, 1942, Churchill decided to buck up the C.O.S. He gave Brooke more authority by making him chairman, and added Mountbatten as a permanent member— and spark plug. At the same time Lord Louis was given new authority as *Chief* of Combined Operations and promoted to acting vice-admiral. In a simultaneous recognition of the interservice nature of his command he was also made lieutenant general and air marshal, the first man ever to hold "triphibious" rank.

It is generally agreed, even among his least ardent admirers, that Mountbatten was an excellent addition to the C.O.S. Sir Frederick Morgan says, "He was not dulled by defeat. He was more like an American. I believe he was the only man on the C.O.S. who really believed that we would be able to invade Hitler's Europe."

Though Sir Alan Brooke thought Mountbatten's presence at C.O.S. "rather a waste of time," he welcomed him with warm courtesy and paid tribute to his achievements at Combined Operations: "He played a remarkable part as the driving force and mainspring of this organization."

Lord Louis himself said, "If I had not been a member of the Chiefs of Staff Committee it would have been impossible to have staged "Overlord" [the invasion of France] as soon as it was, for it was my membership which made it possible for me to get the landing ships and landing craft built, the military camps and airfields built for combined training centers, and my techniques accepted by the three services."

There is no false modesty in that statement, but it is undoubtedly true.

On December 7, 1941, British morale got a tremendous shot in the arm, delivered by the Japanese bombers that blasted the American Fleet at Pearl Harbor and brought the United States into the war. Not that the English were pleased by the destruction of American ships; but before Pearl Harbor, they had only tried to believe England would win the war; now they *knew* she would. When he heard the news Winston Churchill danced around Harry Hopkin's bed at Chequers at three o'clock in the morning. Mountbatten was equally elated. He had tremendous confidence in the Americans, and now they were completely committed as England's allies. He may also have derived intellectual, though not any emotional, satisfaction from seeing his assessment of the Pearl Harbor defenses totally verified.

He was less joyful two days later when news came that one of the newest and finest British dreadnoughts, the *Prince of Wales,* together with the battle cruiser *Repulse,* had been sunk off the Malay Peninsula by a couple of squadrons of Japanese planes. Admiral Tom Phillips, who had gone down with his ship, had been a violent opponent of the Oerlikon-Gazda guns and had replaced them with pom-poms in his command. Lord Louis sorrowfully relived the memory of that last happy cruise with his father in *Repulse.*

Now that America was with England everything was suddenly possible. Both Churchill and Mountbatten saw that what had been scarcely more than a daydream of invading Europe was now completely realistic, though it took another two years to convince the other Chiefs of Staff.

Sir Frederick Morgan said, "Though I was in charge of planning the invasion, I never really believed it would come off until I went to Washington and saw the tremendous surge of American power and the confident thinking of the American officers of all ranks."

Things began humming at Combined Operations. Suddenly Lord Louis had much less trouble getting what he needed. There were now several big training centers, one at Achnakerry on the Scottish coast; one at Westward Ho in Devonshire, where they cooked up the scheme to overcome German underwater obstacles on the beaches. Another was in East Anglia where he had the trick tanks—amphibious, flame-throwing, and those equipped with flails. There was still another center for naval units whose headquarters was the Royal Yacht Squadron's Clubhouse at Cowes. How it must have amused Lord Louis to be received there with full naval honors!

Inevitably, he had a perfectly wonderful time. He was never so happy as when going flat out. Here he was running a completely freewheeling show, surrounded by the hell-for-leather types he chose himself and got on with splendidly. An American attached to Combined Operations, Jock Lawrence, said, "He made his men feel they were an elite. He always picked top dogs, particularly people of his own class. His Commandos had tremendous *esprit de corps*. No one was ever punished in Combined Ops. If they misbehaved they were just posted 'Return to Unit.' Tough men would burst into tears when they were posted."

Mountbatten knew how to handle his Americans, too. Lawrence describes one occasion when the King was coming to inspect the headquarters. Lord Louis gave his unruly crew a little talk on royal etiquette. "Stand at attention," he said. "If the King speaks to you, bow your head while listening." Then he grinned and said, "I know you Americans don't like to bow your heads to kings but bow them to my cousin."

Lawrence added, "Dickie acted the democrat, but he was always royal underneath. It was an act. Wherever he commanded there was always an Alligator Club. This was made up of his own sort of people. When they dined together, no matter where, they always had the finest wine, finest food, finest service. Aristocratic people. Snobbery of all snobberies!" (One wonders if Ian Fleming was a member.)

Naturally Lord Louis had a wonderful time trying out all the weird vehicles invented for Combined Operations. General Morgan describes a hair-raising ride at Achnakerry in a new American amphibious DUKW: "With Mountbatten at the wheel we went in and out of bunkers on the golf course, and then down to the beach. We tore over the shingle and smashed into the sea at full speed, shifting to propeller as we banged into the waves."

As the Americans began to arrive in London, Lord Louis took them on. General Alan Brooke describes a sherry party given for General Marshall, at which the King was present. Mountbatten buttonholed the American general and got him enthused by his plans and techniques for assault landings. "You've got the right idea," Marshall said.

Quick to take advantage of the moment Lord Louis said, "Then cable tonight and double the order of landing craft we've ordered."

Marshall grinned. "Anything else?"

"Yes," said Mountbatten. "We need a landing ship capable of carrying two hundred or more troops and tanks across the ocean and landing them on a beach."

"Is there any such ship?" Marshall asked.

"No." Mountbatten said, "but this is what it should be like." On a piece of paper he made a rough sketch of what became the Landing Ship Tank. "Order 150 for us and 150 for you as a starter," he said.

Mountbatten received a tremendous compliment from another American who came over that April. General of the Army Dwight D. Eisenhower described it to the author: "I met Mountbatten on the first trip I made to England, before I was appointed to command there.* At the first C.O.S. meeting we were talking about a possible landing in France. I said, 'The big thing about a combined operation of that sort is to have a single commander. If we do this soon the British forces will be much greater than ours so it would be reasonable to have a British general in command.'

"They looked quite astonished. Then they said, 'Can you name one?'

"That stopped me. I said, 'Of course I'm not very familiar with your generals, but I've heard a lot about a man called Mountbatten. He knows a bit about this, I hear, and seems to be gallant. I know he's Navy but that doesn't matter. I'd be willing to serve under him.'

"Alan Brooke at the head of the table smiled and pointed to an admiral sitting across from me, saying, 'I'd like you to meet Lord Louis Mountbatten.'

"I said, 'How do you do? I still stick to my story.' "

Although the American generals had plans for landing in France in 1942, they were totally unrealistic. There was simply not enough of

---

* This was in April, 1942.

anything—troops, guns, tanks, and especially landing craft—to make it possible to take and hold even a limited beachhead in France. But under very strong pressure from Russia to open a second front, the Americans were insistent.

So Churchill and the Chiefs of Staff decided to send Mountbatten over to explain the facts to President Roosevelt and the American Joint Chiefs of Staff. The idea appears to have been, "They won't believe us, but if Dickie tells them it won't work, they'll believe him."

Mountbatten, using all his charm and bolstered by his daredevil reputation made a considerable dent in the Americans' overconfidence, though he did not convince them entirely. It was the first of many similar errands he was ordered to undertake.

He came home to command Combined Operations' greatest disaster.

Chapter 10

JUBILEE?

F<small>AILING TO ATTEMPT THE IMPOSSIBLE SECOND FRONT</small> Churchill and the
C.O.S. decided to appease Russia by a dramatic gesture. This was the
political thinking behind the bloody raid on Dieppe. The military
justification was the necessity of practicing the new techniques of assault
landings—there had been none since Gallipoli in World War One. A further, rather brutal reason was that the Canadian Corps, who had been in
England for about two years with absolutely nothing to do, were getting
unruly. "They need to be bloodied," the British generals said. But they
rather overdid it.

There is no doubt that Mountbatten was somewhat over-optimistic
about the chances of success of assault landings in force on the Continent. As early as March 9, 1942, when the Chiefs of Staff had definitely
told Churchill that an attack on France was impossible that year, Lord
Louis had said, "I and my staff do not agree. We think it possible to
take and hold Cherbourg."

Fortunately the opinion of the other Chiefs prevailed, but it was on
that very night that Churchill promoted Lord Louis to vice-admiral,
and made him a permanent member of the Chiefs of Staff Committee.

Mountbatten's optimism was reinforced further by the brilliant
success of the raid on St. Nazaire in late March, 1942. This daring
operation had been planned by Combined Operations Headquarters
(C.O.H.Q.), directed by Navy Captain John Hughes-Hallett, Major

Jay C. Haydon, and Lord Louis himself. Its purpose was to destroy the large dry dock at St. Nazaire, originally built for the *Normandy*, which was the only one on the French coast large enough to repair the huge new German super-dreadnought *Tirpitz*. By putting it out of commission the *Tirpitz* would be confined to German and Norwegian waters.

So desperate did the enterprise seem that when Mountbatten said good-bye to Navy Captain R. E. D. Ryder, who was to lead it, he said, "I want you to be quite clear, this is not just an ordinary raid. It is an important operation of war. It is also a very hazardous operation. I am quite confident that you will get in and do the job all right. But frankly I don't expect any of you to get out again.

"If we lose you all, you will be about the equivalent of one merchant ship, but your success will save many merchant ships . . . for that reason I don't want you to take anyone who has any serious home ties or worries. No married men. . . . Tell all your men that quite openly, and give every man the opportunity of standing down. No one will think the worse of them." Before Mountbatten spoke to the men he said to Jock Lawrence, "Tell me some dirty stories to tell them. They have to laugh before they die."

The raid on the night of March 27–28 was a smashing success. Ryder led his squadron of three destroyers and a group of motor torpedo boats five miles up the heavily fortified Loire River to St. Nazaire, blew the dry dock to smithereens, wrecked the German installations at the port—and got home safely, with more than half his men.

Other, smaller raids planned by Mountbatten and C.O.H.Q. on Vaagso in Norway and Brunéval on the Channel coast had been equally successful. No wonder he was overconfident. Perhaps he did not realize how great a part luck had played. At Dieppe the luck ran out.

To begin with the plan proposed by Mountbatten for Rutter (the code name) was frustrated by the Chiefs of the three services. It was to land 1,000 commandos and 5,000 Canadian troops with tanks under cover of heavy naval and air bombardment on either side of Dieppe and close in from the flanks. Paratroopers were to take other objectives. The troops were to stay ashore for about fifteen hours and then withdraw. Everything was changed. Sir Alan Brooke gave Lieutenant General Bernard L. Montgomery overall command of the troops, with Canadian Major General John Hamilton Roberts as field commander. Monty refused to accept the flank attack and insisted on a frontal assault from the harbor. When Mountbatten demanded a battleship to bombard the German defenses, old Sir Dudley Pound nearly had a stroke at the thought of risking one of his precious capital ships in the Channel. He gave Lord Louis eight small destroyers and a few gunboats. The Royal

Air Force, backed by the Government, refused to sanction the bombing attack because of the danger of killing Belgian and French civilians. This refusal came about at a conference presided over by Montgomery, while Lord Louis was in America. Mountbatten, perhaps foolishly, accepted these limitations. The final planning was done by Hughes-Hallet, Montgomery, and Mountbatten.

Vigorous training began on the Isle of Wight in May, while detailed planning went on at C.O.H.Q., with maps and aerial photographs and a mock-up model of Dieppe on which were pinpointed enemy defenses. On June 7 Montgomery ordered a full-scale rehearsal on the beaches at West Bay and Bridport in Dorset, which vaguely resembled the area around Dieppe. It was calamitous. Naval officers commanding the landing craft got lost and landed the troops on the wrong beaches. The tanks were an hour and a half late. Indeed, the whole timetable went to hell, and if there had been any German troops around the entire force would have gone there, too.

When Mountbatten got back from the United States, he said, "This isn't good enough. We'll postpone Rutter until July [from June 14]."

When the order was telephoned to Montgomery, he said, "I'm not surprised. The Admiral may have had three ships sunk under him, but he has some good sense."

The second rehearsal for Rutter was held on June 23–24, with Mountbatten himself watching. It was considerably better than the first, though still far from perfect. Montgomery and Mountbatten decided it would have to do, and ordered the real thing for July 4. On the night of July 3, Mountbatten inspected the troopships lying off Cowes, and raised morale aboard to frantic heights by his electric presence. He returned to H.Q. at the Royal Yacht Squadron to receive a bitter blow. Major General Frederick Browning, commander of the 1st Airborne Division, had received a dubious weather report and refused to go. Lord Louis got on the telephone and raised hell, but it did no good. The operation was postponed. Sadly, the troops disembarked.

Postponed or canceled? That was the question. The next time tides and moon would be favorable was August 19. Since 10,000 men now knew that Dieppe was the objective, security was shot to pieces.

On the night of July 8 a grim Mountbatten met in secrecy with his brilliant young commanders at his elegant headquarters in London. He even ordered the secretary out of the room. They were all furious with "Boy" Browning of the Airborne Division. Hughes-Hallett wanted to ask for an official inquiry and make the reason for postponement public. Mountbatten sensibly overruled him. The final decision was to re-schedule the operation for August, and take a chance on security.

Mountbatten presented this decision to the C.O.S. on July 12. Under heavy pressure from Churchill to do something in Europe to appease the Russians and satisfy the Americans they agreed. Mountbatten, of course, had secured Churchill's support in advance.

The operation was renamed "Jubilee," which became bitterly ironical. Planning began at once. The paratroopers were out; no one wanted them balking again. Fifty U.S. Rangers were added for experience. In order to preserve as much security as possible the Canadians were not to be retrained, and would be given a surprise order to board ship the morning of August 18.

The command set-up was changed. Mountbatten assumed overall responsibility. General Montgomery, who wanted no part of it, was replaced by Canadian Lieutenant General A. G. L. McNaughton, with Major General Roberts still in command of the Canadian troops on the scene. The former Naval commander, Rear Admiral H. T. Baillie-Grohman also wanted out, so Mountbatten gladly replaced him with Hughes-Hallett. Air Vice Marshal Trafford Leigh-Mallory would command the fifty-six squadrons of R.A.F. fighters—more than won the Battle of Britain—who would provide air cover. Though prodigal with fighters Air Marshal Sir Arthur Harris' Bomber Command refused to provide any big bombers, but there were some fighter bombers for close ground support.

At 10 A.M. on August 18 Lord Louis Mountbatten gave the order, "Go!" There was a tremendous confused scramble embarking the troops, but somehow they all got aboard the heterogeneous collection of 237 ships, including everything from destroyers and transports to MTBs and mine sweepers that made up the armada. At 4:30 P.M. there was a great flap. Another bad weather forecast came from the Admiralty with an almost tearful plea to call it off. Mountbatten called a quick conference with Leigh-Mallory, Roberts, Hughes-Hallett, and a few others. He told them the news and put it up to them. They all knew that if Jubilee did not go that night, it never would. Their local weatherman was more optimistic than the Admiralty. All except Roberts were young and daring. Roberts merely said, "If the Navy can get us there we'll fight." They voted, "Go!"

The expedition sailed at 9:30 of a calm and lovely evening. Mountbatten, Leigh-Mallory, Canadian Lieutenant General H. D. G. Crerar, and their personal staffs went to temporary Combined Operations Headquarters at No. 11 Fighter Group Command at Uxbridge, from which they could be in constant touch with the field commanders via the elaborate radio set-up on the headquarters ships, the destroyers *Calpe* and *Fernie*.

The huge convoy converged from various Channel ports and were formed into the proper order without mishap. The mine sweepers swept a clean road for them to Dieppe and marked it with lighted buoys. The weather remained calm and clear. Everything was perfect.

Then, at precisely 3:47 A.M., August 19, the luck broke. A small German convoy running along the coast to Dieppe sighted the left column of the armada. Everybody began shouting and the sound of guns alerted the German troops at Dieppe.

It was too late to stop now; 3 A.M. was the hour of no return. The attack began at 5 A.M.

Back at Uxbridge, as first reports of landings began, Mountbatten was very gay; the end of waiting and beginning of action always made him so. Crerar was also confident. Leigh-Mallory, the only one who had anything constructive to do, was grimly busy, sending off his fighters. Those first fragmentary reports were good. The landings seemed to be going forward as scheduled, and from where Mountbatten sat it looked as though he had again achieved complete tactical surprise and would have a smashing success. Even as late as 7:30 A.M. the messages from the *Calpe* were optimistic.

This was only because things were so bad that Hughes-Hallett and Roberts in the command ship did not know how bad they were; the simple reason being that a great part of the communication equipment with the assault force had been smashed by German fire. The truth was that the Germans, alerted by the sound of the sea fight off Dieppe, were waiting and ready. The Royal Regiment of Canada that was supposed to surprise and take the powerful German battery at Puits on the east headland of the harbor, were slaughtered on the beach. Out of 554 men who went in only 65 came back; of these 33 were wounded.

To the west of Dieppe the commandos did secure their first objective and got quite a way inland. But the untaken battery at Puits enfiladed the main mass of troops landing on the beach in front of Dieppe. They were joined by cannon concealed in caves in the cliffs, about which British intelligence knew nothing, and by direct machine-gun fire for the unexpectedly strong defenses on the waterfront. The carnage on the shingle in front of the sea wall was horrible. Those troops that got ashore were for the most part pinned down in the shelter of the wall and raked by the artillery from caves and headland behind them. Hardly any of them got into the town and not one tank got off the beach.

From 8 A.M. on the reports received at Uxbridge got grimmer and grimmer. Message after message used the word "confusion." Then at 9:30 they got the flash from *Calpe* ordering "Vanquish" (the code word for retreat) at 11 A.M. This was followed by frantic appeals from

Hughes-Hallett and Roberts for more air cover, for bombers, for smoke-laying planes.

Leigh-Mallory met them with everything he had. He was the only commander who could take any satisfaction from that fatal day, for the Royal Air Force held the sky over Dieppe, and prevented the Luftwaffe from making any significant contribution to the battle.

The retreat was even more costly than the attack. Fresh German troops arriving at the scene added their fire power to those already there. Under the hot August sun landing craft overloaded with troops that piled aboard any old way were sitting ducks for German gunners. Communications almost totally disintegrated. Only the British gift for improvisation and the desperate valor of soldiers and sailors, like that of the naval division under young Earl Beatty, son of the great World War One admiral, saved the forces from total destruction.

As the story of disaster unfolded at Uxbridge in cryptic messages, mutilated dispatches, and fragments of intercepted radio reports from shore to ship, Mountbatten, for the first time in his life, knew the ultimate bitterness of high command, of watching his forces defeated from a safe place, unable to join them and go down fighting. He bore it very well. Grim and haggard though he looked, he never lost his cool air of command, never said or did a foolish thing. His manner throughout that interminable day and the unhappy night, when shattered remnants of Jubilee were arriving at Portsmouth, was grave but calm. Neither then nor later did he publicly blame anyone or try to evade his responsibility.

Though the full count of casualties were not known for several days, the final score was worse than Lord Louis' gravest fears. The 6,086 soldiers and commandos who were engaged in the actual fighting had 3,623 casualties, or 59.5 per cent—the pre-battle estimate had been 10 to 20 per cent. Worse than that, the 4,965 Canadians engaged had 3,367 casualties, an appalling 68 per cent. Not a single main objective was achieved.

Mountbatten called a conference of the surviving officers at Combined Operations Headquarters for August 20—the day after Dieppe. His force commanders were furious at not having a chance to interview their men first in the traditional order. Leigh-Mallory protested violently. Hughes-Hallett being directly under Mountbatten could do nothing, but he was most unhappy. General Roberts even yet did not know exactly what had happened to the Royal Canadians. Lord Louis paid them no heed; he wanted the truth hot off the griddle.

Never had so strange a company gathered under the Duke of

Buccleuch's crystal chandeliers. Many of the participants came just as they got off the ships, with bloody bandages and tattered clothes, the grime of battle in their skins, the bitterness of defeat in their eyes. Only thirty hours earlier they had been in that crazy hell under the sea wall of Dieppe.

To meet them came the spruce, red-tabbed brass. Though Mountbatten's blue-shadowed eyes showed the fatigue of forty-eight hours without sleep, he was, as always, spectacularly elegant, with all his battle ribbons and gold braid.

As the commanders came in Lieutenant General McNaughton started to take the chair. Lord Louis said firmly, "No, I'll run this meeting." Sulkily, the Canadian stepped down.

As Mountbatten opened the meeting the atmosphere was tension-charged; tempers were high. Leigh-Mallory stood up and forbade the R.A.F. officers present to say anything. Hughes-Hallett then told the naval officers that they could report what they had actually seen but, like witnesses at law, they must not repeat hearsay or express opinions. Lord Louis controlled his feelings, knowing that a spark would fire the emotional powder keg.

Captain Dennis Whitaker of the (Canadian) Cameron Highlanders, who was one of the few who actually penetrated into the town, nearly touched it off. He stood up and said, "I am convinced the Huns knew all our plans. We were betrayed."

Mountbatten curtly cut him down with, "I am convinced there was no breach of security. We'll hear no more of that."*

Then Lieutenant Commander H. W. Goulding, who had landed the Royal Canadians at Puits, said they failed because they were afraid to leave their landing craft. Hughes-Hallett shut him up, and another explosion was narrowly averted.†

Then Mountbatten took command, and set the tone of the dialogue in two sentences. In a strong, confident voice he said, "Gentlemen, the purpose of this meeting is not tears but lessons learned. We have lost nothing if we have learned these lessons; everything if we have not."

After that Mountbatten had full control of the meeting which proceeded in an orderly manner. There, and at subsequent inquiries, the lessons were fully explored and truly learned.

.   .   .

---

* The Canadians always remained convinced that they had been betrayed, but captured German documents prove that they had absolutely no warning of the raid until they heard the firing at sea.

† It was later proved that once the Royal Canadians recovered from the first shock of the terrible barrage that greeted them, they fought with superb courage almost to the last man.

Even today the Battle of Dieppe still rages on the printed page.

Captain Roskill, in *The History of the Royal Navy in World War II*, and Terence Robertson, in *Dieppe: The Shame and the Glory*, both blame Mountbatten. Lieutenant General Sir Frederick Morgan said categorically, "It certainly was not the fault of Mountbatten's planning." Winston Churchill and Sir Alan Brooke both absolve him, as do many others.

Though Mountbatten as the commander must take his share of the blame, there are many things in his favor. The original plan of Combined Operations for a flank attack on Dieppe was the right one. This is confirmed by the highest authority. The German commander in chief, Field Marshal von Rundstedt, wrote that had the British attacked on the flanks and with paratroops they might have taken Dieppe. It was General Montgomery who insisted on the frontal assault, but after he left Jubilee Mountbatten did not try to change it, probably because there was not time.

The first question then is: In view of the fact that his plan was mutilated, and the forces given him were inadequate, should Mountbatten have called the whole thing off?

It would appear not. He had been chosen for this sort of thing by Churchill because he was both persistent and daring. Because of the political pressures of Russia and the Americans something had to be done. With the information he had, it looked like at least a fifty-fifty chance of success. There was no way of learning the terrible lessons except by trying.

The second question is: Given the resources at hand could the planning have been better? The answer to that is, of course it could— in the light of hindsight. But again hindsight has the advantage of those lessons.*

Finally, the 4,500-total-casualties question: Was it worth it?

The answer is an unqualified yes.

In the first place the cost in absolute figures was not as terrible as it seems. Three-quarters of the casualties consisted of wounded and prisoners, most of whom eventually came home. This leaves only about 1,200 to 1,300 men killed. General Eisenhower's comment was, "They had mistaken a skirmish for the battle."

The value of the knowledge these lives purchased was incalculable, for never again was an assault landing launched in Europe without battleships or heavy cruisers to provide covering fire—there were six battleships and many cruisers off the beaches on D-Day—and never

---

* However it is generally agreed that the planning was too rigidly detailed and inflexible, probably due to Mountbatten's Germanic thoroughness.

again was one launched without intensive air bombardment. The other changes made because the lessons *were* learned are so numerous as to make up an entire military treatise.

All the leading authorities agree with this answer. Lord Louis Mountbatten said, "For every life lost at Dieppe ten were saved on D-Day."

He is a prejudiced witness. But Sir Frederick Morgan, the chief planner of Overlord—the invasion of France—said, "Without Dieppe Overlord would have been impossible."

The final witness is the cable sent to Mountbatten—then commanding in Southeast Asia on D-Day + 6. It was written by General Marshall, but it is easy to see that he had some editorial assistance from a master of English prose:

TODAY WE VISITED THE BRITISH AND AMERICAN ARMIES ON THE SOIL OF FRANCE. WE SAILED THROUGH VAST FLEETS OF SHIPS WITH LANDING CRAFT OF MANY TYPES POURING MORE MEN, VEHICLES AND STORES ASHORE. WE SAW CLEARLY THE MANEUVER IN PROCESS OF RAPID DEVELOPMENT. WE HAVE SHARED OUR SECRETS IN COMMON AND HELPED EACH OTHER ALL WE COULD. WE WISH TO TELL YOU AT THIS MOMENT IN YOUR ARDUOUS CAMPAIGN THAT WE REALIZE THAT MUCH OF THIS REMARKABLE TECHNIQUE AND THEREFORE THE SUCCESS OF THE VENTURE HAS ITS ORIGIN IN DEVELOPMENTS EFFECTED BY YOU AND YOUR STAFF OF COMBINED OPERATIONS.

ARNOLD,[*] BROOKE, CHURCHILL, KING,[†] MARSHALL, SMUTS.[‡]

---

[*] General H. H. Arnold, USAF
[†] Admiral Ernest J. King, USN
[‡] Field Marshal the Rt. Hon. J. C. Smuts, Prime Minister of South Africa.

Chapter 11

FIVE SHINING STARS

EVEN BEFORE THE DIEPPE RAID—or "Reconnaissance in Force" as Churchill christened it after the event—Lord Louis was deeply involved in the planning for Torch, the operation to take French North Africa by British-American forces under the command of General Eisenhower. It was decided upon at rather rancorous meetings of the Combined British and American Chiefs of Staff together with Churchill and Harry Hopkins (representing Roosevelt) in London on July 20–25, 1942. The Americans were still for Sledgehammer, a proposed attack on the Continent in 1942. When the British rightly refused to try it before 1943, the Americans dubiously settled for Torch.

The plan called for simultaneous landings against the Vichy French at Algiers and Oran on the Mediterranean, and Casablanca on the Atlantic in Morocco. Mountbatten was a key figure in the planning because he was considered the leading expert on how to conduct an assault landing. After Dieppe he was considered the leading expert on how *not* to conduct an assault landing. Thus the lessons of Dieppe proved of value almost immediately.

The landings took place on Sunday, November 8, 1942. Against rather sporadic French resistance they were immensely successful. Within a few days all of North Africa from Tunisia to Casablanca was in Allied hands. Meanwhile General Montgomery's 8th Army scored its great victory at El Alamein and drove Rommel's Afrika Korps out

(276)

of Egypt and westward along the coast. In these happy circumstances it became necessary for the Allies to plan the next moves. The first great summit conference between Roosevelt and Churchill, with their respective staffs, met at Casablanca on January 13, 1943.

Mountbatten, like the other British Chiefs of Staff, was uncertain how he was to get there until he actually took off. At first they were all to go in a cruiser, but the violent activity of U-boats made it too dangerous to risk the best British brains in a ship. Then they were to go in an American flying boat, but the water was too rough to land at Gibraltar. Finally, at 7:30 on the evening of January 12, a motorcade carrying the whole party, including the Prime Minister, rendezvoused in London and dashed through the night to an airport. It was all so secret that even Mountbatten wasn't sure which airport he was at. After a long wait they embarked in converted American Liberator bombers. They were most uncomfortable.

Sir Alan Brooke wrote in his diary: "I slept on the floor of the little cabin at the rear of the plane and had Dickie Mountbatten sleeping next to me. I did not find him a pleasant bedfellow, as every time he turned round he overlay me and I had to use my knees and elbows to establish my rights to my allotted floor space."

They all arrived safely the next afternoon, and were taken from the airport in olive-drab staff cars, their windows crusted with mud so nobody could see who was in them, to Anfa, a suburb of Casablanca.

It was a most pleasant place to hold a summit meeting. On the top of a little circular hill stood a modern hotel from the roof loggia of which there was a superb panoramic view of the glittering white buildings of Casablanca, surrounded by low brown hills; the brilliant blue of the Atlantic, with long, white-crested waves breaking on the beaches where General George S. Patton's Americans had landed; and the harbor with black-gray American battleships and cruisers riding at anchor, and the sunken wreck of the powerful French battle cruiser *Jean Bart,* which had opposed them. Among them Mountbatten picked out the 6,000-ton liner *Bulolo,* his headquarters ship, with a perfect forest of aerials, sieve-like radar receivers, and other communications paraphernalia draped on her masts.

Below the hotel the road spiraled down, lined with luxurious white villas of the rich French colonists, who had been unceremoniously ousted from their homes. Roosevelt was already installed in Villa No. 1 and Churchill in Villa No. 2. The hill was entirely cordoned off by jungles of barbed wire and regiments of American troops with fixed bayonets.

Lord Louis paid a brief visit to Churchill who said, "Randolph is somewhere in Africa with some of your commandos. Please get him here, I'd like to surprise him."

Mountbatten had quite a time finding the Prime Minister's son, who was touring around in a jeep he had bought from the Americans for a bottle of whisky. When he finally arrived, Lord Louis said, "Do you know why I sent for you?"

Young Churchill grinned and answered, "Well, Dickie, my guess is the old man is here."

"You guessed right," said Mountbatten, "but he wants to surprise you. So be surprised!"

"Right, Dickie!"

One evening Lord Louis had a tête-à-tête with the American President, who, delighted by his dash, daring, and gaiety, kept him much longer than he was supposed to. They sat drinking the horribly strong, syrupy old-fashioneds, which Roosevelt proudly mixed himself, while the President plied him with very acute questions about landing techniques. Like Churchill, Roosevelt knew a little about everything and a great deal about seafaring.

Casablanca was, on the whole, an amicable conference. With the first delicious taste of victory on their parched lips they were all in a sunny mood, except the jealous French generals, De Gaulle and Giraud, who stalked each other like fighting cocks. There were, of course, sharp arguments among the Combined Chiefs of Staff about whether to invade Europe in 1943, or postpone it until 1944 in favor of another attack in the Mediterranean. However, the Americans were rather shaken by the slaughter at Dieppe, and so they did not put up much of a fight. Mountbatten's arguments based on first-hand experience helped to convince them that 1943 was too early.

The next argument concerned the Mediterranean landings: Whether they should be made on Sicily or Sardinia. Lord Louis lost this one. Churchill says, "I was myself sure that Sicily should be the next step, and the Combined Chiefs of Staff took the same view. The joint planners, on the other hand, together with Lord Mountbatten, felt that we should attack Sardinia ... because it could be done three months earlier. ... I remained obdurate. ..."

So the invasion of Sicily was decided upon and code-named Husky. Churchill, who had just coined the phrase, "the soft underbelly of Europe," wanted to call it Belly, but he was overruled.

In return for American agreement on Husky, the British solemnly promised that they would make no objection to the invasion of France early in 1944. That operation was named Overlord.

.   .   .

With two invasions to plan for—Husky and Overlord—Combined Operations became more frantically busy than ever. Though the British and Americans had not yet agreed on a Supreme Commander for Overlord they realized that detailed planning must begin. To carry it forward Churchill appointed Lieutenant General Frederick E. Morgan Chief of Staff to the Supreme Allied Commander (who did not exist). General Morgan's outfit was called COSSAC; the Americans nicknamed him Lord Overlord.

Mountbatten and Morgan were soon working hand in glove. Freddie Morgan was one veteran of World War One who had not lost his fighting edge. He was both erudite and gay, with an open mind and a combative spirit combined with a friendly nature and—most wonderful!—a great sense of humor. Lord Louis liked him immensely, and he warmly reciprocated. Together they conspired to undermine the resistance of the regular Chiefs of Staff to new things.

General Morgan said, "Winston co-opting Dickie into the Chiefs of Staff was very clever. He sat there at all meetings and he got things done. He had a nautical sense of humor and enjoyed a good giggle but he wasted no time. He was flat-out all the time.

"He used to work with me on all sorts of things at Storey's Gate*— new inventions and schemes, unorthodox things. Dickie was always bringing in various acts that were coming on, because we discussed many things, and each thing we discussed had its own experts. For instance I would be waiting to talk about Overlord in the little anteroom outside the offices where the Chiefs of Staff met. Dickie would bustle in and out with his experts. As he went by me he might say, 'You want to watch out for them today, they're in a bad mood!'

"Dickie and I sometimes rehearsed conversations we were about to have with Brookie [Sir Alan Brooke]. Dickie would say, 'Now I'm going to say this, and I know Brookie's going to answer that, objecting to it. Then you come in with so and so.'

"He had them pegged. It often worked out just the way we planned it. I have always felt that there were hundreds of useful things that would not have been invented or used if he hadn't been there. And he attracted wonderful people—he attracted the venturesome."

One of those "useful things" was code-named Mulberry. When Dieppe proved that it was insanity to attack a defended city from the sea, the planners realized that the landings must be made on open beaches. That meant the enormous supplies required by a modern army —six hundred tons a day for each division—must also be brought in over

---

* The rambling, ancient building of the Ministry of Defence.

the beaches. To do that, piers to land them on and protection for the shipping were needed.

In *Crusade in Europe* General Eisenhower wrote, "The first time I heard this idea [constructing artificial harbors] tentatively advanced was by Admiral Mountbatten in the spring of 1942. At a conference attended by a number of the service chiefs he remarked, 'If ports are not available we may have to construct them in pieces and tow them in.' Hoots and jeers greeted his suggestion, but two years later it was to become reality."

The Mulberries were actually the brain child of Hughes-Hallett, and were brought to fruition by Mountbatten. They were a complete harbor based on a series of big, box-like concrete "ships," which were towed to Normandy and sunk end to end, forming breakwaters which sheltered the cargo ships. Cargo was brought ashore using piers on pontoons that floated up and down with the tides.

Since Husky was ordered for July 10, 1943, nearly a year before Overlord, planning for that was even more pressing. On this Mountbatten worked closely with the American and British planners and with his old polo-playing friend Captain Lambe, now Director of Planning for the Admiralty. He also went to Africa to consult with Eisenhower and General Sir Harold R. Alexander, who was to be the ground commander, as well as the two army commanders, Montgomery and the American General Patton. There was one bad flap when Lord Louis was told that the Sicilian beaches shelved so gradually that his new LSTs (Landing Ships Tank) could not get near enough to land tanks.

Captain T. A. Hussey of C.O.H.Q. said doubtfully, "I hear the Americans have a thing called 'naval landing pontoons,' a sort of floating causeway that might work."

"Get over there on the first plane," Lord Louis said. "If they're any good send some over in time for Husky." This was done.

Meanwhile Churchill sent Mountbatten on a flying trip to Washington, to use his charming persuasiveness to soften up Roosevelt and the American Chiefs on his strategy of exploiting Allied successes in the Mediterranean rather than Overlord. He was not very successful.

By May 13, 1943, all the Axis troops left in Africa—240,000—had surrendered; and on July 10, the American 7th Army under Patton and the British 8th Army under Montgomery landed in Sicily. German and Italian resistance was far stiffer than that of the Vichy French in Africa, but after some pretty breathless moments beachheads were secured. Mountbatten was there to see how it all worked and on D + 1 he went ashore with Montgomery. It was a tremendous thrill to watch the techniques he had worked on so long meet the test of battle. It was good to hear the sound of guns again.

In thirty-eight days the Germans were cleared out of Sicily, and the Italian Government sued for peace. With their best bases gone the Luftwaffe no longer could interfere with the vital shipping lanes. Once again the Mediterranean became a British lake.

Victory in the Mediterranean required a new assessment of Allied strategy. Though the matter of an invasion of France in 1944 had supposedly been settled at Casablanca the British C.O.S. opposed it. Instead they wanted to exploit the Mediterranean victories and reduce Germany by aerial bombardment and encirclement, avoiding great land battles. Sir Alan Brooke was the leading proponent of this strategy. General Eisenhower wrote, "Brooke told me [privately] that he would be glad to reconsider the cross-Channel project, even to the extent of eliminating that bold concept. . . . Any suggestion . . . of abandoning Overlord could always be guaranteed to bring Marshall charging into the breach. . . ."

The truth is that Brooke had nightmares of an infinitely ghastlier Dieppe, and partly sold Churchill, who talked about "The Channel clogged by the corpses of our Allies." This and other fundamental disagreements required another full-scale conference. Roosevelt and Churchill decided to hold it at Quebec, beginning on August 14, 1943.

On the night of August 4 Mountbatten boarded a special train for Waverly on the Clyde. There were over two hundred people in the British delegation, including all the Chiefs of Staff, their staffs and planners, intelligence, transportation, scientists, and eccentrics. In the morning a small steamer took them out to the *Queen Mary*, towering up in her black-gray war paint and filled with five thousand German prisoners, a large contingent of refugees, and a host of bedbugs and lice left aboard by the troops she had carried to England. The entire main deck had been closed off and refurbished for the Prime Minister's party. Churchill soon arrived with his wife and daughter Mary, Averell Harriman and his daughter, and an extraordinary, mad military genius in dirty battle dress, who was introduced as Brigadier Orde Wingate. The military-politico Noah's Ark sailed immediately.

Lord Louis had a good time on the voyage over. To be on a ship again, even an overgrown transatlantic ferry, was joy enough; but in addition he was exploiting two of his maddest schemes. One consisted of a breakwater for the Overlord beaches, consisting of huge bags of air and cement to be anchored off them. He got Churchill and all the Chiefs crowded into a bathroom to demonstrate a small model. Dudley Pound and Portal made waves, while Brooke held the bag and Mountbatten discoursed on its efficiency. They had more fun than boys with a toy submarine.

The second scheme was Mountbatten's most fantastic. It was to make an unsinkable aircraft carrier or landing field out of ice—2,000,000 tons of it—propelled by motors, and carrying planes, hangars, repair shops, and a freezing plant. He and Churchill had dreamed up the idea during one of those brilliant, liquefied evenings at Chequers, and Mountbatten had brought along Professor G. Pyke, who had invented a nonshatterable ice called Pykrete, a mixture of water, sawdust, and other ingredients. Churchill named the project Habakkuk, after the Biblical prophet who said, "Behold . . . and wonder marvelously: for I will work a work in your days which you will not believe, though it be told you." This exactly described the reactions of the C.O.S.

There was, of course, a lot of planning work to get ready for the all-out push to counter the Americans' "risky" strategic ideas, and also to co-ordinate strategy in Southeast Asia. Though victorious in the Mediterranean and moving forward in the Pacific the Allies were in a terrible mess in Burma. The Japanese had taken all of Southeast Asia, right up to the India-Burma border, and were threatening an invasion of India itself. They controlled most of the Indian Ocean. Churchill was highly dissatisfied with the performance of his generals there, the former Commander in Chief India, Sir Archibald P. Wavell, whom he had kicked upstairs to Viceroy to get him out of the way, and his successor Sir Claude Auchinleck. He was considering setting up a separate Allied Southeast Asia Command and making Mountbatten Supreme Allied Commander. Lord Louis knew about the proposed command, but not that he was being considered for it. Churchill casually broached the idea to Sir Alan Brooke on the way over. Brooke wrote: "This was the first time I had heard of Mountbatten's suggested appointment. . . . He had never commanded more than destroyers. . . . What he lacked in experience he made up in self-confidence. He had boundless energy and drive. . . ." In his private diary Brooke wrote: "He will require a very efficient Chief of Staff to pull him through."

Standing on the bridge of the *Queen Mary*, with the Churchill family and the other Chiefs of Staff, Lord Louis watched her maneuver into Halifax Harbor; having been built to the scale of New York Harbor the liner seemed gigantic in any other port. Then they all took a beautifully appointed train to Quebec, where they arrived on August 10. The luxurious Château Frontenac Hotel had been taken over in its entirety for the Combined Chiefs and their staffs. Churchill and Roosevelt were to stay in the ancient Citadel on the Plains of Abraham, the upper floor of which had been prepared for the President, with ramps laid over all steps to accommodate his wheel chair.

The next day Churchill left to spend the weekend alone with President Roosevelt at Hyde Park. Both the British and American Chiefs regarded the confabulations between those two venturesome gentlemen with even greater horror than Dickie's visits to Chequers.

At Hyde Park Churchill made a deal with Roosevelt that changed Mountbatten's whole life. It had been understood that a British general would command Overlord, and Churchill privately had offered the post to Sir Alan Brooke. But he may have realized that it would be inviting failure to give command of that great enterprise to a man who only half believed in it. In any event at Hyde Park he offered to let an American command Overlord and asked in exchange that Alexander be made Supreme Commander in the Mediterranean and Mountbatten Supreme Allied Commander in the new Southeast Asia Command. Roosevelt accepted fast. He liked Mountbatten better than any of the British Chiefs.

So Churchill came back to Quebec and summoned Brooke to the Citadel to hear that he was not to command Overlord. Poor Brooke was stunned. He wrote: "We walked up and down the terrace outside the drawing room of the Citadel, looking down on to that wonderful view of the St. Lawrence River and the fateful scene of Wolfe's battle for the Heights of Quebec. As Winston spoke all that scenery was swamped by a dark cloud of despair. . . ."

Then Churchill summoned Mountbatten to a happier meeting. Lord Louis still had not the faintest inkling of what was afoot. He went into the room where the Prime Minister sat at a huge desk covered with a mass of telegrams about the India-Burma Theater. Genially waving Lord Louis to a seat Churchill said, "Do you think you can straighten this thing out?"

"I'd be glad to help you sort them," Lord Louis answered.

With a great *umph* of amusement, Churchill said, "No, Dickie, I don't mean these papers. I mean can you straighten out the mess in Southeast Asia? You're going to be Supreme Commander there."

It took a moment to comprehend. Mountbatten's regular rank was still only captain; he was not yet forty-three years old. Supreme Commander! Yet he says he was disappointed not to receive a fighting command: "I was sucking up to the First Sea Lord like anything."

Then a shrewd second thought suggested the necessity of securing his rear. "Thank you for the honor and your great confidence," he said. "But I will have to get the approval of the Chiefs of Staff before I accept."

"President Roosevelt has already agreed," Churchill said. "In fact he is enthusiastic. But you're quite right. Go talk to the Chiefs and let me know what they say."

Mountbatten saw Portal first. The Air Chief Marshal said, "I had someone else in view, but since I can't have him I'll take you. After all you can't sit around twiddling your thumbs or just have a little aircraft carrier after being Chief of Combined Operations."

Alan Brooke said (no matter what he thought), "It's a maritime thing out there, amphibious stuff. I think you should do it."

Admiral Sir Dudley Pound, true to form, said, "This is the only chance the Navy will have of getting a Supreme Commander. You've got to take it!"

Unlike Casablanca, Quebec was acrimonious. The Americans and British clashed violently on everything from Overlord to Burma. But eventually they reached quasi-agreement, mostly on American terms. They were a tough lot those Americans. Admiral King was a new-fashioned martinet, open-minded to innovations of both matériel and tactics, but determined to run his own show, the Pacific, in his own way. Roosevelt said, "King is so tough he has to shave with a blow-torch." Poor Pound was no match for him.*

Marshall, though a courteous, kindly gentleman, was far more confident and convinced than Alan Brooke. He was bound and determined that nothing, but nothing!, should detract from Overlord. The two "Air boys," Portal and General H. H. (Hap) Arnold were about a stand-off, but had less to say about overall strategy than the heads of the older services.

One thing on which they were all—temporarily—agreed was the necessity of getting North Burma back to protect the air supply line to China over the Hump. Roosevelt wanted to save China. Churchill said, "All right, I've got the chap to do it."

This was Brigadier Orde Wingate. Bearded, disheveled, rumpled, and fiery-eyed, Wingate looked like a revolutionist, which he was at heart. Mountbatten had become enthusiastic about him in the *Queen Mary*. The previous winter Wingate had conducted a very successful

---

* Admiral of the Fleet Sir Dudley Pound collapsed with a stroke shortly after the conference. He had literally worked himself to death.

raid in the Burmese jungle behind the Japanese lines. Now he proposed a much larger raid in division strength.

There was a private meeting in the map room of the Citadel. Wingate eccentrically wore British Navy battle dress; Mountbatten was spotless in whites and his rainbow of ribbons. Churchill was there, and Roosevelt, in a black mohair jacket and white velveteen trousers, was pushed through the door in a wheel chair. Wingate stood in front of a large map of India-Burma and told them what he proposed to do. He won them all by his audacity. Mountbatten proposed that this time they be supplied by air. Wingate said, "If we could only get the wounded out. The last time we had to leave them behind to the Japs."

Mountbatten said, "We'll find a way. Small aircraft can land in jungle clearings."

Lord Louis went to General Arnold and asked for a large mixed air group to operate with Wingate's Chindits, as his guerrilla forces were called. In the general enthusiasm for Wingate, Arnold said, "You've got them. That's a promise." He was the only Chief, British or American, who delivered what he had promised to Mountbatten in Burma.

The acrimony of the Quebec Conference was relieved by one farcically comic scene that occurred on a day of enormous strain. Before the meeting of the Combined British-American Chiefs Mountbatten said to Brooke, "Can I explain Habakkuk to the Americans at the end of the meeting?"

In most un-Brooke-like language the harassed General said, "To hell with Habakkuk! We are about to have a most difficult time with our American friends and won't have time for your ice carriers."

"Well, if there should be time," Lord Louis pleaded.

The meeting was even more violent than Brooke foresaw. The opposing Chiefs began shouting at each other, while their sixty or more experts, banked in chairs behind them in the great ballroom of the hotel, were "a quivering audience with silent, gleaming eyes." Finally Brooke ordered the room cleared. The younger officers left and stood nervously in the corridor, listening to the angry voices that penetrated the heavy doors.

Then there was a long period of rather ominous silence, suddenly broken by a yell of pain. A little later two pistol shots made everyone jump. "My God," said an American, "they're shooting it out!"

Inside the room a compromise agreement at last had been reached. As the meeting was about to break up, Mountbatten, like a small boy begging for a treat, whispered to Brooke, "Habakkuk!"

Smiling, Brooke asked the indulgence of the Americans for an experiment Vice-Admiral Lord Louis Mountbatten wished to show them. Genially they agreed.

Lord Louis shot from the room and returned followed by a string of attendants pushing two rolling tables on each of which was a block of ice about four feet by three. He explained that one was ordinary ice and the other Pykrete, suitable for the construction of an aircraft carrier. Then selecting General Arnold as the strongest man in the room he handed him a small ax and said, "See if you can split the ordinary ice."

Arnold marched up to it and swung, neatly halving the block of ice. "Now try the Pykrete," Lord Louis said.

Obediently Arnold went to the other piece. He raised his arm and brought it down with a mighty blow. The ax rebounded, twisting from the ice; Arnold howled in pain.

While Arnold stood rubbing his injured wrist Mountbatten said, "One more demonstration." He whipped out a .38-caliber service revolver. "Look out for the splinters!" he warned, and shot at the riven piece of ice. It fairly blew up, showering the Chiefs with ice splinters. "There!" said Lord Louis. "That is just what I told you. Now I shall fire at the block on the right to show you the difference."

In Alan Brooke's words: "There certainly was a difference. The bullet rebounded out of the block and buzzed around our legs like an angry bee." Admiral King says it went through his trousers; but, luckily for Anglo-American relations, not through the Admiral. If Mountbatten did not convince anybody, he at least followed the vaudevillian's favorite maxim: "Always leave them laughing."

Though Mountbatten's appointment was not announced immediately, rumors got around. One evening Captain Lambe said to him, "Dickie, are you hiding something? I notice you always used to be against sending any landing craft to the East, but at the last few meetings you have argued for more of them for that new SEAC thing. Does that mean you are it?"

"Maybe," Mountbatten said.

Churchill finally made the public announcement on August 31, before which he cabled the news to the Viceroy of India:

WE HAVE NOW FORMED AND SET UP THE SOUTHEAST ASIA COM-
MAND, SEPARATE FROM THE COMMAND IN INDIA. . . . AFTER A GREAT
DEAL OF CONSIDERATION I DECIDED TO PROPOSE LORD LOUIS MOUNT-
BATTEN . . . FOR THIS VERY IMPORTANT POST. MOUNTBATTEN HAS
UNIQUE QUALIFICATIONS IN THAT HE IS INTIMATELY ACQUAINTED WITH

ALL THREE BRANCHES OF THE SERVICES, AND ALSO WITH AMPHIBIOUS
OPERATIONS. HE HAS SERVED FOR NEARLY A YEAR AND A HALF ON THE
CHIEFS OF STAFF COMMITTEE AND THUS KNOWS THE WHOLE OF OUR
WAR STORY FROM THE CENTER. I REGARD THIS AS OF GREAT IMPOR-
TANCE ON ACCOUNT OF THE EXTREMELY VARIED CHARACTER OF THE
SOUTHEAST ASIA FRONT BY LAND AND SEA. MOUNTBATTEN IS A FINE
ORGANIZER AND A MAN OF GREAT ENERGY AND DARING. HIS APPOINT-
MENT HAS BEEN CORDIALLY WELCOMED BY THE PRESIDENT AND BY
THE AMERICAN CHIEFS OF STAFF, AND WAS HAILED WITH DELIGHT BY
SOONG ON BEHALF OF THE GENERALISSIMO [Chiang Kai-shek]. . . .

So much for Churchill's official reasons, which were valid. There
remained one more; his debt of conscience to Prince Louis of Battenberg was in a measure repaid.

Chapter 12

SEAC

Mountbatten's Southeast Asia Command (SEAC) began under the happiest auspices. General Morgan once said, "Remember Dickie has to be loved. He tries desperately to make people like him. If they don't or won't, he turns on them."

In those first weeks everybody seemed to love Dickie. Sir Alan Brooke gave him General Sir Henry Pownall, who had been Commander in Chief Persia and Iraq, as his Chief of Staff. Lord Louis regarded this as sheer generosity, though it was really to make sure he had a "damn good C. of S. to pull him through."

On August 26 Mountbatten flew to Washington with Orde Wingate, and reported to the American Chiefs of Staff, who received him most cordially. General Marshall made him the fine present of Major General Albert C. Wedemeyer as his Deputy Chief of Staff. Wedemeyer, a thin, tight-lipped man, was a splendid organizer. Though he was one of those unreconstructed Americans who dislike and distrust the British, he liked Mountbatten, whom he had known since 1942 and whom he described as "charming, tactful, a conscious gallant knight in shining armor. . . . Later on I was to come to know and respect Mountbatten as a conscientious, energetic Allied Commander."

To Wingate's complete astonishment General Arnold repeated his promise of an air support group for the Chindit "Long Range Penetration Group." He christened it First Air Commando Group.

The next day, August 27, Mountbatten and Wingate flew back to London where Lord Louis began organizing his personal staff for SEAC at Combined Operations Headquarters in Richmond Terrace.

Meanwhile General Arnold appointed Air Corps Lieutenant Colonel Philip Cochran to head the Air Commandos, with Cochran's great pal Lieutenant Colonel John Allison as his co-commander. After explaining the long range penetration idea, General Arnold said to Cochran, "Your job is to support this man Wingate. Support him in any way you think possible. I'll take your ideas. I'll see that you get everything you want."

The next day Cochran left for England. At C.O.H.Q. Cochran says, "They got my function mixed up and I ended up at a super-secret meeting with Lord Louis at the head of a long table and me on his left. I'd never seen so much brass in my life, and they were talking about things I'd never heard of. They were pretty embarrassed when they found they'd put me in the wrong meeting."

When Cochran and Mountbatten got alone together they hit it off at once. Cochran was the romantic ideal of an American fighter-pilot, short and wiry, with wavy blond hair and bright blue eyes that would laugh at the devil himself. He was already famous in America as the dashing airman Flip Corkan in his friend Milt Caniff's cartoon strip, "Terry and the Pirates." Cochran was immensely taken with Mountbatten: "He was so handsome, and sort of boyish."

Lord Louis liked the American and his ideas so much that he invited him to a dinner party that night at Chester Street. Cochran had seen many things in his young life but nothing like that. Lady Louis in all her regal beauty sat at the head of the table; the new Viceroy of India (now Lord Wavell) was on her right, the Russian Ambassador to Britain, on her left. Cochran was a bit awed but remained unfazed.

Wingate reacted less favorably to Cochran. As he looked at him through piercing eyes the American knew that Wingate thought, "They've sent a boy. This kid can't deliver the goods."

"Mountbatten had none of that feeling," Cochran says. "He took me as the representative of General Arnold who would fulfill everything Arnold had promised him. Wingate didn't think I had rank enough—a typically British attitude. Mountbatten believed in me. I would say that he had a sort of American attitude, an easy way. He didn't like red tape. He was a doer. He *is* a doer."

The next day Mountbatten asked how Cochran had got on with Wingate. "I don't believe he thinks I'm for real," the American answered. "He thinks I can't deliver the goods. But you know my orders, and we'll do everything we can."

Mountbatten grinned. "Don't worry," he said. "I'll tell Orde you're okay."

Then with typical generosity Mountbatten, who was going to the hospital to have an old polo injury to his hand repaired, lent Cochran his car and driver so he could see London in style.

In the event Cochran soon won Wingate over with his brilliant ideas on air support for jungle fighters. The Chindit leader asked him about using gliders for silent landings behind Japanese lines. Cochran knew of a new method of snatching gliders off the ground by low-flying aircraft. That set Wingate aglow—a way to get the wounded out.

From these discussions, on which also shone the light of Mountbatten's imagination, arose the new Wingate concept of establishing "strongholds" in the jungle, supplied by air. It was a happy collaboration.

On October 2, 1943, Admiral Lord Louis Mountbatten left London for his new command. He spent his last night in England drawing a phoenix for the SEAC shoulder flash. The design sent to him had been copied from the jacket of a first edition of *Lady Chatterley's Lover*. Lord Louis said, "It looks to me like Lady Chatterley's plover," and drew his own, which he remarked symbolized "The transition from the futile fumblings of the past into the flaming fantasy of the future."

Mountbatten flew to New Delhi in a C-47 transport named *Marco Polo*. Like the Venetian, he was to see some remarkable things, not the least of which was his own command set-up. The Combined Chiefs had handed their new Supreme Commander an organization that seemed designed to cause maximum trouble with minimum efficiency. A diagram of the chain of command looked like an intricate cat's cradle in which someone had blundered.*

To begin with SEAC included Burma, Malaya, Sumatra, Ceylon, Siam, and French Indochina, but *not* India. So the Delhi headquarters was in the area commanded by Auchinleck. Most unusual! For his Deputy Commander in Chief the compromising Combined Chiefs had given Mountbatten Lieutenant General Joseph W. Stilwell, USA, known throughout America as "Vinegar Joe" because of his acid disposition. He hated all "Limeys." Stilwell theoretically wore at least five gold-laced hats—he actually wore a sort of Rough Rider hat *circa* 1898. He was Generalissimo Chiang Kai-shek's Chief of Staff and he was also Commander in Chief of all United States troops in China. In addition he

---

* Alan Campbell-Johnson says, "Quebec both created and destroyed the command at the same time." In Burma people said that SEAC stood for "Supreme Example of Allied Confusion."

wore the derby hat of Lend-Lease Administrator to China, Burma, and India. Finally, he had field command of the Chinese Army fighting in North Burma. This should have brought him under the command of Mountbatten's Commander of Ground Troops Lieutenant General Sir George Giffard, but it didn't. In fact Stilwell was not inclined to take orders from anybody—not even the American Chiefs of Staff.

Mountbatten's service commanders in chief were General Giffard, Ground, a good man, but old and difficult; Air Chief Marshal Sir Richard Peirse, who had been kicked upstairs, to get him out of the Bomber Command—Colonel Cochran described him as "archaic"; and Admiral Sir James Somerville commanding the British Eastern Fleet, whose area included the Indian Ocean and the east coast of Africa in addition to the SEAC Theater. When he was in the Indian Ocean, he was on his own. When in SEAC he was supposed to be under Mountbatten, but he never admitted it.

Finally there was Orde Wingate, who had his own private army. He also had the right to jump all the traces and communicate directly with Churchill. Gaily Mountbatten charged into this wasp's nest, determined to make everybody love him, but also to run the show.

Orde Wingate met Mountbatten at the airport in New Delhi. Lord Louis took one look at him, haggard, pale and shivering with fever, and sent Matron MacGeary to nurse him through a bout of typhoid. General Stilwell was also in New Delhi. Their first meeting was auspicious. Evidently the Mountbatten charm worked even on the tough little Limey-hater, for Stilwell wrote, "Louis is a good egg . . . full of enthusiasm and also of disgust with inertia and conversation. He and the Auk [Auchinleck] are not hitting it off too well. Louis is hot for the 'one happy family' idea and very cordial and friendly."

The first thing Lord Louis did on arriving at New Delhi was to borrow a palace from the Maharajah of Faridkut to live in. It was an ostentatious pile built in bastard Indian-Palladian style, with marble floors, a forest of potted palms in brass pots, and fourteen tiger skins adorning the dining-room walls. The plumbing, however, was modern, and the palace was very comfortable. SEAC's skeleton staff were housed in one of the palatial, red-sandstone secretariat buildings directly across the broad Processional Way from Auchinleck's Headquarters, India Command. The junior officers lived in quite luxurious tents on the grounds of the Viceroy's House.

Mountbatten stayed long enough to see Wavell installed officially as Viceroy, then took off for Chungking to try to straighten things out between Stilwell and the Generalissimo who were at swords' points.

After the long, dangerous flight over the Hump, with the over-weighted little plane dodging ice-covered Himalayan peaks 20,000 feet high, Mountbatten found a fine stew simmering in Chungking. Generalissimo Chiang Kai-shek, who acted as if he were the lineal descendant of the Manchu emperors, had received permission from Washington to dismiss Stilwell, and was about to do it. When Stilwell met Lord Louis at the airport he refused to have a picture taken with him. "Why?" Mountbatten asked.

"Because it will get you in wrong with the G-mo. He's going to fire me."

"Then we'll certainly have a picture," Lord Louis said.

At Stilwell's house Mountbatten met the famous Soong sisters, Madame H. H. Kung and the brilliant, beautiful, and vixenish Madame Chiang Kai-shek, who was the Empress Theodora of Chiang's Byzantine Empire. She was decidedly bored with her husband's obtuseness and determined to keep Stilwell. This was going to be difficult, because though Vinegar Joe was a fine fighting officer, he was probably the world's worst diplomat—his habit of referring publicly to Chiang as "the Peanut" is enough to prove this. Mountbatten also wanted Stilwell to stay on, and said he would work on the Generalissimo.

Chiang kept Mountbatten waiting for three days before he received him. Very few people in the world would treat Lord Louis that way, but since he was determined to make this thing work, he kept his temper. Finally, on the third day, he went to Chiang's fortress-like stone house on the ridge above the bomb-battered city of Chungking. The tall, bullet-headed Generalissimo received him with minimal courtesy and maximal impassivity. Madame Chiang, vibrating with Chinese charm, translated her husband's greeting into good American English.

Mountbatten went into his act, and laid on a barrage of flattery that would have made a basilisk blush—such things as, "Sir, I have come to see you before even setting up my own staff in Delhi. You have been fighting the Japanese so much longer than we have that I felt I must have your advice at the earliest possible moment. . . . I shall have to rely on your counsel. . . ."

Positively subservient, but it worked. The merest firefly flash of expression came into the Generalissimo's face; here was a man who appreciated his military talents! As Mountbatten continued in this vein the temperature of the conference rose rapidly. During it—and several others—Chiang agreed to keep Stilwell and to place the Chinese troops in Burma under a unified command. In fact he promised nearly everything Mountbatten asked of him. That he did not keep his promises was beside the point. Almost no one kept the promises they made to Mountbatten in Burma.

. . . .

A highly elated Lord Louis flew back to Delhi, and set up a joint planning staff, modeled on Combined Operations, composed of officers of all three services and a rainbow of nationalities. This thoroughly infuriated his commanders in chief who wanted their own staffs to make separate plans. They were also irritated by one of the new Supreme Commander's most constructive moves, the setting up of a medical research staff to study and combat the tropical diseases, which were taking a far greater toll of men than were battle casualties. One supposes they disliked it simply because it was a new idea. It was brilliantly successful and eventually cut losses due to sickness by almost 90 per cent.

But if he annoyed the top echelon, his field commanders greeted Mountbatten's arrival with enthusiasm. Lieutenant General Sir William J. Slim,* an Indian Army officer, who had just taken command of the new Fourteenth Army, first met Mountbatten on the brick-floored airfield at Barrackpore. Slim has said, "When I met him I was terribly pleased because I realized that his manner and appearance would be a tonic for morale. The fact that he was a sailor did not bother me. I was pleased because I hoped we'd have amphibious operations. Of course, he was over-optimistic but that was not his fault. His plan to retake Burma from the south by an amphibious operation instead of slogging down from the north was the right thing."

Mountbatten was indeed over-optimistic. At that first meeting, when Slim asked him where the naval covering force for his amphibious operations was to come from, he said, "We're getting so many ships that the harbors of India and Ceylon won't be big enough to hold them."

Leaving the Joint Staff in Delhi planning busily for a number of operations that never came off, Mountbatten took off for Burma and a flight along seven hundred miles of front, if the clumps of troops in more or less isolated jungle encampments could be called a front.

The Supreme Commander knew that his supreme objective was neither strategy nor tactics, but giving his army back its soul. For these Gurkhas, Indians, South Africans, and splendid old-line British troops had known almost two solid years of defeat. Outnumbered, outgunned, outaeroplaned, and outmaneuvered they had been driven back through seven hundred miles of jungle, fighting bravely against enemies who seemed to burst out of every tangled swamp and mountain. Sick, starving, dying of thirst and fever they had somehow gotten back to that last sheltering ridge of mountains on the Burma-India border to which they

---

* Now Field Marshal the Viscount Slim.

now clung, a mere nail-paring of the empire they had lost. Just surviving intact as an army had been a tremendous triumph of courage and tenacity.

But it was not enough, for never once had these troops defeated the Japanese. They had been beaten in every battle; pursued and harried through jungles and over rivers with never a pause from Rangoon to Mandalay, and then westward across the waves of mountains running north and south along the Burmese peninsula to that last thin edge. They stopped there only because the Japanese had outrun their supplies. No wonder they thought the Japs were supermen, invincible in jungle fighting. It was Mountbatten's ardent intention to show them otherwise.

His method was personal leadership. Wherever a plane could land or a jeep could take him he went. His technique was artful informality. The orders went ahead, "The Supreme Commander is coming and will talk with the troops. No reviews or official inspections. He will talk to the men informally standing on a box. Be sure there is a good strong box accidentally lying around."

Stage-managed? Yes and no. Though the props were pre-arranged the thing itself was real—as real as the captain of the *Kelly* singing the "Beer Barrel Polka" on a raft off Crete. For Mountbatten never condescended to the men he led, never tried to fool them, never was insincere. He meant every word he said.

The jeep, flying his personal flag and standard, pulled into a jungle clearing. Mountbatten jumped out, wearing khaki shorts and a shirt with rolled-up sleeves, on which, however, shimmered his battle ribbons and the shining stars of his rank, and ER and GR—the initials of the Kings he had served as Naval Aide. In the steaming heat he looked crisp and confident. Stepping on that accidentally-on-purpose box he shouted and gestured the troops to come near until tightly packed around him stood a crowd of sweating, half-naked men of all colors, faiths, nationalities— Chinese, Indians, Burmese, Americans, British, Negroes from Africa, Sikhs and Gurkhas from Northern India and Nepal—the entire multi-faith, multicolored, multi-racial collection of men who had in common one loyalty and one leader.

"Men!" he shouted in his rather high thin voice that still carried surprisingly well, "Men! You probably think that Burma is the forgotten front. You're wrong! It's never been heard of!"

What a roar of laughter that crack got! Here was a man who didn't give you the old malarky. This Louis must be a straight shooter.

After that he talked to them knowledgeably about the special problems of their area and the techniques of jungle fighting, not forgetting to run down the Japanese as generally inferior creatures inspired only by a sort of low cunning for this particular primitive type of warfare. "Now you've learned it, you'll beat them at it, because basically you're better men than they are."

After one of these speeches, in which Mountbatten talked of a planned offensive, one fine old British sergeant shouted from the back row, "Don't worry, sir, we're all behind you!"

With his humorous, deprecating grin Lord Louis answered, "Unfortunately, I'll be behind *you*."

The exactly right thing to say; not phony right, but right because he meant it.

Of course Mountbatten could not talk to every man in those scattered forces of hundreds of thousands of men, though he came as near to it as one human being could. But word went out from those who did hear him and the word ran through the armies with an effect like a shot of grog on the crew of a British ship. Their hearts came up out of their boots.

This was testified to by every officer and man to whom this writer, or anyone else, has talked about the Southeast Asia campaign. However much they may dislike Mountbatten and denigrate his strategy, they all admit, "He was a leader of men."

From the inspiring business of being with troops in the field Mountbatten returned to the frustrations of high command. Never in any theater anywhere were they so maddening. For Burma was, in fact, the stepchild of all the theaters—the expendable one, rightly so in the light of global strategy, but that fact made it no easier to bear.

By Churchill's express wish Mountbatten first made plans for Culverin, an amphibious attack on the northern tip of Sumatra. That was canceled within two weeks. He was not too disappointed because he knew all along the British Chiefs of Staff did not like it. Then he planned for an amphibious attack, code-named Buccaneer, on the Andaman Islands in the Bay of Bengal. His heart was really in that one, and by a tremendous effort of all hands he was able to fly to the Cairo Conference on November 21, 1943, with an excellent, carefully detailed plan to lay before the Combined Chiefs.

The capital of Egypt was the scene of another of those glittering summits that settled the fate of the world—not always wisely. Beside President Roosevelt and Churchill and all their people, China had been added in the persons of Chiang Kai-shek, his Madame, and old Vinegar Joe, who wrote, "A brief experience with international politics confirms in me my preference for driving a garbage truck."

Relaxed in the warm Egyptian sunshine and their luxurious white villas the high and mighty approved all Mountbatten's plans, which, beside Buccaneer, included ground advances in Burma co-ordinated with the Chindit operation, and an advance from the north by General Stilwell's Chinese Army in India toward the northern Burmese rail center of Myitkyina; another Chinese Army was to advance eastward from Yunnan Province. The Generalissimo agreed to the latter move only on condition that the amphibious operation went through. President Roosevelt, a China-lover, was eager for anything that would help Chiang. The Combined Chiefs promised Mountbatten almost as many warships, planes, landing craft, and matériel as he asked for.

Then Roosevelt and Churchill, with their gaudy traveling circus, moved on to Teheran for the first great triple summit with Russia's Marshal Josef Stalin. Chiang returned to Chungking and Mountbatten dashed back to Delhi.

On December 7 Mountbatten got the first of a series of shocks that would certainly have destroyed a less exuberant commander in chief. It came in the form of a cable from the Combined Chiefs of Staff to the effect that due to the overriding priority (which Stalin had insisted on) given to the European Theater in general and Overlord in particular, more than half the landing craft in SEAC must be returned to Europe. The promised battle fleet also vanished. Buccaneer was out.

After a brief, despairful period of less than twenty-four hours, Mountbatten reanimated his woebegone planners, and set them to planning the use of his remaining landing craft in an amphibious operation against Arakan on the west coast of Burma—operation Pigstick. He hoped this would satisfy the Generalissimo. But Chiang, raging against the "breach of faith" by Churchill and Roosevelt, canceled the attack from Yunnan. Mountbatten kept on planning for Pigstick anyway.

A month later, on January 7, 1944, Mountbatten took a second blow to his solar plexus. The Chiefs of Staff cabled, ordering him to abandon all amphibious operations in SEAC and to return *all* his remaining landing craft to Europe. Later he was even ordered to send back a lot of the 25-pounder ammunition.

Since the purpose of appointing the former Chief of Combined Operations to Supreme Command in Southeast Asia had been to conduct amphibious operations, this was bitter tea for Lord Louis. Of his treatment at this time Lord Slim said, "The real trouble Dickie had was that none of the plans he made were ever used. He had the rottenest luck of any commander we had. There was no other commander we had in the later stages of the war, who was told to plan relying on certain things, and then had them taken away from him."

With reasonable pride Lord Slim added, "Luckily, Dickie had the old Fourteenth Army which kept going along with its pedestrian plans."

However desperate Mountbatten may have felt he did not allow himself to show it. With inimitable energy he started everyone planning for more limited offensives with the matériel that remained. He also succeeded in straightening out his weird command set-up. He had no use for the committee system of waging war, and intended to be, in fact, the Supreme Commander.

To this end he decided that the 10th United States Army Air Force under Lieutenant General G. E. Stratemeyer must be integrated with the larger British Air Group under the overall command of Air Chief Marshal Peirse. Stilwell howled in anguish, but the Combined Chiefs sustained Mountbatten's right to reorganize his command. It was, in fact, an indispensable move; and co-ordination of air forces was considerably improved. It became even better when Lord Louis finally got rid of Peirse, and replaced him with Air Marshal Sir Guy Garrod.

On the ground there was inevitably a violent clash between Stilwell and the British. To settle it Mountbatten called a conference at Delhi, on January 31, between Giffard, Slim, and Stilwell, at which he presided. According to Slim, Mountbatten opened the conference by "very politely suggesting" that as his own headquarters was not designed for operational control of an army in the field, Stilwell's Chinese Army in North Burma should come under the command of SEAC's ground commander in chief, General Giffard.

Stilwell went through the palatial roof. In the course of the argument that followed he changed hats like a Chinese juggler. First, as the Generalissimo's Commander in Chief, he could take orders directly only from the Supreme Commander. In a twinkling he became an American general, who could not serve under a British commander without permission from General Marshall. "Then the redoubtable old man changed hats again." As Mountbatten's Deputy Supreme Commander it would be ridiculous for him to serve under his own subordinate. He had something there.

The plain truth is that Stilwell hated Giffard's guts and was damned if he would serve under him in any capacity. Slim says, "The more Admiral Mountbatten, showing infinite patience, reasoned with him, the more stubborn the old man became."

It looked like a dead end. Giffard was dignified, but naturally unhappy. The other Americans were terribly embarrassed. Mountbatten, under tight control, was still sweetly reasonable, but beginning to wish he had let Chiang fire Stilwell in the first place. As unexpectedly as sunlight in a hurricane, Vinegar Joe came up with the solution. He would serve technically under Slim but not Giffard.

Since Slim was Giffard's subordinate this was the zaniest arrangement yet—but they all jumped at it. Laughing with relief Mountbatten queried the others with his eyes; then accepted. It actually worked for Slim had a great sense of humor and no false sense of importance. Throughout their association he never sent Stilwell a written order but always went and talked to him privately—"He was perfectly reasonable when you were alone with him." Stilwell was actually fond of Slim, even though he was British. Furthermore, to salve Stilwell's pride about taking orders from a "Limey," and also because the situation was so absurd that it would look silly in print, this quirk in the chain of command was never officially promulgated. It was treated as a gentlemen's agreement, and all parties honored it as such.

However, from that time forward Stilwell became very ambivalent about Mountbatten, calling him "Glamor Boy" one day and the next saying, "Louis and I get on fine even if he has got curly eyelashes." Mountbatten "just laughed at his insults and jollied him along."

One night when Slim was at Stilwell's jungle headquarters Vinegar Joe ranted for two hours against Lord Louis, calling him everything from a "a welcher" to a "treacherous Limey." He ended his harangue by looking over the top of his spectacles and saying, "But I can't help liking the son of a bitch."

The Ground and Air thus being settled, Mountbatten tried to bring in the Sea. He got nowhere. The people who most resented Lord Louis' spectacular rise were senior naval officers. The Army and Air Force people were much more flexible and were accustomed to out-of-seniority promotions; for example General Slim's permanent rank was only colonel when, as acting Lieutenant General, he took command of Fourteenth Army. So they cheerfully accepted Mountbatten at his real worth. But seniority was a naval shibboleth, and woe to him who broke the line! And especially woe to a royal sprig who could be accused of accepting favoritism.

Admiral Somerville was particularly obdurate. He hated Mountbatten's planning staff and would never feel himself bound by any of their plans.* He also hated Mountbatten with jealous intensity. No matter how hard the Supreme Commander tried to win him over he would not give an inch, and even in small things he behaved meanly. He objected to the Supreme Commander issuing communiqués about naval

---

* Somerville even advanced the extraordinary doctrine that a Supreme Commander is *constitutionally* obliged to take the advice of his commanders in chief. He wanted Mountbatten to be a mere royal figurehead.

movements. When Mountbatten went aboard his ship without notifying him Somerville was infuriated.

Lord Louis, not one to turn the other cheek, certainly reacted by fighting Somerville with all his ingenuity and influence. *He* too could be vicious. But in all fairness Somerville seems most at fault. Even Captain Roskill, who tends to blame Mountbatten's "Teutonic dictatorial mentality" for some of the frictions in his command, says, "I must admit that Somerville was petty in his actions toward Mountbatten. He could have made things easier." And Admiral Sir Arthur J. Power, Second-in-Command of the Eastern Fleet, remarked, "That was not James at his best."

When Admiral Sir Bruce Fraser replaced Somerville in the summer of 1944 there was no more trouble. Mountbatten was never unreasonable or dictatorial with reasonable people, and was always ready to listen to their ideas. Fraser was the type who would accept a plan if it were good, no matter who made it. They got on famously.

Perhaps Mountbatten's worst failing as a Supreme Commander was his obsession with detail. This had been fine with the destroyers, and not too bad with the Combined Operations, where his inventive mind played so great a part in developing new engines of war. But in SEAC the general opinion of his people was that he wasted their time fussing for perfection in minor things and "hunting hares that didn't matter."

Another criticism leveled at Mountbatten concerns his lavish headquarters establishment and flamboyant style. There was an enormous staff at New Delhi, far larger than was needed. On the other hand the operations originally envisioned were of infinitely greater scope than Mountbatten was finally permitted to carry out. The staff lived on a sumptuous scale, with swimming pools, officers' clubs, and the best of everything; while Lord Louis lived in royal style even by Oriental standards.

When, in the summer of 1944, Mountbatten moved his headquarters to Kandy on the island of Ceylon to get out from under Auchinleck's aegis, the thing became really grandiose. He sent an order to Admiral Sir Geoffrey Layton, commanding in Ceylon, to prepare accommodations for a staff of about three thousand people, including his personal band of thirty musicians. Layton's remarks were spectacular.

Kandy was two thousand feet up in the hills about forty miles from Colombo. Driving up the winding road through the jungle at night in the heavily scented darkness, with mysterious sparks of light flashing through the trees, was a magical introduction to the uplands on which stood luxurious villas in parks embellished with brilliant tropical flowering trees and bushes. Mountbatten's big white headquarters were in the Paradeniyce Botanical Gardens at the end of a superb avenue. There were four tall flagpoles flying the Allies' flags in front of it, and the grass behind it sloped down to the brown Mahaweli River. Other shining buildings were scattered around in which were administrative offices, and palm-thatched huts housed the overflow of staff.

Lord Louis himself lived in the King's Pavilion—a classic, white miniature palace, with large, airy rooms and balustraded terraces, set in exquisitely beautiful grounds complete with white peacocks strolling around pools covered with lily pads, the blaze of hibiscus flowers, and the glimmer of wild orchids on the trees. There was a little white temple at the end of every vista. There was also a nine-hole golf course.

Mountbatten entertained a lot. Nearly every day he would bring a group of young officers home to lunch with him, and ply them with very acute questions. On many evenings there were big formal dinners for the top echelons and visiting V.I.P.s, who would be entertained by first-run American movies, which Lord Louis loved. Sometimes the Supreme Commander gave garden parties in true Buck House style. During one of these Sydney Dillon Ripley* of the American OSS was shaving, when he saw a rare green woodpecker in the garden. Ripley, a dedicated ornithologist, grabbed a .22-caliber shotgun, wrapped a towel around his waist, and set out after this precious specimen. *Bang!* went the gun; down dropped the bird—and the towel. Ripley retrieved his prize and turned to see the Supreme Commander strolling toward him in full rig accompanied by a group of ladies in filmy dresses and cartwheel hats. An OSS man is trained to aplomb under any circumstance. Holding his gun in one hand and the bird in the other Ripley bowed politely to the company and retired to his quarters at a dignified walk.

The Supreme Commander's style of travel is described by Ralph Arnold in *A Very Quiet War*. He writes, "A siren blared and our car drew to the side to allow a terrific turnout to sweep past. First came motorcycle outriders; then a vast American car bristling with flags at every point." The flags were those of all the Allies represented at headquarters. In the car sat a handsome, laughing young man, in an immaculate white uniform covered with ribbons and gold braid. "Does Supremo always travel that way?" Arnold asked.

Not always, was the answer. For longer trips he traveled in his personal plane, the *Sister Anne*, whose elegant green cabin contained a comfortable bed and a writing desk, with an escort of twelve fighter

---

* Mr. Ripley is now director of the Smithsonian Institution in Washington, D.C.

planes.* In Kandy he went tearing around at the wheel of his own jeep, with only his admiral's flag and SEAC standard, which he drove in *grand prix* style. It was generally full of good-looking WRENS. Then word rang around, "Look both ways before you cross the street, Louis is out in the jeep."

Arnold continues: "Supremo was impressive, there was no doubt about that. Nor was there any nonsense about hiding his light under a bushel. . . . Everything he did was most carefully planned and organized in advance. When on Saturday afternoon he went away . . . to his week-end bungalow most mortals would have relaxed. Not so Supremo! Every daylight hour of his short weekend was scheduled ahead for some recreational activity. . . ."

Mountbatten's unofficial title of Supremo became Superbo. The Americans—not unaffectionately—called him Louis the Lord. While everybody made fun of what his disgruntled seniors called "Mount-batten's *folie de grandeur*," it was not without deliberate intent as well as being his personal taste. Lord Slim says, "Personally I think it's a good idea to dress the part of a commander. You must be recognized by the troops; you must always appear the same. For example, I always wore my broadbrimmed Gurkha hat. Monty had his beret and MacArthur his gold hat; Patton wore the white pistols and Ike his smile and outstretched arms. Dickie wore a uniform he probably designed himself that had something of all the Services about it. He was always well turned out. When you saw Dickie it was good for your morale."

This can be said: From the time of Mountbatten's arrival in Burma there were no more disastrous defeats. His multifarious collection of troops became inspired with the idea that they *could* beat the Japanese. Of course this was not all Mountbatten's doing. Long, hard preparation and training by such commanders as Giffard and Slim began to pay off; and reinforcements at last were trickling into the area. Also Lord Louis perhaps was lucky that the first few sorties after his arrival took the Japanese by surprise and routed them. But allowing for all this, he did bring an aura of victory with him by the very flamboyance of his personality, his unquenchable optimism, and his incorrigibly youthful sense of high adventure.

---

* The *Mercury*, a C-47 equipped with elaborate radio installations and coding machines, was usually part of the entourage.

Chapter 13

THE BATTLE FOR

BURMA

THOUGH THINGS BEGAN TO MOVE forward early in 1944, they moved desperately slowly. The road ahead was littered with blasted hopes, abandoned plans, and lakes of blood and sweat. In the winter of 1944, when SEAC headquarters were still in Delhi and one operation after another was being canceled by the Combined Chiefs, that slow forward movement began. Naturally it started with the "pedestrian plans" of Fourteenth Army, who slogged down the valleys between the jungle-covered mountains of Arakan on Burma's west coast, driving the enemy slowly before them. A little later Stilwell's Chinese started down from Ledo toward Myitkyina.

Meanwhile Intelligence got reports of the arrival of vast Japanese reinforcements and their plan for an all-out offensive aimed at bursting through the Burma border defenses into the plains of India. If successful it would not only threaten that whole great bastion of Empire, but it would cut off the airfields needed for the air supply over the Hump to China, and the great base at Ledo, from which American engineers were building the Ledo Road into China to replace the lost Burma Road. The most positive direction of the Combined Chiefs to Mountbatten charged him to guard these places above all else.

Lord Louis had hopes of sowing confusion and disorganization in the enemy's rear by Wingate's long-range penetration operation, which was scheduled for March 5, 1944. General Giffard and his 11th Army Group staff were dead against the Wingate adventure. The very sight of Wingate at mess, with his scraggly beard and mad prophet's eyes, reading aloud to them from a tattered Bible passages from "Revelations" which he maintained prophesied his success, was enough to make any Sandhurst-trained Briton consider him absolutely mad.

However Wingate's own subordinates and his British-Indian-Chinese-Portuguese Chindits believed in their leader as an *inspired* prophet. Mountbatten believed in him as a genius for guerrilla warfare and an audacious leader of men.

At the crucial meeting in Delhi in January, 1944, there was a violent wrangle between Wingate and his opponents. Lord Louis stopped it. Banging on the table he said, "Wingate has been promised certain things and while I'm here I'll see that he gets them. I want no more arguments on the subject. His demands must be met so that his first three brigades can be properly equipped. When that is done we can discuss things further."

Shortly before the Chindit jump-off in March Mountbatten paid Colonel Cochran's headquarters at Lalaghat a visit. He admired the Air Commandos, who were a picked lot "with the great arrogance that goes with that sort of thing." He especially liked Cochran, to whom he once said, "My God, boy, you're the only ray of light in this whole Theater!"

But on this visit Mountbatten almost turned the daring airman's hair white in an hour. As Cochran describes the incident, Lord Louis wistfully eyed a small L-5 liaison plane that was standing on the field: "You know, I used to fly a plane like that," he said. "Does it have dual controls?"

Cochran knew what Supremo had in mind. "It has," he answered.

"Could I? Would you do it?" Lord Louis asked.

"Sure," said Cochran, figuring that he could take over the controls if anything went wrong.

Mountbatten turned to his pilot and said, "Colonel Cochran and I are going to a forward maneuver area. I'll fly with him."

They got into the plane and Cochran showed Mountbatten how the controls worked. "When did you last fly?" he asked.

"Seven years ago."

"Oh! oh!"

"Well, you'll take over any time you see me going wrong."

"You're darn tootin' I will."

Cochran says, "We started down the wide runway and suddenly the plane veered to the right, then it swung so sharply to the left that one wing tip hit the ground. We went straight for a G.I. sitting on a jeep. He jumped out and ran like hell but we just missed it. I realized that Louis didn't know about the brakes on top of the pedals and was hitting them. But he was going so fast by now I didn't dare stop. I thought, 'Get him off the ground'; so I shoved everything forward and yelled, 'Get your damned big feet off the brakes!' Then we straightened out and took off."

Mountbatten, flying from the front seat, looked back sheepishly and said, "That was a frightful thing, wasn't it? What did I do?"

Cochran told him. Once in the air Mountbatten flew very well. But it was an hour's flight to the next field, and all the way Cochran was thinking, "My God, what have I got myself into? This is the Supreme Commander of the whole Theater, one of the best known guys in the world, and maybe I'm going to let him kill himself. What will Arnold think?"

Cochran says, "You see I had to let him land it to save face. But I was scared. As we started down I kept shouting, 'Keep your feet off the brakes! Keep your feet off the brakes!'

"He did, and we landed all right. Then he turned to me and said, 'That was fine. I must come down and do this more often.' "

But Cochran and Supremo's staff for once were in accord—never again!

Thursday, as Wingate's operation was code-named, went in on schedule March 5, 1944. It just missed disaster the first day, when Lieutenant Colonel Clint Gaty of the Air Commandos brought in photographs showing that one of the jungle clearings where the gliders carrying the advance guard were to land had been blocked by huge logs. The other clearing, called Broadway, was all right, so the whole landing was put in there.

In spite of great difficulties the operation was a success. Within a few days Wingate had established a fortified "Stronghold" manned by seven thousand five hundred men, with an airfield, artillery, and hospital, *behind the Japanese lines.*

In this moment of triumph Wingate's difficult temper unexpectedly flared up. For security reasons the first communiqué from SEAC concerning the fly-in had made no mention of Wingate or the Chindits. When this reached Wingate he felt sure his "enemies" at Headquarters had been at work. In a mad rage he fired off a telegram and a letter to

Mountbatten accusing him and his staff of jealousy and bad faith. Mountbatten wrote back saying that as soon as the Chindits were well established he intended giving a sensational story on them to the press. Then he let Wingate feel the whiplash of his own temper: "Your astounding telegram has made me realize how you have achieved your amazing success in getting yourself disliked by people who are only too ready to be on your side. Louis Mountbatten."

Perhaps Lord Louis regretted his asperity; for eight days later, on March 24, 1944, while flying from Headquarters at Imphal to Lalaghat to see Cochran, Wingate's Mitchell bomber crashed in the jungle, killing the Chindit leader and all on board. Churchill wrote, "With him a bright flame was extinguished."

With Wingate's death the fire and life went out of the Chindits. They never accomplished a great deal, though had their prophet remained to lead them they might well have raised a very special brand of hell in the long, exposed lines of Japanese communications.

Meanwhile the Japanese began their last great offensive in Burma, which was to Mountbatten's command what the Battle of the Bulge later was to Eisenhower's armies in Europe—a great peril and a great opportunity. But the issue was much more doubtful.

First the Japanese struck in force against Fourteenth Army in Arakan, cutting its lines of communication. Slim was able to restore this situation, but hardly had he done so when on March 8 the main Japanese offensive, a hundred thousand strong, burst across the Indian border in a two-pronged attack against the city of Imphal, and against Kohima, some hundred miles farther north. The attack had been expected and orders given to concentrate forces in the Imphal Valley and at Kohima; but the Japanese achieved tactical surprise by arriving sooner than was thought possible, because the thick canopy of the jungle concealed even the movements of large armies from aerial reconnaissance. At Imphal the Allies were surrounded and badly outnumbered. At Kohima an entire Japanese division of 15,000 men besieged a garrison only 3,500 strong.

If ever there was a moment when a Supreme Commander must function this was it. But Mountbatten lay far to the north in 20th American General Hospital at Ledo, with his eyes bandaged. A few days before, driving his jeep through a jungle trail, he had brushed through a clump of bamboo. A splinter flew out and pierced an eye. When he reached the hospital the doctor took command. The injury was so serious that he ordered Mountbatten to have absolute quiet and to keep bandages over both eyes for two weeks. Lord Louis agreed to the bandages but not to being quiet.

As he lay in imposed darkness his assistant Chief of Staff, Major General Wildman-Lushington, read the dispatches from the Central Front to him. That was pure torture. To lie still was galling enough, but to be supine while his armies were in battle and the whole bastion of Empire in danger was fiendish.

Lord Louis took it for a day or two. Then he ripped off the bandages, and called for his clothes and his plane.

"You may lose your eye," the doctors protested.

"I'd rather lose an eye than Kohima," Mountbatten answered. And took off for Fourteenth Army Headquarters at Comilla. He got there just in time.

When Mountbatten arrived at Comilla he found General Slim and Air Marshal Sir John Baldwin looking very grave. The only possibility of saving Imphal was to reinforce the outnumbered defenders with 5th Indian Division from Arakan. To send it by land might impose a fatal delay. But no air transport was available. "Our only chance is to take American planes from the Hump," Slim said. "Only you can do it."

Mountbatten had no right to do it. The Hump supply line to China was the darling of the Americans. Lord Louis had solemnly promised President Roosevelt and the American Joint Chiefs that under no circumstances would he take any of these planes without first consulting them, and there was no time for that. To order them to Arakan could bring the wrath of the Americans down on his head. On the other hand, if the Japanese won the battle of Imphal they would cut the only railroad by which supplies moved to these American bases, and would probably take those bases, too. There would be no more flights over the Hump. He argued the pros and cons with Slim and Baldwin rather heatedly for some time. They succeeded in convincing him that it must be done. At last he said to Baldwin, "Send a signal to General Stratemeyer requesting him to take thirty C-47s off the Hump and send them to Arakan immediately."

Knowing full well that such an illegal order might cause an unholy row and be countermanded, Mountbatten deliberately waited three days before cabling London and Washington a full assessment of the situation and stating that, unless he heard to the contrary within two days, he would order the planes off the Hump. By the time he sent the message the planes were already moving the 5th Division to Imphal. Then he waited for the storm to break.

The first reaction was immensely heartening. It was a cable from Winston Churchill:

THE CHIEFS OF STAFF AND I ARE BACKING YOU UP TO THE FULL. I HAVE TELEGRAPHED THE PRESIDENT. IN MY VIEW NOTHING MATTERS BUT THE BATTLE. BE SURE YOU WIN IT.

That same day permission came from Washington to keep the planes for one month.

That was the crux of the Battle of Imphal, which could almost be called, "The Battle for India." Not that it was won in a hurry. For almost two months 60,000 British troops stood off over 100,000 Japanese in the Imphal Plain, while at Kohima the devoted 3,500, including convalescent wounded from the base hospitals, retreated to a hilltop and defied 15,000 Japanese for 16 days until a brigade of 2nd British Division fought its way to their relief. They killed 4,000 Japanese. In view of the fact that General Slim had previously considered that he needed a two-to-one preponderance of strength to engage the Japanese successfully, it does appear as though a miracle had been wrought in morale.

At the height of the Battle of Imphal Mountbatten flew in to have a look for himself. As his plane landed the airfield was under long-range fire from enemy artillery on the hills. He found that the Japanese had occupied the wooded mountains around the plain, completely cutting off the British defenders and shooting down at them night and day.

Still as spick and span and elegant as ever Lord Louis tore around the plain in a jeep, cheering the defenders on. Then he flew back to Delhi where he worked twenty hours a day, burning up the wires and hounding his generals to gather together all the forces they could find and rush them to the relief of Imphal.

The Japanese began to retreat at the end of May as the monsoon broke. In that annual season of torrential rains, when "good" roads became gullies and soft roads almost impassable morasses, it was customary for both sides to stand where they were. The Japanese Commander in Chief, Field Marshal Count Terauchi, had counted on this pause to reform and reinforce his troops. Not this time! Slogging through supposedly impassable country Slim's army went on the offensive, turning the Japanese retreat into a rout in which small bands of men starved, sickened, and perished as they fled across those rain-forested mountains toward the comparative safety of Mandalay. The Burma campaign was not over; it lasted another year. But victory was inevitable.

Though the road to victory was in sight, it was a rugged uphill way. There is no room to describe the intricate planning, the courage and discipline, the immense feats of personal valor, the victories and the disappointments of that long campaign. It was far longer and more arduous than it need have been, through no fault of the Supreme Commander or his generals.

For Burma was still the forgotten front. Even while Fourteenth Army was bitterly pushing through that nightmare landscape, and Stilwell's Chinese were doggedly coming down from the north to join hands with them on the Irrawaddy River, which is Burma's main highway and life line, far greater events occupied the attention of the Allies. Eisenhower's successful landings in Normandy and the liberation of France and the Allies' drive up the Italian peninsula in Europe were matched by MacArthur's return to the Philippines and American Admiral Chester W. Nimitz's island-hopping campaign and destruction of the Japanese Fleet in the Pacific. These were not only far more spectacular than Mountbatten's war, but were, in fact, the essential ingredients of global victory. For if the enemy were beaten in the main theaters his forces in Burma were obviously going to shrivel like fruit on a lopped-off bough.

In addition to this strategic reality the national pride and the individual ambitions of the statesmen and their commanders operated to starve SEAC. For example, if matériel were released from the European Theater it was sure to be grabbed either by MacArthur or Nimitz before it ever got to Burma. British warships, which could have been allotted to Mountbatten in the Bay of Bengal, were sent instead to the Pacific to join the Americans, who neither wanted nor needed them, because Winston Churchill and First Sea Lord Sir Andrew Cunningham were determined that the Royal Navy should take part in the final conquest of Japan for the sake of British prestige.

When all these perfectly natural and reasonable factors are considered, it is nevertheless true that the treatment given Mountbatten was both shabby and short-sighted. In September, 1944, he was directed to plan an amphibious operation against Rangoon, code-named Dracula. This made great sense, for the capture of that great port and railway center would cut off all the Japanese forces in Burma and leave them out on the end of a limb, thus avoiding the long weary march of nearly a thousand miles across the mountains to Mandalay and then down the Irrawaddy to Rangoon against fierce resistance all the way. In October the Combined Chiefs changed their minds. Once again Mountbatten was told he would not get the promised matériel, particularly landing craft and transport planes. In view of the thousands of these vessels and planes now available and operating in Europe and the Pacific it seems ridiculous and niggardly not to have allotted him the comparatively few necessary for Dracula. As a result of this myopic decision Mountbatten's land forces had to fight and walk through all of Burma. How many men were needlessly killed, how much suffering was endured, and how much matériel and time were wasted cannot be reckoned.

When the Battle of the Bulge erupted in December, 1944, 250,000 troops promised to Mountbatten were also canceled. This was perfectly proper and sensible, but frustrating nonetheless.

With virtually none of these promised reinforcements Mountbatten cleared the Japanese out of Burma the hard way. By the autumn of 1944 SEAC had been reorganized according to his ideas. Fraser had replaced Somerville in command of the Eastern Fleet. Giffard had been transferred, and Lieutenant General Sir Oliver Leese was made Allied Ground Commander. Peirse had given place to Garrod. Chiang Kai-shek finally succeeded in getting rid of Stilwell. Mountbatten had loyally done his best to keep Stilwell on, but "the Peanut" had had enough. Old Vinegar Joe left, muttering maledictions on all concerned, particularly that "Limey Louis." No fewer than three lieutenant generals took over the jobs that had been handled by that disagreeable but truly remarkable character. His position as Deputy Supreme Commander of SEAC was taken by Mountbatten's former P.A.O. and close friend, Lieutenant General Raymond T. Wheeler, while Wedemeyer was assigned the unenviable post of Chiang's Chief of Staff and Major General Dan Sultan, USA, took over the Chinese Army in Burma. SEAC became at last a well-matched team, one the Supreme Commander could guide rather than drive.

On General Slim, always the wheelhorse of the team, and his superb Fourteenth Army, which was more than half Asian troops, fell the brunt of the last campaign. This suited Slim perfectly. He proceeded contentedly with his "pedestrian plans," which brought the army overland to the decisive victory at Mandalay in March, 1945.

From there to Rangoon it was a downhill race along the Irrawaddy for three hundred miles to beat an amphibious assault, which Mountbatten at long last had been able to mount. The amphibians won by a scant day's march. They entered Rangoon on May 3, 1944, and found that the remnants of the Japanese forces had pulled out.

This was the happiest time Lord Louis had known since becoming Supreme Commander. A minor abrasion of his contentment was a bad attack of amebic dystentery, which would have knocked most people out. Mountbatten refused to stop working and his doctor actually tried to knock him out with an oversized dose of sedative. Lord Louis rose above it and actually worked twenty hours that day.

On the plus side was the arrival of two people very dear to him, Edwina and Patricia Mountbatten. Patricia and her sister Pamela had returned to England after the blitz in 1942. She had joined the WRENS, and by a kindly gesture of the Chiefs of Staff—or Churchill—was assigned to Mountbatten's headquarters in the last year of the war.

Edwina, who had been made Superintendent in Chief of St. John Brigade in 1942, with over a hundred thousand men and women under her direction, had continued her remarkably efficient and dedicated work. Hardly had Eisenhower's army landed in Normandy than she was over there in the thick of it, organizing the medical and recreational services, and spending her incredible energy cheering the wounded in front-line hospital tents. In the course of this trip a German anti-aircraft battery shot one of the engines out of her plane.

Though the overriding demands of the European Theater kept Edwina there throughout the summer and autumn of 1944, her heart was in Southeast Asia. As in the case of the *Kelly* Dickie's people were her people, and the moment she felt things to be sufficiently well organized in Europe she headed for SEAC, arriving in Delhi in the *Sister Anne* in January, 1945.

Though three Mountbattens were now together it was a brief reunion. Almost immediately Edwina took off on an extended tour of her husband's command. That was a rugged trip, covering 20,000 miles in the course of which Edwina visited 172 hospitals as well as medical centers, convalescent homes, canteens, and front-line dressing stations. The conditions of living and traveling were appalling. At one place she came to a small river with no bridge or ferry, so she dove in and swam it.

The hardships took their toll of her beauty, tropical sun and exposure roughened her skin, until John MacDonald of the OSS described it as "looking like brown corduroy." But nothing dimmed her spirit. Sir Gerald Nye, who was making a similar inspection trip, said that the discomforts seemed to him unnecessarily arduous. "When I protested bitterly," he said, "the invariable answer was, 'Lady Louis was here just before you, and she didn't complain.'"

One heart she won completely was that of General Slim. He said:

> Lady Mountbatten was one of the most impressive women I ever met and one of the nicest. She had an absolutely first class mind, unlimited courage, great organizing ability and indomitable determination, all of which she reinforced with the most feminine charm. That made it damned difficult if you wanted to argue with her.
>
> I think she had a bigger hold on those of my soldiers whom she met and talked to than anyone, including me. She could talk to them as well as Dickie or anyone, and she did things for them. Very

few people came to our theater, it was a backwater. But those who did come were horrified at the conditions they saw—privations, lack of supply, lack of necessities, of everything. They went back but they didn't do anything about it. The people who made things happen here—there were just three of them—they were Edwina, and Stella Reading, and my own wife—though you needn't mention that.

The only serious difference I had with Edwina was after the war, when she wanted ships to get our people who had been prisoners of the Japs out and I wanted the space to get my long service men, who had been here four or five years, home. She put up a splendid case for her point of view. When I refused to be swayed by her intellectual arguments she turned on the charm and her compassion and her pity. I said to her then, "Edwina, this isn't fair."

I had unbounded admiration and affection for Edwina. In fact, Edwina would have made a damned good Supreme Commander.

A month before Rangoon fell the war in Europe ended, though even then not much matériel got to Burma. The Americans were closing in on Japan and some of the bitterest fighting of the war was taking place on Okinawa. In addition they were mustering all their resources for the final grand assault on the home islands of Japan.

While Slim's army was mopping up very large Japanese forces that had been bypassed in the rush for Rangoon, Mountbatten set his planners to work on a great amphibious-plus-air assault on the Malay Peninsula, to retake the great British naval base of Singapore (Operation Zipper). Then he took off for England to see what he could do to get his share of the troops and matériel released from Europe. In Cairo he received a message from Churchill, telling him to come at once to the Potsdam Conference.

Lord Louis was warmly welcomed at Potsdam, where Churchill, Stalin, and Harry S Truman, who had succeeded to the Presidency of the United States on the death of President Roosevelt in April, 1945, were gathered to divide the spoils and plan the final conquest of Japan. The night Mountbatten arrived in Berlin Churchill invited him to dine alone with him. As Lord Louis came into his ornate room in Frederick the Great's baroque palace, Churchill acted very peculiarly. Hardly pausing to greet his guest he went to the door and looked up and down the hall. Then he carefully locked the door and made sure of the windows. Finally he motioned Lord Louis close to him and said in an excited whisper, "You will have to change all your plans."

It was another blow in the solar plexus. If Mountbatten felt physically sick who could blame him? Yet there was an almost hectic gaiety in Churchill's manner that made him wonder. "Not again!" he said.

"Yes, because Japan will have surrendered before you can put them into effect."

"How do you know?"

Sinking his voice even lower Churchill said, "You must not breathe a word of this to anyone. Not even the highest. Forget I told you; but the Americans have successfully fired an *atomic bomb*, of such enormous power that a single one will devastate a whole city."

Churchill then described the terrible test blast at Alamagordo that changed the shape of the world.* "Harry Truman just confided in me," he said.

The next morning Lord Louis attended a meeting of the Combined Chiefs. They also told him the Great Secret, but they carried on the meeting as though nothing had happened. Lord Louis observed, "Planning was consequently rather unrealistic."

After that Mountbatten went to luncheon with the new President of the United States. At that time Truman was a lost and lonely person, still staggering under the enormous burden that had dropped on his shoulders. He lacked the wide historical background which informed Roosevelt's mind; in fact, he did not even know what agreements Roosevelt had made secretly with the British and the Russians. But one thing he did know and he could hardly wait to tell it. Dancing around his crowded suite in the security rigmarole, and swearing Lord Louis to secrecy, he confided his great News. Mountbatten was properly astounded.

After lunching with the President, Mountbatten called on Generalissimo Stalin at his headquarters in East Berlin. It was a depressing drive through a city of ruin so fantastic it made the Roman Forum seem new. The eyes of the people, focused on his great American car, with the proud flags of Great Britain and a Supreme Commander snapping in the wind, were the eyes of men dead of despair. An occasional lightning flash of hate was almost a relief.

Stalin, wearing an immaculate white doeskin tunic shaped a little like a Russian blouse and dark-blue trousers, received him genially. His square fortress of a face, with its *chevaux-de-frise* of iron-gray hair and longhorn mustache, wrinkled in a genuine smile of pleasure. When Lord Louis asked him when he thought the Japanese war would end his eyes

---

* The professional soldiers like Sir Alan Brooke refused to recognize the immense significance of The Bomb.

Viceroy of India. The Viscount and Viscountess Mountbatten of Burma leaving Durbar Hall immediately after the swearing-in ceremony, March 24, 1947. (*Wide World*)

The Mountbattens won Mahatma Gandhi's confidence at their first meeting in the gardens of the Viceroy's House, New Delhi, March 31, 1947. (*Wide World*)

The Mountbattens brought warring Indian factions together in New Delhi on July 4, 1947. Left to right, Mohammed Ali Jinnah (President of the Muslim League), Mrs. Henry J. Grady, Lord Mountbatten, Jawaharlal Nehru, Lady Mountbatten, and United States Ambassador to India Henry J. Grady. (*Wide World*)

The first Indian Governor General of India, Chakravarti Rajagopalachari, weeps as he bids Lady Mountbatten good-bye in New Delhi, June 21, 1948. (*Wide World*)

Admiral the Earl Mount-
batten of Burma in full
fig, when he became
Commander in Chief of
NATO Forces, Mediter-
ranean. (*Wide World*)

Six NATO admirals row their departing Commander in Chief to his ship, Malta, Decem-
ber 10, 1955. Left to right, Lord Mountbatten, Vice-Admiral J. Fife, USN; Vice-Admiral
P. G. L. Cazalet, RN; Rear Admiral S. Karapinar, Turkey; Rear Admiral D. Zepos,
Greece; Rear Admiral M. Calamai, Italy. (*Wide World*)

Admiral of the Fleet Lord Mountbatten with the late President John F. Kennedy and General Lyman Lemnitzer. (*Wide World*)

Lady Mountbatten leaving the wedding at Romsey Abbey on January 13, 1960, of her daughter Pamela. The children are her granddaughter Joanna Knatchbull, Princess Anne, and Victoria Martin. (*Wide World*)

Lord Mountbatten throws a wreath from H. M. S. *Wakefield* at the burial at sea of Lady Mountbatten, February 25, 1960. (*London Daily Express*)

H. R. H. Prince Philip, Duke of Edinburgh. (*Photograph by Baron*)

Prince Philip's father, Prince Andrew of Greece, with (l. to r.) his wife Princess Alice of Battenberg and Philip's sisters, Princess Theodora (later, Markgräfen of Baden) and Princess Margarita (later, Princess of Hohenlohe-Langenburg), London, December 27, 1922. (*Radio Times Hulton Picture Library*)

H. R. H. Prince Philip of Greece in England for the wedding of his uncle Lord Louis Mountbatten, July 18, 1922. (*Radio Times Hulton Picture Library*)

H. R. H. Princess Elizabeth on her thirteenth
birthday, April 21, 1939, at Windsor Castle
with her beloved pony. (*Radio Times Hulton Picture Library*)

Princess Elizabeth at Windsor Castle during
the war. (*Radio Times Hulton Picture Library*)

Princess Elizabeth and Prince Philip on their honeymoon at the Mountbattens' estate,
Broadlands. (*London Daily Express*)

Queen Elizabeth II and Prince Philip at Katmandu during a state visit to Nepal, February 2, 1961. (*Wide World*)

Queen Elizabeth II and Prince Philip enjoying a "Philipic" on a drive through London. (*Wide World*)

crinkled at a secret thought as he replied through an interpreter, "Mr. Stalin says, 'Very soon now.' "

From Potsdam Mountbatten flew to England. He arrived on the day of the General Election called by Churchill, who hoped to perpetuate his rule for another five years. The Prime Minister counted on the tide of victory to carry him into office; but the British people had other ideas. The result was a smashing defeat for the Conservatives. Churchill and all his Conservative ministers were out; Clement Attlee was Prime Minister of Great Britain. It was almost impossible to believe.

That night in Chester Street Lord Louis and Edwina tried to realize and assess what had happened. As any man is bound to do in the face of a sudden cataclysmic change—and this news seemed just that—Mountbatten's first thought was, How will this affect me and my plans? Churchill had been his close friend and supporter, and he knew perfectly well that the Prime Minister's strong hand had pushed him forward. Now it was gone. But Mountbatten might well feel that his position was now so assured that the hand was no longer needed.

As to Attlee, Lord Louis knew him well and liked him. Certainly the slim, dapper little gentleman who had become Labour's Prime Minister would never fill the heroic shoes of his predecessor. Strategic military planning would lack the inspired flair of Churchillian imagination; and the level of Parliamentary oratory would suffer a disastrous decline. But there were plusses in Lord Louis' assessment of the future as well.

Politically Mountbatten and Edwina were far closer to Attlee's thinking than to Churchill's. They recognized that the great romantic patriot would fight with all his splendid power to preserve the Empire in its entirety. This, Mountbatten believed, was neither possible nor even desirable. He had felt the surge for independence under the iron crust of armies at war. He knew that the moment peace came the aspiration for freedom would erupt through the attenuating power of military occupation. Even in wartime half of India was in revolt, her great leaders like Gandhi and Nehru in jail. With peace there would be no stopping her, or the independence movements which the Japanese had encouraged in all the occupied territories, from the East Indies to Burma. Their one victory had been destroying the myth of white invincibility.

To Lord Louis' thinking it was wrong to try to keep the lid on; wrong in respect to the just aspirations of the people of those countries; foolish even in the interests of Britain herself, because by acceding magnanimously to the inevitable she might gain the friendship and alliance of the emerging nations. He already had made his plans, and even taken tentative steps in this direction. It would be easier to pursue this course under Attlee than Churchill.

Mountbatten had intended to fly back to Kandy immediately, but he decided to remain in London for conferences with the new Government. Though Churchill could have remained in power until Parliament met he resigned immediately, and Attlee kissed the King's hand. Then *he* went to Potsdam as Prime Minister to conclude the conference.

The Chiefs of Staff seemed stunned. Sir Alan Brooke, who had doubted if he could "stick another moment with [Churchill] and would give almost anything never to see him again . . ." was literally shattered. The joy and savor seemed to have gone out of his life. He wrote, "Attlee as P.M. and who as Secretary of State [for War]? I feel too old and weary to start off any new experiments. . . . What a ghastly mistake to start elections at this period of the world's history! May God forgive England for it."

If Mountbatten was not as despairing, he was certainly deeply affected by the "very, very sad and very moving little meeting" at Number 10 Downing Street, where he went with the Chiefs of Staff to say farewell to England's great wartime leader. Churchill naturally was subdued, but he was in better command of himself than were his military chieftains. Poor Brookie dared not speak for fear of breaking down. With the deep sentimentality of his nature and race, it would be surprising if Lord Louis did not feel tears pricking his eyelids.

Mountbatten was still in England conferring with the new Government and the Chiefs of Staff, when the vaporized mushroom cloud towered to the sky over Hiroshima. He was actually with Prime Minister Attlee at Number 10 Downing Street when the offer of surrender came from Japan.

It took not a moment for Lord Louis to realize that this was the end, and that he must be at his own headquarters in that historic moment. Crash orders for instant departure went to his plane—not the *Sister Anne*, but the converted four-engine York bomber that he used for long-distance flights. Stopping nowhere longer than the absolute minimum for refueling, he made the voyage of 6,345 miles in 31 hours, breaking all records of that time.

Two days after he reached Kandy, on August 14, 1945, Japan surrendered officially. The war was over. But some of Mountbatten's greatest responsibilities—and frustrations—lay ahead.

Chapter 14

BRIEF EMPIRE

On August 14 Mountbatten sent orders to his commanders over his elaborate communications network to cease all operations on land, sea, and air. At the moment fighting stopped his forces had killed 190,000 Japanese, a greater number than any other command, including MacArthur's.

That same day he received orders from the Combined Chiefs to take over responsibility for the entire area of the southwest Pacific south of the Philippines. This huge addition to his area included Hong Kong, French Indochina, the Dutch East Indies, and Borneo. The move had been decided on at an extremely cordial conference between Mountbatten and MacArthur in Manila in June, and confirmed by the Combined Chiefs at Potsdam, in order to release American troops for the occupation of Japan.

On August 15, Mountbatten received a new directive from the British Chiefs of Staff ordering him: (*1*) To reoccupy key areas of occupied territories in order to secure effective control and to enforce the surrender and disarmament of Japanese forces; (*2*) To secure the earliest possible release of British and Allied prisoners of war and internees.

This was a large assignment. There were still about 750,000 Japanese troops in the million square miles of the enlarged SEAC area, and about 130,000,000 more or less restless natives. No one could be sure that the surrender order had reached these Japanese troops, or that the peoples of these countries would not revolt immediately against any restoration of "colonial rule."

Mountbatten moved fast. He ordered Operation Zipper to start immediately for Malaya and Singapore with whatever forces were ready. Vice-Admiral Walker's task force and some mine sweepers actually sailed from Ceylon that very day in the howling storms at the height of the monsoon. Lord Louis ordered other detachments to prepare to fly in and take over all Japanese headquarters, from Sumatra to Hong Kong, including Field Marshal Terauchi's Supreme Headquarters at Saigon. Lord Louis also sent a "most urgent" signal to Edwina in London to come immediately to help with the sick and wounded from the Japanese prison camps.

Four days later the most extraordinary of all the reversals that Lord Louis suffered came in the form of an order from MacArthur, who had been appointed Supreme Allied Commander for Surrender Arrangements, to effect no landings or reoccupations until after the formal surrender ceremony at Tokyo on August 31. (Because of a typhoon that hit Japan it was delayed until September 2, 1945.)

Mountbatten was raging. He thought of those wretched prisoners, of the sick and dying condemned to two weeks more of unnecessary suffering. He thought of the turmoil and chaos in those vast seething lands, for which he had been made responsible, with no recognized authority to keep order. He thought of the thousands who might die in order that pomp and circumstance, protocol and glory might be properly celebrated before the assembled newsreel cameras of the world. And he thought of the little ships already on their way to Malaya and Penang, battling seas lashed by the monsoon. The smallest of them were literally incapable of fighting their way back to Ceylon in the teeth of the southwest gale. Desperately he cabled the Chiefs of Staff.

All the satisfaction he got was noted in Sir Alan Brooke's diary: "August 22. A short C.O.S. meeting at which we decided that Mountbatten must conform to MacArthur's wishes as regards the dates for the process of surrenders. Namely to await the surrender in Tokyo before attempting surrenders in outlying districts."

From MacArthur he also received a message: TELL LORD LOUIS TO KEEP HIS PANTS ON AND NOT WORRY.

This raised his blood pressure even higher—it was so damned undignified. He fired back a cable: WILL KEEP MY PANTS ON IF YOU WILL TAKE HIROHITO'S OFF.

Then Lord Louis began the usual weary business of picking up the pieces and salvaging what could be saved. The ships were ordered to "mark time at sea." Emergency arrangements were made with Admiral

Power, who now commanded the Eastern Fleet, to supply them with food, water, and fuel at sea.

As to other matters, Mountbatten intended to go just as far as he could without actually contravening MacArthur's orders. He ordered Field Marshal Terauchi to send Japanese delegates to Rangoon on August 26 to sign a "preliminary agreement." He appointed Lieutenant General ("Boy") Browning to meet with the Japanese, but decided to be on hand to size them up himself.

On the morning of August 26 Mountbatten flew into Rangoon, circling the golden spears of Schwe Dagom Pagoda on its hilltop, which he had first seen in another age with the Prince of Wales.

The meeting was held in pretentious Government House, which Campbell-Johnson described as looking like Euston Station without the softening influence of London soot. The Japanese, headed by Terauchi's Chief of Staff, Lieutenant General Numata, arrived in spotless white dress uniforms with ceremonial swords. Lord Louis had feared they might be intransigent and want to argue; but they were correct, sad, and docile. In fact they were so nervous that when Lord Louis suggested to Rear Admiral Chado that he would be more comfortable at luncheon without his great clanking sword, the poor admiral almost burst into tears.

Mountbatten noted in his final *Report to the Combined Chiefs of Staff:* "As a result of this meeting, at which it had been obvious that the Japanese High Command intended to obey my orders punctiliously, I decided that I did not have to guard against large-scale opposition, and that I could now take certain risks."

The risks were to go ahead with Operations for the Recovery of Allied Prisoners of War and Internees (RAWPI), whatever MacArthur thought. Planes were sent roaring through the monsoon to drop pamphlets on all known prisoner camps telling the inmates of the surrender and that help was coming. These were followed by transport planes carrying relief personnel and stores. Mercy ships loaded with supplies were sent to the islands, and these supplies were distributed by relief personnel under the guardianship of Japanese troops.

Before any military landings took place 950 tons of supplies and some 120 relief personnel were flown into known prison camps in the command. As Mountbatten said: "If relief stores and personnel had not been sent in at once, the delay of twelve days imposed on me would have resulted in many more deaths each day among the prisoners."

One of those who arrived in the Japanese-held territories before the Allied troops was Edwina Mountbatten. She came to Southeast Asia in answer to her husband's call for help on August 23, and remained for over three months. When she arrived Lord Louis said to her, "I want you to go to those boys wherever they are, and help get them out as soon as you can. I want you to use your own initiative, but you can call on any of my military commanders for help. Nothing less than an all-out effort will do."

Smiling, Edwina said, "You can trust me."

"I know. It's going to be damned dangerous. But no one can do it as well as you."

"Don't you worry, Dickie. And I won't."

So Edwina started on on a trip that covered 33,000 miles, on which she visited uncounted prison camps and hospitals under conditions of unimaginable horror. As she walked through one of the primitive, stinking hospital sheds in the darkness, with the monsoon howling outside, wearing her khaki blouse and kilt-like skirt and carrying a battery-powered hurricane lamp, one prisoner called her the "streamlined Lady with the Lamp." In one of the camps she found her cousin Harold Cassel. After her visit he wrote, "You will realize what a tremendous moment it was for everyone to see . . . a real Englishwoman again after so many years. . . . Somehow now you've come even the restless ones are certain that everything is being done to get us out quickly. . . ."

They were right, at least about Edwina. She was making a tremendous effort—hounding Dickie and General Slim for ships; pressing everybody on with all her influence, energy, and charm, "her pity and compassion," to get things done.

Conditions were worst of all in the Dutch East Indies, where the Dutch were hated by both the Japanese and the natives. Dutch internees, especially women and children, were dying of sheer starvation on an allowance of a quarter of a pound of rice a day in the rickety, waterless, crowded barracks. "Conditions indescribable," Edwina noted.

In Sumatra Edwina not only arrived before any Allied troops, and was looked after by the Japanese Army, but, at least partly, because of her pressure on her husband, "the whole evacuation of the prisoners of war was carried out [by C-47s and light aircraft from emergency strips] before the Allied troops had landed, or even before our ships had been able to reach the coast."

In October she was able to write with enormous pride in her husband's accomplishment: "Just over five weeks since it started active operations the organization for the Recovery of Allied Prisoners of War and Internees had cleared all the areas of South East Asia Command for which it was responsible."

The dismal, frock-coated plenipotentiaries of Japan formally signed the surrender on the deck of the *Missouri* on September 2, 1945. Mountbatten's ships were circling outside Singapore like eager hounds. In the next dawn the mine sweepers went in, followed by the Royal Marines in the British cruisers *London* and *Cumberland*. Mountbatten summoned Field Marshal Terauchi to a formal surrender ceremony there on September 12.

Poor Terauchi was too sick to come. He had suffered a stroke the day Mandalay fell, and the doctor Mountbatten sent to make sure he was not faking reported it would be fatal to move him. "All right," Lord Louis said. "Tell the Field Marshal he can send a delegate. Later I'll drop in at Saigon and receive his personal surrender."

Mountbatten transferred his headquarters to Singapore, and installed himself in his usual magnificent style in Government House, a huge building in "colonial monumental," built as the seat of an eternal Empire.

Thither on September 12 came Terauchi's Supreme Commander Delegate, General Itagaki. The surrender was carried out in the Singapore Council Chamber with maximal fanfare and ceremony in the presence of representatives of all the Allies. Edwina was there, with a group of St. John Ambulance people lately released from prison camps. Outside the building were detachments from as many as possible of the units under Mountbatten's command as well as thousands of ragged released prisoners of war, drinking the satisfying draft of revenge.

After the document was signed, General Itagaki presented his sword of honor in its wooden case to Mountbatten in the time-honored gesture of unconditional surrender. Lord Louis accepted it with perfect courtesy but no magnanimous gesture of returning it. The other Japanese officers also gave up their swords.

The tremendous pomp and formality were, of course, in accordance with Lord Louis' love of traditional style. But they were also deliberately designed to impress upon the Japanese and the whole Asian world the completeness of Allied victory, and thus restore at least some of Britain's lost prestige.

This was the particular reason for enforcing the surrender of the swords. It was contrary to the instructions of MacArthur who feared the Japanese officers would lose face and hence control of their troops, but Mountbatten intended to mete out the full measure of abasement to his defeated enemy. This was due in part to the necessity of establishing his own prestige in the vast chaotic realm in which he must maintain order, and, it must be admitted, due also to his ruthless Germanic philosophy of *vae victis* (woe to the vanquished).

He was absolutely determined to have Terauchi's samurai sword as his own trophy, and when he found it had been left in storage in Japan he insisted that it be produced. Madame Terauchi came all the way from Tokyo bringing *two* superb swords. Mountbatten gave the lesser one to his cousin King George, and kept an exquisitely wrought blade, forged in the thirteenth century, which now hangs in Broadlands.

However, Mountbatten would allow no indignities to be offered the Japanese. In his order to this effect he pointed out that to degrade them was "to lower ourselves to the same level." In his official report Japanese Lieutenant General Numata stated that in all but a few minor cases he "was informed of the just treatment by the Allies of the Japanese personnel."

Though Mountbatten hated his enemies,* he was not vindictive toward the Asian peoples who to some extent had collaborated with them. He realized that they did so to throw off the yoke of colonialism or simply to survive. When the pukka sahibs spoke of them as traitors, Lord Louis said, "They are *not* traitors. They were fighting for their own country."

Even before the war ended he put this policy into effect in his controversial dealings with Major General Aung San and his Burma National Army. The BNA had been raised under Japanese auspices to fight the Allies. In March, 1945, either because he was disillusioned with the Japanese or, more likely, because he wanted to be on the winning side, Aung San offered to bring his army to the side of the Allies. To the disgust of his more conservative commanders and the absolute horror of the Neanderthalic Civil Governor of Burma, Sir Reginald Dorman-Smith, Mountbatten accepted Aung San's offer and incorporated the BNA into his forces. He did not need them, but he felt that when the war ended the BNA would be the only disciplined native body that could maintain order in Burma, and he wanted them on England's side. Lord Slim said, "It was a terrible nuisance having those blue-coated chaps—or chaps with no coats at all—running around in my lines. But I believe Dickie did the right thing."

In fact, all the *political* moves Mountbatten made in his vast proconsulate—probably the largest area with the greatest population ever ruled by a military governor—were inspired by his realistic and humanistic belief that these nations had a right to their independence, that they were going to achieve it in any event, and that his duty was to help them do so and thus win their friendship for Britain.

He adopted the course of conciliation—his enemies called it "collaboration"—with the popular leaders of all the fourteen nations in his domain. Mostly it worked very well. The exceptions were French Indochina and the Dutch East Indies. In the former General Leclerc went in with two French divisions fresh from the Western Front and

---

* During the war trials in Tokyo he wrote to MacArthur, "When are you going to hang some Japs?"

re-established French colonial rule. This resulted ultimately in a revolt in which the French suffered the disastrous defeat of Dien Bien Phu. The northern portion of French Indochina went communist; the southern part—Laos and Vietnam—is still in a terrible mess.

Mountbatten's policy in the Dutch East Indies was the subject of tremendous criticism by the Dutch Government. Partly due to the delay imposed by MacArthur an Indonesian National Government headed by Doctor Ahmed Sukarno took over from the Japanese before the British arrived. Lord Louis negotiated with Sukarno. The alternative was to order the Indian troops of the British Occupation Force to fight him, and this was contrary to Mountbatten's basic principle that Asian troops should not be ordered to fight Asian nationalists. When Dutch troops finally arrived in Indonesia they tried unsuccessfully to oust Sukarno, with the ultimate result that Indonesia is now communist-oriented.

In the former English colonies Mountbatten's policy was extremely successful. They did indeed achieve independence but retained strong links with the British Commonwealth. An example of Mountbatten's wisdom was his handling of Jawaharlal Nehru's visit to Singapore early in 1946. Nehru had spent most of the war in jail, but he was destined to be the Prime Minister of India as soon as the British kept their promise to grant India independence; and the Viceroy, Lord Wavell, thought it wise to butter him up a bit by inviting him to visit Singapore, which had a large Indian colony. Lord Louis heartily agreed.

Mountbatten arrived in Singapore two days before Nehru was due, and he found the place in turmoil. The local military administration was terrified that Nehru's arrival would touch off a revolt of former members of the Indian National Army, which had fought on the side of the Japanese. They had adopted the ostrich technique of ignoring the whole thing except to station guards all over the city.

Mountbatten was furious. He called a hurried meeting at Government House and said, in effect, "This man is our invited guest and a distinguished statesman who one day soon may rule India. He must be treated as such. I hear you haven't even offered him a car. If you don't I'll give him my car. Furthermore, you will send lorries out to bring in Indians from the suburbs who want to see him. Passes are to be issued to the most distinguished Indian residents here to meet Pandit Nehru at the airport. I shall give a luncheon for him at Government House."

Thus it was done. At Government House Lord Louis put on all the panoply of state, with bagpipes skirling and his top brass on hand to meet the Indian leader.

It had been arranged for Nehru to drive in an open car to the Red Cross Indian Recreation Center, where Lady Louis would receive him.

When Mountbatten told his staff that he was going in the car with Nehru they were genuinely distressed. They felt he would enhance Nehru's prestige. They also advised him of the risks he would run. With deep affection they begged him not to go. "There is no way to protect you from assassination," they told him.

This, of course, was the worst way to dissuade Lord Louis; if a thing were dangerous he felt in honor bound to do it. As to increasing Nehru's prestige he said, "Don't be silly. He'll increase mine."

So it turned out. As the big, open American convertible crawled through the people-choked streets, the Indians went wild. Ray Murphy wrote: "The streets packed with Indians seemed to shake with the cries of enthusiasm. . . ." The cheering was not all for Nehru by any means. For the first time Lord Louis heard the shout that, often repeated in years ahead, never failed to thrill him: "*Mountbatten Kai Jai!*"

The thing got really dangerous at the Red Cross Center—not from hate but enthusiasm. As Nehru and Mountbatten got out of the car thousands of Indians stampeded toward them in an almost hysterical effort to touch their clothing. Edwina, standing in front of the hut in her blue dress uniform, was knocked down. Like a team Lord Louis and Nehru jumped forward and, smashing into the crowd, picked her up between them and carried her into the hut. They set her down and Pandit Nehru was presented to the disheveled but still attractive lady. It was a strangely auspicious beginning to a beautiful and historic relationship.

Lord Louis was completely right, and his advisers myopically wrong, about the effect of Nehru's reception in Singapore. For the Indian leader was a man of great good will, only too willing to discard old animosities in favor of new friendship. Furthermore he was both a gentle man and a gentleman, who by inclination and breeding was bound to return politeness with courtesy and confidence with trust. Once again the Mountbatten charm had worked for the benefit of his country, but in noting that, forget not that in this case it was based on honest good will. Had it not been, a politician as shrewd as Nehru would have seen through it. As it was his attitude, and with it in some measure the attitude of all India, was changed and the course of a waning empire charted in a new and beneficent direction.

Gradually Mountbatten's vast domain shrank as the former owners, France and the Netherlands, and the British civil authorities took over the various sections of it. As he relinquished responsibility for each country there were elaborate farewells made genuinely touching by honest regret on the part of its leaders. He dashed around, accepting decorations from them with juvenile delight. Among the baubles he collected were the Grand Cross of the Star of Nepal, the Cloud and Banner (first class) of China, and the Order of the White Elephant of Siam. At the time the King of Siam offered the latter decoration to Lord Louis, Siam had not yet made peace with England.* Mountbatten cabled the Government to ask if he were allowed to accept it. Back came the reply that he might accept it but could not wear it. Looking at the beautiful medallion in its velvet box Edwina said, "If you're not allowed to wear it, it would make a lovely top for a cigarette box."

"No you don't!" Lord Louis said, as he snatched the box and dropped it in his pocket.

The Mountbattens also made an official visit to Australia and New Zealand, designed to strengthen Commonwealth ties as the Prince of Wales had done. The Australians and their Governor General, The Duke of Gloucester, laid on the pomp of a royal progress. It was a delicate situation in the liberal, almost socialistic, country, but the Mountbattens handled it with that ideal combination of dignity and friendliness which only the best kings ever manage. The people Down Under loved them, and the ties of Commonwealth were duly reinforced.

Finally in June, 1946, after nearly three years at his post in Southeast Asia Mountbatten was ordered home. The impending departure of Lord and Lady Louis set off another round of farewell festivities and ceremonies. These were repeated as they passed through India on their way home. Everyone thought it would be a long time before the Mountbattens came that way again.

The sheer physical exertion of the last few weeks in SEAC, the infinite detail of relinquishing his great command, the ceremonies and farewell parties, combined with the emotional stress of parting from people with whom they had shared such great and trying events, would have left anyone but the Mountbattens in a state of utter exhaustion, looking only for a quiet hole to crawl into and recuperate. So thought Air Marshal Sir Charles Strafford, commanding the R.A.F. base at Habbaniya in Iraq. And so they looked, as they disembarked from the *York* at 6 P.M. the same day they left India, after a very rough flight up the Red Sea. Sir Charles said, "Edwina and her daughter, Patricia, had obviously been air-sick. They were absolutely pea-green when they got out of the plane."

Even Lord Louis looked worn and tired. When they reached Strafford's house at the base their host said, "I haven't laid anything on

---

* Mountbatten played a significant part in restoring good relations between England and Siam.

for tonight, sir. I thought you'd like a quiet evening and an early start tomorrow morning."

"Oh?" said Lord Louis. "What is there to do here?"

Since Habbaniya was blanketed by the burning heat of the plains between the Tigris and Euphrates, Strafford truthfully said, "Nothing much here."

Mountbatten looked disappointed. Then he brightened and said, "Let's go to Baghdad. We've never seen it, you know."

"It's seventy-five miles away," Strafford gasped.

"Well," Lord Louis said decisively, "We can't be that close and not see it."

"All right," Strafford said. "I'll give you half an hour to freshen up and we'll start."

Patricia Mountbatten said, "I can't take it. I'm going to bed."

Exactly thirty minutes later the Mountbattens came downstairs crisply fresh—"Edwina looked twenty years younger."

Meanwhile Sir Charles had called up the governor in Baghdad, and laid on a tour with the leading archaeologist. He flew them down in his own plane—"It was still frightfully hot at 2,000 feet although a little cooler on the ground." With the archaeologist as guide they saw all the historic sights of Baghdad, attended a big dinner the governor had arranged in frantic haste, and started back for Habbaniya about midnight. At eight o'clock the next morning the Mountbattens took off for London.

In England, too, there were laurels to be gathered. Of course, Mountbatten was the object of considerable criticism among the ultra-conservatives. The anguished howls of the local satraps who disagreed with his liberal policies in Southeast Asia had preceded him to London, where they echoed in the clubs, in which long ago his father had been crucified, and reverberated through the hostile Beaverbrook Press. But Clement Attlee's Government were well pleased with their proconsul. Not only had Mountbatten pulled together the military monkey puzzle of SEAC and made it a smoothly functioning instrument of victory; but, more important in Attlee's eyes, he had implemented the progressive policies of the Labour Government toward liberating the former colonies without diminishing—and even enhancing—England's prestige. The Prime Minister had feared that the permanent bureaucrats, who because of that permanence play such a great, unseen role in governing Britain and dictating her foreign and Commonwealth policies, would succeed in frustrating the liberal plans of his administration. They had tried, God knows. But above them had stood the radiant royal figure of a man with modern perceptions and immense good will, who thought as Attlee did, and who had been able to win the friendship of the national leaders of the independence movements. He deserved well of England and Attlee saw to it that his services received recognition.

Mountbatten had already been made a Knight Commander of the Order of the Bath. Now Attlee proposed to the King that he create Mountbatten a viscount. King George was especially delighted that a member of his family had won the honor by his own merit. Because Lord Louis had no son, the peerage would be an empty honor ending with him. The King therefore made the unusual provision that it should descend through the female line.

Mountbatten was both pleased and a little sorry—he had a sentimental, perhaps superstitious, feeling about being Lord Louis. But he lost no time in choosing his name—Mountbatten of Burma; and, in consultation with the College of Heralds, he designed a particularly effulgent coat of arms, which had the Arms of Battenberg-Mountbatten and the Royal Arms of the United Kingdom "differenced by Princess Alice's label." The shield within the Garter was surmounted by a viscount's coronet (later an earl's coronet) supported by the Hessian lion. The first crest was the bull's horns of Hesse; the second crest was the ostrich feathers of Battenberg-Mountbatten. The motto: *In Honour Bound.*

The shield within the *Garter!* In St. George's Chapel in Windsor, brilliant with the armorial banners of the Knights, and in the presence of the elect of the Kingdom in their sapphire-blue medieval cloaks and velvet bonnets, King George installed the Viscount Mountbatten of Burma in the Most Noble Order of the Garter. This was the highest accolade; the last great order of chivalry left in a world where the word has almost lost its meaning. Mountbatten was intensely, emotionally aware of its significance. When in a moment of acute perception American General Wedemeyer had called him "a conscious, gallant knight in shining armor," he touched the inner core of Mountbatten's character and recognized the romantic faith by which he lived and which he never would forswear.

It is probable that no other honor in the world would have meant so much to him, not only for himself, but for the Royal Navy. Though he had been operating so far from the sea, the Navy was still his first love and allegiance. He was intensely jealous of its rights and prerogatives. Later on he wrote to Queen Elizabeth II, noting that while three field marshals and one general had been made Knights of the Garter after

World War Two, only one admiral had been given that honor. That he was the admiral was a special source of pride to him, as was the fact that he, by becoming the first Supreme Allied Commander and the only *British* Supreme Allied Commander, had thus brought honor to the Royal Navy. He now proposed to return to it, where he belonged.

Chapter 15

"LIKE AN AMMUNITION SHIP ON FIRE"

AFTER SEVEN YEARS OF WAR SERVICE, the Mountbattens began to reconstruct their peacetime lives. They went at it with their usual exuberance. Lord Louis—he still thought of himself as that and so did most people—had innumerable reports to make, and a great many ceremonial occasions to attend as lesser honors were showered on him, such as honorary doctorates at Oxford and Cambridge, and the Sword of Honor and Freedom of the City of London. He was made High Steward of the Borough of Romsey, and president of the Royal Automobile Club and of the British Institute of Radio Engineers. The survivors of the *Kelly* formed a Reunion Association of which he became the very active president.

The house on Chester Street came alive again, filled with flowers and guests. Lord Louis' nephew, Prince Philip, was in and out constantly. Through him Mountbatten was about to gratify another ambition he had been quietly promoting. For Philip was unofficially engaged to Princess Elizabeth, heiress to the throne.

The Mountbattens spent their weekends at Broadlands. One wing of the house was still a hospital, but for the first time Edwina and her husband could tranquilly enjoy her beautiful heritage. Mrs. Eily Donald, who helped Edwina redecorate it, called Broadlands "the perfect small, big house." Build originally in the sixteenth century, it was rebuilt in 1750 by Robert Adams and Henry Holland in the Palladian style of the eighteenth century. Its classic façade and pillared portico look down sloping lawns, enhanced by ancient trees, to a quiet little English river. Behind it are the formal gardens with clipped yew and a mirror pool. Its large, finely proportioned rooms are embellished with loot brought home from abroad by generations of its owners, not the least of which is that acquired by Sir Ernest Cassel, including his marvelous collection of Chinese jade. Paintings by great artists of each generation, from Van Dyke to Dali, hang on the walls. But after seven years of neglect Broadlands badly needed refurbishing.

Further excitement was provided by the impending marriage of Patricia Mountbatten. In Singapore she had become engaged to young Lord Brabourne.* An officer of the Coldstream Guards, he had been wounded in Belgium in September, 1944, and later sent to SEAC as one of Mountbatten's aides de camp. His father had been a popular governor of Bombay and Bengal, and for six months acting Viceroy of India— another Mountbatten link with the East.

Patricia was to be married in October at Romsey Abbey, with a great reception at Broadlands. It was a time of rigid austerity in England, but for this occasion all stops were pulled out. True to form Lord Louis took intense interest in planning every detail of the wedding. He must have been an even greater nuisance to his wife and daughter than he had been to his staff in SEAC. Of course, they were used to him, but how they laughed when their lord and master—of logistics—woke up at 3 A. M. two mornings before the great day and suddenly realized that his meticulous plan for parking the cars of a thousand guests was fatally defective. He spent the rest of the night waking everybody up, reorganizing the whole thing, and countermanding and reissuing instructions.

Like almost all Lord Louis' plans, in the end the wedding went off perfectly. Though Patricia was not nearly as pretty as her mother she looked quite handsome that day. Among her bridesmaids were Princesses Elizabeth and Margaret, and Pamela Mountbatten. King George and Queen Elizabeth were there, of course, as were dozens of Mountbattens, including Lord Louis' mother, the Dowager Marchioness of

---

* John Knatchbull, seventh Baron Brabourne.

Milford Haven, and his sister Louise, who had married Crown Prince Gustav of Sweden in 1923.*

After the wedding in Romsey Abbey there was a reception in the long dining room at Broadlands, preserved for posterity by pictures of all concerned in their uniforms and wedding finery. Incidentally, it was the first time Princess Elizabeth and Prince Philip were publicly photographed together.

Then the Mountbattens did a typical thing. Leaving a thousand wedding guests regaling themselves at Broadlands, they carried off the entire wedding party, including King George and Queen Elizabeth, to Crossfield Hall in the village of Romsey to a party given by the Mountbatten and Brabourne tenants.

Ups and downs of rank are standard in the services. From acting four-star admiral, general, and air chief marshal, Mountbatten crashed down to his permanent rank of captain, but was immediately promoted to rear admiral. Rumors were running all over London that he was to be made Governor General of Australia or South Africa, or High Commissioner to Palestine. He wanted none of these things. The exigencies of war might swerve but not alter the course of his ambition to be First Sea Lord. Besides, he felt that it would be good for the Royal Navy to have a young and active admiral—he was only forty-six—who had the experience of having been a Supreme Allied Commander. He also thought it would be good for his soul. When someone asked him how it felt to be a rear admiral after having been Supreme Commander, he grinned a little wryly and answered, "Very salutary."

So Lord Louis was delighted when he was ordered to hoist his flag in command of the First Cruiser Squadron in the Mediterranean, in April. He entered the Senior Officers' Technical Course at Portsmouth on January 6, 1947, to brush up for his new job. But by then he was sadly convinced he would not be there long.

In the evening of December 18, 1946, Mountbatten called his old friend and confidant Rear Admiral Charles Lambe† on the telephone. In an unusually agitated voice he said, "Edwina and I want to see you tonight. May we come over?"

"Of course, Dickie," Lambe answered. To his wife he said, "Something big must be up. Dickie sounded very upset."

---

* Now King Gustav VI of Sweden.
† Later, Admiral Sir Charles Lambe.

The Mountbattens arrived at the Lambes' small house in Stafford Place soon after dinner. Though they greeted their host gaily and joked about old times the Lambes could see that their gaiety was febrile. When they had settled down with drinks Admiral Lambe said, "Well, Dickie, what is it?"

Lord Louis dropped his mask and his face looked suddenly taut. "Attlee sent for me today," he said. "He wants me to be Viceroy of India."

It was a shock to Charles Lambe as it clearly had been to Lord Louis. "What did you say?" he asked.

"I put him off. We had a very long talk; and he was most persuasive. But perfectly frank. He said the odds were six to four against my pulling off this independence thing. But he said I was the only one who had a chance of doing it.

"Charles, I don't want to leave the Navy. *You* know that all my hopes and ambitions are there. I feel I've come home. If I leave again I'm afraid I'll never get back."

"You will," Lambe said. "You can make it a condition."

"I suppose so," Mountbatten said. "But I don't think I can do this Viceroy thing." (Lady Lambe says, "He was rather humble about it.")

They talked it over for nearly three hours. As all such discussions go they iterated and reiterated the same points. Edwina did not take sides; she, too, evidently wanted the Lambes' advice. They were in favor of accepting.

Lady Lambe says, "Charles had tremendous admiration for Dickie. He thought it was the best thing for the country, that perhaps he was the only man who could pull the British out of India peacefully, and with dignity and honor. He said, 'You must do it!' "

Possibly Mountbatten had expected other advice from a fellow naval officer. He was clearly shaken, more than half converted. As he left he said he might accept, if he were convinced that he had "a reasonable chance of succeeding."

The situation in India was, in fact, desperate. Agitation for independence had been rising steadily since World War One. When Lord Louis once mentioned to Nehru that in 1922 he had become engaged to Edwina in Room 13 of Delhi University, the Indian, smiling, said, "At that moment I was occupying cell 13 in the nearby jail."

As long as the prospect of freedom from the British Raj seemed dimly distant the peoples of the two great religions of India, Hindu and Mohammedan, co-operated to obtain it. But when, in 1945, the

Labour Government came to power pledged to grant India independence, the Moslems had troubled second thoughts. There were over 255,000,000 Hindus in India and only 92,000,000 Moslems. Naturally the Moslems feared that if a central government for all India were formed on democratic lines they would become a persecuted minority.

The Hindu instrument of political power was the Congress Party, led by the saintly, mystic revolutionary, Mahatma Gandhi, and his more worldly disciple, Pandit Nehru. It claimed to represent all Indians and did contain a few "tame" Moslems. Mohammed Ali Jinnah, an ice-blooded, arrogant fanatic, was the virtual dictator of the minority group, the Moslem League. They demanded that India be partitioned into two states according to religious predominance—India and Pakistan. The word partition produced the same violent reaction in the Hindu majority as it had in the south of Ireland. Those Englishmen who understood and loved India also feared that partition eventually would result in the "Balkanization" of India into a picture puzzle of feeble little states, as she had been before the British unified her.

There were two other elements in this almost insoluble problem—the 5,500,000 Sikhs, mostly in the Punjab, a proud and warlike lot with an esoteric religion of their own, and the semi-autonomous Princely States. There were 565 of these, ranging in size from Hyderabad with 17,000,000 people and vast revenues to little hillbilly states with fewer than 1,000 inhabitants whose rajahs lived on about $250 a year. The princes were not subjects of the British Government of India. They simply acknowledged the paramountcy of the British Crown and swore an oath of personal allegiance to the King.

Had it not been for religious fanaticism India would have received dominion status before the Second World War. In 1927 the Simon Commission, of which Attlee was a member, had gone to India to try to work out a compromise plan. It eventually resulted in the Government of India Act of 1935, which gave Indians a much greater share in their government. Then, in 1942, Churchill's Coalition Government had sent a mission headed by the brilliant student of Indian affairs, Sir Stafford Cripps. It also failed to produce a viable plan. In March, 1946, Prime Minister Attlee made a final, desperate try to achieve Indian independence without partition by sending a Cabinet Mission, consisting of Cripps, Lord Pethick-Lawrence, Secretary of State for India, and Mr. A. V. Alexander. It produced a plan for a federated India, to consist of a Hindu state, a Moslem state, and an almost evenly balanced state—Bengal and Assam. There would be a central government, which however would be responsible only for Defence, Foreign Affairs, and Communications, leaving all domestic matters to the individual governments of the three states.

Due very largely to the untiring, humanitarian efforts of old Lord Pethick-Lawrence and the enormous patience of the Viceroy, Lord Wavell, both the Congress Party and Jinnah's Moslem League provisionally accepted the "Cabinet Mission Plan." The Cabinet Mission left India with high hopes.

Then the trouble began. The Indians on both sides began to talk themselves out of agreement—how they talked! Wavell was no match for them. He was a silent, almost tongue-tied man of immense good will but a little slow of mind—"A plain man and a soldier" he truly called himself. In addition he was violently antipathetic to Gandhi.

The break came on July 10 when Nehru announced at a press conference that he expected the Congress to modify the Cabinet Mission Plan. That was all the suspicious leader of the Moslem League needed. As Leonard Mosley says, in *The Last Days of the British Raj*, "Mr. Jinnah . . . dived for cover, screaming treachery as he did so." On July 27, at Jinnah's demand, the Moslem League unanimously withdrew its acceptance of the Cabinet Mission Plan and passed a resolution setting August 16, 1946, as "Direct Action Day." In a rabble-rousing speech Jinnah said, "This day we bid good-bye to constitutional methods. . . . Today we have also forged a pistol and are in a position to use it."

Soon after dawn on August 16 a Moslem mob poured out of Calcutta's "leprous slums," armed with broken bottles, automobile cranks, miscellaneous ironmongery, and *lathis* (knives lashed to long sticks). Howling through the narrow streets they attacked and dismembered every lone Hindu they could find, from old gentlemen to baby girls. Burning, looting, raping they turned the city into a charnel house. The stunned Hindu minority took a little time to rally. Then their mobs came roaring out, and did the same things to the Moslems. When British troops finally restored order three days later, six thousand Calcuttans were dead and twenty thousand were maimed, disfigured, or raped.

"We who have gotten civilized are somewhat soft," said Sir Frederick Morgan (§). *"We don't understand the power of hatred—of hatred unto death."*

After Calcutta there was never a chance of a unified India. Oh, they still talked and talked and talked. They even went to England—Nehru, Jinnah, Liaquat Ali Khan,* and Wavell—to confer with Attlee and Lord Pethick-Lawrence. The conference only made things worse.

---

* Finance Minister of the Interim Government of India.

In desperation Attlee asked Wavell for a new plan. The old soldier was now completely defeatist. All he could produce was a plan worked out by his Indian Civil Service, which Attlee described as, "A plan for the evacuation of India with everybody moving from where they were by stages right up through the Ganges Valley till eventually, apparently, they would be collected at Karachi and Bombay and sail away. Well, I thought that was what Winston would certainly, quite properly, describe as a sordid scuttle. . . ."*

Poor Wavell had lost the Prime Minister's confidence, and gained the dislike of Gandhi and Nehru. He had to go. Attlee sought for someone to replace him. "Suddenly I had . . . an inspiration," he said. "I thought of Mountbatten.

"Now Mountbatten was an extremely lively, exciting personality," Attlee continued. "He had an extraordinary faculty for getting on with all kinds of people as he'd shown when he was Supremo in Southeast Asia. He was also blessed with a very unusual wife. So I put it to him. Bit of a shock for Dickie, you know. . . ." And Attlee said, "Appointing Mountbatten was one stroke of mine that was entirely successful."

Mountbatten did not give up easily. In his first letter to Attlee he said he would go only at the invitation of the Indian leaders. This Attlee pointed out was impracticable. Lord Louis wrote another letter, warning Attlee that although he proposed to uphold the dignity of the Viceroyalty, he and Edwina intended "to visit Indian leaders and Indian people in their homes." Attlee thoroughly approved.

But Mountbatten still could not bring himself to accept. Finally he went to see the King, whose permission he had to have in any event. Though the interview was, of course, completely private, the course of it is now known. King George VI, though a shy and self-effacing man, had considerable common sense. He realized what many in the Court did not—that India was bound to attain independence. When Lord Louis said, "Bertie, what do you think I should do?" the King replied in substance, "I think you should take it, Dickie. In fact you're the only man who can hope to pull it off. Not only because the Indian leaders on both sides like you and respect you, and will trust you more than anyone else Attlee could send, but there is also the very important matter of the princes. They swore fealty to me, personally; and only one of my own family can release them from their oath."

Lord Attlee said(§), "The King was very good to allow [Dickie] to take on a job that might turn out so badly and therefore bring opprobrium on the Royal Family."

---

* *Twilight of Empire*, the memoirs of Clement Attlee.

Mountbatten's talk with the King left him with no option but to accept the Viceroyalty. However he drove a hard bargain with Attlee. First, he insisted that the time limit when the British should pull out, no matter whether agreement was reached or not, be set at June, 1948. Attlee was in complete agreement. He said, "Mountbatten and I agreed on the timing of Indian independence in that conversation. The wise old birds always tell you to wait a bit, that things will get better. Things don't get better; they get worse. In India things would have gotten worse. The Indian people were getting very impatient. . . . Besides if we had waited the machinery would have run down. . . ." The British were leaving the Indian Civil Service in droves.

Lord Louis' second condition was that he take his own staff with him. He realized that Wavell's staff were committed to Wavell's thinking and that the thinking of the British in the Indian Civil Service was hopelessly out of joint with the times. They would thwart him on every point. If he were to run the show he had to have his own people. He chose them wisely. Lord Ismay, who had proved himself the ablest soldier-diplomat of World War Two, patriotically sacrificed his hard-earned retirement to become his Chief of Staff; Sir Eric Mieville went as Principal Secretary; also, Captain Ronald Brockman, his close friend who had been his Naval Secretary all through SEAC, and Alan Campbell-Johnson, a brilliant young public relations expert who had been with him ever since Combined Operations. All were young men, except Ismay; all under forty. Lord Louis was forty-six.*

Mountbatten's final and to him most important condition was that both the First Lord of the Admiralty and the First Sea Lord must agree that his career in the Royal Navy would not be prejudiced. Therefore his orders, probably unique in the history of the Royal Navy, read: REAR ADMIRAL THE VISCOUNT MOUNTBATTEN OF BURMA SECONDED TEMPORARY DUTY—VICEROY OF INDIA.

There are people in England who say that accepting the Viceroyalty was an example of Mountbatten's inordinate ambition; that he sold his country for a mess of personal glory.† That is the blackest calumny he had to face. He knew he would have to face it when he took the job. It was the exact opposite of his ambition which ever focused on the Royal Navy. The Viceroyalty was sure to bring obloquy upon him. He was almost certain to fail. Lord Ismay said, "It

---

* Edwina took Elizabeth Ward, who had been her aide in St. John Ambulance, as her private secretary.

† Winston Churchill was furious.

was like taking command of an ammunition ship already on fire." And even if, against the odds, Lord Louis succeeded, he knew that to the end of English history he would bear the stigma of the man who consented to preside over the dissolution of the British Empire.

Lord Attlee said, "My own view would be that his real aim was to stay in the Navy; that Mountbatten wanted to be First Sea Lord to redress the wrong done to his father. It was an act of public spirit to accept the Viceroyalty. *I believe it.*"

The fact is, Lord Louis was living up to his high-flown motto.

On March 20, 1947, Mountbatten's old *York* plane was dusted off, and it set out once more for India. Aboard her were Lord and Lady Mountbatten and their daughter. They had taken Pamela, who was not yet eighteen, out of school, because they thought she might be helpful in taking on some of the social burden, and because it would be an unforgettable experience for her.

The Mountbattens landed in Delhi a little after noon on March 22. A large party of officials, including Pandit Nehru, Mr. Liaquat Ali Khan,* and the Commander in Chief, Field Marshal Auchinleck, met them at Palam Airport. After the ceremonial greetings, the Mountbattens motored into New Delhi where they transferred to a state landau with the Royal Arms emblazoned on its panels. With colorful outriders and the Governor General's mounted Indian escort clattering around them, they swung through the great gates into the courtyard of the Viceroy's House at exactly 3:45 P.M. In the blazing sunshine, its façade of red and white stone stretched a block or more in an infinity of pillared porticos, with the Union Jack flying from the fat dome above the massive central section. Lord Wavell, bronzed, sturdy, soldierly, stood with Lady Wavell at the head of the great stairs leading to the Durbar Hall, waiting to greet them. Lord Louis made a low bow to the Viceroy and Edwina curtseyed.

It was a rather delicate moment, for as Mountbatten knew, Wavell had a great grievance. Usually the most courteous of men, Clement Attlee, either through inadvertence or ennui, had treated the Viceroy abominably, never even warning him that he was to be ousted. Wavell heard news of his impending replacement over the radio, after Attlee's announcement of it in the House of Commons on February 20, 1947; the official cable did not reach him until the next morning. It was dismal recompense for nearly four years of untiring, selfless effort in a post of

---

* Later the first Prime Minister of Pakistan.

the utmost difficulty. Wavell said sadly to his private secretary, George Abell, "Well, George, I always seem to get the short end of the stick." After that he is reported to have spoken to no one, except possibly Lady Wavell, for three weeks.

Nevertheless he was too fine and patriotic a man to take his grievance out on the new Viceroy, whom he knew was not to blame. They retired almost immediately to the Viceroy's gloomy, teak-paneled, air-conditioned study for a briefing that lasted until dinner, and was resumed immediately afterward, as Campbell-Johnson wrote in *Mission with Mountbatten*, "with Mountbatten freely and frankly picking Wavell's brains and extracting all possible background information. . . ." This Wavell generously gave.

The Mountbattens drove the Wavells to the airport the next morning at 8:15, and the following day, Monday, March 24, 1947, Mountbatten was invested as Viceroy of India. That morning the circular Durbar Hall, with its 180-foot dome supported by tall yellow-marble columns, was packed with the power and chivalry of India. On one side were the greatest of the princes, glittering in jewels; on the other were the Indian statesmen—Nehru slight and silvery in a white coat adorned by a single red rose, and Liaquat, fat and jowly under his turban; the others in their various national costumes.

Trumpets under the huge dome ear-splittingly announced the approach of the Viceroy and Vicereine. Preceded by the aides in slow procession, they walked toward the two gold-and-scarlet thrones standing on a semicircular dais at one end of the hall. Lord Louis wore the pale-blue, ermine-trimmed robe of the Grand Master of the Star of India over the full-dress uniform of a four-star admiral (acting), crossed by the blue ribbon of the Garter and with all his orders and decorations ablaze in the fierce white glare of movie lights. He looked superbly young and handsome—more royal than any king in living memory. Edwina in a long gown of ivory brocade, across which was the delicate pink ribbon of the Crown of India, walked gracefully beside him. Her radiant vitality triumphed over the harsh lighting and the blaze of diamonds in her coronet and at her throat. Never before had such a beautiful, youthful couple occupied those thrones; and a soft breeze of approbation swept over the emotional Indians as they passed by.

As soon as Sir Patrick Spens, Lord Chief Justice of India, had administered the oath, Mountbatten broke his first precedent by making a speech from the dais. It was typical of his manner of addressing troops —short, straightforward, almost monosyllabic, lacking style and rhetoric, but carrying a clear impact of simple sincerity and good will:

Although I believe it is not usual for a speech to be made at the swearing in ceremony, I should like to say a few words to you, and to India.

This is not a normal viceroyalty on which I am embarking. His Majesty's Government are resolved to transfer power by June, 1948....

I believe every political leader of India feels, as I do, the urgency of the task before us. I hope soon to be in close consultation with them and will give them all the help I can.

In the meanwhile every one of us must do what he can to avoid any action which might lead to further bitterness or add to the toll of innocent victims....

I have many Indian friends. Some I made when I was out here twenty-five years ago—it was here in Delhi that my wife and I became engaged. In the three years that I was with the Southeast Asia Command I made many more among the Indian fighting forces, with whom I am so proud to have been associated.

It will not be an easy matter to succeed Lord Wavell, who has done so much to take India along the path of self-government. . . . I am under no illusion about the difficulty of my task. I shall need the greatest good will of the greatest possible number, and I am asking India for that good will.

When Lord Louis took his seat beside Edwina on the golden thrones the trumpets blew again and artillery in the park and in every British garrison throughout India fired the thirty-one gun viceregal salute as the Viceroy's flag was hoisted on the flagpole atop the dome.

The whole ceremony, speech and all, was over in fifteen minutes. Fifteen minutes after that Lord Louis had shed his finery and was at work.

Chapter 16

"MOUNTBATTEN
KAI JAI!"

To HIS TASK OF RECONCILING the Indian leaders to each other and to an agreement which would make it possible for England to leave India in freedom rather than chaos, Mountbatten brought not only his indispensable, almost inhuman energy, which made an eighteen-hour day normal and a twenty-hour day quite usual—he said, "I never worked so hard in my life, not even during the war"; but he also used all the weapons in his armory. Charm of course—he fairly slathered on the charm—to which Indians are peculiarly susceptible; but also his ruthless determination, his Germanic arrogance, used sparingly but at exactly the right moment. Then there was "Democratic Dickie," sitting familiarly on the ground at picnics with his Indian hosts, winning them all with his easy hail-fellow-well-met humor. When the occasion suited, as at the swearing-in, he put on the royal act as only he could. Lord Curzon was said to have been the most effulgent Viceroy, but it is doubtful if he topped Mountbatten at his grandest—after all Curzon was not Queen Victoria's great-grandson.

Finally there was Lord Louis' secret weapon—Lady Louis. Before they left he had told Edwina, "Your job is to get the women on our side."

The Indian women have enormous unseen power. Until recently

they seldom acted in public; but their influence on their men was perhaps greater than among Europeans. Edwina won their confidence and
friendship—Nehru's sister, Jinnah's daughter, Patel's* daughter, all
powers behind the ruling powers. She accomplished it by doing what
came naturally to her, by her warmth and genuine interest in them, her
deep concern for the unfortunate people whom they too cared about;
and, finally, by the fact that she truly loved India and wished it well.

In fact, Edwina went beyond her instructions and won Gandhi's
confidence and Nehru's heart as well. In England they still talk of
"Edwina's affair with Nehru." That is the greatest lie of all, for the
relationship between them was based on understanding, admiration, and
a mystic confluence of ideals, and was never physical. There was love,
but it was the pure, chivalrous, transcendent love like that of Dante for
Beatrice. It was in sober truth an example of the most beautiful and
delicate bond that can exist between a man and a woman. It was also a
most fortunate circumstance for England and for India.

Many books have been written about the last Viceroyalty—some
favorable, some bitterly critical; most of them in enormous and con-
fusing detail. To give even a synopsis of all the immense and intricate
pattern of personalities, points of view, negotiations, intrigues, treach-
eries, and self-sacrifice would take hunderds of pages and thousands of
footnotes. One cannot even hit the high spots, but must only touch
briefly on the peaks of achievement and tragedy.

The Viceroy's first formal meetings with the Indian leaders were
very important, because they set the pattern for the future. The first
was with Nehru on the afternoon of the swearing-in ceremony. It lasted
three hours. At the end Mountbatten said, "Mr. Nehru, I want you to
regard me not as the last Viceroy winding up the affairs of the British
Raj, but as the first to lead the way to the new India."

Tremendously moved Nehru stood silent for a moment. Then he
smiled and said, "Now I know what they mean when they speak of your
charm being so dangerous."

When Jinnah finally came, two weeks later, the atmosphere was
quite different. The Moslem leader, wearing a British-tailored suit and a
monocle, was skeleton-thin and armored in suspicion. There was no
more give to him than to old bones. When he left Mountbatten said to
Campbell-Johnson, "My God he was cold! It took most of the interview
to unfreeze him."

---

* Sandar Vallabhbhai Patel, an influential member of the Interim Government.

Before that Lord Louis, setting a tremendous pace, had held interviews with all of the members of the Indian Interim Government, with
the Sikh leaders, with Field Marshal Auchinleck and the commanders
in chief of the three armed services, and with the key princes or their
dewans (prime ministers). The most important meeting of all was with
Mahatma Gandhi. He came to the Viceroy's House on the afternoon
of March 31, wearing his famous, sheet-like garment tucked up between
his wizened brown legs. Almost as the Mountbattens greeted him a
wonderful rapport was established between them and the idealistic
keeper of India's conscience.

Fifty photographers in the charge of Campbell-Johnson were waiting in the Moghul Garden to record the historic meeting, so after a few
moments of talk the Mountbattens took their guest outside to face the
ordeal. There was the usual pushing and shouting, dozens of "one
mores!" through all of which Gandhi smiled his benevolent, toothless
grin and chatted amiably with the Mountbattens. Then the Viceroy
ended it. As they turned back toward the house the old Hindu holy
man rested his hand on Edwina's shoulder. It was an immensely touching
gesture of confidence and friendship—almost a benediction. Max Desfors
of Associated Press, who snapped it, got one of the most famous pictures
ever taken. That photograph was published in all the news media of
the world. In every country but one it was regarded as a symbol of a
new and better order in the world, and a new brotherhood between
Englishmen and Indians.

In England it raised an unholy row. The British aristocracy were
outraged that a British Vicereine should permit such a familiar gesture
by "a native." Their blue blood boiled at this final indignity to the
Empire and to English womanhood. Rather would they have had Lady
Mountbatten brush off the old saint's hand like camel dung. But Edwina
was deeply moved and happy and honored by his touch.

During two long interviews that day and the next between Gandhi
and Lord Louis, who sat comfortably in rattan chairs on a shaded terrace,
that first rapport warmed to friendship. In his soft, lisping voice Gandhi
spoke hopefully of the future and sorrowfully of what might happen
in between. For the apostle of non-violence was a realist who knew that
sometimes violence is inevitable. In an effort to avert it, and partition,
he made the amazing offer to have Nehru resign and have the Viceroy
call on Jinnah to form a Moslem Interim Government. "What would
Jinnah say?" Lord Louis asked.

With his engaging grin, the Mahatma answered, "He'd say, 'Aha, it's that wily Gandhi again.'"

"Won't he be right?"

"No," Gandhi said. "I am absolutely sincere."

Then very, very seriously Gandhi told Mountbatten that the old British (Roman) policy of Divide and Rule was coming home to roost. "The policy of your predecessors has brought about a situation in which there are only two alternatives," he said, "either a continuation of British rule to keep law and order, or an Indian blood-bath."

"What must I do then?" asked Mountbatten.

"You must face the blood-bath and accept it," said the man of peace.

The negotiations now began in earnest. Day after day in the blazing heat of an Indian spring Mountbatten held meetings with Indians of all parties that lasted from three to six hours. Both he and Attlee regarded the Federated India plan as the best, and he faithfully put it forward. But the communal massacres, which had traveled up the Ganges Valley from Calcutta like a forest fire, had made it impossible. The Hindus were willing to make many concessions; but Jinnah would have Pakistan or nothing. So it quickly got down to persuading the Hindus to agree to partition, and the Moslems to agree on a plan for it acceptable to the Congress—and above all to frame it so that both states would freely come into the British Commonwealth.

In these negotiations Mountbatten used his knowledge of Indian psychology with great effect. He knew that unlike Western negotiators, who start far apart and usually end with a compromise agreement, the courteous Indians begin by agreeing for politeness' sake and then impose conditions which nullify everything. When, in the round-table discussions, a point was raised and agreed upon, the Viceroy would instantly say, "Good, now that's settled we can go on to the next thing." On the following day when the Indians returned to reopen discussion with their second thoughts they were stunned to find themselves confronted with a *fait accompli*.

To prepare the ground for these meetings Mountbatten met daily with his staff, to which he had added Wavell's former secretary, George Abell. These men, headed by much-beloved "Pug" Ismay, worked like demons, preparing agenda, sounding out Indian opinion in Indian homes, trying out ideas and reporting reactions, and doing preliminary softening up of the leaders for Mountbatten's clinching arguments.

Nor were Edwina and Pamela idle. They were circulating among the women of Delhi, and inspecting hospitals, schools, and welfare projects at a tremendous pace as well as flying to visit refugee camps and hospitals in riot areas. It was so hot that Edwina had to wring out her long hair three or four times a day.

She was also managing the enormous Viceregal establishment, which contained over 5,700 specialized servants, gardeners, stablemen, engineers, mechanics, and whatnot. This enormous staff was due not to Mountbatten's *folie de grandeur*, as is implied in critical books. In a land where labor was so cheap and different castes so proud that one servant would not perform another's function, it had grown up naturally. Lord Louis inherited it from his predecessors and accepted it for the brief time he intended to be there.

Because social life was so important to the Indians the Mountbattens entertained seven or eight times a week—state banquets in the great dining room that could seat 105 guests, huge garden parties, small, delightfully intimate dinners and luncheons, and one entirely non-political affair, a gay supper-dance in the walled garden by the swimming pool, in honor of Pamela's eighteenth birthday.

But never for a moment did Mountbatten relax his pressure on the politicians to come to some agreement soon. This terrific drive has been violently criticized, but he believed that if it were not done quickly it never would be done. Communal bitterness was rising, rising, rising; the longer the wait the bloodier the bath. As a result of his determination he was able to take a rough plan for partition back with him to England on May 18.*

In London Mountbatten drove the British statesmen as hard as he had driven the Indians. He told Attlee it was essential that he have a Cabinet-approved plan to take back to Delhi with him and that an Indian Independence Act must be ready to be passed before the session of Parliament ended in August. Attlee said it could not be done in less than six months. Mountbatten said it had to be. He and Attlee brought Churchill and the other Opposition leaders into conference and got their reluctant backing, and Mountbatten personally swung the King's influence as well. He returned to Delhi on May 31, with an approved plan. The top Indian leaders were summoned to meet at the Viceroy's House on Monday, June 2, 1949.

At ten A.M. the big black American limousines of the Indian statesmen began rolling into the Viceroy's courtyard—Nehru, Patel, and Acharya Kripalani for the Hindus; Jinnah, Liaquat, and Sardar Nishtar for the Moslems; Sardar Baldev Singh represented the Sikhs. They

---

* The British governors of all thirteen provinces were unanimously agreed that independence must come quickly.

greeted each other with unexpected cordiality in the Viceroy's study, which Mountbatten had redecorated in light green, because he said, "The dark paneling makes everybody dismal and discouraged."

Jinnah arrived last. Then Mountbatten took the chair and presented the approved plan, which called for the Indian people themselves, through their respective legislatures, to decide for or against partition; setting up the method of voting; and then the plan for a separate India and Pakistan if the vote in the Moslem areas went for partition as it was certain to do. Everyone agrees that Mountbatten handled the meeting skillfully. The key words were that he asked the leaders not for agreement with but only *acceptance* of the plan. After two hours of expertly fielding questions and replying to objections he secured qualified acceptances from all concerned. What is even more astonishing, all three principals agreed to go on the radio with him the following evening and announce their acceptance. They also agreed to meet again next morning.

But in another room of the Palace Mahatma Gandhi was waiting to see the Viceroy—Gandhi, whose dearest desire was Indian freedom *with unity*. As Lord Louis greeted him, the Mahatma wrote on a scrap of paper, "Monday is my day of silence. . . . I am sorry I can't speak. . . . But I know you don't want me to break my silence." In his memoirs Lord Ismay commented, "As luck would have it . . . Mountbatten was able to do all the talking. He succeeded in convincing the Mahatma that the plan was in fact a 'Gandhi conception,' and [that no other] arrangement would command general acceptance."

Campbell-Johnson says that on Gandhi's part it was " a great act of political renunciation and self-control."

So far so good. But Jinnah was coming back in the evening with his final word. Before that Mountbatten gave a Burma Star party, for former members of SEAC and recipients of the Burma Star, at which he frolicked around wearing his old bush jacket as though he had nothing else on his mind, which for the moment was true.

Jinnah arrived at midnight, "in one of his difficult moods," according to Ismay. He described the plan as scandalous. He said he would urge it on the Council of the Moslem League, but could guarantee nothing.

Lord Louis took his imperious role. He told Jinnah that unless he accepted in the morning the Hindus and Sikhs would pull out. "Chaos will follow and you will lose Pakistan for good."

Jinnah shrugged.

Sternly Lord Louis said, "Mr. Jinnah, I do not intend to let you wreck this settlement. . . . Since you will not accept for the Moslem

League I will speak for them myself. I will take the risk of saying that I am satisfied with the assurances you have given me. I have only one condition, that you will under *no circumstances* contradict me . . . and that when I look toward you, you will nod your head."*

Jinnah nodded.

The plan was announced officially by the Viceroy over the radio the following evening in a very matter-of-fact speech. Nehru followed with an emotional and moving oration. After him came Jinnah, cold, critical, but grudgingly agreeing. He paid an unexpected tribute to Mountbatten as being "actuated by the highest sense of fairness and impartiality." He closed with, "Pakistan Zindebad!" However he said it so quickly that some of his listeners thought that he had expressed his triumph by saying, "Pakistan's in the bag." The Sikh spoke last and sadly, foreseeing the bloodstained future.

Thus the Plan was launched. On sea, land, or air it was Mountbatten's greatest victory.

It might be supposed that the Mountbattens and their overworked staff could now take a breather. Not at all! At Mountbatten's insistence the date for Indian independence had been set for August 15, 1947, a little over two months off—two months in which to disentangle the complex political, economic, and military ties that bound together united India, with her 400,000,000 people. Lord Louis had a calendar made, each sheet of which said, "72 [or 71 or 70] Days to Independence"; each day he tore off one sheet. The pace became more frantic than ever, as they worked with the newly formed Partition Council.

One of the saddest aspects of partition to the British officers, and to Mountbatten, was that the magnificent Indian Army had to be divided. Lord Louis had done his best to keep it intact to serve both Pakistan and India, but Jinnah had said, "No! I must have my own army even if it is one sergeant and one private."

Regiments whose standards bore the names of some of England's greatest battles consisted of Hindus, Moslems, and Sikhs serving together in perfect loyalty. They had to be broken up and reconstituted according to religious affiliations. At the farewell regimental dinners, officers of the three major religions wept on each other's shoulders and swore eternal comradeship.

More dangerous and difficult was the necessity for partitioning the Punjab, Bengal, and Assam, where the populations were almost equally

---

* Alan Campbell-Johnson, *Mission with Mountbatten.*

divided among the religious groups. A Boundary Commission worked hard and impartially on this, but it was the weakest link in the plan and produced a bloody harvest.

Finally there was the unsolved problem of the Princely States. Under their treaties with the British Crown paramountcy did not revert to the governments of India or Pakistan, but simply lapsed. When the British Raj ended the states became independent nations. According to the Independence of India Act, which was passed by Parliament on July 18, 1947, their rulers could choose to join either India or Pakistan. But what if they did not? Chaos loomed. There would be 565 nations governed by absolute rulers, of whom a few were wise and progressive, but many more as willful, extravagant, and barbarous as the sport-loving Maharajah of Alwar, who, when one of his thoroughbred horses lost a race, poured gasoline over it and set it afire. When paramountcy lapsed men like these would have the power of life and death over their subjects. With such potential centers of anarchy scattered throughout the sub-continent, cutting across main roads and railway lines with national boundaries, India would not be a viable nation. It would be Balkanization with a vengeance.

It was up to Mountbatten to cajole or dragoon the reluctant princes into joining the nation of their choice. Not only was it what the British Government wanted, but the Indian Government begged for his help, and the King had privately charged Mountbatten to do his utmost to this end. But Sir Conrad Corfield, the British political adviser to the princes, who was ten times as royalist as the King, had been undercutting him by advising the princes to retain their sovereignty and unite in a bloc or third force. He intended "to make it as difficult as could be for the ... States to be absorbed."* Corfield had even gone to London to lobby for the princes, which caused Mountbatten to refer to him as "that son of a bitch Corfield." Lord Louis could not completely prevent this mischief; but he got rid of Corfield.

Such was the situation when, on July 25, Mountbatten went to the Council House to meet with some seventy-five of the greatest princes or their representatives and persuade them to sign the Instrument of Accession. Though it was an incredibly hot day—some statistician noted that the mercury stood at 108.4 degrees—he wore his white dress uniform with the royal aiguilletes draped over his shoulder and his breast ablaze with all his orders and decorations; he looked every inch the King's cousin. The tall, black-bearded Maharajah of Patiala and little V. P. Menon, Nehru's representative, met him on the ceremonial red

---

* Leonard Mosley, *The Last Days of the British Raj.*

carpet and escorted him to the antechamber where they presented him to forty of the most important princes. Then he went into the dark, wood-paneled circular chamber and took his place on the throne-chair facing a semicircle of Indian royalty.

Of Mountbatten's performance that day even critical Leonard Mosley says that it "was probably the most spectacular example of Mountbatten's skill, charm and tremendous arts of persuasion." And Campbell-Johnson wrote, "I cannot imagine a more difficult assembly for any man to have to address. . . . Once again Mountbatten's morale-raising talent was seen to full advantage. For somehow he managed to infect them with his own spontaneous enthusiasm and powers of decision."

Speaking without notes in a short, clear, informal manner he told the princes the plain facts of the advantages of accession and the impossible situation their states would face as independent enclaves within a great nation. Slyly he pointed out to these decoration-hungry gentlemen that since both India and Pakistan had opted to join the Commonwealth they could still receive honors from the King of England. Then he opened the meeting to questions from the floor.

They came in—rapid-fire acute questions, stupid questions, and some rather insulting questions. He fielded them with such dexterity and wit that he soon had the formerly glum princes smiling in appreciation. After a couple of hours of this semantic tightrope walking, Mountbatten called for order. Turning to his old friend the Maharajah of Bikaner, whom he had met with the Prince of Wales, he said, "Will you be the first to sign?"

"I will," replied the prince. And so he was.

Next came the Maharajah of Baroda, who signed and then threw his arms around surprised Menon's neck and burst into tears. Another rajah had a heart attack after signing. But not all were willing. When Mountbatten called on the dewan who represented an important prince who was out of the country, the man said, "I have received no instruction from my ruler and cannot sign."

"Surely you know His Highness' mind and can take the decision on his behalf," Lord Louis said.

"I do not know his mind," the dewan said stubbornly, "and cannot reach him by cable."

Mountbatten picked up a round glass paperweight from the rostrum. "I will look into my crystal and give you the answer," he said.

For long seconds he gazed, while the princes began to grin. Then Mountbatten solemnly said, "His Highness directs you to sign the Instrument of Accession."

A perfect roar of laughter and applause shook the Chamber. The rest was easy.

Mountbatten has been accused of betraying the princes; and in one sense he did. For he knew that the guaranties of local self-government and personal privileges offered them by the Governments of India and Pakistan would probably be broken as soon as those governments found it convenient—which they were. Lord Louis was, in fact, contemptuous of the princes. He regarded them as anachronisms left over from feudal days and privately referred to them as "that bunch of nitwits."

On the other hand he believed, quite accurately, that they could not stand alone. The British had agreed in the treaties to keep them on their thrones, and order had been maintained in the Princely States by British soldiers. Once they were withdrawn it was absolutely certain that the people would rise against their dissolute rulers in most of the states. At best they would be kicked out, at worst thrown off their parapets or torn limb from limb. There was really no choice.

In addition, Mountbatten owed a higher loyalty—to his King, to the British Government, and to the peoples of India and Pakistan. If indeed he sacrificed the princes, it was to a greater good.

Three of the princes held out for a while, those of the great states of Hyderabad and Kashmir and the little west-coast principality of Junagadh, which had only a nuisance value. The intransigence of Kashmir caused grave trouble. Nevertheless, 562 out of 565 rulers signed—an excellent score. Laughing, the Indians said, "Mountbatten not only charms birds off the trees, but princes off their thrones."

An extraordinary event, without precedent in the history of liberations, showed the confidence of the Indians in Mountbatten. Nehru's Government begged him to become the first Governor General of the Dominion of India. For a time it looked as though the Pakistanis would also do him this extraordinary honor. Mountbatten hoped they would, for he thought that as Governor General of both countries he could exert a unifying and conciliatory influence. However, Jinnah astonished everyone by deciding to become the Governor General of Pakistan himself, coupling almost dictatorial powers with the office.*

When this decision reached Mountbatten, he had serious doubts about accepting the Indian offer, for he feared that it might seem like

---

* However, both countries asked Mountbatten to become the impartial Chairman of the Joint Council of Defence.

taking sides; it was also a splendid excuse to get out and back to the Navy. There were very serious discussions with his staff and with the Indians and the Government at home. All were in favor of his accepting in any event. Even Jinnah said, "We want you to take it. We feel you will be a moderating influence." Yielding to this pressure Mountbatten agreed to become the first Governor General of the Dominion of India.

On Wednesday, August 13, 1947, Lord and Lady Mountbatten flew to Karachi for his final official duties as the last Viceroy of united British India. Jinnah gave a great dinner and reception for him that evening with sweet soft drinks and sweet soft music furnished by a band of bearded warriors in kilts. Jinnah, in his turban and immaculate, long white coat, with that very British monocle glittering in his eye and the cancer which was to kill him within a year gnawing his entrails, was a curiously aloof and lonely figure among his guests celebrating the birth of the nation he had created almost single-handed.

The next day came one of those hair-raising drives through a vast uncounted and unaccountable multitude. Jinnah's security people had uncovered a plot to throw a bomb at the open carriage in which he and the Viceroy were to ride in the state procession, and advised him to call it off. Jinnah said grimly, "If Mountbatten is willing to go through with it, I am." Of course Mountbatten was willing.

They drove separately to the Assembly. In the Chamber Jinnah made for his accustomed seat of honor as President of the Assembly. Mountbatten stopped him with smiling determination. "After all, Mr. Jinnah, I am still Viceroy and the representative of His Majesty the King."

Jinnah gave way in some embarrassment. Then Mountbatten read a message of congratulations to the new Dominion from the King, and spoke himself in his unoratorical style, which yet managed to be very moving. After offering his congratulations he said, "There is time only to look forward," and expressed the hope that both Pakistan and India would honor their commitments "to safeguard the legitimate interests of all citizens irrespective of religion, caste, or sex . . . and the exercise of liberties such as freedom of speech . . . [and of] worship. . . ." He said, "Now the time has come to bid you farewell—on behalf of His Majesty's Government, and on behalf of myself; also on behalf of my wife, whose thoughts and prayers will be so much with the women of Pakistan.

"This is a parting between friends who have learned to honor and respect one another even in disagreement. . . .

"May Pakistan prosper always . . . and may she continue in friendship with her neighbors and with all the nations of the world."

Then the Viceroy and Jinnah got into the state carriage. In the carriages behind them rode Lady Mountbatten and Miss Jinnah, followed by Mrs. Liaquat and Pamela Mountbatten. At a dead walk they drove through the wildly turbulent streets of Karachi. As the horses turned through the gates of Government House, Jinnah made a surprising, emotional gesture. Putting his hand on Lord Louis' knee he said, "Thank God I have brought you back alive!"

The actual passing of the British Raj was singularly quiet and informal. Indian independence was to begin at one second after midnight, August 15, 1947. The Mountbattens flew back to Delhi on August 14. For almost the first time since reaching India Edwina and Dickie had dinner alone together. They had been raised by the King, on Attlee's advice, to the rank of the Earl and Countess Mountbatten of Burma for their services in India.

After dinner Lord Louis went to his study with Campbell-Johnson and worked quietly on last-minute cables and papers. At a few minutes before twelve he was finished. He glanced at the clock and continued to sit at his desk, chatting with Campbell-Johnson, who described him as "serene and detached." As they sat there the clock struck midnight. Mountbatten quietly took off his glasses, and locked up the dispatch boxes emblazoned with the Viceroy's Arms. The British Empire had joined Nineveh and Tyre.

About twenty minutes later Nehru and President of the Constituent Assembly Doctor Rajendra Prasad arrived from the Assembly where at midnight Nehru had said, "Long years ago we made a tryst with destiny . . . and now the time comes when we shall redeem our pledge. . . ."

Photographers and reporters filled the room, and some of them jumped onto the big circular table. In the confusion "friendship completely burst the bounds of formality."[*] Prasad began his little speech inviting Mountbatten to be Governor General and got stuck in the middle; Nehru smilingly prompted him. With deep emotion Mountbatten gravely said, "I am proud of the honor and will do my best to carry out your advice in a constitutional manner."

Things were very different the next morning. The great Durbar Hall was filled again with a vast, colorful crowd; crimson and gold predominated. At eight-thirty the silver trumpets sounded for the

---

[*] Alan Campbell-Johnson, *Mission with Mountbatten.*

Governor General and his Lady. This time Lord Louis wore his white dress uniform, though with all his orders; Edwina wore a long gold lamé dress. As they took their seats on the golden thrones a flashbulb exploded like a rifle shot. A thousand eyes recorded that neither of them quivered. This time the swearing-in was done by Indian Lord Chief Justice, Doctor Kania. After the ceremony the band played "God Save The King," followed by the Indian National Anthem "*Jana Gana Mana.*"

Then the scene shifted to the Council House. A quarter of a million wildly enthusiastic people were besieging it. Somehow a way was cleared for the Governor General's landau drawn by four beautifully trained horses ridden by erect, white-haired postillions. Within the Council Chamber Mountbatten read a message from the King. Then he gave a concise, logical summation of the steps by which agreement on Indian independence had been reached so rapidly, followed by his tribute to their statesmen who had made it possible, with a special appreciation of Gandhi, who was not present. Finally came his pledge as Governor General to be "One of yourselves, devoted wholly to the furtherance of India's interests. . . ."

No one doubted that he meant it.

Again, by a miracle of order in utter confusion the Mountbattens' unwieldy equipage was cleared through the ever more excited crowds, yelling in fantastic volume, "Jai Hind!" "Mountbatten Kai Jai!" and "Lady Mountbatten Kai Jai!"

But the day was far from over. After lunch the Mountbattens drove (in an automobile) to the Roshanara Gardens where they surprised five thousand Indian schoolchildren, mingling with them, apparently enjoying the Indian side shows and magic tricks in the blazing heat, and handing out sweets to all the children who could get near them. Then back to "Government House"—it had changed its name that day—with just time to dress for the ceremony of raising the new flag of India at the War Memorial in Princes Park at six P.M.

Thirty thousand people had been expected; three hundred thousand were there. The Mountbattens, in their state carriage surrounded by the mounted bodyguard, got stuck in the happy, laughing crowd before they reached the dais. They were mobbed so completely that all that could be seen of them were the lances of the bodyguard, waving like trees in a wind above the tossing people. Nehru rescued Pamela Mountbatten from the crowd as he had her mother. Campbell-Johnson wrote, "In this maelstrom, rank and race, sex and caste were all lost in one vast unison . . . on all sides there was laughter and good humor. . . ."

The formal ceremony was abandoned. Nehru gave the order to hoist the gay new flag of India. As it climbed the pole Mountbatten stood in his carriage at salute; cannon began to fire the salute; a light rain started falling; and across the sky appeared a rainbow which almost matched the yellow, green, and red of India's flag. That universal omen of God's blessing raised joyous abandon to a frantic pitch.

Now to get away! Struggling horses, guards, and outriders somehow got turned around. Seeing Nehru caught in the crowd Lord Louis pulled him into the carriage and he sat on the open top like a boy in a crowded convertible. They also rescued a whole Indian family. With twelve people in it the state landau looked like a gypsy caravan at Epsom Downs.

As the horses got straightened out and began to trot back to Government House the crowd followed at a run, yelling with their last breaths, "Jai Hind! Mountbatten Kai Jai!"

Say what you will. Try to be detached and critical; yet you must recognize that it was a strange and marvelous and moving thing that the bitterness of forty years of revolution, repression, intrigue, and bloodshed should culminate in that scene of love for the man who represented the British King. Stranger yet that he could bring the British Empire to its end with neither the bang of cannon nor a whimper of dismay, but with half a million Indians shouting "Mountbatten Kai Jai!"

Chapter 17

GOVERNOR
GENERAL

INDEPENDENCE DAY was almost perfect, but the next day brought trouble that deepened into tragedy on a continental scale. That afternoon Mountbatten presented to the Government the Award of the Boundary Commission fixing the lines of partition in Bengal and the Punjab. It had been drawn by Sir Cyril Radcliffe with the help of two Moslems and two Hindus (who were no help, since they could agree about nothing). Radcliffe, a famous British jurist, knew nothing about India, and for this reason he had been accepted by the leaders of both sides who thought he would be impartial. He did, in fact, make an enormously conscientious effort to be just.

But the Angel of the Lord himself, assisted by the Lord Buddha and Mohammed, could not have produced a satisfactory division between the intricate tangle of population groups. The Indian leaders were shocked into sullen misery by the Award. The Moslems were furious, and the Sikhs, who had voted for the partition of the Punjab, raged in despair. Even as Mountbatten was presenting the Radcliffe Award news came that the Sikhs were rising in the Punjab.

The next few weeks saw the most enormous mass migrations and the most terrible massacres of modern times. Hindus, who had lived peacefully for generations in predominantly Moslem territory, fled for their lives; the Moslems in Hindu lands were no better off. Not content to let their "erring" brothers go in peace both sides attacked the helpless caravans of emigrants.

The Sikhs began it. Seeing their holy places of Amritsar and Nonkana Sahib given to the Moslems, forced to abandon their rich lands and vital water supply in the West Punjab, they went berserk and thought only of killing Moslems. They attacked them in the cities and in the caravans heading west from territory awarded to the Sikhs. Railway trains packed to their roofs with refugees arrived at their destinations with hundreds of corpses aboard. Painted on their sides was the legend A PRESENT FROM INDIA. Moslems, of course, did the same to fleeing Hindus.

Almost as appalling was the fate of the refugees who survived. They emigrated in millions. Flying over the Punjab plains, Mountbatten saw columns of refugees, with their oxen, cattle, and household goods, over sixty miles long moving in opposite directions, and open to attack from each other and from bands lying in ambush in the tall wheat.

Nor was the trouble in the Punjab alone. All along the borders of East and West Pakistan the vast migrations and the killings took place. Four hundred thousand refugees descended on Delhi alone, and the conditions in their makeshift camps were indescribable. Cholera broke out in Amritsar and in the refugee caravans.

In all, over ten million people migrated—some say fourteen million. About half a million people are reckoned to have been murdered, and Mosely states that approximately a hundred thousand girls were stolen and sold to the highest bidder.*

The one bright spot was Calcutta, the scene of the previous massacre, where the worst had been feared. There Gandhi persuaded the Moslem leader Shaheed Suhrawady to join him in appealing to men of both religions. By the moral force of his fragile person he kept the peace. Mountbatten called him "The one-man Boundary Force."

In the Punjab Mountbatten had set up a Punjab Boundary Force of 50,000 troops to keep the peace, built around the superb 4th Indian Division, under the command of Major General T. W. Reese. Completely overwhelmed by the millions engaged in communal strife, and cursed by both sides for every attempt to restore order, it was ordered disbanded on August 29. This relieved Mountbatten of his last executive responsibility. He was now theoretically in the position of a constitu-

---

* These figures are wildly unreliable. For example estimates of the dead range from two hundred thousand to three quarters of a million.

tional monarch obliged to heed the advice of the government on all matters.

Even Lord Louis was exhausted by his tremendous exertions. With the end of the Boundary Force he decided to take ten days of desperately needed rest at Simla in the foothills of the Himalayas. The Mountbattens arrived at the Viceregal Lodge there on August 30. It was an ugly, gray stone pile whose architectural style might be called Victorian Gigantic. But it was perched on a hilltop and surrounded by lovely gardens. Best of all it commanded a superb view of the towering, snow-shrouded Himalayan Range from which the snow-conditioned air flowed sweetly down.*

What a fool Lord Louis was to dream of ten days of rest! On the fifth day Deputy Prime Minister V. P. Menon telephoned to say that the communal situation had become so desperate that Nehru and his Government felt that only Mountbatten could save it. "Please come back to Delhi!" Lord Louis was in Delhi the next afternoon. After hearing Nehru's report he advised the Indian Government to form an Emergency Committee with powers to act effectively. Nehru said, "I will only take your advice on one condition—that you will become Chairman."

So Mountbatten was back in harness, working harder than ever.† Meanwhile Edwina was flying thousands of miles to inspect the scenes of the worst communal strife, visiting dozens of refugee camps and hospitals in the monsoon downpours, making suggestions from her vast experience, organizing the Indian Red Cross services, cheering the workers on and cheering up the stricken people, moving tirelessly, fearlessly through the overwrought, dangerous crowds. Pamela, who had been working for six months at the improvised free dispensary in Delhi set up in tents to provide medical services for the influx of refugees, became her father's personal assistant on the Emergency Committee.

At first the Indians on the Committee were aimless from despair— Nehru stricken by the horror of the first month of independence, Patel furious with frustration, the others bewildered. Campbell-Johnson wrote: "But for Mountbatten . . . the occasion called forth all his powers of objective and dynamic decision, and he at once radiated confidence and a sense of purpose where none had existed before."‡ One of the first acts of the Emergency Committee was to set up a relief committee under

---

* The Mountbattens' only other vacation was their trip to England for the wedding of Prince Philip and Princess Elizabeth.

† During his service in India Mountbatten also managed to complete his *Report on Southeast Asia* and begin *The Mountbatten Lineage*.

‡ Alan Campbell-Johnson, *Mission with Mountbatten*.

Lady Mountbatten, which she handled with "a perfect blend of charm and strength."*

The Emergency Committee and Edwina's United Council for Relief and Welfare did magnificent work. Mountbatten efficiently organized a regular war staff to bring order out of chaos, and even brought about a most peaceful and profitable meeting between Nehru and Liaquat, who was now Prime Minister of Pakistan. But it was Gandhi who finally stopped the killing. On January 13, 1948, he announced the last of his famous fasts—"A fast to death"—which would end only "if and when I am satisfied that there is a reunion of hearts of all communities brought about without any outside pressure, but from an awakened sense of duty...."

The extraordinary power over Hindus and Moslems alike of Gandhi's fasts, and particularly his last one, is difficult for Westerners to comprehend. It was as though the beloved *Bapu* (Father) transcended religious and national divisions, and in purifying himself by fasting took upon himself the guilt of all, purifying them as well. As the days passed and the old saint grew weaker, profound emotions were stirred in both communities.

In the midst of his fast the Mountbattens went to call on the Mahatma at Birla House, in the Untouchables' quarter of Delhi. Edwina had been there several times before but Lord Louis had always seen Gandhi at Government House. As he entered the bare room where Gandhi, weakening rapidly, lay on his little cot, the Mahatma, with a faint replica of his famous grin, said, "So it takes a fast to bring the Mountain to Mohammed." Then Mountbatten squatted on the floor beside him and they talked of the conditions on which Gandhi would end his fast.

The first material effect of the fast was when Nehru decided at Gandhi's urging to pay the 550,000,000 rupees India owed to Pakistan, which he had been withholding as a bargaining point. This produced a *détente*, and in the relaxed atmosphere an Intercommunal Peace Committee was set up headed by a Hindu and a Moslem and backed by all. When he heard this the Mahatma broke his fast—which had lasted five days.

However, amid the general rejoicing there were harshly discordant notes. Hot-headed Sikhs picketed Birla House with black banners proclaiming, GANDHI MUST DIE! They considered him to be soft on Moslems, and so did the Hindu Mahasabhas, an extremist group comparable to British Silver Shirts or American John Birchers. One night, as Gandhi was holding his regular prayer meeting, a bomb was thrown into

---

* *Ibid.*

the garden of Birla House. No one was hurt, and when Edwina rushed over to see Gandhi, he smiled at her and said, "I thought it was military maneuvers."

In the early afternoon of January 30, 1948, Mountbatten returned from a tour in Madras with Pamela and John and Patricia Brabourne, who had arrived for a long visit before Christmas. Edwina had stayed there, indefatigably inspecting hospitals. Hardly had he settled to work in his study when Chakravarti Rajagopalachari* telephoned the terrible news that Gandhi had been shot and killed as he walked from his house to the evening prayer meeting. He said that he did not know who had done it or any of the details. It shook Lord Louis as no other news could have.

First there was the shock and horror of such a death for so great, so gentle, so saintly a man. Then, after a few moments of numbness, Lord Louis tried to assess the consequences. They seemed unutterably dark. For it was Gandhi's divine spirit which had held India together and held down communal killing. His was the most pervasive influence for moderation and sanity, and without him the lid might blow off—especially if it were a Moslem who had killed him.

Mountbatten groaned and ordered his car. By the time he reached it he was in command of himself, but the strain showed by the way he snapped out orders more like an admiral commanding a fleet in action than a civilian governor general. Campbell-Johnson rode with him through the slums of Delhi to the Sweepers' quarter.

Birla House was surrounded by an enormous emotional multitude, straining against the doors, peering in the windows, tapping against the glass. They were stunned rather than angry; but the slightest spark could explode them for they were as volatile as fulminate of mercury. Mountbatten shouldered his way into Birla House. As he pushed through, a man shouted at him, "It was a Moslem who killed him!" In a flash Lord Louis snapped, "You fool! It was a Hindu." He did not know whether it was or not, but he did know that if the assassin had been a Moslem everything he had worked for, all chance of communal peace, would be lost in such spurting of blood as the world had never seen.

The large, bare rooms of Birla House were quiet compared to the immense susurration of the crowd outside. People were standing about listlessly, not knowing what to do. Mountbatten and Campbell-Johnson

---

* Governor of Bengal. Later, the first Indian Governor General of the Dominion of India.

pushed through to Gandhi's bedroom. Outside the door was a pile of sandals people had taken off before entering. The room smelled of incense. Thirty or forty cabinet ministers and high officials of the Indian Government stood there, weeping quietly. Gandhi's body—so slight that the form was hardly perceptible—lay on his bed in a far corner, covered with a large blanket. A sobbing woman was fondling his head and others chanted a dirge. The Mahatma's face was serene as though in a deep sleep.

As Mountbatten looked down reverently at Gandhi's quiet face he was charged by emotion, yet no longer in despair. As Campbell-Johnson wrote, "[There was] also a sense of victory rather than defeat; that the strength of this little man's ideas and ideals, from the very force of the devotion he was commanding here and now, would prove too strong for the assassin's bullets and the ideas they represented."

After standing for some time in respectful homage Mountbatten moved into the room where the Indian Cabinet were now gathered. Nehru and Patel were standing a little apart from each other—they had been feuding violently over policy. Lord Louis went up to them and said, "The last time I talked to Gandhiji he said that his dearest wish was to bring about a full reconciliation between Nehru and Patel."

With tears streaming from their eyes the two leaders embraced each other.

Then V. P. Menon told Lord Louis the first good news of that mournful day. It was not a Moslem but a Mahratta belonging to the Rashtriya Swayam Sevak Sangh, the storm troopers of the Hindu Mahasabha, who had killed Gandhi. His name was Vinayak Goodse and he was the editor of a small provincial newspaper. His act appeared to be part of an organized conspiracy. This fact awoke in Mountbatten the hope that it would arouse the conscience of the Hindu world and thus sublimate communal bitterness.

Gandhi's body was taken to the burning ghat the next morning, through scenes of tumultuous grief. Lord Louis and Edwina, who had returned from Madras, their children, and Mountbatten's closest advisers went first to Birla House to attend the placing of Gandhi's body on the funeral carriage. There his head lay among flowers, and his sons and granddaughters sat beside him, the girls still weeping and stroking his still face. The crowd was so dense that the escort of 4,000 troops and the sailors drawing the carriage could not move. Nehru and Mountbatten walked into the crowd exhorting them to give room. Finally the cortege began to inch forward.

After returning briefly to Government House, the Mountbattens drove by a circuitous route to the Raj Ghat. As they approached the place of burning their motorcade was swallowed by the multitude moving toward it. However, they reached the Ghat before the cortege and walked up the bare mound toward a small brick platform piled with logs. From there they could see the crowd of close to three quarters of a million people, a quivering ocean of white robes* and brown faces stretching to infinity. A thin line of Indian Air Force men held them back from the cleared space around the pyre.

Sizing the situation up with a military eye Mountbatten realized that the line would never hold if the crowd surged forward. He told his family and staff to sit down on the bare, dusty ground and persuaded part of the crowd nearest them to do likewise, thus forming a human barrier.

As the cortege moved almost imperceptibly in an irresistible flood of humanity, the noise and confusion became almost unbearable. Everyone within reach attempted some final act of devotion. In the most democratic scene India had ever known, statesmen and untouchables, old peasant women and high officers struggled up to throw flowers on the pyre.

While priests chanted prayers logs were piled up on top of the tiny body and ghee for kindling the fire was poured over them from tin cans. The ceremonial rites seemed to take forever as the enormous pressure of the crowd increased. When, finally, Gandhi's sons lit the pyre with a torch of sacred fire and the flames leapt high, a tremendous mass groan arose from three quarters of a million throats. The multitude surged forward from four directions. Mountbatten, alert to the danger, said, "It's time to go now."

He grasped Edwina's hand and told the others to clasp hands and hold tight. So linked they gradually forced their way through the people, who braced themselves against the pressure to give them a narrow way. As they reached the cars and looked back over the crowd, now frozen motionless by the pressure of body against body, they could see the pillar of smoke and fire rising from the body of the man who had been the incarnation of the soul of India.

There were a few more crises during the remainder of Mountbatten's service as Governor General. As the unofficial envoy of the Indian Government, he failed to cajole the Nizam of Hyderabad into signing the Instrument of Accession though the Nizam did later. Kash-

---

* White is the Indian color of mourning.

mir was even more difficult. The Hindu ruler of the state, which was over 80 per cent Moslem, refused to take Mountbatten's advice to consult his people. He acceded to India and fled from his furious subjects. Pakistanis and Indians rushed into the vacuum. The Indians took the best part of the country including the rivers which were the life-springs of West Pakistan. Nehru promised a plebiscite which was never held. Kashmir became the bone of contention which has made enemies instead of allies of the two countries which have so many interests in common.

Naturally the Pakistanis blamed Mountbatten, the handiest object for their reasonable wrath. All their good will for him turned to such bitterness that the man who made Pakistan possible without civil war cannot now even visit that country. Jinnah attacked him vitriolically. Yet just before he died Jinnah said to an English friend, "Mountbatten was one of the few men I have ever known who had *nur* [divine radiance]."

Mountbatten had also been blamed for everything else that went wrong, as he expected he would be. The most serious charge was that his impatience was responsible for the Punjab massacres. Even people who agree that he was right in forcing through the agreement on partition so fast, maintain that his deadline for independence of August 15, 1947, did not allow time for proper precautions and arrangements to be made. Maurice Zinkin, formerly of the Indian Civil Service, says(§), "Wavell represented the Indian point of view in England. . . . Mountbatten was not basically interested in India but represented British interests. His hurry to get out was partly due to his own desire to get back to the Navy before he got hopelessly behind. He did the job with dash and deftness but without compassion. Lady Mountbatten supplied the compassion."

Leonard Mosley also accuses Mountbatten of being too anxious to get back to the Navy, and therefore of the haste that he claims resulted in the Punjab massacres.

On the other hand Mountbatten did not have to accept the Governor Generalship. Even Edwina was against it. Had he been in such a mad hurry to get home, he could have left on August 16, 1947, instead of remaining until June 21, 1948.

Others point out that had Mountbatten waited instead of rushing the agreement on partition, Jinnah, master of the policy of denial, would have been dead, and a united India might have been possible. Mountbatten's reply to that was, "I am not an astrologer."

It must be accepted on the evidence that Mountbatten, rightly or wrongly, believed that speed was essential to achieving Indian independence with the minimum of bloodshed, and there is much to support his opinion. Certainly communal bitterness was rising and in a long period of uncertainty it might well have gotten completely out of hand. Then instead of being fairly well localized in the Punjab the whole of India might well have gone berserk. Millions instead of thousands might have died. What of Calcutta if Gandhi had already been dead? Would the princes have agreed to accession if they had been given time for typically Indian second thoughts? Would it have been possible to hold the Indian Army and Civil Service together much longer? The experts say not.

In his speech to the East India Association after his return to England Mountbatten stated that on the question of when the transfer of power should take place, "There was absolutely no difference of opinion. . . . Everybody wanted the greatest possible speed, everybody wanted the transfer of power to take place quickly. Indeed, why wait? For in waiting there would be the risk of continued and increasing riots. There would be increasing friction and difficulty in keeping the Indian Coalition Government together. . . . So we went ahead and fixed a date. It took two years to separate Sind from Bombay. We separated 400,000,000 people in two and a half months. . . ."

Certainly Mountbatten performed the operation coolly and decisively in accordance with the hard core of his character. But should a surgeon maunder over the cutting of his patient, what a messy operation would result. In this event, the patient lived although he sadly lost a great deal of blood.

Attlee strongly backs Mountbatten's decision on the need for haste. "I think Mountbatten was right in hurrying the takeover," he said(§). "There is no virtue in hanging around when it's time to leave. If after agreement had been reached there had been communal disturbances, it might have upset the whole show. Mountbatten was right to cinch it."

Even the doubting Captain Roskill says(§), "When Mountbatten got out to India, he and Lady Mountbatten acted with enormous courage. Picture the Mountbattens walking hand in hand amongst those enormously dangerous crowds. The Indian knot had to be cut. . . ."

Finally there was the prophecy of India's most peace-loving man: "You must face the blood-bath."

The assessment must remain forever in the twilight zone of opinion. Like every human endeavor, it might have been better. But it certainly could have been infinitely worse.

.   .   .

June 21, 1948. The four-horse state carriage waited in front of Government House, surrounded by the Governor General's bodyguard. The Ghurkas lined the King's Way. Beyond the gates a quarter of a million Indians waited patiently to say good-bye.

The Mountbattens had been saying good-bye for months at official ceremonies and private parties in a triumphal tour all over India culminating on June 20 in the farewell in Old Delhi when the Mountbattens' carriage was buried in flowers thrown by half a million cheering Indians, and the final state banquet where Nehru, almost in tears, had spoken from his brimming heart of Lord Louis as his friend and the friend of India who had won the people's "love and affection"; of Lady Mountbatten's "beauty and high intelligence, grace and charm . . . and even rarer than those gifts, the human touch, the love of humanity, the urge to serve those who suffer and who are in distress, and this amazing mixture of qualities resulted in a radiant personality and the healer's touch. . . . The Indian people love you and look upon you as one of themselves. . . ."

Now everything was said and there remained only the last drive. The three Mountbattens came down the broad steps of Government House in the blazing sunshine while the crowd beyond the gates swayed and shouted, begging them not to leave. Lord Louis inspected the Guard of Honor and then the Mountbattens got into the open landau. The turbaned footmen jumped up behind, the Mounted Guard moved forward, and the old postillions in their scarlet and gold uniforms clucked at the horses.

At that point a curious thing happened. One of that beautifully trained team went crazy as even the best trained horses sometimes do. He reared and plunged, bucked and almost rolled over. There was nothing for it but to unhitch him. As he was led away the crowd shouted, "Even the horses refused to take you from us. . . ."

Prime Minister Attlee and Prince Philip were waiting at Northold Airport to meet the Mountbattens when the faithful *York* landed there two days later. There was a flurry of greetings and congratulations. Attlee was fairly beaming with joy—he had not really believed that Mountbatten could pull it off. He admitted it, and said, "In my opinion no other man could have carried out this tremendous task." For the first of perhaps a hundred times Lord Louis said very seriously, "I never could have done it without Edwina."

Chapter 18

MISSION
ACCOMPLISHED

THE MOUNTBATTENS were flat broke. In fact they owed tens of thousands of pounds. In order to perform properly the function of the Viceroyalty they had entertained 7,605 guests at luncheon, 8,313 at dinner, and 25,287 at garden parties and so forth—a very grand total of 41,205. One can see how far the Viceroy's entertainment allowance of £13,000 (about $50,000) a year went. Since Edwina's fortune was in trust she could not touch the principal, and the income tax in the highest bracket was nineteen shillings sixpence on the pound.* In addition the capital tax levied by the Labour Government was more than her entire income.

Clement Attlee was most helpful, as indeed he should have been. Rather than have him put through a bill for the Government to reimburse them, the Mountbattens suggested that a private bill be introduced to allow Edwina to anticipate her capital. Attlee pushed it hard. The Lords were sympathetic, but an anti-Mountbatten group in the House raised such a ruckus that the bill was abandoned. Ultimately a general bill allowing married women to anticipate inheritances was passed in 1949, so the Mountbattens finally got out of hock.

---

* There are twenty shillings in a pound.

Meanwhile they managed to live in the grand manner. The house on Chester Street was good enough in wartime but very small for their peacetime way of life. They began looking around for another London residence. They spent a good deal of time at Broadlands, where Edwina worked energetically on the house and gardens while Lord Louis brought back the shooting which he loved.

Mountbatten had, of course, reverted to his regular rank of rear admiral. There was a great deal of speculation as to what his new job would be. Various ambassadorships and governor generalships were rumored. The Beaverbrook Press thundered invectives against him, both as the man "who had given away India," and a dangerous influence on the monarchy—because Philip was married to the Heiress Apparent.

Mountbatten paid no heed to any of these things. He knew what he wanted and he got it—command of the First Cruiser Squadron in the Mediterranean. He was ordered to report for duty in October, 1948.

One would think that the Mountbattens would have enjoyed relaxing at beautiful Broadlands and playing with their new Brabourne grandson during this four-month interval. But no! Their inner springs seemed always wound too tight. In August they were off for a holiday in Ireland at Mullaghmore near Classiebawn Castle, which had not yet been reopened. In September they dashed down to the Riviera for a couple of weeks—then back to London to entertain Nehru who had arrived for the Dominion Conference. At Broadlands they had a perfectly delightful evening with their Indian friend—no cares of state, no temperamental Maharajahs or obdurate Pakistanis to worry about, nothing but the joy of friendship renewed. They taught the intellectual Nehru to play Racing Demon.

In October Rear Admiral the Earl Mountbatten of Burma, K.G., etc., etc., at long last hoisted his flag aboard H.M.S. *Newcastle*. Commissioned in 1936, she was a light cruiser of 9,000 tons, mounting twelve 6-inch guns in six turrets, eight 4-inch guns and a lot of anti-aircraft stuff. Her 75,000-horsepower engines drove her at 32 knots. She was, in fact, a handsome, old-fashioned yacht-like ship rather akin to the *Drake* which Prince Louis had commanded.

There was a great deal of curiosity among service people as to how Mountbatten would react to serving in a subordinate position after having been Supreme Commander and Viceroy. To make it more interesting the Commander in Chief Mediterranean was Admiral Sir Arthur Power who had commanded the East Indies Fleet under him in SEAC. Second-in-command was Admiral Douglas-Pennant who had also been under him in SEAC. Mountbatten ranked fourth in the naval pecking order.

Having neither false pride nor false modesty Lord Louis managed things very gracefully. He was properly respectful to his superiors, which was like playing a game according to the rules, for he and they knew that he would always outrank them on the rolls of history. In fact Admiral Power could not get over the habit of calling his old chief "sir." Mountbatten, of course, called the commander in chief "sir." Everyone else was highly amused to hear them sir-ing each other.

The Mountbattens stayed at the Phoenecia Hotel in Valletta while Edwina went house hunting—the Casa Medina had been turned into an apartment house. She rented the Villa Guardamangia and went to work redoing it with her usual energy. On December 29 she announced that it was ready and they all moved in. However, the move was slightly premature. The next morning Lord Louis took a bath, and when he pulled the plug the water poured into the kitchen, nearly drowning the cook. The happy Maltese had forgotten to connect the drain.

The Mountbattens spent five of the next eight years in Malta—perhaps their happiest years ever. It was wonderful to see how the island had regained its gaiety and beauty. The devastation that had made Lord Louis groan as he sailed the *Kelly* in under the Nazi bombs had almost been erased. Houses had sprung up out of the rubble, built of the same soft, golden stone so they looked old. The blue, blue sea was dotted with fishing boats with pastel-tinted lateen sails, and the harbor was filled with pale-gray warships flying the White Ensign, among which native *dghaisas*, like miniature Viking long ships, plied. Garrison life was back to normal, with parties for the opera, picnics in the hills, and polo ponies galloping again on the Marsa Ground.

Edwina had made the Villa Guardamangia into an exquisite tropical-style house done in cool pale greens and pale blues, and of course there were masses of flowers in the big airy rooms. As usual the Mountbattens did a lot of entertaining, but not so lavishly as to give cause for jealousy—though inevitably some were jealous because the Mountbattens were who they were.

Among those who came to visit them were David Milford Haven and his American fiancée, Mrs. Romaine Dahlgren Simpson. "Uncle Dickie" took a great fancy to dark-haired, vivacious "Toody" Simpson and helped smooth the way for their marriage to which David's mother objected violently. Lord Louis undoubtedly hoped that a wife would calm young David down a bit, but he was disappointed. They were married in Washington in 1950 and divorced four years later.

Then, almost at the end of that tour of duty, Prince Philip, recently a proud father, arrived to report for duty aboard the flotilla leader

Chequers. Princess Elizabeth soon followed him. They stayed at hospitable Villa Guardamangia.*

Mountbatten remained in command of the cruisers for nearly two years. It was not a very challenging job compared to the ones he had held. Though he loved Malta, he was delighted when, late in 1949, he was promoted to vice admiral and ordered to Whitehall as Fourth Sea Lord. That was a big step toward his ambition, and a job he could get his teeth into.

During Lord Louis' two years at the Admiralty he pushed the post into a position of importance it had never had before—an empire within the larger sphere. His enormous energy, refreshed by the fallow years at Malta, burst out in a spate of new ideas and reforms. First he completely reorganized his department. Then the Fourth Sea Lord took over the responsibility for ordering all the armament supplies for the Fleet from the Third Sea Lord. Finally he was given the job of all administrative planning for the Royal Navy. There was no end to the amount of work he could do and the motto around the Admiralty seemed to be, Let Dickie do it.

Dickie was willing. Not only did he enjoy the pressure, but he was consciously fashioning the machine he had every intention of running some day, and building himself into the indispensable man.

Meanwhile Edwina was busy running St. John Ambulance. Every year she made a trip to West Africa and the Far East to inspect the work there with special attention to the Indian Red Cross, which she had helped to organize into the most efficient one in Asia.

In England she was also busy reorganizing the Mountbattens' life on its customary magnificent scale—the bill that allowed her to touch capital at last had been passed. She sold the house on Chester Street and bought two houses rebuilt into one on Wilton Crescent, just off Belgrave Square. The outside was rather ordinary but with the help of Mrs. Donald she made its interior into a gay and exquisite classical setting for small entertainments.

She also went to work on Broadlands, part of which was still unreconstructed from wartime use. In the wing that had been used as a hospital the walls were sheathed in protective plywood, and many of the great pictures remained in a bank vault. The incentive came in the summer of 1950 when King George and Queen Elizabeth proposed themselves for a visit. Edwina sent for Mrs. Donald. "Can you give us a good plan for redecoration?" she asked.

---

* When the Mountbattens left, the Edinburghs rented the villa for themselves.

"Of course," Mrs. Donald said. "But I'd like time to think it over."
"It must be done in three weeks."

"I'll never know how we managed it," Mrs. Donald says. "The job included laying four thousand yards of carpet, having ten sofas re-covered and everything else in proportion. That was just like Edwina. She always wanted everything done the same week."

Lord Louis also did a bit of redecorating. In his own room he had the beautiful Adam mantlepiece ripped out and the whole thing re-decorated in the modern style with functional furniture, and, of course, all his beloved mechanical gadgets. For a man who sets such store by tra-dition and ancestry this passion for modernity in his physical surround-ings superficially represents an amazing dichotomy; but it is actually fundamental in his thinking, which always insists on having the best of both worlds.

King George VI had been in poor health ever since 1949. However he seemed so much better in January of 1952, that Princess Elizabeth and Prince Philip started off on an official Commonwealth Tour. Lady Pamela Mountbatten went in attendance on the Princess. On February 5, they were in Kenya at Treetops, the famous observation lodge built in a huge fig tree in the jungle.

That day the King had some fine shooting at Sandringham, and went to bed early. On the morning of February 6, 1952, the valet who came to wake him found that the King had died in his sleep.

The English people who loved their gentle, conscientious King very much were truly sorrowful. Lord Louis was even more affected, for Bertie had been a friend since childhood and youth, and had confided in him in times of trouble. On the afternoon of February 7, he and Edwina went with Prime Minister Winston Churchill and the Duke of Gloucester to the airport to meet Queen Elizabeth II and Philip.

The big blue and silver plane *Atalanta* had hardly come to a stop when Gloucester and the Mountbattens went aboard—Churchill tact-fully waited to greet the Queen until she had seen the family. The royal couple were with Pamela in their stateroom at the rear of the plane. The Queen was stony calm, facing up to things in the manner dictated by her tremendous sense of duty. Philip was stunned. He had hoped and planned to make a real career in the Navy, like his uncle and grandfather, and he was well on his way. Now that was done for. He knew that the tradi-tional, rigid British protocol, which prevents the Sovereign and her Consort from taking a really constructive part in any phase of British life that could possibly be construed as "political," would make it impossible. His honorary title of Admiral of the Fleet would choke him.

The Mountbattens gave what comfort they could and rode with the Queen to Buckingham Palace where Queen Mary was waiting for them.

As the King's personal Naval Aide Lord Louis walked beside the coffin in all the mournful pageantry that followed, as his father had done for Victoria and Edward. The ceremonies ended as they had those other times with the bagpipes skirling "Flowers of the Forest" in Windsor Great Park.

In 1951, Clement Attlee's Labour Government fell and Winston Churchill came again to power. In view of Churchill's fulminations against Mountbatten for his part in giving India independence, this might have been expected to have an adverse affect on his career. Quite the contrary. Churchill recognized that Mountbatten had acted from conviction and a sense of duty. He may even have been glad that his Government did not have to cope with the Indian problem. He retained all his old affection for his young protégé and his keen anxiety to advance his career.

In fact both political parties sympathized with Lord Louis' basic ambition. Lord Attlee said(§), "I always hoped he would become First Sea Lord." Churchill's new First Lord of the Admiralty, Mr. John Thomas, gave him a big push forward by appointing him Commander in Chief Mediterranean in 1952. It was next to the last of his father's footsteps.

In Malta again the Mountbattens settled into Admiralty House. It was another example of the British Government's genius for ostentatious discomfort. Almost the only large house in Malta without a view, it had grandiose state rooms for entertaining and only five bedrooms. Edwina sorely missed the Villa Guardamangia, but as usual managed to make the place livable.

In 1953, almost a year after setting up headquarters in the Castile—known as H.M.S. *Venetian*—Mountbatten was appointed to command the NATO forces in the Mediterranean as Allied Commander in Chief. He was also promoted to admiral and made Naval Aide-de-Camp to the Queen. His new post gave him overall co-ordinating power for naval and air movements in the Mediterranean, including jurisdiction over the great United States Sixth Fleet and warships of France, Italy, Turkey, and Greece. Brian Connell correctly comments in *Manifest Destiny* that, "It is doubtful whether the Americans would have been willing to yield such powers to any other Englishman."

This was the sort of challenge Mountbatten loved, calling for all his powers of organization and diplomacy. Before taking it on Lord Louis talked over the make-up of his staff with many senior British and American naval officers, among them his new chief of staff, Rear Admiral Sir Peter Cazalet, and his old friend, Rear Admiral Royer Dick. He said to them, "I am going to have an admiral for every country represented in the fleet, and have them on the staff. I must have somebody with rank from each country who can go back to his country and bang the table and say, 'This is what we think is right!' A young captain wouldn't be able to do that."

Admiral Dick said to the author, "Although I opposed this set-up for fear there would be criticism of Dickie being, as usual, overstaffed, I now know, and say, Dickie was right—it worked."

Mountbatten adopted the same system he had used in SEAC of holding almost daily staff conferences with everybody present, and bringing them to a consensus, unanimous if at all possible, on problems and plans. It is a rather cumbersome system but it did work—mainly because Lord Louis had lost none of his persuasive power.

Since there was no war on, the actual decisions of the staff were not of earth-shaking importance. However, as General Sir Michael West, Chief of the British Military Mission in Washington, pointed out to the author, "Its political implications—men of all nations working together —were a fine thing."

That political sense of Mountbatten's often riled his critics, and he gave them cause for complaint in Malta—perhaps he had not quite metamorphosed from Viceroy into Admiral. The population of the island, like the people of virtually every other colonial possession, began agitating for freedom, or at least representation in their Government. Lord Louis' sympathetic attitude toward such aspirations led him first into warm friendship with some of the leading Maltese politicians and then into advocating integration of Malta with the United Kingdom, with Maltese representation in the British Parliament. The Maltese Labour Party were for it; the Conservatives wanted Dominion status.

Lord Louis' intervention shocked conservative British opinion on two counts. The first shock grew from the idea of Maltese members sitting in Parliament, which it was said would open the way for all the other little colonies to do the same, thereby turning the House of Commons into a particolored League of Little Nations. But the British were even more shocked that an Admiral, and a member of the Royal Family at that, should express a political opinion.

As Lady Lambe said, "Dickie is frightfully good at bringing people together. He is always being criticized for entering too much into politics, but if you are passionately interested in the well-being of the world you have to take part in politics. He entered that situation in order to try to help the Maltese."

Of course nothing came of the integration plan, but many authorities think that it might well have been a good solution for Malta.

In addition to this piece of politicking Mountbatten took an active role in diplomacy. He rightly regarded strengthening the ties of the NATO Alliance as being part of his job. He and Edwina paid official visits to all the Allied countries within his area of command, and to most of the smaller nations bordering on the Mediterranean as well. As might be foretold from their success in the Far East, they generated an extraordinary amount of good will.

Perhaps their most successful foray occurred during the earthquake in Greece in 1953. The moment the news reached Malta the Mountbattens were off like firehorses to the scenes of disaster. There they worked tirelessly to help the victims. Lord Louis used all his authority to produce relief supplies and Edwina's know-how saw to their efficient distribution, while together they visited and comforted thousands of homeless, desperate people.

On the other hand their official visit to Emperor Haile Selassie of Ethiopia showed quite a different side of Mountbatten's character. Soon after they arrived at the great, cold, comfortless palace in Addis Ababa, Lord Louis said to the British Foreign Service officer who accompanied him, "You know it would be nice if the Emperor decided to give me the Grand Cordon of Solomon. Why don't you drop a hint in the right quarter?" Utterly amazed, the diplomat replied, "It really isn't done, you know."

When Lord Louis was on the trail of another glittering decoration to add to his extensive collection he was not easily discouraged. That evening he personally dropped such a forceful hint to the Ethiopian Foreign Minister that the astonished gentleman secretly cabled the British Foreign Office asking if it would be advisable to present Admiral Mountbatten with the Grand Cordon of Solomon. Back came the undiplomatic reply: "Certainly not."*

Frivolous, brash, and juvenile as Lord Louis' try was, it is not entirely offensive. That a man who had earned so many honors and held the highest of them all—the Garter—should still be ingenuous enough ardently to desire one more, shows a rather endearing, if somewhat prolonged, youthfulness.

· · ·

* The author reserves the right not to disclose the source of this anecdote.

Mountbatten served as Allied Commander in Chief until December, 1954, when he was recalled to England. He could feel satisfied with his work. The Maltese loved him, and loved Edwina even more for the many services she had rendered them; at her office every morning at 8:30 she had chaired, presidented, and pretty much run every welfare activity on the island. Mountbatten's subordinates certainly adored him as they did wherever he served. Most important of all was the impression he made on the commanders from the other NATO nations, which they showed in a tribute unique in naval history.

When the good-byes had been said and it was time to leave, Lord Louis looked for his Admiral's barge. Instead he found a whaleboat waiting, with six admirals of six nations manning the oars. Misty-eyed, Mountbatten took his place at the tiller ropes. Across the blue water, splashing, catching crabs, and making very heavy weather of it, but with enormous gusto, they rowed him to his ship.

Winston Churchill decided that it was time Lord Louis achieved his ambition. He had earned it more than most men who have held the post. Early in 1955, Admiral the Earl Mountbatten of Burma was appointed First Sea Lord. So were amends made, a debt discharged, and honor satisfied. In addition the Royal Navy got a damn good First Sea Lord.

Lord Louis' appointment met with almost universal approval in England—Conservatives and Labour alike applauded. The exception was the vindictive Beaverbrook Press. As early as 1952, when it was rumored that Mountbatten might become First Sea Lord, the *Sunday Express* ran an editorial entitled "Can We Risk It?" After paying lip service to Mountbatten's charm, dash, and courage, it alluded to his command of Combined Operations, and said:

> He left an imperishable monument of that Post—the Dieppe Raid. In one short day that raid practically wiped out a Canadian Army. . . . Lord Mountbatten accepted full responsibility for the plan.
>
> He next moved East to be Supreme Commander South-East Asia. . . . [After] Rangoon fell without a fight, general disintegration set in. . . .
>
> Two years later Lord Mountbatten went to India as Viceroy to carry through the political decision to give self-government to the sub-continent. He achieved the handing over with a speed that had historic consequences. . . .

What were the consequences?

The two hurriedly torn-apart halves of India are today in a state of most bitter enmity. . . . The abrupt removal of Britain's steadying hand was followed by a slaughter of still incalculable dimensions, but which knowledgeable people say involved a million lives.

Before Lord Mountbatten is made First Sea Lord we might profitably ponder over the thought that if the mind that moved so swiftly with the task of partitioning India sets to work on shaping the new Navy with the same degree of energy and judgment, we in our turn may suffer as terribly.

When Mountbatten actually became First Sea Lord the *Sunday Express* carried a cartoon showing Edwina Mountbatten in profile and the Queen behind her. It was captioned: THE POWER BEHIND THE THRONE. The lead article was practically a rerun of the 1952 editorial.

Exactly what caused Lord Beaverbrook's hatred of Mountbatten is a matter of conjecture. Since he was a Canadian the Dieppe Raid undoubtedly fanned the flames. In an emotional moment Beaverbrook is reported to have said of Mountbatten, "He murdered my Canadians."

But the vendetta was probably of a more trivial origin. Mountbatten's own theory was expressed in a letter he wrote to Admiral John Godfrey on January 17, 1952. In it he describes Beaverbrook as a close friend from 1924 until 1942. That year Noel Coward's film *In Which We Serve* appeared. It was a stirring story of a fictional destroyer, which was almost a documentary on the *Kelly*. Near the end of the film, as the *Kelly* sinks beneath the Mediterranean, the camera pans down to a copy of an old newspaper floating among the debris. In huge black type is an actual headline from the *Daily Express* of August 7, 1939, that reads:

NO WAR THIS YEAR

In his letter to Godfrey, Mountbatten says that at a dinner with Averell Harriman, Lord Beaverbrook accused him of having "engineered this" and said he "would neither forget nor forgive this hostile act." Lord Louis assured him that he had nothing to do with it; that, in fact, when he saw the preview of the film he had urged Noel Coward to cut it out, but Coward had refused to do so.

Rather wryly Mountbatten commented that, "Max Beaverbrook has been as good as his word," and he added that he did not believe there was any larger reason for Beaverbrook's campaign against him.

The Beaverbrook attack brought Mountbatten an "unexpected mass" of telephone calls, personal visits, and letters expressing sympathy and confidence.

Ambition achieved can produce relaxation. Not in Lord Louis. Hardly had he settled himself behind the big desk that had been his father's than his keen eyes sighted on a higher goal. They also observed a great many things that were wrong with the Royal Navy. He set to work putting them right.

The postwar impoverishment of Britain had necessitated stringent economies in her defense establishment. The cuts in the Navy had been carried out in a haphazard manner without any overall plan or strategic conception of what the functions of the fleet should be in the terribly changed circumstances in which England found herself.

Mountbatten had a very clear concept of the kind of Navy which would best serve her needs. He proposed a small, modern, *balanced* fleet which could take care of anything except another world war, in which case it would be up to the United States. He did not believe in Britain's having a nuclear deterrent because he felt that it would absorb large amounts of money that would be better spent on ships—that, too, should be left to the Americans. But he did favor a tactical nuclear strike capability.

Above and beyond all this he envisioned as an ultimate objective the unification of Land, Air, and Sea into a single Defence Department. This was completely in line with his thinking ever since Combined Operations. It was, indeed, the logical extension of the interdependence of the three services that had been demonstrated to be essential during World War Two and in Korea. While modernizing the Navy he was building with this greater plan in view. Also in view was his intention of becoming the head of this combined Defence Establishment.

The fact that some of his ideas differed from the thinking of the Conservative Government, and even more sharply with the ideas of most senior British naval officers, did not stop him from making an energetic beginning at putting them into effect. The first step was to get rid of the dead wood. Captain Roskill said to the author, "I think Mountbatten shocked us all by his Fisherlike ruthlessness at scrapping old ships. We wanted to keep the escort vessels in mothballs in case of another Battle of the Atlantic. However, the Board of Admiralty was generally in favor of scrapping them."

In addition to modernizing the physical Navy by concentrating on aircraft carriers, anti-aircraft ships, submarines, and anti-submarine vessels, Mountbatten made significant changes in the education of naval officers—giving it a more scientific direction—and also in providing better conditions, less stringent discipline, and more amenities and benefits for the lower deck.

Apparently the Government generally felt that Mountbatten was doing a good job. In 1956, he received the final accolade—promotion to Admiral of the Fleet.

Mountbatten served as First Sea Lord until July, 1959. He was then made Chief of the Defence Staff. The post had been created in 1958, in conformance with the plan to unify the Armed Services. In this capacity he wore three hats: Chief of the Defence Staff, Chairman of the Joint Chiefs of Staff, and Chief Staff Officer of the Ministry of Defence. As his First Sea Lord, Mountbatten was determined to have his old collaborator and friend Admiral Sir Charles Lambe, who had succeeded him as Commander in Chief Mediterranean for two years.

The difficulty was that two other men, Admirals Sir Guy Grantham and Sir Michael Denny, were senior to Lambe. The problem was resolved by both men's reluctance to accept the post because they felt it would be impossible to implement an independent Admiralty policy under such a determined Chief of the Defence Staff. Mountbatten cheerfully accepted their decision, and Lambe became First Sea Lord.

Mountbatten and Lambe made a splendid team. They had worked closely together throughout the years in everything from the tactics of polo to global strategy. When they were both in London, Lambe usually had breakfast with Mountbatten, during which they threshed out their problems.* Their ideas were very similar, though Lambe exercised a restraining influence over Lord Louis' more flamboyant fancies. He was one person who could tell the Admiral that he was crazy and get away with it.

Evaluating their collaboration Captain Roskill said, "Our Admiralty is conservative like all navies. They [Mountbatten and Lambe] changed all sorts of things . . . things like education, discipline and so forth. For example the Director of Naval Education is now Charles Darlington, a nuclear physicist. They shook the Navy out of the first half of the Twentieth Century and propelled it into the Nuclear Age."

.   .   .

---

* Lord Louis almost always came home from the Admiralty to lunch with Edwina. According to Mrs. Donald, who was often there, "He would tell Edwina everything he had done that morning. It was rather sweet, like a little boy recounting his adventures at school."

Broadlands never looked more beautiful than in the clear white whirling snowstorm on January 13, 1960, the day Pamela Mountbatten was married to David Nightingale Hicks. Neither, say those who knew her well, did Edwina Mountbatten. During the past few years the toll of her numerous activities, the thousands of hours under tropical suns, and the daylike nights of social life, had dimmed her beauty and weathered her complexion. On that day, however, according to Mrs. Donald, "Edwina was dressed in gold and looked perfectly radiant. All the lines and signs of age, and the worn look, had disappeared. I don't know what she did, but she was fresh and beautiful."

Lord Louis also looked extraordinarily young and handsome for a man of nearly sixty. They were in fact still one of the best-looking couples in England.

The wedding was another great Mountbatten occasion done in smashing style. Although David Hicks did not have the social eminence of the bride, he was a slight, good-looking, charming young man, and the Mountbattens very properly ran the show as though their daughter were marrying a duke at least.

Queen Elizabeth II was not there due to the imminent birth of her third child, but most of Lord Louis' other royal English cousins were: Prince Philip and the young Prince of Wales, Princess Margaret, the Queen Mother, and the Queen of Sweden, as well as the Duke and Duchess of Gloucester and the Duchess of Kent. Little Princess Anne was a bridesmaid for the first time in her life. Lord Brabourne was best man.

The festivities followed the form of Patricia Brabourne's wedding, though they were even more lavish since austerity had vanished from the English scene. The ceremony in Romsey Abbey was followed by one reception at Broadlands and another at Crossfield Hall for the tenants and staff of the estate, which most of the royalty also attended.

Four days after the ceremony the indefatigable Edwina started on her annual tour of the Far East in her capacity as Superintendent in Chief of St. John Ambulance Brigade and Chairman of the Red Cross Service Hospitals Welfare Department, and also for the Save the Children Fund. Her schedule called for a ten-week tour which included Cyprus, India, Malaya, Singapore, North Borneo, Hong Kong, and Korea.

Edwina arrived at Government House in Jesselton, North Borneo, from Singapore, on Thursday, February 18, 1960. According to Mr. R. M. Turner, the Administrative Officer of North Borneo, "She appeared in excellent health and spirits." She took a drive to see the sights of Jesselton and went to a gay private dinner that night. The next day she went with Mr. Turner to visit the Army Training Center at Kota Belud. That night there was a St. John Ambulance dinner. Edwina looked pale and shaky. She spoke for only ten minutes or so, and then went back to Government House. She said she felt terribly tired and had a splitting headache—it was most unlike her.

On Saturday, Edwina cut her morning engagements and stayed in bed—that, too, was unlike her. But in the afternoon she made three official appearances, and in the evening appeared for about twenty minutes at a reception for a hundred twenty people at Government House rather than disappoint so many people—that was very like her.

Late Saturday evening she went to bed and, gratefully, to sleep. Edwina Mountbatten never woke up.

The incredible news of Edwina's death came to Lord Louis at Wilton Crescent that Sunday morning, February 21, 1960. It almost literally broke his heart. The younthful jauntiness, high spirits, and good looks of the man who had given Pamela in marriage a little over a month before disappeared forever. As long as a year afterward he said to an intimate friend, "There is nothing left for me but work."

During the twenty years since the war began the Mountbattens had been far closer than most husbands and wives. Their few holidays together had been most precious because they were so brief. But it had been the comradeship in their work which welded them so close. They had been partners and allies.

In many matters supposedly beyond the province of women, Mountbatten had relied on his wife's advice, trusting to her clear realistic brain balanced by her loving heart. This was, of course, especially true of the Viceroyalty. Then and since then he has repeated almost like a refrain, "I could never have done it without Edwina."

From Buckingham Palace the Queen announced her sorrow and a week-long period of family mourning. From Wilton Crescent Lord Louis announced: "At Lady Mountbatten's special wish expressed in her will, the private funeral will take place at sea. The Board of Admiralty have made H.M.S. *Wakefield* available for this purpose and she will sail from Portsmouth on Thursday afternoon. . . ." From all over the world came tributes to Edwina, especially from India where both houses of the Indian Parliament observed a minute's silence in her memory.

On the afternoon of Thursday, February 25, 1960, the frigate

Wakefield sailed out of Portsmouth Harbor escorted by the Indian Frigate *Trishul*. On a steel-gray bier on her quarterdeck in a coffin covered by the Union Jack was Edwina's body. It had been flown back to England the day before and rested at Romsey Abbey that night. A short service was conducted there the next day before six hundred of her family and close friends from Romsey. Then the funeral cortege went on to Portsmouth.

Four miles south of the Nab Tower, the *Wakefield* backed her engines and hove to. On the quarterdeck around the coffin in the gray wintery twilight were gathered Lord Louis and Prince Philip in their naval uniforms, Patricia and Pamela with their husbands, Philip's mother in her gray nun's habit, and three or four of Edwina's closest women friends.

The Archbishop of Canterbury, Dr. Geoffrey Francis Fisher, read the brief, beautiful service of Committal to the Deep. Then, as the boatswains' pipes squealed, the bier was tilted forward and the coffin slid into the sea. Lord Louis, looking terribly old and haggard, kissed his wreath of white roses and leaning far out over the rail tossed it into the water. Each of the others in turn threw a wreath overboard, as did the officials aboard the *Trishul*. The marine buglers sounded the Last Post, and then Reveille to which Edwina had awakened so often in far-off dangerous places.

Chapter 19

"NOTHING LEFT FOR ME BUT WORK"

THOUGH LORD LOUIS felt as though the best part of his life had ended when Edwina died, the years of his greatest service to his country, with the possible exception of his Viceroyalty, lay ahead.

Many conservative people in England, especially senior service officers, think of the integration of Britain's Armed Service as a *disservice*, but it was, in fact, an absolute necessity imposed by the limitations of economics and the exigencies of modern warfare. The plan, which was finally presented to Parliament in the White Paper dated July, 1963, though sponsored by the Minister of Defence, Mr. Peter Thorneycroft, was Mountbatten's brain child. Of course, this does not mean that it was his alone. For several years he worked very closely with the then Minister of Defence Mr. Harold Watkinson. Their main objective at first was to get the fighting services switched from conscription to voluntary enlistment, because they felt that a modern, integrated defense force had to be based on an elite of professional servicemen with long-term enlistments. Conscripts with a year, or even two years of service were no good. While working on this Mountbatten also sponsored a "time-motion study" that gave him a scientific basis from which to work.

When these things were done the plan could be formulated provided the Chiefs of Staff could be brought into agreement on it. According to Mr. Watkinson, Mountbatten accomplished this difficult task with skill and finesse. In fact, the collaboration between Mountbatten and Watkinson appears to have been a happy one. The former Minister of Defence told the author that he found Mountbatten flexible, farsighted, and an easy man to work with because "men who want to get things done *are* easy to work with." Watkinson added, "If I had to fight a battle, I know of no man I'd rather fight it with than Mountbatten."

By the time Mr. Watkinson retired and Mr. Thorneycroft took over, the military details of the plan were pretty well settled. Mr. Thorneycroft worked out the political aspects of it with Mountbatten.

In addition, the thinking of many able men—naval, military, and civilian—went into it, but the conception, the inspiration, and the drive that put it across came from Mountbatten.

In this endeavor he suffered another irreparable loss that was also a heavy personal blow. Charles Lambe died suddenly of a heart attack in 1960. Mountbatten was in Edinburgh taking the salute at the famous Tattoo when the news reached him. He immediately telephoned Lady Lambe saying, "I'll come at once!" Paying no heed to her protest that he need not upset his schedule, Lord Louis ordered a plane and arrived early the next morning.

"He was so kind to me when Charles died," Lady Lambe said. "When he came into the house he said, 'Don't worry now, I'll do everything.' He made all the arrangements—the number of sailors, the order and ceremony of the funeral, everything. He put all his great jobs aside to do it."

The bitterness of the blow to Mountbatten was compounded by the fact that the First Sea Lord he now had to work with was Admiral Sir Caspar John, son of the famous painter, Augustus John. In addition to the fact that Sir Caspar was not in sympathy with his great design, there was a clash of personalities, an oil-and-water relationship. Sir Caspar's term ended in August, 1963. The new First Sea Lord was Admiral Sir David Luce with whom Mountbatten was able to work closely, though he still missed his old teammate of Malta days.

The reorganization plan for the Defence Department that was submitted to Parliament by Thorneycroft was drastic indeed. Based to some extent on the unified defense set-up adopted by the United States after World War Two, it went much further in concentrating power in the hands of the Minister of State for Defence and the Chief of the Defence Staff. The White Paper states categorically that:

A unified Ministry of Defence will be set up. Authority and responsibility will be vested in a single Secretary of State for Defence.

The new Ministry for Defence will absorb the present Ministry of Defence, Admiralty, War Office and Air Ministry. . . .

The object is to improve the central control of defence policy without impairing the efficiency and morale of the fighting Services. Their separate identities will be preserved. . . .

The Secretary of State for Defence must have complete control of both defence policy and the machinery for the administration of the three Services. The lines of authority and responsibility from the Secretary of State run unbroken through military, scientific and administrative staffs throughout the Ministry. . . .

The Chiefs of Staff Committee will remain in its present form. . . .

The collective advice of the Chiefs of Staff Committee will be tendered to the Secretary of State *by the Chief of the Defence Staff.* . . .*

In addition, promotions above the rank of rear admiral or its equivalent in the other services were taken out of the hands of the Service Chiefs and given to the Chief of the Defence Staff. In other words he would have the power of professional life or death.

As though this enormous concentration of power were not enough to curl the hair of the traditionalists, the plan called for downgrading to the rank of junior ministers the Ministers of State for War and Air. The First Lord of Admiralty would become a hallowed memory replaced by a Minister of State for Defence for the Royal Navy. Also, the Board of Admiralty would be "abolished"; and replaced by something banally titled the Navy Board.

To appease the tradition-minded, and also in line with his romantic objective of enhancing the Sovereign's prestige, Mountbatten proposed to make his astounded Queen the Lord High Admiral of the Royal Navy.

In September, 1963, Mountbatten took a trainload of over a hundred unhappy admirals, generals, and air marshals down to the Royal Naval College at Dartmouth to be lectured at by professors of history, psychology, economics, politics, and nuclear science in a seminar inappropriately called Unison. *The Times* noted that it was "a subject for which serving officers . . . have no noticeable inclination."

When the bill was introduced in the autumn of 1963, Parliamentary waters were badly roiled by the "Profumo Scandal," which had resulted in the resignation of the Minister of State for War, Mr. John Profumo, and by the illness and resignation of Prime Minister Harold Macmillan.

---

* Italics added. This is especially important because the British Service Chiefs are never publicly questioned in Parliament as they are in the United States Congress and therefore cannot make their personal views known.

With an untried Government under Sir Alec Douglas-Home (formerly the Earl of Home) a bill making such revolutionary changes in the Defence Establishment might have been expected to have heavy going. On the contrary, the Labour Party was, if anything, more enthusiastic about it than the Government, for they were vitally interested in paring defense expenditures in order to have more money to spend on welfare when the political merry-go-round brought them into power again.

The Labour leaders may also have been influenced by Mountbatten who was on very friendly terms with them. He and Edwina always voted Labour. During the general election of 1955, a Conservative fund raiser called at Broadlands. In answer to his plea Mountbatten said with a grin, "We're on the other side you know. You'll have better luck in the servants' wing. They're all Tories."

In any event the bill had very smooth sailing. Some changes, for the better it would appear, were made in the House. For example, the Ministers for the Army, Navy, and Air Force were upgraded from junior to senior rank; and the House of Lords reared back on its haunches at changing the Admiralty to the Navy Board. In a debate as courtly as a quadrille Lord Teynham moved to retain the old form saying, "The sea is in the heart of every Briton. . . . It would be a sorry day for England if the time-honored Admiralty were allowed to disappear into the limbo of forgotten things."

Loyally, if rather halfheartedly, Earl Jellicoe of Scapa Flow, the last First Lord of the Admiralty, defended a change that would have sent his famous father into a sinking spell. Lord Attlee, who did not agree with his colleagues of the Labour Party in support of the bill, stood firm for tradition. The Amendment was carried, 65 to 57. The Commons accepted the Amendment—what's in a name, as long as the substance remains? But the First Lord of the Admiralty succeeded in abolishing himself.

On Tuesday, March 31, 1964, at a rather pathetic little ceremony at the Horse Guards, the Admiralty Flag was hauled down for the last time. Though the Admiralty had kept its name, it had lost its power, its flag, and its First Lord. The next day, April 1, the vast, reorganized Ministry of Defence came into being. *The Observer* called it "A Bureaucratic Monster," and there were plenty of people who pointed out that the change was made on All Fools' Day.

Part of Mountbatten's plan was to move the whole shebang into one building on the theory that propinquity would lead to love and closer co-operation. It hardly worked that way at first. The place chosen was a big, nondescript modern building on Whitehall Gardens between Whitehall and the Thames. It was promptly nicknamed the "Quadregon." For weeks the old Admiralty and Storey's Gate echoed to the snorts and grunts of senior admirals and generals as they were dug out of their uncomfortable, tradition-encrusted lairs and moved into the efficiently automated, comfortable, convenient, and soulless new offices.

Meanwhile the mutterings of discontent among the junior service officers and civilian bureaucrats made the "Quadregon" sound like a hive full of large, angry bees. But the Chief of the Defence Staff, whose term of office had been extended an unprecedented length to July 1, 1965, because no one else could possibly get the machinery running, serenely presided over the meetings of the Chiefs of Staff in the new Defence Operations Room equipped with enough modern gadgetry to appease even his appetite.

In all fairness to Mountbatten, and fooling aside, the changes he made, drastic though they were and ruthless though he was, were essential and long overdue. It was all very well for the greatest and richest empire in the world to muddle through crisis after crisis, war after war. The new Britain simply could not afford it. She had to be efficient or perish.

As to the discontent in the fighting services it was inevitable. Even in comparatively traditionless America the unification of the Armed Services caused an unholy row. So violent did the quarrel become that, in 1949, President Harry S Truman called General Dwight D. Eisenhower back from retirement to referee the battle royal and try to make peace. The infuriated American soldiers, sailors, and airmen gave him such a rough time that it may have contributed to his first attack of ileitis.

If that could happen in a country that prides itself on its modernity, no less could be expected in England. But, as happened in the United States, the warriors will become accustomed to the pace of progress and even come to take pride in the increased efficiency and scientific advancement of the integrated services. All it takes is a man at the top with a firm hand, certainty in charting a course, the hide of an elephant, and the persuasive charm of the Devil himself. Fortunately Lord Mountbatten has all these qualifications.

In contrast to his full and frantic official existence Lord Louis leads a rather sad and lonely private life. Certainly he has many devoted friends, almost as numerous as his enemies. He has the joy of Broadlands, where the pheasant shooting is now excellent, the exquisite house in

Wilton Crescent, his fast motorboats and fine cars, and his Rube Gold-
berg inventions. In fact he has everything but zest.

Age, which overtook him so suddenly, is written on his careworn
face and evidenced by an unwonted bulge at the belt line. Make no
mistake, he is still a remarkably handsome man—a handsome *older* man.

Lord Louis enjoys most of all the company of Patricia Brabourne,
and "playing the fool with my grandchildren"—two Brabourne boys
and two girls. His few moments of carefree gaiety in recent years have
come when he has taken them all for a summer holiday to Classiebawn
Castle, which stands on a rocky cliff on the wild west coast of Ireland.

The castle looks grim and Gothic, but it was built by Lord Palmerston during the Romantic Revival period of the nineteenth century.
Edwina made it livable again during the fifties, and she and Lord Louis
spent many strenuous holidays there together. The fishing is excellent,
the shooting superb, and the weather usually foul.

Mountbatten also has his hobbies—mechanical gadgets, the more
eccentric the better, and collecting baubles. One object that he is still
after is a field marshal's baton. The last Admiral of the Fleet to have
one was Queen Victoria's son, Alfred, Duke of Edinburgh. Recently
Lord Louis wrote a little historical essay for his Queen, entitled "The
Sovereign and the Navy," in which he recounts some very interesting
curiosities concerning the relations between them throughout the years.
For one thing the uniforms of the Royal Navy were traditionally submitted to the Sovereign for approval; but in 1920 the Admiralty reduced the width of the gold lace on an admiral's sleeve from five eighths
of an inch to a half inch without consulting King George V. The King,
who prided himself on his professional career in the Navy, was furious,
and refused to recognize it. He and his sons all continued to wear the
five-eighth-inch lace. The Admiralty later ordered the standard width
increased to nine sixteenths of an inch. But Lord Mountbatten and the
Duke of Edinburgh still wear gold lace a sixteenth of an inch wider
than regulation.

The point of Mountbatten's essay on royal prerogatives appears to
be that in former times batons as symbols of authority were given to
Admirals of the Fleet as well as field marshals, but the right to give them
was reserved to the Sovereign as a special mark of honor. Nobody had
told Queen Victoria about this until Prince Louis of Battenberg mentioned it to her. She promptly gave a baton to Admiral the Duke of
Edinburgh.

King George V refused to continue the custom saying, "Afloat I
always carry a telescope and ashore it would be in my way."

Mountbatten's essay seems to be a veiled suggestion that Her

Majesty should revive the giving of naval batons, preferably beginning with himself. So far she has not taken the hint.

Perhaps the most endearing of Mountbatten's traits is his loyalty to people who have served under him. He will go to any lengths to honor them or help them with their problems and even to take the blame for their mistakes. In 1942, in the midst of the most urgent affairs at Combined Operations, he went specially to London to be godfather to Alan Campbell-Johnson's first child. No one knows how much time and money he has spent for the people who have served him, for he never tells and will not allow them to. But it is certainly a great deal. One thing is known positively: Any man who ever served in the *Kelly*, even for as little as one week, can have anything within his captain's power to give.

During these mellowing years the Beaverbrook feud was finally ended. It happened at a dinner given by Mr. Roy Thompson, another Canadian newspaper magnate, who apparently knew no better than to invite them both to the same party. However, they were seated some distance apart on opposite sides of the long table.

When dinner ended, and the two lines of men began to make their way toward the door, Mountbatten saw that chance would bring him face to face with Beaverbrook. He began to wonder what he could say to his enemy, for a direct snub was a discourtesy contrary to his nature. What he did say when they met in the doorway was, "It's a long time since I've seen you, Max. I want to thank you for the way your paper handled Edwina's death."

According to Randolph Churchill(§), who was close to them, "Beaverbrook seemed greatly touched—almost confused," by Mountbatten's words.

Since that day the Beaverbrook papers have been "most kind," to Mountbatten though they continue to blast Prince Philip at every opportunity.

While a man yet lives and holds a position of great power he is fair game for critics. Lord Mountbatten is a shining mark. His pride, his blazing ambition and subtle arrogance, his foibles—love of pomp, vanity, wealth, luxurious tastes, and his lack of humor about his own shortcomings—invite brickbats. So he gets them in full measure.

But when these trivialities are noted and forgotten, there remains an extraordinary man. Emotionally he is youthfully simple and forthright; but his mind is capable of dealing with all the complexities of the modern age. He has compiled a splendid record of courage, loyalty, high intelligence and farsighted vision, and great things accomplished.

Of the Earl Mountbatten of Burma, K.G., and all the et ceteras, a future historian may write that no man in his time served England more devotedly or to better purpose.

III

PRINCE PHILIP

Chapter 1

CONCERNING
CERTAIN GREEKS

Prince Philip is an admiral *manqué*—lost to the Royal Navy and to himself. He has all the qualifications for that career—intelligence, courage, good health; a love of the sea and an excellent understanding of the techniques it requires of the men who sail it. He even has the keen ambition that is necessary to rise in any profession. Of him Prince Bernhard of the Netherlands once said(§), "It is a pity that the English waste Philip's great abilities and knowledge of naval matters."*

Most Britons would not agree that Prince Philip is wasted. They believe that his role as husband of the Queen is more important than any contribution he might make as a naval officer. Possibly it is; yet one must feel a certain regret in seeing a fine mind stultified, a good man cut down to size.

Is this necessary? In England it seems to be. One constantly hears about the "Mystique of the Monarchy"—the mystical relationship between the British people and their Sovereign. It is compounded of love and censure. The English attitude toward their monarchs is rather like

---

* In easygoing Holland the Queen's husband is allowed far more scope for creative work.

that of over-doting parents toward an only child—adoration coupled with horror if the child shows any sign of having a personality or will of its own.

If the Sovereign happens to be a handsome young woman this adoration takes on almost religious overtones. The attitude of the British people toward their Queen resembles in some slight degree that of Catholics toward the Virgin Mary, except that the Queen is not supposed to exercise the power over her subjects that Mary may evoke in answer to the prayers of her supplicants.

There lies the nub of the matter, that which makes the royal mystique so very mysterious to outsiders. The Sovereign must not exercise any power or influence. She is there only to be adored, not heard from.

It was not always thus. Indeed, as has been noted before, Walter Bagehot, the greatest authority on Great Britain's unwritten constitution, specially reserves to the Sovereign the right to be informed, to encourage and to warn. These rights gradually have been eroded by the pressure of politicians and public opinion, and by the acquiescence of the Sovereigns, who by now appear to have abdicated even the right to think.*

Yet, at least since the last of the Hanoverian Kings was mercifully interred, the interposition of the Sovereign usually has been highly beneficent. In 1861 Queen Victoria, on the advice of her husband, unconstitutionally refused to sign a letter written by Lord Palmerston which would have meant war between England and the United States, and probable victory for the Confederate States of America. King Edward VII's influence in forming the Triple Entente between England, France, and Russia, and his encouragement of Admiral Fisher's modernization of the Royal Navy, indubitably saved England from defeat in World War One. King George V, by calling the conference at Buckingham Palace on the Irish Crisis in July, 1914, saved England from civil war at the time Germany was about to attack her. King George V also warned vehemently against recalling Lord Fisher as First Sea Lord in 1914. Had he been heeded the disaster at the Dardanelles would have been, instead, a great victory.

But Bagehot takes no heed of a Prince Consort, and such a man has always had a difficult role. Prince Albert was wise and good, and he managed to make his influence felt because Queen Victoria not only loved and honored him but also quite literally obeyed him. But by so doing he aroused the suspicion and hostility of the English, who only

---

* King Edward VIII was sacked, not only because he loved unwisely, but because he thought too well.

recognized his good qualities after he was dead. It was inevitable that Philip should have an even thinner time.

Perhaps he should have realized that when he took on the job. He should have, but he did not—completely. In the first place, when he began courting Princess Elizabeth there was no reason to suppose that King George VI would not reign another quarter century or so—he was less than fifty years old. Philip reckoned that he had time to make a name for himself in the Navy before his dignified retirement as the Queen's husband, which, after all, is a happier lot than is usual for a retired admiral.

Also, Philip may have had dreams of glory, of playing Albert's role, which were totally unfounded in reality but may have been encouraged by his Uncle Dickie. That of course is what the Mountbattens' critics mean by the phrase, "Trying to move in on the Monarchy."

However disappointed and frustrated he may be, Philip on the whole has done his job with dignity, dash, and a sense of humor. It has not been easy. He is rather like the unfortunate Light Brigade, with critics instead of cannon on every side and the big guns of the inimical Beaverbrook Press forever manned by epithet-happy editors.

The fact that Prince Philip of Greece grew up to be a fine, up-standing young man with an outgiving nature and no apparent neuroses, should confound the exponents of environmental predestination. For his youthful surroundings and upbringing were hardly calculated to pro-duce this result. In fact they would have turned Doctor Spock's hair white.

Born in Corfu on June 10, 1921, while his father, Prince Andrew of Greece, was fighting the Turks in Asia Minor, he was the child of his parents' middle age. Prince Andrew was thirty-nine years old and Philip's mother, Lord Mountbatten's oldest sister, was thirty-six. The pretty little princess who had been the center of that carefree royal wedding in Darmstadt in 1903 had become an eccentric and somewhat terrifying older woman. Though she had been born a deaf-mute, she certainly was not dumb; for she had learned to lip read and to talk in three languages, speaking slowly in a deep, unnatural voice. She had always been extremely religious, and as she grew older she became al-most fanatically so, perhaps because her deafness dropped a curtain between her and the world. In addition, Philip had four much older sisters to spoil him.

The books say a child should be given a sense of security, but there was little chance of this for baby Prince Philip. During his childhood his family, the Schleswig-Holstein-Sonderberg-Glücksburgs of the Royal House of Denmark, were climbing on and off the throne of Greece like players in a game of musical chairs.

Philip's grandfather, King George I of Greece, was assassinated at his victory parade in Salonika after the Balkan War in 1913. He was succeeded by his eldest son, King Constantine I, who was married to Kaiser Wilhelm's sister, Princess Sophia of Prussia.

When World War One broke out King Constantine, influenced by his strong-minded wife, was definitely pro-German. Since the majority of his people were pro-Ally under the leadership of Prime Minister Eleutherios Venizelos, this showed poor judgment. Every time Venizelos moved to assist the Allies, the King sacked him; invariably he was re-elected. Finally the Allies' patience gave out. One morning in June, 1917, Constantine woke up to find a British fleet off Piraeus lobbing shells up the hill into Athens. While Princess Alice and her four little girls took cover in the deep cellar of the old palace, King Constantine departed hurriedly for Switzerland. The Allies made his second son, Alexander, King, skipping the eldest son, Prince George, who was too closely associated with his father's policies. Venizelos became Prime Minister again. Greece declared war on Germany just in time to reap the spoils of victory, which unfortunately for her included Smyrna on the Turkish coast of Asia Minor.

During the short happy reign of King Alexander I, Greece settled down to enjoy her affluence. But Prince and Princess Andrew, who had also been exiled, lived in straitened circumstances in Switzerland.

Then, in 1920, that famous pet monkey bit King Alexander. The King died of blood poisoning; history does not record what happened to the monkey. Venizelos offered the shaky throne to the King's younger brother, Prince Paul, who said, "No! Thank you very much, but no!" So there was an election and a plebiscite which surprisingly, threw Venizelos out and brought King Constantine triumphantly back to the throne.

Prince Andrew and his family also returned and settled down in the family villa on the island of Corfu, called, like ten thousand suburban cottages, Mon Repos. It was a pretty little house perched on top of a hill whose rocky sides dropped almost straight down to the wonderfully blue Ionian Sea.

Like those old Bourbons, King Constantine could neither learn nor forget. In a few months he succeeded in alienating the Allies. Then, despite their disapproval, he went to war with Turkey to enlarge his bridgehead in Asia Minor. Prince Andrew, who had no great military experience, was made a lieutenant general and given command of an army corps. It was that kind of war.

When Philip was only three months old he made his first trip to England, where his mother went for the funeral of his grandfather, Prince Louis of Battenberg. He went again the following year for a happier occasion, the wedding of his uncle, Lord Louis Mountbatten. Of course, he attended neither ceremony, but remained in the care of his English nanny "Roosie" (Miss Roose), who had nursed his mother.

Meanwhile, things went badly for Greece in Asia Minor. After a brief taste of victory, the Greek Army was defeated and thrown back to the coast by the Turks, who rallied under a *real* general, Mustapha Kemal. The Greeks hung on there for over a year. But hardly had Princess Alice and Philip returned from England to Corfu, when the bad news arrived. The Turks had smashed the Greek Army again on August 26, 1922, and taken Smyrna, which they burned. A month later the remnants of the Greek Army, thoroughly disgusted with their leadership, staged a revolution in Athens. King Constantine left hastily, this time for Palermo, and his son, King George II, nervously ascended the throne.

The army wanted blood to avenge defeat. In October soldiers came knocking at the door of Mon Repos with a demand from the new Minister of War, Mr. Pangalos, that Prince Andrew come immediately to Athens to give evidence at the trial for treason of three ex-premiers, two former ministers of state, and the ex-Commander in Chief of the Army, General Papulas. To the ineffectual Andrew the summons seemed ominous. He suspected that he, too, was slated for a sacrificial role. Sadly he kissed his family good-bye, and left them crying in the doorway as his armed escort drove him down the twisting road.

When nothing was heard from her husband for several days, Princess Alice contacted his brother Prince Christopher, who lived in the United States and just happened to be making an ill-timed trip to Athens. He was willing to take a risk and help. Christopher learned that Andrew had been imprisoned and all communication with him cut off. He was to be tried for his life on the trumped-up charge of having deserted his command. Poor Andrew found out what the verdict was intended to be when Pangalos questioned him. "How many children have you?" he asked.

"Four girls and a boy," Andrew answered.

"Poor little things—to be orphaned so young," Pangalos remarked.

But Princess Alice went into action. She rushed to Athens to see King George of Greece. He was hanging onto the throne by his fingernails and fearful for his own life. He said he could do nothing, which was probably true. But Alice held some better kings in her hand. Frantically she wrote to her cousins, King George of England and King Alfonso of Spain, and for good measure she appealed to the President of France and Pope Pius XI. In addition she sent a stream of letters to all her royal relatives throughout Europe.

Meanwhile the general and the unfortunate Greek statesmen, who had only followed the dictates of *vox populi*—the Greek people had been ardent for war with Turkey—were all tried and shot. It was Andrew's turn next.

But Princess Alice had gotten results, and notes of protest poured in to the Greek Government. The British sent something more substantial. In 1922 the rulers of the British Empire still remembered Palmerston's proud phrase that every British subject, like the Romans of old, should be able to say, "*Civis Romanus sum!*" And after all, Alice was Queen Victoria's great-granddaughter.

Prince Andrew was tried and found guilty, but the sentence was not death. He was stripped of his rank and nationality and exiled from Greece forever. The fact that justice was thus tempered with mercy possibly is due to the fact that H.M.S. *Calypso* was lying off Piraeus with her guns pointing upward at an acute angle. It made Pangalos so nervous that he personally drove Prince Andrew and Princess Alice down to the port and saw them safely aboard.

The cruiser immediately headed for Corfu to pick up the rest of the family. Mon Repos hardly justified its name as Princess Alice hurriedly scrambled a few family treasures together under the glowering eyes of Greek soldiers, and took them down to the cruiser. The girls and Roosie, carrying Philip in her arms, came with her.

Aboard *Calypso* the officers vacated several cabins, but even so they were rather crowded. The baby slept in an orange crate, which the sailors had padded so he would not hurt himself. It was Prince Philip's first voyage in a British man-of-war.

The family headed for London where they stayed with Princess Alice's mother, the Dowager Marchioness of Milford Haven, in her apartment in Kensington Palace. Everybody made a great fuss over them and especially admired Philip, who was a fat, almost white-haired, blue-eyed little boy.

Leaving him in England Prince and Princess Andrew took a trip to America to visit Prince Christopher and his wife, who was the widow of William B. Leeds and had millions of tin-plate dollars. Their stay at Palm Beach must have been a relaxing change, for Prince and Princess

Christopher lived in tremendous luxury, and Americans were still un-sophisticated enough to make a great fuss over royalty, even those with-out a country.

For that, in fact, was Prince Andrew's—and Philip's—situation. Greek no longer by government decree, they sought a nationality and found it through the courtesy of Andrew's cousin, King Christian X of Denmark, who made them Danes.

That solved one problem, but a greater one remained—they were almost flat broke. Prince Andrew managed to get a little money out of Greece from an indirect interest in farming lands, and when King Con-stantine died in January, 1923, he left his brother a small bequest. George Milford Haven gave his sister a small allowance and perhaps Lord Louis helped out, too—it was not the sort of thing he talked about.

Another of Andrew's brothers, Prince George of Greece, had also married a rich woman, Princess Pauline Bonaparte, whose mother was a daughter of François Blanc, the man who owned the bank at Monte Carlo. They offered Andrew a whole floor of a house, now converted to apartments, they owned on the Rue Adolphe-Yvon near the Bois in Paris, which he gratefully accepted. Later the Andrews moved into a cottage on George's own rather extensive property in the Rue du Mont Valérien in St. Cloud.

Princess Alice started a little boutique in Paris, called *Hellas,* where she sold Greek embroideries, tapestries, and antiques for the benefit of Greek refugees. It appears really to have been a charitable venture from which she derived no personal profit.

The hand-to-mouth, vanished-glories atmosphere in which Philip grew up does not seem to have traumatized him. From childhood on he was a handsome, happy extrovert, who loved people, animals, and games, especially games. At six he began going to the Country Day and Board-ing School at St. Cloud, where the pupils were mostly the sons of rich American businessmen in Paris. He was probably the poorest boy in the school, but this did not bother him. Some people had plenty of money and others did not. He did not. But at quite an early age, from family talk and serious little homilies delivered by his father, who hoped his son might yet be King of Greece, Philip was conscious of being royal. That did not bother him either.

After all, except for his schoolmates, almost everybody he knew was royal. Like the Battenbergs in Lord Louis' youth, his father and mother were continually taking him on a round of visits to the castles of his ruling relatives. Among others they went to the Hesses' at their summer villa in Panka where the dark forests came down to the Baltic

Sea. Philip loved the life there and made great friends with the Baltic fishermen.

In Controcene in Rumania they stayed with King Ferdinand and Queen Marie, whom Philip called Aunty Missy. Even when only the family were there for dinner, the Queen, whose beauty was as famous as her egotism, always appeared in full evening dress and great jewels, with a crown-like diamond tiara glittering regally on her hair. She enchanted Philip as she did all males of any age. Her grandson Michael, who became King when Ferdinand died in 1929, was the right age to be Philip's playmate. They liked to ride together along the shore of the Black Sea, and to sail on it. By the time he was eight years old Philip knew that his favorite sports were riding and sailing.

By then his own family were breaking up. Prince and Princess Andrew had grown less and less compatible. During the next few years they managed to get their four daughters married off to four German princelings. In order of age: Margarita married Prince Gottfried of Hohenlohe-Langenburg; Theodora took Prince Berthold, Markgrave of Baden (son of Prince Max of Baden, the amiable last Chancellor of the German Empire); Cecile married her first cousin, Prince George of Hesse (later the last Grand Duke of Hesse); and Sophia also got a Prince of Hesse. That made a lot more castles where Philip was welcome to visit.

Having done their parental duty Prince and Princess Andrew separated—not officially but tacitly—Princess Alice to devote herself to the monastic life to which she had increasingly inclined; Prince Andrew went in quite the opposite direction. Philip must remember his father as an aging, royal *boulevardier* with a bald, dome-like head, and a long, thin face embellished by a neat little mustache and a monocle. Despite his reduced circumstances he always managed to have a pretty lady around his bachelor dwelling.

Princess Alice forswore feminine fripperies for ever more severe clothing which evolved finally into the gray nun's habit she designed as the uniform of the Greek Orthodox Nursing Order she joined. Neither of them seems to have felt much responsibility for raising their only son.

This was certainly fortunate for Philip. When he was nine years old his Uncle George Milford Haven invited him to stay at Lynden Manor and go to the Tabor School at Cheam in Surrey, with his own son David Mountbatten.* Like his Uncle George, Philip was a great success at Cheam. He was a born athlete with that superb timing and co-ordination that his other uncle, Lord Louis, lacked. Before he finished at Cheam he became diving champion, the best high-jumper, and the

---

* By courtesy, Earl of Medina; later, the third Marquess of Milford Haven.

star of the soccer team. He was also quite good at his studies and won prizes in French and history.

Lord Louis Mountbatten is supposed to have played the greatest part in guiding Prince Philip's career. Though this is true, the influence of George Milford Haven was very important in forming his character. It was at Lynden that he grew to love England and to feel like an Englishman. George, charming and amiable and very good with boys, became a foster father to him. In the long talks they had together he gave Philip something of his own tolerant attitude toward other people's shortcomings and points of view. More important, he nurtured the boy's inclination toward a career in the Royal Navy. Philip never got tired of hearing his uncle tell what it was like in the forward turret of the *New Zealand* on that dangerous afternoon at Jutland, when the two great 12-inch guns under his command were firing so fast they got red hot and three sister battle cruisers blew up from shell hits on their turrets. Quite naturally, too, George never got tired of telling about it.*

Though George loved the Navy so dearly, he was forced to resign in 1932 while Philip was still in Cheam. He simply could not maintain Lynden and his wife Nada, who had inherited a bit of her grand ducal father's way with money, on his small inherited income and an officer's pay. He restored his fortune by taking a job as British representative of the Sperry Gyroscope Company of America.

When he was graduated from Cheam in 1933, Prince Philip went to his family in St. Cloud to spend the summer. There was a general family council as to where he should go to school next. His sister Theodora, who had recently married the Markgrave of Baden, was wildly enthusiastic about the school that Doctor Kurt Hahn and her father-in-law, Prince Max, had founded in a wing of Schloss Salem, Max's castle in the forested hills around Lake Constance. Philip wanted to stay in England, but to his disgust Theodora won and to Salem he went in October, 1933.

It was indeed a remarkable school. Prince Max and Doctor Hahn had founded it soon after World War One to give German boys a new and more liberal sort of education which combined the English public schools' ideal of developing fine physiques and individual initiative, with German thoroughness in education. By a system of graduated tuition fees they made it possible for boys from all walks of life to attend Salem.

By the time Philip got there, the school had grown from four boys in 1920 to five hundred at its peak. Doctor Hahn worked the skin off his

---

* According to Lord Mountbatten, at the battles of Heligoland Bight, Dogger Bank, and Jutland, the turret commanded by George Mountbatten fired more heavy shells at the enemy than any turret of any other ship on either side in World War One or World War Two.

boys. In the thin, cold light of early dawn they had to get up and run 400 yards before breakfast. Then came the typically German, rigorous grind of studies that no English or American boys would tolerate. In the afternoons there were sports or such hard labor as building a cinder running track or pouring concrete for a jetty. This was followed by supper and homework. The last thing at night, when the boys were all thoroughly exhausted, they had to do setting-up exercises. Philip came prepared to hate it; and did.

Note the date: 1933—a blood-red-letter year for Germany. Adolf Hitler had become Chancellor in January, and immediately the iron rule of Nazism was clamped down on German life. The liberal Doctor Hahn was arrested and jailed as a communist in March. Luckily, Prince Berthold was able to swing his influence with senescent President Paul von Hindenberg. Hahn was released, and he headed for England where he founded a similar school in a big country house belonging to Sir Alexander Gordon-Cumming at Gordonstoun in Morayshire, on the east coast of Scotland, where the climate made life even more rugged for the boys than in Baden.

Salem was the only place where Philip did badly. During his three terms there he was too miserable to make an effort—his participation in both sports and study was purely mechanical. Oddly enough it was his sense of humor that rescued him.

His British background and Uncle George Milford Haven's liberal thinking had thoroughly unconditioned Philip for life under a totalitarian regime. The sight of fierce-eyed, brown-shirted young men solemnly stamping by in the stiff-legged, high-kick goose step gave him the giggles. And the Nazi salute made him roar with laughter, because of his English-schoolboy notion of the meaning of an upraised arm: "They look as if they all want to go to the bathroom at once," he sputtered.

Theodora and her markgrave decided that they had better get Philip out of Germany fast, for his safety and theirs. In 1934 he was packed off to England and Gordonstoun.

Getting back to England was like coming home for Philip. He immediately recovered his high spirits and will to win. He did not even mind the rigors of Gordonstoun; in fact he enjoyed them. It was not the hard physical and mental work that got him down at Salem but the depressing atmosphere and those humorless, militant German youths. English voices, English views, and English irreverence for authority were his dish.

The physical work was also more to his taste. The boys helped build and repair boats in the little shipyards nearby, and worked with the coast guard. They also did a good deal of sailing in misty, windy Moray Firth. Philip won a merit badge for seamanship and was one of the few boys allowed to take a sailing dinghy out alone. The seamanship instructor said, "He was a cheerful shipmate.... Thoroughly trustworthy." In fact, he was shaping up nicely in the Mountbatten tradition.

Doctor Hahn has written, "Philip's ... most marked trait was his undefeatable spirit.... His laughter was heard everywhere. He had inherited from his Danish family the capacity to derive great fun from small incidents.... He showed lively intelligence.... Once he had made a task his own, he showed meticulous attention to detail and pride of workmanship."

During holidays it was much more fun to go back to Lynden Manor with his Uncle George or to visit Uncle Dickie in Brook Street than it was to move to another part of the Schloss with Berthold and Theodora. But one of his finest holidays was at a family funeral.

Weakling King George II was restored to the throne of Greece in November, 1935, by a questionable plebiscite engineered by the reactionary Prime Minister, General Kondyles. By November, 1936, George was so firmly established that it was proposed to exhume the bodies of King Constantine and Queen Sophia and his grandmother, Queen Olga, from the alien soil of Florence in which they lay, and bury them properly with their ancestors in the royal burying ground at Tatoi. Prior to interment they lay in state in the Athens cathedral for six days.

It was an excuse for a joyous family reunion—after all, the principals had been dead and buried long enough to dull the edge of sorrow. Best of all from Philip's point of view, he got a special leave from school to attend the ceremony.

According to Philip's cousin, Queen Alexandra of Yugoslavia, who was a girl of the same age, the Greek people entered gaily into the spirit of the occasion: "Aunts, uncles, cousins, and all the kith and kin arrived to drive through streets draped with flags and lined by cheering people...."* They took over the entire Grand Bretagne, the best hotel in Athens. Even Prince Andrew, who had not set foot in Greece since he got out of jail, came in a very good mood.

The funeral service was properly solemn, with black draperies of mourning replacing the gay flags along the streets, and four Greek princes—Nicholas, Christopher, Paul, and Andrew—standing with bowed heads as a guard of honor for the three coffins.

---

* *Prince Philip. A Family Portrait.*

Philip, resplendent in his first morning coat and a shining new high silk hat, rode to the funeral with his fifteen-year-old cousin Alexandra, who openly admired his dashing appearance. However, having gorged himself on unaccustomedly rich food the night before, Philip was feeling anything but dashing. Right in the middle of the elaborate Greek Orthodox ritual he turned green and whispered to Alexandra, "I'm going to be sick!"

Somehow he managed to last through the service but when he got into the car with Alexandra for the procession back to the palace, he was sick, right into his beautiful new topper. Alexandra describes their youthful agony as to what to do with that hat. As they drove up to the palace Philip solved the problem right royally by simply handing it to a dumfounded aide.

Philip got a chance to wear his new finery again at the wedding of his cousin Prince Paul of Greece* to pretty, vivacious—and naughty—Princess Frederika of Hanover. With David Mountbatten and young King Michael he officiated at the wedding. Since the other boys were about two years older they got to hold the traditional golden crowns over the heads of the bride and groom as they exchanged vows, while Philip stood behind them, trying to look dignified while doing nothing.

Another wedding at which Philip hoped to frolic with his amusing royal cousins was that of Prince Louis of Hesse to Lord Geddes' daughter, the Honorable Margaret Campbell-Geddes in London. Two days before the wedding Doctor Hahn came to Philip's room, his kindly face working with sympathy. He told Philip that the private plane bringing his sister Cecile and her husband to the wedding had smashed into a factory chimney in a fog at Ostend, killing all on board. Among the dead, in addition to Cecile and Prince George, were the bridegroom's mother, Grand Duchess Eleonore of Hesse-Darmstadt, and Cecile's two little sons, Louis and Alexander of Hesse.

It was the first great tragedy of Philip's life.†

An even greater personal loss to Philip was the death of George Milford Haven, of cancer, in the autumn of 1938, for he felt far closer to his uncle than to his own father. George was both kind and witty, which rare combination made him beloved by everyone who knew him. Had he possessed the ambition of his younger brother he might have gone as far, or even further. But then, perhaps, he would have been less lovable.

---

* Later, King Paul I.

† Lord Louis Mountbatten took charge of the distraught family and decided that the wedding should take place privately in his apartment.

Lord Louis promptly took on the responsibility for his nephew. This was vitally important in making Philip the person he became, for his close association with the restless, brilliant, dynamic Mountbatten brought out these same qualities which were latent in him. It was the beginning of manhood.

Chapter 2

FROM DARTMOUTH
TO TOKYO BAY

WHEN PHILIP GRADUATED FROM Gordonstoun in 1938, he was Guardian
of the school (head boy), captain of the hockey and cricket teams, and
had qualified as a coast guardsman. He had also qualified as cook in the
cutter *Prince Louis,* named for his grandfather, on a stormy cruise
around Cape Wrath. His qualification was that he did not get seasick in
the smelly galley. According to his shipmates he was an awful cook.

In his final report Doctor Hahn wrote: " Prince Philip's leadership
qualities are most noticeable, though marred at times by impatience and
intolerance." (He is still impatient with fools and reporters.) Doctor
Hahn added: ". . . . He will need the exacting demands of a great service
to do justice to himself. His best is outstanding; his second best is not
good enough. Prince Philip will make his mark in any profession where
he will have to prove himself in a full trial of strength. . . ."

After Lord Milford Haven's death Philip's real home became the
Mountbattens' fabulous apartment on Brook Street. He liked it, if
anything, more than Lord Louis did. He took the same delight in the
mechanical gadgets with which it was crammed, and he loved its

(400)

abundant luxury. In this he was very much like his uncle and his grand-father, who never minded the most rugged conditions, but never lost an opportunity to live in high style.

Best of all was his close association with Uncle Dickie. Though Philip had had such a deep affection for his Uncle George, he indubitably had greater admiration for Lord Louis, who was both more dashing and a doer of deeds. Uncle George was a man to love, but Uncle Dickie was one to emulate. In fact Philip's temperament and tastes were very much like Lord Louis'. And if Philip thought of Milford Haven as his foster father, Mountbatten came to regard Philip almost as the son he never had. Thus his influence over Philip became paramount.

This being the case there was never much doubt as to the service in which Philip's strength would be tested. Under the aegis of Lord Louis, and by his own inclination, he was headed straight for the Royal Navy. His father and other Greek relatives tried to persuade him to join the Hellenic Navy where, he was assured, advancement would be rapid. Like his grandfather, Prince Louis, he chose to become an Englishman.

Philip took a cramming course for the Navy entrance examination. He was coached by Mr. Mercer, and stayed with the Mercers at Cheltenham a good part of the winter of 1938–39. In the spring of 1939, he took the competitive examination for the Royal Naval College at Dartmouth as a special entry cadet from a public school.* He passed it sixteenth among thirty-four who qualified. But in the stiff oral examination he scored 380 points out of a possible 400. He entered Dartmouth on May 4, 1939. That was the last summer before the war everyone knew was coming, no matter how passionately most of them longed for peace. Uncle Dickie was spending almost all his time at Tyneside attending the outfitting of the *Kelly*. But he took time off for a brief cruise in the royal yacht with the King and Queen and the little princesses.

The gold and white *Victoria and Albert* pointed her elaborately gilded figurehead into Weymouth Bay on July 21, in a gentle summer rain, and anchored in the River Dart. The next day was fine and the plan was for the Royal family to go to the eleven-o'clock service in the chapel at Dartmouth. The yacht's launch landed them at the dock—the King and Queen, Lord Louis, and the princesses attended by their faithful Crawfie.† They climbed the long flight of steps toward the red-brick buildings of the college. At the top they were met by the commandant, Rear Admiral Dalrymple-Hamilton, and taken to watch the cadets march past in review. Then the college doctor, an unconscious instru-

---

* In America, a private or boarding school.
† Miss Marion Crawford, the princesses' governess.

ment of fate, upset their plans. "Your Majesty, two of the boys have come down with mumps," he said. "I am sorry, but I don't think it would be wise for Their Royal Highnesses to attend the service."

That produced a hurried conference, which ended with Crawfie being asked to take the princesses to the Captain's House where the Dalrymple-Hamiltons lived. As they went off, Lord Louis, a very conscious instrument of fate, said to the Queen, "Perhaps we could get Philip out of church to amuse the girls."

So it was arranged. The children had only been in the comfortable, red-brick Captain's House for a few minutes when Philip appeared, tall, blond, and very blue-eyed, in his immaculate summer "whites." Crawfie, who is rather sentimental, describes him that day in *The Little Princesses*, as, "A fairhaired boy, rather like a Viking, with a sharp face and piercing blue eyes."

Philip and "Lilibet" played with a toy railroad until Philip got bored. They had some lemonade and gingersnaps, and then went out to the tennis courts where Philip showed off by jumping the net. Miss Crawford appears to have found him rather a smart aleck, but Elizabeth, who was thirteen years old, said, "How good he is, Crawfie! How high he can jump."

Philip was invited for lunch aboard the *Victoria and Albert*, and spent the afternoon with Crawfie and the girls. They all got soaked in a summer shower and had a glorious time. The next day Philip came to the yacht again for lunch—credit Lord Louis with E for effort. By now Elizabeth, by every account, had caught a disease more dangerous than mumps; she had an advanced case of puppy love. And Philip appears to have been extremely attracted to his pretty little third cousin who looked at him with adoring blue eyes. Lord Louis' mind may have been working like a computer; but Philip was too young to be able to calculate and simulate emotions he did not feel.

When the *Victoria and Albert* sailed that afternoon half of Dartmouth College followed her out into the bay in all sorts of craft from launches to sailing dinghies and rowboats. They continued until the King nervously said to Captain Sir Dudley North, "This is ridiculous and quite unsafe. You must signal them to go back."

At the signal all the little boats turned back—except one. Philip continued to row madly after the yacht. Elizabeth watched him fondly through an enormous pair of binoculars. The King watched him with angry apprehension; he did not know what a fine sailor Philip was. "The young fool," he said, "he must go back, otherwise we'll have to heave to and send him back."

That set everybody bellowing at Philip to turn around. The chances are that it was Uncle Dickie's high-pitched but commanding voice that he obeyed. At any rate, he waved gallantly and turned his rowboat's bow toward shore. Lilibet was still watching him through the huge binoculars.

This occasion is often referred to as the first meeting between Philip and his future wife. It was not. They had met at the wedding of Princess Marina of Greece to the King's younger brother, the Duke of Kent, at the Coronation, and at many other family gatherings. But it was the first meeting at which they took cognizance of each other. If it had not happened then, it might never have occurred; for that historic cruise of the *Victoria and Albert* took place less than six weeks before the outbreak of war.

On September 1, 1939, the royal yacht and all the other luxurious toys that a nation at war cannot afford were put away as the British people tightened their belts for the stark struggle for survival. At Dartmouth the young cadets knew it would be only a matter of months until they were sent out to the fleet as midshipmen; indeed the senior class went immediately. A stern, no-fooling atmosphere replaced summer's gaiety.

Philip became one of the most intense cadets. He threw himself into his work with unquenchable energy and burning ambition, very like his uncle, Lord Louis. He evinced that spirit of leadership Doctor Hahn had noted, and also the "impatience and intolerance." His classmates remember him as a bit of a bully—that Germanic arrogance of command. He was saved from priggishness by his sense of humor, which was much keener than his uncle's—he could even laugh at himself.

Energy plus intelligence are unbeatable. By the end of his eight months at Dartmouth Philip was again top man. His training at Gordonstoun had put him a long way ahead of his classmates in seamanship; and his intense application took care of his studies. He won the King's Dirk, as the best all-round cadet of his term, and the Eardley-Howard-Crockett Prize, as the best cadet in the college. On January 1, 1940, Prince Philip of Greece was rated midshipman and posted to the old battleship *Ramillies*, then at Colombo, Ceylon, to convoy Australian-New Zealand troops to Egypt.

The appointment did not please Philip. He realized that he was being sent to a safe post because he was a Greek prince. When the war began Lord Louis had advised him to apply for British citizenship, which he had enthusiastically done. But in spite of all the Mountbatten pull, the wheels of bureaucracy were so clogged by the confusion of war that in matters of this sort they had simply stopped turning.

Nor was Philip's way among his fellow midshipmen smoothed by a special order from the Admiralty that he should be addressed by all ranks as Prince Philip. He disliked the title and the "of Greece" that made him palpably un-English. When asked his name he answered, just Philip. Just Philip he became to all his shipmates, in spite of the Lords of the Admiralty.

Philip served in the *Ramillies* for four months, going to Australia in her and convoying the troopships back to Alexandria, where he had another disappointment. Greece was still neutral and the British Foreign Office did not want a Greek prince getting killed in a British ship. When the *Ramillies* reached the scene of action in the Mediterranean Philip was transferred to the *Kent* en route to South Africa, and then to the *Shropshire,* which he joined at Durban in September, 1940. They were both old County Class light cruisers, good only for convoy duty.

It was all most frustrating for a mettlesome, hell-for-leather midshipman who wanted to see the big guns shoot for real. So Philip must have been more pleased than sorry when, on October 28, 1940, Italy invaded Greece—now that his native country was at war he could get into the fight. With Uncle Dickie in London pulling the strings Philip was transferred to the *Valiant* of the Mediterranean Fleet in December, 1940.

The *Valiant* was one of the splendid Queen Elizabeth Class, which were the last word in World War One. With her eight great 15-inch guns and fourteen 6-inch guns, to which had been added a vast amount of anti-aircraft armament, she was still a first-class battleship. Philip was put in command of a section of the searchlight control—a fine exposed place from which to watch a battle. He had been aboard her only three days when he saw the great guns shoot at the bombardment of Bardia.

In 1941, as has been noted, the Mediterranean was the hottest scene of action. Hitler's Luftwaffe, operating from Italian and African bases, had almost succeeded in making it a Nazi lake. The Royal Navy, beleaguered in Alexandria and Malta, could only make occasional dangerous forays to guard harassed convoys running the gauntlet to supply the British troops in island outposts.

One such trip took Philip to Athens. He arrived in high spirits wth a couple of days leave to see his royal relatives. He found the lot of them gathered in the great, ugly, stone barn of a palace—King George II and Queen Elizabeth, of course, Paul and Frederika, Philip's mother Princess Alice, and little Alexandra—a grown-up lady now. They, too, were in fine fettle, for the Greek Army had done surprisingly well against the Italians.

The night Philip arrived there was an air raid. Instead of going to the dungeon-like air-raid shelter they all went up on the palace roof to watch the show. Searchlights crisscrossed the sky, colored tracer bullets and shell bursts from anti-aircraft guns made a fine fireworks display, and shrapnel fell like metal rain while Philip showed off a bit by making knowledgeable comments on the action.

He left Athens to take part in one of the significant sea fights of the war. At the Battle of Cape Matapan, the British surprised part of the elusive Italian Navy. Philip, high in the upper works of the *Valiant*, directed the long white beams of the searchlight as they fingered the Italian cruisers *Zara* and *Fiume*. Caught like moths in the blinding light, they never had a chance as *Valiant*'s 15-inch guns blasted in splendid salvos. The ship reeled to their recoil, but the searchlights held steady on their mark. Meanwhile British Swordfish planes dive-bombed through the Italian anti-aircraft fire, sowing destruction. The Italian Fleet never again ventured out of safe harbor, except to surrender.

After the action the Commander in Chief Mediterranean, Admiral Sir Andrew Cunningham, mentioned Philip in dispatches, and Rear Admiral Sir Charles Morgan stated, "Thanks to his [Philip's] alertness and appreciation of the situation we were able to sink in five minutes the two 8-inch gun cruisers."*

That was the last victory for a while. The German Army stormed into Greece—quite a different matter from the Italians. Despite 60,000 British troops sent to bolster the Greeks, the Germans went through them like butter. The Greek Royal Family fled to Alexandria, some by air, King George in the destroyer *Decoy*, escorted by the *Valiant*. Only Princess Alice refused to leave Athens, but remained to care for some twenty orphans she had taken under her wing. Philip did not worry overly that the Germans would bother her, because two of her sons-in-law, Prince Hohenlohe-Langenburg and the Markgrave of Baden, were high-ranking German officers.

Thus, Philip was unexpectedly reunited with his cousins in Egypt. Despite the unhappy circumstances they seem to have had a feverishly gay time. Philip was happy to be fighting at last; and, like his uncle and grandfather, never shirked a duty and never lost a chance to have fun. On leave in Cairo he managed to get hold of a little sports car and took Alexandra out to see the town and to the Ghezire Sporting Club which was still functioning with pre-war gaiety.

---

* King George II gave Philip the Greek War Cross for this action, starting him on Uncle Dickie's road.

Then the *Valiant* sailed to take part in the Battle of Crete. In the smoke and bitter fighting of May 22, 1941, *Valiant* was hit by a big bomb that shook up the ship and all on board. Philip was functioning at top efficiency. In spite of the horror of spattered blood and human flesh, and heart-stopping screams of wounded men, he had an exhilarating sense of power. This was the real thing—not shooting fish in a barrel like Cape Matapan, which Philip said was, "as near murder as anything could be in wartime."

A little later Philip, in *Valiant*'s upper works, had a brief glimpse of Uncle Dickie's low-slung *Kelly* knifing through the sea at the head of his flotilla to join the fleet. Then she veered off, still at full speed, to her appointed destiny.

The battleships withdrew that night. The *Valiant* was at anchor in Alexandria by the time the battered *Kandahar* came limping in with David Milford Haven aboard. The next day Philip stood on the deck of the *Valiant* cheering his heart out as the *Kipling*, carrying Lord Louis and the ragged survivors of the *Kelly*, steamed slowly through the fleet, receiving the tremendous roaring ovation of its massed crews.

He got a boat ashore in time to greet Uncle Dickie as he landed at the base. Though he must have been terribly moved and shocked by the sight of Lord Louis, oil-smeared, exhausted, haggard with grief, he greeted him with typically British casualness-in-emotional-moments with that crack about "looking like a nigger minstrel." Lord Louis promptly gave him hell for not writing more often, for Philip was a lazy correspondent, while his uncle poured out letters literally by the thousands.

In June, 1941, Philip, who was due for promotion to sub-lieutenant, was ordered back to England to take his qualifying examinations. With other midshipmen in the same position, he traveled in an ancient coal-burning troopship. Since the passage through the western Mediterranean was interdicted by enemy aircraft, she took the long way around, through the Red Sea and Indian Ocean to the Cape of Good Hope. In Capetown Philip found some of the royal Greeks who had settled in South Africa for the duration. He got leave, and with pretty, adventurous Freddie,* went off in her car for a tour of Cape Province.

From Capetown the transport crawled diagonally across the Atlantic en route to Halifax to pick up Canadian troops. Her captain made the mistake of stopping at Puerto Rico where the Chinese stokers jumped ship in a body. The midshipmen were paraded on deck in the blazing semi-tropical sun and ordered to "volunteer" for stoking.

---

* Princess Frederika of Greece, the present Queen Mother.

Like Prince Louis coaling the *Dreadnought* at Smyrna, Philip found himself in the antiquated boiler room of the old transport, in a pair of dirty shorts, his hair, face, and strong bare body black with coal dust and streaked with sweat, swinging an iron shovel to feed the furnaces that blasted out unbearable heat each time the doors clanged open. It was a rugged experience; but Philip was tough. When he finally reached England he received a certificate as a "trimmer," which is proudly displayed in his study.

Prince Philip of Greece was promoted to sub-lieutenant on February 1, 1942, and posted to the destroyer *Wallace* in which he served for two years. In her, he endured the cold, dangerous job of patrol and convoy work in the North Sea and the Channel. It was very similar to the same duty in the *Kelly*, though not nearly as dramatic and glorious—after all, the *Wallace* was not commanded by Lord Louis Mountbatten.

Philip was promoted to first lieutenant in June, 1942, and was made second-in-command of the *Wallace* in October of that year. At twenty-one he was said to be the youngest officer in the Royal Navy holding such a responsible position.

None of these promotions was the work of Uncle Dickie. They were earned the hard way by efficiency, responsibility, courage, and initiative. Philip also won the respect if not the affection of the lower deck. The last promotion was made at the personal request of the captain of the *Wallace*, who certainly wanted the best second-in-command he could get.

In July, 1943, the *Wallace* was in the Mediterranean covering the landings in Sicily. Though the fighting was stiff and the Luftwaffe still dangerous it was vastly different from that forlorn fight off Crete two years earlier. In October the *Wallace* was ordered home to refit. Philip had eight months in England.

Though Philip was such an erratic letter-writer, he quite surprisingly kept up an intermittent correspondence with Princess Elizabeth. She received exciting letters and post cards from all the far places he went. It is ridiculous to say, as some do, that Philip was faithful in mind and spirit to his child-princess through all those years. Full-blooded men are seldom faithful in wartime, even to those who have a far stronger claim. But he does appear to have felt an affectionate responsibility toward the little girl who had so obviously admired him. Since he was a Mountbatten and a disciple of Uncle Dickie, the fact that she was the

Heir Apparent to the Throne may have reinforced this feeling, or it may have had nothing to do with it. Certainly Philip is not about to clarify this point, and it is possible that even he does not know.

The Princess, on the other hand, appears to have nourished a sentimental attachment for her handsome correspondent. She answered all his letters and sent parcels of goodies to him, which made her feel very grown-up and in the swing of things, since nearly every woman in England was writing and sending parcels to a man in the service.

Though the King and Queen made a point of staying in London to share the risks of their people all through the war, even when a bomb wrecked part of Buckingham Palace and blew them halfway across a room, the princesses were kept in the country, mostly at Windsor Castle, and sometimes at Sandringham or Balmoral. A battalion of the Grenadier Guards was stationed at Windsor, and Elizabeth and Margaret saw quite a bit of the handsome young officers at meals or impromptu parties; but Elizabeth seems never to have wavered in her affection for Philip. She is a steadfast sort of person.

Because she was always off in the country and Philip's leaves were brief, he seldom if ever got a chance to see Elizabeth until Christmas, 1943, when he was between ships. Then he was invited to Windsor to spend three nights and see the pantomime the princesses and the children from Windsor town put on for the benefit of the Queen's Wool Fund.*

That was the real beginning of the story of which that summer day at Dartmouth had been only a prelude. Philip found his Princess was a little girl no longer. At seventeen Elizabeth was an extremely attractive girl with a charming figure, her mother's high coloring, and intense blue eyes. She was indeed an intense sort of person, as strongly devoted to the ideals of goodness and duty as a young knight. At this time she had insisted on joining the Auxiliary Territorial Service, learning to drive an ambulance and taking the regular course in mechanics. She often drove herself to exhaustion in her work, because she was so conscientious and because her strong sense of being who she was thus obligated her to set an example. In spite of her seriousness she had real gaiety, though no great sense of humor.

But though she seemed quite mature for her age she was truly an innocent. Even in the most democratic of countries, even in England, even in wartime, royalty still lived behind the Cellophane Curtain, through which all the world could look, but which sealed them off from life in a protected, make-believe world. Old Queen Wilhelmina of the Netherlands used to call it The Cage, and, strong-minded as she was,

---

* Charging a top admission price of seven and six (about $1.) they raised about £900 ($4500).

never quite succeeded in breaking out. Small chance, then, for the gentle, loving Princess, whose Crawfie was alert to shield her from every shock.

Philip arrived at Windsor on Christmas Eve looking more than ever like a Viking, though a drawn and weatherbeaten one. He had been through a good deal.

The pantomime was given in the Waterloo Room of the Castle in which, a long time before, Queen Victoria had built a stage with superb blue velvet curtains for the household theatricals, of which she was very fond, and for the occasions when she commanded a London company to present the latest hit for her amusement. Around the huge, ornate room hung heavy gold frames which had contained pompous portraits of former kings and queens, now stored in vaults for the duration. At Princess Margaret's suggestion gaudy pantomime posters had been stuck up in the empty frames, which certainly enlivened the atmosphere.

Prince Philip sat in the front row with the King and Queen, never taking his eyes off Elizabeth who was indeed a charming Principal Boy in the role of Aladdin whose wonderful lamp shone no more brightly than her eyes. In fact, Philip's effect on Elizabeth was electric. According to Crawfie, "There was a sparkle about her none of us had ever seen before."

It was a carefree holiday. In the evenings the young people rolled up the rugs and danced to the "gramophone" which fortunately had just been mended. The last night was the best of all. David Milford Haven arrived and a group of young officers who commanded the Bofors guns around around the Castle joined them, in addition to the staff on duty which included the new Equerry, Commander Pilly-Fry. They played charades and clumps; and then "danced and danced and danced." According to a letter Princess Margaret wrote to Crawfie, "David Milford H . . . and Philip went mad."

After that evening Philip's photograph was placed on the dressing table in Elizabeth's room, never to be removed; her photograph traveled the China Seas in Philip's cabin.

In February, 1944, Philip was appointed first lieutenant of the new destroyer *Whelp*, which had been launched but not yet commissioned. His orders were to stand by while she was fitted out, which meant that he was in London off and on for several months. When there, he lived in a tiny bedroom in the Mountbattens' house on Chester Street. Lord Louis was in Southeast Asia, but Edwina was there while she organized the Red Cross and St. John services for D-Day.

During this time Philip managed to see quite a bit of Elizabeth. There were other weekends at Windsor Castle, and the Princess came up to London frequently for her ATS training, though she seldom spent the night there. On her eighteenth birthday, April 21, 1944, Queen Mary gave a little party for her at Marlborough House, to which Philip, of course, was invited.

An eighteenth birthday is a coming of age for British Royalty. After it Elizabeth was made a member of the Privy Council and given more freedom and many more duties, among them visiting the wounded in the hospitals in and around London. It was a stomach-turning, heart-rending ordeal even for older women; for the protected young Princess it must have almost been unbearable. But since it was clearly her duty, she did it, and did it very well, hiding her distress and pity beneath a lovely smile that she never allowed to become frozen with horror.

The compensation was that she could now see even more of Philip. It had become "of course" for them to be asked together for any suitable occasion. But King George did not view his daughter's choice with any noticeable enthusiasm. When King George of Greece stupidly brought up the subject one day at Buckingham Palace the King said testily, "Tell Philip to stop thinking about anything like that, at least for a while."

Philip's nights in London appear to have been spent in much more raucous company. As in all wars, the "tomorrow we die" philosophy prevailed among soldiers and sailors on leave, sharpened in this case by the new German buzz-bombs and V-2 rockets which made it quite possible that some of them would die *tonight*. Philip was a leader of this wild young crowd and their girls, though his high spirits seem to have taken the innocuous form of the family fondness for rather silly practical jokes, like tripping up dowagers or ringing up total strangers at 4 A.M. It was a phase he mostly outgrew.

On the serious side he watched over the progress of the *Whelp*, and made another effort to become a British citizen, by filling out form S—"for aliens in the Fighting Services." It has been stated that he did not try to use any special influence. This is nonsense. When the Mountbattens wanted anything really badly they used every ounce of pull they had. Uncle Dickie wrote from Southeast Asia asking King George to take an interest in Philip's case. The King pointed out that Philip first should get permission from George II of Greece. By the time that reluctant monarch came through, the *Whelp* and Philip were in the Mediterranean, backing up the Allied landings in the South of France in August, 1944. So the matter was dropped once more.

From the Mediterranean the *Whelp* sailed to join the 27th Flotilla based in Australia as part of Admiral Somerville's East Indies Fleet. This brought Philip under the overall command of his Uncle Dickie. Philip had a grand time in Australia. Those final months of the war were neither terribly arduous nor very dangerous for the Royal Navy. Since Philip had abundantly proved his manhood in more perilous seas he could enjoy this relaxation. He grew a fine bushy reddish beard that made him look rather like his grandfather Prince Louis. Of course, all big, bearded men have some resemblance, but there was rather more to it than that—something about the cut of his jib, as Prince Louis might have said.

Moreover Philip got on splendidly with the Australians. He liked their informal, matey style, their sporting proclivities, and their genuine warmth. The Australian girls liked him—and why not? He was so dashing, so good-looking, such fun, and an authentic Royal Prince to boot. Such were rather rare birds Down Under, so the girls' natural inclination to glamorize royalty was not sated by overexposure. Naturally, their mothers shared their enthusiasm. Pretty girls who were also great heiresses were hurled or hurled themselves at his curly, bearded head in large numbers. In vain! Philip was remarkably discreet. He flirted; he had fun; and just as some young lady thought she was making progress, she found he was not there. He became a master of evasive tactics. Doubtless it seemed strange to their worldly mothers that so impoverished a prince as they knew him to be should seem utterly impervious to the advantages of a wealthy marriage. But, of course, they did not know that there was a letter from the greatest heiress of all in every mail.

Philip's admiration for Australian men got him into trouble with his kinsman, the Duke of Gloucester. The Australian press was sniping at the Governor General about some of his actions. Philip, who had not yet suffered the barbed arrows that were to make him one of the world's foremost journalist-haters, took the Australian side of the small tempest in conversations that were reported to Government House. Humorless Gloucester let his fresh young cousin know what he thought of that. Philip was not perturbed.

When the war ended with that deadly flash at Hiroshima, Philip in the *Whelp* was escorting Admiral Fraser's flagship, the *Duke of York*, which had joined the vast American Fleet off Okinawa. Uncle Dickie's long arm reached out across the seas to pluck him out of the *Whelp* to stand on the crowded deck of the U.S.S. *Missouri* in Tokyo Bay on the historic morning of September 2, 1945.

Afterward Lord Louis appointed Philip to his own effulgent staff, where he served with John Brabourne, Patricia Mountbatten, and all the other bright, gay, hardworking young people who were helping Proconsul Lord Mountbatten settle the affairs of his vast Oriental satrapy. It was not only tremendously interesting and tremendous fun, but a very valuable experience for a future Consort. In that time he learned more about the people of Asia, and, from Lord Louis, how to win their confidence and loyalty, than he could have in any other of life's schools.

Chapter 3

A
DIFFICULT
COURTING

Philip returned to England in the *Whelp* in January, 1946. The first night he got leave he made straight for Buckingham Palace. Still bearded* and bubbling with gaiety he had dinner with his radiant Princess in her sitting room, chaperoned by Margaret, who at sixteen was much livelier, wittier, more artistic—and precocious—than her older sister, though not as pretty or as amiable.

The three of them had a glorious time together. The high-ceilinged room echoed to Philip's roars of laughter and his cousin's soprano giggles. After dinner they chased each other up and down the long corridors of the palace. Philip and Elizabeth were so happy to be together again that they did not think about the future at all, or if they did, it looked smooth as cream. They were, of course, mistaken.

However, for the time being things did go smoothly. Everyone, including Crawfie, appears to have liked Philip a good deal more than

---

* Elizabeth soon made him shave it off.

they had before. He had matured and though still full of rampaging spirits, he was kinder and more thoughtful.

Even King George was impressed. After a long talk with Philip as they drove out to Windsor one afternoon, he remarked, "I like Philip. He is intelligent, has a good sense of humor and thinks about things the right way."

All of which did not mean that the King was reconciled to the idea of Philip marrying his daughter.

The *Whelp* was laid up with a skeleton crew and Philip in command for two months, and then decommissioned. Philip was posted first to the naval training center at Pwllheli in Wales, officially known as H.M.S. *Glendower*, and then sent as one of two officers to start a training school for petty officers at Corsham in Wiltshire—H.M.S. *Royal Arthur*.

The school was a pretty dismal place, consisting of a group of temporary Nissen huts set down amid fields and muddy lanes outside the little town. It had two advantages: First, the challenge of being responsible for inaugurating an important program for updating the education of the petty officers from the age of sail, which naval tradition had clung to as the best possible preparation for a sailor, into the atomic era in one huge jump.

The second advantage, probably the more important from Philip's point of view, was that Corsham was only ninety-eight miles from London. He is known to have made the run in his black and green MG in one hour and forty minutes, an average of almost precisely a mile a minute, which, allowing for country lanes and suburban traffic, might give Phil Hill something to think about.

In London, as his secret courtship of Elizabeth continued, difficulties multiplied. They did everything possible to throw people off the scent, except stop seeing each other. Their theme song was the sunny tune from *Oklahoma!*, "People Will Say We're in Love." But there was no hiding place behind the Cellophane Curtain.

Reporters noticed Philip's car driving into a back entrance of Buckingham Palace. When they went out dancing in the evening, always with a group of people, no matter how careful he was to obey the song's injunction, "Don't dance all night with me," a columnist always spotted them and made the most of it. The press became their great enemy which no evasive tactics could escape.

The papers were, in fact, not kind to Philip, especially those owned by Lord Beaverbrook who enlarged his campaign against Lord Louis to include his nephew. Even after Philip finally succeeded in becoming a British citizen, they referred to him as "Phil the Greek," and ran polls to determine whether the British people would approve a marriage of Philip and Elizabeth. Only 40 per cent were in favor, not surprising considering that the English were in the midst of their habitual postwar xenophobia and were particularly annoyed with the Greek King who, from his precarious perch on the throne, was encouraging rather repressive measures against his leftist subjects.

Though 40 per cent was thus pretty good, it was disturbing to King George and Queen Elizabeth since the British Monarchy aims for 100-per-cent approval of their acts, and usually comes close to the mark. It was subtly evident that they did not favor the match. Whether or not they ever tried to dissuade Elizabeth is not, and probably never will be, known. They certainly used delaying tactics. But being genuinely devoted parents, they took no overt steps to separate Philip and Elizabeth. Had they done so, Elizabeth would probably have obeyed them. But they knew that in breaking up the match they would probably break their daughter's heart.

Even so there was a good deal of tension and very little privacy in the palace. Behind its solid, guarded walls they were hardly ever alone together. "Buck House" resembles Grand Central Station in more ways than its somber-colossal school of architecture. The officials of the Court and the staff are always popping in and out, and it takes the equivalent of a World War One regiment of servants to run the place. For example, there are fifty housemaids and large numbers of footmen, butlers, pages, chefs, electricians, and such specialized characters as the clock winder, the vermin man, and the table decker (flower arranger), who wander about performing their various functions.

And there was Margaret; the classic little-sister-you-can't-get-rid-of, old enough to enjoy Philip's company, not wise enough to realize he would be happier without hers.

Naturally there were many kind people who tried to help them. Marina of Kent, whose husband had been killed in an air crash during the war, often asked them to lunch at her flat; and other people asked them to their homes. One of their few opportunities for privacy was walking or riding together in Windsor Great Park—Elizabeth, like her namesake the Great Queen, was a fine horsewoman and Philip was much more expert than his Uncle Dickie. But even there they had to be as wary as hunted deer.

It was not at all Philip's way of doing things and he was unaccustomed to it. He would have liked to come out and tell the world above his love, and then tell it where to go. But it was good indoctrina-

tion for the life he would have to lead if his hopes—and Elizabeth's—
were realized. The fact that he controlled himself so well and put up
with it so patiently and, on the whole, decorously gives considerable
credence to the theory that he really was in love with the girl and not
her dazzling prospects. Unlike his uncle, Philip had not the ruthless
determination to endure distasteful circumstances for pure self-advancement without a higher motive. Besides, he may well have come to realize
that to marry a future Queen was more in the nature of self-sacrifice
than self-interest.*

During this period Philip made a trip to Monte Carlo to wind up his
father's affairs.† It was a melancholy business, for Prince Andrew's poor
possessions and shabby quarters showed how unhappy his last years must
have been. When funeral expenses had been paid and debts settled, his
estate completely disappeared. Philip's patrimony amounted to a few
mementos of his father, and a rather handsome suit which he had altered
to fit him, and an ivory-handled shaving brush.

In June Lord Mountbatten came home from Burma wrapped in
clouds of glory, shot with flashes of diamond decorations which the
King soon capped with the Garter. The house on Chester Street quivered with activity and almost burst with guests.

Lord Louis made no secret of his pleasure at his nephew's past
record and present activities. If anything were to come of the latter,
Philip must become British—the sooner the better. Mountbatten threw
his whole enormous influence and executive ability into expediting the
matter. There was no nonsense about letting the law take its ordinary
course. This was no ordinary case; and it looked to be getting more extraordinary every moment. Prime Minister Clement Attlee and Winston
Churchill, now Leader of the Opposition, got into the discussions, but
there were so many complications that the matter dragged on for almost
a year longer.

Late in the summer the King, who deeply loved and greatly admired his elder daughter, decided that her happiness should be his first
consideration and that she could be trusted to choose wisely. Certainly
a penniless Greek prince was no great match and unlikely to be popular
with his subjects; but he recognized that in her gentle loving way Lilibet
yet had some of her great-great-grandmother's constancy and determination. He decided to let her find out if Philip was the man she really

---

* When Prince Albert accepted Queen Victoria's proposal of marriage the
young Queen recorded in her diary that she thanked him for, "his self-sacrifice."
† Prince Andrew died at Monte Carlo on December 3, 1944.

wanted, and if he were, so be it. Philip was invited for a long visit at Balmoral.

He realized that this was to be both a time of testing and, hopefully, of acceptance. He must have been rather nervous as he made the journey to Scotland, but that feeling did not last very long. With his extroverted nature, he expected people to like him, particularly if he wanted them to, which in this case he certainly did. So almost at once he was completely at home in the relaxed yet tradition-bound atmosphere of Balmoral.

Most people would find this a bit difficult. The castle Queen Victoria had built in the romantic, Sir Walter Scott manner was still very much as she had left it. There were gigantic halls with groined ceilings and walls covered by forests of antlers and the moth-eaten hides of dead animals; thirty-foot-square sitting rooms were crowded with red-plush furniture, their floors covered with tartan rugs matched by tartan doilies and tartan mats, all in Albert's execrable taste of which Victoria had been so proud.

Philip's bedroom was a large room crammed with furniture, including a brass double bed above which was a brass lamp embellished by a fussy lace shade. The nearest bathroom was a good city block away.

Art was represented by Scottish landscapes and noble Landseer dogs and stags. Everywhere were statues and portraits of Victoria's Albert, whose melancholy hazel eyes, seeming to warn Philip of the difficulties of the job, failed to dampen his gaiety.

Always in splendid physical condition, Philip actually enjoyed the traditional deerstalking, crawling on his belly through the rocky hills and glens in the pouring rain that Scots call mist. Luckily for his popularity with the King he was a naturally good shot.* More trying were the formal dinners, when led by a piper they all marched in to the long table groaning with silver plate—though not with food, because this was a time of austerity. The King and most of his gentlemen wore the kilt with a white buckskin sporran and a black velvet jacket with crested silver buttons. Philip's national kilt was the pleated white skirt of the Greek Evzone, so he wore a naval mess jacket.

Philip stayed at Balmoral nearly a month. Sometime during that period he became—very unofficially—engaged to Elizabeth. She did not follow Queen Victoria's precedent of proposing to him. Philip asked her to marry him as they sat in the heather beside a small blue lake. It was a mere formality, more in the nature of a mutual declaration of the love of which both were sure.

---

* Elizabeth was much better. One day in 1961 she killed four stags with four shots.

King George and Queen Elizabeth accepted Philip as their future son-in-law and toasted the young couple in champagne. But it all had to be very tentative. There were so many difficulties to be ironed out and negotiations to be conducted. Not only must the all powerful Parliament agree and the British people be won over, but some of the King's conservative advisers were set against the match.

Naturally the press made a Roman Holiday of Philip's month in the country. As time dragged on speculation gave way to acrimonious suggestions that the Royal Family ought to stop shilly-shallying. Either the engagement should be announced or Philip should go home.

The first royal reaction was negative. In September Buckingham Palace officially denied the rumor that Her Royal Highness the Princess Elizabeth was engaged to Prince Philip. This was soon followed by the announcement that Their Royal Highnesses, the Princesses Elizabeth and Margaret, would accompany Their Majesties on their scheduled official visit to South Africa early in 1947.

King George's reasons for postponing the announcement of his daughter's engagement until after the tour were sound, and partly political. The South Africans were in a rather touchy and ambivalent state of mind about remaining in the British Empire, and the main purpose of the royal visit was, of course, to arouse their loyalty. The King wanted no distractions or discussions to dim its effect. On the personal side he may still have had his reservation about Philip. Since propinquity had not changed Elizabeth's mind, perhaps absence would. Many a doubting parent has tried this cure.

But in October, at Patricia Mountbatten's wedding to Lord Brabourne, King George allowed Elizabeth to be photographed with Philip for the first time. In the original her father was also in the picture. Virtually every newspaper and magazine in the world printed the photograph, and almost all of them cut out the King.

This was followed by an invitation to Philip to spend Christmas at Sandringham, which really made him one of the family. It also left no doubt in the British people's minds that the official spokesman of Buckingham Palace was lying in his teeth when he denied the engagement.

The winter of 1946–47 was miserable for every inhabitant of the United Kingdom, and particularly miserable for Philip. The final pleasant moment was a family dinner at the Mountbattens' little Chester Street house late in January, with the King and Queen, and Elizabeth and David Milford Haven. They all drank champagne, except the King, who drank Scotch all through dinner. Lord Louis was in tremendous form, preparing to be Viceroy of India. Philip and Elizabeth were rather wet blankets.

On February 1, 1947, the Royal Family sailed for South Africa in the huge new battleship *Vanguard*, which Princess Elizabeth had christened in one of her first official acts during the war. The 40,000-ton *Vanguard* was the last and greatest dreadnought ever launched in England. Obsolescent before ever she hit the water, she was nonetheless a fine, dignified vessel for a royal pilgrimage.

Hardly had Philip waved his sad-eyed Princess off from Portsmouth, than England was turned into an excellent facsimile of the ninth circle of hell by one of those frightful Arctic invasions that come once in a decade, breaking through the beneficent barrier of the Gulf Stream and bringing another Ice Age. Howling blizzards and near-zero temperatures persisted day after day. Roads were blocked, trains stopped running, fuel ran low. The shaky, war-wracked economy of England faltered and ground to an almost complete stop. Factories shut down, electricity was shut off for several hours each day, lights went out, and everybody was miserably cold.

At Corsham it was particularly dismal. The Nissen huts, uncomfortable under the best conditions, were barely warmer than outdoors; in fact the wind hardly paused as it blew through them. There were of course neither central heating nor fireplaces, and when the electricity was cut off there was no heat at all. When the sailors were not digging themselves out of snow drifts, Philip, wearing bad-weather gear, lectured to them by the light of a few candles. Unable to indulge in the strenuous sports he loved, his only amusements were drinking beer and playing darts and skittles at the local pub, the Methuen Arms. Even the house on Chester Street was shuttered and dreary, for the Mountbattens had gone to India. War was never like this—at least for Philip.

One bright spot was that he finally became a British subject on February 28, 1947.* He renounced his tenuous claim to the Greek throne and, of course, his title, thereby incidentally leaving himself without a last name. This had, of course, been foreseen. Before the King and Queen left for South Africa there had been numerous conferences about it. "Just Philip" would not do; nor did Glücksburg seem either euphonious or appropriate. The King offered him a British title, which he refused at that time. Other family names of the Danish Royal House were suggested. Finally he made the logical choice—Philip Mountbatten. He knew that it would please Uncle Dickie enormously. It did.

. . .

---

* The Home Office paid the £10 fee.

Though it seemed never-ending, winter reluctantly gave way to spring; and in May Elizabeth came home. On July 10, 1947, there was an official announcement:

Buckingham Palace, July 10, 1947

It is with the greatest pleasure that the King and Queen announce the betrothal of their dearly beloved daughter, The Princess Elizabeth, to Lieutenant Philip Mountbatten, R.N., son of the late Prince Andrew of Greece and Princess Andrew (Princess Alice of Battenberg), to which union the King has gladly given his consent.

From that moment Philip was involved in what he called, "the royal rigmarole." The deserted house on Chester Street was considered too undignified and unprotected—from the press—so he moved into his grandmother's, the Dowager Marchioness of Milford Haven, spacious but shabby apartment in Kensington Palace. Princess Alice was also there, and gave him some diamonds for Elizabeth's engagement ring. The atmosphere of the place would have been unendurably gloomy if naughty David Milford Haven had not also been there.

Now that he was such a public figure Philip desperately needed help. Miss Lees, the Mountbattens' secretary, came over to help answer the mail, and John Dean, the young butler from Chester Street who had often washed Philip's extra shirt and socks when he came up from Corsham to court Elizabeth, came as his valet. There is not much doubt that Lord Louis continued to pay their salaries.

Even so, things were pretty difficult for Philip financially. There were many expenses involved in being the official fiancé of the Princess. Philip's minuscule salary of $33.60 a week as a Royal Navy lieutenant got him nowhere. Just where the money for clothes, tips to servants, and all the other things came from is a mystery to which Uncle Dickie probably holds the key.

The press was a greater problem than ever, and Philip compounded it by being a little too frisky with the MG one night. He turned it over in a ditch. It scared Elizabeth, irritated the King, and gave the newspapers a chance for pious sermons on imperiling the happiness of the Heiress Apparent by reckless driving. Then one day when he was driving Elizabeth, one of those London taxis, who respect neither man nor monarch, crumpled his fender. Elizabeth burst into Crawfie's room to tell her all about it and say like a little girl: "How are we ever going to convince Papa and Mama that it really wasn't Philip's fault this time? They'll never believe it!"

Naturally no one could be convinced that it was not Philip's fault.

He was typed, not without some justification, as a reckless driver. A campaign was started to forbid him to drive Elizabeth. That got nowhere. The papers said that the royal chauffeurs were afraid to drive with him. Most likely they were. A royal chauffeur is by definition a very cautious driver. Old King Edward was always shouting, "Faster, Stamper, faster!" to his driver back in 1909. They certainly were grumpy whenever Philip wanted to drive one of the immaculate royal cars.

The King thought it would be nice if they had a June wedding. Elizabeth, ardently backed by Philip, showed a flash of Great-Great-Grandmother's spirit. They had waited long enough, she said. It must be soon. The King yielded and set November 20. Let the English weather do its worst!

As a sort of engagement present, the King gave his daughter an old "grace and favour" country house, Sunninghill Park, near Windsor Castle. When the young people went to look it over they found that it had precious little grace and was a small favor. Sunninghill had been used as an army barracks. The soldiers had battered its interior, and what they had omitted to do was accomplished by a bomb through the roof. The place was such a wreck that only one wing could be made habitable. But Philip and Elizabeth gaily made plans for its restoration and decoration.

Then, in August, the place mysteriously burned down. Sabotage was suspected, though the police never admitted it. But if arson it was, the arsonist did the young couple a great favor. In its place the King gave them Clarence House on the Mall in London, a dignified and beautiful home.

As the time for the wedding approached pressures piled up. Philip had to be received into the Church of England. There was not much difficulty about this, for the Greek Orthodox Church and the Anglican Church recognize each other's sacraments. It was accomplished at a private ceremony conducted by the Archbishop of Canterbury.

Much more controversial were the plans for the wedding. England was at her economic nadir, and in view of the hardships of the people the Royal Family and the Government wanted to keep the ceremony as simple as possible. It was proposed at first to hold it in St. George's Chapel at Windsor, where King Edward VII had been married, or in the Chapel Royal at St. James's Palace, where Queen Victoria had married Albert. It was also suggested that the Guards wear battle dress as they had ever since the war.

The people would have none of it. They were sick to death of austerity and wanted their Princess to have a proper wedding, with all the trimmings, in Westminster Abbey. The Conservative Party raised such a rumpus in the House of Lords and in the Commons, and the people themselves wrote so many angry letters to *The Times*, that the King and his Government backed down and decreed that the Abbey should be the place and full dress should be worn. Clement Attlee was rather pleased. In spite of being a Labour Prime Minister he was a traditionalist at heart.

So the scarlet or blue uniforms came out of mothballs where they had been for eight dismal years. Helmets and breastplates were polished, jackboots shined, and bearskins fluffed up. The Irish State Coach was freshly gilded and the eight grays assembled and trained.

One worry was eliminated. The English love a lover as much as the rest of the world. It was common knowledge that the King and Queen had not been too keen on the match. So it must be love. Philip's popularity soared.

The invitations went out for November 20, 1947, and tens of thousands of presents poured in; many of them superb, like the great diamond parure sent by the Nizam of Hyderabad, others touchingly simple sent lovingly by poor people.

Meanwhile Philip continued to teach the petty officers at Corsham, virtually commuting between there and London. The strain of this plus the wedding preparations, the attentions of the press, and the sight of Wilhelmina's "cage" closing around him made him rather short-tempered with his friends and servants, though not with Elizabeth. Every so often he and Milford Haven had to have a night out drinking and playing cards at the Thursday Club. Occasionally they returned via the roof of Kensington Palace rather than arouse the sleeping dowagers.

November 19, 1947, the eve of his wedding, was a full day for Philip. At a family ceremony in Buckingham Palace, which included the beaming Mountbattens temporarily back from liquidating the British Empire in India, King George provided him with the rank and status suitable to his new position.

First, the Garter! The one right which the Sovereign has won back from ever-encroaching Parliament is that of bestowing this order *without* the advice of his Government.* In 1946 King George VI had a

---

* Lord Melbourne once remarked: "The nice thing about the Garter is there's no damn merit about it."

long and very earnest talk with Mr. Attlee, in which he pointed out that the order was becoming a mere political reward. It seemed to him unfortunate that this symbol of chivalry should be debased. Unexpectedly Attlee agreed with him. He returned it to the Monarchy and gallantly threw in the orders of The Thistle and St. Patrick. King George's first installations on his own were Lords Addison, Cranborne, Alanbrooke, Alexander, Montgomery, Portal, and Mountbatten.

Now, having carefully installed his daughter eight days earlier so she would be senior to her husband even here, King George made Philip a Knight Companion of the Most Noble Order of the Garter.

Then the King, with the expertise of long practice, touched Philip's shoulder three times with the blue steel blade of a naked sword, creating him Baron Greenwich (for London and the Navy), Earl of Merioneth (for Wales), and Duke of Edinburgh (for Scotland). The latter title was particularly well chosen since it was Alfred, Duke of Edinburgh, who had talked Prince Louis of Battenberg into joining the Royal Navy. The King also authorized Philip's use of the prefix His Royal Highness; but he did not make him a British prince. This was later referred to as "an omission," implying oversight. It was nothing of the kind, but done on the advice of Mr. Attlee and others who feared the popular effect of too much too soon.

That night, while Philip had his bachelor dinner, Elizabeth dined alone with her parents and sister, a solemn, nostalgic meal. Afterward, the choirmaster of the Abbey arrived to go over the wedding music. Elizabeth wanted to have the Scottish paraphrase of the Twenty-third Psalm sung to the tune of Crimond. The choirmaster did not know it, and they all tried to teach it to him. Residents of Buck House heard remarkably discordant sounds emanating from the music room—Margaret was the only member of the family who could sing on key, although Elizabeth could play nicely on the piano.

Commander Norfolk, who had been captain of the *Whelp*, gave Philip his bachelor dinner at the Dorchester Hotel on Park Lane. All his raffish pals were there—David Milford Haven, his best man; Lieutenant Michael Parker; Baron, the Court photographer who had introduced him to the Thursday Club; many other young naval officers, and, of course, Uncle Dickie in tearing high spirits.

The party started decorously with sherry followed by champagne at dinner with lots of toasts. Around midnight some of the guests "unfortunately switched to beer."* However, it was still orderly enough so that the press and photographers were let in, probably to scotch any rumors of bacchanalian revels. The photographers broke the thing up,

---

* Geoffrey Bocca, *Elizabeth and Philip*.

leaping on chairs, shouting for "one more," and trying for odd angles—while the guests grabbed their cameras and took pictures of them. As one photographer raced around the table for a side shot, Mountbatten yelled, "I'm being outflanked!"

The party ostensibly ended then. Actually it adjourned to the privacy of the Thursday Club where everybody except Philip got roaring drunk. One rather insulting episode is reported to have taken place. A certain actor stared drunkenly at Philip and said loudly, "I think you are an absolute bastard to do this thing." Then he walked out. It is not possible to obtain any confirmation of this incident; but whether it happened or not, that thought was in the minds of a certain super-sophisticated group. They simply could not accept the gush about a royal love story. Even they believed that the Princess was madly in love with Philip, because there was no other conceivable reason for her to marry him. However, they thought he was coldly taking advantage of her infatuation to advance himself and his family.

While this is a tenable hypothesis it does not seem in tune with Philip's character. Though he needed money, he never cared that much about it; and if he had there were plenty of heiresses who would have supplied it without the onerous responsibilities. Power? Perhaps; for all the Mountbattens love power. Yet how far could a man, who knew the position of royalty from the inside, fool himself about their having much real power? Finally, Philip was quite aware of his considerable ability. He was confident of making a great career in the Navy; and would have valued the earned power of the First Sea Lord above the similitude of power accorded the Queen's husband.

So it seems reasonable to conclude that Philip really loved his Princess. Admitting that the glamor surrounding her may have been a factor, more important ones were her youthful beauty, her sweetly amiable nature, and above all her immensely touching love for him. This he returned, if not in equal measure, at least as much as his tougher nature permitted.

When Philip got home to Kensington Palace after his bachelor party, he lit a cigarette. As he stubbed it out he said to Milford Haven, "That's the last one."

Philip gave up smoking forever that night. Elizabeth did not smoke but she had no objection; after all her father smoked a pipe and she was used to it. Philip's act seems to have been symbolic, a testing of his strength of character, and a renunciation of the frivolities of youth.

Chapter 4

ELIZABETH II

❧

JOHN DEAN SAYS THAT WHEN he went to wake Philip at seven o'clock the next morning, he found him in "great form [and] extremely cheerful,"* which certainly indicates a remarkably hale constitution. After breakfasting on toast and coffee, Philip dressed in his regular naval uniform with his few decorations and the Star of the Garter, though not the blue ribbon which was only properly worn with dress uniform.

He chose to be married wearing Prince Louis of Battenberg's beautifully wrought sword, in which Lord Mountbatten had been married. The story goes that he borrowed it because he was too poor to buy one of his own. This is nonsense, since he had to get one immediately in any event for ceremonial occasions. He wore it from sentiment.†

David Milford Haven had more trouble getting up, but he finally came in, and they sat and drank a gin and tonic together, which David needed badly. Then they started for the palace.

It was a typical London November day, cold and miserable, but at least it was not raining. Enormous crowds filled the streets; and Westminster Abbey was packed with all that was left of the beauty and chivalry of England, together with such distinguished foreigners as had

---

* John Dean, *Prince Philip.*

† Another misconception about this sword is that Prince Louis wore it at his wedding. He was married in the uniform of the Royal Hessian Artillery and wore a sabre, not a naval officer's sword.

been invited. Five kings and eight queens—not all of them still reigning—eight princes and ten princesses were there, but next to the bride and her immediate family it was the new Earl and Countess Mountbatten who attracted the most interest.

They arrived from the palace with the Royal Family, and as they walked to their seats they were probably the handsomest couple in the great church. But many of the eyes riveted on them expressed not admiration but dislike and scorn. For most of the old aristocracy regarded Mountbatten as the man who had collaborated with their enemies to give away India and the Empire of which they had been so proud. They thought him a traitor to his class and to his country.

Lord Louis had discounted this when he took the distasteful duty; and secure in the knowledge of a job well done and the approval of his King, did not let it dim his happiness. Unfortunately, however, some of this hostility spilled over onto Philip as he came in quietly with Milford Haven to wait by the altar for his bride.

All ill feeling evaporated in tremendous emotion as the music and the clash of singing bells announced the arrival of the bride. First the bridesmaids, wearing rather simple dresses in deference to austerity, among them Pamela Mountbatten. Then Margaret walked gracefully alone, very grown-up and serious, followed by the King, in his favorite uniform of an Admiral of the Fleet, with Elizabeth on his arm. Not a great beauty by classic standards, she was beautiful that day by any standard, but especially in the blue-eyed, pink-cheeked, innocent English way as in her exquisite wedding gown she walked sedately beside her father through the tall Gothic forest of Westminster's nave.

The Archbishop of Canterbury married them with the regular Anglican service which included Elizabeth's promise to "love, honor, and obey." As she and Philip started back down the long aisle, Elizabeth made a low curtsey to her father and mother with all her love and gratitude in her shining eyes.

The solemnity and order of the ceremony at the Abbey gave way to complete confusion and noisy greetings as the high-spirited royal cousins poured into the State rooms at Buckingham Palace. Here it was all in the family and they could let down their manners and burst out of the "royal rigmarole." There was not even a formal receiving line. It was a difficult business getting them all formed up properly for the official group photographs. Margaret rushed around saying, "Come along everybody. Pictures!" They had trouble putting properly dignified expressions on their faces. The immediate wedding party had to keep rushing out to make appearances on the balcony amid the cheers of the cold but enthusiastic crowds.

The wedding breakfast was served, on the famous gold plate at small tables in the magnificent ball-supper room, by dozens of footmen in long scarlet and gold-braided coats and knee breeches. Coffee was served in the Blue Room. Having bitten the bullet, King George was as merry as a monarch could be, cracking his funny Victorian jokes with everybody. Some said that Queen Elizabeth was prettier and gayer than her daughter. This may be true, for Elizabeth was very anxious to be off.

At last it was time to leave for Broadlands, which Lord Louis had lent them for the first part of the honeymoon. By now it was nearly dark outside and raining, but they had to drive in an open carriage; Elizabeth in a pretty pale-blue dress and blue wool coat smiled and waved, with chattering teeth, to the cheering people.

The two-car special train took Elizabeth and Philip with her maid, Miss "Bobo" MacDonald, and John Dean to Winchester. The Princess had fifteen suitcases. Philip had two for his two extra uniforms, his one good gray suit of civvies, his shooting clothes, and dinner jacket.

There were more receptions at Winchester and a great cheering crowd in front of the gates of Broadlands. But at last they got up to their suite. It was Edwina Mountbatten's and as different as possible from Balmoral, being decorated in white and pale gray with delicate eight-eenth-century furniture and Dali sketches on the walls. In line with the Mountbatten fondness for following in each other's footsteps it was the same suite in which Lord Louis and Edwina had begun their honeymoon.

Broadlands was a mistake. It was much too close to London, and the best efforts of the local constabulary reinforced by security men from London could not cope with the hordes of people who came down in chartered buses, or the do-or-die photographers hanging like monkeys from the splendid old trees. Sunday church going in Romsey Abbey was a shambles.

Philip got more and more annoyed. One day when they were out shooting pheasants it took all his self-control not to add two photog-raphers in a tree to his bag. When he took Elizabeth for a ride in his new Humber roadster, he went down the drive flat-out and zipped through the gates with reporters and photographers leaping for their lives. By the time they recovered and thought of following, Philip and Elizabeth were in the next county.

When they returned to London on their way to Scotland Philip dictated a statement which expressed their feelings with delightful ambiguity: "The reception given us on our wedding day and the loving interest shown by our fellow countrymen . . . have left an impression that will never grow faint. We can find no words to express what we feel, but we can at least offer our grateful thanks to the millions who have given us this unforgettable send off in our married life."

How they must have laughed over that!

In Scotland, Philip and Elizabeth stayed at Birkhall, a small ancient manor house near Balmoral, which the Prince Consort had bought a long time ago. The weather was frightful, but they had escaped at last. They had a glorious time.

They came back in time to spend a Dickensian family Christmas at Sandringham. It was Philip's second one there, but now that he was a member of the family he had to wear the kilt. The King offered him a choice of several which had belonged to King George V, and Philip chose the Stuart Hunting Tartan. Because he was so much taller than the late King it was much too short for him. As he came down to dinner the first night with several inches of pale skin showing above bony knees he felt like a fool and so he acted the fool. As he greeted his father-in-law he dropped a curtsey.

King George had a nice sense of humor, but on this occasion he was not amused, and he told Philip so in a roar of quarterdeck language.

Unlike Prince Albert, Philip had a period of grace before "the cage" snapped shut. During the first months of his marriage he worked from nine to six at the Operations Division of the Admiralty. While Clarence House, which had been badly bombed, was redone he and Elizabeth lived in her apartment at Buckingham Palace. Then, when the Duke of Athlone left to be Governor General of South Africa, they took over his apartments in Kensington Palace.

This was much better than the heavy atmosphere of Buck House; but they both loved the country, so for weekends they rented Windlesham Moor in Surrey, not far from Windsor. It was a small white country house with fine gardens containing a famous stand of rhododendrons and brilliant herbacious borders. On its fifty acres of rolling moors there was a small golf course and a grass tennis court which Philip turned into a cricket pitch. They drove over to Windsor most mornings to ride in the park.

Naturally Philip could not keep his end up on a lieutenant's pay, nor was he expected to. The King sent a message to Parliament, "Relying on the liberality and affection of my faithful Commons" to make provision for Philip. A committee was appointed, which, after worrying over the matter for weeks and consulting innumerable precedents, voted thirteen to five that the Duke should receive an annuity of £10,000 (at that time $48,000) a year.

At the same time Elizabeth's allowance was raised to £40,000 a year. But considering the fact that these incomes were subject to the high British income tax the King did not think "the liberality of his faithful Commons" exactly spectacular. He helped the young couple out by giving them £100,000 (tax free), which he had saved by economizing on his Civil List.

Philip and Elizabeth earned their salary. They were continually being sent off on tours and inspection trips to various parts of the country. True they traveled very comfortably in the royal train; but those long days in small cities, with municipal receptions, endless speeches, and tours of factories, housing projects, dockyards, or what have you, usually in the pouring rain, were not only exhausting but boring. A further annoyance were Philip's squealing teen-age fans. Philip enlivened the boredom for his wife in private by his rather biting wit, which shocked her slightly and made her giggle.

The interruptions to his work at the Admiralty disturbed Philip. At Sandringham he had made it plain to Uncle Bertie that he was deadly serious about continuing his naval career. The King sympathized as one who had seen his own cherished ambition wrecked, and he promised to help all he could. Philip was much relieved when he was ordered to take the Naval Staff Course at Greenwich. This was a prerequisite for high rank and showed that the Admiralty had not written him off. At Greenwich Philip studied hard, and lived in most of the time, returning home for weekends.

On November 14, 1948, Philip and Elizabeth reached the height of their pre-coronation popularity with the British public as their first son was born in Buckingham Palace. In naming him Charles they overturned a tradition of three hundred years' standing—no heir to the British throne had been christened Charles since the Stuarts were sent packing.

Only four days after this joyful event they received the first shocking intimation that "the cage" might finally close much sooner than they hoped. On November 18 the King suffered the collapse of an artery in his right leg. He was in terrible pain and the doctors in their cautious official bulletin spoke of "risk to the limb." In plain fact they were convinced that it would have to be amputated.

Elizabeth was filled with anxiety for the father she loved so dearly and for her worried mother to whom George was the very pattern of all that a man and a King should be. Philip not only sorrowed with them, but also in less unselfish moments could not help wondering what this would do to his career in the Navy.

Fortunately the doctors, as they so often do, underrated the strength of their patient's constitution. Instead of getting worse the King slowly improved. On December 15 he was able to attend his grandson's christening, and shortly after Christmas he was able to go to his beloved Sandringham. In February, 1949, he returned to London in his special train. The waiting crowd noted that the first person off the train was a page in the blue battle dress with gold buttons, the uniform of the palace since the war, carrying six of the red dispatch boxes on which the King had never ceased to work all through his illness.

Though he held an investiture at Buckingham Palace on March 1 it did not indicate King George's recovery, but only his fortitude and sense of duty. Ten days later a team of seven doctors operated on the King to bypass the affected artery, and restore normal circulation. The manner of it was typical of King George. The doctors unanimously urged him to go to the Royal Masonic Hospital, to which their patient replied crossly, "I have never heard of a King going to hospital, and I don't propose to be the first. Do it here!"

An operating theater was set up in Buckingham Palace and the operation was performed successfully. From that time on the King began a real recovery, but it was many months before he was able to perform the more arduous of his ceremonial duties.

With Princess Elizabeth recovering from childbirth and involved with the care of her baby, it was up to Philip and the Duke of Gloucester to attend most of the ceremonial occasions which the British consider total losses unless a member of the Royal Family blesses them by his presence. This had the exact effect on Philip's naval career that he had gloomily foreseen. He went on half pay and his hope of getting to sea again seemed infinitely remote. However, he, too, had a strong sense of duty, and cheerfully tore around the country laying cornerstones, cutting ribbons, smashing bottles of champagne, eating badly cooked and indigestible banquets, and making charming little speeches which he wrote himself with the aid of Mike Parker, who had become his secretary. Unsurprisingly his oratorical style was strikingly similar to Lord Louis'—a plain, humorously underplayed, straight-from-the-shoulder manner of speech.

Philip's greatest personal interest was the National Playing Field Association in which he followed his uncle as president. His own love of sport and the ideals fostered as Gordonstoun made him passionately enthusiastic about the work of the Association. When Philip took over, the N.P.F.A. was broke, in debt, and senescent, in need of money and vigor. Philip supplied the vigor and raised the money—£500,000 in four years. He did it by dragooning all his friends in industry, the theater, and sport into giving money or their services. Frank Sinatra flew to London for a show at Albert Hall that raised £16,000 for the fund. Philip himself co-starred with Bob Hope in a movie, about poor London boys with no place but the streets to play, that raised £84,000.

Philip, in fact, would make an appearance that he thought would help, at any event great or small. He said, "I'll go anywhere to open a new playing field," and proved it by dashing from the Shetland Islands to Land's End.

By May, 1949, the King was much better; and in July Clarence House was ready at last. Both Philip and Elizabeth were glad to give up their gypsying from Windlesham to Kensington and Buck House for a home of their own. Elizabeth's nesting instinct was strongly motivated, and Philip had a lot of fun introducing all the mechanical gadgets he could think of. The closet where his greatly amplified wardrobe hung was arranged so that when he pressed a button the desired suit shot out. And his study, like that of Uncle Dickie at Brooke House, was decorated like the cabin of a ship.*

Nor did Philip have to content himself with this simulacrum of naval life for long. In the autumn the King was so much better that at last Philip was able to go to sea. On October 17, 1949, he reported for duty as First Lieutenant of the flotilla leader *Chequers* at Malta, where Elizabeth soon joined him.

The time Elizabeth and Philip spent in Malta was probably the happiest time of their lives, for it was the nearest they ever came to living like other people. When Philip arrived Lord Louis, who was commanding the First Cruiser Squadron, met him at the airport, "as an uncle not an admiral," he carefully explained to the press.

Some photographer caught them striding away from the plane in intimate humorous talk—so very much alike in their identical uniforms and jaunty, raked caps, with the ribbons on their breasts. Like those uniforms, they were cut from the same cloth—tall, bold, charming, determined men. That picture must have done them a lot of harm, reinforcing the legend of their conspiratorial oneness. But the legend is

---

* General Sir Frederick ("Boy") Browning became comptroller of their Household.

wrong. They were too boyishly naïve to be dangerous conspirators. Both still believed in ancient ideals, the obligations of nobility, and the code of chivalry. They were emotionally simple men, who, despite their intellectual modernity, spiritually belonged in an earlier age.

Philip and Elizabeth stayed with the Mountbattens at the Villa Guardamangia. When Lord Louis went back to the Admiralty to become Fourth Sea Lord, they took over the house. They made it seem as home-like as possible by bringing their own silver, their Daimler for state occasions, and a Hillman Minx to drive themselves in the narrow streets.

When Philip's ship was in port he slept at home and got up at 6:30 every morning to be on board early. Most afternoons he played polo on the Marsa Ground. Lord Louis coached him. Mountbatten was a better teacher than player, and his pupil soon surpassed him.

In the mornings Elizabeth often did her own shopping, and she always went to see Philip play polo. In the evenings there were little dinner parties, or they went dancing at the Phoenecia Hotel. On week-ends there were picnics in the hills or swimming in the warm sea, all just as it used to be.

But, of course, they were not really living like other people. Ashore, for example, Lieutenant the Duke of Edinburgh took precedence over his commander in chief; and Elizabeth was always the guest of honor and was always being asked to open bazaars, inspect welfare projects, and be a patroness of local charities. They were still involved in the royal rigmarole; their life in Malta just seemed normal to them by comparison with that in England.

Philip's greatest embarrassment was on shipboard, but he handled it very well. He was dead keen on his work and there was no nonsense about it. In the *Chequers* he was called simply Number One, as first lieutenants usually are. He called the captain, sir, but on shipboard the captain did not sir him.

Elizabeth had to fly to England after Christmas, but she went back to Malta for a longer stay in April, and returned to London for the birth of Princess Anne on August 15, 1950. Philip got home on leave for the event.

Just previously, on July 29, he had been promoted to Lieutenant Commander and in September he was appointed to command the frigate *Magpie*,* then at Malta.

Philip loved every moment of his first, and last, command. She was a smart little ship and he set out to make her Cock of the Fleet—had

---

* A frigate in the British Navy is similar to a destroyer escort in the United States Navy.

not Grandfather Louis and Uncle Dickie earned that distinction? He would have a taut ship, for by temperament he was a martinet. At Corsham he had written on the blackboard for his entering class of petty officers:

DISCIPLINE

The force which causes a man to play the part required of him in the organization to which he belongs. It is:

A Guiding Force
An Inspiring Force
A Driving Force
A Controlling Force
A Comforting Force.

But from Lord Louis' example he knew that he must also win the confidence of the lower deck. He must command; but he must lead not drive. So as soon as the ceremony of taking over command ended and the inevitable reporters and photographers had left, he called the crew of 186 men together and made one of those humorous, confidential, gung-ho Mountbatten speeches. He told them that *Magpie* was going to be the best ship in the fleet, and, he said, "It will be up to you. And up to me." He warned them that he was going to be tough, but that he would be just, and always willing to talk with them about things that bothered them.

Then he told them that he knew they might be razzed by other crews ashore because they were serving in "the Duke of Edinburgh's yacht." "Don't you take it!" he said. "Any man who comes up before me on a charge with two black eyes can be sure I'll be on his side."

The crew of the *Magpie*—they called her "Magger" and, in private, they called her captain "Dukie"—had no easy time. Philip worked them dizzy, but he got results. In the annual regatta *Magpie*'s boat crews won six out of ten events, with Philip himself stroking one of her boats to victory. That and her record in maneuvers made her Cock of the Fleet, with a huge plyboard rooster hoisted arrogantly on her single mast. So Philip proved Doctor Hahn's prediction of his potential for leadership.

But though Philip won the confidence of his crew he never won their affection as Lord Louis had. One of them is reported to have said, "He stamped about like a ——ing tiger looking for trouble." And another proclaimed he'd rather be dead than serve on that ship again. Perhaps they sensed his Germanic arrogance and the fact that he did not really love them as Lord Louis certainly loved the men of the *Kelly*.

If he drove his crew hard, he drove himself even harder, because he had another and more important job than commanding the frigate. He was still president of the N.P.F.A., and in the midst of his money-raising campaign. In addition there were his many other honorary posts and obligations, entailing an enormous mass of correspondence. In Malta Mike Parker was there to help him; but there was no place for a secretary in a frigate at sea. Yet letters must be answered. So late at night in his cabin Philip laboriously hand wrote his replies.

Nor was he able to concentrate on the routine of an ordinary ship. The Government found Philip's presence in the Mediterranean convenient for improving relations with bordering countries. They were continually ordering *Magpie* here and there for ceremonial occasions or state visits.

One of the pleasantest of these was a semi-official visit he and Elizabeth paid to King Paul and Queen Frederika in Athens in the early summer of 1951.* Since there was no accommodation for the Princess in the *Magpie*, she went in the dispatch boat *Surprise*, escorted by *Magpie* and a destroyer. The captain of *Surprise* radioed Philip every morning as to his wife's health. One message was: "Princess full of beans"; to which Philip replied, "Can't you give her something better for breakfast?"

It was Elizabeth's first visit to Athens, and in the intervals between entertainment, Philip had a fine time showing her the glory of ancient temples and the modern places where he had fun in his youth.

Philip also made official or semi-official visits to Gibraltar, Cyprus, Saudi Arabia, Algeria, and Egypt. Since *Magpie* also took part in all the fleet exercises, and Philip had a heavy schedule of training afloat and sports and entertainment ashore, it is lucky he had inherited the Mountbatten energy.

It could not last. King George was not well enough to undertake any arduous ceremonials; and Elizabeth was constantly flying back to England to perform them and see her children. Then the Government decided that she and Philip should make a tour of Canada with a side trip to the United States. In July, 1951, Philip was ordered home.

During his last days in Malta he was more depressed than at any other time in his life. Everyone who knew him then comments on his oppressive gloom. He seemed to know intuitively that this was the end of his naval life. As he sadly bade good-bye to *Magpie*'s crew, ranked in

---

* King George II of Greece died in 1947, and was succeeded by his brother, Paul, who died in 1964.

gleaming whites in the sunshine of Lazaretto Creek, he said, "The past eleven months have been the happiest of my sailor life."

Ambitious for more than an ornamental role, Philip had accepted the honorary position of president of the British Association for the Advancement of Science. He realized that this, too, was supposed to be ornamental, but he had other ideas. During his last weeks at sea, he worked on his speech almost every night. His little cabin in the *Magpie* was an appalling mess of reference books, treatises, and scribbled notes. The title of his speech was, "The British Contribution to Science and Technology in the Past Hundred Years." It was quite a subject, but as Philip once remarked, "I am not noticeably reticent about talking about things about which I know nothing."

Two thousand people, some of them scientists, gathered in the assembly hall of Edinburgh University and two thousand more watched on closed-circuit television. They hardly expected to be enlightened. Rather the mood was that of people watching a man walk a tightrope over Niagara Falls.

"Your kind invitation to me to undertake the office of your president," Philip began, "could not but startle me. . . . The high position which science occupies . . . contrasted strongly in my mind with the consciousness of my own insignificance. . . ."

Then smiling he told them that this was a quotation from a speech by Prince Albert on a similar occasion. That set them back a bit, but they were due for more. After lauding the contributions of British scientists in mid-nineteenth century for almost an hour, he spoke his mind in a manner most unlike the bland royal way.

Since that splendid start, he told them, British industry had coasted on its admitted supremacy, not making use of scientific progress. At the present time he said, "The rate at which scientific knowledge is being applied in many industries is too small and too slow. . . . Our physical resources have dwindled but the intellectual capacity of our scientists and engineers is as great as ever, and it is upon their ingenuity that our future depends. . . ."

He pointed out that scientific knowledge had reached a point where it could either free the world from drudgery, fear, hunger, and pestilence, "or obliterate life itself.

"It is clearly our duty as citizens to see that science is used for the benefit of mankind. For what use is science if man does not survive?"

That was strong meat coming from a man who stood in the shadow of the Throne. Philip's audience sat stunned, then burst into tremendous applause. Their approval was echoed in the British press next day. For the first time, Philip had stature in the eyes of England.

The Canadian trip was a foretaste of the future. In the planning stage it was short and simple, calling for visits to three cities in ten days. But it escalated to an enormous schedule of 10,000 miles requiring at least thirty-five fourteen-hour days.

Shortly before they were to leave, King George, who had apparently been suffering from a heavy cold, learned that he had cancer of one lung. Elizabeth was stunned. All was confusion. Should the trip be canceled?

The King was firmly opposed to disappointing the Canadians. He asked them to wait until after the operation to make their decision.

The King's whole lung was removed, but with his usual fortitude he rallied strongly. The last thing in the world Elizabeth wanted to do was to leave her father at this time; but he pointed out to her that it was her duty. He wanted her to go. On October 8, a few days after the operation, Philip and Elizabeth flew to Canada.

From the first reception—at which she had to appear carefree and smiling while hiding her secret knowledge of her father's condition—to the final stormy passage in a small tender to the *Empress of France* in St. John's Roadstead, it was a grueling trip. The fourteen-hour days of the schedule sometimes stretched to sixteen and eighteen hours of unremitting public appearances. The enthusiasm of the Canadians was unbounded. Every man, woman, and child was determined to get a glimpse of the Princess, and most of them did.

The obvious fact that it was all worth-while pulled Elizabeth through; that and Philip's solicitous care of her. On that trip he was a model of everything a Consort should be. He did not even get very cross with the reporters who were more rambunctious than usual.

Toward the end of the trip they made a brief incursion to the United States to pay a state visit to President Truman. That, too, was highly successful. Half a million people turned out in Washington to see them drive from the airport. The crowd, barricaded behind lines of police and troops, were not as demonstrative as the Canadians, and their shouts were drowned by the roar of half a hundred motorcycles of the escort. Philip thought that the security was greatly overdone, but he was unfamiliar with the unfortunate American predilection for shooting at their Chief Executive and his guests.

Oddly enough the British Ambassador gave them their worst time. Under tremendous social pressure from the royalty-mad Americans, he invited hordes of people to his reception for them. In two frantic hours Elizabeth and Philip shook hands with eighteen hundred people.

The success of the Canadian trip made it inevitable that Elizabeth and Philip should undertake the Australian-New Zealand Tour, which King George had twice been obliged to cancel because of illness. Christmas at Sandringham was made especially gay by the King's amazing recovery. Another factor was that Churchill had been returned to power in the General Election of October 1951. Though King George never gave the slightest indication of political preferences, he could not help but feel that with Winston Churchill at Number 10 Downing Street all was well with the world.

On January 30, 1952, the whole Royal Family went to see *South Pacific* (as indoctrination?). On January 31 Elizabeth and Philip took off for Nairobi in BOAC's blue and silver aircraft *Atalanta*. With them were Pamela Mountbatten as lady-in-waiting, Lieutenant Colonel Martin Charteris, Mike Parker, Bobo MacDonald, and John Dean.

Though it was a bitterly cold day the King and Queen saw them off, as did Margaret, the Mountbattens, and the Gloucesters. King George seemed reluctant to leave the *Atalanta*. "Look out for yourselves," were his last words to Lilibet and Philip. He stood bareheaded in the icy wind waving good-bye as the aircraft moved away from the ramp.

On Wednesday, February 5, Philip and Elizabeth arrived at the famous Treetops Hotel, built in a huge fig tree in the forest in Kenya. They walked along a narrow path through the noisy jungle, noting with amusement the ladders placed at intervals just in case they had to climb a tree to escape a wild animal. The little four-room hotel, with its observation platforms overlooking a water hole, was reached by ladders which were pulled up at night.

That was an enchanted evening for Elizabeth and Philip. All sorts of wild animals came down to drink at the water hole. Wild elephants trumpeted madly, and Elizabeth kept her movie camera going as long as light lasted. She caught a cow elephant nursing her baby, and another teaching a little elephant to swim. Two water bucks obligingly staged a duel with their long, delicate horns, and baboons frolicked around.

Finally after dinner a herd of rhinoceros moved in, their sides and snout-horns silver in the moonlight.

They went to bed very late and were up again at first light so as not to miss a moment of the unstaged animal act. The memory of those hours at Treetops made so strong an impression on Philip that it motivated one of the major enterprises of his unofficial life.

Philip was having a nap in the noontide heat when Mike Parker knocked and came hesitantly into his darkened room. Philip woke up instantly alert, as a naval officer must. He sensed a crisis. Speaking with unusual formality Parker said, "Sir, a press report has been received that the King is dead."

"No!" Philip said. "No. It's not possible!"

Parker told him it was a Reuters dispatch. It was unlikely that that great agency would be mistaken.

"Don't let my wife hear of this until it's confirmed," Philip said.

He knew better than anyone how close were the ties between Elizabeth and her father. Everyone who knew King George loved him—he was so completely good and so very kind. Elizabeth worshiped him. Because of their unique position there was a special bond between them, the King and the future Queen. George had never wanted to be King. "This is terrible, Dickie!" he had said to Mountbatten. Knowing that his daughter must take up the burden he regarded her with infinite tenderness; and with infinite pride he had watched her grow up and prepare herself to assume it.

To Elizabeth he was more than a loving father—he was an ideal, and he was also her King. To a girl brought up in the great tradition of Britain's Royal House there was still, today, a mystic radiance about the King, even one who happened to be her father, that gave additional strength to filial love, lending it almost the quality of religious devotion.

Philip must have thought of these things as he waited for confirmation of the tragic news. He also had time to think about himself; perhaps to pity himself a little. For this was the end of his beloved career. Never again would he command a ship at sea; never again be a man among men on his own feet. Certainly he had been prepared for this; nevertheless the swift finality was stunning.

It was two hours before confirmation came from Buckingham Palace; perhaps the longest two hours Philip even spent. When it came at last, he took the cable and went softly into Elizabeth's room. Despite his hardness Philip could be very gentle with those he loved—never more so than now.

.   .   .

All those years of training, all the discipline and self-control were evident in Elizabeth that day. Her whole life had been a prologue to this bleak hour when she became Queen. Almost automatically she assumed her role. She was given very little time to gather her forces.

Philip had been with her but a few moments when there was a knock on the door. He opened it and Colonel Charteris came in. He bowed very low to Elizabeth saying, "Your Majesty, forgive me for intruding at this time, but there is one question I must ask."

"Yes?" she said.

"By what name will Your Majesty be called?"

The answer she had known almost all her life. In a low, firm voice she said, "Elizabeth. Elizabeth II."

Chapter 5

A NEW AGE

Twenty-four hours later the *Atalanta* landed at London Airport. As the propellers stopped turning the Mountbattens and Gloucesters came aboard and went to the private stateroom aft where the Queen and Philip waited with Pamela Mountbatten. What was said is not known, but Lord Louis gave Philip's shoulder a hard squeeze of comfort.

Then the Queen in somber black came down the steps. At the bottom stood Prime Minister Winston Churchill with the former Prime Minister, now Earl Attlee, and some of the Cabinet. The Prime Minister bowed very low over the Queen's hand; but for once his power of speech was lost in emotion. Tears rolled down his cheeks and he managed only a hoarse rumble. Elizabeth greeted him with a few words spoken clearly with disciplined composure. After greeting Attlee and the others she turned to thank the *Atalanta*'s crew. Then she got into the royal Daimler with Philip and the Mountbattens to drive to Buckingham Palace, resisting the temptation to go directly to Sandringham where her mother and Margaret had remained. At the Palace Queen Mary, who also knew how to restrain her emotions, is said to have remarked, "Lilibet, your skirts are far too short for mourning."

From the palace Philip and Elizabeth drove to Clarence House. There she had no more than time to greet her children when she must see the officials waiting with pressing problems, among them her father's private secretary, Sir Alan Lascelles, who said, "Ma'am, the Boxes are in your office."

The Boxes were those same dispatch boxes containing state papers that only the Monarch can see, and which neither in joy nor sickness nor mourning can she avoid.

On the morning of Friday, February 8, the Queen held her Accession Council in St. James's Palace. After the Council the Garter Principal King of Arms, accompanied by the Earl Marshal of England, three more Kings of Arms, and heralds and trumpeters in scarlet and ermine of medieval pageantry, proclaimed that the King is dead and, "the Crown is solely and rightfully come to the high and mighty Princess Elizabeth Alexandra Mary, who is now become Queen Elizabeth II by the Grace of God, Queen of this Realm and all her other realms and countries of the Commonwealth, Defender of the Faith to whom all her lieges do acknowledge all faith and constant obedience with hearty and humble affection. . . . God save the Queen!"

Only then could Elizabeth go to Sandringham to be with her mother and sister.

Elizabeth and Philip arrived in Sandringham that afternoon. Shortly afterward, in a coffin made from an oak tree grown on the estate, King George's body was placed on a farm wagon and taken to the little church. Pipers marched before it, the Queen and Philip walked behind, followed by her mother and Margaret, and a few of the old servants.

After lying there that night the King's body was taken to London to lie in state under the wide, bare arches of Westminster Hall. When he had been placed upon the bier a photographer caught a terribly moving picture of the three Queens who had loved him paying him homage in their long black veils of mourning, their faces tearless but eroded by grief.

Nine days after he died, King George was buried at Windsor. During those agonizing days Elizabeth, knowing that her father would wish it, never lost her composure in public, not even during the last awful moment when she scattered earth from a silver bowl on her father's coffin as it sank slowly through the floor to the Crypt of St. George's Chapel at Windsor. Philip was constantly with her, attentive to her every need, giving her strength by a touch on her arm, a whisper of encouragement.

In addition he had the duty of greeting all the royal cousins who poured in for the funeral, and making sure that they were properly taken care of. There was not a moment to himself, not a moment to think. Perhaps this was fortunate. Later he confided to his cousin Alexandra that all through those days he felt stunned, deprived of feeling as though he were anaesthetized.

. . .

The weeks that followed were hardly less trying, though emotion was no longer deadened by shock. There were many things to be done, among them the melancholy business of moving from gay and beautiful Clarence House to the gloomy grandeur of Buckingham Palace. Oddly enough, it was Philip's health that broke under the strain. He came down with yellow jaundice, possibly a light case of hepatitis, and was forced to spend three weeks in bed. That was bad enough for a man of Philip's burning energy. His sick room made it worse.

Because the Queen Mother was understandably reluctant to move out, Philip was temporarily bedded down in a large, ground-floor room of the palace. The furniture was heavy, ornately black and gold and marble-topped—except his bed and television set which had been brought from Clarence House. The red silk walls were covered by somber portraits of Spanish kings and infantas. The bright yellow of Philip's face ironically completed a décor of Spain's national colors.

He was hardly up again when an unpleasant though sub-rosa row began with the Government. At the time of her marriage Elizabeth had taken her husband's name; and under that name she began her reign. Now Winston Churchill advised her that the feeling of his Government reinforced by public sentiment was that she should drop the Mountbatten and reign under her father's name of Windsor. This was an extraordinary proposal and quite unprecedented, for it had not even been thought of in Victoria's time. Most likely it was due to that underground agitation about "the Mountbattens moving in on the Monarchy."

Because of her love for Philip and her pride in him, Elizabeth tried to keep his name. Philip was annoyed to be made even more of a cypher, and Lord Louis was furious. The pressures against them were too great. The Queen dutifully bowed to her Prime Minister's "formal and insistent advice." On April 21, 1952, by an Order in Council, she decreed that she and her immediate descendants would bear the name of Windsor.*

The Mountbattens, however, had the satisfaction, as Lord Louis points out in *The Mountbatten Lineage*, of knowing that though the House of Mountbatten reigned for only two months, it has taken its place historically among the reigning houses of the United Kingdom. But a purist might say it was the House of Glücksburg.

When the dust of controversy had settled the Queen restored at least some proper dignity to her husband's position. In order of precedence he ranked behind the royal dukes and his own children. In September, 1952, she ordained by Royal Warrant that, "His Royal Highness, Philip, Duke of Edinburgh, henceforth and on all occasions . . .

---

* In 1964 the Queen changed this so that only her two oldest children are named Windsor and her two younger sons are called Mountbatten-Windsor.

have, hold and enjoy Place, Pre-eminence, and Precedence next to Her Majesty."

At almost the same time Parliament, after the usual querulous debate, raised Philip's salary to £40,000 a year, still subject to tax!

In the light of his prospects Philip had made an intensive study of the life of his most successful predecessor, Prince Albert. Not that he expected to emulate him. It is hard to imagine two more opposite characters than Elizabeth's dynamic, witty, impatient, fun-loving, rather naughty husband, and Victoria's deeply religious, humorless, self-righteous, conscientious, intelligent, and deadly solemn Albert.

Then, too, circumstances had changed tremendously. Soon after Albert married Queen Victoria, the Prime Minister, Lord Melbourne, actually urged the Queen to communicate all foreign dispatches to her husband. He clearly trusted Albert's judgment more than that of the somewhat flighty young Queen. In 1840 Prince Albert wrote to his father, "Victoria allows me to take much part in foreign affairs, and I think I have already done some good. I always commit my views to paper, and then communicate them to Lord Melbourne. He seldom answers me, but I have often had the satisfaction of seeing him act entirely in accordance with what I have said."*

Thus, in spite of his pious determination of "sinking his individual existence in that of the Queen," Albert actually succeeded in sinking hers in his. He became the real power behind the Throne.

Whatever dreams of glory Philip may originally have had of shaping the course of Empire, he knew by now that he never could. The rebuffs of Parliament in making him such a miserable allowance and in the matter of his own children bearing his name were broad hints that he took realistically. He was aware of the distrust the Mountbattens excited in British minds. No Prime Minister would be caught dead acting "in accordance with what *he* said." They would rather trust the judgment of his dutiful, solid wife. And in any event, there was damned little scope left to the Monarch for the exercise of judgment.

In planning his role Philip also consulted the greatest living expert on the subject, Prince Bernhard of the Netherlands—as Bernhard once remarked, "After all there are only two of us."

The advice of the Dutch prince, who was very fond of Philip, was sound, but small comfort. "You are new at this thing, Philip," Bernhard has reported(§) he said, "and you probably don't realize what you are up

---

* Queen Victoria, *Memoirs of the Prince Consort.*

against. Practically everything you do will be a subject of criticism. You can't ignore it because some of it may be justified, and even if it isn't, it may be politic to heed it.

"But don't let it get you down. In this job you need the skin like an elephant."

In handling the job Philip decided to try to emulate Bernhard rather than Albert. In other words, instead of sinking his personality in that of the Queen, to try to make a career for himself outside of political and royal circles in the area of international understanding, science, culture, conservation of the world's resources, and sports. That he has not been as successful as Bernhard is due to no lack of ability, intelligence, or good will—he has quite as much of these qualities as his Dutch counterpart. What thwarts him is the British "Mystique of the Monarchy," the iron-bound tradition of England that makes the British apprehensive of anyone connected with the Royal Family having any ideas about anything. The Dutch welcome Bernhard's truly valuable contributions to their military, industrial, and cultural life, and to bettering international relations. Every time Philip tries to do anything constructive the British look at him askance.

In the first months of Elizabeth's reign, however, Philip devoted himself almost completely to helping his wife through a difficult time. She in turn gave him an important job that occupied some of his excess energy; she made him Chairman of the Coronation Commission. The Duke of Norfolk, as hereditary Earl Marshal, was in overall charge of the arrangements—and very good at it he was, having arranged the coronation of George VI when he was only thirty. But the Commission was the working committee and was also in charge of Commonwealth participation.

Philip worked very compatibly with the Duke, who was a close friend of Elizabeth's, due to their great mutual interest in the Turf. Philip, too, was very good at this extremely specialized sort of organization. The Mountbatten love for tradition and ceremonial coupled with the Mountbatten energy and love of detailed planning made his contribution truly valuable. He studied descriptions of previous coronations, meticulously following tradition where it seemed valid and changing things for the better where they appeared foolish. He even went into the detail of ascertaining the chemical composition of the oil with which the Sovereign is anointed, and succeeded in finding a flask of the very oil used for Queen Victoria. He personally engineered the lighting of the interior of the Queen's coach in case it should be a dark day.

The fact that Philip could immediately get the Queen's reaction to any proposal made him very much her representative in the planning. He could say, "I know the Queen won't like that" or "Her Majesty would want us to do this." In addition, his first-hand knowledge of distant parts of the Commonwealth, and his enthusiasm for holding it together, gave him an authoritative voice in the arrangements for the participation of its members.

There were many additional outlets for Philip's drive. Elizabeth made him Chief Ranger of Windsor Great Park, and even during the period of court mourning he was continually being asked to inspect shipyards, factories, and coal mines. He always did it thoroughly because of his intense interest. In one coal mine he not only descended to the lowest level, but insisted on crawling through a hundred yards of tunnel to the cutting face.

This, however, was not enough to occupy him. His naval career had ended, though in July, 1952, he was promoted to his earned rank of commander. That he valued. The fact that he would soon have to accept the phoney ranks of Admiral of the Fleet, Field Marshal, and Air Chief Marshal embarrassed him. He wanted to do something more on his own and decided to become a pilot.

Elizabeth, very understanding of her husband's ambitions and frustrations, made no objection. However, the Prime Minister did—if anything happened to Philip he knew his Government would bear the blame.

So Philip asked Winston Churchill to come to the palace and talk it over. He argued that when he became an air marshal he would feel silly unless he had earned the right to wear wings. He also pointed out that he could save a great deal of time and money if he could fly himself from one engagement to another. Furthermore, there was a precedent— Prince Bernhard was a pilot. It is doubtful if Churchill fell for these rather disingenuous arguments. But being a pretty adventurous chap himself he sympathized with Philip. Also, he probably felt that it was wise not to keep too tight a rein on this ambitious and impetuous prince lest some day he burst out with something really outrageous.* Besides these things there was Churchill's fondness for the Mountbattens and the fact that he understood them so very well. Risking his own political neck, Churchill gave his consent.

With his quick reactions and automotive expertise Philip was a natural pilot. He started his flying lessons in November at White Wal-

---

* Ex-King Peter of Yugoslavia wondered aloud how long Philip could last, "bottled up like that."

tham, getting up before dawn to fit them into his heavy schedule. When he was at Windsor he flew from Smith's Lawn, a nice long stretch of smooth grass. He soloed his little Chipmunk plane before Christmas and looped the loop in February. Then he went on to faster, heavier military planes. He won his wings a month before the Coronation.

In June, 1952, Elizabeth had set the date of her Coronation for June, 1953. A year was hardly time for all the preparations. At one moment it seemed a long way off; the next the stands were going up along the procession route; flags, bunting, and illuminations were hung all over the place; every house was being decorated and people were pouring in from all parts of the Commonwealth and the world.

Final rehearsals of the crowning were held in Westminster Abbey. At one point Philip was supposed to kneel before his wife and swear to become "Your liege man of life and limb and of earthly worship, and faith and truth. I will bear unto you to live and die, against all manner of folks. So help me God." Feeling a little foolish he mumbled the words at high speed, jumped up; gave the crown a mere flip of his hand, pecked at the air a foot from the Queen's cheek; and backed off rapidly. With the amused exasperation of a mother with a wayward child Elizabeth said, "Come back, Philip, and do it again—properly!"

At the Coronation itself he did very properly, indeed, with the sincerity of real emotion.

There is no intention of describing here what was seen by millions on television and the screen, and relayed to everyone who could read in a hundred thousand newspapers and magazines. As all could see the Coronation was a superbly staged and genuinely inspiring pageant, made intensely moving by the beauty, grace, and touching earnestness of the young Queen. In his supporting role Philip performed with high serious-ness, leavened by his admittedly dashing good looks.

The Coronation was, in fact, more than the installation of a new monarch; it marked as sharply as a black boundary line on a map the division between two eras—austerity and recovery. Winston Churchill's Conservative Government had been in power for twenty months. They had loosened the economic bonds by which the oddly puritanical Labour Government had bound British life and stifled British enter-prise, allowing it suddenly to bound forward. In England's history it was rather like the restoration of Charles II after the dun years of Crom-well's rule. In glorious color and unshadowed gaiety, in splendor, pomp and glory, and religious exaltation, it was the brilliant sunrise of what the British people hopefully looked forward to as a new Elizabethan Age.

Chapter 6

THE QUEEN'S HUSBAND

NOTHING IS EVER AS GOOD as it looks at the peak of enthusiasm. The new Elizabethan Age was due for its peck of troubles great and small, of which Philip had his full share. For a time, though, the impetus of enthusiasm carried forward as Elizabeth and Philip paid official visits to Scotland, Wales, and Northern Ireland. Then, in November, 1953, they started on a tremendously successful Commonwealth Tour that spread the wave of euphoria all around the world.

Philip was at his best on such tours. The excitement of new places and new faces, and the constant pressure of a tight schedule kept him in high humor. His private wisecracks enlivened the deadly boredom of official speeches; and he would take on endless toil to relieve the strain on Elizabeth. The only thing on which he could be faulted was his attitude toward reporters. He never acquired the philosophy of "they've got to eat, too." Rather it would be, "I don't see the necessity." On this and other trips he made some really unpleasant remarks, such as that on being shown the apes at Gibraltar. "Which are the apes and which the reporters?" Or, when a photographer fell backward out of a tree, "I hope he broke his neck!" On another occasion, the Chelsea Flower Show, he turned a water sprinkler on members of the press.

It was an extremely shortsighted, bad-tempered attitude, and it boomeranged into bad publicity—or none. On one recent tour the reporters had a competition among themselves as to who could mention him least. However, with all the other contretemps and bores encountered on such a tour as that in 1953–54, he was extremely courteous and good-tempered. He could be as matey with a Maori or Watusi as with a fellow naval officer, and this had no small part in the success of the tours.

But trouble was already churning up in England. As early as April, 1953, Princess Margaret had told her sister that she wanted to marry Group Captain Peter Townsend of the Royal Air Force. It was perfectly natural. Townsend was a first-rate fellow, good-looking, charming, intelligent, and conscientious, who had been the late King's favorite Equerry and was now Equerry to the Queen. Margaret had known him since she was a young girl, and among all the beaux and suitors of her rather giddy debutante days she had found no man she liked so well. There was only one difficulty. Townsend had been married to a charming but amoral lady, whom he had divorced in 1952. The Divorce Court stated that he had been granted the decree *nisi* "on the grounds of misconduct by his wife, Rosemary."

Townsend was so completely blameless that the Queen was willing to keep him as her Equerry despite the traditional ban by the British Court of divorced persons; and the Queen Mother confirmed him as Comptroller of her Household at Clarence House where Margaret and she now lived. But it was one thing for the Queen to accept a blameless divorced man at Court and quite another to let her sister marry him.

Elizabeth's attitude toward Margaret had always been that of a mother hen with a chick who liked to swim and preen in dangerous waters. On one occasion, when she was especially fussy, Margaret said to her, "You tend to your Empire and I'll take care of myself."

More important, Elizabeth had deeply religious as well as social objections to divorce. She went all the way with the Church of England's canon that those whom God had joined together no man could put asunder; and she had expressed her concern for the social consequences of divorce in a speech to the British Mothers' Union, in which she said: "When we see around us the havoc that has been wrought—above all among children—by the break-up of homes, we can have no doubt that divorce and separation are responsible for some of the darkest evils in our society today.

"I do not think you can perform any finer service than to help maintain the Christian doctrine that the relation of husband and wife is a permanent one. . . ."

Elizabeth meant this with all her heart. It accurately expressed what Geoffrey Bocca, in *Elizabeth and Philip,* termed her "highly aggressive sense of virtue."

Naturally, the sensational press added to the Queen's distress with wild speculations about Margaret and Townsend. The matter was temporarily shelved for the Coronation summer, during which the Queen Mother and Margaret went off on a tour of Rhodesia. Hardly had their plane taken off when the Queen sent Townsend off to be attached to the Embassy in Brussels, though she had promised Margaret not to do so until her return. She was trying the absence cure. As in her own case, it did not work.

The following year Townsend returned. He and Margaret met at Clarence House, and at the Bonham-Carters' in the country; and spent a famous weekend with Lord and Lady Rupert Neville at Uckfield House in Sussex. They were truly in love, and determined to marry. Elizabeth was implacable, and rallied all the tremendous forces of Anglican morality, from the Prime Minister to the Archbishop of Canterbury. Even Philip.

One might have thought that Margaret could count Philip in her corner. The contrary was true. His sense of propriety was outraged, his belief in discipline flouted, and his strong sense of loyalty betrayed. He felt that Margaret was letting the side down, thus he had far less sympathy for her than did the troubled but understanding Queen Mother.

It was all too much for poor Margaret. After a final heartbreaking interview with Townsend at Clarence House she issued a sad little communiqué stating that: "I would like it to be known that I have decided not to marry Group Captain Townsend. . . . Mindful of the Church's teaching that Christian marriage is indissoluble, and conscious of my duty to the Commonwealth, I have reached this decision entirely alone, and in doing so I have been strengthened by the unfailing support and devotion of Group Captain Townsend. . . ."

There is little doubt that the final decision was, in fact, Margaret's. In spite of her frivolous ways she is a deeply religious person. The thought that her action might induce many others to disregard the teaching of the Church was undoubtedly the compelling reason. She would certainly have given up her right of succession and even risked her immortal soul for Peter Townsend; but she would not contribute to the delinquency of her sister's subjects.

For several years Margaret was subdued and melancholy. Then she fell in love again. This time with Anthony Armstrong-Jones, an attractive though "Bohemian" young man, who had replaced Baron, who died in 1957, as the Court photographer. Though he was quite well connected, "Tony" Armstrong-Jones was hardly a brilliant match; but at least he had never been married. Elizabeth and Philip could not stop it this time; they had shot their bolt. And the Queen Mother was on Margaret's side. However, their attitude was exemplified by a letter the Queen's secretary wrote on her behalf to the Garter King of Arms in answer to his query as to whether the Heralds were to attend the wedding. The Secretary stated that, "While Her Majesty appreciated the loyal feeling of the Officers at Arms, they would understand that for obvious reasons she did not want the wedding to be made more of an occasion of State than was absolutely necessary."

Margaret's wedding was quite an occasion nonetheless. But millions of television viewers noted that the Queen never once flashed her usual radiant smile.

Philip has managed his own marriage with a minimum of difficulty as far as the outside world knows. The one occasion on which a rift appeared may or may not have been deliberately manufactured by sensational journalism. In 1956 Philip was invited to open the Olympic Games in Australia in October. He decided to take advantage of the opportunity to visit many other Commonwealth countries coming and going, and set off happily with Mike Parker and his usual entourage.

It was a long trip covering nearly 40,000 miles, partly made by air and partly in the Queen's splendid new yacht, the *Britannia*, over whose design Philip had worked with the late King, suggesting such modern conveniences as a landing deck for helicopters. In the course of it, in addition to Australia and New Zealand, he visited such tiny British outposts as the Falkland Islands, where he won a sailors' horse race; Gough Island; St. Helena and Ascension Island, whose inhabitants had never seen a member of the Royal Family. He even took the research ship *John Bistoe* down through the ice floes of Antarctica to pay a visit to Base W on Deception Island, and eleven other research bases. Things went right almost everywhere and Philip had the feeling of having accomplished a great deal for his Queen and country.

Then, early in 1957, as *Britannia* was sailing homeward from Gambia—where the Moslem natives had greeted Philip with astonishing shouts of "Welcome, Duke, and Jesus keep you for the Queen!"—things went very wrong indeed. A columnist in England wrote that Mrs. Michael Parker was about to divorce the Duke's secretary for cause. It was true enough, and it made a front-page story with the usual embellishments.

The story was that the Queen was upset and demanded that Philip dismiss Parker. Since Elizabeth was so intense on the subject of divorce it may have been true, or it may have been pure imagination. In any event, Parker felt he must resign, and left the *Britannia*. Now Philip, who was intensely loyal to his friend, was upset. All the fun and satisfaction went out of the trip. But worse was to come.

In the world of London's clubs, where all too many people longed to believe anything deleterious about the Mountbattens, the gossip was that Parker and Philip had gone in for wild parties at the Thursday Club, with Baron procuring pretty models for their amusement. This seems to have been impure imagination. As far as anyone really knows Philip had kept his nose remarkably clean where women were concerned. But floating across the Atlantic the gossip fired the brain of a little English columnist on the *Baltimore Sun*, Joan Graham, who earned that day's bread by tapping out a tale of London seething with rumors of a serious row between the Queen and the Duke of Edinburgh.

So far so bad. But at least none of the the British papers picked it up, until a reporter from the Associated Press in London had the nerve to call up Buckingham Palace. Unfortunately he was put through to a press officer who should not have been allowed to do public relations for a dog show in the Shetland Islands. Instead of laughing it all off this solemn fellow issued an official denial. That broke it wide open. The British papers had to print an official denial from the palace, and therefore to describe what was being denied and why. They had a Roman Holiday feeding Philip to the lions.

According to plan Elizabeth was to fly to Lisbon to meet Philip in the *Britannia*, and then make a state visit to Portugal. She took off right in the middle of the hullabaloo and the whole journalistic world waited with baited breath and cocked cameras for the great "reconciliation" scene.

It is certain that the Queen found a very embittered Prince aboard *Britannia*—all he had worked so hard for on this trip, all his splendid accomplishments, shot to ribbons by sixteen-point headlines. But he was not bitter with her—nor she with him. There was no reconciliation, just a joyful reunion. Perhaps, after a little while they could even laugh at the stories, though the incident certainly left a residue of gall in Philip's system.

And the aftermath was equally offensive. The gooey sob stories of the royal reconciliation—"Radiant Queen" and "Smiling Prince"—were even more sickening. It was one cross that Philip had not foreseen, and one Albert had never had to bear.

At the Mansion House luncheon, shortly after his return, Philip himself spoke of his "sacrifices," though in a different connotation. He said, "I believe that there are some things for which it is worth-while making some personal sacrifice, and I believe that the British Commonwealth is one of those things, and I, for one, am prepared to sacrifice a good deal if by so doing I can advance its well-being by even a small degree. This Commonwealth came into existence because people made sacrifices and offered their services to it. Now it has been handed down to us, and if we don't make sacrifices for it we shall have nothing to hand on to those who follow us, and the world will have lost something of much greater value than just a grand conception. . . ."

Elizabeth's way of showing her love and confidence in Philip came in an official announcement: "The Queen has been pleased . . . to give and grant unto H.R.H. the Duke of Edinburgh the style and titular dignity of a Prince of the United Kingdom. The Queen has been pleased to declare her will and pleasure that the Duke of Edinburgh shall henceforth be known as His Royal Highness the Prince Philip, Duke of Edinburgh."

Thereby she rectified that accidentally-on-purpose omission.

Philip's life has been so varied that, paradoxically, it becomes monotonous to describe, and possibly to live. The frequent state visits and tours with the Queen have been supplemented by innumerable personal tours all over the world in the course of which the *Britannia* has furrowed every sea and his planes have roared down all the skies. *Plus ça change, plus c'est la même chose.*

There is no question that Philip meant with all his heart his words at the Mansion House luncheon about making sacrifices for the Commonwealth. He has proved it by being absolutely indefatigable in promoting its welfare and other things which he believes contribute to it, and to the welfare of all human—and even animal—beings. He is the most traveled prince ever, having covered at least 30,000 miles a year; and he averages from sixty to eighty major speeches and any number of off-the-cuff talks.

Though his speeches are never profound they are extremely effective in their direct, man-to-man, informal style. In his introduction to a collection of his speeches* he wrote, "I try to say something which I hope might be interesting or at least constructive. To do this and at the same time avoid giving offense can sometimes be a ticklish business. I have come to the conclusion that when in doubt it is better to play safe —people would rather be bored than offended."

---

* *Prince Philip Speaks: Selected Speeches, 1956–1959.*

Fortunately, Philip frequently does not follow his own rule. When he feels something ought to be said, he hews away even if the chips fly into some people's eyes. For example he recently told a meeting of British airline experts that "British safety standards are lower than those of several other countries"; and he asked the Coal Board: "How much longer can we go on exploiting every feature of this country purely for gain?" To a group of scientists he said, "Progress is undiscriminating. Progress gives us better medical science, but it also gives us better bombs. How do you relate computers to compassion?"

In a speech to the Chamber of Commerce and Manufacturers in Edinburgh, trying to blast them out of their customary inertia, he echoed iconoclastic Bertrand Russell: "America has invented the phrase 'Yes-Men.' . . . In England we are more troubled by No-Men, who make it their business to employ clever ignorance in opposing and sabotaging every scheme suggested by those who have energy, imagination and enterprise.

"I am afraid our No-Men are a thousand times worse than the American Yes-Men. . . ."

This sort of thing infuriates the unfortunate objects of his comments and a great many others who consider that a prince should always be bland. Philip replies that criticism "is a very important function of any free country." He quite evidently does not intend to be deprived of the inalienable right to try to make people think.*

Such remarks have not bettered his relations with the press. The late Lord Beaverbrook's truce with Lord Mountbatten did not include Prince Philip. There is open, declared war between him and the *Daily* and *Sunday Express*. In a bitter article in the *Sunday Express* in 1963, Colin Cross dredged up every instance of Philip's tactlessness with journalists and then bitterly attacked him for daring to say *"in private conversations"* that he still thought it desirable and inevitable that Britain should go into the Common Market. This was politics!

On the other hand Philip frequently refers to the *Daily Express* as "a bloody awful newspaper" and "a newspaper full of scandal" or "full of lies."

Because of his many trips one newspaper carried the headline, "The Duke Visits Britain." However Philip plays a very active role in his own country. He conceives his function to be to modernize the Monarchy as far as possible. At the luncheon of the Foreign Press Association in London on February 25, 1964, in answer to a loaded question, he

---

* These quotations are from a column by John Crosby in the *New York Herald Tribune* entitled, "Philip the Frank."

said, "What you are implying is that we are old-fashioned. Well, that may easily be true. I do not know.

"One of the things about the Monarchy and its place, and one of its great weaknesses, is that it has to be all things to all people and, of course, it cannot do this when it comes to being all things to people who are traditionalists and all things to people who are iconoclasts.

"We therefore find ourselves in a position of compromise and we might be kicked by both sides. The only thing is that if you are very cunning you get as far away from the extremists as you possibly can because they kick harder.

"I entirely agree that we are old-fashioned; it is an old-fashioned institution. The interesting thing about the Monarchy is that it is not a monopoly of old people. . . ."

Within this realistic framework of what is possible, Philip has done his best to bring this peculiar institution up to date. It is difficult because the opposition is entrenched in a Maginot Line of traditionalism that is very difficult to outflank. Nor is the Queen a very enthusiastic idol-smasher. Her whole temperament and training, and her father's teachings, are to keep things as they have always been. But she is a reasonable person and when Philip's ideas are plainly sensible she backs him up.

So he has been able to initiate some streamlining into the royal residences, especially Buckingham Palace; things like modern kitchens, an intercom system, and the ordering of a time-and-motion study that resulted in reorganizing the service—there are now only thirty housemaids. He has also tried to put the huge agricultural estate of Sandringham on a paying basis. In these and other ways Philip has saved quite a lot of money. Having been so poor so long he is a careful spender.

Philip has also been able to reorganize the Court's social life to some extent. He got rid of the costly and slightly ridiculous "drawing rooms," at which hundreds of wide-eyed and nervous debutantes, dressed in long trains and ostrich feathers, waited in line for hours to curtsey to the Queen. But he encouraged the huge garden parties held rain or shine in the rather barren grounds of the palace—the Queen cares little for its gardens—because they give people from all over the Commonwealth a feeling of belonging. He also instituted small luncheons at the palace for interesting people of all professions, especially scientists, who would never have gotten beyond the gates in the old days.

However, there have been some minor reversals. For example, soon after she came to the Throne, the Queen ordained that Knights of the Garter, when appearing at Court with the ribbon of the Order, must wear knee breeches. King George would have approved!

Perhaps Philip's most valuable function has been as a sort of liaison man between his sheltered, reticent Queen and her subjects throughout the Commonwealth. He has the common touch—it is acting, but convincing acting—and he can get people to open up and say what they really think. Then he comes home and tells his wife how the currents of thought are running in far corners of her realm; and the near corners, too, like, for instance, Cheapside. It is good that she should have this information. Though he officially avoids the implication of advising her politically, his opinions based on his wide-ranging experience must command her attention.

In this connection a great deal too much is made of Lord Louis' influence on his nephew. It was paramount in Philip's youth; but politically their paths have diverged. Despite the fact that in their respective positions they are supposed to be completely apolitical, both are intelligent, well-informed men who have strong opinions. Lord Louis is, and always has been, very liberal. Philip is much more conservative. Once he is reported to have remarked to a South American dictator that it was "a pleasant change to be in a country that wasn't ruled by its people." This sort of flippant, offhand remark, if it was ever made, certainly does not reflect Philip's political philosophy, but merely his irritation with the restraints of his position. Nevertheless he is far to the right of his uncle.

This divergence of political views is a practical guarantee against the two Mountbattens ganging up to exercise political influence. It is also a good thing for them, because it means that no matter which party wins an election one of the Mountbattens is sure to have friends in power.

Within the British Isles Philip has accepted all sorts of positions, some honorary, many onerous, where he thinks he can help. They range from heading scientific and industrial bodies, in which he takes an intense interest, to such sporting posts as Admiral of the Royal Yacht Squadron, Grand Master of the Guild of Air Pilots, President of the Marylebone Cricket Club, and many others.

He is a great conservationist and heads many British organizations for this purpose. His own pet project is the World Wildlife Trust. To raise money for the preservation of wildlife he is willing to go anywhere in the world, and often does.

Because he is so fond of field sports Philip is forever running afoul of the small but vociferous minority of English people who abhor hunting. In public they damn him and in private they wonder at what they call his "dichotomy" in being so keen on both conservation and hunting. There is, of course, no dichotomy. Does the chicken farmer hate chickens or the rancher hate steers because he slaughters them? The true sportsman, which Philip is, loves all wild things and never kills them in such numbers as to threaten their survival. He will also go to great lengths to avoid cruelty. Since the wildest duck must die, there is nothing cruel in bringing him down in his pride of strength rather than letting him live on to die of sickness and old age, provided it is well and cleanly done. Philip is an excellent shot.

Even his other favorite sport, polo, brings criticism on Philip's head every time he falls on it, or even plays on Sunday. Naturally he pays his critics no heed. The Queen loyally supports him, always coming to see him play if it is at all possible. He is not as faithful to her favorite sport of racing—she is one of the world's great experts on blood lines. It bores Philip to tears and except for such mandatory state occasions as the Derby and Royal Ascot, the Queen goes racing without him.

Philip has made himself a good, though not great, polo player with a handicap about in the middle of the spectrum. He could be better if he had more time for it.

In Philip's crowded life time is, indeed, the essence. Finding time to be a good father to his four children, the Prince of Wales, Princess Anne, and Princes Andrew, born in 1960, and Edward born in 1964, is a major problem. Considering the pressures on him, he is rather successful, because he tries hard. Whenever he has a free moment, he likes to spend it with them. He taught Charles to swim, and gave him his first riding lesson, his first sail, and, when the boy was old enough, took him stalking at Balmoral where Charles shot his first stag—what a row that caused with the anti-hunting crowd!

Philip's most important function as a father was planning his oldest son's education. The heirs to the British throne have been underprivileged in this important department. Prince Albert set such a ferocious schedule of studies and exercises for his eldest son as gave King Edward VII a life-long distaste for intellectual effort. The half-hearted attempts to modernize the education of both George V and George VI were pretty much of a failure. What those Kings learned was largely self-taught or, perhaps, acquired by osmosis in later life, rather than through formal instruction. Even Elizabeth had a far from normal schooling.

Philip was adamant that his son should have the normal opportunities of an upper-class English boy. As a result Charles followed his father's footsteps, first to Cheam and then to Philip's beloved Gordonstoun. This might be Philip's finest contribution to the Monarchy.

In spite of his glittering, busy, and genuinely useful life Philip impresses some of his closest friends as a bitter man. Certainly he fumes against the restrictions imposed upon him and the unfair publicity he gets. Sometimes this bitterness even appears in his public speeches. In India, in 1959, he said, "I have had very little experience in self-government. In fact, I am one of the most governed people in the world." For all his admiration of discipline, the yoke galls him. It is, indeed, overly restrictive.

Yet it would be a mistake to think of Philip as permanently embittered. Rather these periods of anger against the world and himself can be regarded as the downswings of a mercurial nature. The Germanic temperament tends to be slightly manic-depressive, and Philip's is no exception. There are times when his life seems to him full and fair and significant; and others when his mouth is full of ashes, and he thinks angrily of the things he might have accomplished.

But despite his self-doubts and occasional bouts of self-pity, soon dispelled by his sense of humor, Philip is as successful in his line as were his famous uncle and beloved grandfather in theirs. Recently he has become, next to Lord Louis, the leading liquidator of the British Empire, for he has been chosen to represent the Crown at the Independence Day ceremonies of several former British colonies. One famous scene shows why.

At five minutes before midnight on December 11, 1963, Prince Philip—his white uniform crossed by the blue Garter ribbon and brilliant with decorations, though even now not as many as Mountbatten wears—arrived at Uhuru (Freedom) Stadium in Nairobi, the capital of Kenya. The stadium was filled to overflowing by a wildly enthusiastic crowd of townspeople and tribesmen, gathered to see Kenya receive her independence. All week long Mau Mau leaders had been drifting down from the hills in which they had been hiding for a decade to carry on their campaign of terror and assassination; "Field Marshal" Mwariama and fifty of his "generals" came—very few privates. All week, too, the representatives of many nations had been arriving: from the Soviet Union and Communist China; Indira Gandhi came from India, and most of the Western powers had sent representatives, among them Secretary Stewart Udall from the United States.

Immediately after Prince Philip entered the stadium Prime Minister Jomo Kenyatta, who as Burning Spear had been the greatest Mau Mau of all, arrived in a white Lincoln Continental presented to him by a group of American businessmen. Black, powerful, and dedicated, the African statesman wore a colorful robe that flapped loosely on his tall, broad-shouldered body and a round, beaded hat crowned his wrinkled face with its fringe of grizzled beard and dark piercing eyes. Though Kenyatta had waged relentless warfare against the British and had spent seven years in an English jail, he was not embittered. He had opted to bring Kenya into the Commonwealth and already written was the conciliatory speech in which he promised white men and Asians equal protection and opportunity with Africans in the new nation.

Kenyatta joined Prince Philip and British Governor Malcolm MacDonald, and together they walked toward two flagpoles in the center of the arena, from one of which flew the Union Jack. As they stood there the hour struck. Kenyan soldiers and the British African Color Guard stood rigidly at attention; the saluting cannon were loaded and cocked; bandsmen held their instruments at the ready. In that moment of tremendous emotional tension Philip had an impish thought. Turning to Kenyatta he asked, "Are you sure you want to go through with this?"

The old African leader's eyes glinted with amusement and smiling he nodded his head. Prince Philip gave the order to lower the Union Jack. As the brilliant lights of the stadium dimmed, a courteous gesture by Kenyatta to spare British feelings, the flag started slowly down the pole. The band struck up "God Save the Queen," and the sharp, spaced reports of the cannon saluted the passing of another fragment of Empire. Philip stood at attention, the brief flash of humor replaced by solemnity befitting the occasion.

The Union Jack reached the bottom of the pole and a white-uniformed, turbaned British soldier gathered it tenderly in his arms. At that instant all the lights blazed on and the black, red, and green flag of Kenya was hoisted on the other pole. As it reached the peak and blew out proudly a hurricane of sound greeted it—the band playing the new anthem, cannon firing, fireworks banging and flashing in the sky and fifty thousand ecstatic people shouting, "Uhuru! Uhuru! Uhuru!"

Philip still stood at salute, very tall and fair in the brilliant light that cannoned off his white uniform and sparkled on the jeweled insignia of ancient chivalry. The eyes of many in that wild, eager crowd were on him, not in hatred of a tyrant overthrown, but in perhaps unwilling admiration of him as a fitting symbol of the greatness that was Britain, and the grace with which she accepted her reduced role in this new, if doubtfully better, world.

The ability to accept defeat with humor and turn it into a moral victory is also a form of success.

Bibliography

Alexandra, Queen of Yugoslavia, *Prince Philip: A Family Portrait* (Copyright © 1959, 1960, by Opera Mundi, Paris; reprinted by permission of the publishers, The Bobbs-Merrill Company, Inc.).

Ralph Arnold, *A Very Quiet War* (London: Rupert Hart-Davis, 1962).

Herbert Asquith (The Earl of Oxford and Asquith), *Moments of Memory* (London: Hutchinson, 1937).

Margot Asquith, *Autobiography* (New York: Doran, 1920).

Clement R. Attlee (Earl Attlee), *Twilight of Empire* (New York: Barnes, 1962); *Empire into Commonwealth* (London: Oxford University Press, 1961).

M. A. K. Azad, *India Wins Freedom* (New York: Harcourt, Brace, 1962).

Walter Bagehot, *The English Constitution* (London: Oxford University Press, 1933).

E. F. Benson, *Queen Victoria's Daughters* (London and New York: D. Appleton-Century, 1938).

Geoffrey Bocca, *Elizabeth and Philip* (New York: Holt, 1953; by permission of Holt, Rinehart and Winston).

Hector Bolitho, *A Century of the British Monarchy* (London and New York: Longmans, Green, 1951).

The Countess of Brecknock, *Edwina Mountbatten: Her Life in Pictures* (London: Macdonald, 1961).

Arthur Bryant, *The Turn of the Tide* (New York: Doubleday, 1957) and *Triumph in the West, 1943–46* (London: Collins, 1959), based on the Diaries of Field Marshal Lord Alanbrooke.

Alan Campbell-Johnson. *Mission with Mountbatten* (New York: Dutton, 1953).

Winston Churchill, *The World Crisis* (London: Butterworth, 1923; by permission of Charles Scribner's Sons, New York); *The Second World War* (Boston: Houghton Mifflin, 1959; by permission of Cassell and Co., London); *The Grand Alliance* (Boston: Houghton Mifflin, 1950; by permission); *Closing the Ring* (Boston: Houghton Mifflin, 1951; by permission).

Brian Connell, *Manifest Destiny* (London: Cassell, 1953).

Marion Crawford, *The Little Princesses* (New York: Harcourt, Brace, 1950).

John Dean, *H. R. H. Prince Philip, Duke of Edinburgh, A Portrait by his Valet* (London: Hale, 1954).

Anthony Eden (The Earl of Avon), *Full Circle: The Memoirs of Anthony Eden* (Boston: Houghton Mifflin, 1960).

Dwight D. Eisenhower, *Crusade in Europe* (New York: Doubleday, 1948); *Mandate for Change* (New York: Doubleday, 1963).

Bernard Fergusson, *The Watery Maze: The Story of Combined Operations* (London: Collins, 1961).

Bibliography

J. A. Frere, *The British Monarchy at Home* (London: Gibbs and Phillips, 1963).

Alden Hatch, *General Ike* (New York: Holt, 1945–52); *George Patton: General in Spurs* (New York: Messner, 1950).

James Hilton, *The Story of Philip, Duke of Edinburgh* (Boston: Little, Brown, 1955).

Ileana, Princess of Romania, *I Live Again* (London: Gollancz, 1952).

Hastings L. Ismay (Lord Ismay), *Memoirs* (New York: Viking, 1960).

Jane's Fighting Ships (published at irregular intervals in London).

J. R. Jellicoe (Admiral the Viscount Jellicoe of Scapa), *The Grand Fleet 1914–16* (New York: Doran, 1919).

Mark Kerr, *Land, Sea and Air* (London: Longmans, Green, 1927); *Prince Louis, Admiral of the Fleet* (London: Longmans, Green, 1934).

Sidney Lee, *Edward VII* (New York: Macmillan, 1925–27).

Eric Maguire: *Dieppe: August 19* (London: Jonathan Cape, 1963).

Arthur J. Marder, *Fear God and Dread Nought: The Correspondence of Admiral of the Fleet Lord Fisher of Kilverstone* (3 vols., London: Jonathan Cape, 1952–59; by permission); *From the Dreadnought to Scapa Flow* (London: Oxford University Press, 1961; by permission).

Princess Marie Louise, *My Memories of Six Reigns* (London: Evans, 1956).

Madeline Masson, *Edwina* (London: Robert Hale, 1958).

John Masters, *The Road Past Mandalay* (London: Michael Joseph, 1961).

Sir Frederick Morgan, *Overture to Overlord* (London: Hodder and Stoughton, 1950); *Peace and War* (London: Hodder and Stoughton, 1961).

Leonard Mosley, *The Last Days of the British Raj* (London: Weidenfelt & Nicholson, 1962).

The Earl Mountbatten of Burma, *The Mountbatten Lineage* (privately printed in London, n.d.); *The Sovereign and the Navy* (privately printed in London, n.d.); *Time Only to Look Forward: Speeches 1947–48* (London: Nicholas Kaye, 1949); *Report to the Combined Chiefs of Staff by Supreme Allied Commander S. E. A., 1943–45* (London: H.M.S.O., 1951).

Ray Murphy, *The Last Viceroy* (London: Jarrolds, 1948).

Harold Nicholson, *King George V* (London: Constable, 1952).

Frank Owen, *Tempestuous Journey, Lloyd George, His Life and Times* (London: Hutchinson, 1954).

Oscar Parkes, *Some British Battleships* (London: Admiralty Library, n.d.).

George S. Patton, Jr., *War As I Knew It* (Boston: Houghton Mifflin, 1947).

Sir Frederick Ponsonby, *Recollections of Three Reigns* (London: Eyre & Spottswood, 1951).

Kenneth Poolman, *The Kelly* (London: William Kimber, 1954).

Philip, Duke of Edinburgh, *Prince Philip Speaks: Selected Speeches, 1956–1959* (London: Collins, 1960).

C. E. Lucas Phillips, *The Greatest Raid of All* (Boston: Little-Atlantic Monthly Press, 1960).

Terence Robertson, *Dieppe: The Shame and the Glory* (London: Hutchinson, 1963).

George Rock, *The History of the American Field Service* (privately printed in New York, 1956).

S. W. Roskill, *The War At Sea* (London: H.M.S.O., 1954).

William Slim (Field Marshal the Viscount Slim), *Defeat Into Victory* (New York: McKay, 1961; by permission of David McKay Co., New York, and David Higham Associates, agents for Cassell Publishers, London).

C. E. Stacey, *The Canadian Army 1939–45* (Ottawa Admiralty Library, 1948).

Christopher Sykes, *Orde Wingate: A Biography* (London: Collins, 1959).

The Times (London), *The Times History of the War* (London: 1914–18); *The Times File 1868–1963* (London).

Harry S Truman, *Memoirs*, 2 vols: *I. Years of Decisions, II. Years of Trial and Hope* (New York: Doubleday, 1958).

Barbara Tuchman, *The Guns of August* (New York: Macmillan, 1962).

Queen Victoria, *Memoirs of the Prince Consort* (New York: Harper, 1867).

Loelia, Duchess of Westminster, *Grace and Favour* (New York: Reynal, 1961).

Albert C. Wedemeyer, *Wedemeyer Reports!* (New York: Holt, 1958; by permission of Holt, Rinehart and Winston).

Theodore H. White (ed.), *The Stilwell Papers* (New York: Sloane, 1948; by permission of William Sloane Associates and William Morrow and Co.).

The Duchess of Windsor, *The Heart Has Its Reasons* (New York: McKay, 1956).

The Duke of Windsor, *A King's Story* (New York: Putnam's, 1951).

Index

THE MOUNTBATTENS

The Last Royal Success Story